THESIXTHFAMILY

THE SIXTH FAMILY

THE COLLAPSE OF THE NEW YORK MAFIA AND THE RISE OF VITO RIZZUTO

Lee Lamothe &
Adrian Humphreys

HarperCollins*PublishersLtd*

HarperCollins Publishers Ltd
2 Bloor Street East, 20th Floor
Toronto, Ontario, Canada
M4W 1A8

www.harpercollins.ca

Library and Archives Canada Cataloguing in Publication
information is available upon request

ISBN 978-1-44342-802-6

Printed and bound in the United States
RRD 9 8 7 6 5 4 3

To the memory of my mother
Elsie Mae Lamothe (December 4, 1919 – March 20, 2006)
— L.L.

To the memory of my grandfather
H.G. Humphreys (March 12, 1905 – June 19, 2001)
— A.H.

CONTENTS

Q: How many organized crime families are there in New York?
A: Five.

Q: What are the names of the five New York crime families?
A: Lucchese, Gambino, Colombo and the Genovese.

Q: And what's the fifth family?
A: Us, the Bonanno Family.

> —*Testimony of Salvatore "Good-Looking Sal" Vitale, former underboss of the Bonanno Mafia family, United States Courthouse, Brooklyn, New York, June 28, 2004.*

"For the past 25 years, Montreal has been the key that turns the lock of America. The one holding that key becomes the pinnacle. … The Rizzuto family was able to promise a transport between the Mafias of Europe and the Mafia of America. Riches were promised for all."

> —*A leading anti-Mafia investigator with the* Carabinieri, *Italy's federal police force, 2006.*

PROLOGUE

BROOKLYN, MAY 5, 1981

"Don't anybody move. This is a holdup."

The words were clear despite the muffling effect of a woolen ski mask pulled down over the long, thin face of Vito Rizzuto, a 35-year-old Sicilian who called Canada's French-speaking city of Montreal his home. Vito was slumming it in New York City this day, more accustomed as he was to receiving nods of respect in Canada and Sicily as the son of a powerful mafioso, or relaxing on the coast of Venezuela, where his family controlled massive drug-trafficking interests. On May 5, 1981, Vito found himself bursting from a closet in a rundown Brooklyn social club, waving a pistol and shouting out stick-'em-up clichés.

It was a casually dressed but powerful group of men who suddenly stopped their chatter and, startled by the sudden appearance of masked and armed men, looked up at Vito and three colleagues as they emerged from the narrow confines of the darkened closet. Gathered before them were the top men in the Bonanno Mafia Family, perhaps the most deadly and storied of New York City's notorious Five Families, which between them control much of the continent's underworld. The Bonanno captains, each a leader of crooks operating under the family's banner, had been summoned to an "administrative meeting" by Joseph Massino, a senior Bonanno captain often called "Big Joey" by his mob colleagues, a nod at first to his substantial girth and later to his position of power. Officially, peace was the sole item on the meeting's agenda, talks meant to mend an unseemly rift between factions within the family that had grown from quiet disdain to open hostility and brought it to the brink of out-and-out warfare.

Among those in the social club, feeling particularly uncomfortable, were three leading captains who formed the core of opposition to Joseph Massino within the family: Alphonse "Sonny Red" Indelicato, Dominick "Big Trinny" Trinchera and Philip "Philly Lucky" Giaccone. Other gangsters milled about uneasily with them.

Earlier, before the guests started trickling into the private, two-story Brooklyn club, Vito Rizzuto had arrived to make dark preparations with Massino and Salvatore Vitale, a slender New York mobster known as "Good-Looking Sal." At the time, Vitale was a mere mob associate, but he would go on to become the underboss, the second most powerful position in a Mafia family. Vito allegedly brought with him from Montreal two close mob friends of his own, Emanuele Ragusa, whose daughter would later marry Vito's son, and a veteran gangster identified by informants only as "the old-timer," who was likely a Rizzuto relative with ties to the New York underworld.

The club was small and simply laid out; utility was chosen over decor for such private mob moments. Visitors passed through a narrow foyer into an unadorned room with a cloakroom to one side and stairs leading up to an area that was equipped to handle catering but in fact, primarily used to host a modest gambling racket by the club's ownership group. This group included Salvatore "Sammy Bull" Gravano, who would soon become underboss of the Gambino Family under its notorious boss John Gotti and, later, a spectacular mob turncoat.

"The minute I walked into the club, in the foyer, Vito, Emanuele and the old-timer, we were issued the weapons, told to have ski masks that we'd put [on] in a closet in a coat room," said Vitale. Vito and Ragusa took pistols and were appointed lead shooters. Vitale was handed a heavy-duty machine gun, what he called a "grease gun" because it blasted automatic gunfire, and the old-timer suitably went old school, taking a sawed-off shotgun. Playing around with his new toy, Vitale accidentally squeezed the trigger, wildly spraying bullets around the club.

"Don't shoot unless you have to," Massino scolded him. "I don't want bullets flying all over the place." Even mobsters get the jitters.

"We were in the closet, we all had our weapons loaded. We sat there and waited for the doorbell to ring," said Vitale. "We left the door open a smidge to look out."

The ringing of the bell at the club's entrance signaled the arrival of the first of the invited guests.

Vito crouched low, peeking out from his vantage point. Through the swelling crowd and loud chatter from tough men all accustomed to having their say, Vito kept his eyes on one man, Gerlando Sciascia, a fellow Sicilian who was a longtime Rizzuto family friend. Sciascia was easy to pick out because of his thick, silver hair, brushed back off his forehead in a bouffant hairdo that any aging Hollywood hunk would envy. Everyone in the room knew Sciascia; the Americans called him "George from Canada" because he was Montreal's representative in New York, while the Canadians stuck simply with "George."

Breathing deeply beneath his mask, Vito watched for the secret signal that would draw him from the closet, a signal that came when Sciascia slowly ran the fingers of his lean, right hand through the silver hair on the side of his head.

That simple act of preening brought mayhem to the social club and radically changed the balance of power. This was not about robbery, despite Vito's words when he confronted the gangsters. Nothing would be taken but three lives and the rights to an underworld throne.

"Vito led the way," said Vitale, who was the last to scramble out of the closet. While Vito and Ragusa pointed their guns, Vitale and the old-timer jogged past them to block the club's exit.

Big Trinny, one of the rebellious captains, seemed the first to realize they had been set up. Bellowing loudly, he threw his full 300 pounds headlong at Vito, who reacted by firing his pistol, making Big Trinny the first to die, although his flab-fueled momentum kept his body hurtling forward while other bullets pounded into him. Philly Lucky appeared to surrender, placing himself against a wall, his hands out-stretched. His submission was in vain. Peppered with bullets, he slid to the floor, dying from multiple bullet wounds to his head and chest.

Sonny Red turned on the heels of his brown cowboy boots and made a go at fleeing. In his bright orange T-shirt, however, he was an easy target. A shot to the back sliced through his backbone and burst out his chest. A second bullet hit him in his left side and whistled under the skin across the length of his rib cage before breaking through the flesh on his other flank; with its momentum suddenly sapped, the battered .38-caliber slug could not even pierce the fabric of his shirt a second time, falling instead into its blood-soaked folds. Sonny Red stumbled to the ground. Sciascia, anxious to join the fray, pulled out a pistol he had tucked in the back of his pants, pointed it down at the struggling gangster and fired it once into his left ear. The bullet tore downward through Sonny's head, whipped out through his right cheek and grazed his right shoulder before slamming into the floor. The rebellion was over.

When the gunfire stopped, all the survivors except Massino and Vitale raced out of the club.

"The only one standing in the room other than the three dead bodies was Joseph Massino," an amazed Vitale said, recalling the scene. "Everybody else was gone."

————

Time has not been kind to those involved in the murder of the three captains, an act that has since become a rich part of popular lore, forming the core of a multitude of trials and police investigations, and being colorfully re-created and immortalized on film in the Hollywood movie *Donnie Brasco*.

Several of the notorious men involved would later be imprisoned, likely for the rest of their lives. Others would go on to shatter their oath of *omertà*, the Mafia's vow of silence, and cooperate with government agents to far-reaching effect. Still others would, themselves, be killed in the continuing gangland intrigue; one would die in a plane crash and another under even more unusual circumstances—hanging, face-to-face with his son, both officially declared to have committed suicide. One by one, each of them would fall—at the wrong end of a gun, through life imprisonment or in a freak incident. All but one.

Vito Rizzuto is the last man standing.

"The significant factor surrounding these murders is that Vito Rizzuto, Nick Rizzuto's son, is suspected of being involved," concludes a confidential FBI report from 1985—almost prescient as it was written 20 years before there were informants filling in the extensive blanks of what authorities knew of the mysterious murders. The same report outlines with some amazement the Rizzuto family's central role as a hub for extensive criminal interests in America, Italy, Canada, Mexico, Brazil, Venezuela, France and Switzerland, noting Vito's and his father's relationships with some of the world's most significant drug barons. More recent investigations would add China, Saudi Arabia, Cuba, Haiti, Belize, Bahamas, Aruba, Dominican Republic and Panama to the list of the family's international interests. Two decades ago, FBI special agents wrote with a growing sense of alarm that Vito, a shadowy mob figure based in Canada, was not only trusted to carry out this most sensitive bit of internal Bonanno business but also operated with seeming autonomy and impunity around the world. Compared to what New York–based authorities were used to looking at, largely homegrown gangsters lording it over turf they could drive across in a leisurely afternoon, the breadth of geography and intertwining connections of the Rizzuto organization surprised even seasoned investigators.

Within the blood-splattered walls of the Brooklyn social club, the Sixth Family had emerged with a deafening crescendo. The Canadian connection had been made.

The New York mob had gotten a taste of a gangster who would eventually eclipse them all.

———

This is the story of a war, of a family and of a man. It documents a hard struggle for the biggest prize in crime—the New York drug market. At the same time, it reveals the hidden history of the family that helped wage and win that war. Finally, it tells the story of the man who heads that family and how he runs the family business, an enterprise that grew within three generations from a small operation in rural Sicily to a mammoth, North American–based crime corporation with grasping hands reaching around the globe.

Vito Rizzuto is a man of many parts. He is the product of a strong family from a tough place. Without the drugs and the murders, the story of the Sixth Family would be an illustrious and celebrated tale of success, drive and ambition; a story of tradition, culture, love and hate. But the story cannot be told without noting the movement of massive quantities of drugs and the copious murders, because the vast, alarmingly successful global operation that the Sixth Family built, expanded and assiduously protects is a franchise for drugs: heroin at the outset, then cocaine, hashish, ecstasy—whatever the market demands, whatever turns a profit. This book, however, is not meant to be a tawdry account of the day-to-day life of a gangster, but rather a probing and lasting examination of a criminal dynasty that made "Rizzuto" one of the most important names in the world of crime.

The Sixth Family is as much a genuine family as it is an organization. A careful examination of the major players shows that blood ties and marital links are an integral part of its operation. It grows slowly and carefully, often absorbing new members when an acolyte, or one of their children, marries a child or sibling of another key operational player, suggesting either the insular nature of the families or a crafty, purposeful plan. The result is a family tree that in its roots and in many of its branches closely mirrors police reports on important criminal networks. It is a hallmark that distinguishes the Sixth Family from the Five Families of New York, which recruit neighborhood crooks based on a pattern of high-paying scores, a materialistic standard of loyalty that has proven to be a weak foundation.

The Sixth Family is not a term the organization uses to describe itself. Rather, it is a name coined by the authors of this book to describe the network of clans that has gelled around the Rizzuto organization, a term chosen to highlight both the close ties between its members and its place in the underworld alongside the Five Families of New York City.

The Sixth Family is a blend of unvarnished capitalism and globalization, tempered only by loyalty and a deep criminal culture more than a century old, although it is bound more by its own personal relationships than by archaic Mafia rituals. The Sixth Family is a tight web of drug-trafficking clans. Instead of maintaining a geographic base in Sicily, like traditional Mafia families, they consider the globe their village; instead of beating a profit out of the streets of New York, like many of their Mafia confederates, they make the world their marketplace.

While New Yorkers retain memories of colorful mobsters such as John Gotti, Chicago clings to the legend of Al Capone, and Montreal still reminisces about its old Godfather, Vic Cotroni, the entire world can claim the Sixth Family. For the Sixth Family lays claim to the world.

Chapter 1

AGRIGENTO PROVINCE, SICILY, 2006

A narrow road, carved from the chalky hills of southern Sicily, cuts north at Montallegro from the coastal highway that links the major cities of Agrigento and Trapani. As the road bends and twists its way some seven miles north and 600 feet up, sun-bleached vistas alternately rise and fall from the sides of the pavement. Scrub brush and thin bunches of long green grass poke out of dusty soil that clings tenuously to rocky, mountainous hilltops. An occasional farmhouse dots the land, set behind hard-won fields of grapevines and hardy crops such as pistachio trees, olive groves and ancient almond orchards.

Enchanting, tranquil, rustic—a host of adjectives can describe such Old World scenes, and on a map, Cattolica Eraclea looks like any one of the hundreds of hilltop villages that define Italy's island of Sicily. On the outskirts of town, as the road flattens, a recently erected sign comes into view, offering travelers hospitality in three languages: "Benvenuti," "Willkommen" and "Welcome" to Cattolica Eraclea. The sign then lists the location and phone numbers of the Carabinieri, the federal police force, and the Polizia Municipale, the local police detachment.

Around a bend, set on a small traffic island, there is another sign announcing the town. This sign is rusted, pockmarked and marred with graffiti, suggesting a certain malaise has set in, an idea reinforced by the absence among the tall, orange-tiled houses of the low cranes and scaffolding that signal new construction and remodeling in most Sicilian towns. The inordinate number of newer high-end automobiles navigating the narrow streets—with BMW the favorite and Alfa Romeo not far behind—belies the appearance of Cattolica Eraclea as a poor village with few prospects.

Small-town Sicily is known to hospitably welcome the children and grandchildren of émigrés to the Americas who make a pilgrimage back to the old country to see where their ancestors came from and to visit the graves of known and unknown relatives—in Sicilian terms, to respect the tradition of *sangu de me sangu*, "blood of my blood." In Cattolica Eraclea, however, responses to questions about how old the church is or how to get to the cemetery are not met with a smile and a dizzying monologue about the town. Despite the welcoming roadside sign, answers provided to strangers are abrupt and precise. Instead of the usual friendly inquisitiveness about one's family—when they left and where they went—you are likely to be followed by a sinister-looking man in one of those BMWs, a person to be encountered three or four more times as you walk among the graves of the town cemetery, allowing you to leave his sight only when you reach the town limits.

The residents' suspicions probably spring from the simple fact that the town and its surrounding province of Agrigento have, over several decades, given the world some of its most rapacious drug-trafficking clans.

Cattolica Eraclea is a community of some 6,000 people that is missed by a wide margin on each side by the twin highways and rail lines connecting the cities of Palermo and Agrigento, infrastructures that look as if they have made considerable effort to bend around the town. This no doubt contributes to the rarity of tourists, a fact that speaks to the absence of hotels. It is as if the people just wish to be left alone. That is not to say the town is without its visual charm. The old Town Hall, for instance, and the original Borsellino palace, built in 1764, the town's clock tower, the powerful architectural statement of the Fascist-era Palazzo Municipale and the Mother Church Dedicated to the Holy Spirit, with its lofty bell tower and double-decker stone columns, are pleasing marvels.

Another church of some beauty is la Chiesa della Madonna del Rosario, the Church of the Madonna of the Rosary. It is a testament to the religious roots of a town named for its faith—Cattolica is Italian for "Catholic"—that a village of such size would have so many churches. The Chiesa del Rosario, as it is commonly known, features an imposing stone facade broken only by a circular window set with a stained-glass portrait of the Virgin Mary praying over the infant Jesus. Built in 1638 and topped by three bells in an open tower, the formidable exterior of the church gives way to a surprisingly bright nave inside, where rows of wooden pews lead to a sunlit apse and intricately carved altar. Parishioners still gather in this venerable church that casts its wide shadow over Via Ospedale, a narrow street near the center of Cattolica Eraclea.

In modest homes along Via Ospedale, a short, dead-end street, the nucleus of the Sixth Family began to form. It was in a house here that Nicolò Rizzuto was born on February 18, 1924, and it was here also that Nicolò would marry and would welcome the birth of his first child, a son. Born on February 21, 1946, that beloved *bambino* would be called Vito, in honor of Nicolò's long-dead father—a man who gave Nicolò his start in life as well as a criminal pedigree, but a father he would never personally know.

Nicolò Rizzuto's father, Vito, was born to Nicolò Rizzuto and Giuseppa Marra on April 12, 1901, and grew up in Cattolica Eraclea. And just as the names would be handed down through the ages—with the Vito Rizzuto of today being the son of Nicolò who is the son of Vito who is the son of Nicolò—a desire to move to the New World also extended through the generations.

CATTOLICA ERACLEA, SICILY, 1924

The previous generation's Vito Rizzuto was slim and fit, standing 5-foot-6 with a strong jaw, brown eyes, a full head of chestnut-colored hair and a modest scar low on the left side of his forehead. He decided to leave Cattolica Eraclea in 1924.

Rizzuto had moved into a home on Via Ospedale in 1919, months after the close of the First World War. He appears to have then completed a post-war stint in the Italian army—but even there he could not resist his outlaw urgings. On June 23, 1921, he was sentenced by the Military Tribunal of Rome to two months' incarceration in a military jail for theft. At the age of 22, on March 9, 1923, he married Maria Renda, a family friend, relative and neighbor who was three years his senior. Just 10 months before he left Sicily—never to return—he and Maria had their first and only child, Nicolò.

There was no doubt sadness and uncertainty at leaving his young family behind, but both husband and wife must have taken some comfort in knowing that the other would remain among family despite their separation. Maria Renda and baby Nicolò would live on the same short street, perhaps even in the same house, as the Rizzutos. For her part, Maria knew that her husband was leaving Sicily accompanied by her brother, Calogero Renda. Calogero was two inches shorter and a year younger than Rizzuto. With a darker complexion and a mole on his left cheek, Calogero appeared to be a man of some means—he owned fashionable clothes and had the ability to travel internationally. (On February 1, 1923, police in Agrigento issued him a passport, #126/241107, allowing him to travel to Buenos Aires, Argentina.) Calogero also lived on Via Ospedale in Cattolica Eraclea, with his mother, Grazia Spinella. By 1924, his father, Paolo Renda, was already dead.

Vito Rizzuto and Calogero Renda planned their departure during extraordinary times in Italy. Benito Mussolini, the Fascist leader, was turning the crisis over the murder of socialist leader Giacomo Matteotti, his most potent political rival, into an opportunity. Matteotti disappeared in June 1924 as he was delivering withering denunciations of Mussolini. A month later, Matteotti's decomposing body was found in a shallow grave outside Rome. The political storm that followed this obvious assassination at the hands of the Fascists weakened Mussolini and for months there was doubt about his ability to retain power. In December, he promised to reconvene parliament after Christmas to discuss electoral reform. In the New Year, instead of concessions, however, Mussolini seized full dictatorial powers.

It was at that very time of political uncertainty that Rizzuto, Renda and four close friends planned their departure, heading north past Rome. By December 1924, they had crossed the border into France. A few days after arriving in Boulogne-sur-Mer, a northern port city near Calais on the English Channel, the six friends bought third-class tickets for passage to America. It was a meandering trip, more a tourist cruise than an immigrant steamer. The S.S. *Edam* left Rotterdam, its home port with the Holland–America Line, and stopped in Boulogne-sur-Mer on December 14, 1924, to collect Rizzuto and his pals before crossing the Atlantic over Christmas and New Year's. The ship arrived in Havana, Cuba, on January 5, 1925, and then left for Tampico, Mexico, arriving there on January 16, before finally heading to America.

It was a suspiciously unusual and expensive route for supposedly simple laborers from rural Sicily immigrating to America. Rizzuto and Renda, however, seemed to have unusual reasons.

NEW ORLEANS, JANUARY 19, 1925

When the S.S. *Edam* drew into port at New Orleans, Louisiana, U.S. immigration officials were far more concerned with two Cuban stowaways who had crept aboard the ship in Havana than with Vito Rizzuto and his entourage, all of whom presented American officials with the required paperwork and visas. The rules for immigrants from Italy had recently changed as the United States grew increasingly concerned about the continuing waves of new arrivals. As of July 1, 1924, a quota system was imposed on Italian immigrants, sharply limiting the number that could legally enter America. Every Italian émigré needed an immigrant quota visa issued prior to their departure by the U.S. State Department.

As Vito Rizzuto led his small group off the S.S. *Edam*, Immigration Inspector J.W. McVey examined the quota visas and identity papers for each of them.

Giving his occupation as "laborer" and falsely declaring himself to be single, Rizzuto listed his next-of-kin as his father, Nicolò, in Cattolica Eraclea. He said he was able to read and write in Italian and was arriving in America for the first time with the intention of becoming a citizen. As required, he declared he was not a polygamist, an anarchist or an advocate of overthrowing the U.S. government; he had not been in prison or an insane asylum and was not "deformed or crippled." He was in good health and carried with him $40 in cash to fund his new life. His final destination, he claimed, was New Orleans, where he was joining his cousin, Pietro Marino.

Next to present himself to Inspector McVey was Calogero Renda. Like Rizzuto, he declared himself a laborer suitable for immigration and intent on becoming a citizen. He gave his next-of-kin as his mother, had $35 with him and, like Rizzuto, had plans to stay with Pietro Marino, whom he described as his uncle.

Also traveling with Rizzuto were four other men, one more from his hometown of Cattolica Eraclea and three from Siculiana, a Mafia stronghold just 12 miles to the south. The two towns were closely linked, socially and criminally, and citizens from each would later work together to build the Sixth Family into one of the world's most successful criminal enterprises.

Mercurio Campisi was the next to be inspected. He was a friend of the Rizzutos who lived on the same street, Via Ospedale, in Cattolica Eraclea. His father, Salvadore, remained there. At the age of 37, Campisi was an experienced traveler. He had lived in the U.S. from 1911 until 1915 and again in the early 1920s and appears several times in passenger manifests and immigration records, shuttling back and forth between Sicily and the United States. Unbeknownst to officials in New Orleans at the time, just a year earlier he had been detained and deported after arriving illegally in New York. This time, Campisi had $50 with him and said he was heading to Seattle to join his uncle, Alfonso Vaccarino.

Next off was Francesco Giula, 32, from Siculiana. The men from Siculiana all carried more cash than their Cattolica brethren, in Giula's case, $75. Like Campisi, Giula had also lived in Detroit in the early 1920s. He said his final destination was the home of his cousin, Sam Pira, in Los Angeles.

Giuseppe Sciortino, also from Siculiana, was the youngest traveler among them, just 19. His father, Salvadore, was listed as his closest relative. With $70 in his pocket, Sciortino, too, was heading to Los Angeles, he said, to the home of his uncle, Giovanni Marino.

At 43, Vincenzo Marino was the oldest of the S.S. *Edam* group. He also carried the most money: $90. Also from Siculiana, he had married into one of Sicily's preeminent Mafia clans when he took Giuseppina Caruana as his wife. Marino, too, said he was heading to Los Angeles and the home of Giovanni Marino, whom he described as his cousin.

Of these men, only Francesco Giula would be lost in the mists of time. The other five would each show where their true interests lay in America. Between them, they would find their way into bootlegging, counterfeiting, arson, fraud, perjury and murder.

The Sixth Family had arrived in America.

Chapter 2

HARLEM, 1928

The Cotton Club, the most famous of New York's nightclubs, was offering fabulous floor shows and musical revues exclusively for white patrons in the heart of Black Harlem. On stage were some of America's greatest black performers: Duke Ellington, Louis Armstrong and Ethel Waters among them. The bustling nightlife at this and similar swanky clubs catered to rich and famous patrons who motored uptown from Manhattan, while most of the people actually living in Harlem's tenement apartments could not hope to enjoy the shows. Strictly enforced policies ensured that the only blacks inside were on the stage and the white locals were kept at bay by steep prices and a dress code. The action of Harlem's main strip, packed with speakeasies, taverns, cafés, supper clubs, dancehalls and theaters—often controlled by America's emerging mobsters—was just a few blocks from where Vito Rizzuto, a young man in his late 20s, settled soon after arriving in America from Sicily.

Contrary to what this Vito Rizzuto—the grandfather of the Vito of today—told immigration officials when he arrived aboard the S.S. *Edam*, he had no intention of staying in New Orleans. His brother-in-law, Calogero Renda, was well settled in New York by 1927, so it is likely that both men wasted little time in Louisiana before heading north, where the American Mafia was getting properly organized. Rizzuto was living in east Harlem, just across the Harlem River from the Bronx, when, on February 9, 1928, he declared his intention to become a naturalized American citizen, the first step in obtaining citizenship.

His financial fortunes seemed to be improving. Seven months later, he was able to leave the crowded streets of Harlem for a house at 94 Ridgewood Road in Oradell, across the Hudson River in New Jersey. The suburbs did not bring him peace.

At 8:35 p.m. on September 25, 1930, Rizzuto was shot inside his Oradell home. Police arrived quickly and took him to Hackensack Hospital, where he was treated by doctors while detectives questioned him about the attack. With his friend Giovanni "John" Chirichello at his side, Rizzuto told police: "I was shot by my best friend, Jimmy Guidice." He said little else, other than insisting that he had no wish to pursue charges. Police believed the dispute was the result of a love triangle, with a detective later noting that Rizzuto and Vincenzo "Jimmy" Guidice were involved with the same woman. Officers also noted that Guidice was never again seen in Oradell. Two days after the shooting, despite his injury, Rizzuto filed his petition for American citizenship at the Court of Common Pleas in Hackensack. Calling himself a "contractor," Rizzuto swore the oath of citizenship and renounced his loyalty to Vittorio Emanuele III, the King of Italy. The event was witnessed by two of his friends, a carpenter and a laborer. This time he came clean with authorities, stating on his application that he was married to Maria Renda and finally revealing the existence of his son, Nicolò, likely the first notation in U.S. government files of a man who would, decades later, cause investigators great concern by bringing the Sixth Family to true prominence. Certificate of Citizenship #3455682 was soon forwarded to Rizzuto by the U.S. Bureau of Naturalization. He was now an American.

Police records on this early Vito Rizzuto are complicated by the carelessness of recording foreign names during that time. There were Vitto Rizzuttos, Vito Rizutos, Rissutos and even Riuzzitos turning up in police notes throughout the late 1920s and 1930s in the area, mostly involving bootlegging and violence. Even when the name was spelled correctly in police files, the newspapers of the day were notoriously sloppy, with reporters drawing the names phonetically from policemen who had no interest in the intricacies of Italian pronunciation. As Rizzuto would soon learn, however, not everyone in the local media was so lackadaisical about who he was.

PASSAIC, NEW JERSEY, 1931

Max L. Simon was an aggressive entrepreneur who had started his newspaper career as a streetwise cub reporter known for his exposés of scandalous behavior. Described as having "ability, energy and intelligence," Max Simon became a powerful and prominent newspaper publisher. A lawyer by education, he was feared by businessmen and politicians for his skill at muckraking, mudslinging and manipulation. It was widely known that he kept secret files on the misdeeds and peccadilloes of powerful people in the community. In fact, he had once suffered a severe beating when one of his blackmailing schemes went awry.

By 1931, he was owner of the moribund *Elizabeth Daily Times* and deeply in debt. Operating from the Passaic, New Jersey, area, Simon seemed to take too many cues from the gangsters and thugs he had once reported on and to prove that he was himself a crook at heart. Finding himself in increasing debt, Simon turned to the underworld. He called on John Chirichello, Rizzuto's close friend. The pair were part of one of the dozens of arson rings operating across America, a rare growth industry in those desperate times, as more and more businessmen found themselves suffering from the financial cancer of the Great Depression. As the economy melted, so did well-insured business premises under suspicious circumstances.

Chirichello was invited to Simon's printing plant for a discreet conversation.

"I'm hooked up to my neck," Simon told Chirichello, complaining of his financial straits. How much would it take to "make a good job" out of the newspaper's printing plant, he asked, intimating he wanted it torched to the ground.

"How much is it insured for?" Chirichello asked.

"Between $30,000 and $40,000," Simon replied. "I must have this place burned down. It's the only thing that will save my neck." For some reason Chirichello resisted, perhaps suspicious that Simon was drawing him into a trap. "I told Max I didn't want to do this job because I had just got out of a scrap, but he pleaded and told me if I got into trouble, he'd help me out," Chirichello later admitted to authorities. Eventually, Chirichello contacted his gangster buddy.

"I spoke to Vito Rizzuto about the job and I took him down to the plant," Chirichello recalled. There, Simon offered them 10 percent of the insurance money. "He paid me $300 as an advance payment," Chirichello said. "This was to buy materials to set the place on fire." With their front money, Chirichello and Rizzuto bought 100 gallons of liquid celluloid and 200 gallons of turpentine. "We put it into six barrels and moved it in my Chevrolet truck to the plant in Elizabeth," he said. On the morning of October 17, 1931, the firebugs were ready.

"Rizzuto and myself got tin pails and dipped them into the barrels and threw the stuff over the first and second floors. When we couldn't dip any more, we rolled the barrels over the floor. We spread about thirty yards of gauze bandage around." To the gauze wicks he tied a sulfur stick, the type used to purify wine barrels. Chirichello and Rizzuto then pulled a length of electrical cable from the wall; they shut off the main power so Chirichello could safely scrape the cable to bare the two wires inside. He put a nail between the wires and twisted them around it, making what would become an electrified spike when the power was turned back on.

"I then threw the switch and lit the sulfur stick." Calmly, the men left the plant and jumped onto a streetcar heading towards Newark. As they rode away they heard sirens and then saw fire engines racing towards the printing plant. Looking back, they could see flames emerging from the building. They knew their job was done.

The operation seemed successful but Max Simon was unimpressed—or, at least, feigned disappointment. "It could have been a better job," Simon complained when Chirichello and Rizzuto went to his office to collect their money. He then declined to pay them. Rizzuto was enraged.

"Rizzuto was going to shoot him," Chirichello said. Rizzuto was not making idle threats. Shortly after the meeting, Simon called a policeman he was friendly with and said Rizzuto was armed and stalking him. The officer tracked Rizzuto down and took away his gun. The disagreement festered. Simon was clearly able to make life in New Jersey uncomfortable for Rizzuto and he soon fled, hidden by Stefano Spinello, a gangland friend from the Bronx, in a shack near the Patterson Stone Quarry in Patterson, New York, about 80 miles northeast of New Jersey. At the quarry, Rizzuto spent his days carrying water from a deep hole that formed a natural pool in a nearby swamp to make cement blocks, working to fill an order of 200 for a local company. Rizzuto was to lie low until the problem with Simon could be settled. It was the perfect place to hide: he could keep busy, Spinello would visit him and Rizzuto could pass his time chatting with a friendly watchman. Best of all, only one man from his gang knew where he was—Spinello—and he was a trusted *paisan*.

Meanwhile, the vindictive Simon, appalled and frightened by Rizzuto's threats, decided to settle this problem in the same anti-social way he dealt with his mounting debts. He reached out to his underworld contacts.

———

Vito Rizzuto was sleeping on his cot when three men slipped into his hideaway shack during the night of August 12, 1933. They wasted little time before bashing his head in with a cement block tamper, a heavy metal device made for compacting uneven concrete. The tamper was brought down again and again, up and down his body. Ropes were then looped around his neck and yanked, an unnecessary precaution as he was already dead. The assassins cloaked his body with cement bags and wrapped it again in the canvas cover of a cement block machine before dragging it into the nearby swamp, to the very spot where Rizzuto had been drawing water for the cement. They pushed him into it and left. He was 32 years old.

When the watchman at the stone quarry realized he had not seen Rizzuto for several weeks, he went to the shack to check on him. He found the door open and no sign of Rizzuto, although his "good" clothes had been left behind. Fearful, the watchman called the local sheriff, who arrived and immediately noticed a trail leading to the swamp; something heavy had been dragged from the shack. The sheriff then "sounded" the water in the swamp by poking down with a long steel bar. When foul-smelling bubbles arose, he dragged the water and soon found Rizzuto's submerged corpse.

The autopsy report spares little detail: "[The victim's] mutilated and battered body was found buried in a hole in a swamp near an abandoned stone quarry. Chief cause of death: fracture of skull—comp[ound]. Other causes: rupture of liver; internal hemorrhage; simple fracture of fifth, sixth, seventh, and eighth ribs on left side." Coroner Dr. Robert Cleaver, who conducted the examination, concluded: "Homicide by crushing instrument."

When the victim was identified as Vito Rizzuto, police were not surprised. The activities of the arson ring had already come under investigation. A month before Rizzuto's body was found, the New York State Police had received an alert from officers in Passaic County to be on the lookout for him. He was wanted for arson after a small hotel was torched.

The police investigation moved quickly. People who knew plenty were talking too much, particularly John Chirichello, Rizzuto's friend, whom Simon had first approached with his arson scheme. Chirichello told police the details of the printing plant fire, as well as Simon's subsequent dispute with Rizzuto over payment. Investigators, meanwhile, had determined that Stefano Spinello was the only person in New Jersey who knew where Rizzuto had been hiding.

Max Simon, Stefano Spinello, and a third man, Rosario Arcuro, another of Rizzuto's friends, were charged with his murder. The theory of the prosecutor was that Simon had hired the other two to track down Rizzuto and kill him. They had killed Rizzuto either to protect Simon from Rizzuto's revenge or to shut him up in the face of an investigation into the arson ring. The names of Rizzuto's killers remain provocative: Spinello is also sometimes spelled Spinella—the last name of Calogero Renda's mother's family—and Arcuro has an alternate spelling of Arcuri—the name of a Sixth Family clan from Cattolica Eraclea who would remain close to the Rizzuto family to this day. Could he have been killed by kin? Answers do not come easy.

In response to the charges against him, Max Simon pulled every string he could wrap his crooked fingers around. After being convicted of the arson, he had a soft landing, editing a newspaper and writing columns from his jail cell and, able to acquire steaks and a stove to cook them on, maintained his rich diet. He only served nine months of his three-year sentence and was released after a special session of the New Jersey Court of Pardons. The murder charge was then dropped.

Stefano Spinello was not as lucky. He had originally pleaded not guilty to first-degree murder, but after a few days of hearing the damning testimony of Chirichello in court, he pleaded guilty to manslaughter. He was sent to Sing Sing prison for a 7-to-20 year sentence. Rosario Arcuro was never captured by police or brought to trial. He did, however, get a taste of what he had meted out to Rizzuto: he was murdered in the Bronx in August 1934.

Vito Rizzuto, one of the Sixth Family's first North American pioneers, who would give his name and a criminal culture to a grandson he did not live long enough to see, died as a fugitive arsonist at the hands of his friends. American police could find no family who needed to be notified of his death and he ended up in a grave at the Methodist cemetery in Brewster, New York.

The American government, however, was far from closing its file on Vito Rizzuto.

WASHINGTON, D.C., 1932

Even before his murder, Vito Rizzuto had earned unwanted attention from the U.S. federal government. On Halloween, 1932, a memo marked "CONFIDENTIAL" was sent from Washington, D.C. to the New York director of the U.S. Bureau of Naturalization, asking that Rizzuto's immigration file be pulled and forwarded. Someone had questions about the visa that had allowed Rizzuto entry into the United States.

On November 7, 1932, the quota visa that Rizzuto had presented when he disembarked in New Orleans in 1925 was found in the archives and sent to Washington. An official also dusted off the 10-year-old pages of the passenger manifest for the S.S. *Edam* that recorded his arrival in America.

To everyone's eye, even now, Rizzuto's visa looks perfect. Apparently issued by the American Consular Service in Palermo, Italy, certificate #2226 shows it was duly processed, approved, signed and stamped on November 19, 1924. The nine dollars' worth of fee stamps were affixed and appropriately canceled to acknowledge payment for the visa, which bears the signature of Robert E. Leary, the diplomatic post's vice consul.

The visa, issued under the American government's recently imposed quota system that tightly controlled the number of Italians that could immigrate, carries the photograph and name of Vito Rizzuto, allowing him a coveted way into America. His paperwork to obtain the visa also seemed in order.

He had a *Certificato Di Identita Personale*, his personal identity certificate. Issued by the Italian government, featuring his photograph and signature and bearing the stamp of the commander of the Carabinieri station in Cattolica Eraclea, it acted as a passport.

He had a medical certificate: "I, the undersigned physician and surgeon, hereby certify that Rizzuto, Vito, son of Nicolò, of Cattolica Eraclea, has no contagious disease and has a sound mind and perfect physical constitution," reads the letter, dated November 13, 1924, and signed by Dr. Mario Bellina, of Cattolica Eraclea. The letter was witnessed and notarized as authentic by P.A. Margiotta, the mayor of Cattolica Eraclea, and stamped with the seal of the town's municipal office.

Finally, he had a *Certificato di Penalita*—a penal certificate testifying that he had never served a term in prison—signed by the vice chancellor of the court in Agrigento, the provincial capital. Everything appeared authentic, but U.S. officials were suspicious.

In October, 1934, more than a year after Rizzuto's murder, all of Rizzuto's documents were gathered together by the Department of State in Washington, D.C. and sent in a diplomatic package to its consulate in Palermo, in what was being classified as "the fraudulent visa case of one Rizzuto, Vito." The government was trying to "ascertain the circumstances and facts in the case," the accompanying letter says. The inquiry, however, did not stem from Rizzuto's messy murder. The diplomatic note ends: "The Department also wishes to learn whether or not Vito Rizzuto is in Italy at present or still resides in the United States." A joint investigation by U.S. and Italian authorities was launched into the visa, which found that a good portion of the documents Rizzuto used were brilliant forgeries or corruptly obtained versions of the real thing.

Alfred Nester, the U.S. consul in Palermo, reported in sworn statements that the quota immigration visa carried by Rizzuto when he arrived in New Orleans was not issued by the consulate. Further, Nester said, there was no record of the money for the fee stamps that are affixed to Rizzuto's visa ever having been paid. Italian authorities found similar duplicity in his paperwork. They examined copies sent by the Americans and declared that Rizzuto's medical certificate and identity papers were false because there had never been a Dr. Bellina nor a mayor named Margiotta in Cattolica Eraclea. The penal certificate, however, was genuine. (Rizzuto's theft conviction was not listed on his record because, in accordance with Italian regulations, it was a first offense for a period of less than three months' imprisonment, investigators reported.) When authorities went to Rizzuto's home town in 1935 looking for him, they interviewed his wife, Maria Renda, who told them that her husband had never returned to Sicily after leaving for America and he had died there in 1933. Italian authorities could not confirm the death, however, as the vital statistics office in Cattolica Eraclea had not been informed of his death.

"Taking into consideration the circumstances," wrote Inspector G.M. Abbate of the director general's office of the Italian Ministry of Foreign Affairs, "there is no doubt but that Rizzuto emigrated clandestinely."

U.S. immigration investigators then painstakingly retraced Rizzuto's steps in America, with the mandate of interviewing him as part of their probe. It was not until July 1935, that Frank Steadman, a federal investigator, learned of Rizzuto's murder at the stone quarry two years earlier. In his report Steadman noted that other men had traveled to America with Rizzuto and that perhaps their visas should be looked into as well.

Indeed, with Rizzuto dead, the U.S. government went after the men who had arrived with him aboard the S.S. *Edam*.

Investigators found that Calogero Renda's documents were also false. The same fictitious doctor and the same imaginary mayor had signed his papers and the U.S. consulate had no record of issuing his quota visa. Investigators found that after Renda's arrival he had applied for U.S. citizenship in 1927, giving his home address as Morris Avenue in the Bronx. He had returned to Cattolica Eraclea in 1929, however, to marry Domenica Manno, the young sister of Antonio Manno, the most powerful Mafia boss in the area. On April 6, 1930, he'd returned to his home in the Bronx without her, presenting a fresh U.S. quota visa at the port of New York. He then applied for a U.S. immigration visa—legally, this time—for his bride. It was rejected. After Renda's U.S. citizenship was granted in 1932, he again went to Sicily to spend time with his wife, returning to New York on March 24, 1933, five months before Rizzuto was murdered. In the summer of 1935, after Rizzuto's death, Calogero Renda went to the Oradell street where Rizzuto had lived—a few weeks ahead of the U.S. immigration investigators—asking neighbors which house his brother-in-law had lived in. By the time U.S. Immigration Inspector Jacob Auerbach went looking for Renda in 1936, in the widening probe of the fraudulent visas, Renda was back living in Cattolica Eraclea with his wife, Domenica Manno.

The Manno name would prove to be important, although no one realized its significance at the time. This was one of the first official recognitions of the closeness of the Rizzuto–Manno–Renda family clique—the base of the Sixth Family. On March 17, 1937, Renda's U.S. citizenship was canceled and, 11 days later, an arrest warrant for immigration violations was issued against him, removing any chance that he could legally return.

Mercurio Campisi, who had arrived at New Orleans with Rizzuto and Renda, was also found to have traveled on false documents. He fought to remain in America but was ultimately sent back to Cattolica Eraclea in 1938. Pleading destitution, he forced the U.S. government to pay for his return trip.

Giuseppe Sciortino, another of the S.S. *Edam* bunch, was also found. After he arrived in New Orleans he married and settled in Buffalo with his wife, where they had three children. Sciortino earned money selling bootleg alcohol made in an illicit still in his home. In 1936, police found counterfeit U.S. banknotes in his car. When the Secret Service questioned him about it, Sciortino was adamant about what kind of criminal he was: "I am not a counterfeiter, I am a bootlegger." When quizzed about his travel documents, he claimed he properly paid the fees at the American consulate. Later, when pressed at a deportation hearing, he admitted he had bought them for about 3,000 liras from a man at the Concordia Hotel in central Palermo.

"First, he told me to go to the municipal authorities to get my penal certificate, then birth certificate and after I got them I turned them over to him," Sciortino said. Eight or 10 days later, the man delivered the false visa. His proffered revelations brought him no slack. He was deported to Siculiana, but his wife, Jennie Zarbo, refused to go with him. He then began a 15-year letter-writing campaign—including flowery missives to President Franklin D. Roosevelt and his wife, Eleanor—to convince U.S. officials to allow him back to be with his family. The government denied all requests. The letters end in 1950 on a sad note: one of Sciortino's children had died and he himself had savagely lost an arm. "My condition requires a woman to help me out in the house," he wrote. Since his wife was steadfast in not moving to Sicily, he begged the U.S. Attorney General to "abolish" his marriage so he could remarry. The government replied: "I am unable to offer any advice in the matter."

Vincenzo Marino, the oldest of Rizzuto's companions aboard the S.S. *Edam*, had more success at disappearing. An arrest warrant for Marino was issued on February 19, 1935. The search started in Los Angeles, where he had said he was going to settle. Two years later, however, Los Angeles police were still making "intensive efforts" to find him. Detectives concluded that Marino had never actually traveled to California.

The elaborate visa fraud was an important investigation for the American government. Reports on its progress were sent directly to Cordell Hull, President Roosevelt's famed secretary of state. Curiously, documents uncovered show the government solving the visa crisis by clamping down on the gangsters who they found had used them. There is little evidence of what investigators discovered when they inevitably probed how the visas and fee stamps got out of the consulate and into their hands in the first place.

Although this Vito Rizzuto's criminal activity led to his murder, that gruesome lesson did not dissuade his son or grandson from pursuing an outlaw life. As for Calogero Renda, he would continue to work closely with the Rizzuto family for the rest of his life. The offspring of these two men, who had tried but failed to move their clan to New York, would soon form the innermost core of the Sixth Family. And if it could not be based in America, then it would settle for the next best thing—Canada.

That would have to wait, however, for the next generation.

CHAPTER 3

CATTOLICA ERACLEA, 1940s

Back in the Sicilian town of Cattolica Eraclea, the son of the murdered Vito Rizzuto, Nicolò, came of age amid the death and tumult of the Second World War without ever knowing his father, although he had a stepfather for guidance after his mother, Maria Renda, remarried. That second marriage, to Liborio Milioto, gave Nicolò a half-sister, whose offspring remain close to the Rizzutos to this day.

At the close of the war, having grown into a strong and industrious man, Nicolò Rizzuto started a family of his own.

Nicolò's choice of bride was not merely a matter of falling in love with the robust and determined Libertina Manno. Winning the hand of such a woman and—perhaps more important—gaining the approval of her father to marry her, would have been an intimidating but important affair, more so than for the average man navigating a relationship with a future father-in-law. Nicolò's romantic success brought him more than a wife, lifelong companion and future mother of his children. Marrying Libertina brought Nicolò closer into the family of Antonio Manno, the head of a family of great note in the area, one designated in Italian police files as the Famiglia Manno, the "Manno Family."

The Mannos were the pre-eminent Mafia clan in the southwest of the province of Agrigento, ruling a territory that stretches out in a long triangle linking the towns of Cattolica Eraclea, Siculiana and Montallegro. Antonio Manno, who was born in 1904 and died in 1980, was the undisputed *capo mafia* of this important area. He is also ground zero for the formation of the Sixth Family and a showcase for the intermingling of the clans that would become notorious: his mother was a Caruana; his wife was a Cammalleri; his sister married Calogero Renda, who had earlier traveled to America with the Rizzuto patriarch.

When Nicolò married Libertina Manno, he "married up" in the underworld. With Antonio Manno as her father and her mother being Giuseppina Cammalleri, a woman from a prominent clan with similar outlaw traditions, Libertina was from rich Mafia stock. To be allowed to marry her was a crucial sign of acceptance and approval of Nicolò on many levels.

As a young couple, Nicolò and Libertina Rizzuto moved through Cattolica Eraclea in a social milieu that included friends and family; the distinction between who was merely a friend and who was family continued to blur and, indeed, be erased as the Manno clan expanded, by entrusting their many daughters (they had surprisingly few sons) to well-chosen grooms who were often "Men of Honor," as the mafiosi call themselves. In Cattolica Eraclea, and within the Mafia triangle of nearby towns, the Famiglia Manno met and married a number of like-minded people from a few—a very few—families. Perhaps because of the smallness of their village and the insular clique they built for themselves within it—but likely by a clever plan to protect the family from betrayal—the closeness of the group was tightened further by marriages amongst these families. It is a family where the lines of connection stretch backwards and forwards simultaneously—with first and second cousins intermarrying—making it common for members to describe their relationships to each other in several ways, such as being both a cousin and a son-in-law. From the Manno clan springs a family tree with branches that would spread briefly to entangle a new family name, only to fold back in on itself.

The list of names and interweaving relationships is often hard to follow but each would distinguish itself in Sixth Family deeds: the Rizzuto, Manno and Renda families are joined by the Cammalleri, Sciascia, LoPresti, Ragusa, Arcuri, and Sciortino families—among others. Members of the sprawling clans of the Caruanas and the Cuntreras from nearby Siculiana, who are renowned for their drug prowess, and the Vella and Mongiovì families would also woo and be wooed into the Famiglia Manno through marriage, one of the strongest bases of power among the Sicilian clans. This is the traditional base of the Sixth Family.

After the ill-fated move to America in 1925 by Vito Rizzuto and Calogero Renda, other Sixth Family members also left Sicily under a cloud. Sometime during the night of August 14, 1955, the first democratically elected mayor of Cattolica Eraclea, Giuseppe Spagnolo, lay sleeping outdoors, in the rural stretch between his home town and Cianciana, a village seven miles north on the other side of the Plátani river. Spagnolo was heralded as the "peasant mayor," the first and only peasant to be so elected, propelled into office by the popularity of his radical land reform policy. After his election in 1946, Spagnolo raised the ire of the Mafia by refusing to hand the most fertile land over to the local mobsters. Instead, Spagnolo insisted that the best land go to the neediest—and that clearly did not include the Famiglia Manno. Spagnolo soon faced their wrath. His own farm was vandalized, his barn set ablaze and threats made against him. He did not waver, although he appears to have moved into hiding, preferring outdoor sleeping quarters over his farmhouse. The move did not protect him.

From the darkness of the night emerged several men, each holding a *lupara*, the distinctive shotgun of Sicily. Seven shots rang out, tearing into Spagnolo where he lay. It was a shocking crime. The open assault on civility and democracy outraged the government and the townspeople. By the time authorities identified four men suspected in the assassination, three of the men had fled, apparently after hiding in a local church. Undeterred by their absence, the government moved to prosecute them. The accused included Leonardo Cammalleri and Giacinto Arcuri, who were found guilty, *in absentia*, of murder and handed life sentences. The sentences were later upheld on appeal. But the men were still not to be found. They had fled to Canada, where—despite an arrest warrant issued against them by the Italian government—they settled in Montreal and Toronto. When the Italian government was wrongly informed that Arcuri had died, the arrest warrant for him was canceled. In Canada, Arcuri, whose mother was a Cammalleri, joined up with his Sixth Family associates and remains free in Toronto where he is considered an important man of influence within the underworld. Similarly, Leonardo Cammalleri would somehow avoid prosecution, settling in Montreal and then Toronto, where he raised his family, including his daughter, Giovanna, who would later marry Nicolò's son, Vito Rizzuto.

The deep relationships the clans forged in the lean years in Cattolica Eraclea would remain intact for generations as the family strategically spread across the globe.

———

Sitting on a hilltop along the Mediterranean coast, the city of Agrigento is both the capital and main urban center of the province that shares its name. The city has gained international recognition for the ancient Greek ruins of Akragas, the Valley of the Temples, an extensive and awe-inspiring site built along a sea-facing ridge, considered the best-preserved Greek ruins outside of Greece. Sandy beaches to each side of Agrigento draw locals from their homes on the warmest weekends and the rutted medieval streets exude the Old World feel sought by tourists. The nearby Porto Empédocle runs regular ferries to the Pelagic Islands, a pair of bleak rocks in the Mediterranean Sea that, since they lie closer to Africa than to Europe, place the historical remoteness of Sicily in acute context. These tourist draws do not translate into community riches, however. Agrigento, government statistics show, is one of Italy's poorest cities.

Despite its poverty, the province of Agrigento has an old and sophisticated Mafia. Over generations, a small number of families, or *cosche*, emerged to dominate their towns along the coast and into the interior, engaging in crimes that seem almost quaint in their reflection of time and place—cattle rustling, stealing farm produce, misdirecting irrigation, organizing hired farmhands and thievery. Gradually, public institutions also fell under the control of the leading Men of Honor, who were grabbing and stealing what little there was to take, all the while accepting nods of "respect" from their victims. Their criminal ingenuity and prowess continued to evolve.

"Agrigento's type of criminality," an Italian judge said of the local Mafia clans, "is a form of almost scientific crime, especially if compared to the Mafia in Palermo. The latter is vulgar because it doesn't think twice about shooting in a public street; it acts on impulse. The one from the province of Agrigento is sophisticated: it studies and plans crime with a scientific perfection."

Similar to the ruins in the Valley of the Temples, there is another archeological site along the Mediterranean, just southwest of Cattolica Eraclea. Eraclea Minoa shares a portion of its name with the Rizzutos' home town. In contrast to the community in Cattolica, leaders in Minoa try hard to attract tourists visiting the more famous ruins of Agrigento. The Sixth Family has not helped that cause. As late as the 1990s, the Famiglia Manno was accused of plundering the sites and selling archeological objects of historical value.

In Mafia circles, this passes for living off the land.

While such tawdry thievery certainly helped line the pockets of family members who remained behind in Sicily, the real family money would be generated abroad and the real family power stems from the men who left Agrigento for richer prospects in the New World.

As a geographic location, Antonio Manno's Mafia triangle is as remote and insignificant to legitimate global commerce as any in Italy, but its impact on the international trade in illicit drugs would be unparalleled. This rural triangle became an incubator for a resource crucial to the mass transit of drugs—that resource being the skilled and strong Men of Honor who would leave their family homes and set down roots in North and South America and parts of Europe to build an interwoven and seemingly impenetrable family-based organization that is the modern-day Sixth Family.

In Agrigento province, the Famiglia Manno—sometimes now called the "Famiglia Manno–Rizzuto," as a nod to Vito Rizzuto's prominence in international underworld affairs—is still tracked by the Direzione Investigativa Antimafia, Italy's anti-Mafia investigations department, and by organized crime investigators with the Carabinieri and the Polizia di Stato, the national police. The real concern, however, is with the diaspora that spread these gangsters around the world: to Venezuela, Brazil, Germany, Canada and the United States.

When it came time for Nicolò Rizzuto to wrap up his affairs in Cattolica Eraclea and to pack up his family for relocation, it was to Canada that he went. There he would forge a bold outpost in Montreal. Over time, the Rizzutos would be joined by members of the cluster of interconnected families Nicolò had known all his life: Sciascia, Renda, LoPresti, Ragusa, Cammalleri, Arcuri, Sciortino and Manno. Each would be welcomed into an organization forming in the New World, as the Famiglia Manno became the Sixth Family.

It was a move of strategic brilliance, in keeping with their "scientific perfection" of crime.

CHAPTER 4

HALIFAX, CANADA, FEBRUARY 1954

There was just a trace of rain falling over Pier 21 in Halifax, the major seaport on Canada's Atlantic coast, when 774 passengers who had started their voyage in Palermo, the principal city of Italy's southern island of Sicily, disembarked in the New World. For people acclimatized to the heat of southern Italy, this was something of a lucky break as, just four days before, nearly five inches of snow had blanketed the city, and two days after that a deluge of rain had washed it into the ocean. Among that crush of travelers, mostly new arrivals with plans for permanent immigration, was Nicolò Rizzuto, following his father's footsteps in leaving the family home in Cattolica Eraclea for brighter economic prospects in North America. Unlike the trip of his father some 30 years earlier, however, Nicolò came not with criminal colleagues but with his family.

Their 24,000-gross-ton ship, the M/S *Vulcania*, considered one of the finest transatlantic passenger vessels ever built, arrived from Palermo on February 21, 1954—young Vito's eighth birthday. A future full of anticipation and promised opportunity might well have been gift enough for the boy.

Like most immigrants to Canada, the Rizzutos quickly headed to one of central Canada's largest cities. A bustling and colorful city along the St. Lawrence River, with a large port of its own, Montreal was dominated by its French-speaking population and offered a European feel that English-Canadian cities could not match. In Montreal, a thriving "Little Italy" had evolved as waves of immigrants settled close together, enjoying the labor opportunities and social freedoms of the New World without giving up their culture, one complete with grocery stores carrying familiar food and churches and social clubs mimicking life in their former homeland.

Nicolò Rizzuto's interest in Montreal, however, was not the abundance of imported meats or even the comfortable social setting. Along with the family he adored, the 30-year-old Nicolò brought with him to Canada an impressive underworld pedigree that gave him easy access to the world of crime.

That Nicolò would choose Canada, rather than America, as his new home was likely a consequence of the poor reception his father and his friends had received when the Sixth Family first eyed the New World back in 1925. Nicolò certainly knew that the U.S. government had uncovered his father's visa fraud, particularly after American and Italian officials arrived in Cattolica Eraclea to question his mother about it. He also likely knew of his father's involvement in the arson ring and, particularly upsetting, of his untimely and unpleasant death. Further, Calogero Renda, his uncle and most trusted mentor, was the subject of an arrest warrant in America after the massive visa fraud probe and had retreated back to Sicily. Nicolò's brother-in-law, Domenico Manno, had also tried to make America his home, leaving Cattolica Eraclea and arriving in New York in 1951, only to face expulsion, according to U.S. immigration files. Canada must have seemed a far more welcoming place for the clan. Nicolò already had at least one friend settled in Montreal. Canadian immigration records show that, on August 10, 1953, six months before the Rizzuto family arrived in Canada, Giuseppe Cuffaro had settled in the city. The future master money launderer for the Caruana–Cuntrera clan was from Montallegro, another of the Agrigento towns in the Famiglia Manno's Mafia triangle. Cuffaro would form both a friendship and partnership with Nicolò. As a sign of his growing sense of ease in North America, Nicolò soon started to be known almost exclusively by the natural anglicization of his name: Nick.

MONTREAL, 1950s

Post-war Montreal was a thoroughly corrupt city. Every level of government was riddled with the vexing influence of crime stemming from bribery and blackmail; from police who were sometimes in the pockets of gambling kings, drug traffickers and bootleggers to municipal politicians who relied on gang bosses for vote rigging and election-day goonery. The crooks were quietly repaid with lucrative kickbacks, untendered and inflated contracts, political cronyism and tacit permission to operate. Periodic bursts of public outrage would usher in a wave of law enforcement that would soon relax back into the old routine. From September 1950 to April 1953, 15 high-ranking police officers were fined, suspended or demoted for tolerating illegal activities such as gambling dens, brothels and speakeasies. Scandal was the order of the day, and almost every day, scandal was delivered.

The city's underworld was a complex network of overlapping gangs: Jewish and francophone mobs, Italian and Irish gangsters and Corsican trafficking rings. The port was riddled with corruption as well, facilitating the movement of illegal goods into North America. Outside influence on the underworld of Montreal came from Paris and Marseilles, where Corsican and French smuggling rings saw it as their North American gateway. Since the early days of the French Connection—drug-smuggling networks that started in the mid-1930s when heroin laboratories were built near France's port of Marseilles— virtually every major drug importation scheme originating in Europe used Montreal as a transit point.

Twenty years before the Rizzutos arrived in Canada, another nota- ble family had immigrated to Montreal from Italy. In 1934, the Cotroni family of Mammola, Calabria, had made the city their new home, and 14-year-old Vincenzo Cotroni had quickly taken to its streets. A per- ceptive lad, he soon realized there was good money to be made from bootleg alcohol, prostitution, gambling and drugs—the mainstays of the underworld service industry.

For Vincenzo Cotroni—typically called "Vic" or "Vincent"—vice crimes were a fast and sure way to wealth and power. By 1945 he had emerged as a significant force in Montreal, with his fingers in an ar- ray of criminal activities, from theft and extortion to organizing votes and intimidating polling stations during elections. His two brothers, Giuseppe (called "Pep") and Francesco (called "Frank") would become increasingly active in the drug trade.

All of this activity was duly noted by Joseph Bonanno, the boss who in 1931 took the reins and gave his name to the Bonanno Mafia Family, one of the Five Families that had emerged in New York City as a powerful and controling criminal elite. By the close of the Second World War, the Bonannos were making moves on Montreal.

In 1945, Carmine Galante, a formidable senior representative of the Bonanno Family in New York, started crossing the border into Canada on business trips to Montreal, trips that increased in frequency and length.

"We used to have a lot to do with Canada," said Salvatore "Bill" Bonanno, son of Joseph Bonanno. Now 73 years old and a retired *mafioso*, Bill said his father's relationship with Montreal began in the 1930s, soon after he became the boss and years before the Bonanno Family's interest in the city was officially sanctioned by the Commission, the American Mafia's board of control. "Toronto was the bailiwick of Buffalo and Montreal was apportioned to us after the Second World War. I don't know why they did it like that, probably to keep some balance along the way. The guys in Canada were always old school," Bonanno said recently. On this point, Bonanno and the Federal Bureau of Investigation agree.

"Joseph Bonanno assigned his underboss, Carmine Galante, to Montreal to establish a close working relationship with elements of organized crime already operating in Canada," a report by the FBI said. Galante liked what he found in Montreal. Mature as the city's underworld was by Canadian standards, it was a shadow of what Galante envisioned it could be: nightclubs and restaurants were not being shaken down thoroughly enough, pimps and madams operating brothels were paying a mere pittance and back-alley abortionists had somehow escaped altogether the underworld imperative of paying kickbacks to the mob to be allowed to work in peace. These were things Galante was in the process of changing, but most important, he saw first hand the substantial profits flowing from the France–to–Montreal–to–New York heroin trade. After the Second World War, when American ports were under scrutiny, Galante recognized that the port of Montreal could provide an easier and safer route to get heroin to the burgeoning American market.

This discovery would consume him for the rest of his life.

———

The diminutive Galante was well suited to muscle his way into the Canadian underworld. He had a record that went from the mundane— petty larceny and bootlegging—to the significant: he was suspected of killing a police officer in New York, wounding another officer and assassinating a prominent editor of a New York political newspaper. Police would unofficially pin 80 murders on Galante. Nicknamed "Lilo," Galante was described by a prison doctor as "neat in appearance but dull emotionally."

"He had a mental age of 14-and-a-half and an IQ of 90. He was shy with strangers and had no knowledge of current events, routine holidays or other items of common knowledge," the psychiatric assessment continued. Galante was diagnosed as a "neuropathic, psychopathic personality; emotionally dull and indifferent." The doctor's prognosis for any chance of improvement was expressed in one word: "poor."

In Canada, Galante did not let his emotional dullness or his supposedly low IQ get in the way of his progress. In the underworld, he flourished, marshaling all of his anti-social tendencies to great effect. Stories abound of his appetite for cruelty masquerading as comic relief, such as the time he smashed beer glasses on the floor of a restaurant and forced a young busboy to dance barefoot on the shards. He opened several businesses, including the Bonfire Restaurant on Decarie Boulevard, for which he partnered with Sicilian-born Montreal gangster Luigi Greco and local hoodlum Harry Ship. The Bonfire was a large eatery that was popular for offering customers a choice between its spacious dining room and a drive-in service. Hungry drivers would park their cars in the parking lot, facing the restaurant's front windows, and flash their headlights for car-side service. As car culture gripped North America, this was seen as the pinnacle of modernity.

Part of Galante's mandate from Joe Bonanno was to bring Montreal's illegal gambling under control. Galante pressured American bookies, who had moved their operations to Canada when the U.S. Senate's Kefauver committee was probing organized gambling. Galante's message was clear—the bookies could leave New York but they could not escape the Bonannos.

"[Galante] dictated policy, set rates and tariffs for the American gambling syndicate in Montreal," reads an FBI intelligence file from the time. Although he met with great success in bringing the gamblers to heel, he drew less and less satisfaction from such work. Soon, everything except the heroin trade ceased to fully engage him.

The French Connection was made famous by a book and two movies; as such, it is popularly seen as a Europe–to–New York network that ran for several months in the early 1960s until it was busted by a couple of colorful New York cops. In reality, it was a decades-long series of narcotics networks with Montreal as its hub. The Corsicans at the front end of the network in Europe included businessmen, spies and politicians. The American end of the network comprised relatively low-level operatives who shuttled the dope to the end users. In the middle, tying the conspiracy together, were Montrealers.

With so much heroin passing through his Canadian base, Carmine Galante felt he had found a better home. He even applied for permanent resident status on February 26, 1954, telling officials in Montreal that he had $5,000 to invest in a Montreal restaurant. He was told to get a medical examination, which he did. On March 1 he returned to fill out his forms and, when he was asked if he had a criminal record, he answered yes; further inquiries would have to be made about that, he was told. Four days later, Galante's lawyer informed immigration officials their client had changed his mind and was returning to the United States. It was a preemptive move—any serious inquiry by Canadian officials to American police about his past would destroy any chance of him being ever considered as a suitable candidate.

Back in New York, however, he by no means cut his close ties to the growing Canadian drug connection. In fact, he jealously guarded them, attempting to rule by proxy through other trusted New Yorkers sent to Montreal in his place. By the spring of 1956, Canadian authorities were starting to crack down on the American bookies and gangsters in their midst and issued a list of undesirables who, if they were ever found in Canada or stopped at the border, were to be deported. On that list was Galante and his New York colleagues whom he had asked to look after Montreal in his absence.

Joe Bonanno and Galante then settled on a new tactic. They established a local two-man board of control to mind the Montreal store for New York. The Sicilian, Luigi Greco, who was close to Galante and shared his interest in drug trafficking, and the taciturn Calabrian, Vic Cotroni, were entrusted to jointly run the Montreal rackets on behalf of the Bonanno Family. It was a shrewd move, one that quelled the rivalry between the Sicilian and Calabrian factions within the Montreal Mafia and would bring nearly 20 years of relative peace and prosperity to its members. Montreal became an official satellite of the Bonanno Family, with Cotroni's and Greco's men becoming a crew of Bonanno soldiers operating in Canada.

Competition between the two men arose almost immediately as they jockeyed for favor with New York. Both men had strong qualities, but when it came to leadership, Joseph Bonanno gave Cotroni the edge.

"Cotroni was the head honcho. He was the captain of the crew. Louie was his right-hand man. We had to have a couple of sit-downs to straighten that out but we got it down. They trusted and listened to my dad," said Bill Bonanno. "They had a sit-down at some place on Jean-Talon and the decision was that Vincent [Vic Cotroni] was the captain and Louie, you be the right-hand man. Louie was big enough to respect that. Louie knew it was best for everyone. Now, Louie had guys he was responsible for, but Vincent was responsible for everyone. If any of Louie's guys made trouble, Louie knew he had New York to answer to."

As agents with the U.S. Bureau of Narcotics and Dangerous Drugs stepped up their investigations into the myriad Canadian connections they were uncovering, and as the FBI continued to track increased north-south interaction between Montreal and New York, federal authorities started to better understand Galante's interest in Montreal.

"Although the precise reasons for this move into Montreal are not known entirely, it is fair to assume that a primary reason was to establish an elaborate narcotic smuggling network," an FBI agent wrote in an internal report. (Bill Bonanno insists neither he nor his father had anything to do with drugs, describing Galante as a "loose cannon" and a "rogue element" within their organization.)

Among those who quickly pledged allegiance to Greco, and who grew more and more appreciative of the new opportunities brought by Bonanno's organizational intervention in Montreal, were Nick Rizzuto and several of his kin. The changing landscape put him at an increasingly important nexus: he was a Sicilian Man of Honor who had just become part of a major American Mafia family.

"I knew Nick. I met him in Montreal back in the 1960s," said Bill Bonanno. "He was a young guy then. Another from the old country who had a lot of the same ideals as us and we accepted him. You can almost feel another Sicilian when you meet him—it is something that comes from the cradle."

The Old World and the New World then came together in Nick, precisely at a time when the underworld elites on both sides of the ocean were arranging a similar intersection. It was an important time in the global development of the underworld. Decisions being made elsewhere among criminal cartels, led by the Bonanno Family, would have unimaginable consequences for crime, politics, economics, public health and social stability when mafiosi living in Sicily and America started working together. It was a partnership personified by Nick Rizzuto.

CHAPTER 5

PALERMO, SICILY, OCTOBER 1957

With a four-post colonnade at the entrance and intricate Art Nouveau details in its high-ceilinged foyer, the Grand Hôtel et des Palmes in downtown Palermo, an aristocratic home that was turned into a luxury hotel at the turn of the last century, has attracted many visitors of wealth and fame. Italian prime ministers have wined and dined in its restaurant and lectured in its meeting rooms. The German composer Richard Wagner wrote his final opera, *Parsifal*, while a guest here in 1881. Today the hotel continues to put on a good show for tourists, but even by the mid-1950s it had become a bit of a cliché destination for well-to-do travelers, a bit like the Waldorf Astoria in New York—it still had the reputation but was a little tired around the edges for those seeking true luxury.

The waning tastes of trendsetters meant nothing, however, to a group of visitors who filled its suites from October 10 through 14, 1957. The guests in this entourage reportedly indulged extravagantly in food and drink but their primary purpose was one of serious business, and the hotel staff were kept well away from that. From the United States and from across Sicily, this was a gathering of leading gangsters. The intricate and often delicate discussions between them continued into the night, with an adjournment that saw them pause only long enough to travel to the Spano restaurant, a chic seafood emporium on Palermo's waterfront. The Spano, long since closed, was sheer elegance. At the Spano and the Grand Hôtel, the cream of the Sicilian underworld met with the Bonanno leadership to discuss a partnership.

None of the attendees ever fully disclosed what was discussed, but years of analysis by police intelligence agencies show that one of the major items under discussion was the heroin trade. The French Connection was coming under increasing law-enforcement pressure— an assault led by the United States, which was reeling from the flood of high-quality heroin. American mobsters and European traffickers had long had pieces of the French Connection, but no one had made an effort to bring the entire trade under control. That proposition seems to have been the focus of the talks at the Grand Hôtel et des Palmes.

The architect of the gathering, the man who brought together these American and Sicilian mafiosi, was the deported American Mafia boss Charles "Lucky" Luciano. Joining the discussions as one of the Bonanno representatives was Carmine Galante, who became the primary liaison between Montreal, New York, Sicily and mainland Europe when the Bonanno Family decided to forge ahead into drugs.

Among the notorious mafiosi from Sicily who arrived for the meetings were Gaetano Badalamenti and Tomasso Buscetta. Buscetta later denied knowing anything about meetings at the Grand Hôtel but told of the elaborate dinner party at Spano, one that went on for more than 12 hours, he said. Buscetta, who much later in life became an important *pentiti*, or "repentant" mobster who cooperated with authorities, denied until his death that he—who was clearly one of the world's most industrious drug traffickers—had ever dealt in narcotics. Despite Buscetta's denial, the conclave seems to have had two major achievements. The first was the creation of the Cupola, to monitor the internal affairs of Sicily's many Mafia clans. The Cupola is the equivalent of what the American Mafia calls the Commission, and while most of the traditions that bind the Five Families are imported wholesale from their Italian homeland, the idea of an underworld oversight board was a gift the American mob gave in return.

The second achievement was a formal transatlantic heroin accord. A transit route was being planned; supply and distribution chains were being arranged; problems were being identified and ironed out. The Men of Honor in Sicily were borrowing and buying the expertise of corrupt French chemists who had mastered *l'école française,* "the French school" of production that sent the off-white powdered morphine base through the 17-step process of turning it into the pure-white crystals of European heroin. To consistently get it right, without wasting the precious substance through over-cooking or contamination, took the knowledge of a scientist and the touch of a chef. The Mafia were building clandestine heroin production facilities directly under their control in the western portion of Sicily, bypassing entirely the raucous French port of Marseilles. They were now looking for new ways to send ever greater amounts of the world's most valued drug into North America, particularly New York City, the largest drug market. Although often portrayed as a merger of two monolithic organizations—the American Mafia and the Sicilian Cosa Nostra—it would be more accurately described as a cabal of select gangsters from a number of clans which were hungry for the immense profits attainable through the drug trade.

The two achievements—the Cupola and the heroin accord—did not stand in isolation. Both were necessary for the orderly running of a permanent narcotics pipeline. Unless some measure of peaceful cooperation existed at each end of the pipeline, the entire enterprise could collapse through rivalry and jealousy.

Such divisive emotions, however, emerged almost instantly.

Gaetano Badalamenti, a dour and brooding mafioso in Sicily, quickly recognized that the U.S. marketplace would provide unparalleled profits for the Sicilian families willing to sell heroin to the Americans. He capitalized on his own contacts in America and sought a little added action. Through family—a cousin was a member of New York's Profaci Family, later to become the Colombo Family, and other relatives lived in Canada—and through contacts he made during an ill-fated 1946 trip to the United States that resulted in his deportation to Italy in 1950, Badalamenti directed Tomasso Buscetta to head to North America. Rather than deal strictly through the Bonanno Family receivers, Buscetta was instructed to create a parallel pipeline from Sicily to Montreal, Windsor and Toronto and, from there, into the United States. Both networks would pass through Canada en route to America.

Rivalries among the Five Families were well known in Sicily, mostly through Bonanno relatives who made up a Mafia group in Sicily's Castellemare del Golfo, a fishing village midway between Palermo and Trapani. Joe Bonanno was seen in America as an arrogant man who considered himself an aristocrat, an offspring of Mafia royalty, which was an offensive contrast to the false humility preferred by many old-school mafiosi.

Bonanno's inflated sense of self was not pure delusion. He had come from good Mafia stock and was an educated, cosmopolitan man who had certainly made something of himself in his adopted homeland. By comparison, the other American leaders had little family Mafia history and only modest strategic visions for the future. The contrast was never lost on Bonanno and it fed his egoist's feelings of grandeur, which grated on and frustrated the other bosses. Bonanno caused constant strife with the other American bosses, including his cousin Stefano Magaddino, who ran the Buffalo Mafia. Magaddino had his own outpost in Canada, firmly rooted in Hamilton, a tough steel town on Ontario's Great Lakes waterfront. Magaddino's man in Canada was Johnny "Pops" Papalia, who also earned the nickname "The Enforcer." Papalia himself would grab a piece of the French Connection in the late 1950s, a move that would land him in an American prison, charged alongside his partners: Joe Valachi, the future Mafia turncoat; Alberto Agueci, a Sicilian mafioso from Trapani who had moved to Toronto; and Vinnie Mauro, a Greenwich Village soldier in the Genovese Family. Clearly, while the Sicilian Men of Honor were struggling to ensure that their clans had a place in the heroin trade, so too were the other American Mafia families.

Bonanno and Galante retained a key card to play, however, in their bid to be central figures in the emerging transatlantic heroin business: they had a competent crew in Montreal ready to handle importation, and a large organization in New York ready to aid in distribution.

NEW YORK, 1960

With Montreal in pocket and the Sicilian–American alliance in place, it was not long before Galante's efforts started paying him dividends. His Montreal colleagues were proving to be prodigious smugglers and his extensive network in New York was off-loading vast amounts of heroin to a populace with a voracious appetite for the drug. As quickly as the tap had been turned on, however, its flow was restricted, temporarily, by federal agents.

On May 3, 1960, the U.S. Attorney General for the Southern District of New York announced a sweeping indictment against 29 men for a massive conspiracy to import large amounts of heroin into the United States from Canada. Among them was Carmine Galante.

"The conspiracy consisted of a group of Canadians, headed by Guiseppe 'Pep' Cotroni, who handled the exportation of the drugs from Canada. Couriers brought the narcotics across the Canadian–United States border and into the New York metropolitan area," court documents say. In New York, distribution centers had been established where the high-grade heroin was received, unpacked, diluted and repackaged for further sale.

"Overall responsibility for the continuing operation rested in its 'chief executive,' the appellant Carmine Galante," a New York judge ruled. During the trial, the court heard riveting testimony from a cooperating government witness. Edward Smith, until then a little-known criminal, described meetings with Galante, Vic, Pep and Frank

Cotroni, and others, as far back as 1957. In a Montreal apartment Galante picked up a suitcase, put it on the coffee table and opened it, Smith said, describing an early encounter with the group. Inside were rows of clear plastic bags containing white powder. Smith's partner counted the bags, shut the case and left with Smith for a drive south to New York City, where they took the suitcase to Frank's Bar & Grill in Brooklyn. From there, colleagues would head out every week on a regular delivery route that took them to bars and nightclubs throughout the city.

For more than three years, the U.S. Bureau of Narcotics and Dangerous Drugs, working with city police and the Royal Canadian Mounted Police (RCMP) in Canada, burrowed their way into the conspiracy. Smith started to secretly cooperate in 1959 and introduced an undercover agent, Patrick Biase, into the group posing as a major buyer. The greedy Canadian mafiosi quickly agreed to sell him large quantities of drugs, despite it being in direct competition with their partners in Brooklyn. In June, Pep Cotroni and René "Bob" Robert, his driver and drug partner, were arrested by Canadian police in what was at that point the largest drug case in the country's history. Pep Cotroni pleaded guilty a few days into his trial and accepted a 10-year prison sentence.

The case against Galante in New York would not be tied up so neatly. The trial against the defendants arrested in the United States began on November 21, 1960, after several delays, including a postponement when one of the defendants fled the night before the trial was scheduled to begin. For six months it staggered along, sagging under the weight of "every conceivable type of obstruction and interruption," an appeal court judge would later rule. In May, on the eve of summations to the jury, the trial was halted after the jury foreman suffered a broken back. The judge could not help but note that the mysterious injury was the result of an unexplained fall down a flight of stairs in an abandoned building in the middle of the night. With the pool of alternate jurors already expended, a mistrial was declared.

A retrial got under way on April 2, 1962. It, too, was a mess from the start, reaching "violent and bizarre extremes," a judge noted. The jury had not even been selected when Salvatore Panico, one of Galante's co-accused, started shouting abuse. Panico would later climb into the jury box and walk from one end to the other, pushing the jurors in the front row and screaming angry slurs at them and the judge. Anthony Mirra, who decades later would be killed by his own kin for unwittingly introducing an FBI agent into the Bonanno organization, was also charged. He took the stand in his own defence and, under a testy cross-examination, picked up his witness chair and hurled it at the prosecutor who was grilling him. It narrowly missed the prosecutor and shattered against the jury box. Some of the defendants sat through the remainder of the trial shackled and gagged; 11 were later convicted of contempt of court.

"More abhorrent conduct in a federal court and before a federal judge would be difficult to conceive," the appeal court judges noted. The gangsters' disruptive efforts were in vain. Galante was sentenced to 20 years in prison.

While Galante had other things on his mind, what most concerned Vic Cotroni was that the removal of Galante from the streets stripped the Montreal boss of his conduit into New York.

MONTREAL, 1960s

Against the backdrop of international underworld intrigue, the city of Montreal continued to grow and to bleed as the newly reorganized Mafia tightened its stranglehold. An emerging presence in the milieu was a man who shared Joe Bonanno's belief in the power of Sicilian stock: Nick Rizzuto.

Considered a soldier in what police were then calling the "Montreal Bonanno Faction," Nick had quickly become something of a lightning rod, attracting around him a tough, tight crew of transplanted Sicilian gangsters. Nick was a good earner, a contributor who was ambitious and strong, respectful and aggressive—depending on what the circumstances required. Within the Sicilian wing, led by Luigi Greco, Nick carried himself a noticeable cut above the rabble, drawing on his connections to his father-in-law, Antonio Manno, and his network of Agrigento clans to further his criminal interests. In these early years, Nick formed his Mafia organization in Montreal with support from his extended family, such as Calogero Renda, his uncle who had arrived in America in 1925 alongside Nick's father, and Domenico Manno, Nick's brother-in-law. The Sixth Family was starting to make its mark.

As Nick's criminal organization grew, so, too, did his personal family. At the time of the Palermo meetings, Vito Rizzuto, Nick's only son, had not yet turned 11, his daughter, Maria, was a year younger. The Rizzuto children were growing up in Montreal's Villeray district and in Saint-Léonard, two largely Italian neighborhoods. Vito was plodding his way through school in Montreal and would eventually complete Grade 9 at St. Pius X High School, an English-language Catholic school. He was also being tutored in what would become his true calling. Young Vito was immersed in outlaw culture from the day he was born and, as he grew, he assimilated the accepted and expected behavior of his family. Everywhere Vito looked, on both sides of the family, he encountered outlaw role models (just as his own children would a generation later). Vito was carefully groomed in the old ways, while having in his grasp all the latitude and promise of the changing times.

At every turn, he was taught the importance of staying close to his kin.

CHAPTER 6

BOUCHERVILLE, QUEBEC, MAY 16, 1968

The fire alarm sounded a little after 1 a.m. at the Centre d'Achat Place-la-Seigneurie, a small shopping mall in Boucherville, a suburb of Montreal on the south shore of the St. Lawrence River.

The clamor roused members of the town's fire department, who quickly arrived in force; 23 firefighters would respond that night, hauling out the six hoses they would need to attack the flames that were thickest around the Renda Barber Shop, which seemed to be the center of the blaze. The first contingent of firefighters to arrive, however, were confronted by an even more alarming sight: two men burst through the shop's back door and ran frantically into a field, their clothes ablaze. As the startled firefighters watched, the men dropped to the ground and started rolling in the dirt to extinguish the flames. The firemen rushed to help, but before they could reach them, one of the men jumped to his feet and dashed away in the other direction. The firemen watched as he disappeared into the night, his clothes still smoldering. The other man, apparently in too much pain to keep running, remained on the ground, where firefighters and, soon after, the police found him.

The young man was rushed to hospital where he was treated for serious burns. Police would later identify him as Paolo Renda, 28, of Montreal, owner of the barbershop and known to the other businessmen at the shopping center as a simple barber. Detectives suspected that the mystery man who had fled would be in similar need of medical care, and police officers started visiting nearby hospitals. Hours later, they found a man who had arrived at Montreal's Santa Cabrini Hospital seeking treatment for severe burns. He fit perfectly the description given to them by the firefighters.

The man identified himself to police as Vito Rizzuto.

Then 22 years old, Vito at first dismissed questions from suspicious investigators by saying he had suffered the burns when the gas tank of his car exploded that night. That explained both the damage to his skin and the unmistakable smell of gasoline, of which he reeked. After police learned that Renda was Vito's brother-in-law, the weak alibi soon crumbled and, under questioning, Vito eventually admitted that, yes, he had in fact been at the Renda Barber Shop in Boucherville that night. But he insisted he had absolutely nothing to do with starting the fire. Detectives remained dubious.

By morning, back at the fire scene, the last of the flames had been extinguished. The damage was significant. Renda's Barber Shop was completely destroyed. A neighboring business was largely consumed by the flames and 16 other businesses were damaged by either the smoke or the water from the fire hoses. Damage was calculated at $115,000, a large sum by 1968 standards. Fire investigators quickly determined that the blaze had been deliberately set. They found that the two men had been pouring gasoline on to the floor of the barbershop with the intention of setting it ablaze. While they were pouring, however, the gas ignited prematurely, sending a fireball roaring through the shop and enveloping Vito and Renda. This was not the first time the business had been set on fire; the previous December, a smaller fire was doused before it could destroy the premises.

Police slapped both Vito and Renda with serious criminal charges. More than three years elapsed before the case went to court. Judge Georges Sylvestre heard how the fire at Renda's Barber Shop had been set by the two men in a bid to fraudulently collect an insurance claim. Renda apparently was ready for a change of career.

He was well-positioned for a move into crime. A native of Cattolica Eraclea, Paolo Renda is the son of Calogero Renda, the man who had made the ill-fated moved to America in 1925 before returning to Sicily to marry into the Manno family. Paolo, who immigrated to Montreal in October, 1958, later solidified his Sixth Family standing by winning the hand of Maria Rizzuto, who was Nick's only daughter and Vito's younger sister.

Had the gasoline in Renda's barbershop not ignited before the men could flee, they might well have gotten away with it. As it was, they were found guilty of a raft of charges: arson, criminal conspiracy, two counts of fraudulently burning property and nine counts of being negligent with fire. Renda, the business owner and beneficiary of the insurance policy, was found to be more culpable than Vito, who was seen as having been brought into the scheme merely to help out Renda. A dutiful member of the Sixth Family, Renda did not protest that view.

On January 29, 1972, Vito was sentenced to two years in prison for the arson and conspiracy charge and nine months on each of the other counts, to be served concurrently. Renda was handed four years for arson and conspiracy and 18 months on each additional charge, also to be served concurrently. For Renda, it was his first—and only—criminal conviction. Vito, however, had one previous—tiny—stain on his record, a conviction for disturbing the peace in the summer of 1965 when he was the tender age of 19. He had been fined $25 and spent eight days in jail.

It was a decidedly inauspicious start for the future head of the Sixth Family.

———

By the time young Vito was playing with matches, his father, Nick, had built a formidable criminal coterie in Montreal. He had a loyal core that, although officially pledged to protect and contribute to the Bonanno organization, maintained a distinct loyalty to their own flesh and blood. Along with marriage vows and blood ties, the growth of the Rizzuto clan into the organization that is the Sixth Family can most suitably be described in business terms, in that they doggedly adhered to a winning strategy of carefully selected mergers and acquisitions. As with most aggressive corporations, what they sought first was a mutually agreeable assimilation of a smaller corporate entity that allowed for profit for all parties. If that failed, a hostile takeover was almost inevitable.

The first significant merger in Canada for the Rizzutos came in the 1960s when Nick forged a bond with the Caruana–Cuntrera family, a clan from the Sicilian town of Siculiana, just a winding 10-mile drive from Cattolica Eraclea. For decades, back in the Mafia triangle of Agrigento, the clans had been friendly, interrelated, and occasionally comrades-in-arms. When Nick's father first arrived in the New World in 1925, he arrived with two men from Cattolica Eraclea and three men from Siculiana; most, if not all, of the men were related in some way. One, Vincenzo Marino, was married to a Caruana, and another, Giuseppe Sciortino, was related to Calogero Renda, who in turn was related to Nick. In Canada, these bonds were strengthened. Fusing the Rizzutos with the Caruana–Cuntreras was a strategic alliance of immense value to both parties, who were keenly interested in the same sorts of commodities. The merger gave Nick a significant boost, increasing his international presence and his access to drugs and money-laundering services. The Caruana and Cuntrera families, who formed a single criminal organization, also had considerable influence within the Sicilian faction in Montreal. On the flip side, having the Rizzutos as partners offered the Caruanas a form of physical protection and a far more robust presence on the streets of Montreal as they concentrated on matters abroad. While the Caruanas boosted the Rizzutos' contacts in Europe and South America, the Rizzutos gave the Caruanas direct contact with New York.

"When the Caruanas and Cuntreras moved to Montreal in the mid-1960s, they became affiliated with Nicolò Rizzuto and his son Vito Rizzuto. They began to work together in drug trafficking activities," an FBI report says.

The internal structure of the Sixth Family—by itself—was starting to mimic the vast transatlantic structure that had taken more than two dozen mafiosi from two countries four days of heated discussions at the Grand Hôtel et des Palmes to achieve. Next came another merger and acquisition of a distinctly non-hostile nature.

MONTREAL AND TORONTO, NOVEMBER 1966

Late in the day on November 28, 1966, two Montreal police constables asked three men who were sitting in a car parked on a side street to slowly get out of their vehicle. The officers' concern was palpable, as the men, despite their neat short hair, suit jackets and expensive clothing, still looked like tough customers and, far more alarming, three .32-caliber handguns were clearly visible on the car seats. The men were arrested and additional police officers soon arrived, as did a second car full of civilians who were likewise asked to get out of their vehicle. When a starter pistol was found under the seat of their car, the four new arrivals were also arrested.

At a Montreal police station, the seven men stood about impatiently, smoking cigars and asking that the proceedings be moved along more quickly. Police were taking their time, however, because of the unusual cast of characters before them and the many questions they had for them. Most of the officers were personally familiar with only one man in the group: Luigi Greco, whom they knew as a local hoodlum whose fortunes in the underworld had been soaring of late. The remaining men were all American. Wearing a casual and slightly

wrinkled dress shirt, unbuttoned at the neck, and black pants, Bill
Bonanno towered over Greco. With them were Vito DeFilippo and his
son, Patrick DeFilippo. Patrick, who became known to fellow gangsters
as "Patty from the Bronx," would go on, more than 30 years later, to orchestrate the execution of one of the key members of the Sixth Family,
a rare attack on the clan. Peter Magaddino, of Brooklyn, Joe Bonanno's
cousin and close ally, was also identified by police. He wore a suit almost identical to Patty DeFilippo's but filled it out considerably more,
in all the wrong places. Also identified by police were Carlo "Buddy"
Simaro, of New Jersey, and Peter Notaro, of New York, both Bonanno
bodyguards. (Notaro later joined Joe Bonanno when he was deposed
and went into exile in Arizona.) Bill Bonanno recently said he came to
Canada with the soldiers who remained closest to his father, Joseph,
during an acrimonious split within the organization in New York.

"They were loyal to us. Patty was there with his father, Vito
DeFilippo. Vito DeFilippo was one of our closest confidants. He was
very loyal to us," said Bonanno.

Had the approach by the constables been accidental, the officers
would likely have been stunned to find Bill Bonanno and his cronies
in Montreal. It was, however, part of an extensive police surveillance
operation. Throughout the day, investigators had secretly watched as
the men met with Vic Cotroni, Paolo Violi, who was Cotroni's favored
young gangster in Montreal, and Giacomo Luppino. Luppino was an
old boss of the 'Ndrangheta, the Mafia organization originally formed
in Calabria, the southern part of mainland Italy, who had moved to
Hamilton, Ontario, and had recently become Violi's father-in-law.
Police had seen Bill Bonanno, with Notaro and Cotroni, in a shopping
plaza making dozens of telephone calls, one after another, from a public pay phone. In police custody, however, they were far less talkative.
Grilled by detectives about drugs and illegal immigrant smuggling,
gambling and extortion, the mobsters feigned ignorance of it all. They
had only come to Canada, they insisted, to attend a wedding.

In a way, they were not lying. It was a wedding that had drawn
them across the border and it was their own paranoia and precarious
situation in New York that had prompted the Bonanno men to so heavily arm themselves. But in the world of the Mafia, social engagements
and criminal business blur into one impenetrable mix.

Two days earlier, on November 26, 1966, a half-day's drive to the west of Montreal, Vito Rizzuto was married in an elegant ceremony in Toronto. It was part of a thoughtful reorganization of Vito's life that suggests he was starting to take his role in the Sixth Family more seriously. This was two years before his botched arson at the barbershop but two months after he obtained his Canadian citizenship; on September 27, 1966, he had been granted government certificate #947663, allowing him all the considerable privileges of citizenship in his adopted homeland.

In accordance with Sicilian tradition, the groom, his family, friends and supporters traveled to the hometown of his bride and her family, in this case Toronto, for the wedding ceremony and reception. Those friends and supporters apparently included the six-man Bonanno contingent from New York.

The day before leaving for Toronto for their wedding, however, Vito and his bride-to-be signed a prenuptial marriage contract in Quebec, witnessed and notarized by Gaétan Reid, stipulating that each spouse remains the exclusive owner of his or her property, administers that property alone and assumes responsibility for their own debts. Should their marriage fail, each retains their own property, providing they can prove ownership, the contract states.

Vito's bride was Giovanna Cammalleri, his first cousin once removed, on his mother's side. The Cammalleri family had made their home in Toronto after leaving Cattolica Eraclea. The Cammalleri family, like Vito's, has a long history of outlaw behavior and Mafia involvement, police say. Officers have tracked at least two generations of Cammalleri family members. Along with others, they formed what police dubbed the "Toronto Sicilian Group," a Mafia organization suspected by police of running illegal gambling, extortion and drugs. One RCMP report notes the group's ties in New York, Detroit and Montreal.

The newlyweds were young. Vito, who had grown into a tall, lanky man just shy of 6-foot-1 with brown eyes and hair so dark it appeared to be black, was 20; Giovanna, who was four inches shorter than Vito and slim, with chestnut hair, was just 18.

Organized-crime investigators often refer to Vito's nuptials as a "marriage of convenience," suggesting the sanctity of his vows and love for his bride are secondary to his family's larger interests. But who is to say it was not both love and good sense? Certainly, photographs of the couple show them engaging each other and seemingly happy in each other's company. Nonetheless, good sense it was, since it built an important bridge between the Cammalleri's Toronto base and the Rizzutos in Montreal. The two most populous cities in Canada were crucial hubs for the country's economic activities and its illicit enterprises. What is more, Vito's wife was a bright and lively woman with a good head for numbers and finance, who was often ready with investment advice for both sides of her family.

One facet of Vito's wedding that was almost pure diplomacy, however, was the selection of the men he asked to stand with him on this important day. There was Frank Dasti, then 52, one of the most respected figures in Montreal's underworld. He was one of its oldest active members, but was far from preparing for retirement. (A few years after Vito's wedding, Dasti would step up his efforts to move narcotics through Canada into the United States, only to be caught in 1973 and sentenced to 20 years in a U.S. prison. He has since died.) Also standing up for Vito was Angelo Sauro, 30 at the time, a Montrealer whose lengthy criminal record was peppered with minor convictions through every decade, from the 1950s to his most recent in late 2002. Orlando Veri, a friend of Vito's, was the youngest, at 23, and the least involved in criminal activities, although he, too, would later be convicted for a drug conspiracy. Most strikingly, Paolo Violi, then 34 and a Calabrian mobster being groomed for Mafia success by Vic Cotroni, was also included in the wedding party, according to a Montreal police report.

That Vito would invite Violi to assist in his wedding is a clear sign that, although there were tensions between the Cotroni–Violi faction and the Greco–Rizzuto faction, the relationships had not yet so seriously deteriorated that they could not at least pretend to be civil and respectful to each other. However, the fact that Bill Bonanno would meet separately with both Montreal factions during his visit suggests the Montreal mobsters were not exactly a model of solidarity. Such suppressed feelings of distrust would hardly have been noticed by Bonanno, for he was in the midst of the "Banana Wars," a far more open dispute that had officially split his father's family in two. While Bonanno factions were shooting it out on the streets of New York, the more intimate interactions between the Bonanno loyalists and both the Sicilian and Calabrian sides of the Montreal group suggested that Joseph Bonanno retained the support of his Canadian wing, the outpost he had created, while most of his New York family thundered away from him. Bill Bonanno does not dispute he may have been at Vito's wedding on his ill-fated trip north.

"It could have been," he said. "But that's not why we came up. It was about what was happening in New York. New York was in turmoil in my world. We needed to meet with our friends and allies in Canada."

The "Banana Wars" almost had seismic consequences for the Mafia in Canada. During a conversation on June 10, 1965, Simone "Sam the Plumber" DeCavalcante, the boss of a small New Jersey Mafia family, was discussing the problems in the Bonanno organization with Joseph "Joe Bayonne" Zicarelli, a Bonanno captain who lived in New Jersey. DeCavalcante had been acting as something of a go-between for Bonanno loyalists and the Mafia's Commission. He confided to Zicarelli that Carlo Gambino, the boss of the Gambino Family at the time, had told him of the problems the Commission had with Joe Bonanno. Recording the chat at the boss's plumbing business was a secret FBI listening device known as microphone NK 2461-C. After ousting Joe Bonanno as the boss of the family and replacing him with Gaspar DiGregorio, Gambino said the Commission almost went further. One form of punishment the Commission considered, DeCavalcante revealed, was redistributing Bonanno's territory.

"You know, they were gonna give the guys in Canada away to Buffalo," DeCavalcante said, referring to a proposed transfer of the Bonanno's Montreal group to Buffalo's Magaddino Family. Had the plan gone forward, it would have had far deeper ramifications for organized crime in North America than anyone, except perhaps for the mischievous Stefano Magaddino, probably realized. It would have put the important drug hub of Montreal under the control of Magaddino, who already held sway over Southern Ontario, including Toronto. Had Montreal and Toronto been joined into a single mob territory so early in the game, it could well have made Magaddino's boss in Canada, Johnny "Pops" Papalia, one of the richest and most important gangsters on the continent. In the end, Montreal remained Bonanno territory, but Joe Bonanno would lose his struggle to retain control of the Mafia organization that bears his name to this day. He left New York and retired to Tucson, Arizona, where he died of heart failure in 2002 at the age of 97. Almost to his end, the exiled boss kept his ties to his Canadian mob friends. Late in his life, FBI agents tracked him to hundreds of telephone calls made from public pay phones in Tucson into the Montreal area code.

Not many Mafia bosses embroiled in such harsh disputes get the luxury of a long life and non-violent death. By contrast, the cordiality between Vito Rizzuto and Paolo Violi at Vito's wedding would acutely wane and their dispute would not have such an idyllic ending.

CHAPTER 7

MONTREAL, 1969

Mauro Marchettini was an Italian immigrant who brought with him to Canada modest entrepreneurial dreams. He put his plans into action in 1969 when he opened a small pool hall in Montreal's Saint-Léonard neighborhood. He signed the papers to take control of a vacant store-front location on Jean-Talon Street East, just east of Lacordaire Street, and sank his life savings into buying the needed equipment and redecorating the small facility. What he failed to account for in his business plan, however, was that his pool hall was a mere 400 feet away from the Reggio Bar at 5880 Jean-Talon East, an address known to many in Montreal as the headquarters for Paolo Violi, who had become the right-hand man of the city's Mafia boss, Vic Cotroni.

For Marchettini, it was a disastrous oversight. Emissaries sent by Violi soon paid him a visit.

"I was told I could open a business of this kind but not on Lacordaire Street, not on Jean-Talon Street, east of Lacordaire," Marchettini said. He was told that if he chose another spot, Violi would help him to secure it. However, Marchettini seemed set on his little spot on Jean-Talon. The nature of the entreaties then changed. Violi sent his younger brother, Francesco, to take Marchettini for a ride, during which the businessman was savagely beaten with an oddly memorable weapon, a four-foot-long wooden paddle most restaurateurs use only to make ice cream. With his body bruised and battered, a tooth snapped in two and both eyes blackened, Marchettini finally understood; he could not maintain his pool hall in Violi's neighborhood without Violi's permission.

It was a sad scene, variations of which were repeated for decades throughout Montreal's Italian community. Small businessmen and independent contractors, typically Italian, were bullied and beaten by Violi and his henchmen. The battered pool hall owner was one of hundreds who had learned first-hand the efficiency, reach and persuasive power of Paolo Violi over portions of Saint-Léonard, an area he controlled with uncommon thoroughness and viciousness.

For several years, Violi had held a favored status in the Montreal mob, one bestowed upon him by Cotroni, who had, over the years, moved to the pinnacle of the city's underworld, while Luigi Greco, his Sicilian counterpart, had slipped into a secondary position, something akin to underboss, while he concentrated on heroin deals. With Cotroni's considerable backing, Violi's standing in Montreal continued to rise to the point where, in 1975, an underworld figure who was compelled to give testimony before a government commission spoke of Violi's position with shocking clarity.

"My Lord, his name, it's like a god ... everyone is afraid of him. Violi, he's not one man—he's a thousand men," he said.

Not everyone in Montreal would capitulate so easily to Violi's will. One man in particular did not recognize his authority, succumb to the fear of Violi's name nor bow to the power of his "thousand men."

Nick Rizzuto, the Sixth Family patriarch, would never accept Violi's position of supremacy. If Violi was "like a god," then Nick Rizzuto was a heretic. Their distrust and dislike of each other caused alarm from the moment Cotroni signaled that Violi was his right-hand man—even when Luigi Greco was still there to maintain some semblance of a Sicilian–Calabrian balance. While problems between Cotroni and Greco were noticeable to all who looked for such things, Greco, at least, was still willing to go along with the game. He was so thoroughly acclimatized to the American way of doing things that he had little stomach for an out-and-out fight with the boss. He bowed low to New York, to the Bonannos and, when it was required, to Cotroni. Any direct showdown would have to come from someone who had not been a party to the *pax Mafia* created by Carmine Galante and Joe Bonanno. That accord finally crumbled, but not through gunfire. It was broken by a chemical fire.

MONTREAL, DECEMBER 1972

Luigi Greco was a short and stocky man with a brooding face that betrayed a life spent on the wrong side of civility. He had dark brown, piercing eyes, a nose bent from a nasty break and a noticeable scar on his forehead. Born on September 19, 1913, he was still a teenager when he was convicted of assault; at the age of 23, he was sentenced to 11 years in prison for armed robbery. His time in prison only solidified his criminal interests, and in 1954 he was leading a squad of strong-arm goons who marched to Carmine Galante's orders.

"Luigi Greco—we called him Louie—was quite a character. He was an old-timer. He was loyal and tough. Once he made up his mind on something you couldn't move him on it," said Bill Bonanno. "He had a right hand that you wouldn't believe. He was out riding a horse one day and it threw him. He fell hard to the ground but he pulled himself back up, dusted himself off, straightened his shirt. He walked up to the horse, looked the horse in the eye and said: 'How dare you do that to me.' And he punched the horse in the head—knocked it to its knees."

Greco's business holdings had grown alongside his stature in Montreal's underworld. He owned several nightclubs and restaurants, including joint ownership of the Bonfire restaurant with Galante. He also controlled a pizzeria that was officially owned by other family members. By the late 1960s, flush with heroin profits, he had smoothed over part of his rough image and was dressing sharper, sometimes even strutting about with a swank silver-tipped cane.

The competition between Greco, a Sicilian, and Cotroni, a Calabrian, took a toll on their relationship, even after Joseph Bonanno settled their positions of authority. They were both strong-willed men, with Cotroni relying more on his brains, and Greco on his brawn. Police had become increasingly interested in Greco's extensive travel: he routinely visited Detroit, Chicago and New York, trips that suspiciously followed travel to Mexico and France. Greco even accompanied Bill Bonanno on trips throughout Europe in the 1960s. Greco's career, however, was tripped up early by his heroin dealings for Galante and, as a result, much of his international travel came to an abrupt end in 1962 when he was indicted on a narcotics charge in the United States. Although he remained safe in Canada, the indictment gave him "fugitive" status in America, clipping his wings considerably. Accordingly, his value to New York slipped substantially and, soon after, so did his standing in Montreal. At every turn, Greco had been outmaneuvered by Cotroni, who easily assumed leadership of the Montreal organization. This did not sit well with the Rizzutos, who maintained that a Sicilian should be at the top. Nick was not shy about expressing that opinion.

Cracks in the Sicilian–Calabrian alliance were already noticeable by the spring of 1967, with news of the "disharmony" between Greco and Cotroni even making it on to the front page of *The New York Times* that year. Although Greco had once had the upper hand in Montreal,

Cotroni had eclipsed him to the point where a senior Canadian police officer was quoted in the *Times* as saying: "Greco is only a door opener for Vic Cotroni." Still, even opening doors for Cotroni, in those years, made one a master of the Montreal underworld.

Greco's businesses, appreciable underworld position and growing interest in the heroin trade did not mean he put himself above getting his hands dirty when it came to tending to his family's Montreal restaurant. This is rarely a bad trait, but for Greco it brought unexpected disaster.

On a Sunday evening, December 3, 1972, he arrived at Gina's Pizzeria, an outlet near the Jarry Park police detachment, to the south of Saint-Léonard. Greco and his brother, Antonio, were renovating the establishment. That evening, contractors were to lay new ceramic tiles over the worn asphalt floor. Greco first asked the workers to help him clear the furniture from the area to be tiled and then, while the contractors prepared to lay the new floor, Greco and his brother set about scrubbing the old one. For this Greco chose a mop dipped in kerosene to be used as a solvent and a metal scraper to remove the stuck-on gum and accumulated filth. It proved an unstable combination. The ensuing explosion and flash fire was brief but devastating. Greco was horribly burned and, four days later, died in Sacré-Coeur Hospital. Such an unusual death for someone in Greco's line of work naturally led to lingering suspicion, but an official probe of the fire declared it to be the result of a careless tangle with a volatile solvent rather than underworld intervention. The death of the boss of the Sicilian faction was a stunning shock to the underworld of Montreal, a sentiment reflected in his funeral, which was a large, old-style mob send-off.

The loss of Greco was deeply felt by his family, close friends and criminal allies, Nick Rizzuto among them. Despite any lingering sadness, however, Greco's death also presented an opportunity. Nick's crew had grown mightily in the almost two decades since his arrival in Canada. He had gathered together a diaspora of Sicilian expatriate mafiosi who had come to Montreal to reap gangland spoils. As a wave of immigration continued, the few who arrived with references from mafiosi known to the Sixth Family immediately gravitated toward the Rizzutos. The family found them work—both legitimate, to aid in their bid for residency and citizenship, and otherwise—as Nick expanded his criminal empire. In the landscape of Montreal's burgeoning underworld, Nick was now the obvious Sicilian candidate to replace

Greco. It was not vanity that led Nick and his supporters to think he was the rightful heir to Montreal's underworld, or at least to Greco's share of it. In addition to his increasing power and presence on the streets of Montreal, his family's merger through the marriage of his son, Vito, into the Cammalleri family of Toronto gave his organization a strong domestic presence and, more important, his alliance with the Caruana–Cuntrera clan had enhanced his position abroad.

"This Italian Sicilian Mafia family, with its international expertise in drug importation and money laundering, puts the once Cotroni-lieutenant Nicolò Rizzuto in a new position to lead the Sicilian faction on Canadian soil," notes a private RCMP briefing on the early days of the family.

Nick had also put his Sixth Family links to good use elsewhere in Canada and around the world. Hinting at his wide-ranging criminal interests and international activities, for instance, is a curious arrest in Paris on June 22, 1972. Nick, along with unnamed others, was found in the French capital with approximately $1 million in counterfeit U.S. currency, according to U.S. Drug Enforcement Administration files. The arrest appeared not to have impinged on him too much, as no conviction or period of incarceration in France can be found in his records. All of this suggested that Nick was a superior earner and a leading figure in Montreal, certainly worthy of being an underboss to Cotroni, in keeping with the Sicilian–Calabrian accord imposed by Galante. It was not to be.

Likely recognizing how deep the erosion was in his relationship with Luigi Greco in recent years, and the increasing push by the Rizzutos to open the city to their Sicilian drug-trafficking partners, Cotroni did not seem interested in bringing Nick closer to him; nor did he seem concerned with maintaining the delicate Sicilian–Calabrian balance. Instead of Nick—or any other Sicilian mobster—he chose Paolo Violi as his heir. Violi accepted both the position and Greco's illicit operations, which came with the post. Underworld sources said that all of Greco's mob assets were assigned by Cotroni to Violi: not only the soldiers in his crew but all outstanding debts owed to Greco and all of his on-going scams were put on record under Violi's name. It was a significant promotion for Violi, one that Nick and his kin did not much approve of. Many Sicilian gangsters felt slighted and insulted. For Nick Rizzuto, the stakes were much higher than the anticipated take from frightened businessmen and the gambling enterprises in Saint-Léonard.

In his long existence in the mob, Nick had hidden many things, but something he did not—or could not—hide was his feelings for Paolo Violi.

The sentiment was mutual, of course, with Violi and Cotroni frequently cataloging Nick Rizzuto's many sins when chatting privately with any influential underworld figure who would listen. Both Cotroni and Violi accused Nick of acting inappropriately. Cotroni was heard complaining that Nick was a "lone wolf" who was more interested in the private internal affairs of his Sixth Family kin than in contributing to the Montreal organization. Cotroni complained that Nick failed to show adequate respect for his administration, especially for Violi. The catalog of complaints continued: Nick lied about his intentions within the family; he bypassed the proper chain of authority; he acted on his own initiative without seeking or obtaining permission from the administration, even on important matters. Violi complained that Nick and his inner circle came and went without deigning to inform him, or anyone else outside their clique, what he was up to and whom he was working with. That, Violi said, made him dangerous.

Their complaints were not without merit. After the death of Greco, Nick did blatantly ignore Cotroni and Violi wherever and whenever he could. Nick showed his disdain for the administration by avoiding its gatherings altogether, making himself noticeably absent from family-related functions. Whenever Nick did cross paths with Violi, he failed to display the expected deference that Violi's position demanded—however forced or insincere it would have been for him to do so. There were plenty of underworld figures with grievances against Cotroni—and even more who disliked the bellicose Violi—but almost everyone managed to bite their tongue and go through the motions of accepting and respecting the position, if not the person. Nick was not so diplomatic.

Nick had complaints of his own. He objected to Violi interfering with his right to govern his own clan and he maintained that he had been personally insulted when Violi's thugs had stolen presents from a Cuntrera family wedding. The wedding-theft story could be true, as it was a well-known scam that Violi had concocted, stealing the thick envelopes filled with cash that were typically given as gifts at large Italian weddings. The complaint about the Cuntrera wedding theft even appears in files of the U.S. Drug Enforcement Administration.

Through it all, Nick was acting as if he were the boss of a completely separate organization. Which, of course, was precisely how Nick was beginning to see things.

"What is known is that there was a traditional rivalry between then-underboss Paolo Violi and Rizzuto," an FBI report says. "RCMP reports indicate that Rizzuto was a lieutenant in the Cotroni organization until he became disenchanted with the hierarchy of the group."

Despite the petty complaints and personal disregard between Nick and Violi, this was not the real meat of their disagreement. The core of their rivalry was not hubris or insult or being denied a promotion, or whether one was a Sicilian Man of Honor or the other a member of the Calabrian Honored Society. All of this helped to fuel the ensuing melee—and charge the emotions of supporters and detractors who were already hot and bothered even before Greco's death. This masked, largely to this day, the real impetus for the fight, which was the unfettered access to the drug markets of America. The Sixth Family needed to have Montreal as its transit point in the movement of heroin out of Europe and into the United States. With Sicilian mafiosi in Europe shipping the product, and Sicilian mafiosi set up in several New York enclaves to receive it, the key transit route through Montreal, Nick felt, needed likewise to be controlled by Sicilians. And he knew that whoever held the keys to Montreal would become wealthy, powerful and important on the world stage.

Unlike the businessmen and junior mobsters in Montreal, however, Nick Rizzuto was not a problem Violi could easily manage. A stickler when it came to traditional Mafia etiquette, Violi knew he could not simply have Nick killed. Nick, as both a made man in Sicily and a fellow Bonanno Mafia member, was officially immune to such a dire action unless Violi sought and received permission in accordance with Mafia rules. Obtaining such permission would not be a simple thing. Because of Nick's involvement in wider concerns—as an increasingly important link in the Sixth Family drug chain and a key part of the immense revenues associated with it—such a move would require permission from both New York and Sicily. Violi felt he was up for the challenge.

Rarely has a dispute between rival mafiosi been allowed to fester as long as it did with the Violi–Rizzuto feud, with so much effort expended in finding an amicable solution by mobsters on two continents. For seven years, senior mobsters from Italy and New York would make many trips to Montreal to listen to Violi and, separately, to Nick or his supporters, looking for common ground and a way to resolve the widening gulf between them. It represented a significant investment in trying to mediate an end to their feud. The seriousness with which the dispute was seen, the difficulty in finding a resolution and the involvement of such important players affirmed the tremendous value of both the city of Montreal and the men who controlled its underworld. It also suggests the power and respect that the Sicilian Mafia and the Calabrian 'Ndrangheta accorded each other in such matters, something that did not transfer so easily to the New World.

NEW YORK, EARLY 1970s

The Bonanno Family in New York City, as short-sighted as it seems, was comfortable with the evolution of leadership in the family's Montreal outpost. New York was probably too consumed with its own internal chaos to give much thought to the noises coming from its reliable money-maker to the north. As Violi was settling into his new, expanded role in Montreal, the New York end of the Bonanno Family was only just recovering from serious disarray. The longtime boss, Joseph Bonanno, had made so many enemies among rival Mafia families that in the mid-1960s the Commission had moved to depose him. A brief period of dissent and contested leadership followed, a tense time that sparked occasional shoot-outs. A quick succession of bosses were installed by the Commission but none lasted long in the job. Within a few years two of them had stepped down for health reasons, falling far short of the nearly 35 years that Joseph Bonanno had held the reins of power for.

By 1970, Natale "Joe Diamonds" Evola, a convicted heroin trafficker, had ascended the shaky Bonanno throne. Among Evola's inner circle was Philip "Rusty" Rastelli. Rastelli had a modest personal obligation to the Montreal mob—although probably not directly to Violi—because, like so many other Bonanno members who ran into trouble with the police, he had hidden in Canada while on the run from the law. Around 1961, Rastelli was on the lam in Montreal, protected and accommodated by the Montreal mobsters, until the heat died down.

It was not the first or the last time the New York mob looked to Canada to hide its fleeing felons. It is one of the fringe benefits of having family outposts abroad. Joe Valachi, an old-hand soldier in the Genovese Family who partnered with Canadian-based mobsters in the heroin trade—and would, just a few years later, become a seminal Mafia turncoat—slipped across the border into Canada in 1959 and hid out in Toronto. And in July 1964, Joe Bonanno himself arrived in Montreal. His stay was intended to be a semi-permanent relocation, an escape from the pressure and threats from the other New York crime bosses. Like Carmine Galante before him, he even applied to the Canadian government for permanent resident status, trying to pass himself off as an honest businessman interested in cheesemaking and dairy products. In support of his claim, he presented a letter from the owner of the Saputo cheese company of Montreal, which offered him a partnership in the company, with one-third of its shares. (Such an offer was startling. Had Bonanno secured his immigration status and a piece of the Saputo cheese and dairy empire, it would have been a lucrative move. Saputo & Sons has gone on to become an international corporate juggernaut. Saputo is one of the largest dairy and cheese producers in North America, with 45 plants and 8,500 employees in the United States, Canada and Argentina that generated revenues of $1.03 billion in the 2005 fiscal year. The company founder, Giuseppe Saputo, later said he was unaware of any mob connections of Joe Bonanno's at the time.)

Cotroni and Violi had built up substantial good will within the Bonanno hierarchy in New York, both institutionally and personally, through such ventures. They were connections both sides would remember and seek to profit from. A decade after Rastelli's return to New York from Canada, when he was named Bonanno underboss, Violi would not be shy in trying to cash in on the favor. Rastelli, likewise, reached out to Violi when he needed work done north of the U.S. border. In April 1971, soon after Evola and Rastelli's installation as the new Bonanno Family administration, Montreal police began intercepting telephone calls between Violi and Rastelli. On May 14, 1971, Rastelli called Violi directly, asking him to help "deal" with someone in Toronto who owed him a significant amount of money. On January 21, 1973, Joseph Napolitano, from Pointe-Claire, Quebec, met with Violi at the Reggio Bar and passed on a request from New York for him to find and return a recalcitrant debtor who had fled to Canada from New York, where he owed $30,000, some of it to Evola. Violi, not missing an opportunity to curry favor with the boss, promised he would handle the matter personally.

Violi helped New York where he could. Such requests were an affirmation of his authority in Montreal, and he basked in the recognition.

All the while, he used the contact to continually push his concerns over the growing impertinence of Nick Rizzuto. Violi showed he was as intent on countering Nick's challenge as Nick was on pressing it. A colossal showdown seemed inevitable. If the Rizzutos could triumph, it would be a crucial step in their personal and organizational history.

It would decide what the family was to be—a support player in an American Mafia group glued to its own narrow city turf, or a leading player in a global underworld enterprise. But first, they had to survive.

CHAPTER 8

CATANIA, SICILY, 1972

On the eastern edge of Sicily, hugging the Ionian coast, the island's second-largest city, Catania, bustles in the shadow of Mount Etna, the highest and most active volcano in Europe. Many visitors are drawn to the city for its baroque architecture, blackened by the volcanic dust, and ancient Roman relics, some of them encrusted in lava from Etna's periodic eruptions. For Paolo Violi, who was on something of a pilgrimage to his native country, Catania's antiquities held little interest. It was people he was interested in—or rather, one person. Before Violi indulged himself with a trip to his native Calabria, he had serious business to attend to in Sicily.

In Catania, a city close to the narrow straits that separate Sicily from Calabria, Violi had sought out Antonino Calderone, a mafioso who was the boss in the port city before he went on to become an informant. He granted Violi an audience, and the Montrealer inquired about other Men of Honor. Whether Violi was seeking to build new international enterprises of his own, to compete with those of his rival, Nick Rizzuto, or, as was later suggested by Calderone, trying to reconnect with Mafia traditions, the quest drew derision.

"Paolo Violi, the well-known Canadian mafioso and a native of Calabria, arrived in Catania," Calderone later recalled. "He came to my office for half an hour, enough time for us to have a cup of coffee together and for him to ask me if I knew any men of honor in Calabria. Violi was a native of Sinopoli, a small town in the province of Reggio Calabria, and he explained to me that he was the boss of a *decina* [in Canada]." (*Decina*, Italian for "ten," was a name for Mafia cells that were often divided into groups of 10 men. It is now more often used to denote any sub-group of mobsters within a family.)

Violi said his New York boss "didn't want to hear anything, he just wanted dollars from his *decina*," Calderone said. "Violi could do as he pleased ... but at the end of the year, Violi had to bring him cash," he added. "Paolo Violi didn't make a great impression on me. He was a braggart, a big, fat man who didn't seem to have much upstairs. In any case, he was going to Calabria because he thought there were 'men of honor' there. Things are different, in fact, in America. American 'men of honor' aren't just Sicilians, but even Calabrians and Neapolitans. It doesn't matter," the old don said. "The Calabrians would talk, talk, talk. They talked all the time. Not to others, of course, but among themselves. They would have endless arguments about their rules, especially in the presence of us [Sicilian] Men of Honor. They felt uneasy because they knew that in reality they were inferior to the Cosa Nostra [the Sicilian Mafia].

"We've always considered the Calabrians inferior, garbage. Not to mention the Neapolitans, who we've never trusted much." These were harsh words that spoke volumes about the contempt some Sicilian mafiosi felt for their Calabrian counterparts. It was certainly a view held by many in the Sixth Family, even while they built alliances and close ties with those Calabrians powerful enough to aid their cause or dangerous enough to threaten it. Calderone's thoughts on Violi would have mirrored—and perhaps even been tainted by—those held by friends of the Rizzutos. News could travel quickly through underground whispers and Calderone was not the only Sicilian Man of Honor Violi had met on his trip. In Agrigento, the heartland of the Rizzutos' Sicilian base, Violi met with Giuseppe Settecasi, a meeting he requested as a way to personally and directly make complaints about Nick Rizzuto. Violi was aware of the sway the old don had with the Sixth Family.

Settecasi was an imposing presence; taking a complaint to him might have given most people pause, but Violi seemed excited at the prospect, apparently reveling in the idea that it was a meeting of minds, a gathering of two great mafiosi. It is doubtful that Settecasi shared his enthusiasm.

Settecasi avoided colorful or embarrassing nicknames during his life in crime. As a sign of his success at balancing extensive underworld activity with his public persona, he was invariably called "Mr. Settecasi" in and around Agrigento. He was a gentle-looking figure, but looks can deceive. In his younger years, Settecasi was the epitome of the peasant mafioso: quiet in demeanor, thoughtful in action. His violence was legendary, although police had little success proving any of it. His name was whispered in talk of murders, extortion, political corruption, mysterious disappearances and cattle rustling. In several decades as a member of the Sicilian Mafia, Settecasi reached the rank of *capo-provincia*, or boss of the province. For those living in the original hometowns of the Sixth Family, there were few higher authorities.

Settecasi's business increasingly involved heroin. He appeared at meetings in Montreal, weddings in Toronto, conclaves in New York, underworld conferences in Palermo. Almost without exception, his contacts were fellow Sicilians of the expatriate Mafia—like the Rizzutos—who were stitching together a drug network across the Americas and across the Atlantic, regardless of conflict arising from established organized crime interests. Settecasi recognized the power of the American Mafia families in the U.S. and Canada on their home turf, but he had little use for them.

By his late fifties, Settecasi was considered a Mafia statesman. His position in Agrigento was secure. When his position in the Mafia of western Sicily was noted by a parliamentary commission, it was greeted with mock surprise by local officials, who protested that Settecasi was simply an elderly gentleman who spent his days with other retirees, playing cards and talking about the good old days. The denials persisted even after his murder, in 1981.

Despite the popular image, throughout the late 1960s and 1970s, Settecasi was very much consumed by criminal affairs, much of it on matters of policy and the settling of disagreements between the codes of the Sicilian Men of Honor, the 'Ndrangheta of Calabria and the American Mafia. The question of compatibility or equivalency between the old Italian criminal fraternities—a question put in acute context by Calderone, the old Catania boss—was a vexing one that was eroding once-cordial relationships. Such problems were arising exponentially in North America as the Sicilian traffickers, particularly members and associates of the Sixth Family, found themselves in conflict with existing organized crime groups. It was happening in all of the important drug transit points—in New York, Montreal and, to a lesser degree, South America. These were early days for such disputes and Nick Rizzuto and Paolo Violi were on the cutting edge of a dangerous trend that would repeat itself wherever the expatriate Mafia landed. Everyone should have been paying closer attention.

Paolo Violi's complaints about Nick Rizzuto were nothing new to Settecasi. A skilled diplomat who kept a poker face, he listened patiently to Violi and promised to come to Montreal to deal with the situation directly. His show of concern, and even a measure of sympathy, was certainly a charade. It is inconceivable that Settecasi would have considered siding with Violi against the Rizzutos. All evidence suggests that, behind the scenes, Settecasi was biding his time while putting on the expected show in a bid to accomodate the old codes.

While the Sixth Family in Montreal was struggling with the frustrating obstinacy of Violi, Settecasi was maneuvering to arrange a made-in-Agrigento heroin pipeline. Drug intelligence analysts have long documented Settecasi's interest in international drug trafficking at the highest levels: "Settecasi is said to have been one of the few Sicilian Mafia Men of Honor present at both Apalachin and Grand Hôtel et des Palmes in October and November 1957," a police report reads, referring to the two seminal "Mafia summits" during which the world's heroin networks were mapped out—the Palermo hotel meeting that went off without a hitch, and the disastrous follow-up meeting in Apalachin, in rural New York State. Canadian police believe Settecasi and other attendees fled into the woods when the gathering was uncovered by authorities. Police scooped up dozens of men that day who held rank in the American Mafia, but others are believed to have escaped. Among those noted by police was Pasquale Sciortino, from Cattolica Eraclea. Montreal was represented by Luigi Greco and Pep Cotroni, some police investigators believe. Despite repeated and largely speculative references to Settecasi and the Montreal mobsters being at the Apalachin meeting, it seems unlikely that these three would be among the lucky few who escaped without being caught and identified by U.S. authorities. It seems more likely that the Sicilians and Canadians met with American mafiosi involved in their budding heroin partnership in separate meetings in the lead-up to the Apalachin debacle.

Certainly there is an intriguing timing to an early notation U.S. authorities made on Nick Rizzuto: his first registered crossing into America. Just nine months before the infamous Apalachin Mafia meeting, Nick traveled by land into New York State on February 9, 1957, crossing the border from Canada at Champlain, less than an hour's drive south of Montreal. (The crossing apparently caused no alarm on either side of the border and, for a decade, the single record on it lay dormant in the voluminous U.S. border files. On May 10, 1967, the crossing record was retrieved and the file on Nick was restored into an active investigation file by U.S. law enforcement in St. Albans,

Vermont, another city near the border with Canada, about a 90-minute drive from Montreal.)

Violi's position as a leader within the New York Bonanno Family in the 1970s—and his status as an 'Ndranghetisti with strong family ties to powerful Calabrian criminal figures in North America and Italy—made negotiating a solution a delicate situation, even for someone with Settecasi's power and experience.

Settecasi did not much care for Calabrian gangsters, whether in Italy or in North America, but there had been a formal recognition of the codes of the Sicilian Mafia and Calabrian 'Ndrangheta, an acceptance that both were steeped in history, honor and mutual respect. To old Sicilian Men of Honor like Settecasi and Calderone, the Mafia of Calabria consisted largely of peasants who talked too much, were loose in whom they allowed to join and had no vision of the world outside their often tiny fiefdoms. Nonetheless, they were recognized as legitimate outlaws, part of the same *malavita*—the "bad life." Because of this, just as Violi was having difficulty getting permission to take care of Nick Rizzuto, Nick likewise needed to show more restraint toward Violi. So the problem, which would normally have been sorted out by a late-night assassination—by either party—required some adherence to procedure. Added to the mix was the fact that the Montreal *decina* was under the protection and guidance of the Bonanno Family—the most Sicilian of the American Five Families and the leading architect of the Mafia heroin summits of 1957. Except as a channel for receiving heroin, the American crime families meant little to hard-core Sicilian Mafia traditionalists. Already, several dozen Sicilian Men of Honor had made their way into the United States, often through Canada, in preparation for the planned heroin pipelines. The Sicilians might have disdain for the American mobsters, but their guns and manpower had to be acknowledged. It was a growing international problem, an internal strain on the world's foremost criminal groups.

While professing to be in search of a solution on Violi's behalf, as early as February 1973, Settecasi was in fact meeting in Rome with two powerful members of the Caruana clan: the up-and-coming Alfonso Caruana and Giuseppe Cuffaro, a money launderer who had moved to Montreal and helped forge the Caruana–Cuntrera clan's alliance with the Rizzutos. One of the issues discussed was Violi's leadership in Montreal and his increasingly aggressive behavior toward the Sicilian faction.

Tomasso Buscetta, the once-powerful Sicilian mafioso (later a star government informant), said that Violi did not approve of the heroin ventures the Sixth Family was putting through Montreal. It is debatable, though, whether it was opposition to drugs on moral or principled grounds—as it is often presented in popular accounts—or just resentment over the wealth his rivals were accumulating from it. Evidence that Violi himself was involved in drugs comes not only from the extensive involvement of the Cotroni family in major drug-smuggling operations under Violi's watch, but from evidence presented in an Italian court in 1979. Two U.S. drug investigators, working undercover in Italy as major narcotics buyers, had sought to purchase large quantities of cocaine and heroin from Saverio Mammoliti, a mafioso in Calabria. Mammoliti said any amount of cocaine was available, so long as he secured the consent of two other 'Ndrangheta bosses in neighboring territories; as for the heroin, he said he would have to contact Montreal and speak with "his friend Paolo Violi, a well-known Italo–American mafioso."

Settecasi promised Violi he would travel to Montreal to examine the situation personally. Before arriving, however, he apparently traveled to Venezuela and Brazil, touching base with all of the branches of the expatriate Sicilian Mafia that were aligning with the Sixth Family.

In spite of Settecasi's promise of a fair hearing for Violi, it is far more likely he was merely going through the motions of adjudication, satisfying the required protocol before Violi could, as a last resort, be eliminated. Settecasi's true motive seemed to be a firming up of the Sicilian clans in Canada, the United States and South America, an action in direct opposition to Violi's request.

But Violi's trip to Italy was not the only flank to his diplomatic offensive against Nick. He was keenly aware of the importance of bringing both Agrigento and New York to his side if he wished to triumph over the Sixth Family. He also likely recognized the futility of expecting Settecasi to turn on one of his own.

Early in 1972, within months of his visit to Sicily and Calabria, Violi traveled to New York and met personally with the Bonanno boss, Natale Evola. During meetings in Brooklyn and Manhattan, Violi spoke openly and disparagingly of Nick's inappropriate behavior. Like Settecasi, gangland disputes were not new to Evola, who had sat through his share of "sit-downs"—the face-to-face mediation sessions used to settle "beefs" between "wiseguys." Like Settecasi, Evola was prepared to settle the Montreal dilemma, a beef he seemed to understand as a simple matter of listening to both sides, then making a pronouncement that all would accept. Evola nonetheless needed more time; he had become boss during a period of great uncertainty for the family and he told Violi he needed first to put New York affairs in order.

With the internal feud turned over to outside forces, Montreal became the focus of intense underworld attention and intrigue.

CHAPTER 9

MONTREAL, MAY 1972

Agrigento's Giuseppe Settecasi was the first to respond to Paolo Violi's diplomatic entreaties, and he arrived in Montreal to aid in arbitration. Over several days in May 1972, Settecasi held high-level talks with Cotroni and Violi about their complaints. He brought with him a man well known in both Sicily and Montreal—Leonardo Caruana, a Sicilian-born mafioso who had come to Montreal from Agrigento in 1966 after the Italian courts issued a preventative custody order against him for Mafia association. Settecasi valued his input as a trusted man with deep and direct ties to Agrigento, who at the same time had an intimate familiarity with Montreal. Caruana's presence was a distraction for Violi; he knew well the strong ties the Caruana family maintained with the Rizzutos. One thing Violi could count on was that anything he said to Settecasi in front of Caruana would soon be repeated to Nick Rizzuto. On May 11, 13 and 21, 1972, Violi, Settecasi and Caruana spoke at length. At the May 21 meeting, at Violi's Reggio Bar, Cotroni joined them. Not long after, Settecasi and Caruana seem to have sought further counsel on the matter. As with many mob matters in Canada, that meant traveling west to Hamilton. The ostensible occasion for the Settecasi–Caruana visit was an important Mafia wedding of a Luppino daughter to the son of a Commisso, a powerful Calabrian 'Ndrangheta clan in Toronto. The visit did not go smoothly, however, as Caruana, who was in Canada illegally, was arrested at the City Motor Hotel in Hamilton and deported to Italy.

Far more meaningful meetings for Settecasi during his visits to Canada—and certainly the sessions were held in greater secrecy—were his discussions with several Sicilian Men of Honor: Guiseppe Bono, whose wedding would later be the focus of intense police attention; Giovanni Gambino, of the Sicilian Mafia clan that became known as the Cherry Hill Gambinos in New Jersey (not the same family of Gambinos that are one of the Five Families); and members of the

Caruana–Cuntrera clan. That these people would emerge years later as some of the world's most important drug traffickers suggests where their common interest lay.

These 1972 sessions in Montreal were not even known to have taken place until, some two decades later, an informant named Giuseppe Cuffaro was debriefed by Giovanni Falcone. Cuffaro, not the man of the same name who laundered money for Montreal mobsters, was arrested in 1988. He outlined for authorities the Sixth Family's bridge between Montreal and Venezuela, the activities of the expatriate Mafia on the island of Aruba and links to the Colombian cartels that were in the process of offering a "license" to the Sicilians to market their cocaine in Europe. Cuffaro, who ended up in the U.S. witness protection program, said much of the planning for the emerging heroin routes was done in Montreal with Settecasi present.

With these meetings revealing Settecasi's true objective, it was a surprise to no one when he offered no assistance to Violi.

———

By September 1972, Natale Evola had got his New York house in order sufficiently to send representatives north to listen to what Violi and Nick had to say about their quarrel. Evola chose Michael "Mikey Z" Zaffarano, a tall, heavy-set man, to kick off New York's arbitration efforts. Zaffarano was a senior mobster with a long history of dealing with disputes and internal mob hostilities. He'd had a front-row seat in a similarly acrimonious split in New York in the 1960s, during the ouster of Joseph Bonanno. Zaffarano survived that period of instability and indeed thrived, becoming a major earner for the family when he led the mob into the pornography business, first dominating distribution of "stag" films and directing the nationwide chain of Pussycat Cinema adult theaters. When porn went mainstream, with such films as *Debbie Does Dallas* and *Deep Throat*, he made a killing. (It also later killed him: on Valentine's Day, 1980, the FBI crashed into his New York office to arrest him on federal obscenity and racketeering charges; Zaffarano died of a heart attack, clutching a raunchy reel of film that agents believe he was trying to destroy.)

Despite Zaffarano's keen interest in pornography, Violi was more comfortable dealing with him than he was with Leonardo Caruana. Like Philip Rastelli, Zaffarano likely felt a modest personal debt to both Cotroni and Violi; the two Montrealers had gone to considerable trouble to hide Zaffarano's brother-in-law, Joseph Asaro, when he was on the lam for 13 years from American police. Asaro, a Bonanno soldier and a second-generation mobster (his father worked under Al Capone, Chicago's legendary mob boss), was hidden by Cotroni for years. He earned his keep by working in Cotroni-controlled nightclubs in Montreal. On June 21, 1966, his impressive run ended when police burst into a home in Repentigny, Quebec, and found Asaro sitting with Vic and Frank Cotroni. The location of the arrest was embarrassing for Vic Cotroni, as it was the home of his mistress. He offered police a $25,000 bribe to arrest him somewhere else to keep his presence secret from his wife. The offer was doubled when it was refused. Cotroni was then charged with bribery.

In Zaffarano, Violi felt he had regained the upper hand he'd lost when Settecasi chose Leonardo Caruana as his advisor. Zaffarano was but one of the New Yorkers weighing in on the matter. Over months, Nicolino Alfano, who was the Bonannos' *consigliere*, Nicholas "Nicky Glasses" Marangello, who would later become a Bonanno underboss, Nick Buttafuoco and Joseph Buccellato would each come to Montreal to try their hand at mediation. Violi used each meeting to press his two related requests—not only did he want Nick Rizzuto sanctioned for challenging his leadership, he wanted permission from New York to induct more members into the organization.

"Look, we need a couple [more] *picciotti*," he told Zaffarano during an early visit, using the old Calabrian term for what the Americans called soldiers. It appears Violi wanted to bolster his ranks in the brewing feud with Nick. Violi was growing frustrated. As other conversations revealed, he thought the Rizzuto side was being unfairly inflated with new, mobbed-up immigrants from Sicily who did not seem overly concerned about their status with Violi.

"Paolo, we can't do nothing for the time being. Make do with what you got for right now, later we'll talk about it again," was Zaffarano's reply. Violi next moved on to his more immediate concern, his troubles with Nick.

"He goes from one thing to the other—here and there—and says nothing to nobody. He does things and nobody knows nothing," Violi complained of his rival.

"If things are really like that, everyone's safety, even ours ..." came Zaffarano's unfinished reply, likely accompanied by a concerned shrug. "So, if he's pigheaded, he don't wanna change, okay, when the others get here, Angelo and Nicolino, they're going to talk to Vincent [Cotroni] and all of you and discuss all your problems. Say exactly what's going on," Zaffarano said, arranging yet another round of diplomacy. Violi was then told the best news he had heard yet in his efforts to bring the Rizzutos to heel: Zaffarano told him to tell the Rizzutos that New York was now on the case. He carefully outlined the message to be passed directly to Nick. Violi was to tell him: "We [Violi and Cotroni] got nothing more to do with you, go to New York. We got no time for you here. Go explain yourself to them." Violi was ecstatic. It was a message he would deliver with relish and relief.

Not long after one of the meetings with the American visitors, Violi updated Cotroni on changes in the gangland landscape of New York. "Joe [Evola's nickname], he's the *capo* [boss], Mike [Rastelli's Montreal nickname] is the *sotto capo* [underboss]," Violi said, using the more traditional forms of address that had long been anglicized by most other North American gangsters.

"Who's the counselor?" Cotroni asked.

"Don Nicolino," said Violi, referring to Nicolino Alfano. "He don't like it too much, 'cause he's old and he's gotta travel all over … Counselor's a big job," Violi said, recounting the chatter from the Americans. "He told me, when [Nick Rizzuto] comes [to New York], those guys would talk to him." said Violi.

The New Yorkers had regaled Violi and Cotroni with tales from the streets of Brooklyn, and the Sicilian visitors had updated the Canadians on significant comings and goings among the island's Men of Honor. These talks were conducted in utmost privacy and were to be held within the strictest bonds of secrecy. Unknowingly, however, it all went far beyond the ear of Paolo Violi. The Montreal meetings with the American and Sicilian mobsters had serious ramifications for the future of Violi, his organization and many of the men he had met during his diplomatic entreaties.

Unbeknownst to anyone but a tightly controlled group of investigators and top police brass, Montreal police had pulled off a considerable investigative coup. Robert Menard, an undercover Montreal police officer, had posed as a young electrician looking for an apartment to rent and managed to cut a deal with Violi to move into a room directly above the Reggio Bar. Once installed in his new home, Menard and his surveillance and technical team began to wire the downstairs bar for sound.

Violi's inner sanctum had been penetrated. With secret electronic bugs now picking up conversations inside, and their agent, Menard, maintaining his nerve-racking double life upstairs, Canadian police suddenly had a front-row seat watching the mob action not only in Canada but in New York and Sicily. For six years, Menard persevered in his daring charade, living among the violent mobsters. All of the whispered conversations, explosive outbursts and secret negotiations were being absorbed by Canadian investigators, who were forwarding the salient information to the FBI and Italian authorities. The tapes would soon come to wide, and embarrassing, attention in Canada.

On September 15, 1972, Cotroni and Violi laid out their final positions with the New York mobsters. Cotroni defended his right to punish Nick Rizzuto. If he could not kill him because of outside sensibilities, he still had some power to act.

"Me, I'm *capo decina*," Cotroni said, asserting his preeminence within the Montreal organization. "I got the right to expel."

MONTREAL, SEPTEMBER 1972

Friday, September 22, 1972, was a day of tremendous distraction across Canada. The nation's much-loved hockey team took to the ice that afternoon in Moscow for a pitched battle with the Soviet team; it was the first of the historic eight-game Cold War series to be played in Russia and Canada's pride was being battered by an unexpectedly strong opponent.

As the nation was glued to televisions and radios for Game 5 of the series—at first loudly ecstatic at Canada's early 3-0 lead and then deeply distraught as the Soviets rallied to a 5-4 win—mobsters in Montreal had other things on their minds. Domenico Arcuri was driving to Montreal's Dorval airport to meet a plane arriving from New York, according to police surveillance reports. At the airport, Arcuri greeted Nicolino Alfano and Nick Buttafuoco, two-thirds of an important delegation from the New York Bonanno leadership. The greeting was eased by the apparent kinship between the Arcuris and the Alfanos.

The Arcuri family held a strategic position in underworld affairs; three closely related Arcuri men, all born in the Sixth Family's spawning ground of Cattolica Eraclea, had moved to North America and settled in three heroin transit hotspots; all maintained close ties to the Sixth Family. Domenico Arcuri, born in 1933, settled in Montreal and was considered by police to be a close friend of the Rizzutos. Police believe

Domenico married a niece of Nicolino Alfano and they identified him as a guest, alongside Vito Rizzuto, at an important Mafia wedding in New York in 1980. Another Arcuri relative, Giacinto Arcuri, born in 1930, immigrated to Toronto alongside Leonardo Cammalleri, Vito's father-in-law, after both men were named by Italian police in the shocking slaying of the mayor of Cattolica Eraclea, police intelligence files and Italian court records note. Police say Domenico and Giacinto are brothers but a source close to the family insists they are, in fact, first cousins. In Canada, Giacinto remained close to Sicilian mafiosi associated with the Sixth Family, including Vito and the Cammalleri clan in Toronto. When Gerlando "George From Canada" Sciascia, the Montreal Mafia's representative in New York, visited Canada, he sometimes stayed with Giacinto. The third man, said by police to be a cousin of the other two, Giuseppe Arcuri, also born in 1930, arrived in New York and was closely aligned with both the Bonannos and the Sixth Family as a partner with Sciascia in a Long Island pizza outlet. Giuseppe would later post bail for Sciascia when he and Joe LoPresti, another of the Sixth Family's key men, were arrested for heroin trafficking.

Giuseppe Arcuri would go on to be identified as a Bonanno soldier and, when he died in New York in June, 2001, FBI agents watched more than a dozen Bonanno members, including at least five captains, pay their respects at his wake. These many links with New York were likely the reason Domenico Arcuri was the one asked to pick the New Yorkers up and why the Americans felt at ease staying in his home during this time of trouble. Arcuri's link to the Sixth Family likely, however, made Violi nervous.

The following day, as the nation chewed itself up over the third-period collapse of its hockey heroes, Alfano and Zaffarano, the other member of the New York delegation who arrived separately in Montreal, sat together in Violi's Reggio Bar, quietly discussing how they would proceed at the "hearing." Later that day, Alfano and Zaffarano traveled back to Arcuri's house to host the long anticipated sit-down with Nick Rizzuto, Paolo Violi and Vic Cotroni. The Calabrians pushed for Nick's expulsion from the Montreal *decina*. Nick resisted. The New Yorkers slept on it before visiting Violi at his home on Sunday to deliver their verdict: Nick could not be expelled. He was, however, to be more forthcoming to the bosses about his business, particularly with others outside their organization. The Bonanno delegation then returned to New York.

If there was anger or disappointment with the ruling by either Rizzuto or Violi, they showed little of it. As well-raised and well-schooled *mafiosi*, they knew decisions at sit-downs were rarely negotiable until circumstances fundamentally changed. Both men likely planned for the day the decision could be revisited but accepted it at the time in accordance with the old codes they lived under. On the morning of September 26, 1972, just two days after the decision came down from New York, Nick and Violi chatted in the Reggio Bar, with music playing softly in the background, both amicable, both getting down to business and both ignoring their festering dispute. There had been a shooting that almost hit one of their mob colleagues and the Montreal *decina* needed to know who was behind it before they retaliated.

"These young guys are our responsibility," said Violi.

"These people must be found and I do not think that they are guys from the other world," said Nick. "I think we can come to an agreement."

"But I don't think that they can fuck us," said Violi. Business was business. Even when you hate the man you're doing it with.

Despite that restrained show of unity, Nick, a deeply suspicious Sicilian, was not happy deferring to Violi. He did not trust that Violi would adopt a live-and-let-live philosophy. And such a definitive expression of dislike from Vic Cotroni, about wishing to expel him, clearly carried weight, even with Nick Rizzuto. Nick decided to move to a safer location. If he could not move about as he liked in Montreal, he would go elsewhere.

The hasty exit, however, was not an admission of defeat. It was not even a full retreat. While portrayed at the time, both on the streets and in police intelligence files, as a clear, if temporary, victory for Violi, hindsight suggests that Nick's relocation was also a well-timed opportunity to build another important Sixth Family drug outpost. This base was in neither Italy nor North America but rather in a country that seems to have been carefully chosen for its geographic location. Despite the pleasingly warm weather in the region, it was the accommodating political climate that was the more important draw.

CHAPTER 10

CARACAS, VENEZUELA, 1973

Whatever pangs of homesickness Nick Rizzuto might have felt for the city he fled and the family he left behind, he nonetheless found a comfortable and accommodating place to resettle. Slightly more than twice the size of California, Venezuela is a beautiful and vibrant country on the northern coast of South America with hot and humid weather that might well have reminded Nick of his Sicilian homeland. It offered something else, as well.

In Venezuela, the expatriate Mafia was gathering.

The people of Venezuela have lamented the "problem of geography" that has brought the narco-mafiosi into their midst. What is seen as a "problem" for those interested in a healthy community and good governance is, of course, the very reason the drug lords so love the country. Venezuela is positioned between Colombia—the world's largest producer of cocaine, with which it shares a rugged, difficult-to-monitor, 1,274-mile-long land border—and the United States—the world's largest cocaine market, just a short voyage away, across busy shipping lanes and seas dotted with small islands, several of which are under only nominal international oversight. As such, Venezuela is a natural transit point linking North and South America. But geography alone is not to blame for Venezuela's dubious distinction as a haven for drug barons. It has another key attribute.

"It's a very corrupt country," said Oreste Pagano, a significant cocaine trafficker, member of the Camorra and an associate of the Sixth Family in large-scale drug deals. Before his arrest in 1998, Pagano divided his time between South America, Mexico and Miami, with periodic visits to Montreal, from where most of his business would come.

"Money will buy you everything, and without money you can have nothing," Pagano said of Venezuela. This was a subject he knew something about. Pagano owned 1,544 square miles of mineral-rich land in the interior of Venezuela, near Bolivar City, which is close to the border with Brazil. The land came to him complete with titanium, gold and diamond mines, and even an indigenous village. Pagano knew well the connections that the Caruana–Cuntrera and Rizzuto organizations had built and maintained in that country and the protection those connections brought.

Venezuela had by the early 1970s become a drug trafficker's paradise. All the main players of the expatriate Mafia seemed to have a presence there, some hiding from Italian justice, others because they had abandoned Sicily, with its constant waves of violence. Starting in the late 1950s—shortly after the Grand Hôtel et des Palmes meetings—and continuing through the 1960s and 1970s, members of the Sixth Family and its associated clans left Sicily to land comfortably elsewhere. While the Rizzutos settled in Montreal, others headed for Brazil and Venezuela, forming an expatriate Mafia. These were decidedly genuine Sicilian Mafia clans no longer based in Sicily—Men of Honor who surrendered geography in exchange for profit.

Wherever they landed, they quickly made a place for themselves in the underworld, zeroing in on whatever that location could offer in the orderly transit of drugs. They chose their destinations with care and foresight. Since America was their primary market, Montreal was a crucial transit point to the north and Venezuela an impeccable outpost to the south. Canada meant control over the smuggling routes into the United States, and Venezuela was about product acquisition and transit. Plus, a safe place to live. Sometimes moving rapidly and forcefully, at other times creeping along—like rust—the expatriate Mafia clans have over the past half-century created several valuable criminal satellites that have consolidated their dominance over the drug franchise. After leaving Sicily, these foreign outposts were often disposable, with the clans taking on a nomadic existence, ready to move at a moment's notice. While many of the outposts would later crumble, Montreal has retained its value and standing with the Sixth Family—and the Sixth Family has remained true to Montreal.

In Venezuela, three brothers—Pasquale, Gaspare and Paolo Cuntrera—established a strong base. The Cuntrera clan were from Siculiana, part of the Manno Mafia triangle in Agrigento, and they were the leading edge of a single Mafia organization known as the Caruana–Cuntrera. They had spent time in Montreal after leaving Sicily and were friends, allies, partners and, in some cases of cross-marriage, family of the Rizzutos and other members of the Sixth Family. And so, when Nick

Rizzuto joined the Cuntreras in Venezuela, the mutual trust and inti-macy had long been established. They joined once again in business enterprises, both drug-related and seemingly legitimate. Nick was soon at the helm of several businesses, establishing companies that dealt in powdered milk, cheese, chicken production and furniture manufac-turing, his wife later told authorities. With the Cuntreras, he opened a nightclub that suggests they retained a sense of humor about their cho-sen profession: they called it Il Padrone, Italian for "the boss."

In 1972, Tommaso Buscetta joined with Nick in illegally importing a fine white powder into Venezuela. Buscetta insisted until his death that it was powdered milk. Given Nick's interests in food-related busi-nesses—as well as drugs—this might even have been true.

Along with these endeavors, Nick Rizzuto and the Cuntrera broth-ers started arranging heroin- and, later, cocaine-trafficking operations, government documents from several countries show. Their presence in Venezuela, if not their underworld operations, was sanctioned by corrupt government officials, much to the frustration of the U.S. gov-ernment, which badly wanted them in custody, as most of the drugs ended up in the arms and up the noses of American citizens.

———

Major Benedetto Lauretti, a specialist in organized crime and drug operations with Italy's Raggruppamento Operativo Speciale (ROS) Carabinieri, said Italian authorities have long tracked the activities of the Sicilian mafiosi who arrived in Venezuela by way of Canada.

"We're talking about the existence of a Mafia family called the Venezuelan Mafia Family, which is composed of people linked to the Mafia of Siculiana, who emigrated into Canada and Venezuela starting in the 1950s," he said. Lauretti said the growth of the Venezuela Mafia Family was bolstered by the arrival of Nick Rizzuto and the subsequent involvement of Nick's family, including Vito, in the Venezuelan oper-ations. Citing a firm called Ganaderi Rio Zappa, a cattle company that owned a massive ranch—including a private airstrip—near the border with Colombia, Lauretti named Nick Rizzuto as one of the founders.

Now that they could connect directly to South American cocaine suppliers and heroin sources, the Sixth Family and their expatriate Mafia allies began to be an increasingly important part of one of the world's most profitable businesses.

It is testament to both the secrecy of the underworld and the cleverness of Nick Rizzuto that top investigators on three continents still argue over the nature of his relocation to Venezuela, even with the broad hints captured on the Reggio bar wiretaps. The FBI calls it an "apparent expulsion" from Montreal, on orders from Cotroni. The Bureau then notes: "It is also possible that Rizzuto was planted in Venezuela to further develop narcotics trafficking." RCMP files describe the relocation as a strategic move initiated by Nick to avoid being killed by Violi.

"Rizzuto escaped this fate," an RCMP briefing says, "exiling himself and his family to Venezuela where he consolidated links between his family and the Caruana–Cuntrera group as well as the Colombian cartels."

In Venezuela, Nick himself confided to Buscetta that he had left Montreal under threat because Violi wanted him dead.

Although he had physically removed himself from Montreal, Nick had neither abandoned his position nor ceded his interests there. He quietly returned to the city periodically, when business or family demanded it, or when the occasional health concern prompted a trip north to take advantage of Canada's skilled, and free, health care system. Violi was incensed whenever he heard of Nick being spotted in town. Usually the information came long after Nick had returned to the safety of his South American compound, highlighting further the disconnect between the Rizzutos' men and Violi's men on the city's streets. Canadian gangsters would also "holiday" in Venezuela only to be seen meeting privately with Nick around Caracas, or nearby Valencia, but rarely swimming or sunning at the beach.

Nick ensured that his significant business and other interests in Canada were nursed through his absence. For this he turned to one of his most trusted associates—Calogero Renda. Renda was a mainstay of the Sixth Family, having accompanied Nick's father in their ill-fated 1925 foray into America, and the father of Paolo Renda, who would continue the family tradition of being at the Rizzutos' side. Calogero's appointment as Nick's representative and authority in Montreal gave him proxy over the day-to-day running of the family's affairs.

———

Despite the growth in the Rizzuto family's interests abroad and Renda's steady stewardship of its interests in Montreal, these were nonetheless trying times for the Rizzutos. The organization was virtually at war with the powerful leadership of its own *decina* in Montreal and seemingly losing the battle of opinion with the boss in New York. Vito Rizzuto and Paolo Renda were both in jail for the botched barbershop arson. The Rizzuto women also suffered as a result of the difficulties in the lives of their men. Nick's wife, Libertina, and daughter, Maria Renda, lived together in a house Nick maintained in Montreal. The two women bided their time while their husbands remained beyond reach.

Nick's absence from the streets of Montreal, however, did not end his quarrel with Violi or cede his claim to his throne. How could it? It was precisely the need for the Sixth Family to control Montreal that was at the root of the dispute. For an outsider to retain power in such a key location—even one with an 'Ndrangheta background and American Mafia membership—would have created a situation of insecurity for the Sicilian gangsters, who trusted few who were not kin. Perhaps if Violi had stepped back and allowed the Sixth Family to run heroin unfettered through "his" town, he might have avoided his fate. Perhaps not. The ferocity of the Sixth Family, their acquisitiveness and distrust of those outside their group likely would have meant that, in time, they would have to overpower him. Besides, Violi rarely, if ever, stepped back. Time seemed to be on the side of the ever-expanding, ever-consolidating Rizzutos. This was something Nick seemed to fully understand. He could be a man of immense patience and planning.

Violi might well have breathed a sigh of relief at Nick's departure. He certainly felt he had triumphed in this war of nerves and words, and he gave himself credit for the diplomatic coup. Violi was starting to feel he had regained a firm handle on affairs in Montreal. But just as he began to feel secure again, his hold would start to crumble.

The uncertainty began in New York and gradually made its way to Montreal.

CHAPTER 11

MANHATTAN, AUGUST 1973

Paolo Violi's progress in pulling New York to his side was thrown into jeopardy when the strain of the job as Bonanno Family boss got the better of Natale Evola. On August 28, 1973, his short reign as boss ended when he was felled by cancer, not rival gangsters. The search for a replacement was on and Violi started pushing for Philip "Rusty" Rastelli as the man to fill the void. Violi feared that someone with whom he had no personal ties, or—worse—someone who was too tight with the Sicilian mafiosi, might move into power. Violi, more than most in the American Mafia, knew the true intentions and interests of the Sicilian mafiosi.

On October 20, 1973, John DeMatteo, a Bronx-based member of the Gambino Family, visited Violi at the Reggio Bar and passed along a message from New York. Violi was told to attend a meeting at the Americana Hotel in Manhattan. On November 6, Rastelli himself called Violi, inviting him to the same meeting and telling him to bring Vic Cotroni's brother Frank with him. The next day, Violi updated Cotroni on the development. Cotroni, a man with a sound mind for strategy, immediately balked at the idea of his brother attending such a delicate meeting. Frank was not to go, Cotroni said, "since he is so closely watched by the police." This was a nod to Frank's increasing drug involvement, although Frank's drug connections might well have been why Rastelli wanted him there in the first place.

By Friday, November 9, Violi had a plan in place and asked Joe DiMaulo, a trusted and loyal mafioso, to stand in for Frank. Violi and DiMaulo would head to New York separately, in case one of them was stopped at the border. The two discussed their cover stories if they were questioned by police or border guards and, early the next afternoon, DiMaulo left in a car driven by Raynald Desjardins, his brother-in-law. Violi left by plane on the Sunday. Both car and plane made it safely to New York and the Montreal representatives met with at least three New

Yorkers—Rastelli, Nicholas "Nicky Glasses" Marangelo and Joseph Buccellato. Largely because of the advance warning from Canadian police who were listening to the Reggio Bar wiretaps, FBI agents secretly monitored the gangsters coming and going from the Americana Hotel, photographing them as they walked and talked. Violi later complained of the agents' presence. He had spotted someone snapping his picture inside the hotel.

Behind closed doors, Rastelli told Violi that the Commission had installed him as the acting boss of the Bonanno Family. Rastelli also declared his intention to secure the job permanently at an election by Bonanno captains to be held in New York in a few weeks' time. Montreal would have a vote and Rastelli wanted Violi's support. Violi, rarely shy, immediately asked for permission to induct new soldiers into his organization. Rastelli said it was impossible at that time. Despite the rebuff, Violi was thrilled to help propel into high office someone with whom he had a solid relationship.

Later, on March 19, 1974, in his office at the Reggio Bar, Violi had what was likely a rare encounter with Nick Rizzuto that he actually enjoyed. For once, Violi felt he had the upper hand and likely spoke with braggadocio when updating Nick, who was on one of his occasional visits from Venezuela, on recent events. Things were changing in New York, Violi told Nick. He said that Rastelli had been elected as the new boss, Nicky Marangello as underboss and Stefano "Stevie Beef" Cannone as the new *consigliere*. Violi said he had sent Roméo Bucci, whom he described as a "senior" member of the *decina*, to New York to register Montreal's vote. And, he could not resist adding, shortly after Rastelli's ascension Violi himself went to New York, on February 25, 1974, to meet with the new boss and his administration.

Nick knew what subject would have dominated the conversation. The distance between Montreal and Venezuela had eased none of the animosity.

MONTREAL, 1974

With Nick Rizzuto living in exile, if not in fear, Violi was feeling more comfortable in Montreal, freer to exert his power. At a meeting with Pietro Sciarra and Leonardo Caruana, two mobsters of Sicilian birth, Violi decreed that all outsiders would have to follow his orders while they were in his territory—a clear shot aimed at reducing the sudden influx of Sicilian Men of Honor into Montreal.

In April 1974, Pietro Sciarra arranged for Giuseppe Cuffaro and another Sicilian mobster to travel from Sicily to Montreal to meet with Violi and Cotroni. They updated the Montrealers on recent changes in Agrigento. At a meeting with Violi on April 22, the Sicilian mobsters passed along news that Leonardo Caruana, the one-time Montreal resident who had been repeatedly deported from Canada back to Agrigento, had been elected *capo-de-madamento*, or district boss, on the Cupola, the ruling panel of the Mafia in Sicily. The movement of mobsters between Italy and North America was becoming a difficult issue for crime bosses everywhere. How were they to be treated? Could a Sicilian Man of Honor set up shop in North America as if he were an inducted member of one of the Five Families? Could an American gangster expect to be considered a made man in Sicily? Could a gangster be made in both countries? If so, where did his loyalty lie? As globalization came to the Mafia, these issues were openly debated at senior levels of the underworld.

The Rizzuto faction that remained in Montreal continued to push Violi to officially recognize some of their newly arrived colleagues from Sicily. They wanted full "working privileges" endorsed by Montreal and New York. Violi outlined his view on the Sicilians to Sciarra and Cuffaro: "I know all about how it is here in America. Someone who comes here from Italy—it's orders and you better believe it—he has to stay here for five years under us. After the five years are up, then everyone can see what he's like."

Not long after, the Sicilian mobsters were back sipping coffee with Violi at the Reggio Bar and again bringing news of Leonardo Caruana; his ascension to the ruling board in Sicily was causing controversy because some in Sicily considered him an outsider after his long exile in Montreal. Suspicions between the New World and Old World mafiosi, despite their deep links and ongoing dealings with each other, were evident on both sides of the ocean. It led the men to again discuss the issue of membership. The visitors wondered: If a Montrealer could sit on the ruling board in Sicily, under what conditions could a mobster arriving from Sicily become part of the Montreal organization? Violi reiterated his position: visiting Men of Honor would be accepted; those who wanted to permanently relocate were a different story. They needed to prove their loyalty to Violi.

"He comes here, he moves his home, he comes, he comes to us here, he has to stay with us for five years, and after, he can move up—if there's an opening and we can give it to him. That's how it's done," Violi said. The visiting Sicilians were unimpressed.

"In our mob," the visiting Sicilian mafiosi said, in apparent dismay, "it's a friend and we got to recognize a friend and that's that." The rebuff from Violi was an insult.

If the Sixth Family was by that point growing ever more impatient with Violi, they would soon get a helping hand in ending his reign from an unexpected quarter. With Nick Rizzuto ensconced in Venezuela and his son, Vito, still in jail for the botched arson, the offensive was not directed by the Sixth Family but it nonetheless greatly aided their cause.

MONTREAL, 1975

Le commission d'enquête sur le crime organisé was a public investigation ordered by the provincial government of Quebec. The sessions, some held in private, others sensationally public, began to shine a light into some shadowy places for Montreal's mafiosi and other homegrown gangsters. The hearings were similar in style and protocol to the 1951 Kefauver commission hearings of the U.S. Senate, which forced Frank Costello, one of the leading bosses of the Five Families—a man dubbed "the Prime Minister of the Underworld"—to take the stand. There were also echoes of the 1963 U.S. Senate Permanent Sub-Committee on Organized Crime, chaired by Senator John McClellan, that put Joe Valachi on display as a Mafia turncoat.

From September 27, 1972, to March 31, 1977, the Quebec organized crime commission was given the power to subpoena witnesses, question them at length and present its findings in a quasi-judicial forum that carried the weight of the government. It also had the power to issue contempt citations for those who refused an order to appear, or who refused to give truthful and meaningful testimony.

The first target of the commission was the Cotroni–Violi organization.

The prospect of a commission that would dig up dirt but not have the teeth to lay serious criminal charges was at first a source of ridicule and amusement among the Montreal mob. Shortly before Christmas in 1973, Violi was heard lampooning the commission: "Their balls are in an uproar because they don't know anything." What he did not know was how deeply his organization was about to be exposed. Nor did he know of the profane and embarrassing police recordings of him and his closest advisors and co-conspirators in his inner sanctum. One man who did seem to realize what was at stake was one of Violi's closest confidants, Joe DiMaulo. On September 19, 1974, when DiMaulo was being questioned by police on another matter, he asked directly whether his trip to New York the year before to help install Philip Rastelli as the Bonanno Family boss was going to be entered as evidence at the commission hearings.

"DiMaulo thought that public disclosure of the election of a head of the American Mafia would be a disaster for him and for the family. For DiMaulo, this would be a serious breach of the rule of silence with respect to all family business," says one of several reports issued by the commission.

The toll of the inquiry on Violi and his organization was profound. In 1974, the commission sought first to hear from Vic Cotroni. Responding to a subpoena, Cotroni put on a show of befuddlement, gently rebuffing question after question in what he hoped would come across as benign ignorance. The charade did not hold. After eating up more than a thousand pages of commission transcripts he had revealed nothing of importance, prompting one commentator to describe him as "impassive as the Sphinx."

"I have no authority," Cotroni said in a whisper to the three-judge panel. The commission was not pleased. Cotroni was sentenced to a year in jail for contempt of the proceedings. The sudden jailing of the boss sent Violi into action. Likely expecting a renewed challenge for leadership by the Rizzutos, he took the initiative of formalizing his position with New York. On January 9, 1975, he called Pietro Sciarra into his office and told him to go immediately to New York to ask what should be done.

"You're gonna talk," Violi told him, preparing him for an audience with Rastelli. "The best thing is to explain your case before. You're gonna say to him: 'Paolo sent me here, actually, and seeing as Vincent's inside all that time ... somebody's got to take responsibility now.'"

Rastelli knew what Violi was really asking for and gave it to him: "When Vincent gets out, have him call me, and if a change has to be made then, I'll talk to Vincent. But for the time being, you take over," Rastelli told Violi. Just days later, Violi was heard bragging to Joe DiMaulo of his appointment by New York as the acting boss. His joy was short-lived.

After Cotroni testified, Violi was also ordered to appear before the inquiry. His appearance was a media spectacle. Dressed in a sharply tailored light gray suit and fashionably wide, striped tie, Violi appeared as a stern, brooding man who stood authoritatively and defiantly in the witness box. His dark hair, with a hint of gray at the temples, was neatly combed and glistened in the television lights. In contrast to Cotroni, who seemed to shrivel before the commission, Violi seemed to swell beyond his natural size. His testimony was as unhelpful for the commission as Cotroni's had been but—as with everything else Violi did—he was less subtle than his mentor.

"I don't refuse to testify," he said on the stand. "I have a lot of respect for the court but I don't have anything to say." Those words— and his refusal to take the oath before testifying—prompted the inquiry chairman to slap Violi with a one-year jail sentence for contempt.

Although Violi had nothing to say at the inquiry, he had plenty to say in private, and the secret police recordings were replayed for the commission in all their color. The words were shocking, not only to the public, who were riveted by media coverage of the hearings, but to Violi's associates and rivals, who were the most astute of listeners. The scandal started to erode his respect. As would happen years later to John Gotti, the New York boss of the Gambino Family, who also made incriminating pronouncements on tape, Violi's own words amounted to an unintentional breach of *omertà*. It was something his rivals did not ignore. Rizzuto supporters quickly used Violi's lapse in security to stir up discontent. Complaints about breaches in mob etiquette suddenly shifted into reverse—Violi was now on the receiving end of the whispers.

The FBI noted the increasing "dissension from within its ranks" of the "Montreal family" in its internal reports.

"Although Nick Rizzuto had been banished to Venzuela, there remained a number of Sicilian figures in the Montreal organization," an FBI report said. "Other organized crime groups in the Montreal area began to take more control of organized crime."

Violi, through his own words, had suddenly made himself vulnerable, with little help from the Rizzutos. It is said that a mafioso is most at risk of attack when he is either dangerous or isolated. Violi was both.

The conversations recorded on the bugs captured an important problem that was cropping up within key Mafia centers all over the world. The issue of Sicilian Men of Honor operating criminally in the territory of the American Mafia was one that would arise wherever the expatriate mafiosi encountered an established mob presence: in New York, Montreal, Philadelphia and Toronto, in particular. It would take years for the full ramifications of the Sicilian penetration to be felt in New York. Had the situation between Violi and the Rizzutos and their Sixth Family allies properly made its way into police files and been fully understood by intelligence analysts, it might have saved investigators in New York years of confusion.

If the New York mediators from the Bonanno Family dismissed the Rizzuto–Violi dispute as a mere annoyance, or as yet another petty gangland squabble, they were not looking carefully enough. Had they paid more attention and compared the situation in Montreal to the changes on their own streets they might have been more prepared for what was to come in New York.

There is nothing to suggest that they did.

CHAPTER 12

QUEENS, NOVEMBER 4, 1976

At 11:30 p.m. on a cool autumn night, 70-year-old Pietro "Peter" Licata swung his long 1974 Cadillac to the foot of the driveway of his New York home, one of many tidy, well-kept houses in Middle Village, Queens. He and his wife, Vita, had just returned from a late meal at a restaurant. Before Licata could swing open the gates of his home, however, the tranquility and quiet were broken by the reverberating boom of a shotgun blast. Seven hot metal pellets shredded Licata's head and upper body as his wife watched in horror from the passenger's seat. A deeply distressed Vita told police detectives that a man had stepped out of a yellow car, possibly a Cadillac, and approached her husband before calmly firing the shotgun, aiming for his head. The gunman had jumped back into the yellow car and was driven from the murder scene by an accomplice.

Speculation abounded about the motive for the murder. Licata, ostensibly a retired businessman from the knitwear industry, was an old-time American gangster—one of the few remaining "Mustache Petes," a term for the older, more traditional Italian gangsters. Homicide detectives and organized crime investigators wondered what was at the root of Licata's demise. Was it the death three weeks earlier, through natural causes, of Carlo Gambino, the head of the Gambino Family? Or the distinct rise in influence and avarice of the Bonanno's Carmine Galante? Or perhaps it was tied to the murder, four years earlier, of a Licata relative who was involved in gambling?

Later events offered more substantial clues. Licata's murder was rooted in far wider shifts in crime than a neighborhood gambling den or even the death of an important crime boss. There was a shake-up under way in Mafia centers around the world and two of the most important New World mob outposts—New York and Montreal—were facing the same dangerous demographic shift.

———

Knickerbocker Avenue in Brooklyn is a long, cluttered street that runs through the Bushwick section of the borough, near the border with Queens. With Knickerbocker and its surrounding streets as his base, Pietro Licata had operated a crew of Bonanno soldiers and associates. He was the epitome of the Italian-American mob boss. The longtime turf of the Bonanno Family, Knickerbocker was Licata's personal fiefdom, just as Montreal's Saint-Léonard was Violi's.

"Anything moving in there, even a tree, they got to say to him: I want to move the tree. Nobody moves nothing," said Luigi Ronsisvalle, a former enforcer for Licata, who worked Brooklyn's streets for years at the behest of the Bonanno organization. Ronsisvalle described Licata as an old-style street boss involved in low-key money-making ventures, loan sharking and gambling. He owned—legitimately or by hidden interest—several businesses in the area, including Italian cafés where organized card games were run, with Licata getting his "end"—a piece of each hand wagered. On a good night, a single café could make thousands of dollars in profit.

Licata stood out from other neighborhood residents because he always wore white. Legend had it that when his daughter was deathly ill, he went to church and prayed that if God spared her, he would from then on wear only white clothing as a sign of gratitude for the divine intervention. The child recovered, and thereafter Licata walked like a living ghost through Brooklyn.

Licata kept his crew busy, leaving them enough money to live on. All they had to do was to show traditional respect, obey him without question and keep away from drugs. Drugs, as many old-timers like Licata believed, were not only evil but would destroy the underpinnings of the Mafia's traditional breadwinners. Gambling, loan sharking and other activities were illegal, but accepted by large segments of society. No one, however, could put a good face on drug trafficking. Licata and Ronsisvalle both had a nostalgic—if delusional—view of the Mafia.

"Like an American kid falls in love with baseball, I fall in the love with Mafia," Ronsisvalle said in halting and broken English. "A Man of Honor no go around stealing and killing for money. A Man of Honor, he kills for some reason; to help people." He himself had murdered 13 people during his time in America, which he no doubt felt had contributed to some greater societal benefit. Ronsisvalle established himself in Brooklyn in time to see the last vestiges of his beloved Mafia evaporate—if it had ever existed. When he arrived in America in 1966, he headed straight to Knickerbocker Avenue, on the advice of a connected friend in Sicily. Ronsisvalle would join Licata on collection runs, helping to convince debtors to quickly turn their money over.

But the old routine, which had played itself out for generations, was becoming a little archaic. Licata and Ronsisvalle found their precious Mafia was undergoing slow but distinct changes. It started with Carmine Galante.

After the death in 1976 of Carlo Gambino, the powerful boss of the Gambino Family, Carmine Galante started to believe he might finally achieve his dream of being the head of a pan-national heroin enterprise, not to mention boss of bosses in the American Mafia. It is hard to tell which he wanted more, although he probably saw them as related propositions. Upon his release from prison in 1974, after serving 12 years for his heroin conspiracy with Montreal's Pep Cotroni, Galante's outsized dreams became dangerously well known. The Bonanno Family leadership seemed an open question. Galante, as a former *consigliere* and underboss, felt himself to be more qualified than anyone for the job. The police and the public braced for a new wave of violence as Galante moved to regain his place as the key man in the Sicily–Montreal–New York heroin axis.

Like most theories and legends, there were kernels of truth scattered among the hyperbole and speculation. Galante did seem to have insane designs on becoming a boss without peer in the American Mafia. But he was really yesterday's man. Internationally, the underworld had realigned in his absence: the French Connection, along with Galante's Corsican and French colleagues in Europe and Canada, was unraveling. The European traffickers had spread through Europe and South America and formed direct alliances with the Bonanno and Gambino families in New York City—if not the other families as well—without Galante. Elsewhere, heroin laboratories in Sicily were starting to churn out product at an alarming rate. It seemed that all of the Sicilian Mafia clans were involved in the drug trade and the expatriate Mafia in Venezuela and Brazil were forming their own alliances. In Montreal, the Sixth Family was conspiring to eliminate the blockage caused by Paolo Violi, putting Galante's longtime Cotroni connections at risk.

The Bonanno Family had also changed drastically in Galante's absence. There were new players on the scene, tough young imports who had immigrated—legally or not—from Sicily over the years. Their loyalty was to the clans of Agrigento, Palermo and Trapani.

It was these young cadres of Sicilian traffickers in Brooklyn who, like the Rizzutos in Canada, were bumping up against the older, established American Mafia. And, just as in Canada, here was an old-style gangster trying to stand up to them, believing that tradition would trump the allure of drug wealth. It was a dangerous position for Licata.

BROOKLYN, 1977

Men like Pietro Licata would have been the first to notice the change in the underworld landscape.

As Licata surveyed his territory, he saw the influx of new Sicilian immigrants who had set up shop and burrowed into the heartland of the American Mafia. In New York, they gathered around the most Sicilian of the families, the one named after Joe Bonanno, who was in turn the most Sicilian of the New York family bosses. The new players caused a stir among American-born Mafia members, who referred to them as "Zips," probably for the fast-paced dialect they spoke. Behind their backs, though, the Americans were as likely to refer to the Sicilians by a grossly insulting term: "greaseballs," according to Kenneth McCabe, a former New York City police detective who died in 2006. The Knickerbocker Avenue Zips were part of the Bonanno Family. Several were "made," and all—in theory—answered to Licata or other Bonanno captains. Most of the American-born Mafia members were leery of them: they kept to themselves, spoke an indecipherable dialect and were involved in schemes American gangsters could only speculate about. They were considered to be a breed apart.

"The Zips stood alone," said Sal Vitale, a longtime Bonanno member and former family underboss. Frank Lino, a former Bonanno captain, echoed the sentiment: "I recognized them as Zips. You could detect a guy from Italy." How? "The way they looked," Lino said.

———

Salvatore "Toto" Catalano was the boss of the Bonanno Sicilian faction—the Zips—in Brooklyn. Born in 1941 in the Sicilian town of Ciminna, south-east of Palermo, Catalano and his two brothers, also Mafia members, had been sent to the United States in 1966 by old-country traffickers intent on expanding the Sicilian drug trade. The state crackdown on the Mafia in Italy, following the 1963 massacre of policemen in Ciaculli, south of Palermo, had sent members of the Sicilian Mafia fleeing around the world.

In Brooklyn, Catalano had relatives—including a cousin of the same name who was nicknamed "Saca"—who had been in the drug trade since the 1950s. Catalano lived a quiet, modest life, operating a shop on Knickerbocker Avenue. Capitalizing on his membership in the Sicilian Mafia, and on his family relationships, Catalano became a small businessman, with partnerships in bakeries and several pizzerias. All of his partners were mafiosi; all the businesses were fronts for the emerging heroin network that would later be known as the Pizza Connection. Those who met Catalano came away with a feeling that he was a deeply self-controlled man who wrapped himself in an aura of steel. He displayed none of the braggadocio and swagger of his contemporaries in the American Mafia—even though he was a "made" member of the Bonanno Family, like Nick and Vito Rizzuto in Montreal. His role in America, as with the Rizzutos, Caruanas and Cuntreras in Canada and Venezuela, was to conduct the Sicilian heroin franchise, although, as good mobsters, all the factions were reluctant to turn their back on any profitable opportunity that came their way. Six months after Licata's murder, Catalano was made a captain in the Bonanno Family and handed Licata's old turf, likely revealing his role in the slaying.

Among Catalano's early contacts for heroin distribution was Carmine Galante, who, even though his parents were Sicilian, was thoroughly a product of the American Mafia. For many newly arrived immigrants like Catalano, Galante's expertise and contacts were crucial in building those first bridges to American crews who were willing to get involved in the drug distribution business. Galante was tough, had spent a lifetime in the drug trade and had deep contacts in the United States, Canada and Italy. More important to the Zips, Galante was willing to let them in.

The influx of the Sicilian gangsters is often seen, from the American perspective, as an initiative on the part of Galante, who is said to have "imported" the Zips to do his heavy lifting. Evidence now suggests, however, that the Zips in fact perpetrated a quiet invasion. They were sent from Sicily, rather than called for by America. It is a significant distinction.

The American Mafia, largely the powerful Five Families of New York, had over the decades developed quite differently from its progenitor in Italy.

"Originally it was a simple franchise of the Sicilian organization, born in the rut of migratory movements from southern Italy toward the New World," wrote Giovanni Falcone, the Italian investigative magistrate, who spent more quality time with turncoat mafiosi than perhaps any other investigator. "The two organizations have evolved their habits and their way of thinking according to the country in which they developed. This separate evolution has, in practice, caused a progressive autonomy on the part of the American Mafia which, today, is complete," Falcone wrote.

Once a new generation of Sicilian Men of Honor had infiltrated the American Mafia in New York and Montreal, distinct differences between the Zips and American mobsters became clear to all.

"With the establishment of heroin laboratories in Sicily, there was a need to organize North American distribution capabilities," said Tom Tripodi, a former leading agent with the old U.S. Bureau of Narcotics and Dangerous Drugs and, later, with its successor, the Drug Enforcement Administration. Tripodi, a man with extensive overseas experience and a keen world view—he had previously debriefed such key Mafia informants, in both Italy and America, as Joe Valachi and Tommaso Buscetta—said it was a Sicilian Mafia overture, not an American Mafia initiative, that brought the Zips to New York and Montreal in such numbers.

"With the French traffickers on the wane, the Sicilian sphere of influence was growing, a development that appealed to mafiosi both in New York and Palermo," Tripodi said. "The Sicilians wanted to restore order in the ranks of their American brethren, as well as reassert, through diplomatic means, the supremacy of the traditional strongholds in Sicily."

Regardless of why the Zips arrived, one thing is certain: Carmine Galante liked them. They appealed to his ideal of all that was good and right with the Mafia—loyalty, strength, cunning and a ruthless interest in the drug trade. He personally inducted many of the Zips into the Bonanno Family, even though that role was usually reserved for the boss.

In 1977, Galante conducted an initiation ceremony in Brooklyn for Frank Coppa. Twenty-five years later, Coppa would wreak devastation on the Bonanno Family, but even his induction was something of note: Coppa was sworn in on the same day as a pair of the most aggressive and active Zips.

"They took me to an apartment in Brooklyn," Coppa said. Waiting in the apartment were Carmine Galante and other Bonanno captains.

"We waited," Coppa went on. "Me and the other fellow—I can't remember his name offhand—waited in the bathroom while they were inducting two other people." Through the thin walls, he could hear Galante in the living room leading the ancient induction rite for Cesare Bonventre and Baldassare "Baldo" Amato.

"They were speaking Italian, so I didn't understand," the Brooklyn-born Coppa said. "They left and we came out of the bathroom, went into the living room. And at that point they asked if you didn't want to be inducted you had the right to leave, and if not, you join hands and you commence the meeting to be inducted into the Bonanno crime family. ... We were led to believe that Carmine Galante was boss."

The Sicilians were inducted separately from the Americans. And since Bonventre, and likely Amato, too, had been inducted into the Sicilian Mafia before emigrating, the issue of dual membership or competing loyalties was not something Galante seemed much bothered about. He appreciated the boost in power these new soldiers gave him on the street, thinking they would help to propel him to further heights. Galante felt they depended on him as well. He saw the Zips as his men; the Zips had other ideas.

———

Catalano's drug organization, newly emerging in Brooklyn, consisted of a host of Sicilian-born and, more important, Sicilian-made Mafia members. Among them were men with strong ties to the Sixth Family: Bonventre, Amato, Giovanni Ligammari, Santo "Tony" Giordano, Filippo Casamento and Giuseppe Baldinucci. Bonventre and Amato arrived in New York through Canada. Much later, Casamento and Baldinucci would both return to New York after being deported to Italy, arriving after first visiting with Sixth Family associates in Canada. Ligammari had also been seen meeting and working with key Sixth Family leaders.

Not only did the Zips start flooding New York with heroin, but they supplied traffickers in Philadelphia, Boston, Chicago and Detroit.

Repatriating the profits out of America to Europe and Canada, the Catalano faction utilized legitimate money-moving channels, including the Royal Bank of Canada and the Bank of Nova Scotia, both huge Canadian banking institutions with branches around the world. Other profits were channeled to the Sixth Family, who moved the bulk of the cash through Montreal's far looser banking system and on to Switzerland and Liechtenstein.

By the mid-1970s, Catalano was being unmasked to authorities by several informants. Still a man of some mystery, he was, however, turning up in several investigations, mostly as a passing, collateral target when other Bonanno members were under surveillance. In 1975, he had been arrested while riding in a car with two other Sicilian mafiosi; an unregistered handgun had been seized and Catalano was convicted, serving three years of a five-year sentence. Around the same time, he was already in a dispute with Licata: tradition had it that the baccarat game that Licata ran "floated," meaning that it moved once a year through a circuit of mob-controlled cafés in the area. Licata, however, was resisting the move. He did not much like the Zips and was particularly disdainful of Catalano. Licata was working to undermine the Zips any way he could.

Despite Catalano's growing presence in Brooklyn, which was not going unnoticed by police, he was just another name in the broad Bonanno Family tree; his true role and importance in the underworld would not be revealed until after the Sixth Family completed its takeover of Montreal.

It would appear that for Catalano, membership in the Bonanno Family was a convenient formality. He had a job to do, and that was to move heroin. He seems to have had no loyalty to the Bonanno bosses, and he had little to do with fellow made members from America, who watched in envy as he amassed power and respect that seemed out of proportion to his quiet life.

"The highest American boss in the Mafia here is beneath the newest recruit in Sicily, both in stature and power," said a trusted old associate of a major Sicilian-born mafioso drug trafficker. "Each member of a family in Sicily carries with him the weight of the entire family." When told what Frank Coppa had said of the induction ceremony of Bonventre and Amato, during which they would have vowed to protect the Bonanno Family to the death, the man shook his head.

"If this is true, you can bet the Sicilian had his fingers crossed," he said with a smile. "The loyalty only goes to one place: Sicily."

As heroin profits poured in, Catalano and his crew began showing signs of unusual prosperity on the depressed strip of Knickerbocker Avenue. They drove expensive cars. They bought homes that were the envy of local mobsters who, in some cases, were living hand-to-mouth. Cesare Bonventre, in particular, caused a stir with his high fashion designer clothing in the style of the day, favoring open-necked striped dress shirts and tinted aviator glasses—outdoors and in. Along Knickerbocker Avenue, a $2,000 designer suit was difficult to ignore. What is more, at the nightly card games, the Sicilian gangsters—the Zips—were slapping down money at a dizzying rate.

Money was the very thing that men such as Pietro Licata in Brooklyn and Paolo Violi in Montreal could not control, contain or suppress. And it was drug trafficking that was bringing in the cash. Licata, like Violi, tried to intervene.

"He no like drugs," Ronsisvalle said of Licata. "He say: no, no no [to heroin] on Knickerbocker Avenue. They say, 'Okay.' Then they kill him."

Licata, despite his longevity in the mob, had only the code of the American Mafia to protect him from the Zips. It was not enough. Licata was dispatched, and the Zips quickly moved in to fill the void. As would happen in several similar cases, the murders of American mobsters drew no retaliation against the Zips.

Despite Luigi Ronsisvalle's old-school view of the Mafia, he was certainly more flexible than Licata, and he soon found himself fitting in well within the new regime. He became a heroin courier. From Knickerbocker Avenue he started making dozens of trips to Florida and Los Angeles, carrying the Zips' drugs. One load totaled 45 kilos; another, four kilos, he said. His life was planes, trains and automobiles. He made more than a dozen trips to Chicago on Amtrak, each time carrying about 40 kilos of heroin in his luggage. Ronsisvalle detailed another 15 heroin loads he ferried from the Bonanno Family to the Gambinos. After a brief interruption in his travels owing to a shortage of supply, trafficker Felice Puma, Carmine Galante's godson, told Ronsisvalle that the drugs were once again flowing.

"We are in business again," Puma told him. "Do you know, Luigi, the pipe from Canada that brings oil to the U.S.? We got the same thing—with heroin."

MONTREAL, 1977

The tension that led to Pietro Licata's murder mirrored in almost perfect symmetry the situation between Violi and the Sixth Family in Montreal. To the chagrin of the Sixth Family, Violi could not be eliminated as quickly or with as much ease as Licata had been in Brooklyn. While the code of the American Mafia was often trampled on by the Zips, the 'Ndrangheta code was something entirely different. Still, the spike in large-scale heroin trafficking that arose after the Licata murder has to have impressed upon them how profitable clearing the blockage could be.

With violence on the horizon, the Sixth Family went into war mode. Their core group drew closer, and they stepped up security. Intrigue was rife, as the loyalty of underworld figures was assessed and reassessed. Weapons were secured and kept at hand. And Vito, the future of the family, was moved out of harm's way.

In 1976, after his release from jail, when tensions in Montreal were reaching their zenith, Vito joined his father in Venezuela, where he would be shielded from rival mobsters and police. He would stay in South America for the next three years, while war drums pounded in Montreal.

CHAPTER 13

MONTREAL, FEBRUARY 1976

Valentine's Day, when romance is in the date book if not always in the hearts of long-married couples, was a time for Pietro Sciarra to put aside the consuming intrigue of the Rizzuto–Violi power struggle in Montreal and snuggle close to his wife. He had been in the hot seat lately, and the pressure had been intense. In some ways, there was more pressure on him than there was on Paolo Violi and Nick Rizzuto, for Sciarra was caught in the middle of these two indomitable forces. Even though he was Sicilian he was a trusted advisor to the Calabrian Violi—police describe him as Violi's *consigliere*—and had openly sided with his boss. Several attempts had been made by the Sixth Family to bring Sciarra into their new Sicilian-centered reality. These were entreaties he had explicitly refused.

Sciarra was a Sicilian mafioso Violi had embraced and welcomed when he fled to Canada. Violi valued Sciarra for his ability to listen and for offering sober, sound advice. Violi shared with him some of his most private thoughts and trusted him with serious business, particularly when it involved interactions with those outside his milieu. Sciarra was, in a way, Violi's minister of external relations. When Vic Cotroni was jailed by the Quebec organized crime commission, it was Sciarra that Violi sent to New York to plead his case for being named acting boss of the Montreal *decina*. And when a man named Frank Tutino ran for public office in the 1974 city election, it was Sciarra that he sent to suggest to Tutino that he withdraw from the race, after Violi had thrown his support behind a rival candidate. (Tutino refused, but was trounced at the polls.) And it was Sciarra that Violi relied on for advice on how to deal with the Rizzutos and his Sixth Family kin. Sciarra was repaid with respect and a fond nickname from Violi, who was often heard calling him *Zio*—"Uncle."

Even though he was skilled at diplomacy, Sciarra was not all talk. In Italy he had been declared by a judicial tribunal to be a member of the Mafia and sentenced to preventive detention under anti-Mafia laws. To avoid prison, he had fled to Montreal. His status as a fugitive and a mafioso, however, did not prevent him from traveling easily back and forth, entering and re-entering Canada and Italy, seemingly at his pleasure. Although deportation orders were eventually issued against him in Canada, he filed repeated court appeals, extending his stay by years. He was free on bail from ongoing immigration proceedings when, just weeks before the Valentine's Day movie date with his wife, he was called to testify before the Quebec crime commission. Smartly dressed in a dark pinstripe suit and spotted tie, Sciarra was asked about his links to organized crime.

"Do you know what the Mafia is?" Judge Jean Dutil, the commission's president, asked Sciarra, after hearing extensive evidence about his involvement with Violi in running the affairs of the Montreal mob.

"No," Sciarra said, looking perplexed.

"You don't have any idea of what Mafia means?"

"No," he said, with a straight face.

"But you were designated by the anti-Mafia law!" the judge exclaimed.

"I don't know what anti-Mafia means."

With all of these tensions, Sciarra's desire for a quiet, relaxing night out with his wife is understandable. For their Valentine's date, however, he chose an American classic dubbed into Italian—*Il Padrino parte seconda*, or *The Godfather, Part II*. Many a mafioso has expressed admiration for the famous series of Mafia movies that presents their traditions in such a romantic light. After the couple watched two generations of the fictional Corleone family solve their mounting problems with acts of murder, they left the small theater that was something of a family holding, owned, as it was, by Palmina Puliafito, sister of Vic Cotroni.

If a director were looking for a location to film a mob rub-out, he would have to look no further than the area around this theater, with its faded, inner-city feel that came from being nestled in the shadows between expressways. Arm in arm, Sciarra and his wife were walking to the parking lot when a hooded man stepped from the darkness. The masked figure quickly drew a 12-gauge shotgun and leveled it at Sciarra. There must have been a sudden moment of panicked understanding by the mobster before the blast wrenched him from his wife's arm and knocked him to the ground, where he lay dying.

If Sciarra had thought his Sicilian blood offered him some insulation from the Sixth Family, or if he felt his patron, Violi, was powerful enough to protect him, he was terribly shortsighted on both counts. Straddling two worlds had made Sciarra particularly vulnerable: he was a member of the Sicilian Mafia and, as such, the Sicilian Mafia had no need to go through diplomatic channels or take into consideration another mob group's code. They could deal with him in the way they wanted.

The blast that killed Sciarra was the opening shot in a war that had really been declared three years before. In the wake of Sciarra's murder, police investigators and mobsters of all stripes braced for an all-out war in Montreal.

———

A careful chess player might take out an opponent's strong supporting pieces before advancing on his king. It weakens the opposition, makes the final assault safer, with fewer casualties and, most important, saps the opponent's ability to raise an effective counter-attack. Such moves by a tactician—a careful planner who thinks before moving, never rushing—might take more time, but are calculated to lead inexorably toward the final, decisive victory. It is this strategy, that of a chess player, that police ascribe to the Rizzuto organization when it finally moved against Violi. The removal of Sciarra was a sound opening position; it garnered attention, made a clear point and removed a valuable strategic asset from the enemy. But there were other obstacles blocking the path to power, and additional targets in this creeping, rather than sweeping, coup d'état.

Francesco Violi was nine years younger than Paulo Violi and yet was the tallest and most physical of the family. The top of Paolo Violi's head barely made it past Francesco's ears, and while Paolo Violi had a certain girth, his center of gravity was lower in the gut than that of Francesco, whose shoulders were broad and muscular. Francesco's physical attributes had been put to good use; he had accepted his role as an enforcer, the most trusted of the family's muscle, and dutifully did much of the dirty work, seemingly without question or compunction. He would do anything to protect his brother and the family name. He could be cruel and stern, quick to hit and slow to relent. Francesco was considered even more volatile than his brother, who was known for his temper. If Paolo Violi went to war, he would want Francesco in the front lines. And if Paolo was hit, Francesco could be expected to explode with bloodthirsty rage and exact an awful revenge as a matter of honor. This family dynamic did not go unnoticed.

On February 8, 1977—just six days shy of the anniversary of Sciarra's murder—Francesco Violi was working in the office of Violi Importing and Distributing Co. Ltd., a family firm located in an industrialized stretch of Rivière-des-Prairies, on the northern shore of the Island of Montreal. Francesco was apparently alone and talking on the telephone at his desk, set well inside the office, when assailants marched in and opened fire. The attackers—police believe there were at least two—did not wish to botch the job; besides a shotgun blast to the face, Francesco's body was peppered with bullets from a pistol.

"Although it was not proven," says an FBI report from 1985, "Nick Rizzuto is suspected of ordering this murder."

Paolo Violi was in jail at the time, serving the last of his sentence for contempt. He had been greatly shaken by the murder of Sciarra, and was no doubt terribly upset by the death of his brother. He would have known by then, if not before, that he was a marked man. And yet, upon his release from jail, he remained impassive and restrained. There is no indication he was rallying his troops for war. He maintained many of his old routines and old associations, visiting gangsters and friends alike along the familiar streets of Saint-Léonard. And even though the Reggio Bar, his old headquarters on Jean-Talon, had been sold to a pair of Sicilian mobsters, he continued to visit and could often be seen there sipping espresso.

———

Despite the felling of Sciarra and Francesco Violi, there was—unbelievably—still talking to be done. A last-ditch effort was made to settle the dispute. It is unknown who insisted on the meeting, for it is difficult to imagine anyone believing that things could now be settled in any other way than more bullets and blood. And yet, there it was, a face-to-face meeting arranged in 1977 between Nick Rizzuto and Paolo Violi, a rarity since Nick's relocation to Venezuela.

His other failings aside, few could accuse Violi of cowardice. It must have taken significant internal fortitude for him, at such a heated, vulnerable time, to willingly return to the Arcuri home.

For this final sit-down, Nick and Violi arrived separately. With the Reggio wiretaps now removed, such private moments were once again closely guarded secrets. As such, it is impossible to say how sincere either was in proffering peace. Violi brought no offer of abdication; Nick, no sign of submission. Neither apparently was conciliatory. Perhaps Nick wished to formally deliver to Violi—*faccia-a-faccia*—something of an ultimatum. For his part, Violi likely wanted to show he was unmoved, unafraid and unprepared to waver from his position that he was the rightful heir to the Montreal *decina*. Whatever was said between the two men that day did not erase their disagreement or ease its tensions. They had, in the parlance of the modern divorce court, irreconcilable differences.

"The meeting held in Montreal did nothing to stem violence," an FBI briefing paper noted.

MONTREAL, LATE JANUARY 1978

Police realized something was amiss when the tone and tenor of underworld talk about Paolo Violi slipped from derisive to malevolent. Within the inner circle of the Sicilian coterie, thoughts were shifting from merely wishing calamity upon him to actively plotting it. Police were hearing rumors from street sources and wiretaps that Violi's position was precarious.

If the plot against Violi was obvious to investigators, Violi himself surely knew of it. In fact, police tried to discuss it with him, but he rebuffed them, just as he had refused the Quebec crime inquiry. Violi was not one to run, nor to seek the aid of the state, even if it was his best—or only—chance of survival. When word reached Montreal police that several Rizzuto men were plotting Violi's murder, surveillance officers started keeping a close eye on the suspects. Much of their time was spent watching the comings and goings at Mike's Submarines in Saint-Léonard. After weeks of police surveillance, often late into the night, nothing happened.

On Friday, January 20, 1978, the police surveillance teams were called off for the weekend, an officer involved in the surveillance said. It was about money. The overtime bills were getting too high and the officers had gotten nowhere in their search for information that might result in the laying of charges, he said. The anniversary of Francesco Violi's murder was 19 days away. The second anniversary of Sciarra's murder was six days after that. Thoughts of mortality must have been on Violi's mind.

On Sunday evening, January 22, two days after police were told to suspend their watch of Mike's Submarines, Violi was at his old headquarters, the Reggio Bar on Jean-Talon. He had received the invitation by telephone, after dinner with his family. Perhaps a dozen familiar faces milled about inside. A game of cards was under way and Violi, wearing a wide-lapeled leisure suit over a white shirt, a popular style at the time, sat in a plastic and steel-tube frame chair, pulled up to a wood and Formica table at the back of the wood-paneled bar.

Someone at the bar placed a phone call: "The pig is here."

Shortly afterward, at 7:32 p.m., a masked man carrying an Italian-made shotgun called a *lupara*, a stubby, double-barreled weapon, crept toward Violi from behind. The masked man shoved the barrel into the back of Violi's head and fired. His body slumped to the fake marble floor, where he lay sprawled, arms and legs outstretched, in a growing pool of blood.

There followed a second phone call.

"The pig is dead."

———

Although the hit was successful, it was by no means carried out without flaws. Police had more clues to work with than in most Mafia murders, which are notoriously hard to solve without cooperating witnesses. Circumstantial evidence gathered before the killing was compelling. Police issued arrest warrants for five suspects. Three men were quickly arrested in Montreal: Domenico Manno, Vito Rizzuto's uncle on his mother's side; Agostino Cuntrera, a proprietor of Mike's Submarines who was a cousin of Alfonso Caruana; and Giovanni DiMora, a brother-in-law to both Agostino Cuntrera and Liborio Cuntrera, one of the patriarchs of the Caruana–Cuntrera clan. Another man arrested was Vincenzo Randisi, one of the new owners of the Reggio Bar and a friend of Nick Rizzuto's, but he was quickly released and the charges against him dropped for lack of evidence. The remaining official suspect became a fugitive. Paolo Renda had left Montreal for Venezuela, where he remained out of reach of Canadian authorities.

The Sixth Family had struck.

On September 15, 1978, Domenico Manno, Agostino Cuntrera and Giovanni DiMora pleaded guilty to conspiracy to murder Violi. They were issued modest sentences, the judge having been convinced that their efforts to establish legitimate careers and firm community ties made them good candidates for rehabilitation. In the end, the killing of Violi was strictly a family affair. All of those convicted were related by blood or marriage, a key marker of Sixth Family success. Curiously, when Manno was arrested, he was quick to distance Nick and Vito Rizzuto from the crime, telling authorities they were not implicated in the plot.

"After his arrest, Dominico Manno signed a written declaration that notably mentioned that Nicolò Rizzuto is his brother-in-law and that Vito Rizzuto is his nephew," a report by the Montreal police says. "He says that both of them have been in Venezuela for about two years. It is important to underline that [Vito] Rizzuto has maintained ties with people associated with the murder of Paolo Violi over the years." Indeed, over the following years, the trio of conspirators remained close to each other and to Vito and Paolo Renda as well. When police raided the Club Social Consenza, the Sixth Family's headquarters, a little before 10 p.m. on March 3, 1983, among the 22 people inside were Vito, Renda and Agostino Cuntrera. In December of that year, at a boxing match at the Montreal Forum, Vito was seen talking with all three men convicted in the death plot. They were seen together again on March 25, 1984, at a boxing match that pitted Dave Hilton, Jr., against Mario Caisson. Vito sat with Cuntrera and Renda, with DiMora seated nearby, at the end of their row. And Manno and Cuntrera were also invited to the June 3, 1995, wedding of Vito's son, Nicolò, to Eleonora Ragusa, daughter of Emanuele Ragusa, another figure in the constellation of Sixth Family clans.

"[Nick] Rizzuto is suspected of authorizing the murder," an FBI report says. "Other suspects were Paolo Renda, Rizzuto's son-in-law, and Joseph LoPresti, another member of the Sicilian faction in Montreal."

After the convictions, authorities seemed satisfied; the only outstanding arrest warrant in the case, the one against Paolo Renda, was canceled and he returned to Montreal a free man. LoPresti remained untouched, despite deep and enduring suspicion by police.

The end of Paolo Violi, however, was not entirely the end of things between the Sixth Family and the Violis.

It was two and a half years after the death of Paolo Violi when Rocco, the last of the Violi brothers (another brother, Giuseppe, who was Rocco's twin, had died in 1970 in a car crash), realized that the mob was not yet finished with his family. Rocco was in the driver's seat of his Oldsmobile, idling at a red light in Montreal, when a motorcycle pulled alongside him. A sawed-off shotgun was lowered and fired. The blast narrowly missed Rocco, who, despite the shock, jammed on his accelerator. The motorcyclist caught up to him and fired again, catching him in the head with a splatter of pellets. Almost miraculously, he survived, but then, like his brother, declined the assistance of the authorities.

Summer slipped into fall and Rocco perhaps thought he had been given a reprieve. He was not, after all, a major player in the mob, had no apparent designs on the leadership in Montreal and had not sought revenge over the death of his brothers.

On October 17, 1980, Rocco was seated with his family in the kitchen of their Saint-Léonard home when a single sniper's bullet, from a high-powered rifle, punched through a window and killed him. No one can accuse mobsters of not being thorough when they put their minds to it. The Violi boys were all dead, buried together at Notre-Dame-des-Neiges cemetery, on the imposing heights of Montreal's Mount Royal, a generation destroyed.

If New York had finally turned its back on the Violis in their dispute with the Rizzutos, at least one old mafioso remembered the family's hospitality. A wreath sent to Rocco Violi's funeral bore the name of Joe Bonanno.

The FBI attributed Rocco's slaying to the war with the Rizzutos: "Nick Rizzuto is believed to have ordered this killing as well. This murder is described by the RCMP as yet another act of revenge by Rizzuto for his expulsion to Venezuela," an FBI report says.

Though the blame may lie with the Sixth Family, it was not about revenge. It was about the future, not the past.

––––––––

With Violi and his brothers eliminated, the Sixth Family's primary irritant and impediment was removed—just as Pietro Licata had been removed in New York. The ensuing transformation of organized crime in Canada was unequivocal.

Despite the seemingly interminable delays, the mob had secured Montreal in time to allow the Sicilian expatriate clans on both sides of the U.S.–Canada border to put the final pieces together in what would become the Pizza Connection. This drug-smuggling and distribution enterprise brought in high-quality heroin that had been processed in clandestine laboratories in Sicily. Much of it was channeled through Canada and sent on to New York, where it was distributed through storefront retailers, many of them pizzeria owners for whom the restaurants were legitimate fronts that hid their criminal activity. The billion-dollar Pizza Connection would go on to eclipse the famed heroin rings of the past, including the French Connection. And, like its antecedent, it was really a system of intersecting, meandering routes that at once competed and complemented each other.

The end of the Sixth Family–Violi feud brought two changes that Canadian police noted in internal reports. The first was the return to Montreal of Vito Rizzuto. Vito returned from Venezuela "to slowly take over," RCMP documents said. The second was an increase in drug activity in the city.

"After the Paolo Violi murder," says an internal Canadian police intelligence report from 1990, "the Sicilians took the dominant role in Montreal. The Sicilians quickly and quietly began a large drug importing operation. They transformed the port of Montreal into the gateway to North America for hashish shipments from Pakistan and Lebanon and large heroin shipments from Sicily and Thailand. They sold most of their heroin in New York and New Jersey."

Nick and Vito, however, did not immediately seize control of the city's rackets. The official boss of the Montreal *decina* was still Vic Cotroni, who had left the day-to-day business to Violi. Even if the Sixth Family had wished to kill him, it would have been frowned on. It was not necessary for the Sixth Family to remove Cotroni. The wise old don seemed to know better than to try to hem in the Rizzuto organization. As long as the Sixth Family could fulfill their obligations in the drug pipeline, their patience seemed endless. Although Cotroni kept his job as boss, the demise of Violi allowed a reordering of power that would continue to tip in favor of the Sicilians.

"The already tenuous alliance between Calabrian and Sicilian factions worsened. The 'Sicilian faction' began its take-over of Montreal," a private RCMP briefing says.

If the changing of the guard was slow to manifest itself on the streets of Montreal, it was strikingly evident elsewhere. The Rizzutos were active with major Sicilian mafiosi, South American drug lords and leading New York gangsters in the years immediately after Violi's murder. The Sixth Family seemed content to concentrate on building its international infrastructure, shoring up its networks and conducting private business until Montreal was formally cleared for them. They knew the wait would not be long, as Cotroni was dying of cancer. Nick and his family had their official mob status restored in Montreal, although Nick still spent much, if not most, of his time in Venezuela and Europe in the years after Violi's death. Vito was the family's face in the city and he prepared for a future where the Sixth Family would be soundly and securely in control. Cotroni was often said to be in semi-retirement when Violi was running things on his behalf; with the Rizzutos running free, there was little that was "semi" about it. His title remained and little else.

———————

By September 1981, Nick, Vito and other family members, along with some of their closest associates, had bought a long strip of property along Antoine-Berthelet Avenue, in an exclusive Montreal neighborhood near the waterfront on the southwestern edge of the city. Here they built several large, posh homes and moved in, signaling not only their return, but their triumph.

Along the far side of the street at the end of the secluded sub-division was a short string of mansions. Near one end was Nick and Libertina's house, in a Colonial-revival style of red brick with white decorative accents and dramatic circular porch featuring two-story columns. Over time, the evergreen trees planted in front would grow to tower over the pagoda-like roof. Next door was the home of their daughter, Maria, and her husband, Paolo Renda, with a wraparound front porch, double front doors, white stone facade and a terracotta tile roof, an outsized version of the roofs typical in their old village in Sicily. Beside that was the home of Vito and his wife, Giovanna, the most spectacular on the street; a colossal structure that was part Tudor style, with decorative half-timbering, and part Medieval revival, with imposing dark stone and recessed doorway. It was with an eye to Vito's interest in expensive automobiles that the design included an impressive three-car garage, larger than the entire area of most homes. Toward the end of the block, on the other side of Vito's house, was another impressive home, with a two-car garage and white brickwork. Joe LoPresti and his family would move in here. Beside the LoPresti property at the time was an empty lot that was awaiting construction of yet another home, this one for Gerlando Sciascia. It would never be built. Although only a few people on the street are linked to the mob, it is still often called *Rue de Mafia*, "Mafia Street," in Montreal.

As their business was to be largely kept away from their homes, they also established a headquarters where more unsavory people could visit. Long before Cotroni died, the Club Social Consenza, on Jarry Street East in Montreal, was in full swing as a gambling den, organizational headquarters and social club in the New York City Mafia tradition.

Like his Godfather, Joe Bonanno, Cotroni enjoyed a relative luxury among mob bosses who had lost a showdown with a rival. His life was claimed by nature, not man. He died of cancer on September 16, 1984, apparently while watching television coverage of Pope John Paul II's visit to Canada. It was a serene end for a man who had seen so much vice and violence during a career at the top of the underworld. Cotroni's funeral, in north Montreal, was a send-off fit for minor royalty, complete with a 17-piece brass band and a road-choking number of limousines just to carry the flower arrangements. Among the many mourners were two tall, neatly dressed men who showed the appropriate respect and sadness at the passing of the Godfather.

Police identified them as Vito Rizzuto and his loyal Sixth Family colleague Joe LoPresti.

———

With Cotroni's passing, the Rizzutos' control over Montreal was complete. The rank-and-file members and associates of the Mafia quickly fell into line, easily flipping their allegiance and answering as smartly and respectfully to the Rizzutos as they had to Cotroni and Violi.

Leslie Coleman, for instance, had been a young enforcer for Luigi Greco in the 1950s and was "inherited" by Violi when Greco died. After the deaths of Violi and Cotroni, Coleman was frequently seen flexing his muscles beside members of the Rizzuto organization. Similarly, Joe DiMaulo, who was such a close and personal part of Violi's inner circle that Violi asked him to represent the entire Montreal organization in meetings with the Bonanno leadership in New York, seemed just as content to ply his trade under the Rizzuto banner. Most surprising to many, even the remnants of the Cotroni family bowed to Nick and Vito Rizzuto. In 1979, Frank Cotroni was released from a U.S. prison and returned to a Montreal that was vastly different from the one he had left. As a good mobster, Frank accepted the changing of the guard and settled in to play his part in the new order of the Montreal *decina*. As an enthusiastic drug trafficker, Frank fit in far better with the Sixth Family than with Paolo Violi. He died in 2004, also of cancer, at the age of 72.

The taking of Montreal was a significant feat in the context of global crime.

"For the past 25 years, Montreal has been the key that turns the lock of America," said a high-ranking anti-Mafia investigator in Italy who has spent a career probing organized crime and the drug trade as an officer in the Carabinieri. "The one holding that key becomes the pinnacle. You can ship the narcotics, but if there is no one to facilitate the reception of the drugs and the transition into the marketplace, you have no profit. The Montrealers have long held that position." From the 1970s on, expatriate Sicilian Men of Honor—many of whom made up the Sixth Family drug consortium—"smothered" the American Mafia in both Canada and the United States, the Carabinieri officer said.

"They are beguiling. Little of what transpired in America is known, but from the activities of Catalano, Salvatore, it's clear he was able to make significant profits for the bosses of [the American Mafia]," he said of the Zip leader who had taken over Brooklyn. (Italian investigators typically state the last name of a person first, and then the given name.)

"In Canada, things are a little more transparent, thanks to the Violi transcripts: the Rizzuto family was able to promise a transport between the Mafias of Europe and the Mafia of America. Riches were promised for all. Codes meant nothing in the onslaught of finance. It was a situation of cynicism. If the Violi situation had evolved in the 1990s, its resolution would not have taken years. He would have been killed instantly."

The final transfer of power to the Rizzutos had indeed taken far longer than anticipated—six years of battling with Violi followed by six years of waiting for Cotroni to pass away. During those in-between years, the Sixth Family would have an explosive impact on the American Mafia as they continued to work closely with the other expatriate Mafia clans, Sicilian Men of Honor and members of the Five Families to hammer out a new form of international organized crime.

The prominence and significance of the new Montreal organization in New York City would far exceed anything Paolo Violi likely ever dreamed of.

CHAPTER 14

MANHATTAN, JULY 1978

"Why the hell are we standing here?" a newly recruited associate of the Bonanno Family asked, as he milled about in the oppressive summer heat in front of Casa Bella, a restaurant on Mulberry Street in New York's Little Italy. Half a dozen Bonanno soldiers were on the sidewalk with him, all having similarly been summoned to this spot.

"We're out here to make sure nothing happens to the Old Man. He's in there," the associate's mob mentor answered.

The man asking the questions was known to all on the street that day as Donnie Brasco, a jewel thief with great mob potential. He was, they would later be horrified to learn, really FBI Special Agent Joseph D. Pistone, posing as a bad guy in an unprecedented undercover operation. The man answering his questions was Benjamin "Lefty" Ruggiero, a made man in the Bonanno Family, a prodigious killer and an inveterate gambler. The "Old Man" he spoke of was Carmine "Lilo" Galante.

"What's the big deal? What's gonna happen to him?" Brasco asked.

"Things are going on. There's a lot of things you don't know, Donnie. Things I can't talk about," Lefty said. "You don't know how mean this guy is, Donnie. Lilo is a mean son of a bitch. A tyrant. That's just me telling you, it don't go no further. Lot of people hate him. They feel he's only out for himself. He's the only one making any money. There's only a few people that he's close to. And mainly that's the Zips, like Cesare [Bonventre] and those that you see around Toyland," Lefty said of the Toyland Social Club, a Bonanno hangout on the outskirts of Little Italy.

"Those guys are always with him. He brought them over from Sicily and he uses them for different pieces of work and for dealing all that junk," Lefty continued, using the mob slang for heroin. "They're as mean as he is. You can't trust those bastard Zips. Nobody can. Except the Old Man. He can trust them because he brought them over here and he can control them. Everybody else has to steer clear of him. There's a lot of people out there who would like to see him get whacked."

Lefty Ruggiero was a soldier of great loyalty who had killed many times for the family. His enduring legacy as a mobster, however, will forever be his introduction into the Bonanno Family of "Donnie Brasco." For Lefty, and for any number of other made Bonanno soldiers, Galante was the boss. It highlights the disarray within the family at the time that its leadership was such an open question. Others insisted Philip "Rusty" Rastelli, who was in prison, was still the boss, having been picked for the post in 1974 during a meeting that included Paolo Violi's representative from Montreal. Lefty had it right that Galante's gruff presence and monomaniacal plans were causing dissent within the family—and outside it as well—but he was misinformed about Galante's true rank.

"He wasn't the boss. I guess he wanted to be the boss, but he didn't make it," said Frank Lino, a former Bonanno captain. "He was a captain of the Montreal crew. At one time, he just wanted to take over Montreal, didn't want anything to do with New York."

Sal Vitale was equally emphatic: "He was never the official boss. ... [Galante] was a captain with the Bonanno Family, [a] very powerful individual."

What Galante wanted to do was to use that power to gain control of the family, unify it under his banner and then flood America with high-grade heroin. The profits would flow ever upwards until they reached him. And then, likely, go no further: not to Sicily, not to Canada and not to the other New York families. As it was, although he was not the official boss, Galante was already demanding a "boss's cut" from all Bonanno wiseguys. Echoing the attitude of Nick Rizzuto in Montreal toward Violi, Galante just ignored the fact that the family already had a boss.

Galante was able to hijack the boss's position not only because of his strength but because of Rastelli's weakness. For the captains and soldiers on the street, it put them in an uncomfortable position. Galante was forcing the issue, telling them to choose sides, and Galante was a hard man to say no to. Mobsters and cops alike tell of how frightening it was just to look into his cold eyes.

Among those ambitious Bonanno soldiers and captains trying to navigate the situation was Joseph "Big Joey" Massino, a mobster who was bright and had a keen mind for strategy. Massino was broad and plump, with thick, fleshy arms and a double chin. Even with the plush exterior, however, he did not look soft. He wore his dark, wavy hair longer than most mobsters, which, coupled with his preference for T-shirts that showed his panther tattoo on his left arm, made him look less like a stereotypical Mafia leader and more like a petty thug. Just as the gentlemanly air of "Mr. Settecasi" was deceiving, so, too, was Massino's look of being a dumb tough. If his hair and clothes rubbed older mobsters the wrong way, there was one thing Massino did that erased any concern—he was an earner. He proved himself to be resourceful, smart and careful. Born in 1943, Massino grew up in Queens and, like Sal Vitale, his childhood friend and future mob colleague, attended Grover Cleveland High School. Massino first met Vitale as a young boy when Vitale's sister, who was friendly with Massino, introduced them. Four years older, Massino taught Vitale how to swim at the local swimming pool. Leaving school early, Massino made good money hijacking trucks and selling the stolen cargo before he moved into other mob activities. By the late 1960s he was running snack trucks around construction sites from which he sold food and drink as a cover for the more profitable activities of gambling and loan sharking. He franchised one of these routes out to Vitale for $16,000.

"It was a catering truck, a coffee wagon. Serves coffee, cake, sandwiches, lunch—so it's a roach coach. They call it a roach coach," Vitale said. When Vitale started breaking into factories and pulling off petty heists with two friends, it did not take long for Massino to hear of it. Vitale was unloading his deli truck one day when he was approached by Massino.

"I heard you're doing scoring," Massino announced.

"That ain't true," was Vitale's reply.

"Don't lie to me. Philip Rastelli sent me word, if you're going to do scores, do it with me," Massino said. From then on, Vitale was put on record as working for Massino, and he could lie to his mentor no more. At the time, Vitale was ignorant of the larger concerns of organized crime.

"I did not have the foggiest," Vitale said. "There is no book. You try to follow a person that you respect, admire and he would teach you." Massino gave him "on-the-job training," and it was the beginning of a long partnership between the two men. Vitale had hitched his wagon to an impressive star. In the mid-1970s, Massino was inducted into the Bonanno Family at the invitation of Rastelli.

"He was friends with Louis Rastelli. Louis Rastelli was nephew of Philip Rastelli, Philip Rastelli being the boss, that's how he got close to Philip Rastelli," Vitale said of Massino. Massino even called Rastelli "Unc," short for uncle, displaying the same affection his friend Louis had for his Uncle Phil. Massino worked first as a soldier in the crew headed by James Galante, Carmine's nephew, and later, in the crew headed by Philip "Philly Lucky" Giaccone.

By the time Carmine Galante was eyeing the tarnished Bonanno throne, Massino needed all the support he could muster, especially given his known ties to the true boss. With Rastelli in prison, Galante was anxious to sever all his contact with Bonanno soldiers on the outside. One day in the late 1970s, Galante called Massino to a meeting. Vitale drove him to see Galante and waited in the car, parked nearby on a corner, for his mentor to return.

"This guy is going to kill me," Massino said to Vitale when he got back into the car. "He doesn't want me to visit Phil Rastelli in jail." It was a request Massino felt he had to refuse. "He is like my uncle. He raised me, baptized me. I can't abandon him; I have to go visit him," Massino said. Massino, after all, owed his mob existence to Rastelli; the "baptism" was a reference to his induction into the Mafia. Despite his support for Rastelli, behind closed doors Massino was often less than adoring.

"How smart can Rastelli really be?" he once complained to Vitale. "He spent half of his life in jail."

Others cut Rastelli a little more slack, particularly the conservative forces on the Commission. If there was one thing the bosses of the Five Families tended to agree on, it was that killing bosses was not a good idea. It was a move aimed more at their own safety than honor, but it was a pervasive—although not always strictly adhered to—rule of thumb. When Rastelli complained of Galante's preemptory activities, he had a sympathetic audience. When the other bosses started hearing stories of Galante's ambition to be the first among equals in New York, their desire to see him dead only heightened. With the loss of support from the other bosses, Galante lost any safety net that the Commission might have provided him. He was shedding friends left and right in New York but seemed hardly to care, primarily because he placed his faith so deeply in the Zips, men he knew—even if the FBI and the other gangsters did not—would pay little heed to the whims and wishes of the Commission. Like Violi before him, Galante was becoming increasingly isolated.

His faith in his own worth and the fealty of the Zips was grossly misplaced. It was not to him that the Zips were pledged, it was to themselves, to their Sicilian kin and to their heroin franchise. The heroin pipeline was starting to flow. The Sicilian clans had expatriate outposts in South America and their own clannish operatives in America. The Sixth Family, meanwhile, had taken Montreal, severing the firm ties Galante had had with the city under Violi. What need was there now for Carmine Galante and his grabbing, controlling demands?

Contrary to Lefty's private summation of the lay of the land to Donnie Brasco, crediting Galante's success to the loyalty of the Zips, the Sicilian gangsters seem to have had their own secret mission.

Galante had opened the door, inviting the Sicilian Men of Honor in. Once there, they were perfectly at ease attacking their host.

VALLEY STREAM, LONG ISLAND, JUNE 5, 1979

Cynical developers often say that they name their construction projects after whatever natural feature they demolished to make room for bricks and mortar. This was perhaps how the Green Acres Mall in Valley Stream, Long Island, got its name. One of the largest shopping malls in New York State, it contained dozens of retail stores, food outlets and three large department stores. Only one shop, however, was of interest to two plainclothes police officers in an unmarked Plymouth Valiant. California Pizza offered hot pizzas, cold drinks and—at this outlet, at the time that it was run by the Sixth Family's Gerlando Sciascia—a lot of heroin on the side. Drug sales exceeded anything running through the cash register from the food.

The Valiant entered the mall parking lot at around 9:30 p.m. on Tuesday, June 5, 1979, and made a slow sweep across the darkened pavement. In a parked car, facing the storefronts, were two men in a blue Cadillac. As the Valiant passed, the men in the Cadillac turned their faces away, but it was too late—one of the officers recognized the man sitting behind the wheel as Baldo Amato. Beside him was Cesare Bonventre. These were two of the most aggressive Zips in the Brooklyn Sicilian faction and Carmine Galante's favorites. The Valiant continued past, out of sight of the Cadillac, and then did a wide turn and crept in between a cluster of cars near Gimbel Brothers Department Store. Hidden, the officers watched the Cadillac for half an hour until it moved closer to Sciascia's California Pizza. The officers continued their surveillance on foot, one man watching the Cadillac, and the other the pizzeria. That was when they noticed a second Cadillac idling in the parking lot.

By now it was closing time. Through binoculars, an officer saw a man and a woman locking up. The man, silver-haired and stocky, was, in all likelihood, Sciascia. He left the pizzeria and went to a third Cadillac parked in front of his store. That car turned around near Gimbels and met the second Cadillac that was idling there. There was a shuffling about of Cadillacs and two of the cars sat, driver's door to driver's door, almost touching. After a minute, the second Cadillac sped away, racing through the parking lot behind Gimbels; Sciascia's Cadillac—number three—headed north and stopped suddenly in the middle of the lot. Meanwhile, the first Cadillac, the one the officers had spotted with Amato and Bonventre inside, cut a sharp turn of its own and ended up facing south. All the curious movement piqued the officers' curiosity. They radioed for backup and a short time later another unmarked police car cruised into the lot and stopped out of sight behind a steakhouse. Everyone waited.

"I observed [Cadillac] number three flash its high beams," one of the officers recalled, referring to Sciascia's car. "I observed [Cadillac] number one do the same," meaning Bonventre and Amato's car. "Number three then proceeded up to number one." In a quick sequence of moves, Bonventre hopped out of one car carrying a package close to his body and climbed into the rear of Sciascia's car; when he got out again, he was carrying his leather jacket wrapped around an object about three feet long, the size and shape of a sawed-off shotgun. He stopped briefly at the other Cadillac, apparently passing the long package over, before returning to Amato's car. Then, as if by agreement, the three cars suddenly lurched into motion. The officers in the Valiant went after Sciascia's Cadillac but it was gone, traveling "at a tremendously high rate of speed," an officer said, "as fast as the car can go starting from a dead stop."

Similarly, Cadillac number two with its unidentified occupants sped away from the plaza and was lost to the officers. The backup police car, however, went after Bonventre and Amato's Cadillac and managed to pull it over near the exit to the westbound Sunrise Highway. The men inside identified themselves: the 28-year-old Bonventre said he was a pizzeria operator from Brooklyn; Amato, 27, said he owned a deli. Both said they were originally from Castellammare del Golfo, Sicily, and were cousins.

In the car, police found the tools of assassination. Poking out from inside a paper bag was a revolver, loaded and with the serial number stripped. In a pouch hanging from the back of the front seat was another loaded pistol. Officers also found a switchblade, bullets, two black ski masks, rubber gloves, a rubber Halloween mask and other knives. Bonventre had $1,800—all in $50 bills—in his pockets; Amato, just a few hundred. Written on what officers call "pocket litter"—scraps of paper, notes, matchbooks and so forth found in pockets—were the names and telephone numbers of the cafés in Brooklyn run by various gangsters associated with the Zips, and there were the names of heroin traffickers in America and Sicily. It would be 10 years before these names and numbers became significant—when they were linked to the defendants charged in what came to be known as the Pizza Connection case. At the time, though, the officers merely noted the numbers, as they were more interested in where the shotgun that appeared to have been passed from Sciascia's car, had got to. Bonventre and Amato were arrested on weapons charges, granted bail and returned to whatever business they had that required guns, masks and rubber gloves. The missing shotgun might well have made an appearance the following month.

BROOKLYN, JULY 12, 1979

A stifling heat had enveloped New York when Carmine Galante stepped out of a black Cadillac, having been dropped off at the door of a favored eatery on Knickerbocker Avenue by his nephew, James Galante. Joe and Mary's Italian-American Restaurant offered good food and was family-run, both of which were appreciated by Galante, who enjoyed eating and was related to the proprietor. The "Joe" in the restaurant's name was Giuseppe "Joe" Turano, Galante's cousin and a made Bonanno member. Galante sat near the door on the open-air patio, on one of a hodgepodge of mismatched chairs. He was flanked by his favorite bodyguards—two Zips, Cesare Bonventre and Baldo Amato—and joined at his table by Turano and Leonardo Coppolla, a Bonanno captain. It was late for lunch, about 2:45 p.m., but the mobsters nonetheless ate their fill.

As Galante finished his meal, a blue Mercury Montego, a car that blended in better on Knickerbocker Avenue than Galante's black Cadillac, pulled up in front of the restaurant, blocking the roadway by double parking. One man stayed seated at the steering wheel while four others, carrying guns and wearing ski masks, climbed out. One of these stayed beside the car looking up and down the street while the three others filed into the restaurant. Inside, they again split, with one training a shotgun on the kitchen staff, telling them to shut up and stay still, while the remaining two rushed through to the backyard. From the patio came a shout, the voice of restaurant owner Joe Turano.

"What are you doing?" Any other words were drowned out by gunfire.

After the fusillade, the gunmen left as quickly as they had arrived. Leaving with them, unscathed in the melee and seemingly unperturbed, were Bonventre and Amato. Out back, Galante, Turano and Coppolla lay dead. Galante's body was sprawled in a heap, his head resting on a concrete curb, his left eyeball popped by a bullet or shotgun pellet, his famous cigar still clenched between his teeth and his blood slowly seeping into an iron-grated drain on the patio floor.

———

The murder of a man as notorious as Galante sparked as much frenzy within the mob as it did in the New York tabloids. Special Agent Pistone, still undercover as Donnie Brasco, was in Miami when Galante was killed. The next morning, he received a phone call from Lefty, his mob mentor, telling him to go out and buy a New York newspaper. Pictures of Galante's corpse were on the front of most papers.

"There's gonna be big changes," Lefty told Brasco. Indeed there were. At a face-to-face meeting soon after—for such things could not be said over the phone—Lefty brought him, and, inadvertently, the FBI, up to date.

"Rusty Rastelli is the new boss even though he is still in the can," Lefty said, still unaware of the true nature of Galante's position at the time of his death. "We're gonna be under Sonny Black. He was made captain." Dominick "Sonny Black" Napolitano's promotion was one small part of the vast reorganization within the Bonanno Family after Galante was removed from the equation. Those who had let Galante get away with his charade as boss, particularly the official underboss, Nicky Marangelo, and Mike Sabella, a captain who ran the Casa Bella restaurant where Galante sometimes held his meetings, were busted down in rank, narrowly escaping death sentences by becoming mere soldiers. Those who had remained loyal to Rastelli were rewarded with promotions. And those who had helped kill Galante were blessed above all.

Cesare Bonventre, one of Galante's bodyguards, was clearly in on the murder conspiracy and undoubtedly one of the shooters. For his act of betrayal he was made a captain. At 28, he was the youngest captain anyone could remember. Shortly after the murder, Bruno Indelicato—Sonny Red's son—was similarly made a captain, as was Joe Massino. Sal Catalano, Lefty told Brasco, was made "the street boss of the Zips." The reorganization was one of the strongest acts of leadership Rastelli had ever managed. He shook up the way his family was run on the streets and worked to ensure that the people in key positions supported him. Looking back, it shows that Rastelli had, in fact, rewarded those who had rid him of Galante. And despite the danger they presented, he accepted the Zips into the family as an official power to be reckoned with. If Galante was the one who had let them in the door, it was Rastelli who offered them a seat at the table.

The masks covering the gunmen's faces protected their secrets for many years. That Bonventre and Amato were in on the assassination, however, seemed obvious to police.

"Baldo Amato and Cesare Bonventre, both present in the back yard with Galante at the time of the shooting, are still prime suspects," says a 1981 update on the case, that was sent by the FBI Special Agent-in-Charge of the Brooklyn–Queens office to federal prosecutors with the Organized Crime Strike Force. The suspiciously timed flight of Sal Catalano to Italy, where he stayed for five months, suggested that he, too, had something to hide. When the getaway car was found, police lifted prints from the middle and ring finger of Santo Giordano, another Zip, from the inside driver's window. Years later, new technology allowed police to identify another print found in the getaway car, a palm print from Bruno Indelicato. Indelicato was already a suspect because, immediately after the murder, he had arrived at the Ravenite, a social club in Little Italy run by Aniello Dellecroce, the Gambino underboss. Waiting at the club was Stefano "Stevie Beef" Cannone, then the Bonanno *consigliere*. Bruno seemed to report some news and then receive a hero's welcome—all of it caught on film by a police surveillance team investigating another matter.

The murder of Galante, U.S. federal prosecutors wrote in court documents filed in 1985, was engineered "to ensure that the Sicilians would enjoy the [narcotics] importation franchise," which Galante had "threatened to disrupt." Prosecutors said that Galante was "trying to control the emerging narcotics traffic from Sicily into the United

States," and that the Zips—particularly Catalano and Bonventre—conspired "to eliminate people who are obstacles to the flow of narcotics." As proof, the government outlined how Galante had been "hoarding a large share of both power and profit," and that after his death "the Sicilian faction succeeded to a significant portion of both his power and his profits. ... So great was the dissension within the Bonanno Family resulting from Galante's refusal to share the Sicilian drug profits with other factions of the family that the survival of the Sicilian faction and their drug business depended on their forming new alliances and killing Galante," the government said. Could that explain the rise in power of Bruno Indelicato, Joe Massino and Sonny Black, all of whom had been bumped up to captain in the wake of Galante's murder?

Frank Lino, a former Bonanno captain, said that these men—and others—were behind the bold assassination of Galante. Bruno Indelicato was indeed one of the masked shooters that afternoon, Lino said. Bruno shot Joe Turano and Coppola, according to what Bruno told Lino. Russell Mauro, a Bonanno soldier who was tight with Sonny Red, was another of the men pushing their way to the back patio. Mauro shot Galante; Bonventre and Amato were in on it; Big Trinny was the masked man inside the restaurant who threatened the kitchen staff with a menacing shotgun, Lino said. Joe Massino, Philly Lucky, J.B. Indelicato and Sonny Red were stationed outside the restaurant to ensure nothing went wrong.

If Lino was right, then the murder of Galante was not the work of rogue gangsters or even a vengeful Zip faction. It was an uprising. The Zips, Sonny Red, Joe Massino—the three main factions—had joined together to end Galante's oppression. The slaying would by no means spell the end of the bloodshed in the war for the New York heroin market. Nor would it immediately restore stability at the top. For a short while, though, there seemed to be some spirit of cooperation.

With Galante out of the way, the new distributors of the heroin were waiting for the Sixth Family and their expatriate Mafia allies to turn on the tap.

CHAPTER 15

MANHATTAN, NOVEMBER 16, 1980

The wedding was set to be a splashy and memorable affair from its religious start to its debauched finish. Giuseppe Bono had booked St. Patrick's Cathedral on Fifth Avenue in Manhattan—the largest Roman Catholic church in the United States—for a solemn ceremony below the great rose window, a marvel of stained glass. The 300 invited guests would then walk behind the happy couple along the inlaid Italian marble floor and down the worn front steps beneath the cathedral's twin spires, and travel 10 blocks northeast for a lavish reception at the Hotel Pierre. The Pierre is a refined-looking Georgian building, a grand 44-story tower topped with an octagonal copper-clad roof overlooking Central Park.

The invitations drawing the well-wishers from across New York and its surrounding suburbs and cities, and from Canada, Italy and England, were simple and elegant: "Miss Antonina Albino and Mr. Giuseppe Bono request the honor of your presence at their marriage on Sunday, the Sixteenth of November, Nineteen Hundred and Eighty at three o'clock. St. Patrick's Cathedral, Fifth Avenue, New York, New York."

Many of the guests skipped the ceremony entirely, however, heading straight to the reception, where the mixed drinks, hard liquor, champagne and wine were flowing freely. It was a tough crowd, after all, filled with men who had spent more time before a judge than before a priest. Brandy and Scotch were popular choices, even before dinner had been served. As a clear sign of bygone times, on each table—amid the ostentatiously oversized bouquets of tropical ruby anthuriums and white trumpet lilies—was a blown-glass cup holding piles of cigarettes for guests to help themselves. And help themselves they did, filling ashtrays in the signature Hotel Pierre china pattern, set among the bottles of San Pellegrino spring water and red wine.

Despite the formal surroundings, this was not a tuxedo-clad crowd. The men opted instead for business suits, white shirts and typically

wide striped ties, and the women for evening gowns, most in conservative styles, suggesting the mobsters were accompanied by their wives,
not their girlfriends.

For Giuseppe Bono, it was a full day spent with his closest friends
and most important and trusted business associates. He obviously
wished it to be memorable. Even with a discount, the cost of the reception—paid for in money orders—climbed to $63,120. And yet he
still set aside $4,746 to pay a professional photographer to capture the
event on film. The guests took turns posing with the bride and groom,
mixing and matching the portrait groupings among friends, relatives
and spouses. The guests posed again as the photographer moved from
table to table with the guests standing or sitting stiffly while grinning
for the camera.

Later, as they flipped through them, the photographs may have
provided Giuseppe and Antonina Bono with many happy memories.
But it is difficult to imagine that even they would have studied the images more closely than hundreds of police agents on three continents.

———

Giuseppe Bono, a short, weedy-looking man with black, thinning hair,
large glasses and crooked front teeth, was 47 at the time of his wedding. When happy, he looked downright impish, like a good-natured
college professor. When well-dressed and serious, he could easily pass
as a banker. When angry or annoyed, however, he appeared oddly
bloodless; his features took on an icy quality that hinted at the dangerous milieu in which he moved. Bono, it was learned by FBI agents
a year after the wedding, was a prodigious, skilled and exceptionally
well-connected drug trafficker, a leading Mafia boss in Italy and a major money launderer. An FBI dossier later described him as "one of the
most knowledgeable men operating abroad in international drug trafficking." His guests that fall day in New York, astonished agents would
learn, were some of the most significant mafiosi and narcotics barons
in the Western world. It was perhaps the largest single gathering in
memory of high-level international mob-linked drug traffickers.

Even to these men, the roving photographer caused no alarm. They
were thoroughly comfortable among friends. And it was not the first
time most had wined and dined at the Pierre. Like many New Yorkers
who enjoyed their wealth, mobsters had long used its facilities for

parties, including a reception in 1975 that Carmine Galante had hosted for his daughter.

When the FBI and DEA learned that a wedding had brought the world's drug-rich mafiosi to New York, they hunted down details of the event. And then, in an intelligence coup that is still exploited by agents to this day, they came upon the wedding photographs.

"They were obtained through a subpoena from the photographer who took them," said Charles Rooney, now the acting deputy assistant director in the FBI's Criminal Investigative Division. In 1981, when the authorities were learning of the Bono wedding, Rooney was an agent in the Bureau's Brooklyn–Queens office and the case agent for what would become the Pizza Connection heroin case.

"We subpoenaed the wedding photographs because we began hearing about a large wedding that took place in the New York City area with a number of different people from various countries, and that got us to start looking for the location of the wedding," Rooney said. "We learned that Giuseppe Bono was a boss of an organized crime family in Milan, Italy. That he arrived here in the United States."

The stack of photographs was huge.

"I think it was at least a hundred photographs, probably more than that," Rooney said. Before the discovery, however, Bono was a man of significant mystery for FBI and DEA agents embarking on fresh investigations into a shadowy group of Sicilian gangsters who had moved into New York with friends galore and money to spare. Bono had, until recently, been listed only as "unknown male" on surveillance photos taken by agents watching the Brooklyn haunts frequented by the Zips. Shortly before his wedding, he was photographed visiting the bakery run by Sal Catalano. Agents tailed the mystery man to a newly built 14-room mansion in Pelham, a New York suburb, and they uncovered the identity of its owner. They now had a name to go with the pinched and bespectacled face: Giuseppe Bono.

It meant nothing to them.

———

The cross-pollination and enhanced relationships between international crime groups in several countries is one of the most important and defining developments in crime. The Mafia of New York were working with Men of Honor in Sicily who, in turn, were working with Asian overlords and corrupt Middle Eastern officials. It was globalization at its most efficient, and these gangsters were early leaders. Certainly, their links were established long before law enforcement had similar arrangements. Many police officers in the United States eyed Italian authorities with suspicion, and anything outside Western Europe was beyond the pale.

American and Canadian interaction was better, as had been shown in previous cases, but even there, some of the best and most sensitive information was jealously guarded. The suspicions went both ways. Foreign law enforcement and security agencies were uncertain how their information might be used. The Cold War, and overarching American political interests abroad, sometimes created a conflict between sound global law-enforcement priorities and the imperatives of U.S. national security interests. Foreign police forces often wondered whether the information they passed along was being used by the FBI to fight crime or by the CIA in pursuit of other interests, and they acted accordingly. Even between U.S. agencies—such as the FBI and the DEA—the trust was not deep and the sharing of information was sometimes done reluctantly, with certain pieces held back. There was always competition among the agencies.

These attitudes helped the emerging expatriate Mafia immeasurably. Strangely, even when information was shared between national police forces, it was not always given the attention it merited. The recordings secretly made at the Reggio Bar during the 1970s, for instance, which had captured Paolo Violi in secret conversation with senior mafiosi, were shared by Canadian authorities with Italy and the United States. By 1976, transcripts of the most relevant conversations had been given to Italy's Ministry of the Interior, where they were slowly passed through government offices until they reached the courts in Agrigento, where Carmelo Cuffaro, a Sicilian mobster caught on the tapes, was on trial. Incredibly, the transcripts were simply filed away and forgotten. It was not until 1984, according to Giovanni Falcone, the famed anti-Mafia magistrate who would later be assassinated for his efforts, that a junior Agrigento magistrate stumbled across them and, realizing their significance, passed them on to Falcone's office. In the right hands they proved explosive, helping to bring dozens of accused men to court almost a decade later in one of Italy's famed maxi-trials. Law enforcement was finally catching on to the value of cooperation.

It started with unofficial, back-channel interaction between individual officers in one police agency talking directly to a contact they had made in another. An FBI agent would talk to an RCMP officer; an RCMP officer would talk to an officer in Rome or Milan. An investigator in Palermo would call an agent in the DEA, and everyone would feed off the street knowledge and expertise of a small cluster of New York City police officers who had been tracking organized crime figures for decades. The unofficial channels expanded as more cases netted more crooks in more countries. The value of these interactions became clear to the young FBI agents starting to probe the influx of Sicilian gangsters into Brooklyn and the movement of money out of the country.

It seemed a simple question, put to the Italian authorities by two inquisitive agents in the FBI's Brooklyn–Queens office. All Special Agents Charles Rooney and Carmine Russo wanted to know was: Did the name Giuseppe Bono mean anything to Italian police? The question hit like a hurricane. When Italy's anti-Mafia investigators heard that Bono had turned up in New York, they were astounded. They knew him well, as a significant Mafia boss who had disappeared when their investigations of him started to gain traction. He was considered a fugitive, whereabouts unknown, although police suspected he was hiding out in Venezuela with Nick Rizzuto and the Caruana–Cuntreras. Bono had worked with Montreal's mobsters for decades, at least since 1964, according to Tomasso Buscetta, the Sicilian *mafioso*.

The FBI then realized it needed to pay close attention to the Zips.

In Italy, the probe into the Bono organization was rejuvenated. In both countries, the investigations—and criminal indictments—would prove to be expansive. But that was a long way off.

The FBI discreetly started to share the Bono wedding pictures with the DEA, New York City police, the RCMP and several Italian agencies. For those officers in the loop, it became something of a parlor game—pin the name on the mobster. The FBI wanted to know the identity of each and every attendee at Bono's wedding. For years, the wedding photos were shown to almost every informant who agreed to cooperate with authorities, each being asked to put a name to as many people as he could.

The list that slowly emerged was incredible. Almost every adult male present at Bono's wedding was involved in organized crime and the drug trade. Bono, it seemed, opened up his Rolodex of international drug contacts and sent each of them one of his elegant invitations.

Perhaps even he was surprised by the number of positive responses. It suggests the interest they all had in maintaining a relationship with him and his colleagues. The Bono wedding photographs became an illustrated guide to the world's Mafia-run drug trade.

"Anyone who was anyone in Italian organized crime was invited," said Tom Tripodi, the former U.S. drug agent.

The Sixth Family was there, of course. Featured in several of the photographs was a tall man with dark hair and long face who was among the most tastefully dressed of all the guests; in a black two-piece suit, crisp white shirt and soft silver tie dotted with black was Vito Rizzuto.

In one photograph, Rizzuto stands smartly with the smiling bride, who is splaying her fingers over his arm to show off her new diamond ring and thick gold band. With her other hand, she clutches the hand of Vito's wife, Giovanna, who in turn has her free hand draped over the shoulder of Giuseppe Bono. The portrait exudes an air of warmth and familiarity, as they stand in front of a trellis draped with fresh-cut Shasta daisies. Another photograph features a smiling groom, as if he is just at the end of enjoying a good joke, standing with Vito and his lieutenant, Joe LoPresti, a towering man who is one of the few in the room taller than Vito.

A third photograph shows Vito and his wife standing with the guests assigned to their dinner table. Standing with them is LoPresti and his wife, Rosa Lumia. Seated at the same table was Gerlando Sciascia with his second wife, Mary Elizabeth Macfadyen. Sciascia was also close to the groom, so much so that Bono had asked Sciascia's daughter to be a flower girl in his wedding party. In Vito's entourage was Domenico Arcuri, the Montrealer who had hosted the final sit-down between Nick Rizzuto and Violi. Another invitee from Canada was Michel Pozza, a money man who worked closely with the Cotroni organization in Montreal but quickly moved to support the Rizzutos once he saw how things were going in the power struggle. The presence of the Rizzutos was seen as evidence that Vic Cotroni was not making the same mistake as Violi and getting in the Rizzutos' way. He was giving the Sixth Family free reign in Montreal.

"This event supports the theory that Nick Rizzuto was now directing operations for the Montreal Sicilian Faction, and that he was acting independently from the hierarchy of the Cotroni group," an FBI report says.

Investigators studying the photographs—in particular, the group pictures of the guests at their designated dinner tables—noticed something else. A curious pattern was emerging. Seating arrangements are not an inconsequential matter at any wedding, and deciding where each mobster was to sit, and with whom, must have been a narcotics trafficker's worst social nightmare. Eventually, the invitees seem to have been seated according to their underworld faction.

One photo shows a young Vincent Basciano at a table with Philly Lucky, Big Trinny, Frank Lino, Bruno Indelicato, his uncle Joseph "J.B." Indelicato and Joseph Benanti. Basciano, who was nicknamed "Vinny Gorgeous," would be named acting boss of the Bonanno Family in later and more trying times. This group would be described in court as the early distribution arm of the Sixth Family's heroin in New York. At another table stands a smiling Sal Catalano with Santo Giordano.

The table of the leading Zips in New York was immediately beside Vito's table, suggesting their familiarity and friendliness. A suave-as-always Cesare Bonventre, wearing his tinted aviator glasses, and one of the few men in a tuxedo, lounges at a table with his wife, Theresa, Baldo Amato and Amato's shapely wife. Giovanni Ligammari was also present, beaming a wide smile, wearing a light gray suit and red tie at a table of mostly older men and their wives.

Seating the Zips of New York next to the Sicilian mobsters from Canada was a courteous move. Members from each group knew each other well. The same year as the wedding, Bonventre and Amato made such a mad dash from New York to Canada that New York State troopers stopped them at least three times on the same day for speeding. Each time they were driving at more than 100 miles an hour. For the early fines, the pair pulled out an enormous wad of cash and paid the fine on the spot in $100 bills. At the last stop, the trooper would not allow an on-the-spot settlement and took Bonventre's license and issued a ticket he would have to settle in court. With Amato taking over the driving, they continued on their way. The business in Canada must have been urgent, indeed, as the pair then returned to deal with the traffic matter aboard a Canadian-registered private plane. It speaks to the unusual interaction and disposable income of the guests at Bono's wedding.

"Bono had interested us for years," Tripodi said. "A rising star in the Sicilian Mafia, he had been sent early in his career to Milan to oversee its interests in the banking center of Italy." Bono's diplomatic skills—and his warm relationship with the Sixth Family, as shown by his early meetings in Montreal—made him a good choice as the Sicilian Mafia's emissary in New York. "Bono was the guy chosen to pull everything together. In effect, he acted as Palermo's ambassador to the Italian crime groups in New York," Tripodi said. News of Bono's wedding was a wake-up call for agents probing organized crime and international drug traffickers.

"During this period it also became more apparent that within the Bonanno Family there had emerged a Sicilian faction, similar to the situation in Montreal," an internal FBI report says about the Bono wedding. "The leader of the Bonanno Sicilian Faction, Salvatore Catalano, is heavily involved in heroin importation from Sicily. What is even more significant, however, is the fact that the Sicilian factions from Montreal and the Bonanno Family are criminally aligned. The leaders of both factions, Rizzuto in Montreal and Catalano in New York, are both documented heroin traffickers.

"There is strong evidence that individuals from these groups have met together on numerous occasions to discuss criminal activity," the report continues. "Surveillance from Canada and the United States verify many of these meetings." The meetings had been fast and furious and incredibly productive.

It was happy times for the mafiosi, a mood captured in the cheery photographs from Bono's wedding. Appropriate for the start of a new decade, Bono's 1980 wedding party marked a new era in the underworld. It was as if the wet and garrulous soiree was also a celebration of another achievement: a new heroin franchise had already been built and the men at Bono's wedding at the Hotel Pierre were among its primary architects. The effort had been substantial. And sneaky. It took both police and rival criminal organizations by surprise when the seemingly unrelated events over a decade suddenly gelled into an unsurpassed global heroin enterprise. Much work had been done, though only a few men, even among the guests at Bono's wedding, were truly aware of it all.

The Sicilian Mafia had been busy in New York, Canada, Italy and South America. To get where they wanted to be, they needed people and product. Both had been making their way into Canada for trans-shipment to the United States.

CHAPTER 16

BUCKS COUNTY, PENNSYLVANIA, JANUARY 1973

Tucked in the southeastern corner of Pennsylvania, Bucks County is best described in terms of its neighbors; sitting on the busy New York City–Washington corridor, it is bounded on the east by the Delaware River and Trenton, N.J., and by Philadelphia to the south. It is almost equidistant between New York City and Atlantic City. Such a place could not be immune from the mob.

It was here that a deliveryman stumbled across the body of a man lying face down in plain view behind an abandoned Red Barn Restaurant in Bristol Township, shortly before noon on January 5, 1973. His feet and legs rested awkwardly on the sidewalk and his six-foot, 190-pound body sprawled onto the first parking space. Until this discovery, the old brick building, which had been vacant for six months, had gained notoriety as a hangout for local teenagers. This, however, seemed far beyond anything mischievous kids would get into. The victim's hands had been tied in front of him and he had been shot in the back with a .45-caliber pistol. Police found $21 in his pockets, a set of house keys and a letter from immigration officials.

The murdered man was identified as Stefano Sciarrino, a 27-year-old from Cinisi, Sicily. Police learned that Sciarrino had entered the United States in a time-honored way for illegal migrants with money: in April 1971 with a ticket from Italy to Mexico, he arrived at New York's John F. Kennedy Airport on an Air France jet and, instead of changing planes, simply walked away into New York's teeming streets. He had little contact with American authorities beyond his arrest later as an unregistered alien. Quickly bailed out of custody—he was only one of a hundred Sicilians picked up in the northeastern United States that year—Sciarrino had spent some time in the Bonanno Family's Brooklyn turf before moving to Bucks County, where he took a job in a pizzeria.

Baffled police could uncover no immediate motive for the murder but a subsequent investigation led directly to the Montreal Mafia and the murky world of Sicilian immigrant smuggling.

It did not take long before police determined that Stefano Sciarrino was related to Lorenzo Sciarrino—known as "Enzo the Quarrelsome One" because of his legendary temper. Enzo Sciarrino had long been suspected of running an illegal immigrant smuggling operation, moving people out of Sicily, through Canada and into America. He had two types of customers: those with Sicilian Mafia links who were placed in key parts of the U.S. northeast, and "legitimate" illegal migrants— those who were emigrating in hopes of finding honest jobs. Most of his clients did not arrive in the way Stefano did. The preferred, and cheaper, route was to come through the unguarded border points and Native reserves along the U.S.–Canada border. Once in the United States, because of the poor cooperation and exchange of information between American and Italian authorities, some of Sicily's most active organized crime figures were able to infiltrate the American marketplace, passing themselves off as legitimate businessmen and entrepreneurs.

Canadian police intelligence files showed Enzo meeting with senior mobsters in Montreal, almost all of them Sicilians linked to Nick Rizzuto and Pep Cotroni. At least one meeting, in the summer of 1971, narrowly preceded Enzo's arrest in Italy, where he was later sentenced for Mafia activity. Safe houses in Toronto and Montreal were used to harbor the smuggled mafiosi while en route—in Toronto, in particular, the family shepherding the migrants through was related by marriage to the Rizzutos. The transit route through Canada was busy. American files show that in 1972 alone, as many as 10,000 Sicilians—most of them not part of any drug conspiracy—traveled from Canada to the United States. Those immigrants with no intention of joining the mob were charged $500 to make the crossing. However, they were preyed on at every turn. When they wanted to change their Italian *lira* into American dollars, they were charged a 25-percent service fee. False documents, including social security cards and driver's licenses, were sold to them on a payment plan that often saw them handing over thousands of dollars. When they were given work—almost always in a pizzeria or construction company—the employers clawed back a portion of their salary. When they went for relaxation to gambling houses, they were cheated until they lost, then given loans at extortionate rates. Unable to pay, several agreed to travel back into Canada to pick up a shipment of heroin and return with it to the United States to pay off or reduce their debt.

For Stefano Sciarrino, who came to America with Mafia roots and a criminal record, none of this abuse was an issue. In addition to Enzo the Quarrelsome One, his connections in his hometown included Gaetano Badalamenti, one of the key participants at the Grand Hôtel heroin summit. Badalamenti would later be revealed as a major player in the Pizza Connection. But that was years away. Many of the early clues to its formation, however, emerged from the Sciarrino murder mystery.

In Bucks County, Sciarrino had found work at a pizza franchise that was a thoroughly mobbed-up enterprise, with more than two dozen stores in New Jersey, New York and Pennsylvania—several of them identified later as being owned and operated by the pioneers of the Pizza Connection. As a sideline, the corporation sold basic supplies to other pizzerias. Many of the sales were used to disguise the laundering of heroin profits. The franchise outlet Sciarrino worked at in Pennsylvania was owned by the son of another franchise owner who, in turn, partnered with Frank Rappa, a Queens employee of a pizzeria in the same chain. He was a heroin smuggler whose ring, naturally, used Montreal as a way station.

Around the same time, Luigi Ronsisvalle, the mafioso who had worked for Pietro Licata, the old Knickerbocker Avenue boss, started working for the Zips, which meant dividing his time between smuggling heroin and illegal aliens out of Canada and into the United States. On at least three occasions, Ronsisvalle went to Canada.

"We have some connection to bring passports from Canada and give it to Sicilian people coming to the United States," he said. "The first time I go, we go to Niagara Falls. There were six passports ... which had, I remember, every picture [already] in [the] passport."

By the time of the Bono wedding, the infiltration by illegal Sicilian gangsters was thorough. In a 1981 FBI status report on a probe of Gerlando Sciascia, agents said "an extensive investigation into organized crime's influence on alien immigrants" had been initiated. The report noted that many illegal Sicilian immigrants with dubious pasts were being arrested at businesses owned and operated by a small circle of people with Mafia links. A law enforcement analyst said that background reviews of most of these people found they had first shown up as targets of interest to drug investigators in the late 1950s and 1960s and were traced back to Canada, and before that, Sicily. Sciascia and his Sixth Family kin in Montreal were clearly involved as middlemen, agents noted.

"They poured through Canada," the analyst said of the Sicilian Mafia immigrants. "If you came from Canada you were almost automatically accepted." Also coming through Canada to New York were several of the Zips gathering in Brooklyn, including Cesare Bonventre and Baldo Amato.

While the murder of Stefano Sciarrino was never solved, his slaying started to shed light on some of these other mysteries. It provided a glimpse into where the manpower for much of the new drug enter-prises was coming from and, like the drugs, it was being linked by police to Montreal and the supportive hand of the Sixth Family.

FIUMICINO AIRPORT, ROME, 1980

Because of its highly secretive nature, the success of a drug pipeline can be judged only by its failures. Until seizures are made or people are arrested, there is little evidence to appraise its size, test its purity levels or marvel at its ingenious methods.

By 1965, eight years after the heroin summit at the Grand Hôtel, the signs of success began to appear. That year, a drug and contraband ring—Italian police called it a "supergang linking the Sicilian Mafia with the American La Cosa Nostra"—was broken up. Among those indicted were Giuseppe "Genco" Russo, the head of the Sicilian Mafia, and several American criminal deportees. The following year, police tackled a Sicilian Mafia ring run by brothers Salvatore and Ugo Caneba. Based in Trapani, a provincial neighbor of Agrigento, the Canebas gained notoriety in the closing days of the Second World War when they were caught stealing and refining shipments of opium and morphine sent from America to help injured U.S. soldiers in army field hospitals in Italy. Fat on the profits from this audacious scheme, the Caneba brothers expanded into more sophisticated ventures.

Security concerns over America's border with Mexico have long overshadowed any problems from the long, largely unguarded border with Canada, which has always been perceived as the more gentle neighbor. Almost without exception, however, undercover operatives with the old U.S. Bureau of Narcotics and Dangerous Drugs found significant Canadian connections in their cases. Following the trail even further, they often found some link to the Sixth Family.

The Canadian city of Windsor is to Detroit what Montreal was to New York—a cross-border satellite of American Mafia interests. In the case of Windsor, the strategic value is even more narrowly defined: border access to the United States. Windsor lies just across the river from Detroit and, as such, it is not only Canada's most southerly city and busiest border crossing, but, with a nod to Motor City, the heartland of its automotive sector. Along with seamless links between auto plants on both sides of the Detroit River, Windsor has also long been used by gangsters to move contraband back and forth between the countries.

Prohibition in the U.S., starting in 1920 and stretching until 1933, a law that banned the manufacture, sale, transportation and importation of alcohol, was a gift to gangsters on both sides of the border. Perhaps coincidentally, two of the men who traveled with Nick Rizzuto's father from Sicily to America in 1925, Mercurio Campisi from Cattolica Eraclea and Francesco Giula from Siculiana, said they had previously lived in Detroit during the early years of Prohibition. If this was an early incursion to the area by associates of the Sixth Family, then there have been others in the decades since. During a probe into the Detroit drug market in the late 1960s and early 1970s, agents stumbled across members of the Badalamenti family. In the 1980s, the patriarch of the clan, Gaetano, would be convicted as a linchpin in the Pizza Connection, forever ensuring the clan's notoriety. Earlier, however, Gaetano's cousin, Cesare Badalamenti, was arrested for smuggling drugs into America and, when released from prison, moved to Detroit, where he quickly met up with Giuseppe Indelicato.

Indelicato, like the Rizzutos, left Sicily's Agrigento province to settle in Canada. In the New World he retained his Sixth Family links while settling in Windsor, with an eye on the Detroit skyline across the river. In 1964, an RCMP surveillance team monitoring a meeting in Montreal between the Cotronis and Nick Rizzuto's father-in-law, Antonio Manno—likely an early meeting to smooth ruffled feathers between the families—noted that a vehicle used by the Sicilians was registered to Indelicato.

An early smuggling foray, however, did not go well. Stopped when disembarking in New York City from a ship arriving from Europe, Indelicato was found with a half-million-dollar load of heroin stitched into the lining of his vest. He insisted it was icing sugar to decorate a wedding cake. His inability to explain why the confection needed such secretive transport led to the obvious conclusion and subsequent indictment. It is not known whether the border agents—or the jury—laughed at his feeble explanation; the 31-year-old Indelicato was sentenced to five years in prison. After serving his time, he was deported to Canada and immediately picked up where he had left off in Windsor. With Badalamenti on one side of the Detroit River and Indelicato on the other, they established a modest heroin route.

One of the men in regular contact with both Badalamenti and Indelicato was Nick Rizzuto, who, in 1970, turned up on the telephone records of both traffickers, police said. The Rizzutos were firming up key access points to the United States. Relations with the American Mafia in Detroit and the 'Ndrangheta bosses of Ontario were quite amicable. The Sicilian mobsters were careful to spread their profits around and not to encroach on their other activities. Everywhere accommodations were being made—everywhere but in Montreal.

From each of these successes and occasional missteps, the Mafia learned, perfecting technique, routes and methods. They were not seeking perfection, but something terrifically efficient. The next-generation heroin pipeline, part of which was captured and chronicled in the Pizza Connection case, would dwarf the previous machinations.

Signs of the success of the new pipeline were getting harder to suppress. Large shipments of impeccably pure heroin, leaving Italy and arriving in the United States, were being detected with unprecedented frequency, as production in the new laboratories in western Sicily moved toward capacity. Starting in late 1977, luggage stuffed with heroin, placed aboard Alitalia flights from Palermo's Punta Raisi Airport to New York's John F. Kennedy Airport, was being seized with some regularity. In June 1979, a suitcase arriving for Gaetano Badalamenti in Sicily was found to contain $497,000, with the cash haphazardly wrapped in pizzeria aprons. The Pizza Connection was up, running and immediately profitable.

Then, in 1980, came a seizure in Rome that, more than all of the other finds of drugs and money, highlights the success of the new operation.

Albert Gillet, a Belgian, had arrived at Rome's Fiumicino Airport direct from New York when his luggage was checked at customs. Inside, inspectors made a surprising and perplexing find. There, neatly pack-aged, were 10 kilos of heroin that tests found to be 86 percent pure. In any North American city, such a find would have been almost routine, but in Rome it was unheard of, for the simple reason that the drug was moving in the wrong direction—heroin was supposed to flow from Italy, where it was produced, to New York, where it was being bought and resold at an inflated price. Nobody bought heroin at the premium price in New York and brought it to Italy, where it would have attracted only a fraction of its cost. Giovanni Falcone, the anti-Mafia magistrate, seized on the strange case and soon solved the riddle. The shipment, which had originated with the Sixth Family and been sold to one of their regular New York Mafia customers, was being returned, having been found unacceptable by the American buyer. So successful were the new pipelines, and so good was their merchandise, that the buyers had the luxury of being choosy.

"We did not know that, at the time, the Americans considered 86 percent purity not good enough, which was why the goods were being returned," Falcone later said.

Sending 10 kilos of heroin back from New York because, at 86 per-cent, it was not pure enough? No wonder the men at Giuseppe Bono's wedding were all smiles in the photographs being studied by police. It was a time of heightened congeniality among the men, who were working, by turns together and in competition, on the disparate parts that made this enormous drug conspiracy work so well.

The congenial mood could not last with so much at stake and so many greedy men eyeing the same prize. In fact, Bono's wedding pho-tographs would come back to haunt many of the men pictured in them. Including Vito Rizzuto.

CHAPTER 17

BROOKLYN, SPRING 1981

Despite the fact that Carmine Galante was no longer around to stir up trouble, or perhaps because of this, the situation in Brooklyn by the spring of 1981 was still in disarray. The Bonanno gangsters were beginning to accept the presence of the Zips as a permanent part of the new face of New York, although the Sicilian mobsters were still eyed with suspicion and a degree of distaste. They were not so much outsiders now, but rather one of several factions within the fractured Bonanno Family.

For Philip Rastelli, Galante's murder seemed, at first, to ease some of the pressure on his leadership. Rastelli was a gray, cadaverously gaunt man. He had been a captain in the Bonannos since 1968, before moving up to become underboss under Natale Evola in 1971, and then quietly slipping into the boss's seat some months after Evola's death in 1974. Despite his steady rise, he was not a strong leader. His frequent stints in prison hurt him greatly, but even when free he had difficulty inspiring his men or enhancing his family's position. After Galante's death, Rastelli's position as boss was re-affirmed far and wide. Lefty Ruggerio even pulled Donnie Brasco, a non-member, aside to tell him that Rastelli was the boss. Everyone finally seemed to acknowledge this. Acknowledgment was one thing; acceptance quite another. While Galante's murder seemed a relief for all concerned, it eased little of the internal strife that had afflicted the family since its longtime boss, Joe Bonanno, was ousted by the Commission in the mid-1960s. For 15 years the Bonanno organization, once the proudest of the Five Families, had been in decline. Much of the blame was laid at Rastelli's feet.

New York mobsters have a saying: "You're only as strong as your boss." It is a recognition that the boss of the family is the one who speaks up for the family's interests before the other families and the Commission; who guides the organization as it seeks to expand into new criminal ventures. Many of the Bonannos felt that Rastelli was not leading them to greatness. The drug profits pouring into New York, and the natural jealousy and intrigue it caused, made the stakes even higher and the untenable situation even worse. The idea that someone other than Rastelli might be capable of doing a better job was quickly catching on. Rastelli soon found himself in his perennial quandary— trying to defend his interests within a divisive and wounded family from the confines of a distant prison cell.

From within the family, others started braying for a new boss; Alphonse "Sonny Red" Indelicato was the loudest among them.

The Bonanno Family was splitting into clearly defined factions, with most scrambling to seize what they considered to be their share of the lucrative drug trade, competing to find a role in its operations and calculating where their interests lay on the issue of leadership. Alliances among mob captains were sought, forged and broken; gangsters with a means of distribution were being courted by those with a means of importation, and, through it all, those controlling the flow of drugs were aggressively building strategic alliances that would further their profits, regardless of any mob sentimentality about family structure or arcane rules. A new underworld order was emerging in which contribution to the drug trade was more important than family affiliation, creating strange bedfellows; Bonanno captains grew closer to like-minded Gambino soldiers than to their own family.

The 15 or so captains within the Bonanno Family, who, between them, controlled roughly 150 made men, started taking sides. The Bonannos, at one time the most cohesive of the Five Families, continued to split apart at the seams. Four factions emerged, Bonanno insiders said.

"There was the Zips from Italy, one faction," said Frank Lino, a longtime Bonanno member. "Joseph Massino and Sonny Black was another faction. Sonny Red and Philly Lucky was another faction."

Sonny Red had become the head of the disaffected and dissident faction in this squabble over Rastelli's leadership. He had built a power base around close friendships and family ties. Early on, he had brought his son, Bruno Indelicato, into the mob. After Bruno helped kill Carmine Galante, he was rewarded with a promotion to captain. Bruno was a big supporter of his father; the two socialized and conducted serious mob business together, and, with Sonny Red's youthful looks, he could just about pass as Bruno's older brother. Another family member, Joseph "J.B." Indelicato, who was Sonny Red's brother, was also a Bonanno captain. Also close to him were two captains not related by blood: Dominick "Big Trinny" Trinchera and Philip "Philly Lucky" Giaccone, a distinctly passive-looking mobster. Just six months before, at the Bono wedding, Big Trinny and Philly Lucky had sat with J.B., Bruno and Lino at the Hotel Pierre, their role as distributors of the Sixth Family's heroin having secured them their invitations.

"Philly Lucky, Trinny and Sonny Red wanted to rob the family from Phil Rastelli," said Sal Vitale, who, as Massino's right-hand man, was slavishly devoted to the Massino faction. Lining up behind Massino were Sonny Black, James "Big Louie" Tartagliano, Gabe Infanti and others. The Massino faction was loyal to Rastelli, the titular boss. For Massino, this was his best chance for retaining significant power within the family in anticipation of the day when Rastelli stepped down or passed away, leaving Massino as his heir.

The fourth faction, made up of the old-timers, seemed keen to stay out of harm's way during the troubles. Salvatore "Sally Fruits" Ferrugia, Matty Valvo, Stefano "Stevie Beef" Cannone, Nicholas "Nicky Glasses" Marangello, Nicholas "Nick the Battler" DiStefano and Joseph "Joe Bayonne" Zicarelli remained somewhat passive observers as the younger gangsters faced off.

The Zips faction, who had caused much of the strife with their aggressive move into the heroin market, included Sal Catalano, Santo Giordano, Bonventre, Amato and Giovanni Ligammari. Also siding with the Zips was the Sixth Family.

One member of the Sixth Family was, in fact, at the center of the double-dealing and fury in New York. Gerlando Sciascia had access to a seemingly endless supply of heroin. A burly man with a warm, engaging smile, he held some power and distinction in New York, despite being looked on as something of an outsider.

CATTOLICA ERACLEA, SICILY

In the winding cemetery of Cattolica Eraclea, a casually dressed man ambled among the large mausoleums adorned with images of kneeling angels, whimsical cherubs, crosses and a risen Christ, his pierced hands outstretched. The man, a former Montrealer, had returned to Cattolica Eraclea under circumstances he would not discuss.

"He is the one you should be writing about," he said, pointing to a tomb containing the remains of the Sciascia family. "You know Sciascia? He was the most powerful one who went overseas. But he's dead now." The man squinted at the vast field of tombstones and crypts.

"Killed," he added, needlessly.

Gerlando Sciascia, born on February 15, 1934, in Cattolica Eraclea, was almost 12 years older than Vito Rizzuto and a close family friend. Sciascia was raised just 10 houses down the narrow street from the Rizzuto family home and a similar distance from that of Joe LoPresti.

Sciascia was not yet 25 when he, along with other members of the Agrigento Mafia, followed the Rizzutos to North America. Sciascia arrived a year after the Grand Hôtel heroin summit. By the time he was establishing himself in the New World, heroin was starting to trickle in from the new conduit and, accordingly, Sicilian traffickers were setting up shop in Toronto, Montreal and New York. Sciascia's relocation seems to have been sparked by these new ventures into the drug trade. As it was for Carmine Galante, heroin seemed to be Sciascia's calling.

This was all unknown, of course, when he had his first encounter with American authorities. Arriving in New York City in September 1958, he was listed in U.S. Department of Justice files as "a stowaway." The entry was illegal, but he was nonetheless granted an immigration visa. Sciascia was simultaneously assigned Immigration file #A11628312 and FBI file #726030D; although he had no known criminal record, the Bureau opened a file on him because of the illegal entry. Over the years, that file would grow to an immense and unwieldy size. Little was known about Sciascia when he arrived. He was five-foot-seven, a trim 160 pounds and was said to be vain about his thick head of hair. He listed his birthplace as Cattolica Eraclea and said he had left the middle school there after completing the eighth grade. His father, Giuseppe, died a month after Sciascia arrived in the United States; his mother, Domenica LaRocca, would die in 1974.

Once in America, Sciascia traveled to Montreal to reconnect with the Rizzutos and other friends and family there. He returned to the United States on January 17, 1961, driving a car from Montreal to New York, crossing at Rouses Point, an hour's drive due south of Montreal. U.S. Immigration officials quietly started their own case file on him that day. Back in America, Sciascia moved first to Newark, New Jersey, and worked at Ridoni Gardeners in nearby Summit, and Como Pizzeria on Broadway in Manhattan. Two years later, he worked at Mac Asphalt Contracting Company Inc., in Flushing, New York, while living in the Bronx. That same year, he became a member of Local 1018 of the Asphalt Workers' Union. In March 1974, he moved to 1646 Stadium Avenue, in the Bronx, where he lived for the rest of his life—when he was not a fugitive, or in Canada, or in jail. For some time, Sciascia led a low-key life and did not appear on the radar of law enforcement, although he was seen at Italian social clubs and in the company of people who would later become prime targets of police surveillance.

"We didn't know enough about George. There were a thousand Georges," a U.S. law-enforcement analyst said. "No one knew about the heroin agreements in Palermo. No one knew the Sicilians had gone into the heroin trade. There were just a lot of guys, mostly young guys, who turned up in New York and New Jersey and who had a lot of free time on their hands. In those days, investigations worked from the outside in: you were investigating a crime and the people you were investigating led you to other people, to social clubs or parties. There were no family charts, no integrated intelligence. If you overheard them talking, it made no sense, even to Italian-speaking cops. They spoke dialect and they didn't speak a whole lot."

Like most of the rural Sicilian mafiosi who went into the heroin business, there are huge gaps in Sciascia's biography. There are months, even years, when he dropped out of sight, only to turn up in the midst of increasingly larger drug deals and ever more successful police investigations. But he was always in the best of criminal company: the Sicilian expatriate Mafia, the Bonannos, the Gambinos and the Rizzutos. Like many Zips, Sciascia was inducted into the Bonanno Family. A May 1981, FBI memorandum, noting that a racketeering case was being opened on him, reads: "According to sources, Sciascia is a recently 'made' capo in the Bonanno Family ... involved mainly in drug trafficking."

To the Bonannos, Sciascia was a loyal captain. He was recognized as the New York–based head of the "Montreal crew," the Rizzuto organization that had assumed control over the Bonannos' satellite in Montreal. Sciascia, however, was a man whose loyalty—at a glance—seemed deeply divided. He was a captain in the Bonanno Family but was known among the gangs of New York as "George from Canada." He is described by New Yorkers as the boss of the Montreal crew, but the Montreal crew was answering to the Rizzutos, who were living primarily in Venezuela and addressing interests based more in Agrigento than in Brooklyn. The Bonannos considered Sciascia one of their own, a sworn captain in their family, but he was, at the same time, a wholly absorbed part of the Sixth Family.

Was Sciascia looking out for the Bonanno Family's interests in Montreal, or the Sixth Family's interests in New York?

While Sciascia's loyalty seemed a puzzle, other issues of fraternity and loyalty were once again consuming the Bonanno Family in New York, overshadowing any cursory confusion that might have arisen over his status.

By the time Sciascia had used his Sixth Family heroin connections to become a major player in New York, Rastelli's leadership of the Bonanno Family was again being challenged.

The struggle for primacy within the family is often presented as being about loyalty to the boss or protecting the officially sanctioned hierarchy. It also had a far less romantic and honorable subtext. For many choosing sides, it was largely about drugs and control over a billion-dollar heroin network. Sciascia—and his Sixth Family kin—had just one real concern in the seemingly internecine struggle: which faction would be most useful in their efforts to flood the streets of North America with high-grade heroin?

CHAPTER 18

BROOKLYN, SPRING 1981

Alphonse "Sonny Red" Indelicato was a stocky man, with strong, tattooed arms and dark hair, despite his nickname. He favored large tinted glasses, perhaps taking a fashion cue from fellow Bonanno captain Cesare Bonventre. Any sartorial similarities to the cool and stylish Bonventre, however, ended there. Sonny Red preferred garish, casual clothes—orange T-shirts, bright red shorts, colorful baseball jackets, striped track suits, multicolored socks and faded blue jeans were all part of his wardrobe. He was particularly fond of a pair of brown leather cowboy boots, the looks of which probably made Bonventre cringe. If Bonventre dressed Euro-cool, Sonny Red was American-kitsch.

Despite his clothing, Sonny Red was a powerful force on the streets of New York. Born in New York on February 16, 1927, Sonny Red displayed an early interest in narcotics transactions and stark displays of violence. Charged with heroin possession in 1950, he was quickly convicted. Not long after his six-month stint in jail, he was an aggressor in a social club shooting, on Boxing Day, 1951, that left one man dead and another, a witness to the attack, wounded. The poorly planned hit led to convictions against Sonny Red for murder and attempted murder, followed by a 12-year stay in Sing Sing prison. He was hardly reformed by his incarceration. After his release, despite being on lifetime parole—likely the reason he was not celebrating with his cohorts at the Bono wedding—he was repeatedly named by informants as a major narcotics dealer, according to FBI documents.

In the 15 years since his release from prison in 1966, Sonny Red had built himself into a formidable presence within the Bonanno Family, not only because of his opinionated, charismatic swagger, but because at least four other Bonanno captains supported any move he made. With each captain controlling a half-dozen to a dozen other made men, the tight-knit group presented a significant force, one that seemed in a reasonable position to seize control. Many in Sonny Red's group had proven their deadliness in the slaying of Galante; although they were not alone in its planning and perpetration, Sonny Red's men took the lead. Along with his Bonanno allies, Sonny Red had solid connections to other New York crime families, including senior members of the Colombo Family and a father-in-law, Charles "Charlie Prunes" Ruvolo, who was a Lucchese Family soldier. As such, both the Zips and Joe Massino took the Sonny Red faction seriously. Sonny Red threatened both the leadership of Philip Rastelli, the family boss, and Massino's grand ambitions.

For the Zips, motivation for opposing Sonny Red's rebellion came from more materialistic concerns. Sonny Red was not only cocky toward Rastelli and disrespectful to Massino and Sonny Black, but he appears to have been dismissive of the power of the Zips, a mistake also made by Paolo Violi and Pietro Licata.

Sonny Red and his faction had been happily reaping the profits from distributing the Sixth Family's heroin in New York. In late 1980 or early 1981, he is said to have taken $1.5 million worth of heroin on consignment from Gerlando Sciascia and Joe LoPresti and then declined to pay for it. This endears you to no one in the mob, where men have been murdered over debts a thousand times less. More important, if Sonny Red were to become the boss, he would inevitably cut in on the Sixth Family's lucrative action, perhaps move for exclusive access and put a crimp in the Zips' free-wheeling, wide-ranging heroin sales to any and all comers.

The other New York crime families were well aware of the growing strife. Between chuckles about the chaotic Bonanno Family, seemingly unable to keep its own house in order, each weighed where its interests lay in the struggle for control. Vincent "The Chin" Gigante, the boss of the Genovese Family, was backing Sonny Red and, accordingly, a Genovese soldier was directly agitating on Sonny Red's behalf. John Gotti, then an aggressive captain in the Gambino Family, along with the Gambino underboss, Aniello Dellecroce, and several of his captains and soldiers, were staunch supporters of both Sciascia and Massino. Gotti and Massino had long been pals, since their wayward youth as chronic truck hijackers; the Gambinos were huge buyers of the Sixth Family's heroin who met regularly with Sciascia and LoPresti to arrange lucrative deals. There was little doubt where the Gambinos' support would go. Some Colombo Family members also gave Massino the nod, although some old-time Colombo members had ties to Sonny Red.

Support from within the Gambino and Colombo families was a good omen for Massino, who, on Rastelli's behalf, next took the complaint to the top—the Commission. The Commission was the Mafia's highest authority when navigating the crowded underworld of New York. It was led by Paul Castellano, the boss of the Gambino Family (until he was killed on orders from John Gotti in a 1985 coup d'état within his own family). Castellano listened as Massino made his case against Sonny Red. The Commission seems also to have gone to Sonny Red to hear his side. Later, Castellano passed the Commission's ruling on to Massino. Not surprisingly, the conservative forces on the panel came out in support of retaining Rastelli as the Bonanno boss, but denied Massino the option of striking out against his opponents. The Bonannos, the Commission declared, needed to sort their problems out privately and peacefully.

"No bloodshed," Castellano told Massino.

"The Commission ruled that there should be no gunplay; to work it out among yourselves," said Sal Vitale, who was briefed by Massino on the ruling shortly afterward. In accordance with those orders, a series of meetings between the rival Bonanno factions was planned, ostensibly to find common ground among the contenders and bring a peaceful end to their standoff. For the first meeting, on February 4, 1981, all of the captains were called to Ferncliff Manor, a catering hall on West 11th Street near Avenue U. When Sonny Red was told to meet the other captains at Ferncliff, he asked his men to check it out beforehand.

"When they asked me, am I familiar with this place, I said 'Yes. Only about six blocks from my bar,'" Frank Lino said. Sonny Red decided to gather his men together at Lino's bar before the meeting. Sonny Red, Philly Lucky, Big Trinny and Bruno Indelicato showed up. Curiously, so did Sciascia, LoPresti and other unnamed mobsters from Canada. Together the men walked to the nearby hall, where they joined up with others from the Zip contingent: Salvatore Catalano, Cesare Bonventre and Baldo Amato.

"I walked him to it to let him know where the meeting was, George from Canada, people from Canada, I walked them to the place," Lino said. The first meeting was a bust.

Sonny Red's worries were heightened rather than eased by the truce talks, so much so that before the second gathering, called a month later, he braced for an all-out Bonanno war. The second meeting was scheduled at Brooklyn's Embassy Terrace on Avenue U and East 2nd Street, again close to Lino's bar.

"They thought there would be some kind of trouble and my bar was only two blocks away from the Embassy Terrace, so they came down and we loaded up. We had rifles and pistols," Lino said. Despite the worries of Sonny Red, Lino was unconcerned because the second meeting coincided with a parade through the streets of Brooklyn.

"When they told me where the meeting was, I told them they're having a big parade, going to be loaded with patrolmen for the parade. I doubt if anything would happen that day," Lino recalled. The parade was in celebration of the American hostages who had been released after 444 days of imprisonment in the captured U.S. embassy in Iran. One of the former hostages, oddly, was a cousin of one of Sonny Red's most vicious soldiers. The firearms were not needed for that meeting, but they did not go unnoticed.

"We were at J&S Cake when Tuttie Francese, a friend of Joe Massino, came in and told him that the other side were loadin' up. They were buying automatic weapons, meaning the three other captains were getting ready for war," Vitale said. Francese was a soldier in the Colombo Family.

Massino took this new information to Castellano as well as to Carmine Persico, the boss of the Colombo Family. Massino was a shrewd operator—he knew Persico sat on the Commission and would likely give credence to the information since it came from one of his own men. Massino begged the Commission to untie his hands and let him and his men "defend themselves." Warfare, after all, was bad for business. Uncontrolled blood in the streets—as the gangsters had seen from past bursts of violence—brought unwanted attention from police, politicians and the press, and cut into all mobsters' profits. Faced with the disquieting prospect of Sonny Red trying to seize control of the Bonanno Family in a drawn-out war, the Commission gave in to Massino.

"You have to defend yourself. Do what you have to do," Castellano told him. In mob parlance, that was permission to kill. Massino pounced on the opportunity.

Massino and Sciascia had formed an alliance to purge the three rival captains, and they started making their plans. The challenge they faced was finding a way to kill all of the dissenters at once, so there would be no opportunity for a revenge strike. What they needed was a trap. A third "peace" meeting was called by Massino. Sonny Red had looked at things in pretty much the same way as Massino and Sciascia and was concerned that his opposition was drawing him into an ambush. With good reason. Unbeknownst to Sonny Red, the meeting was purposely called for a Tuesday evening—the night Joe Massino and his cronies habitually played cards and ate a long dinner together at J&S Cake, Massino's private social club.

"Joe Massino felt that we can go there, kill them and come back to the club using that as an alibi," Vitale said.

Through Sciascia, arrangements were made for Vito Rizzuto and two of his closest colleagues to come to New York to help take care of the nasty bits. Vito maintained a relative disinterest in the daily grind of New York's wiseguys when it did not directly affect his business. This job seemed to qualify. He could appreciate the need to purge opposition forces, as the Sixth Family had recently done in Montreal. It might even have been seen as the necessary pay-back to New York for finally approving the Sixth Family's hit on Paulo Violi.

Massino also met with Sonny Black, another influential Bonanno captain, who had been promoted after Galante's murder. Sonny Black had his own interests to look out for, and during his discussions with Massino he sought to have an associate take part, thinking the new recruit would earn a chance to be inducted into the family.

"We should take him with us," Sonny Black said to Massino, indicating Donnie Brasco. Massino dismissed the idea and, in one of many fortuitous and canny decisions he would make in his long mob career, dropped Brasco from the roster. When Massino returned to the car after his meeting, where Vitale, acting as his driver, was waiting for him, Massino said that Sonny Black was now part of the plan.

"Sonny Black is signed with us," Massino told Vitale. "Sonny Black wants to 'straighten out' [induct] Donnie Brasco." His words are an embarrassing acknowledgment of how deeply FBI agent Joe Pistone had fooled the mobsters. Massino also met with John Gotti, Aniello Dellacroce and Angelo Ruggiero, all of the Gambino Family, eliciting their assistance.

May 5, 1981, the night of the third meeting, was a busy one for all concerned. Joe Massino and Sal Vitale met at J&S Cake, just as they did every Tuesday. They were joined by Duane "Goldie" Leisenheimer and James "Big Louie" Tartaglione. Later in the evening, Sciascia and Santo "Tony" Giordano arrived. The two Zips chatted with Massino in the foyer.

Goldie was to be the lead driver that night, shuttling shooters and captains around to where they needed to be. He had also offered his apartment as a crash pad for anyone needing a place to sleep. Massino handpicked Goldie as his counter-surveillance man outside the club. Goldie had been serving Massino since he was a boy, following him around like a puppy dog. It had led more than one mobster to refer to him as "Joey's Golden Retriever." Although he had earned Massino's trust, he could never join the family because of his Irish–German roots. Sciascia, who always preferred to place his faith in fellow Sicilians, was worried about including Goldie.

"Joe introduced Goldie to them," Vitale said. "George made a face, Tony made a face. This kid has blond hair, blue eyes—he's not Italian. Joe says he's the best driver, good with mirrors, good with walkie-talkies, it was a go." (Being "good with mirrors" meant he was able to track vehicles behind him as he drove, often detecting when his car was being followed by police.) Goldie was given a walkie-talkie to allow those outside the club to communicate with those inside. Goldie, Big Louie, Sonny Black and five other trusted members of Sonny Black's crew—including Lefty Ruggiero and John "Boobie" Cerasani—waited at a discreet distance outside the club, watching for police or rival gangsters. They were also to watch for any of the three captains who might escape the trap that awaited them. Goldie was to drive those who were not slated for death away from the club afterward, and the others were ready to swoop in to clean up the anticipated mess.

Well before the scheduled meeting, Vitale drove Massino to the club. He dropped him off in front, drove two blocks farther, parked the car and walked back.

Vitale already knew he had been selected as one of the shooters. When he arrived at the club, Massino introduced him for the first time to the others, all imported from Montreal: allegedly Vito Rizzuto, Emanuele Ragusa and a man known simply as the old-timer. The old-timer had silver-gray hair and was an "elderly gentleman," Vitale said. He later described him as being between the ages of 65 and 70. It was likely one of Nick Rizzuto's mob contemporaries sent to oversee Vito's demeanor under fire. The family had several members who were proficient with a shotgun, such as Domenico Manno, Vito's uncle, who had been convicted in the Paolo Violi hit a few years earlier—although, then 47 years old, Manno was likely too young to be considered a senior citizen by Vitale, who was 33 at the time.

After the introductions, the men armed themselves with guns already inside the club. They were also given ski masks so the other captains "wouldn't know who the shooters were," Vitale said.

"I had a Tommy gun," he said. "They call it a grease gun, an automatic weapon. Fires multiple rounds." Vitale did not remember much about the weapons that had been under his care when he was his company's armorer in the U.S. Army. He examined the gun from the barrel to the stock, fingering its parts. He pushed the safety lock to the off position in the process.

"When I pulled the chamber back it discharged and shot five times into the wall." The rounds narrowly missed a startled Giovanni Ligammari.

"I was shocked. Everyone was shocked," Vitale said. "I got everybody's attention." Massino did not want Vitale to fire his gun during the ambush unless he absolutely needed to. In such a small space, anyone could be hurt during a frantic shootout.

Vito and Emanuele were designated as the lead shooters, according to Vitale. Vitale and the old-timer were told to guard the exit door.

"No one was supposed to get by me and the old-timer," Vitale said. "We were told by Joe and George that if Sonny Red did not show up, they were going to call it off. Prior to them arriving, George Sciascia said, 'If Sonny Red is there, I will put my hand through my hair on the side of my head, that means it's a go.'"

Massino told them to announce that it was a holdup and to try to get everyone to stand up against the wall. He had hoped the captains could be killed in an orderly, execution-style manner to avoid a messy free-for-all gun battle. They were now ready for the arrival of their prey.

"When we entered the closet," Vitale said, "we left the door open a smidge to look out. We were in the closet, we all had our weapons loaded. We sat there and waited."

CHAPTER 19

BROOKLYN, MAY 5, 1981

About the time that the hunters had gathered at the site of the third meeting, the intended prey likewise gathered together. Sonny Red had made plans of his own, although not so elaborate as Massino and Sciascia's.

Sonny Red had called in Frank Lino, a soldier in his son's crew, for a serious chat. He told Lino that they were heading into a dangerous meeting and, to be cautious, wanted to leave Bruno Indelicato out of it. Sonny Red said that Lino would go to the meeting in Bruno's stead.

"They thought they might get killed," Lino said. "They had asked me to go because they thought there would be trouble. I didn't feel too good [about that], but I went." It was a strategic move to guard against having all of Sonny Red's men caught in the same place at the same time. The fact that the one asset to be held in reserve was his own son no doubt made the plan look particularly good to Sonny Red.

If they did not return, the order from Sonny Red to Bruno was clear: "To kill everybody in the Zips, Joe Massino [and] Sonny Black; get them," Lino said. Sonny Red ordered his men who were not attending the meeting to spread throughout the city that night so they could not all be taken out if the anticipated purge widened.

"They were already at their places. Some were in Staten Island. Some were at Tommy Karate's in Brooklyn," Lino said. Sonny Red then had one last order for the men heading with him to the meeting.

"If there is shooting, everybody is on their own, try to get out."

———

Sonny Red, Philly Lucky and Big Trinny arrived at the My Way Lounge, Frank Lino's club, early in the evening, collecting Lino, and then all four set off together. Lino and Big Trinny drove in one car, Philly Lucky and Sonny Red in another. They drove to a diner, where they met up with two neutral captains also invited to the meeting—Joseph "Joe

Bayonne" Zicarelli and Nicholas "Nick the Battler" DiStefano. The pair had been invited to avert Sonny Red's suspicions, although the two old-timers apparently had no idea of the plan. Two members of the Zips joined them at the diner and everyone ditched their own cars at a Nathan's Famous hot-dog outlet to climb into vehicles being driven by the Zips. They wheeled through the streets of Brooklyn until they reached the social club that was on loan to the Bonannos that night from Salvatore "Sammy Bull" Gravano and Frank DeCico, members of the Gambino Family. Lino was familiar with the club from time spent drinking and gambling there with fellow mobsters.

"I used to frequentize it," Lino said. The knowledge would save his life. Sonny Red and his men were not carrying guns as they headed into the meeting. It is one of the arcane rules of the Mafia that a member cannot bring a gun to an administrative meeting; it is largely why such arranged meetings have been known to turn into planned assassinations. Not everyone plays by the same rules.

———————

The club where the captains were gathering was a modest two-story brick building virtually indiscernible from its neighbors. A low wrought-iron fence separated the club's property from the next. As they arrived, the gangsters rang the doorbell at the locked door. This was nothing unusual, as most of the mob's private social clubs, after-hours bars and gambling joints kept tight control on public access.

"When the doorbell rang, we looked through the crack at who entered," Sal Vitale said. Sonny Red and the others walked inside and saw that other Bonanno captains were already there.

"When we first walked in, we walked downstairs and there was a room. Looked like a storage room," Lino said. "There was Joe Massino. There was George from Canada, Anthony Giordano, another couple of Italian guys, I don't know their names, and, you know, and us guys." Giordano greeted Sonny Red and his entourage at the door.

"We're getting everything ready upstairs," Giordano told them. "Give me a few minutes."

Inside the closet, Vito, Vitale and their colleagues watched closely and waited. In the main room, the group was unsettled.

"Sonny Red was holding onto Joe's arm," Lino said. "Like a friend, like two friends, you hold an arm." Rather than a sign of friendship,

Sonny Red likely thought the closer he stuck to Massino, the less likely he was to be hit by a bullet.

"They were talking in the back. Philly Lucky was in the back talking to Joe Bayonne and these two Italian guys. I was talking to George from Canada, Big Trinny and Nick the Battler," Lino said. Sciascia firmly placed his left arm around Lino, who was an unexpected guest at the gathering. Sciascia tried to make it appear like a friendly gesture, but Lino, nervous from the start, did not seem to appreciate it. Then Sciascia deliberately lifted his other arm and slowly ran his fingers through his silver hair.

"Vito led the way," Vitale said. "I was last. Vito entered the room with Emanuele while me and the old-timer guarded the exit door."

"My job was to say 'It's a holdup' when I went in the room, 'so everybody stand still,'" Vito Rizzuto later confided. Vito insists he did not pull the trigger of the gun he admits he was holding. "The other people came in and they started shooting the other guys," he said. Vitale disagrees.

"I seen Vito shoot. I don't know who he hit," Vitale said. Everyone who was in that room, however, likely agrees on Vitale's assessment of what happened next.

"All hell broke loose." Sonny Red and his men were braced for violence but, unarmed, there was little they could do.

"When they came in with the shotguns, Big Trinny charged them. He made a loud noise. They shot him. He died right there," Lino said. "I knocked George down. I don't know, you know, I jumped over Trinny. While I was jumping over him, I see Philly Lucky in the back, ready to get killed, and I see Joe hit Sonny Red with an object, I don't know what it was.

"I was jumping, you know, over Trinny, to get out," Lino said. "I'm jumping over a body—the guy is six-six, 400 pounds." Lino's chance for escape was a sign of Vitale's hesitation.

"I froze for five seconds," Vitale said. "By the time me and the elderly gentleman gets to the door, Frank Lino came flying past us. He was running. And kept running." Meanwhile, Sonny Red had been struck in the back with a bullet that had cut clean through his body and a second time in his side. Injured but alive, he scrambled toward the door. Sciascia saw that their prime target was not yet dead and moved toward him.

"I seen George reach in the back, pull out a gun and shoot him on the left side of the head," Vitale said. "By that time, it was all over."

Outside the club, Lino did not run into the Bonanno soldiers who were supposed to be watching for just such an eventuality. He spent little time weighing his options.

"I got out the door and I ran," he said. "I made a left. I went up 68th Street, jumped over a few fences, went into these people's home. I knocked at their door, elderly people; the man was in a wheelchair. I told him I'm not there to hurt him, if I could use their phone. They were nice, let me use their phone."

"First I called the My Way Lounge. Then I called my house," Lino said. At his club, he spoke with a bartender, then to his brother and a few of his regulars, looking for a quick ride out of the area. "I just told them if they could get somebody to pick me up at this location. Then when I hung up, I called up my house and my son Frankie answered. I told him the same thing. He happened to get there first."

Meanwhile, the remaining captains had also been anxious to leave the scene of the shootings, but Vitale and the old-timer waved their guns to keep them at bay until Vitale got the signal from outside the club. The plotters did not want a panicked crowd spilling out on to the street, drawing attention and, perhaps, calls to the police.

"I wouldn't let them exit. I was calling 'Goldie' in the walkie-talkie, 'Goldie, where are you?' He came around the [street] corner [in the van]; when I knew he was outside, I let the individuals out of the club," Vitale said. The other captains were then hustled into Goldie's van and whisked away. Vito, Emanuele and their Sicilian colleagues, however, seemed to have suddenly and mysteriously vanished.

"I closed the door, I turned around and the only one standing in the room other than the three dead bodies was Joseph Massino," Vitale said. Massino and Vitale had been told that there were no other exits from the club and yet people were gone who did not pass through the guarded door.

"We just looked at each other; 'Where did everybody go?'... Me and Mr. Massino didn't know there was another exit. After the shooting, all the Zips got out through the back door. We were standing in the middle of the room; we didn't know there was an extra exit," Vitale said.

The Canadian crew and their New York–based Sicilian kin seemed to have arranged an alternative route to safety—and kept it to themselves.

The body of Sonny Red lay near the door in the foyer. Big Trinny lay dead in the main room and Philly Lucky's body was near the end wall. Massino and Vitale then left the club.

"We exited the building through the front door, walked to the corner, where we ran into Sonny Black," Vitale said. "Massino and him had a conversation. I had stood to the side. They talked and they said it was time to go back in and package the bodies."

Frenzy soon returned to the club. Sonny Black's crew came in for the cleanup and faced the significant challenge of moving Big Trinny's dead weight. Lefty Ruggiero tried to shift the limp mass but could not budge it. He then watched in amazement as Boobie threw his considerable muscle into the job. Lefty would later regale fellow gangsters with the story of Boobie's surprising strength. The bodies were each wrapped in white bedsheets and tied tight with clothesline—once around the neck, again around the waist and a third time around the ankles.

"The men opened up the drop cloths, placed them on the floor, carried the bodies to the drop cloths, wrapped them up and put rope around them so they could carry them," Vitale said. The bodies were then carted out of the club and dropped into a waiting van and spirited away for discreet disposal. For that part of the job, Angelo Ruggiero (who was not related to Lefty), Gene Gotti and John Carneglia—Sciascia's heroin partners in the Gambino Family—were called into action, Vitale said.

"When I got back to the club with Sonny Black's crew, there was so much blood," Vitale said. "We couldn't clean it up. It was impossible." They turned to a rather primitive form of cleansing. Massino told Vitale to give the club's keys to one of the Montrealers.

"He's going to burn the place down," Massino said.

————

Lino's escape was not the only snag that night. Santo "Tony" Giordano, the Zip who was playing the congenial host for the ruse of a meeting, caught some friendly fire when the gunmen started shooting. Two fellow Zips pulled the injured Giordano from the floor and, holding him between them, rushed him from the club, out through the exit that Massino and Vitale did not know existed.

Giordano was driven to the Brooklyn apartment of his uncle, Gaspare Bonventre. The uncle walked up the stairs from his basement apartment to answer the frantic ringing of his doorbell. It was late, close to 11 p.m., and, before opening his door, he asked who was there.

"Nino, it's Tony," came the reply. Santo Giordano was often called Tony, and he affectionately referred to his uncle as Nino. Opening the door, the uncle saw that his nephew was in deep distress. He was alone, in pain and crumpled against an outside wall—bent over, almost on his knees.

"Uncle, uncle, help me," Giordano said.

"What happened? What's happening?" his uncle asked.

"Give me help. Help me," Giordano repeated. His uncle put his arm around Giordano's shoulder and helped him inside and down the stairs. Giordano could barely move on his own. On one side he leaned heavily on his uncle and to the other he leaned against the stairwell's side wall. At the bottom of the steps, without a wall to offer support, he collapsed to the ground, refusing to be moved any farther. His uncle offered to carry him to a nearby chair but Giordano begged him not to move him or even touch him any more.

"No, leave me here. Leave me here," Giordano cried. He then called out for a doctor.

"Why? What's happened? Why can't you stand up?" his worried uncle asked. What his uncle did not know was that his nephew's associates were already making arrangements for medical attention—arrangements that would be more discreet than a public call to an ambulance or, worse, the police.

Dr. Edward Salerno was in his pajamas and just settling in front of the television for the 11 o'clock news. Salerno was a community doctor whose office and home shared the same building on Suydam Street in Brooklyn, where he had practiced medicine for almost 25 years. Among his patients had been Giordano, who had started seeing him infrequently in 1968, and Sal Catalano. Salerno's home office was near Catalano's bar, the Café del Viale, on Knickerbocker Avenue, where the doctor would go almost every morning for a cup of coffee before his office hours began. Salerno's attention was abruptly pulled away from the nightly news.

"The bell rang and I opened the door and I saw this man that I knew by sight. He asked me if I could go with him because there was an emergency," Salerno later recalled. He knew he had seen the man several times at the Café del Viale but did not know his name. Salerno asked what the emergency was.

"I'll tell you later," came the reply. The doctor was reluctant to go. He was dressed for bed, it was late and the situation seemed mysterious, but the visitor was insistent. Salerno was handed a stack of cash. He did not know how much was there, nor did he stop to count it then, but later he found it was a wad totaling $500. Salerno changed into street clothes, grabbed his medical bag and slipped into the back seat of a waiting car. Sitting beside him was Cesare Bonventre. The car sped away.

"I asked the driver once he took the parkway where we were going. So he told me we're going to Bensonhurst. That's the only conversation I had with him," he said. When the doctor arrived at the uncle's apartment, he was ushered downstairs, where he recognized his old patient, Giordano, who was lying on the floor and screaming out in pain. Salerno checked his pulse, which was weak, and his blood pressure, which was extremely low. His patient was pale and blood flowed freely from a wound to his back. Salerno gave him an injection of morphine to ease his pain.

"He had been shot. I saw there was a bullet lodged in his chest under the skin. So I turned him around to see where the entry bullet [wound] was and I noticed the entry bullet was some place around his back," Salerno said. "It was very fresh. I don't know how fresh it was. There was too much blood on the floor." He quickly realized there was little he could do in the apartment. Giordano's condition was graver than the gangsters had realized. It was not just a matter of stitching up a hole; Giordano needed major surgery, the kind only a hospital could provide. His condition, Salerno told the men, was critical. Their friend was dying.

"I will call the ambulance," Salerno said. Giordano protested, insisting that Salerno treat him personally. The doctor told him that he had to get to a hospital quickly. The hospital where Salerno had privileges, Wyckoff Heights Medical Center, was on the other side of Brooklyn. What Giordano needed was an ambulance to take him to the nearest facility, Coney Island Hospital, for immediate surgery, the doctor said. But even through his agony, Giordano was resolute.

"I advised him, I felt the trip wasn't good for him because of his condition, but he insisted. So I called the private ambulance myself and in the meantime I also called the hospital and the surgery room, to have the operating room ready, and I went with Mr. Giordano in the ambulance," Salerno said.

"He was taken to the operating room immediately. The result of the operation was that the bleeding was stopped. The man was paralyzed and the paralysis was permanent," he said.

Although neither Salerno nor Giordano's associates had called the police over the gunshot injury, as the law requires, an officer in the emergency room at the time noticed the fuss and approached medical staff. A report on the incident eventually made its way to the FBI. A few days after the shooting, FBI Special Agent Carmine Russo, one of the agents probing the Zips' drug activities in Brooklyn, visited Giordano in hospital. Giordano lay bandaged and, in contrast to his screaming panic on the night of the murders, was now calm, collected and even cocky.

"I heard you had some trouble," Russo said to the mobster, who was propped up on pillows on the hospital bed.

"Me? Oh, this? Nah, this is nothing," Giordano replied.

"The doctors say you were shot," the agent said.

"An accident," answered Giordano.

"How'd it happen, Santo?"

"Argument over a parking spot."

"Where?"

"I don't remember."

THE BRONX, MAY 6, 1981

At nine-thirty the morning after the three murders, FBI Special Agent William Andrew was on surveillance duty inside a house, rented secretly by the FBI, that looked out over Catalano Brothers Bakery, a café on Metropolitan Avenue in Middle Village, Queens, that was run by Sal Catalano as a base for his heroin deals. Hidden nearby with his camera and long lens, Andrew waited and watched until his radio crackled with instructions to move his camera across to the Bronx side of the Whitestone Bridge to train his lens on the Capri Motor Lodge. A police surveillance team working on the Pizza Connection heroin investigation had seen Sciascia and Massino driving in a car linked to Catalano. They watched as they switched cars in Queens and headed off in a blue Buick Regal, which had, in turn, been followed to the Capri Motor Lodge. At that point, Andrew and his camera were called in. The agent found a suitably discreet spot outside and was set up by 10:30 a.m. to watch the front of the motel. It was an uneventful vigil until shortly after noon, when four men emerged. Andrew clicked away with his camera, capturing 10 photographs over the next minute or so.

Massino and Sciascia walked out first and headed along the motel's cut-stone and white brick facade toward its parking lot. Massino put his arm around Sciascia as they walked and talked. Two other men, unknown to the agent, followed about 15 feet behind. They also chatted as they walked and one had a garment bag nonchalantly slung over his shoulder and a cigarette dangling rakishly from his lips. The other had bushy, dark hair and wore a suit jacket over a T-shirt.

"I took photographs as they progressed down the front walkway, toward the blue Buick," said Andrew. Massino and Sciascia turned to speak to the other men a moment, before Massino headed toward the passenger door of the Buick Regal while Sciascia hunted for the car keys. "They were followed out by the two individuals and, at some point, they were fairly close to each other and they exchanged words," he said. "They were saying something to them, acknowledging them. I could not hear what they were saying." While Massino and Sciascia climbed into the Buick, the other two men walked past it and got into a red Ford pick-up truck that was parked beside it. Both vehicles pulled away as Andrew shot off one last frame, capturing with his camera Sciascia and Massino driving past him.

Both Sciascia and Massino were well known to the FBI agents, but the other two men were a puzzle. The agents ran the New Jersey license plate of the pick-up truck and it came back registered to Giovanni Ligammari, a New Jersey contractor who was another of the Sicilian men involved in moving heroin through the city. It is not known when agents first identified the man with the cigarette and the garment bag. His identity was likely established when agents compared his long facial features to the profiles of the guests photographed at the Bono wedding. It was Vito Rizzuto.

While Vito, Massino, Sciascia and Ligammari were having a post-ambush meeting and Giordano was realizing he had become an underworld oddity—a paraplegic gangster—Frank Lino remained fearful for his life.

"I thought I was going to get killed sooner or later," he said. It seemed a natural outcome of both his loyalty to Sonny Red and being a witness to the purge. After the murders, Lino went to spend the night at the home of his old mob friend, Frank Coppa, but the evening's intrigue was not yet over for him. Lino's cousin Eddie Lino, who was part of John Gotti's Gambino Family crew, telephoned him at Coppa's house to call him to a meeting. With Eddie, when Lino arrived, was the Gambino gang that had been helping in the plot: Gene Gotti, Angelo Ruggiero, Frank DeCico and Aniello Dellacroce.

"They told me that after the killing, that I wasn't going to get killed," Lino said. Dellacroce asked Lino if he had alerted police to the bloodletting and, after Lino's assurance that he had not, Dellacroce turned toward Angelo Ruggiero: "Tell them to get rid of the bodies," he said. Dellacroce then had one more thing to ask. "Do you know where Bruno is?"

Lino lied, telling Dellacroce that he had no idea where Bruno might be or what he might be up to. The Gambino underboss then told Lino to find Bruno and to kill him.

The next day, Lino was called to yet another meeting, this one with his own crime family, but it started at Angelo Ruggiero's house in Howard Beach. Inside were Sciascia and Nick the Battler. When Lino arrived, they trundled off together to Massino's house, just a short distance away. En route, Sciascia and Nick talked to Lino about his miraculous escape the night before. Sciascia admitted he had placed his arm around Lino on purpose: "He was supposed to hold me down so I couldn't escape; that I was getting killed," Lino said. Nick said simply: "Don't ever do that again. If you gotta die, die." If that conversation made Lino nervous about what might be coming, at Massino's house he felt some relief that other Bonanno captains were there, Sally Fruits, Sonny Black and Joe Bayonne among them. It did indeed look like a family meeting and not an execution, although Sonny Red might have thought the same thing the night before. This time, a direct peace offering was extended to Lino.

"They says they would leave me as the acting captain if I could bring everybody in," Lino said. "The next day I got in touch with Joey D'Amico. He brought everybody in. ... I made them come back into the neighborhood. I told them what happened, that the guys got killed and that they says that if everybody came in and didn't retaliate, you know, it would be forgotten about," he said. "The only ones that didn't come in was, like, Bruno and Tommy Karate."

Massino and Sciascia were willing to let Lino live, but their magnanimity did not extend to Bruno, Sonny Red's son. Massino and Sciascia did not relish living with an aggrieved mobster out walking the streets, likely harboring thoughts of revenge. Massino's orders to his men on Bruno's fate were explicit: "Just kill him and leave him in the street." Sonny Black saw this as yet another chance to earn his favored associate, Donnie Brasco, a Mafia membership. He told Lefty and Brasco to hunt down Bruno and kill him.

Sally Fruits was then named the acting boss while Rastelli remained in prison. He was a candidate that both Massino and the Zips could tolerate. Both knew he would not interfere with their plans.

"The way it was explained to me," Vitale said, "they picked him to be like a figurehead between the Zips and the American guys, just to keep harmony and peace until Phil Rastelli came home."

Soon after the murders, Massino, Sciascia and Sally Fruits went to visit Vincent "The Chin" Gigante, the boss of the Genovese Family. (The Chin was later dubbed "The Oddfather" because of his attempts to dodge indictments by feigning mental illness; to carry it off, he frequently wandered the streets in his slippers and housecoat. The ruse failed; he died in prison in 2005.)

"[They] went to Chin's club to tell Chin that they took care of business," Vitale said. "When they walked into the club to see the Chin, Mickey Divino [a Genovese captain] said to Joseph Massino to sit here. He said, 'I don't want to sit, I'm not sitting,' and they asked George to wait outside." The powerful Genovese Family did not seem to have much trust in Sciascia, and Massino was likely nervous about the Chin's previous support of Sonny Red.

QUEENS, MAY 24, 1981

Shortly before 4 p.m. on May 24—19 days after the shootings—children playing in a vacant lot on Ruby Street in Ozone Park, Queens, were drawn by an odd smell to a section of rough dirt and garbage. The lot, plowed under just two months before, had quickly become an unofficial dump, but this odor, oddly attractive to both flies and young boys, stood out from the usual stench. Kicking at the loosened soil, a neighborhood lad discovered a hand. The boy ran for his parents, who called police. At 4:20 p.m., New York City Police officer Andrew Cilienti arrived at the lot to find a left arm, bearing a tattoo of two hearts and a dagger and bejeweled with a $1,500 Cartier watch, poking out from the dirty bedsheet in which a body had been wrapped. The watch had stopped ticking two days after the captains' murder, with its hands resting at 5:58. The cool pressure of the soil around it in its rough tomb had slowed decomposition of the body, so, prior to autopsy, finger-prints could be carefully taken from the malleable hand. The prints came back to police as a match to Alphonse "Sonny Red" Indelicato. Four days later, Salvatore Valenti,

Sonny Red's 33-year-old son-in-law, had the gruesome task of officially identifying the body.

News of the find on Ruby Street spread quickly through the ranks of the mob. Sonny Black telephoned Massino and said he had some bad news to share. Massino hung up and hopped into Vitale's car for a drive over to Sonny Black's club, where his captain broke the news to Massino in person.

"The body popped up," he said.

Incredibly, despite the involvement of so many people from two Mafia families, the unexpected discovery of Sonny Red's body, the accidental crippling of one of their own and the improbable escape of Frank Lino, the conspiracy by Massino, the Zips and the Sixth Family seemed to remain a secret. Only bits and pieces of the events filtered out. With the high tensions in the Bonanno Family over the purge and the unsavory prospect of an FBI agent being handed a gangland murder contract, the FBI had to pull Special Agent Joe Pistone out of his unprecedented six-year ruse as gangster Donnie Brasco. When Pistone was called in by his handlers, other FBI agents visited the Bonanno leadership and soon-to-be indicted gangsters, informing them that Pistone was an undercover agent and not a mob turncoat; it was a move designed to protect him from vengeful gangsters. While killing rats was fair game in the American Mafia, murdering a federal agent was still beyond the pale. Agents also visited Philip Rastelli in prison, seeking his assurance that Pistone would not be hunted down. As proof of the true identity of "Donnie Brasco," the agents showed Sonny Black and other gangsters photographs of Pistone posing with grinning FBI agents. Pistone's subsequent evidence, however, sketched in only some of the peripheral events to the murders.

The fact that the massacre went unsolved for more than 20 years speaks volumes about the power and cohesiveness of the Mafia when it operates according to plan. The Canadian connection to the murders remained a closely guarded secret.

Those who helped to purge Sonny Red and his dissidents from the Bonanno ranks were well rewarded. Some who helped were later inducted into the family. For Massino, his power widened both within the family and on the streets of New York. His claim as heir apparent to Rastelli was now assured.

"He was very influential. He was one of the strongest captains in the family, if not the strongest," Vitale said.

QUEENS, FALL 1981

Sal Vitale stood at the top of a stepladder, tilting up ceiling panels and peering into the dark infrastructure that housed J&S Cake, a brick storefront-catering facility on a side street in Maspeth, Queens.

J&S Cake, despite its decidedly benign-sounding name, was not a legitimate catering facility. Rather, it acted as a social club and gathering place, dubbed the "Rust Street Club" by the Bonannos, as well as a seemingly legitimate front for the criminal activities of its two proprietors. The "J" in its name stood for Joe Massino and the "S" for Sal Vitale. It was from J&S Cake that many of the participants in the hit against the three captains disembarked, and it was at J&S that, every Tuesday night, Massino would host a sprawling dinner meeting with his underlings, with Bonanno members taking turns doing the cooking, after which they played cards, with Massino taking a cut on each hand played in the high-stakes games of Continental. After the murders of the three rival captains, Massino's position as the first among supposed equals was assured. In a display of respect by ambitious and fearful mobsters, soldiers and other captains would make regular pilgrimage to J&S Cake to ingratiate themselves to Massino.

Anyone in the Bonanno Family who wanted to talk to Massino knew where to find him—at J&S Cake. Likewise, the FBI also knew they could find him at J&S Cake. And, in the cat-and-mouse continuum of the struggle between the Bonannos and the FBI, Massino knew that the FBI knew that he used J&S as his headquarters. Quite simply, this was why he had sent Vitale up the ladder to poke around underneath the ceiling tiles. It had become a routine for Vitale, who periodically searched under furniture, in light fixtures and behind the drop ceiling at the hangout for signs of hidden electronic listening devices installed by government agents. Massino was always cautious, but at that point he was particularly jumpy. The murder of the three captains and his subsequent rise in status within the family meant he was both a greater target for law-enforcement scrutiny and had more to hide.

"I would actually look for the bugs," Vitale said. "I would get up on a ladder and lift the ceiling up—the drop ceiling—look on the furniture. We'd have a Bearcat scanner to pick up voices in the club," he said of a common counter-surveillance technique. Since the electronic bugs carried their intercepted conversations over radio frequencies, they could sometimes be detected that way. Massino even periodically paid for a professional "sweep" to be done.

"I just normally would search every two weeks, three weeks, make it my business to sweep the place and go through the place," Vitale said. The mobsters had good reason to worry. The FBI's Bonanno Squad had targeted Massino for special scrutiny, attention befitting his obvious rise in underworld status. With court authorization, members of the FBI's Special Operations team had managed to break into J&S Cake and secretly place a bug inside. With great anticipation, the squad switched on its equipment and finally had a glimpse into Massino's inner sanctum.

"It lasted maybe 12, 24 hours, then it went quiet," said Patrick F. Colgan, a retired member of the Bonanno Squad, who spent a decade investigating Massino. "We knew we were compromised," he said. Sure enough, just a day after the microphone was switched on, Vitale had made his trip up the ladder and, behind the ceiling tiles above the table where the mobsters typically sat to chat as they played cards, he found a tiny microphone and transmitter.

"I discovered the microphone and left it right where it was in the ceiling," Vitale said. For the agents monitoring the bug, there was concern over the sudden silence. It did not take long for them to realize that the bug in J&S had been discovered. There was little the agents could do but go over and collect the expensive device. While the two mobsters were at their headquarters there was a knock at the front door. Outside was Agent Colgan, whom both Vitale and Massino recognized by sight. Vitale answered it.

"Can I have my bug back?" Colgan said, according to Vitale.

"Hold on, let me find out," said Vitale, who ran over to Massino to check.

"Pat wants his bug back," Vitale said to his boss.

"Give him his bug back," Massino said. Vitale returned to the door with the microphone and its related pieces in hand and passed them over to the agent, who then left. It was an embarrassing turn for the proud agents.

A new era within the Bonanno Family had begun and the FBI's Bonanno Squad clearly had a lot of work ahead.

With the rebellious faction dead or muted, the balance of power in the Bonanno Family had significantly shifted. In accordance with an explicit prior agreement with the Zips, the Massino–Sonny Black faction also took over from Sonny Red the lucrative job of distributing the heroin being brought in by the Sicilian gangsters, including the Sixth

Family. On June 15, 1981, just before Donnie Brasco was unmasked as an FBI agent, Lefty Ruggiero spoke to the undercover agent about the sweeping changes in the wake of the murders. The two men huddled on the street near the Holiday Bar in Manhattan.

"Since these guys got hit," Lefty said, "Sonny [Black] took over all the drugs."

The deal had been consummated. Everyone was happy and the drugs kept flowing. While Carmine Galante and Sonny Red had both been executed for moving to be the Bonanno boss while Rastelli still held the title, Massino managed to balance maintaining power while still respecting Rastelli's title and the Commission's interest in non-violent leadership transition.

For Vito Rizzuto, he had earned respect and favors-owing from his New York colleagues and demonstrated the efficiency and contribution of the Canadian connection in a visceral and explosive way. He had cemented the Sixth Family's relationship with the emerging power within the Bonanno Family in a way that Paolo Violi or Vic Cotroni never could. Sciascia, Montreal's main representative in New York, also experienced a burgeoning of his influence in the Bonanno Family and was recognized by all as a key ally of Massino and as a force to be reckoned with in his own right.

More important, the Canadian assassins had protected the Sixth Family's heroin franchise in New York.

CHAPTER 20

ATLANTIC OCEAN, OFF SAVANNAH, GEORGIA, MAY 6, 1982

The Gates Learjet 23 N100TA—or "One-Hundred Tango Alpha" in air-crew jargon—took off from Teterboro, New Jersey, at 10:28 a.m. on May 6, 1982, which was a good day for flying. Pilot George Morton had been told, when he checked conditions earlier in the day, that there was no hazardous weather on the horizon and it looked like clear flying through to Orlando, Florida.

On board the Learjet, which was owned by IBEX Corporation, Morton was joined by a stand-in co-pilot named Sherri Day and two passengers—a husband and wife—who were described by IBEX management as business associates being flown to a meeting in Orlando. Morton flew the jet while Day handled the radio communications. For more than an hour, the flight was uneventful. Then, from over the Atlantic, Day radioed the Jacksonville, Florida, air traffic control center requesting landing status.

"Descend and maintain flight level three-nine-zero," an air traffic controller radioed to Learjet N100TA at 11:31 a.m., instructing the pilot to lower its altitude from Flight Level 410 to Flight Level 390.

"Three-nine-zero, One-Hundred Tango Alpha," Day responded calmly. The Learjet, however, did not immediately start its descent. A minute and a half later, Day came over the radio again.

"One-Hundred Tango Alpha's descending now," she said. Her voice sounded hurried and the controller could hear a warning horn sounding in the background. Day made another brief transmission, which was unintelligible.

"Say again," the controller directed. There was no response. Not even static.

At noon, the crew of a fishing boat spotted a huge water geyser on the surface of the Atlantic, 12 miles southeast of Savannah, Georgia. The captain sped to the scene and found debris scattered across the surface—bits of skin from the fuselage and pieces of the Learjet's interior—but no survivors.

Ninety minutes after the crash, the National Transportation Safety Board was notified. That same day, a team of three investigators was dispatched from Washington, DC. On May 13, a search team, using sonar equipment, began an underwater scan of the crash site. Visibility underwater was poor and it was not until late in the afternoon the next day that the main wreckage was found, 55 feet below the surface, scattered over 75 feet of the ocean floor. Morton's body and those of the two passengers were recovered from the wreckage. All had suffered multiple traumatic injuries. Day's body was never found. After examining the debris, the NTSB was unable to determine the cause of the crash. The weather was almost ideal for flying—another pilot said he had encountered no difficulties in the area at about the same time. An explosion was eliminated as a possible cause, as was an onboard fire. The pilot and co-pilot were both certified; the jet had been well maintained.

"The National Transportation Safety Board determined that the probable cause for the accident was an uncontrolled descent from cruise altitude for undetermined reasons from which a recovery was not, or could not be, effected," the official Aircraft Accident Report concluded.

Although the NTSB investigation could not solve the mystery of why the Learjet plunged into the Atlantic Ocean, it did resolve a long-standing mystery for the FBI. One of the passengers aboard N100TA was Salvatore Ruggiero. Until his body was identified in a morgue, Ruggiero had been listed as a fugitive from justice, a member of the Gambino Family, a large-scale heroin trafficker and a key customer of the Sixth Family. A year and a day earlier, Salvatore's brother, Angelo, also a Gambino soldier and a childhood friend of John Gotti's, had helped Gerlando Sciascia and Joe Massino get rid of the bodies of the three captains killed in the Bonanno purge.

Ruggiero's flight from justice and his untimely death would mean far more to the Sixth Family than just the loss of a good customer. The search for Ruggiero—and the probe following his death—would bring grief to their American operations.

NEW YORK, EARLY 1980s

The Montreal-to-New York heroin pipeline was pouring product into the United States at such a rate that the supply outstripped any reasonable marketplace demand. Two years after the Bono wedding and a year after the murders of the three captains, the drug supply routes into the major cities of America were running almost flawlessly. The notion that organized crime merely supplies an existing need was put to the lie by the sheer bulk of the heroin shipments. A market had to be created, so the price of heroin was dropped considerably and the victim pool shot up accordingly, tenfold by most estimates. When it comes to street drugs, supply creates its own demand. In New York, the Sixth Family and other Sicilian-backed heroin enterprises were giving drugs on credit to Mafia soldiers and associates who were willing to take it and move it.

"There was no demand for a down payment," a former undercover drug agent remembers. "It was: take it, take it, take it. Just take the fucking stuff. Move it. Pay when you can, just take it off my hands, I got more coming."

Gerlando Sciascia certainly did not hint that his supply was running low. "How about 30 kilos?" he announced at the start of one of his ubiquitous sales calls, this one made to the home of a fellow mobster, whose children were playing in the same room.

"I got 30 things ... that's why I'm here." Take it, take it, take it.

The 10 years from 1975 to 1985 were the golden years of heroin—even more so than during the decades of the French Connection, whose routes seem unsophisticated by these standards. The loads were larger, the market far wider and the facilities for repatriating the dirty money sleeker and more global. The expatriate Mafia families—the Rizzutos, the Caruana–Cuntreras and the Bonos, among others—came to true power in these heroin years, just as the old gangs of the Prohibition-era were built on their ability to move alcohol.

No one could afford not to be in the game: the Sicilian clans and the American Mafia families all recognized the vast profits at hand and had members work their way into the heroin trade just to maintain the status quo in the underworld, if nothing else. The Bonannos were out in front, but the Gambinos were close behind. Any question that selling drugs had been "banned under pain of death" by the senior members of the American Mafia had long since been abandoned, even by those few who actually tried to stick to that code. In Buffalo, for instance, the old Mafia boss Stefano Magaddino reaped huge profits from his soldiers' drug deals while ordering them to sell dope only in the black neighborhoods. Vito Agueci, the Toronto-based brother of the Sicilian trafficker Alberto Agueci, who helped run a piece of the French

Connection, was inducted into the Buffalo family by Magaddino on the strength of his contribution to the heroin trade.

No family was above it. It was a sport without spectators.

———

Sciascia was the Sixth Family's lead player in the New York distribution, lining up customers, keeping an eye on their activities and continually working to ensure that the family's interests were not overlooked. As a captain in the Bonanno Family, he carried weight beyond the kilos he was offering.

With Sciascia was Joe LoPresti, his direct Montreal liaison. Both were close friends and distant family of Vito Rizzuto, and among the inner circle of the Sixth Family. Around them in New York were dozens of well-connected salesmen who had their own networks of buyers along the eastern seaboard and farther afield in American cities. These Sixth Family constituents had been slowly increasing the organization's output and efficiency in New York for at least three years since they first started to make their way onto police radar through street snitches and drug probes. The more business they generated, the more police started to hear of them. To keep the money flowing satisfactorily, however, they needed to boost their sales volume. And that required careful client management.

Sciascia was a consummate salesman. He was always ready with product, always prepared to cut a deal. And he looked after his buyers, wanted them for himself and often lied to them that they were his only customers.

"How'd you make out with George?" John Carneglia, a Gambino soldier, once asked his mob colleague Angelo Ruggiero, brother of the fugitive who died in the plane crash, after Angelo had met with Sciascia to arrange a drug deal.

"Very good," Angelo replied. "Excellent. He doesn't want to do anything with anyone else but us." Both Ruggiero brothers had become well acquainted with Sciascia and LoPresti from their frequent sales calls. Salvatore Ruggiero was Sciascia's first major client in the Gambino Family. Along with Gotti's brother, Gene, the Ruggiero brothers formed an extensive drug-trafficking network within the Gambinos. Ostensibly, John Gotti himself was never involved in the drug trade, but with two of his closest friends and his own brother so tightly involved with Sciascia and LoPresti, it is impossible to believe that he did not know and approve of their activities, and profit from them. Like the other families, the Gambinos developed a heroin wing within their organization; it was often managed by the boss's brother.

Unlike Angelo, Salvatore Ruggiero had graduated from street thuggery and become a multimillionaire, selling a range of drugs, from major shipments of marijuana to heroin and cocaine. Wanted on several charges, he had become a fugitive, hiding out with his wife, Stephanie, under various names in New Jersey, Florida, Pennsylvania and Ohio. His prime heroin supplier was Sciascia.

When the Gates Learjet carrying Salvatore plunged into the Atlantic Ocean in May 1982, Salvatore had been on the run for six years. Being a fugitive had not slowed his drug-dealing activities; at the time of his death, he had yet another shipment of heroin, taken on credit from Sciascia, stored in his house awaiting resale.

After Angelo was notified of his brother's death, he, along with Gene Gotti and Carneglia, went to Salvatore's hideout in Franklin Lakes, New Jersey, searching for the heroin and hidden cash. A few months earlier, however, hoping to catch up with the elusive Salvatore and to gain evidence to indict John Gotti, the FBI's Gambino Squad had thoroughly wired Angelo Ruggiero's home in Cedarhurst, Long Island. Not only was his telephone line bugged, but microphones were placed in his kitchen, den and dining room. Federal agents recorded Angelo's attorney, Michael Coiro, offering condolences to Angelo on the death of his brother, and then saying: "Gene found the heroin."

The talk of heroin in the wake of Salvatore's death—and the connection to a Gotti—seized the attention of investigating agents. The fishing expedition on Angelo suddenly held the promise of reeling in big fish. Targeting Angelo for electronic surveillance had been a perfect call for another reason. Often known as "Quack Quack"—because of his inability to stop talking—Angelo was a constant chatterbox, providing a running commentary on everything going on around him. Everyone who visited Angelo had to endure endless gossip, complaints and general indiscretions. It was ridiculously loose talk, doubly so because he knew he was under investigation. On one of Sciascia's sales visits, he heard how Angelo had suspected he was being monitored and the steps he had taken to ensure he was not; all of it, meanwhile, recorded by the FBI. Angelo had answered the doorbell one day to find a workman from the telephone company outside.

"What the hell do you want?" was Angelo's greeting.

"I come here to fix the phone," the workman said.

"Come here to fix the phones?" Angelo bellowed. "You [were] fixing the phone before!"

"Me? Not me," the confused workman said. "This is my area. Mister, I don't know who those [other] people were." Ruggiero called in a counter-surveillance expert, a retired detective, to check the entire house.

"It was clean," Angelo told Sciascia. Too bad for Sciascia, LoPresti, Gene Gotti and any other gangster who stepped near Angelo's house, that it was not quite true. Tipped off to the planned sweep, the FBI turned its bugs off the day of the scheduled search. With Angelo now relaxed in his supposed privacy, he again started to chatter wildly— and the bugs were turned back on.

Salvatore's death hit Angelo hard. Afterward, he was often heard wistfully speaking of his brother to Sciascia and LoPresti.

"He made money," Angelo said to Sciascia one day. "He knew how to make money." In the mob, there were few more adoring words one could say about someone. Salvatore, clearly making money hand over fist through his connection to the Sixth Family, was a source of awe for Angelo, who tried his best to emulate him.

"He made me make money," Angelo said. "I was in debt six months ago. I'm way out of debt now. I bet you—I'm no fucking millionaire, I got no million dollars—but I know what I got. And I gambled. Gambled. I mean I'm sitting on $400,000. What the fuck has my brother got? If I'm sitting on four, what does my brother got?" Such was the quick return on the Sixth Family's merchandise. The day after the memorial service for Salvatore, a distraught Angelo worried that people who owed money to his brother would renege on their debt and deprive Salvatore's children.

"We're up against lice in this world," Angelo said. "Listen, I ain't no scumbag. I'm not asking nobody for nothing, you hear? All I'm telling you is this: If I find out anybody's lying, a year from now, six months from now, and if anybody is holding back anything from my brother … I promise youse this, youse are gonna die the same way my brother died—in pieces. I give you my word on it. … My brother was good to everybody. My fucking brother helped every fucking one of youse."

The love between the brothers spilled out again as Angelo spoke to LoPresti, who had arrived to discuss yet another shipment and answer a question from Angelo, to which he said he would "refer it to people in Canada." LoPresti also talked about a scheme to double their profit—selling drugs to someone "and then we'll whack him." But Angelo, for once, was not so interested in talking about heroin. The talk of whacking someone seemed to spur in him another bout of wistful regret.

"You know, I lost my brother," he told LoPresti. "I said to myself: 'I'll have to get drunk.' I had two vodkas ... I went in my room, I closed the door and I cried ... If they would have found him in the street and he would have [been] shot in the head, I would have accepted it, because this is a part of our life. Next week, the week after, we would have got even [with] whoever did it, right? We would have accepted it. Not this way. This is ... this is ..." He could not find the words.

To LoPresti, Angelo was like a child, a product of a Mafia that LoPresti, Vito, Sciascia and the rest of the Sicilian traffickers had little use for except as an outlet for their heroin. LoPresti let the distraught Angelo pour out his heartbreak.

"Let it out," LoPresti said. But when Angelo was finished crying, LoPresti was right back at it: How much can you take? Take it, take it, take it.

Had LoPresti known that each of the sales calls made by him and Sciascia were being monitored and documented by the FBI, he might also have felt like crying. So much time spent with a man whose home was so thoroughly penetrated by the FBI could only mean trouble. From an unexplained plane crash, the quiet commerce of the Sixth Family's operations would be partially exposed.

CHAPTER 21

THE BRONX, SUMMER 1981

On July 1, 1981—a national holiday in Canada, marking the creation of the Dominion of Canada in 1867—Gerlando Sciascia remained in New York, with his house secretly watched by the FBI. It was the fifth day of surveillance by agents assigned to monitor the home on Stadium Avenue in the Bronx, and this was the first day the agents had spotted their quarry.

At 11:30 a.m., Sciascia walked out of his home, climbed into his green 1979 four-door Peugeot and drove off along Route 95. Agents tailing him watched as he pulled off the freeway and stopped at a service station to fill up with diesel. He then resumed his journey, south on Route 95, and agents watched him drive through the tollbooths at the Throgs Neck Bridge and soon lost him in traffic. It was a rather inauspicious start to a new federal racketeering investigation into Sciascia's activities. All evidence, however, suggested they should not give up.

Sciascia had been targeted for investigation after several years of reports continued to pile up in the FBI's offices showing that he was an increasingly active part of both the Sixth Family's drug trade and the Bonanno Family. When agents were assigned to take a closer look at him and the people he was working with, they soon found themselves bumping into other investigators from other agencies who had also found their way to Sciascia through their own leads. FBI agents probing the links between the Bonanno Family members and the Sicilian drug traffickers on Knickerbocker Avenue were interested in him; the agents monitoring the wires in Angelo Ruggiero's home were interested in him; the Drug Enforcement Administration was tracking him, as were Canadian police. In 1981, the information was starting to be pooled and a federal racketeering investigation was officially launched.

Sciascia's involvement in heroin distribution in New York preceded the Bono wedding; even before the last of the Violi brothers had been killed. By early 1980, FBI agents were already writing internal reports on Sciascia and his Sixth Family kin, noting suspicious transactions by an import/export company linked to Montreal as well as meetings in New York by Canadian visitors. The Canadians seemed to have a lot of friends in a lot of places, agents noted. An internal FBI report filed in February 1980, noted that the Canadians—in the deadpan bureaucratic argot of the FBI—had "a multitude of telephonic interaction" with contacts in the United States, Italy, France, Switzerland, Venezuela and Canada, particularly Montreal. In November 1980, in the days leading up to the Bono wedding, New York City Police Department intelligence officers had watched Sciascia meet with visiting Sicilian traffickers, who were likely in town for Bono's celebration.

Previous reports of Sciascia's movements were re-examined. There had been meetings in New York's Plaza Hotel and in several homes between Sciascia, other known Canadian traffickers, and American Mafia members of all stripes, some of them freshly released from prison after serving time for narcotics offenses. Each time a visitor from Montreal met with Sciascia, the agents pulled the phone records for their hotel rooms, and each time they were astounded at the scope of their contacts. After one visit in September 1981, calls had been traced to Monaco, Caracas, Rome, Lima and Montreal. On another visit, calls were made to Germany, Paris and Bogotá. Paolo Renda also attracted the attention of agents, apparently in connection with an address to which calls were traced, FBI documents say. A report noted that Renda "from time to time" traveled between Canada and Venezuela.

Canadian police were asked to conduct background checks on the increasing number of Canadians appearing in their investigations. Later, the DEA and the FBI also agreed to cooperate on, rather than compete over, Sciascia. A meeting was arranged between the respective agents who had been monitoring Sciascia; they had so much to say that a follow-up meeting needed to be scheduled a week later.

For one month—from January 8 through February 8, 1982—federal agents intercepted Sciascia's mail, checking it before it was delivered to his home. Registers that recorded every phone number dialed were placed on his home telephones. A corporate records check revealed him to be a founding officer of Pronto Demolition, which appeared to be a through-and-through Mafia enterprise. Joining Sciascia in the boardroom were Giuseppe Bono, Giovanni Ligammari and Giuseppe Ganci, who was the right-hand man of Sal Catalano, the new Zip street boss of Knickerbocker Avenue. The agents' search also led them to

California Pizza, the pizzeria Sciascia ran in the Green Acres Mall in Long Island where Cesare Bonventre and Baldo Amato had been caught with guns in their Cadillac. In the pizza business, Sciascia had partnered with Giuseppe Arcuri, a relative of the man who had hosted the final Montreal sit-down between Nick Rizzuto and Paolo Violi and another of the Sixth Family's staunch supporters in New York. The mingling cut both ways. Police in Canada had noted repeated visits by Cesare Bonventre and Baldo Amato to both Montreal and Toronto. Amato in particular was a frequent visitor.

———————

On the morning of May 17, 1982, 11 days after Salvatore Ruggiero's plane crash, two FBI agents watched Sciascia leave his home, accompanied by a tall, dark-haired visitor. (Two days later, the RCMP showed the agents a photograph of Joe LoPresti and the agents confirmed that he was the mystery man.)

The pair got into Sciascia's second vehicle, a black Jeep Grand Cherokee, a vehicle much-loved by members of the Sixth Family, and drove to a Queens Dunkin' Donuts outlet, where they were met by Cesare Bonventre. After a short chat over coffee at the counter, the three men drove to the Green Acres Mall. While LoPresti and Bonventre walked into the mall, Sciascia headed into his pizzeria. When Sciascia left his restaurant a few minutes later and went into the mall, the agents followed him inside. There they watched Sciascia, LoPresti and Bonventre standing in the center of the busy mall, deep in discussion, in an apparent attempt to thwart being picked up by an electronic bug. LoPresti, who was always surveillance-conscious, spotted an agent watching them from 30 feet away. When he pointed the interloper out to his colleagues, the three men scattered.

"He looked in my direction and he looked back at the other two individuals and said something and at that point the three dispersed and each went in a different direction in the mall," said Special Agent Charles Murray, one of the surveillance officers. "I tried to observe them as best I could," he said. One agent later saw Bonventre making a call at a pay phone; the other spotted Sciascia at a pretzel concession. Sciascia, realizing he was being followed, stopped suddenly and feigned interest in a store window, forcing the agent to continue walking past him. Then Sciascia started to follow the agent. Realizing their folly, the agents left. LoPresti, despite his size, seemed to vanish. He headed for the airport and flew back to Montreal that afternoon.

It was one of several meetings by Sixth Family members that police were aware of. When authorities in Italy learned that Giuseppe Bono was consorting with drug traffickers in New York and in Canada, they rekindled an investigation that had been put on hold when he fled. The Italian probe ran straight into the Sixth Family as well.

On June 12, 1982, Italian police were monitoring Bono as he met at the Gallo Rosso, a luxurious restaurant in Milan, with Michelangelo LaScala, an old Sixth Family contact from Venezuela who had flown to Milan from Caracas. On June 24, the two got together again. This time, while they ate and chatted, Bono took a telephone call. On the other end of the phone was Nick Rizzuto, according to surveillance reports from the Polizia di Stato, the Italian national police. Bono and Nick discussed the movement of a "suitcase," which agents believed was likely traffickers' code for a drug shipment. Investigators determined that Nick had already sent three large shipments of furniture from Italy to Canada, which police believed had drugs hidden inside. Police reports say the listed recipient of the shipments was Maria Renda, Nick's daughter. Nick spent most of that summer in Milan, where he was "in constant contact" with Bono, usually by telephone.

In August 1982, shortly before his departure from Italy, Nick met with Bono in person, but police could not get close enough to intercept their conversation. Nick had a busy time in 1982 and 1983, constantly shuttling between Caracas, Milan and Montreal.

"The suspected purpose of these meetings was to discuss heroin shipments from Italy to the United States," the FBI concluded. The Venezuelan authorities were also helping to build the case, providing the FBI and the RCMP with a detailed report of their investigations into the Sicily–Canada–U.S.–Venezuelan axis, listing several Canadian, Sicilian and American Mafia members.

Taking into account the meetings between Nick and Bono in Italy, the sales calls by Sciascia and LoPresti to the Gambino soldiers in New York and the extensive international telephone contacts made by visiting Montrealers, FBI agents were sure they were on to something huge.

"The targets of these investigations are probably the largest and most significant group involved in importing heroin through Sicily into the United States," states an FBI report dated June 14, 1982. "This group's illegal activities are the most graphic example of internationalization of the Mafia. Their drug importation network is the Cadillac in the New York area, involving staggering amounts of heroin and money."

———

There were clear overlaps between this probe and the massive Pizza Connection case that focused on Sal Catalano, the Zips' Brooklyn street boss, and his coterie. Agents tracking Catalano in Brooklyn and Sciascia in the Bronx were frequently comparing notes. Many of the players overlapped. Telephone records showed members of different groups in constant contact with each other; surveillance reports showed an astounding interplay, as seemingly unrelated and unconnected players from different Sicilian and American Mafia families networked busily. Bonventre, Amato, Sciascia, LoPresti and Catalano; the same names kept surfacing. Giovanni Ligammari, one of the Zips photographed alongside Vito Rizzuto, Sciascia and Joe Massino on the day after the murder of the three captains, was also arranging the payments from investors in the Pizza Connection heroin network.

How did it all relate? And how did all the intermingling trafficking schemes come together? Where did one conspiracy end and the other begin? Agents were befuddled. The investigation into the Zip connection was hampered by the difficulty of penetrating their insular group. Street sources and informants were slim. The people the investigators wanted to get close to did not let strangers get too close. They were, frustrated FBI agents noted, "bound together either by blood or marriage." Another problem was that, despite all of their work, investigators had found precious little heroin. The shortcoming was not lost on them.

Alerted by Italian police to the freight being arranged by Nick and discussed with Bono, the FBI, DEA and U.S. Customs monitored a series of suspicious shipments sent throughout the summer of 1982 from Italy to Montreal, with stops in New Jersey. The link between shipments from Montreal and gangsters in New York was also coming across loud and clear in the Angelo Ruggiero wiretaps.

"I got a call from Montreal. Understand? The people I know," Sciascia said to Ruggiero on June 15, 1982, three days after Nick and Bono spoke about the suitcase. "They want to know, before they do any move, what the profit [is] they gonna get paid," Sciascia said. In the same conversation, he mentioned that they had received the "docked goods."

Agents selected one of the suspicious shipments for interdiction. On the day before the ship was scheduled to arrive at a New Jersey port, a command post was set up at the customs station in Newark.

On August 6, 1982, the MV *Tulsidas* pulled into a New Jersey port and was confronted by customs, FBI and DEA agents. The crew was ordered to unload three large shipping containers whose manifests declared them to contain furniture and antique lamps destined first for Halifax, Nova Scotia, then on to Montreal. Once the containers were on American soil, agents swarmed over the contents. To their dismay, they found no contraband—only furniture and lamps. The red-faced agents repackaged and reloaded the cargo on to the *Tulsidas*, but their investigation did not retract at the misfire.

Police in Montreal and New York continued to follow suspects who were in the Sixth Family, although the FBI complained in internal memos of unspecified problems in Canada that prevented the RCMP from installing electronic bugs on the telephones of its targets. The FBI were convinced that Sciascia, LoPresti—and the Rizzutos as well—had conspired to bring large quantities of drugs into the United States, according to testimony given in a New York court two decades later.

For 19 years, Kenneth McCabe had been a criminal investigator with the United States Attorney's Office in the Southern District of New York, specializing in cases brought against members of the Mafia. Before that, he was a detective with the New York City Police Department, assigned to an organized crime unit in Brooklyn. Testifying at a trial in New York in 2004, shortly before his death, McCabe was asked by the defence attorney for an accused Bonanno mobster about the Canadian connections to the early drug boom. McCabe said that in the early 1980s, Sciascia was a captain in the Bonanno Family.

"His crew was a Canadian crew," McCabe said.

"Would it be fair to say, sir, from your knowledge, [that] Sciascia, Rizzuto and LoPresti were the people who would bring the drugs into the country?" lawyer David Breitbart asked.

"They were definitely involved in importation of drugs, yes."

FBI agents realized that there were related drug networks all pumping heroin into New York, each following a similar pattern—a convergence of New York distributors linked to American Mafia families and Sicilian Mafia suppliers, much of it through Sixth Family middlemen in Canada and Venezuela.

The men they had been tracking, declared an internal FBI report on their investigations into Sciascia, were "the upper echelon of Italian drug traffickers in the world." By late 1983, agents and federal prosecutors started sorting out whom to indict and when, and which people could best be prosecuted in connection to which network. Evidence against the Canadian wing of the heroin pipeline was used to obtain search warrants and arrest warrants in the closing days of the Pizza Connection case. LoPresti and Sciascia were both named in the affidavits used to obtain warrants against others. In the end, however, the Sixth Family would remain untouched when the Pizza Connection indictments were unsealed. On April 9, 1984, their colleagues, including Sal Catalano, Gaetano Badalamenti, Baldo Amato and Giovanni Ligammari, were arrested. Also wanted, but not found, was Cesare Bonventre.

––––––––

Maybe it was Bonventre's ambition or the ease with which he was drawn into murder conspiracies that made people nervous. Or perhaps his arrogance made them angry. Bonventre's self-absorption certainly infuriated Massino. When Massino was on the lam, hiding in the Pocono Mountains of Pennsylvania from an indictment, Bonanno members wishing to curry his favor provided him with money and morale-boosting visits. The Zips, however, stayed away.

"He was just amazed that no one sent him nothing and Cesare didn't send him nothing," said Vitale. "He felt he was on the lam for the Bonanno Family because he killed the three captains," he said. "And the family should take care of him and no one [from the Zips] sent him nothing." Massino seemed to be having second thoughts about his unholy alliance with the Sicilian gangsters, probably realizing then, if not before, that they owed their allegiance to no one but themselves. He was determined not to make the same mistake that had cost Carmine Galante his life. Massino called in Louis "Louie Ha-Ha" Attanasio, who was the acting captain in Bonventre's crew, Duane "Goldie" Leisenheimer, the blonde-haired man who had helped deal with the three captains, and Vitale; then he sat down at the dining-room table at his hideout and mapped out an assassination plot worthy of the suspicious and smart Bonventre.

"What happens if he comes with Baldo?" Vitale asked Massino, knowing that Bonventre and Amato seemed inseparable.

"If he comes with Baldo, kill Baldo too," Massino said. Massino then warned: "He's a very sharp guy. You will have to be careful."

With Massino's dark genius guiding them, a plot suitable for ensnaring the crafty Zip was formulated. Bonventre was to be called to a purported meeting with Philip Rastelli, an invitation he was not at liberty to decline. Rastelli was even asked to actually sit in a diner and wait, just in case the plot went awry and Bonventre actually had to be taken to the meeting—they did not want Bonventre tipped off, so they could try again later. Vitale was to pick up Bonventre and Louie Ha-Ha to drive them to the meeting, Vitale said. Louie Ha-Ha would quickly hop into the back seat, leaving the front passenger seat for Bonventre. As the three drove along near Goldie's auto garage, if the coast was clear, Vitale would give Louie Ha-Ha a prearranged signal. He was to say, "It looks good to me." Louie would then pull out a gun he would be hiding in his boot and shoot Bonventre in the back of the head at point-blank range. Vitale would then quickly turn the car into Goldie's garage and Goldie would be standing out front, ready to pull down the large door as soon as the car pulled inside, giving them privacy to dispose of the body. Louie had earlier told Vitale it would be an easy kill. Whenever he shot into the back of someone's head, death was immediate, Louie allegedly told Vitale. "Whenever I shoot a person, one shot, goes right to sleep," he said, according to Vitale. It seemed a solid enough plan, certainly more carefully crafted than most gangland murders. Such attention to detail was a testament to Bonventre's reputation.

In April 1984, the team moved to execute both the plan and Bonventre. Vitale pulled up in a Dodge K car that he had rented. This, too, was to avoid making Bonventre suspicious—if he saw any of the tell-tale signs that the car was stolen, he would know something was wrong. Vitale collected the pair near Brooklyn's busy intersection of Metropolitan and Flushing avenues, and Louie hopped into the back seat, leaving the passenger seat open for Bonventre. It likely seemed a sign of respect to Bonventre, who accepted the superior seating without hesitation. He was, after all, a captain. As Vitale neared the turning for Goldie's garage, all was clear.

"It looks good to me," Vitale said. Louie Ha-Ha shot into the back of Bonventre's head, Vitale said. Bonventre did not go to sleep.

"That's when Cesare started fighting me for the steering wheel," said Vitale. "I was holding him back with my right arm, he was trying to put his foot on the gas pedal to crash the car and he was trying to

grab the steering wheel. I kept hold of him and that's when Louie
Ha-Ha shot him again," Vitale claimed. Bonventre was still alive and
the struggle for control of the car made it obvious that the plan was
not going smoothly.

"A K-car comes down at a pretty high rate of speed and somewhat
reckless—goes flying down the block," said Leisenheimer, who was
waiting outside of the garage for the car carrying Bonventre's body
to pull in. "When it passed me, it looked like there was a commotion
going on in it, but it passed real fast. In other words, it was just like
something didn't look right." Vitale managed to get the car into the
garage and slam on the brakes.

"When they pulled the body out of the car, the body was still
shaking up and down," said James "Big Louie" Tartaglione, who was
inside the garage waiting for them to arrive. "Louie Ha-Ha takes the
gun and shoots him a couple of more times," he said. Bonventre would
fight no more. As one gangster later said: "The guy didn't wanna die."
Bonventre left behind a wife just weeks away from giving birth to their
first child, a son. The gangsters in charge of the body disposal were
told to make sure that it was never found.

Afterwards, everyone was afraid of the reaction from the Zips,
Louie Ha-Ha most of all. When Bonventre disappeared, his friends
were eyeing Ha-Ha with the greatest of suspicion. Louie Ha-Ha, who
had been promised a promotion to captain in Bonventre's place for
his efforts, was impatient for the move up. He felt that being a captain
would offer him protection from vengeful Zips.

"He was supposed to make me a captain," Louie Ha-Ha complained to Vitale about two weeks after the murder. "Tell him to hurry
up and do it because, if he doesn't, the Zips are going to kill me."
Massino was true to his word and Louie Ha-Ha was promoted. But that
was not the end of the trouble that Bonventre caused for his killers.
If executing him was more difficult than expected, making his body
disappear was equally problematic.

Not long after the shooting, on April 16, 1984, officers with the
New Jersey State Police and agents with the FBI arrived with a search
warrant at T&J Trading Inc., a former macaroni factory that was being
used as a multi-story warehouse. When they entered a room on the
fourth floor, they were hit by a distinct smell.

"There was a pretty pungent odor of death," said Joseph Keely,
a now retired New Jersey State trooper who worked on the crime

scene that afternoon. "Bodies, after they start decomposing, leave a pretty pungent odor and that is what I was smelling." The officers were drawn to three 55-gallon drums with their lids tightly sealed. When opened, the mysterious disappearance of Bonventre, who was then wanted in the Pizza Connection case, was solved. His body had been severed just below the waist. The torso and head were in one drum, the legs were in a second. The third drum contained some personal papers and an attaché case. The body parts had been covered in glue and immersed in lime, a chemical that masks the smell of rotting flesh.

"It was pretty well along in the decomposition stage," said Keely. The combined smell of decomposition and chemicals forced the officers to don gas masks. A gold chain and $1,000 cash were found with the remains. An autopsy showed he had been shot in the head three to five times before being chopped up. Prophetically, when Bonventre had failed to show up in court for arraignment in the Pizza case days earlier, his lawyer said that Bonventre had gone missing and "wasn't likely to return shortly."

The Canadians managed to avoid a Pizza Connection indictment without facing such horror. They had simply been cut loose from the arrest list by the prosecutors at the last minute. It was another stunning bit of the luck that followed the Sixth Family.

Part of the reason for the reprieve was that Sciascia, LoPresti and others were also the focus of a parallel investigation in a neighboring New York judicial district. With the Pizza Connection case already threatening to topple over because of its complexity and size, prosecutors in the Southern District of New York were quite willing to sever some of the defendants who would likely be indicted in the future by prosecutors in New York's Eastern District. It spared the Sixth Family from being caught up in what became—after 17 months of trial—the longest criminal prosecution in U.S. history and one of the most publicized organized crime cases to this day. The case led to 18 convictions against most of the defendants.

Unperturbed by the massive Pizza indictments, the Sixth Family pressed on, after only a momentary reassessment. With Sciascia established in New York and LoPresti moving between Montreal and New York, the Canadian drug connection continued to move large loads of heroin to the American market. For the better part of a year after the Pizza arrests, LoPresti and Sciascia carried on their business.

With police tripping over themselves while watching the pair in New York and Montreal, with the added attention from Salvatore Ruggiero's plane crash and the compromising wires on his brother, Angelo, how long could that luck be expected to last?

CHAPTER 22

MANHATTAN, JANUARY 1985

Joe LoPresti was well dressed in a starched white dress shirt and a long tan cashmere coat when federal agents came for him at a Manhattan hotel, at 1:15 p.m. on Thursday, January 17, 1985. The agents had arrived armed with an arrest warrant, issued when an indictment in the Eastern District of New York was filed against him and Gerlando Sciascia for bringing massive quantities of heroin into the country. At the time of his arrest, LoPresti was on one of his many business trips to New York on behalf of the Sixth Family. Such business allowed him to travel light. His only luggage was a black briefcase and a garment bag.

Despite his size and strength, LoPresti knew better than to resist when approached, and the FBI agents politely informed him of his arrest. LoPresti, in turn, politely acceded to their demands, turning over his briefcase, in which agents found various business cards, photographs, brochures, a car-rental agreement, an Eastern Air Lines plane ticket and a toiletry kit. In his garment bag was a suit, another change of clothing and shaving items. He had $2,143 in a large roll of bills and a pocketful of change totaling $5.05. He wore a gold wedding band and an expensive Cartier watch. LoPresti went with the officers to a waiting car and, during the 15-minute ride to the FBI's office, expressed surprise at the charges.

"What makes you guys think I'm involved with drugs?" he asked.

"If anyone's to blame for the predicament you're in, it's yourself, Ruggiero and Sciascia," an agent said, hinting at the bugs in Angelo "Quack Quack" Ruggiero's house.

"What Angelo does is Angelo's business," LoPresti said. "I don't know his business."

"How long have you known Angelo Ruggiero?" the agent asked. LoPresti quickly changed his strategy.

"I don't know Angelo Ruggiero, I never met him," he said, perhaps too late. He did not deny knowing Sciascia, however, truthfully telling the agents that the two had been born in the same town in Italy and been close personal friends ever since. He did not, he told agents, have any idea where Sciascia might be. He had not seen him for more than a year, he said. The agents knew he was lying. They knew LoPresti and his wife had spent some of the summer visiting with Sciascia and his wife. They also knew of FBI and RCMP surveillance showing the two together on both sides of the U.S.–Canada border.

At the FBI office, while LoPresti was fingerprinted and photographed, he became deeply quiet; his mug shot shows him sullen, with his mouth in a frown and his eyes downcast.

———

Almost two years younger than Vito Rizzuto and 14 years younger than Sciascia, Giuseppe LoPresti was another of Agrigento's favorite sons. Over six-foot-two with a strong build, bushy dark hair and a prominent nose, "Joe" or "Big Joe," as he was often called, had known the two men all his life. LoPresti was essentially born into the Sixth Family, and then, as if to make certain, married into it as well.

LoPresti was born in Cattolica Eraclea, the son of Lorenzo LoPresti and his wife, Giuseppina Sottile, on January 24, 1948, he told FBI agents when he was arrested. (Some police charts, however, list his parents as Giuseppe LoPresti and Antonina Mongiovì; the Mongiovì clan is linked to both the old Agrigento Mafia of Giuseppe Settecasi and the Cuntrera clan.) In true Sixth Family style, he married a woman who was also from Cattolica Eraclea, Rosa Lumia, who was four years his junior. And, like Vito, LoPresti emigrated to Canada, becoming a naturalized citizen, living in Montreal and adding English and French to his language skills. The LoPrestis had two children, one who suffered from a form of bone cancer, he told the FBI. Among his family and friends were the highest-ranking members of the Canadian and Sicilian underworlds.

In Montreal, he owned or had interests in several legitimate businesses: among them, LoPresti Construction, of which he was the sole owner, and a board-game venture in which his involvement was so vague he could not even remember the company's address or phone number when asked. The business connections, however, were sufficient to justify his comfortable lifestyle. LoPresti had made his way into police files in the 1970s as a conspirator in the murder of Paolo

Violi, but was never arrested for it. After he was identified as one of the men posing with Vito Rizzuto and Giuseppe Bono in the 1980 wedding photos, the FBI started to take an interest in him as well. Although Sciascia was known in New York as "George from Canada," it was really LoPresti who made most of the cross-border trips for the Sixth Family's heroin pipeline. LoPresti was a well-traveled man. Police in Canada documented his routine appearance in Montreal at Vito's side, while at the same time American law enforcement frequently tracked him on visits to New York, where he mingled easily with Bonanno, Gambino and DeCavalcante Family mobsters.

"LoPresti is a narcotics trafficker and serves as liaison ... between the Montreal Sicilian Faction and the Sicilian Faction in the Bonanno LCN [Mafia] Family," an FBI report from 1985 says. "LoPresti, despite his frequent role as diplomat, clearly owes his allegiance to Rizzuto and the Montreal Sicilian Faction," the report adds. LoPresti managed to keep a low profile despite the growing police interest and, in fact, had no criminal convictions—which, of course, made him the perfect choice for such frequent cross-border travel.

———

The Eastern District indictments were aimed at both the Montreal and New York ends of the heroin scheme and revolved, in large measure, around the evidence gathered from the bugs in Ruggiero's Long Island home. Along with Sciascia and LoPresti, Gambino soldiers Ruggiero, Eddie Lino, John Carneglia and Gene Gotti were also indicted. While the FBI managed to catch LoPresti during a trip to New York, Sciascia, ironically, was back in Montreal, ostensibly involved in his Canadian construction business, when the New York indictment came down. The U.S. government applied for Sciascia's extradition from Canada and, in November 1986, he was arrested by the RCMP and jailed.

"He was clean," said Yvon Thibault, who made the arrest as a sergeant with the RCMP's Montreal office. "No weapons, no drugs, no fuss. He was a gentleman." Sciascia then began a two-year fight in Canadian courts to prevent his return to the U.S.

Sciascia was concerned about facing trial with someone with the notoriety of the Gotti name, and someone with the mouth of Ruggiero. By October 1988, he saw a more favorable climate in New York: his codefendants had all received bail and the case had been broken into separate trials, effectively distancing him from both the tainted Gotti name and his talkative co-accused. On October 28, 1988, in a letter to Judge Joseph M. McLaughlin of the Eastern District of New York, Benjamin Brafman introduced himself as Sciascia's lawyer and informed the court that his client was returning to face trial. Describing Sciascia as a 55-year-old father of two with a wife of 25 years and no criminal record, Brafman started his campaign to win Sciascia bail.

"At the time of his arrest, Gerlando Sciascia learned that he was one of many defendants named in the same indictment," Brafman wrote to the judge. "Sciascia was advised [by both his Canadian and New York counsel] that it was not in his best interest, as a peripheral defendant, to proceed to trial in the same proceeding with all the other defendants, because of the prejudicial spillover that was certain to result." Sciascia had spent two years in Canada—in detention—rather than risk an appearance before a jury with such bad elements.

The U.S. Attorney's Office did not let the lawyer's spin pass without comment. In his reply letter, prosecutor Andrew Maloney lampooned the idea that Sciascia had voluntarily surrendered. "After his arrest in November 1986, Gerlando Sciascia, in fact, sought to prevent his return to the United States by opposing our application for his extra-dition," Maloney wrote. "For almost two years, Gerlando Sciascia had been unsuccessfully seeking to overturn the order of extradition."

After returning to the United States to await his trial, Sciascia was allowed to return to Canada briefly—for just 28 hours—on the occasion of the January 14, 1989, marriage of his son, Joseph, to Laura Bruno, at the Mary Queen of the World Cathedral in Montreal. While in Canada, he was to stay with his nephew, Luciano Renda. A year later, Sciascia finally secured a little more freedom, although his bail restrictions did not allow him to travel outside Manhattan, the Bronx or Brooklyn nor anywhere near an airport. At his bail hearing, when the issue of organized crime involvement came up, Sciascia looked up at the judge and appeared confused.

"Who's in organized crime?" he asked.

Notwithstanding, he was released on a $2.5-million bond, signed as a surety by Sciascia's wife, son and Giuseppe Arcuri, a relative of both Domenico Arcuri in Montreal and Giacinto Arcuri in Toronto.

Putting Sciascia, LoPresti, Ruggiero and Eddie Lino on trial was, as was becoming the custom for large mob cases, fraught with difficulty. After a mistrial, prosecutors forged ahead a second time, this time without Ruggiero as a defendant. The talkative mobster had died of cancer.

At the trial against the remaining three men, Assistant United States Attorney Gordon Mehler highlighted the clannishness of the Sciascia–LoPresti axis. If the Bonanno hierarchy did not realize where Sciascia's loyalties lay, then Mehler certainly did when he declared: "George and Joe, Joe and George; they are one and the same." Brafman, Sciascia's lawyer, appeared to be playing to the jury's preconceptions about "the Mafia" and his client's Italian ancestry when he used objectionable terms to counter Mehler's contention. "In Agrigento, when they were little greaseballs, they knew each other, too," Brafman said at one point.

Waiting until their cases could be severed from that of Gotti and Carneglia proved its value. Gotti and Carneglia were sentenced to 50 years in prison. On February 9, 1990, however, after a month-long trial, Sciascia, LoPresti and Eddie Lino were acquitted.

"Thank you very much," LoPresti called out to the jury, after the foreman delivered the verdict. "God bless you." At least one member of the jury should have been thanking LoPresti, instead.

Earlier, a captain in the Gambino Family told Salvatore "Sammy Bull" Gravano that the daughter of a customer at his Brooklyn fish store was a member of the jury. The captain said the woman "would be talked to and that for an appropriate gift of $10,000 she would do the right thing," Gravano claimed. Gravano checked first with John Gotti and then turned over the money.

MONTREAL, SPRING 1992

Both Sciascia and LoPresti knew they had dodged a bullet with their acquittals and that their operations would forever be under close scrutiny by American law enforcement. For LoPresti, that did not appear to be an untenable problem. He was Canadian, and he returned to Montreal where he immersed himself in the daily activities of the Sixth Family. It was not long before Canadian police would again hear LoPresti on wiretaps, this time in Canada. On March 21, 1991, at 12:58 a.m., as part of Operation Bedside, one of several RCMP drug probes targeting Vito Rizzuto, officers intercepted a telephone conversation between Vito and LoPresti. LoPresti was back in business.

Something, however, turned sour.

On the last day of April 1992, Montreal police were called to a set of railway tracks that ran through an industrial plot on Henri-Bourassa

Boulevard East. There, wrapped in a large gray dropcloth, the kind used by painters, and tied up with the type of cord commonly used at construction sites, was the body of a tall, dark-haired man carrying a large roll of cash but no identification. He had been shot in the head at close range with a small-caliber bullet. The next day, the body was identified as that of Joe LoPresti. Police later found his red Porsche abandoned at a nearby restaurant. He was 44.

"Joe was involved a lot more in the background and was very discreet in Montreal. Unfortunately, he was not discreet enough in New York," a longtime Montreal drug investigator said. The murder investigation was not helped by LoPresti's grieving family. A lawyer for the family wrote a letter to the Montreal police asking detectives investigating the murder to stop contacting them.

"His point was clear: Lay off. He said for us to stop harassing the family, cease and desist. It effectively shut down the investigation," said André Bouchard, who retired in 2004 as head of the Montreal police's Major Crime Unit. It went unsolved and is periodically reviewed by detectives. "We took a look at it again in the last year I was there," Bouchard said. "Still nothing." Perhaps some members of the family knew more about the murder than the police. Although the murder was never solved in Montreal, LoPresti's killer had revealed himself in New York.

LoPresti was well known to most of the New York gangsters. He spent enough time in the city for the Bonanno captains to know him by name and by sight. LoPresti was officially recognized by the Bonanno administration as Sciascia's acting *capo-regime*, or acting captain, meaning he was second-in-command to Sciascia in New York and was a suitable stand-in for Sciascia, should Sciascia not be available. The New Yorkers had been looking at things only from their perspective and, by their standards, LoPresti was the number-two man in Montreal, behind only Sciascia. They failed to realize that both men were underlings of the Rizzutos and had been sent off to New York to mind the Sixth Family's interests in their primary marketplace. As such, the Sixth Family could deal with both of them as it wished, even if it caused some ruffled feathers in New York.

"George from Canada came to see me and said that Big Joe from Canada was out of control; he was doing drugs, he was snorting drugs, he was using drugs, he was selling drugs," Vitale said. The implication was clear to Vitale. Sciascia was saying that LoPresti was dangerous and had to be killed.

"If that is what you want to do, do it. You have to protect the family," Vitale told him, authorizing Sciascia to "take care of business," meaning the kill would be a sanctioned hit. "But he led me to believe that business was already taken care of," Vitale said. "George, for the sake of this conversation, he was [being] cute. ... He led me to believe he might have already done it." Sciascia previously had the same conversation with Anthony Spero, the Bonanno *consigliere*. When Vitale and Spero compared notes, they knew that they would not be seeing "Big Joe" ever again.

"Me and Spero agreed, when George came to us, the gentleman was already dead," Vitale said. Sciascia, it seems, was trying retroactively to seek official permission to eliminate Joe LoPresti. If Sciascia had followed the American Mafia's rules, he would have needed the permission of the Bonanno administration before LoPresti was killed.

"Big Joe was a made member of the Bonanno Family," Vitale said.

This was another example of how the Sixth Family flouted the accepted rules of the Bonanno Family and operated independently as its own crime group. Vitale, seeming to realize the futility of taking issue with the decree of the Montreal organization in dealing with its own man, did not pursue the issue further. Why Sciascia and, presumably, the Sixth Family administration, would have wanted LoPresti dead is a mystery. One reason he certainly was not killed for, however, was one of the excuses Sciascia had complained of to Vitale: that he had been selling drugs. That was not a problem.

The unexpected, unapproved and unexplained murder of LoPresti, apparently by or with the complicity of Sciascia, was not the only sign of a deteriorating relationship between Montreal and New York. At the highest levels, there were overt signs that the Bonanno administration had already noticed that the Sixth Family was starting to pull away from its expected orbit around New York. That did not mean, however, the Montreal organization was withdrawing from international affairs.

CHAPTER 23

CARACAS, VENEZUELA, 1982

The sparkling reception for Nick Rizzuto and his colleagues in Venezuela first started to tarnish in the spring of 1982—although the mobsters did not yet know it. Venezuelan security intelligence officers had been probing foreign influence in the capital city and were concerned over the volume of overseas telephone calls being made for no apparent or legitimate reason. Tracking the calls led agents to Nick Rizzuto and his expatriate Mafia allies, the Caruanas and the Cuntreras. The country's security forces at first believed the calls were related to espionage activities by a foreign government and, if some in the government were not overly concerned with mobsters investing drug profits in their country, a potential breach of security in this easily destabilized part of the world was not taken as lightly.

The Venezuelan authorities turned to the CIA for help in tracking down this suspected foreign menace but the U.S. agency, realizing pretty quickly that it was drug trafficking, not insurgency, being plotted, turned the case over to the Drug Enforcement Administration. Tom Tripodi, a DEA specialist in international drug trafficking, was sent from Washington to look into the matter. Tripodi met with Venezuelan officials at a coffee shop near the American Embassy in Caracas and from there was taken to the investigators' secret apartment where the telephone calls were being monitored and recorded.

Many of the voices were speaking the Sicilian dialect particular to Agrigento. On one, the caller spoke of "fish" being shipped from Venezuela to Sicily. Each fish seemed to weigh a kilogram and they were putting a thousand of these beasts into a single shipment. Tripodi knew immediately that it was really a 1,000-kilogram shipment of cocaine. The more conversations he listened to, the larger the scale of the operation was uncovered—cocaine was going to Italy and heroin was being returned in huge amounts. Although cracking that part of the traffickers' code was simple, the DEA could not penetrate the system they used for passing on the date and place that the shipments were scheduled to arrive.

While the Venezuelan authorities lost some of their enthusiasm for the case once the non-political nature of the conspiracy was deduced, the DEA's interest remained strong. Their investigation started to focus on Giuseppe Bono, who seemed to be at the root of the activities on the European side of the transactions. A prosecution in Italy would also be far easier than in South America, especially when it was learned that Italian police were monitoring some of the same calls from their end. They traced calls from Bono, through the phone lines of Citam, a powdered milk company used for laundering drug profits, to many members of the Sixth Family. Throughout the summer of 1982, the Italian police also monitored Bono's constant contact with Nick Rizzuto. That the investigation so quickly became a European affair, however, was of great relief to the Sixth Family. Most of their activity at that time was divided between North and South America.

On February 4, 1984, Vito Rizzuto and Sabatino "Sammy" Nicolucci left Montreal for Caracas. Nicolucci, a thin, almost nerdy-looking man who might have been able to pass for Bill Gates's impoverished brother, had a minor drug possession conviction in 1973 and a more serious conviction for possessing $2 million of counterfeit money from 1978. His association with the Sixth Family would eventually lead to more prison time and even more frightful ventures. In 1984, however, his Sixth Family connection meant a winter break from the cold of Quebec. Nicolucci also visited the island of Aruba, a Caruana–Cuntrera stronghold in the Caribbean Sea, off the northern coast of Venezuela. RCMP officers following him later asked the management of the Holiday Inn where he had stayed to let them review the phone records for Nicolucci's room, but no registration could be found for him. Officers discovered that his room had been reserved and paid for by Pasquale Cuntrera, one of the senior members of the Caruana–Cuntrera clan.

A year after his visit to Venezuela and Aruba, Nicolucci was charged in Canada with conspiracy to import drugs and laundering the proceeds of crime. Vito, again, was side-stepped when it came to charges. Nicolucci was sentenced to 14 years in prison but was released on full parole in January 1991. By August 1994 he had stopped making personal appearances at the office of his parole supervisor, as he was required to do. He telephoned in to the office instead, claiming he did not have the money to travel by public transit. Suspicious officials revoked his parole and ordered him back into custody. When he failed to appear, police officers went looking for him. Their suspicion proved to be well founded—he was not even in the country. Nicolucci eventually turned up in Colombia in May 1996.

"According to the police version, you had purchased 280 kilos of cocaine on behalf of Vito Rizzuto. However, you refused to pay for the amount owing for the drug, $1.7 million, to the Colombian cartel, claiming that the drugs were of poor quality," states Canada's National Parole Board records. In August 1994, Nicolucci was kidnapped by Colombian drug traffickers from a Montreal strip club. The Colombians demanded their money and first hustled Nicolucci to the Laurentians, a mountainous area north of Montreal that is famous for its skiing, then smuggled him across the border to Florida, and finally on to Colombia.

In the traffickers' jungle hide-away Nicolucci, who was always a good talker, negotiated a deal with his cartel kidnappers; his life would be spared and he would work off his debt as an indentured servant for the cartel in Colombia. His conditions could not have been too onerous, however, for when he was found by Colombian officials he fought extradition to Canada, a battle he eventually lost. Back in Canada, he faced 437 counts for drug trafficking and money laundering; here he also lost, drawing a second 14-year sentence in 1997.

Nicolucci's Colombian adventures were to come years later; at the time of his 1984 visits to Caracas and Aruba, he was a drug trafficker still in good standing. The RCMP alerted the Venezuelan authorities to the Montrealers' activities, although they undoubtedly already knew of Nick and his business from their probe with the DEA of the shipments of "fish." It is also believed that the intelligence dossiers they gathered were used by high-ranking police officials not to prosecute Nick but to ramp up the bribes they demanded to continue turning a blind eye.

In Venezuela, the expatriate Mafia were as comfortable as they had ever been. Nick and the Cuntrera brothers—Pasquale, Paolo and Gaspare—had been joined by Alfonso Caruana, a former Montrealer from Agrigento, and together they lived in style.

"He had a huge villa looked after by private people, by private police who made sure that he was never disturbed," said Oreste Pagano, a former drug-trafficking colleague of Alfonso's. The Caruana–Cuntrera family, and presumably Nick as well, felt at ease there.

"He felt completely safe and well protected by the big, important friends that he had there in Venezuela. They were friends with the former president," Pagano said of a relationship between Pasquale Cuntrera and Carlos Andrés Pérez. His feeling of security seemed well founded. The Venezuelan government had already rebuffed Italian extradition requests for Pasquale Cuntrera several times.

"They felt as strong as steel," Pagano said.

Protected by officials, the Cuntrera brothers, along with Nick and the Caruanas—the elite of the Sicilian expatriate underworld—organized a drug network that flowed multi-ton shipments of heroin, cocaine and hashish into North America and Europe.

"The fact is that when something happens in Venezuela, there is a lot of commotion at that moment, but afterwards, with money, it is corrected," Pagano said. His words, although not directly referring to Nick, mirrored what apparently occurred when the Rizzuto patriarch finally ran afoul of Venezuelan authorities.

CARACAS, FEBRUARY 1988

As comfortable as Venezuela had been for the Sixth Family, no haven lasts forever. The first cracks in their southern sanctuary opened suddenly and unexpectedly. On February 12, 1988, officers with the Cuerpo Técnico de Policía Judicial, the national police agency responsible for organized crime investigations, arrived at Nick's home. There, officers found a quantity of cocaine. (Official reports say the amount ranged from 700 grams to 1.5 kilos—regardless, it was a relatively small stash for someone in Nick's position and likely constituted only a sample provided to him for assessment before larger loads were arranged.)

Wearing a collared shirt with narrow stripes, unbuttoned at the neck, Nick was arrested and taken to Policía Judicial headquarters in Caracas. He was not happy, and he glowered at officers who processed him.

Nick was not alone in being implicated in a cocaine operation. Arrested with him were four other men, two Montrealers and two Venezuelans: Gennaro Scaletta, suspected by the FBI of being behind several illegal financial schemes in Caracas before he moved to Montreal in 1987 to handle some of Alfonso Caruana's financial affairs; Frederico Del Peschio, identified in RCMP reports as an old associate of the Cotroni organization; Camilio Porchio, another Montreal man; and Nicola Marturano, a resident of Caracas.

The arrests came as a deep shock to the friends and family of the men in Montreal, and in a show of love and concern, some of the wives and daughters immediately flew to Caracas to see what they could do to help. Among their stops in Venezuela, made on their husbands' behalf, the women paid a visit to the Canadian Embassy in Caracas.

The small entourage turned heads as it made its way through the embassy's security and reception area. Dressed in business attire, weighed down by big jewelry and with their hair in perfect order, they had obviously dressed to impress for their meeting with Canada's diplomatic representatives in Venezuela. Although they remained unfailingly polite to all, they were nonetheless firm and assertive. Platitudes and quick assurances would not do. They wanted answers and action.

"Their wives came in the following day, maybe two days later," said a former Canadian diplomat who was serving in Venezuela at the time. They wanted to know what had happened to the men, why they had been arrested and what was to become of them.

"I threw up my hands and said, 'Look, talk to the Solicitor General's department; they'll know far more than we do,'" the diplomat said. "They said, 'Well, what do we do?' I said, 'What you need is a lawyer. Here is a list of the six we recommend, go out and talk to them and see what they can do.'" The women took the list, thanked the staff for their attention to the matter and then left. "None uttered a harsh word or said anything nasty to us, that we were not doing our job. They were all very considerate," the diplomat said.

Representatives of the accused men came to the embassy about two weeks later. "Right, we've talked to a lawyer and he said the only way to get these guys out is to bribe the judge," one of the visitors said, according to the diplomat. "We've brought the money and here it is." The visitors then heaved a suitcase on to a table in an office of the diplomatic mission and snapped it open. Inside was row upon row of American currency.

"I didn't count it," the diplomat said. "I was in shock." The sight of the money brought stunned silence in the office.

"I said, 'Well, look, we're not going to touch that. It's not our business. Don't you give it to the judge, either. You give it to the lawyer; it's your lawyer and if that's his fee, then how he spends it—whether he sends his kids to private school in the United States, takes his wife on a holiday to France or he puts it in an account of somebody else somewhere—that's his business.'

"Don't you touch it, or you'll find yourself in the can as well," the diplomat advised. The entourage then closed up the suitcase, thanked the officials for their assistance, hauled the case off the table and left. Canada's diplomatic officials did not have much more contact with the family, but diplomats maintained a level of contact with Nick.

Perhaps the suitcase almost worked. The prisoners had a near-glimpse of freedom when they were acquitted of the drug charges. Their hopes of release were dashed, however, when they were held in jail under a Venezuelan Minister's Order, an RCMP report says.

Nick Rizzuto and his co-accused were housed in a special administrative prison near Caracas. It was, in fact, just a secure, separate wing of a larger facility where the general population prisoners were held in often overcrowded conditions. While such cells can be a miserable, tense and violent place—"a gringo in there might last a week and then they'd eat him," said a man who has toured several of the facilities—the arrangements for Nick were far more comfortable.

Past the locked and guarded entrance was a long corridor that led to another hallway leading to four separate rooms where Nick and his co-accused were kept. Each man had his own bedroom, with a private bathroom, and the prisoners shared a common area with cooking facilities, a sitting room with a small television and a bookcase stocked with a modest selection of reading material. Apart from the fact that the doors could not be locked from the inside, it was more like a motel than a prison, and the men had regular contact with visitors and private time with their wives, family and friends on weekends. Visitors seemed to come around frequently, in fact.

Some arrived unannounced and, while not invited by Nick, were nonetheless politely received. Embassy officials periodically dropped in on the men, as is the practice of the diplomatic corps, who regularly visit jailed nationals to ensure that they are in good health and not being mistreated, and to see if they are in need of any consular services.

The officials would bring Nick recent copies of *Maclean's* magazine, a Canadian newsweekly, and a couple of pairs of clean underwear to replace undergarments that wore out quickly from repeated hand washing. However, while Nick and his colleagues were always polite, the visits were a little awkward. The men were clearly uninterested in confiding anything to a government official.

"They greeted us and we said who we were and they all said 'Hi.' And we'd say, 'We brought you a pile of magazines from Montreal.' And they said, 'Thank you very much, that's very nice,'" said a diplomat who made several of the visits.

"How are you? How are you being treated?" the men were asked.

"Oh, fine," they answered.

"Everything is okay?"

"Yes."

"We're doing what we can to push this process along," the diplomats assured the prisoners.

"Oh, well, you're wasting your time. We have no confidence in the system here," came the reply. There were a few minutes of forced small talk before the diplomats felt they had done their duty.

"We'll come and visit you every few months and bring you some magazines," one diplomat said, getting up to leave.

"Thank you very much," the men answered.

"Is there anything more we can do for you?"

"No, we're fine here. As you can see we're well accommodated. Our lawyers are looking into this and our wives come and visit us."

As the diplomats were leaving, Nick turned to one of them and said firmly: "Don't worry about us. We're fine."

This was a far cry from the typical Canadian citizen imprisoned abroad, who is usually anxious for diplomatic access and consular support. There are usually plaintive calls for government intervention and pleas to get them back to Canada. Often, the families of the imprisoned parties are a thorn in the side of the government, constantly calling, lobbying and pressing for action.

"Usually with the imprisoned consular cases, they are asking for a lot of things," a former diplomat said. "Whereas these people didn't phone the Canadian government in Canada, ever. They didn't phone us, ever. We had to actually go out and look for them—look for them in the sense that we went out and asked if we could call on them. They never asked for us to come in. They never asked us for anything."

———

It was a time of uncertainty for the Sixth Family in Venezuela. While Nick's arrest was a hostile gesture, the remaining expatriate Mafia remained intact and untouched. In fact, a 1991 U.S. Department of

Justice report states that Vito Rizzuto was residing in Caracas that year as well. He must have been earning frequent-flier points, for throughout the year, the RCMP and Montreal police photographed him meeting with an array of criminals in Montreal. They watched him drive around town in a brown 1987 Porsche 928 S4 two-door sports coupe and monitored him on innumerable local calls with associates in Canada. Still, it was likely he was a frequent visitor to Caracas, meeting with his father, meeting with lawyers who might be able to help with the situation, and conducting the family's business in his father's place.

While Nick was imprisoned, police in Canada launched a large probe of Vito and several of his associates, code-named Project Jaggy, to investigate massive cocaine importation from Venezuela and cannabis from the African coast, a Montreal police report says.

Things were changing in Venezuela, however. There was a reluctant realization by some officials that their country could not be so close to Colombia and remain immune from the cocaine trade. For those in positions of power to whom the accommodation with the expatriate Mafia was merely out of naiveté—as opposed to those for whom it was a profitable arrangement—the realization was a depressing one. The arrest of Nick Rizzuto and his colleagues was a start in cleaning up, the government claimed, although there are certainly many who suggest it was merely a means to extract payments that exceeded what the Sixth Family was prepared to pay. Nonetheless, the arrest of Nick was proof, to those in Venezuela who needed it, that there were extensive links within their borders between the Mafia and the Colombian cartels. Far more shocking cases would soon emerge.

At the 1990 wedding of Pasquale Cuntrera, an invited guest brought with him a friend from the United States who, in turn, brought a couple of additional guests. They were all welcomed with open arms—primarily because they each brought an envelope stuffed with $5,000 cash as a wedding gift. Unfortunately for Cuntrera, two of the interlopers were DEA agents who engaged the host in a discussion of heroin transactions. With this proof in hand, the American government started asking the Venezuelan authorities to act against the Cuntrera brothers. In the backlash against the Mafia after the 1992 murder of Italian magistrate Giovanni Falcone—who had targeted, along with Carla Del Ponte, the Sixth Family's financial undertakings in Europe—the pressure became unbearable. Faced with the possibility of an armed DEA snatch team air-dropping in to grab the brothers in a midnight raid, Venezuelan authorities arrested them and deported them to Italy.

For Alfonso Caruana, who had become the leader of the Caruana–Cuntreras, the writing was on the wall: the Venezuelans had been glad to take his money and exploit his influence, but faced with worldwide pressure, his days were numbered. With the Rizzutos seemingly untouchable in Canada, unscathed by the American investigations into the Pizza Connection and still robust after many other law enforcement initiatives, Alfonso headed back to Montreal.

It was a place where, he said, "I feel safe."

MONTREAL, SPRING 1993

At a swanky downtown restaurant, one of many fine eateries in Montreal, a city that loves its food, Dominico Tozzi was eating, drinking and in a friendly mood during a lengthy business lunch with a man he knew as an underworld money launderer. Tozzi, a Montreal businessman and associate of the Sixth Family, was known as an amiable, if not talkative, fellow to begin with. Perhaps it was the wine, or maybe he felt the need to boast about his close ties to important people, but for whatever reason, at the March 29, 1993, lunch, Tozzi confided to his guest that Nick Rizzuto had been freed from a Venezuelan jail after Tozzi personally had delivered $800,000 to somebody in Venezuela.

The news would have been surprising to almost anyone, but as the lunch companion was, in reality, an undercover RCMP officer, the information was doubly appreciated. Although a close relative of Tozzi's has denied the incident, which is revealed in a sworn affidavit used by officers to obtain wiretaps in 1994, and a lawyer for Vito said a bribe was not paid to free Nick, police took the information seriously. The news was a shock to officers, who did not know that Nick had been freed, although they were pretty certain he had not returned to Montreal.

On May 19, 1993, Canadian passport No. PZ-362199 was issued through the Canadian Embassy in Caracas to Libertina Rizzuto, Nick's wife. With their travel papers in order, she then escorted her husband home to Montreal four days later, where Nick was greeted at the airport by Vito and more than two dozen friends and relatives. The joy of that reunion, however, did not erase the bitterness over the arrest.

A few years after Nick's return to Montreal, Vito still considered some business in Venezuela unfinished. The treatment of his father in Venezuela weighed heavily on Vito, and it came up when he was discussing business in that country with Oreste Pagano.

"He wanted me to do him a favor," Pagano said. "He was very upset over a lawyer in Venezuela that had stolen $500,000 from him for when his father was arrested in Venezuela. Five-hundred-thousand *American* dollars," Pagano emphasized, noting the lower exchange rate of the Canadian dollar at the time. "And he asked me if I could have this lawyer killed," Pagano alleged to police in a debriefing session, although the statement has never been tested in court and remains unproved.

"I said yes to him. But I never did anything."

––––––––

Nick had been imprisoned for more than four years. Despite the loss of his leadership, the Sixth Family had progressed well while he was away, expanding the franchise. The organization had seen growth in its customer base, its product line and its list of suppliers. And, like most businesses, it had experienced a few setbacks and tense moments.

Chapter 24

IRELAND'S EYE, ATLANTIC COAST, OCTOBER 1987

Just off the rugged northeast coast of Newfoundland, Canada's most easterly province, the rocky hills that form the tiny island of Ireland's Eye rise steeply from the seawater of Trinity Bay. From the north, the approach to the tiny island is one of imposing red-and-gray-streaked rock, poking through a green canopy of stubby coniferous trees, that forms a threatening barrier from the sea. To the south, however, lies a narrow sound that cuts its way inland, twisting so deeply into the center that it very nearly cuts the island in two before coiling around to form a tranquil, protected lagoon. The round, dark pool may well have given the island its odd name, but this natural harbor certainly did offer settlers protection from the hard wind and choppy water. Which is why, despite its remoteness, Ireland's Eye was first occupied in the 1600s by fishermen who drew from the teeming cod stocks and hid their meager earnings from Peter Easton, the marauding "pirate admiral" who led an armada of privateers in shaking down these maritime communities, one of North America's first acts of organized crime.

Covering just two square miles, Ireland's Eye reached a population peak of 157 people in 1911 before decline set in. Under a government relocation plan, people living in dozens of tiny outport fishing communities were moved to larger, better-serviced towns and, by the 1960s, Ireland's Eye was abandoned, becoming a picturesque ghost town of well-spaced clapboard houses, some with tiny wharves jutting out into the harbor, a post office, schoolhouse and the once-impressive St. George's Anglican Church, with its tall spire and stained-glass windows. The buildings are now a rubble of weathered planks and stone foundations that are slowly being reclaimed by nature.

It was this unlikely spot, in the fall of 1987, that the Sixth Family chose as its base for another revenue stream, part of a purposeful diversification plan to expand its portfolio. Man cannot live by heroin alone, and, like good businessmen and astute investors, the Rizzuto organization moved diligently to ensure relevancy, profitability and flexibility in an uncertain market. The expansion of the drug enterprises came through a startling array of contacts, both international and local, forming a multicultural stew of global underworld confederacies that would frustrate and bewilder police investigators trying to sort through, and, more important, penetrate them.

Some partnerships were more successful than others.

For the Ireland's Eye enterprise, the Sixth Family turned to Raynald Desjardins, who had his first drug conviction in 1971, and later married the sister of Joe DiMaulo, a veteran Montreal mobster, bringing him into the Sixth Family orbit. Desjardins was one of several men over the years to be described by police and the media as the "right-hand man" of Vito Rizzuto, and his purchase of a home at the far southwestern corner of the Rizzuto clan's exclusive neighborhood was further evidence of Desjardins's standing. His interest in this stretch of Newfoundland coast seems to have been piqued, in part, by Gerald Hiscock, a corrupt Newfoundlander with a criminal past. Between them, police suspected, they worked to arrange the tail end of a series of transactions that started far from Ireland's Eye, in the Middle East.

———

For years, Montreal's mafiosi had been buying hashish by the ton from Christian Phalangist militia factions in Lebanon. The city's underworld connections to Lebanon were both broad and deep. As far back as 1975, police wiretaps on Frank Cotroni's telephone revealed that he made calls directly to the home of Suleiman Franjieh, the then-president of Lebanon. Cotroni was also meeting personally with high-ranking Lebanese government officials. When the Rizzuto organization seized Montreal, they inherited the rich connections in Lebanon as well.

Mostly their business involved straight cash transactions, proceeds from which the militia fighters funded their war efforts in strife-torn Lebanon. Sometimes the drugs were swapped for explosives, high-powered guns and clips of ammunition. Such firepower is rare in Canada, and authorities had long suspected that the Montreal gangsters were using their links to New York gangsters to secure the weaponry in the United States and smuggle it into Canada before forwarding it to the Middle East. This theory was proven in 1980, when the FBI managed to track a large shipment of weapons, including U.S. military assault rifles and matching ammunition, that had been stolen from a Boston armory; it made its way first to Montreal, and then to Lebanon in exchange for hashish.

Some time later, police informants recounted how Montreal mobsters had made a visit to Lebanon to meet with their business partners, swapping samples of their respective wares. During a meeting, automatic weapons were test-fired at the unfortunate residents of a Palestinian refugee camp. As horrific a scene as that was, Canadian investigators also worried about possible ramifications closer to home—for it showed that the Montreal mob had easy access to high-powered weaponry. They worried what might happen if it was ever needed. The Lebanon–Montreal connection flourished and, by the late 1980s, the RCMP estimated that 90 percent of the hashish smuggled into Canada came from Lebanon. Never ones to stand still for long on such matters, though, Montreal gangsters found other sources of the drug to supplement even this rich supply. They were quick to expand supply lines, looking to add to the routes from Lebanon, rather than replace them.

With backing from the Rizzuto organization, Allan "The Weasel" Ross, the boss of the West End Gang, a tight group of Irish gangsters, forged a new supply line for hashish through his connections with the Irish Republican Army and the Irish mob of Boston. The IRA talked loudly about its political agenda against the British, but tried to keep hush-hush its role in international drug smuggling as a means of financing its struggle. Montreal gangsters also forged ties in Pakistan when Adrien Dubois, one of the notorious Dubois brothers, who formed a feared francophone gang in Montreal, introduced a Sixth Family associate to his impressive source for hashish—a corrupt government official in Pakistan who had a ministerial position and a thirst for foreign currency. With financial backing from the Sixth Family, and its assurance that no amount of hashish would be too large, the Montreal organization was able to command the minister's exclusive attention. The official agreed to sell them the entire year's production of hashish from the portion of the Pakistani border region under his watch.

Then, in the early 1990s, yet another considerable source of hashish was secured in Libya. A scheme to import 50 tons of hashish from Libya was intercepted by police, however, and during an extensive investigation, code-named Project Bedside, they traced telephone conversations between Desjardins, Vito Rizzuto, Joe LoPresti and Samir Rabbat, among others, according to Montreal police. Rabbat was once decribed as one of the world's top-10 drug traffickers and was in the process of building a large house in Montreal, just blocks from Vito's home, when he was arrested.

All of that hashish made for a hugely profitable supply, with bulk loads being arranged—sometimes simultaneously—in the Middle East, Asia and Africa, all of it making its way to the Canadian coast and then into Montreal for redistribution across the country and into the United States. High-quality hashish was a cash cow, particularly in Canada, where the drug remains strangely popular. The hashish added another revenue source to Sixth Family holdings, as it continued to diversify from its near-dominant position in the heroin trade.

———

In the fall of 1987, gangsters arranging their latest hashish load from Lebanon's Bekaa Valley thought the toughest part of their operation was over—its purchase in unstable Lebanon, the loading of the drugs onto a freighter and the paying off of harbor masters, Lebanese officials and senior Christian Phalangist militia leaders to allow the vessel to slip, unfettered, out to sea. When word arrived in Montreal that the shipment was en route, the receiving end of the arrangements swung into action. This was supposed to be the easy part.

With past shipments, the Canadian end had gone like clockwork, apart from one disappointment. For at least a decade, large loads of hashish had been smuggled successfully into Canada on foreign freighters traveling from Lebanon and arriving on Canada's East Coast. One such ship certainly passed through the Port of Halifax in 1980. Police learned of a larger shipment—12 tons—that had been secretly offloaded in 1985 from a freighter anchored off the desolate coastline of Nova Scotia and placed onto small boats. When a 1986 shipment into Halifax was discovered and seized by police, the gangsters went looking for more remote drop-offs.

Ireland's Eye seemed perfect. With its hidden harbor and no prying eyes for miles—and with a rudimentary infrastructure, including pathways and wharves—it was a smuggler's paradise. What's more, once a shipment was shifted over to the Newfoundland mainland, the area was not so remote as to make transport by land unreasonable. There was an access road to the Trans-Canada Highway.

Despite all the planning, the operation ran into difficulty.

On October 17, 1987, RCMP officers boarded the *Charlotte Louise*, a 100-foot fishing trawler, while it was docked at Blanc-Sablon, a small port and Quebec's easternmost community, just across from the northern tip of Newfoundland. Despite initial confidence in their tip, a thorough search of the filthy trawler did not uncover any drugs. Even drug-sniffing dogs brought in for a second search found nothing untoward. Officers were feeling a little uncomfortable when two investigators in the bowels of the ship suddenly noticed that a number of bolts were not encrusted with rust like most everything else on board. The officers asked one of the ship's mechanics to come down and remove the fresh bolts, a request he nervously refused, at first declaring the cover to the trawler's drinking water tanks was not meant to come off and then that he did not have the tools to do it. The officers were increasingly insistent and eventually persuaded him to start twisting off a dozen or so bolts. When the metal panel was lifted off, the officers instantly knew they had found what they were looking for.

"When it was finally opened, the odor of hashish burst out and we almost got high on the smell," said Michel Michaud, one of the RCMP officers onboard at the time. Reaching deep into the darkened water tanks, they pulled out bale after bale of tightly packed hashish. "All of the bales of hash were wrapped in many layers of cheesecloth, plastic bags and other materials and all were submerged under the water." When tallied and weighed, the officers found about 500 kilograms of hashish, a load with an estimated street value of $9.5 million. On deck, covered by a tarp, were a small speedboat and an all-terrain vehicle. Officers arrested four crew members, all from Quebec, but Brian Erb, the ship's flamboyant skipper, managed to flee. Erb was a notorious seafarer who had become a modern-day pirate, a freebooter with liberal views on what constituted marine salvage rights.

Erb had gained some fame-cum-notoriety more than 10 years earlier when one of his marine stunts captured world attention. The irascible skipper had hauled a 2,500-ton abandoned freighter out of the St. Lawrence River, patched it up and renamed it the *Atlantean*, a ship that was later impounded because of unpaid debts. After it had been auctioned off, Erb led a ragtag co-ed crew of teenagers to reclaim her. In the middle of a late-February night in 1975, the *Atlantean* slipped her moorings and set off downriver on only one working engine, as Erb defiantly tried to make his way through the ice-clogged St. Lawrence in a slow dash toward open seas. His act of piracy led to a dramatic

11-day chase by police. Daily reports on the ship's progress and evasive stunts were carried in newspapers around the world. Once stopped by police, Erb agreed to head for port, followed closely by the RCMP. During the night, however, Erb slipped a small boat carrying two storm lanterns into the water, turned off the *Atlantean*'s lights and bolted for sanctuary while the police icebreaker continued to follow the decoy's lights. He was soon recaptured, but by then he had been dubbed the "Errol Flynn of the St. Lawrence."

Erb's more recent adventures along the coast of Newfoundland, however, were not the escapades of a lovable rogue. Police were certain the hashish they found in his boat was but a small portion of a much larger load; in fact, it was probably only his payment for services rendered. Weeks before she was seized at Blanc-Sablon, the *Charlotte Louise* had been anchored off the shore of Ireland's Eye while bales of the hashish were dropped on to a small speedboat, whisked to shore through the narrow harbor and then shuttled about the island on an all-terrain vehicle to hiding spots among the ruins.

The allure of fast money and a break from the grueling work of the commercial fishery brought otherwise honest fishermen under the control of gangsters from Montreal. Gerald Hiscock was the alleged Newfoundland contact for the Montrealers, whom police say hired local strong-arm fishermen to help unload the cargo. Their pay of between $17,000 and $20,000 made it an attractive alternative to hauling in fish for a pittance.

The drug trade, however, was hard to swallow for most fishermen. While in the past they may have enjoyed the easy money from Prohibition-era rum-running, few had much desire to be involved in illegal street drugs. They soon confirmed police suspicions about the movement of drugs with tales of unusual sea traffic along the craggy shores of Trinity Bay. Police were starting to get a pretty good idea of what was happening on the supposedly deserted island.

When the RCMP descended on Ireland's Eye, the island had not seen so much activity since Pirate Easton brought his ships to harbor. Three fishermen had already shuttled some of the hashish to the mainland. From there, it had been loaded aboard a truck, hidden under a layer of onions and was en route to Montreal. Police arrested the fishermen, seized the main load of hashish and went patrolling down the highway for a truck with Quebec license plates. They found it, 17 miles east of Gander, driven by a father-and-son team from the

Montreal area. (The Newfoundland town of 10,300 people earned renown years later when, after the September 11, 2001, terrorist attacks, it took in 6,000 passengers from diverted and grounded transatlantic jumbo jets.) The *Charlotte Louise*, with the drugs still in the tanks, was towed by a Coast Guard vessel to Sept-Îles on the Quebec north shore, with two RCMP officers taking turns guarding the dope, despite one being seriously seasick after too heavily celebrating the arrests with his colleagues the night before.

All told, the operation uncovered about 17 tons of hashish, with a retail street value estimated by the police at about $225 million. It was, at the time, the largest drug seizure in Atlantic Canada, but nabbing a handful of fishermen and two truck drivers did not seem to solve the riddle of the huge find.

On Monday, November 30, 1987, police significantly added to their catch of the day, however, when they arrested Vito Rizzuto, Raynald Desjardins and a third man, all in Montreal; Hiscock was arrested in Newfoundland. Vito was then 41 years old. It was six years after the New York slayings of the three captains, five years after Gerlando Sciascia and Joe LoPresti had been charged with heroin smuggling and three years after Vic Cotroni died. Until this arrest, Vito had not been in police custody for 13 years, since his release in July 1974 on the barbershop arson conviction, other than two brief tangles in September and December 1986, when he was charged with impaired driving. Desjardins was then 34 years old and nominally running an auto repair garage in Saint-Léonard. They were charged with conspiracy to traffic in drugs and, after a quick court appearance the next day in Montreal, flown to Clarenville, Newfoundland, where, by week's end, they were sitting with their alleged co-conspirators before a provincial court judge. Authorities were overjoyed at laying such serious charges against operators as renowned as Vito and Desjardins.

As evidence of Vito's collusion in the plot, prosecutors would point to a three-page transcript of a telephone conversation between Vito, in Montreal, and Desjardins, in Newfoundland, in late November. The conversation was oblique. Vito wanted to know when Desjardins would be returning to the city and Desjardins said he would explain everything in person when he arrived. Desjardins then said there was "something happening next week." Police and prosecutors claimed that this was a reference to the unloading of the hash from Ireland's

Eye a week later. Lawyers for the accused men described it as an innocuous conversation between acquaintances.

Vito spent Christmas in jail before obtaining bail in March 1988. He returned to Montreal while lawyers worked on his case.

SEPT-ÎLES, QUEBEC, OCTOBER 1988

Vito was out on bail when, on October 20, 1988, more than 60 officers with the Sûreté du Québec, the provincial police force, fanned out through several rural coastal communities at the mouth of the St. Lawrence. They uncovered a second hashish importation scheme remarkably similar to the Ireland's Eye find. Another modest vessel, the *Jeanne d'Arc*, was searched while anchored at the port of Mingan, near Sept-Îles, Quebec. On board, police found 38 tons of hashish, said to have a street value of more than $450 million, along with lesser amounts of cocaine, marijuana and weapons. This seizure was more than twice what had been found at Ireland's Eye, and was in turn declared the largest ever found in the area. Nine people were arrested, including Normand Dupuis, 38, the boat's owner and skipper.

Dupuis was wealthy by the standards of local fishermen and operated his vessel on the lower North Shore. He was also a self-confessed cocaine addict. Perhaps it was his drug habit that made Dupuis unstable, but his progress through the courts was anything but typical. Within two weeks of his arrest he had already agreed to cooperate with authorities and, to the glee of police, implicated as the mastermind of the venture none other than Vito Rizzuto. His demands in return for his cooperation were as modest as his ship, especially considering the stakes involved. In exchange for testimony against Vito he wanted $10,000 to help him resettle, a new identity, help in obtaining a passport, $120 a month while he was in prison and—perhaps the most sensible demand—drug treatment for him and his girlfriend. The authorities quickly agreed to it all and, on November 4, 1988, Dupuis and government representatives signed a contract for the seaman to become a cooperating witness. Six days later, his case was whisked before a judge and he pleaded guilty for his role in the hashish conspiracy. He was handed a four-year sentence that was to be served concurrently with a 30-month term for possession of 585 grams of cocaine. Dupuis then entered a protective wing of a provincial jail to keep him safely away from the general population while prosecutors digested their new evidence and drafted charges against Vito.

Just after lunch on November 17, 1988—precisely one week after Dupuis's plea deal—Vito drove away from his Antoine-Berthelet home, backing out of his driveway and heading west. Officers with the Sûreté did not let him get far before they pulled in behind him and signaled for him to stop. There, officers broke the news to him that he was to face another court on another charge of large-scale hashish smuggling. He was taken into custody and, the next day, flown from Montreal to Sept-Îles and formally charged with conspiracy to import hashish.

Vito now faced two serious drug charges, stemming from separate, but nearly identical, enterprises. While police wondered how many similar boatloads they might already have missed, or how many more might be heading toward their shores, prosecutors settled down to prepare their cases. Confidence ran high that Vito was down for the count, if not on both of the charges, then at least on one. The government even started making preparations to seize Vito's house and other property under new proceeds of crime legislation, legal actions that were supposed to be unveiled upon his conviction. The resolution of these charges, however, would come in unexpected ways. Both cases would take on the status of underworld legend, but it was Vito's second charge that was settled first.

MONTREAL, SUMMER 1989

Normand Dupuis had not been in jail long when he started to have doubts about his deal with police. As part of his plea agreement, he had asked to be placed in a provincial jail, rather than a federal penitentiary, and as his accelerated parole date drew closer he grew increasingly agitated. One day, while in Parthenais detention center, a fellow inmate approached him and made him a surprising offer—a $1-million cash "reward" if he declined to provide evidence against Vito at trial, Dupuis said.

"I refused," Dupuis said. "Then some time later the same prisoner came back with an ultimatum, warning that I had better cooperate or they would come after my family." Dupuis had three school-age children and the news affected him deeply. He felt trapped. He had already testified at Vito's preliminary hearing, implicating him in the hashish scheme, and signed the cooperation agreement with police.

"I did not want to commit perjury," he said. About to be released from jail and fearing that his deal with police would not adequately protect his family, the troubled seaman started to hatch a scheme that might offer him a better option. "I had decided I wasn't going to testify," Dupuis said.

After his release from jail, Dupuis telephoned Jean Salois, a long-time lawyer for Vito who has handled many of his legal affairs. Dupuis introduced himself to Salois and then asked for a meeting. Salois said he rebuffed the offer as improper, but as Dupuis grew insistent he reluctantly agreed to have the government's star witness against his client meet him in his law office. Salois then made careful plans.

"I hired a private investigator and told him to tape-record everything that was said and to photograph everyone who walked into my office that morning," Salois said. "I feared a trap. I worried that the plan was to attempt to incriminate me or to do something that would force me to abandon the case."

The day that Dupuis arrived at Salois's Montreal office, July 7, 1989, started with a brief thunderstorm, and, although the rain quickly cleared away, the day remained cloudy. As the unsuspecting Dupuis approached the office, a photographer's camera clicked away, unheard and unseen. Dupuis entered the office and announced why he was there: He was ready to disappear before Vito's trial opened, thereby destroying the prosecutor's case. In return, Dupuis wanted "a lifetime pension." No amount was named, but Dupuis no doubt remembered the million-dollar sum the inmate had supposedly mentioned earlier. That might have been his starting point.

To Dupuis's dismay and disappointment, Salois did not seem overly interested. Some time after Dupuis left his office, Salois gathered together the photographs and the audiotapes and went to the authorities, presenting his evidence. Disappointed police then spoke with Dupuis and listened to his story of the inmate in Parthenais and the offers and threats against his family. The other inmates in the protected prison wing where Dupuis had served his time were interrogated by provincial police officers looking for something—anything—to corroborate the story. Finding nothing and faced with the compelling evidence offered by Salois, prosecutors felt they had little choice.

"As a result, we decided to charge Dupuis with instigating the incident," government lawyer Louise Provost said. With a sick, sinking feeling, authorities charged Dupuis, their star witness against their biggest catch, with obstructing justice. It was August 16, 1989. Vito's trial before a jury in Sept-Îles was set to begin in less than a month and the government could no longer call Dupuis as a credible witness.

Fearing again for his own safety, Dupuis agreed to stay in prison until his preliminary hearing, where the key witness against him would be Jean Salois. On August 29, Dupuis pleaded guilty. Provost, the prosecutor, expressed appropriate outrage at the breach of judicial propriety attempted by Dupuis. She argued in court that his actions could encourage other witnesses to put a price on their testimony.

"It's like holding out for the highest bidder," she told the judge, asking for a stiff prison term on top of the unfinished four-year term for drug conspiracy that had been knocked off when he agreed to cooperate with the government, a deal the government now felt no obligation to meet. Dupuis was sentenced to 32 months in prison.

Without the testimony of Normand Dupuis, the case against Vito for the Sept-Îles hashish bust was in tatters, but the government glumly soldiered on.

"After Dupuis's visit to my office there was first a rogatory commission in the Dominican Republic," according to Salois. "After that, the trial took place in Sept-Îles. The authorities dedicated significant resources, going so far as to dispatch to the scene a senior Crown prosecutor."

On December 18, 1989, after several days of trial, all pretense of a prosecution against Vito was dropped. He appeared once more in a Sept-Îles court where he was formally acquitted of all charges related to the 38 tons of hashish found by police aboard Dupuis's boat. Police were deeply disappointed, for this was the stronger of the two smuggling cases against Vito, and the one they thought presented more compelling evidence of his involvement because of the cooperating witness.

Meanwhile, any joy felt by Vito and his family was tempered by the looming approach of his other trial, the one stemming from the Ireland's Eye seizure. With the dismissal of the charges in Quebec, the case in Newfoundland became, for investigators, all the more crucial.

Some might say desperate.

ST. JOHN'S, NEWFOUNDLAND, FALL 1990

In October 1990, three years after police swooped down on Captain Brian Erb's trawler and uncovered the huge hashish stash on Ireland's Eye, Vito appeared in court in St. John's, Newfoundland, to answer his other set of drug charges. Salois represented Vito; Pierre Morneau, another Montreal lawyer who often represents Sixth Family clients, represented a co-accused. With Vito in the prisoners box were Raynald Desjardins, Gerald Hiscock and Michel Routhier, who, like Vito, were contesting the charges. Prosecutors planned to map out the connections: how Hiscock had been seen meeting with Routhier, a Montreal man, a week before the shipment arrived; how Routhier was then seen meeting Desjardins in Newfoundland; and how Desjardins had spoken about "something happening next week" to Vito on the telephone. It placed two men between Vito and Hiscock and three between Vito and the fishermen who would be handling the drugs.

In what was becoming a pattern for Vito, this case would prove another spectacular fiasco for the government. And, as with his previous case, the best drama did not take place in a courtroom. Instead of a secretly recorded conversation in a lawyer's office in Montreal, this one involved similar intrigue at a hotel restaurant.

Newman's, a fine-dining establishment on the ground floor of the Radisson Plaza Hotel in St. John's, attracted hotel guests and city dwellers alike, with its formal service and varied menu. The Radisson, now the Delta St. John's Hotel, was Pierre Morneau's choice of accommodation while working to defending the men against the drug charges. He was a creature of habit. Each night, he reserved Table 6 at Newman's for himself and his fellow lawyers, who were defending Vito's co-accused. Every evening, they retired to the restaurant to dine together, discuss the day's events and prepare for the next day's challenges. The lawyers' chats did not go unnoticed by members of the RCMP. For whatever reasons, investigators—who swore in an affidavit that they were conducting a completely separate investigation from the one at trial—placed electronic bugs in a hotel meeting room, several of the bedrooms and at the lawyers' favored dining spot—Table 6.

For three days, from Monday, October 15, to Wednesday, October 18, the lawyers dined at their regular table while a bug hidden in the base of a lamp secretly captured their conversations. On Thursday, however, before Morneau's party arrived to take its usual place, a New Brunswick businessman named Guy Moreau arrived at the restaurant for dinner. The hostess who greeted him got the similar-sounding French names confused—Moreau? Morneau?—and, quickly scanning the reservation's list, thought the businessman had reserved Table 6. She promptly seated him at the table normally used by the lawyers. By the time the lawyers arrived, Moreau was already settled in and, with apologies offered, the hostess sat the lawyers at Table 3 instead.

The restaurant's manager, who was in on the RCMP operation, noticed the hostess's mistake and was concerned that the secret mission could be in jeopardy. He discreetly called to Greg Chafe, a busboy, and told him to swap the lamps between Tables 3 and 6. Chafe, who could see that both lamps were working fine and that neither customer had complained of the lighting, balked at the strange command. The manager, however, insisted. Chafe realized something peculiar was afoot.

Meanwhile, Moreau, the businessman sitting at Table 6, had an issue unrelated to his seat or his lamp. His roast duck had arrived cold. He asked that the dish be returned to the kitchen and heated. The busboy saw his chance. When he swooped in to retrieve the duck, he also picked up the lamp. Moreau, thinking the busboy planned to use the lamp to heat his duck, objected. Promising that the duck would be properly heated, Chafe was able to make off with both the cold meat and the hot microphone. Chafe was a curious and questioning sort and, while he was carrying the lamp, he noticed it weighed less than the other lamps. Examining it, he saw that the metal base normally fitted to the bottom was missing. Before he could poke around further, the manager pushed him to get it over to the lawyers' table. The lamps were switched and no one at the lawyers' table seemed concerned by the activity. The manager no doubt was relieved that tonight's meal was supposed to be the last night of the police operation, as the court hearings were set to adjourn.

The trial, however, was unexpectedly extended for another day, and so the following evening, the lawyers were back again for dinner. This time they secured their regular table.

It was likely with a wave of panic that the manager realized the bugged lamp had been left on Table 3, after the switch the night before. Again the manager called Chafe over and, just as he had the night before, ordered him to swap the lamps between Tables 3 and 6. Chafe quickly figured out what was going on and, for whatever reason, plunked the bugged lamp down on the lawyers' table along with a handwritten note saying: "Be careful, you might be bugged."

The note was like a bombshell for the lawyers, who knew their conversations were privileged. The real shock over "the zeal of the police," however, came when Salois learned listening devices had also been placed in his suite and in a conference room, he said. "It was in this location that the lawyers talked with their respective

clients or elaborated between lawyers on the strategy they would follow in the hearings," according to Salois. To make matters worse for
the government's case, the defense team called into question the wiretap recording of Vito speaking with Desjardins.

On November 8, 1990, almost three years after he was arrested,
Vito appeared before Newfoundland Supreme Court Judge Leo Barry, a
former provincial government minister. Judge Barry examined the word-
ing of the police request for judicial authorization of the wiretaps, then
made his ruling: The recordings were illegal and, worse, so injurious
to Vito's right to a fair trial that the entire case against him had been
tainted. It was an immense blow to investigators and to the prosecutor.

"You are discharged and free to go," Judge Barry said to Vito.

Vito greeted the news with only the slightest sign of relief. He
stood up, shook hands with the three co-accused seated with him and
walked out of the prisoners' box, taking a seat in the public gallery
near the back of the court to watch the remainder of the day's proceedings. Vito's lawyer then asked for the return of his client's $150,000
bail, posted back in 1987. Plus, he added with a flourish, $40,000 in in-
terest. Afterward, a satisfied Vito Rizzuto walked out of the St. John's
courthouse a free man, having won his second acquittal on serious
drug charges in less than a year.

"One word can mean so much," Vito said, "especially when that
word is acquittal."

Vito's elation contrasted sharply with the mood of an RCMP officer
who watched the cases crumble: "We were devastated."

A month after Vito's acquittal, Hiscock, along with Desjardins and
Routhier, were similarly freed after a judge declared that the illegal
bugs targeting the lawyers in the hotel compromised their defendants'
right to a fair trial. Hiscock then applied to get back his speedboat,
which had been seized by police.

––––––

Vito's pair of stunning acquittals did more than merely enhance his
reputation for being untouchable, although that it did. John Gotti,
the publicity-hungry Gambino boss in New York, had recently been
dubbed the "Teflon Don" by the press because charges against him
never seemed to stick. Vito, in turn, was sometimes called the "John
Gotti of Montreal," a comparison that likely rubbed the unassuming

Montrealer the wrong way. In fact, by contrast, a better name for Vito would be the "Quiet Don."

The two acquittals had another, more important ramification: Prosecutors grew distinctly gun-shy in dealing with Vito. There was a fear of bringing anything less than ironclad charges against him out of concern that more cases would similarly backfire or, worse, suggest a pattern of harassment, incompetence or corruption among authorities. Instead of sparking a renewed drive to slap fresh charges on Vito, the result was that authorities retreated.

"They kept saying, 'Next time, we'll measure twice and cut once,' but from then on they did a lot of measuring but no cutting. It was disheartening," an organized crime investigator said.

A confidential RCMP report from 1990, noting the legal defeats, summarized the fallout a little differently, seeing some measure of success in the failures: "Rizzuto is keeping a very low profile," it says.

Profitable as the massive hashish shipments were, cocaine offered an even better return for invested drug dollars in the 1990s. The Sixth Family was moving to be a leading player in that as well, but after the arrest of Nick in Caracas, the South American outpost was thrown into jeopardy. The Sixth Family was hungry for new sources of supply.

They found it closer to home.

CHAPTER 25

WEST PALM BEACH, FLORIDA, 1993

The arrest of a man carrying 200 kilograms of cocaine in South Florida was cause for conversation but, because the poor wretch had nothing to do with the Sixth Family, no cause for alarm. The arrest was mentioned in passing by Pasquale "Pat Gappa" Canzano, a Montreal truck driver, when he was chatting on the telephone with a woman on April 29, 1993. The woman quickly turned the conversation around to something of much greater interest to her, namely, Pat Canzano.

"And you? How's the Mafia?" she asked.

"Pretty good," Canzano answered.

"You monster," she said.

"Yes, of course," he replied.

"Oh, I'm just kidding."

"It's all right. Hey, hey, the truth never bent anybody's arm."

The conversation, and its obviously titillating effect on the woman, likely seemed amusing to Canzano. Life was good. He was reaping the rewards of being the right-hand man of a bona fide leader in a Mafia-run drug smuggling enterprise, a job that allowed him to travel, mingle with legendary crime figures, impress those women who were attracted to dangerous men and earn far more than his salary from hauling fruits and vegetables, his usual cargo, would ever pay. The enterprise Canzano had found himself involved in, which gave him some right to so indiscreetly claim his Mafia association, was an important and timely venture for the Sixth Family.

By 1992, Montreal was the Sixth Family's northern trafficking gateway and Florida was rapidly becoming its southern front. There was a growing—and increasingly urgent—need for a new southern route.

The 1980s and early 1990s saw an explosion in popularity of cocaine, a sharp, addictive stimulant that was being churned out in seemingly unlimited quantities in South America and hitting the streets of North America, typically through Florida. Thousands of traffickers, mostly relocated Colombians but also expatriate Cubans, ran cocaine networks from within Florida that brought hundreds of millions of dollars into the state. These new gangs also brought a wave of violence, echoes of the carnage in Colombia where well-armed and well-funded drug gangs amounted to full-scale insurgency groups battling for control of portions of the country. Bodies were dumped in the South Florida streets; the "Colombian necktie" was invented, where the victim's throat was slashed and his tongue pulled out through the hole; "war wagons," civilian cars and trucks stuffed with high-powered firearms clutched by high-flying gunmen, roamed the streets, opening fire indiscriminately on perceived threats or targets.

Cocaine profits altered the economy in the southern part of the state. Thousands of businesses were opened, many of them inactive front companies used only to launder drug money, but others, real businesses used as a means of reinvesting the accumulating profits. Colombian drug traffickers were bringing in so much cocaine in the 1980s that they were competing for clients; murders were sometimes not over the drugs or the money, but over the theft of customers. For several years, the wrong parts of South Florida were something of a bloody, narco-capitalist war zone.

The Mafia in Canada looked on this with more than passing interest. For many Canadians, Florida was already well within their comfort zone—it was a winter holiday destination for mobsters as well as the so-called "snowbirds," the Canadians who spend their winters in Florida's more temperate climate. For several decades, the old Cotroni organization in Montreal had members working in Miami, Fort Lauderdale and up the eastern coast. As Canadian representatives of the Bonanno Family, the Montreal mafiosi were welcomed by Gambinos, other Bonannos and members of the New Orleans Mafia family also operating there.

Canadian mobsters showed up with some regularity in investigations, mostly drug cases. William Obront, a Montreal underworld financial genius, was arrested by the DEA in a 1983 drug case in Florida, sparking an emergency meeting between Joe LoPresti, Frank Cotroni and others. It was a huge loss to the Montreal Mafia when Obront was found guilty and sentenced to 20 years. Later, the Caruana–Cuntrera and Vella organizations in Venezuela started landing its cocaine in Florida, often through the Port of Miami, where Oreste Pagano, Alfonso

Caruana's key supplier, worked with Cuban criminals to get the drugs off the ships and out of the port.

"I had my connections in Miami," Pagano said. "[They] introduce me to Cubans who were working very hard and who had big connections at the port and they would be able to pick up any amount of merchandise that would be sent," he said. Never ones to pussyfoot around, once the connection was made, Alfonso Caruana and Pagano shipped in 1,600 kilos in a single load. The interest of the Sixth Family and other expatriate Mafia clans in Florida stemmed not only from the Cuban connection being established in the Port of Miami, but also from the erosion of their base in South America. As a haven, Venezuela was heading into a meltdown. Under pressure from the U.S. government, the Venezuelan government was finally getting cold feet about offering sanctuary to the mobsters. Caruana was preparing to flee the country, Nick Rizzuto—as a sign of the trying times to come—was already in prison on cocaine charges and the Cuntrera brothers had been expelled.

Astute businessmen, the Sixth Family leadership recognized that the evolution of their organization must continue apace and that new sources of supply and bases of operation had to be found and preparations made for the abandonment of its South American outpost. South Florida seemed an ideal replacement.

With Nick in prison, the Montreal hub of the family was in the hands of his son. Vito had strong advisors all around him—Mannos, Rendas and Cammalleris, chief among them. They were family; he trusted them implicitly. He had Joe LoPresti at his side and, in New York, Gerlando Sciascia. The Sixth Family was imposing a more rigorous business approach onto their criminal enterprises. Several members were entrusted to run their own drug operations as best they could, with each network carrying the powerful Rizzuto imprimatur despite its semi-autonomy. It was a lesson drawn directly from corporate America: the franchising of crime. As the organization's hunger for product increased, four new international cocaine smuggling routes were opened, each supervised by a different Sixth Family acolyte. The routes they built spanned the globe: one was built with Montreal contacts living in South America, another was securing its drugs in Texas, a third dealt directly with gangs in Asia and still another formed in Florida.

For the foray into Florida, the job fell on Domenico Manno.

Born on December 27, 1933, in the Sixth Family stronghold of Cattolica Eraclea, Domenico Manno is 11 years younger than Nick Rizzuto and 13 years older than Vito, making him a generational bridge within the Sixth Family. Manno was a true man of the Mafia. In his hometown, he had been born into Mafia royalty, as the son of Antonio Manno and Giuseppina Cammalleri, and the younger brother of Libertina Manno, Nick's wife. Manno joined in the early exodus of the clans from Cattolica Eraclea to Montreal. He had tried to move to America when he was just 17 but faced expulsion in July, 1951. A file was started on him by U.S. immigration officials in January, 1958, and he was registered as driving across the U.S. border from Canada on September 3, 1959, at Champlain, New York. He fell under investigation in St. Albans, New York, in July, 1963, apparently sparked by another border crossing the month before.

In Canada, however, Manno made his first blip on police radar when he was arrested and convicted for running a gambling den in 1967, during a crackdown on vice in Montreal that coincided with Expo '67, the World's Fair that was held in the city as the country marked its centenary year, an event that attracted huge foreign crowds. A decade later, he was a substantial underworld player, a key part of the Sixth Family as it was wrestling Montreal away from Paolo Violi. He had stepped in to help represent the family on the streets of Montreal during some of its most tenuous years, while Nick and, later, Vito moved to the safe haven of Venezuela. He then helped to settle the dispute once and for all, having an active hand in Violi's assassination, a slaying that gave the Rizzuto organization control over the Montreal gateway to the American drug markets. Manno gained additional notoriety when he and his co-accused kin received such mild sentences for the slaying—Manno was handed seven years—that a local newspaper, *The Gazette*, lashed out, saying the sentence served "almost to sanction the planning of executions." The defendants, the judge declared, were "model immigrants who performed the most modest tasks in an effort to earn a living and to slowly and laboriously build themselves a trade." Manno would apply that same ethic to his drug enterprise in Florida.

At the time of his Montreal conviction, Manno was a lean, hard-looking man with close-cropped hair and deeply creased facial features. He quietly did his time in prison, after assuring authorities—in writing—that neither Vito nor Nick had anything to do with the slaying. Clearly, Manno knew his place within the Sixth Family and accepted it. Well respected, he always hovered near the top—but never at the top—of the Canadian Mafia hierarchy. If he ever felt jealous that Vito, not he, was the successor to the family throne, there was no hint of it. After his release, he again offered himself as an advisor to, and protector of, Vito, when Vito returned to Montreal to claim the city as his own while Nick remained in South America. U.S. police intelligence files list Manno as part-owner of a trucking company based in Saint-Léonard that was used as a front for drug trafficking and money laundering. It was this firm that hired Pat Canzano, the Montrealer who seemed to like titillating his friends with his mob association. Manno had also attended major gatherings of the Sixth Family core, including a key organizational meeting in Montreal, in January 1983, where Manno was joined by Gerlando Sciascia, Paolo Renda and many others, police reports say.

For Manno, his connections to career traffickers and ownership in a trucking firm was an opportunity not to be missed. With the Sixth Family's South American outpost in jeopardy, the 59-year-old Manno stepped forward to create a cocaine importing scheme in Florida.

LAKE WORTH, FLORIDA, 1993

Manno was a jovial and polite buyer when dealing with Bertha Lucia Osorio de Reyes, who lived in Lake Worth, Palm Beach County, Florida, a midsize coastal community with the slogan: "Where the Tropics Begin." Reyes liked to be called "Berta" and she responded to Manno's friendly manner by being a charmer in return.

Like Sicilian mafiosi, Berta also believed in keeping business within the family. Her business was using a good connection for cocaine in Colombia through a legendary smuggler named Herbert Luna-Luna to get the drug into the United States. With her son, Mauricio Reyes, her sister and two close associates, Berta specialized in couriering cocaine out of South America and into Florida. A typical Berta operation consisted of sending couriers to South America, where they were given relatively small quantities of cocaine to smuggle back, often hidden in tubes containing rolled-up paintings. One shipment of three such tubes, brought back from Quito, Ecuador, on commercial airlines, totaled a modest 10 pounds. The drugs were delivered to Berta's Lake

Worth home, where the courier was paid. Word would go out that Berta had dope to move and a buyer would come forward.

Increasingly, that buyer would be Manno. Berta's tight little group operated off the radar, the underworld equivalent of a prosperous but not ostentatious mom-and-pop corner store, and the always friendly chitchat between her and Manno, and Manno and her son, reflected that.

"How are you, sweetheart?" Berta, in her South Florida home, said to Manno, who was calling from Montreal. It was November 1, 1992, just before 11 a.m., and both were ready for business but never let the pleasantries pass unspoken.

"Not bad, you?" Manno replied.

"Oh, fine, thank you, your family?"

"Everything's okay," Manno answered. "How's it going there?"

"Oh, everything is fine," she replied. The talk then moved into the typically disjointed terrain of furtive code words used when drug smugglers try to say things without actually saying them, on the off-chance that the conversation is being recorded by police. Berta, Manno and Mauricio Reyes would all appear to be talking about anything other than drugs. On the morning of October 5, 1992, the RCMP, who for two months had been secretly monitoring wiretaps placed on several members of the Sixth Family—with their prime target being Vito Rizzuto—heard Manno answer a call from Mauricio.

"Hey, how are you?" Manno asked.

"How are you doing, sir?" Mauricio politely replied. Manno told him that "his friend," Pat Canzano, was leaving the following day for Florida in his truck.

Did he have any "tomatoes," Manno asked. Mauricio replied that he did.

"Probably gonna get, uh, like five bushels this time," Mauricio said, meaning five kilos of cocaine. Manno was hungry for the product.

"We'll take whatever ya got. It's no problem."

Between them, Canadian police and U.S. federal agents drafted a list of 45 code words that Manno and the Reyes family would use in their conversations, forming something of a guide to drug traffickers' code. "The hard ones" was cocaine, "the soft" was heroin. And sometimes "Cadillacs" meant cocaine and "Hondas" meant heroin. When the product was "like cement" it was in hard, brick form. "Good boys" meant good-quality merchandise. "Documents" meant money. The federal agents were "the bad guys" and "a gentleman" was a trusted drug distributor. "Fifteen cents a square foot" meant the price for a kilo of cocaine was $15,000. It made monitoring their conversations difficult for everyone—including, sometimes, themselves. When two shipments were on their way, one of heroin and the other of cocaine, and one got seized by police, Manno and Mauricio were quickly on the phone.

"How are you doing?" Manno asked, on March 18, 1993.

"I'm doing good and not so good," Mauricio replied.

"Good or no good?" asked a confused Manno.

"Good and no good."

"What's the matter?"

"OK, there are Cadillacs and Hondas," Mauricio started, looking for a way to make Manno understand without being too explicit. Manno knew words beginning with C usually meant cocaine and H words typically referred to heroin.

"Which one's good?" asked Manno.

"The Hondas," answered the boy.

"What about the Cadillacs?"

"The Cadillacs? Well, we're gonna have to wait until another guy can go. ... We're going to have to start all over again with these guys because the guy ... the ... the guy got, uh ... How do you say? He got caught," he said, finally giving up on finding a suitable code word for being arrested.

Despite the occasional setback, business was good for Berta. And Manno was the only buyer she needed. He had endless clients lined up and was constantly demanding cocaine and edging for credit.

"Anything more, I will accept it," Manno said one day. "Whatever you can send me." Berta's sources in South America were increasing not only the size and frequency of their shipments of cocaine, but also introducing heroin, which had begun to be manufactured in labs hidden in the jungles of Colombia. It was all, Manno was told, earmarked for him. Heroin was like a magic word to Manno. He began ramping up his demands for the drug. Heroin was historically the underpinning of the Sixth Family; if cocaine was the modern meat of the criminal body, heroin was the very bones.

Canzano was taking money hidden in his truck down to Florida and returning with cocaine. The organization became so active that Canzano had to find other drivers to assist him. Sometimes the deals were successful and Manno was able to market large quantities; other

times there were backups, arrests of couriers, even a ripoff. One trafficker, known to the others only as "Chico," took more than $70,000 of
Sixth Family money and, instead of delivering cocaine, disconnected
his telephone and vanished. When hunting for Chico, the traffickers
did not know of the police wiretaps but someone had spotted a surveillance agent. With Berta living on a dead-end street in a residential
community, stationary surveillance was difficult for police. Officers
also noted with frustration that the traffickers frequently threw off
their surveillance by conducting "heat runs"—driving through an area
in which a trafficker has associates who watch his car pass and then
look for any vehicles following it. Police had surreptitiously stolen the
trash on several occasions from in front of Berta's home in a search for
additional evidence. Berta and her family were starting to feel the heat.

"Bad guys showed up across the street for days and days and days,"
Mauricio nervously told Manno one day. He believed the surveillance
was on Canzano, who had stayed at Berta's house and made several
telephone calls from there while trying to locate Chico. Manno, fearing
his carefully nurtured source for cocaine and heroin would evaporate
if Berta got too nervous, hastily calmed Mauricio down, telling him
that they had not slipped up on their end. Alas, they had. Between the
RCMP, the DEA and the Palm Beach County Sheriff's Department, the
enterprise had been thoroughly compromised.

Pat Canzano was under heavy police attention when he made a run
to Florida in 1993. During a lengthy surveillance, Canzano met with several notable Florida traffickers. He also met with another Montreal truck
driver being used to transport cocaine back to Canada. Similarly, when
Manno himself traveled to Florida, police were all over him. Manno,
frustrated at the money lost to the elusive Chico, flew into West Palm
Beach airport in late March 1993. For nine days he and Mauricio Reyes
tried to track Chico down. Attempts were made to find him through his
social security number and credit records. Manno said that he had access to a lawyer who could obtain such information for him.

In spite of the loss of the $70,000 and the increasingly obvious
police surveillance, Manno did not slow down. When Berta showed an
interest in obtaining counterfeit money, he sent a sample down, saying
he had a huge amount in Montreal. Counterfeiting U.S. banknotes had
long been a quiet specialty of Montreal crooks under the Sixth Family.

On May 10, 1993, Manno called Canzano in Montreal and told him to go to an address on Bélanger Street to meet a man named "Pietro" to whom Canzano was to simply say he was a friend of Manno's and ask for "some stuff." Later that day Canzano was arrested in Montreal with a kilogram of cocaine. On the same day, RCMP and DEA surveillance teams watched Manno and a man authorities described as his son-in-law, drive out of Montreal and across the border at Rouses Point, New York. The pair ended up at the Marriott Hotel, at New York's LaGuardia Airport. The following day, Berta Reyes, accompanied by two men, also arrived at the hotel, where they found Manno lounging near the lobby elevator. The group had a meeting, then Berta and her entourage left the hotel and easily dodged the surveillance team. Manno and his driver checked out the following day and drove to Manhattan, where they took a room at the New York Helmsley Hotel. On May 13, Manno was followed by agents to the Grand Hyatt Hotel, near Grand Central Station, where he waited in the lobby until Berta and her companions showed up again. Unable to get a cab for all of them, they headed into the subway and were lost by the surveillance team.

The heroin purchase was not going well. In a call to his wife on May 17, Manno said he expected to be "finished" that same day and that someone should leave "it" with her cousin. But the negotiations dragged on. Manno wanted 10 kilos but did not like the $105,000 per kilo asking price; plus he wanted at least partial credit. On the Berta side, there was frustration over the delays in closing the deal. She was in the classic middleman squeeze, caught between the Colombian suppliers and the Mafia purchasers. Mauricio Reyes was told that things were "moving slowly" and there had been disagreements with Manno. The "old guy," Mauricio was told, had become upset during negotiations. At one point Berta told her son that she hoped Manno "would quit being a pain in the ass."

That heroin deal between Manno and Berta never fully came together, although Manno was able to buy a single kilogram for $105,000. Relations between Manno, whom the Florida associates started calling "the little old man," and Berta, became strained, to the point where she began leaving her telephone off the hook to avoid his repeated calls. Such was his hunger for heroin shipments.

In spite of the tension between the Canadian mafioso and the Berta crew, Manno continued to move counterfeit money to her. At one point he sold $85,000 to one of Berta's associates. When the man went to buy cocaine with it, he was arrested—the seller was an undercover policeman. At the end of 1993, Berta herself was arrested when she was found with $10,000 of Manno's bogus bills.

On March 11, 1994, Manno and Pat Canzano—who was already facing a charge of possessing a kilo of cocaine in Montreal—and several members of Berta's organization were indicted in the Southern District of Florida. The U.S. government sought the extradition of Manno from Canada, with court documents identifying Manno as "a Sicilian Mafia member" and Canzano as "his right-hand man." Court papers record that Manno was "responsible for 29.5 kilograms of cocaine, 10 kilograms of heroin and $85,000 in counterfeit currency." These were terribly conservative figures.

It was perhaps then that Pat Canzano started to regret his loose talk to his lady friend about being part of the Mafia. The phone conversation had been recorded and transcribed by police and presented in court, read from the witness stand by a DEA agent. If Canzano did not blush, others in court did it for him. Canzano later said that he "got blinded by stupidity." But he had bigger things to worry about. His lawyer, Eddie Kay, described him in a Florida court as a "tweener."

"[Canzano] was between cooperating and not cooperating," Kay said. "And during that tweener period he told the government about the amounts of cocaine involved … [but] he wouldn't tell the government about Manno. He just won't go against Manno," he said. "I tend to think that there's something to be said for this type of philosophy of being a standup guy, and this is the last standup guy, here." Despite his client's apparent sympathy for Manno's circumstances, Kay was not as forgiving. Manno was not, he said, a "good godfather."

"Manno is all over the tapes. Manno is acting throughout this whole conspiracy, and there's a guy named Rizzuto who's on top of Manno. Now, it would be like Don Corleone going ahead and doing the acts himself," Kay said, referring to the Mafia boss in *The Godfather.* "This is some Don Corleone, you see, who takes his right-hand guy and puts [his family] on welfare." Canzano was sentenced to more than 15 years in prison.

Twenty-two months after the request for Manno's extradition from Canada, he appeared in a U.S. court. His criminal case was wrapped up far quicker than his battle to remain out of the hands of the American authorities. Within six months of returning to Florida in shackles, he struck a plea agreement admitting his role in running a criminal enterprise and a heroin and cocaine conspiracy in return for a 20-year sentence and a $250,000 fine. A pre-sentence report portrayed a broken-down, hardworking Italian immigrant. He said he had never attended school. He lived in a finished basement with his wife, who earned money as a self-employed seamstress doing piecework, and he had an ill daughter who had been institutionalized for more than 25 years, the court was told. He had no assets; in fact, he claimed a negative net worth of $115,097. He owned a truck and other equipment to run his business, but all was heavily encumbered by liens and had no resale value. How he would pay the fine that he had agreed to pay was a mystery.

"Mr. Manno, has anyone used any pressure, threats, coercion, force, intimidation of any kind to cause you to plead guilty?" the judge asked him.

"No, no," he answered. Manno was contrite before the court. "The only thing I want to say is, on my own behalf, to give me as low a sentence out of consideration for my family ... I'm so sorry for all of the problems that I've given to the United States. I feel very bad about it."

The guilty plea—almost a mandatory action by all captured Sixth Family members to try to keep the Rizzuto name out of the public's eye—was a strategic move on Manno's part. Or, at least, so he thought. He had successfully played the justice system in Canada when pleading guilty in the Violi murder. He was going to find American justice a little more equal to his machinations.

Manno and his lawyer had cooked up a plan designed to shave years off his sentence and save him from having to pay the hefty fine. He would agree to the outrageous plea, then quietly apply for the Transfer of Offenders program, a treaty between Canada and the United States that lets citizens of one country imprisoned in the other serve their sentences in their homeland. Once in Canada, Manno knew, the Canadian penal system calculations of appropriate punishment would apply and, under its generous parole allowances, he would likely be out of prison after serving as little as one-third of his sentence. And further, once back in Canada, he had no intention of paying a cent of the $250,000 fine. This turned out to be a bad strategy. While his lawyer, Samuel DeLuca, had advised Manno that it should work out rather nicely, after his plea Manno was informed that he would have to pay every penny of the fine before he was eligible for an international transfer. Disgusted, Manno got new lawyers to appeal his sentence.

"As a result of bad advice, Mr. Manno agreed to a deal which subjected him to a longer sentence than he was willing to agree to serve because he was advised that he would not have to serve it," his new lawyers argued.

In November 2004, his appeal was rejected. Outfoxed at every turn, Manno, the previously crafty mafioso, remains in an American federal prison, due for release in December 2012, when he will be 79 years old.

CHAPTER 26

CENTRAL SQUARE, NEW YORK, SEPTEMBER 1993

Interstate 81, following the path of the Appalachian Mountains, stretches from eastern Tennessee to the Canadian border without passing through any major metropolitan areas, making it a popular route for impatient truckers. Not surprisingly, speed traps are common. It was on the southbound lanes of the northern leg of that highway, as the pavement passes between the sprawling Adirondack Park and Lake Ontario, that a New York State trooper stopped a speeding taxicab in September 1993. While the trooper wrote out a ticket, the cabbie told him a curious story.

He was just returning from Canada where he'd dropped off an unusual fare—an agitated, sweating passenger who had abandoned his car at a diner in a small New York State village. The passenger was exhausted and jumpy, muttering quietly to himself such things as: "Even if they find it, no one can prove it's mine."

It was a bizarrely long and lucrative 185-mile cash fare to Cornwall, Ontario, for the cabbie, who marveled at his good fortune. The driver's luck, however, meant bad news for the Sixth Family. The traffic stop was the first thread to pull loose in what would be revealed as a complicated tapestry: another cross-border drug smuggling plot. In what would emerge as a trademark of the Montreal Mafia's operations, the plot drew together disparate players in the underworld, this time natives living on a reserve that straddles the U.S.–Canada border and members of the Hells Angels Motorcycle Club.

The passenger who had flagged down the cabbie was having a rough couple of days, although his trip started smoothly enough, leaving Cornwall alone at the wheel of a rental car and heading south across the border. During his long drive to Texas he started cursing the fact that no one had been hired to share the driving with him; to compensate, he popped pills to stay awake.

After arriving in Houston, the driver made his rendezvous and loaded the car with duffel bags stuffed with 40 kilograms of cocaine, a $6-million load (at street-level prices). He immediately turned around and headed back. State after state, he made his way north. Pill after pill, he drew closer to home. Then the rental car, pushed to the limit, broke down in Falling Waters, West Virginia, a bedroom community along the Potomac River that had not seen so much action since Union cavalry charged through during the Civil War. Desperate to get back to Canada, the courier went looking for the cheapest replacement vehicle he could find. At a local used car lot, he settled on an old Plymouth Gran Fury, bought it for $300 and transferred the bags of dope into its trunk. This car, however, was in little better shape. About six hours and 355 miles later—tired, wired and paranoid—the courier parked the Gran Fury outside Wilborn's Restaurant, a diner in Central Square, N.Y. When he returned to the car it would not start. That was when he hailed a taxi.

Before the cabbie agreed to drive the courier to Canada, he made the man prove he had the cash to pay the fare—about $350, more than it cost to buy the used Plymouth. The man showed him a large wad of cash and off they drove, with the passenger muttering as he tried to doze, the cabbie later told the state trooper.

With barely 1,500 residents at the time, the village of Central Square was not known for its big spenders, though its easy access from Interstate 81 often brought strangers through town. Suspicious about such an odd taxi ride, the trooper drove to Wilborn's, where he found a Gran Fury parked in the restaurant's only handicapped spot. Diner staff told the trooper the car did not belong to any of its customers. The parking infraction gave the trooper cause to call in a tow truck and, in accordance with laws on police seizures, it was subject to an inventory search. It did not take long to uncover the drugs.

"They realized pretty quickly that with 40 kilos in the trunk somebody would be coming back for the car," said Richard Southwick, the U.S. government attorney who worked on the case. Officers put the Gran Fury back in the parking space and set up surveillance to watch it. A car with Ontario licence plates soon drove into the lot and cruised slowly around the Gran Fury before stopping. Someone got out, looked at it—but did not touch it—and then left. Police still waited. Not long after, a tow truck from the Akwesasne native reserve arrived, hoisted the car up and set off with it. State troopers swooped in but the driver clearly knew nothing of the drugs. There were no arrests, but officers were left with some pretty compelling clues and the largest drug seizure in the region.

It was not hard for U.S. authorities to link the Gran Fury to the Virginia car lot and then to the abandoned rental car from Canada. That led police straight to the courier. Canadian police then traced him to the Travelodge Hotel on Brookdale Avenue in Cornwall, where he worked. A joint U.S.–Canada investigation was launched.

CORNWALL, ONTARIO, AUTUMN 1994

In the autumn of 1994, a young RCMP officer went undercover, hanging around the Travelodge Hotel and an attached bar, meeting the regulars and showing his face. Constable Michel Aubin soon became known at the hotel as an affable man and modest drug trafficker as he watched members and associates of the Hells Angels mixing with the hotel management, local barflies and men linked to the Montreal Mafia. Investigators believed the street-level trafficking at the hotel was connected to the seized cocaine from the Gran Fury, but were uncertain how. After this first taste of Mafia intrigue, Michel Aubin, a quietly efficient officer, would go on to play a startlingly important role—12 years later—in the history of the Sixth Family. Back in April 1995, however, Aubin's undercover effort was more modest; he provided his fellow officers with enough evidence for the RCMP to legally tap into the phone lines of the hotel and the homes of two Cornwall residents: the courier who had bungled the cocaine delivery and the owner of the Travelodge Hotel, Giuseppe "Joe" Sicurella.

Living quietly in Cornwall but from a family from Cattolica Eraclea, Sicurella had avoided legal trouble except for an armed robbery charge 20 years earlier that had been withdrawn before trial.

The Cornwall traffickers could not have known their phones had been tapped, but they were clearly aware of the possibility. As the police monitoring began, investigators found their suspects already using secret codes. When trying to determine the size of an expected cocaine shipment, Sicurella would ask, "How many girls?" The answer from Julian Tabares, alleged to be their Miami supplier, was "Three to four hands," meaning 15 to 20 kilograms, a kilo for each finger on that many hands. They also sometimes identified friends by combining the first two letters of their first and last names: Luis Caceres became "Luca," for instance. For a time, the subterfuge left officers confused. Who were these apparently unknown and unidentified people? Then a call from Sicurella to a colleague at the Travelodge asking for "Luca's" telephone number was heard. A police check on the Montreal phone number given in reply was traced to the pager of Luis Caceres. Their naming code was cracked.

Unknown to police at the time, the conspirators had already brought several shipments of cocaine from the United States into Canada, ranging in size from 10 to 22 kilograms each. Four days after the monitoring began, Sicurella took a call at his hotel from Tabares in Miami. A few days later, Sicurella called a pay phone in Miami that was answered by Tabares and a meeting between the two was arranged. Another load was in the works, police believed.

On May 6, 1995, officers secretly watched as Sicurella left his home and drove across the border at Massena, New York, telling border guards he and his female passenger were just going for breakfast. Meanwhile, Pierre Rossignol, a co-conspirator from St. Joseph du Lac, Quebec, was smuggled across the border by Akwesasne natives. He joined Sicurella and the pair headed to Syracuse airport, where they boarded a flight to Miami under the watchful eye of Drug Enforcement Administration agents. Tabares picked them up at the airport and the two Canadians checked into Room 6912 at the nearby Marriott Hotel. During quiet face-to-face meetings, the two sides haggled over the purchase price for bulk loads of cocaine.

Sicurella and Rossignol then returned to Syracuse, where an Akwesasne resident picked them up and drove them to the American side of the reserve. There they boarded a boat for the short hop across the St. Lawrence River to the reserve's Canadian side. This same easy way of shuttling people across the border without passing through government checkpoints in either country was also being used to move drugs.

Over the next 18 days, details were negotiated and a deal was finally struck in a Laval restaurant, although price remained an issue. Despite the Canadians' hunger for a steady supply, Rossignol announced he would not "go down on his knees" to make the deal.

On June 2, 1995, Aubin, the RCMP's undercover officer, met with the man who had previously bungled the cocaine delivery. Aubin placed an order for one kilogram of cocaine. Such an order could not be filled at the moment.

"We're waiting for things to happen," Aubin was told. A week later, Sicurella headed south in a car that was stopped by New York State troopers as part of the investigation. He told the troopers he was going to Atlantic City to "hang around," and allowed them to search his car.

It was a bold gamble—he had $50,000 as a down payment for cocaine hidden in a box of tissues on his rear window ledge. The troopers' search, however, found no luggage, no drugs and no money, and he was allowed to continue on his journey.

Despite the large down payment, arrangements came in fits and starts, requiring repeated telephone calls. Several calls received by Sicurella came from a man he seemed to answer to: Girolamo Sciortino.

The name Girolamo Sciortino meant nothing to American investigators. In Canada, however, Sciortino had been noted in police files not only because of his criminal record—dating back to 1973 with two convictions for running an illegal gambling operation, followed in 1988 by a conviction for drug trafficking—but also because of the company he kept. Born on September 27, 1941, in Cattolica Eraclea, Sciortino moved to Montreal, where he often went by the nickname "George," dubbed himself "the king of the submarine sandwich" and started a casual submarine and pizza restaurant. He married into Montreal's D'Angelo family, which, in the wickerwork of Sixth Family interrelationship, links back both to the Rizzuto and the Renda families. Sciortino is likely a relative of Giuseppe Sciortino, who arrived in America in 1925 alongside Vito Rizzuto's grandfather and Calogera Renda. The families have remained close. In 1995, his name attracted more interest from police when Sciortino's son, Bernardo, married Bettina Rizzuto, the only daughter of Vito. The lavish nuptials, with Bettina beautifully outfitted in a fairy-tale grown and a string of white pearls, came two years after the Gran Fury stuffed with cocaine was found but two years before Girolamo Sciortino would have to answer for it. (Bernardo Sciortino, often called Benny, has a criminal conviction for assault and manages the family's submarine restaurant, George Le Roi du Sous-Marin, according to police. He and Bettina would later give Vito his first grandchild.)

To investigators in Cornwall deeply embroiled in the Travelodge drug probe, which was given the codename Project Office, Girolamo Sciortino became an important part of their investigation, although his specific role was still a mystery.

On July 18, 1995, Sciortino called Sicurella at his Cornwall hotel, asking, in code, for an update on the planned shipment of cocaine. Sicurella said he was working on it. Three days later, Sciortino phoned again, complaining that Sicurella was not returning his calls. The

Cornwall hotel owner said there had been a number of "fuck-ups," but that Sciortino need not worry. A week later at the Miss Cornwall Restaurant, down the road from the Travelodge, Sicurella received news that the cocaine shipment was finally ready for pickup. His courier arranged to borrow the vehicle of a reserve resident, promising there would be $500 in the glove box when it was returned. The next morning, the courier headed to New York City. Clearly learning from his mistake on the Texas run, this time he brought his wife with him to share the driving. Even so, the drive was a frantic one. His deadline for the pickup in New York was noon and yet he had not crossed into the United States until 9:57 that morning, at the start of a nearly seven-hour drive. Clearly, he was going to miss his pickup time by a wide margin. Repeated calls begging for more time, placed to a pay phone on the sidewalk outside Flushing Auto Salvage, almost in the shadow of New York's famed Shea Stadium, were made during the drive.

"Time is the number one thing," said the voice on the New York end. Once in Queens, the courier was given the keys to a gray Mercury Cougar. Behind the back seats, he was told, 30 kilograms of cocaine had been hidden. This was high-tech subterfuge: the secret compartment was hydraulically operated and could only be activated by tuning the car's radio to a specific radio station's frequency. The courier and his wife climbed into the Cougar. After an overnight stay, they drove it north, arriving at a house on the American side of the Akwesasne reserve where the cocaine was removed from the Cougar. The courier counted 27 one-kilo packages as he placed them in a cardboard box inside a garage. A little after 7:30 that evening, the cocaine was driven to the St. Lawrence River, loaded onto a boat that took it across to the Canadian side of the reserve, and packed into a waiting pickup truck.

The truck then headed into Montreal, an easy 90-minute drive. The driver had noticed a police tail, however, and from Highway 40 made a sudden exit onto St. Laurent Boulevard, disappearing into city traffic. Eventually, police say, the drugs were delivered to Sciortino in Montreal.

Now it was Sciortino's turn to be on the receiving end of haranguing phone calls. He appeared to be having trouble pulling together the final payment, or was purposely reluctant to do so. In a sudden reversal of roles, Sicurella phoned Sciortino, whom he called "George," at his Montreal sandwich shop, asking about the money.

"Don't worry about it," Sciortino told him. But others did. Sicurella's courier was taking calls from the suppliers, asking when he was returning their Cougar and the rest of the money. The suppliers were told they "could not dance," suggesting they were under police surveillance. By July 30, their Miami supplier had lost patience and said he was on his way to Cornwall to collect his car and cash. Under pressure, Sicurella told the suppliers they were all in danger of arrest.

"If he comes here, he'd better be prepared to go in for a long time," Sicurella said, referring to prison. "You guys are gonna make me do something; the mistake of my life."

On July 31, at 10:09 a.m., Sicurella said he was leaving for Montreal to settle the "documents," a common code word for money. Police immediately placed his hotel under surveillance. The RCMP had lost the drugs and were determined not to lose the money as well. An hour later, Sicurella's wife called him from the hotel and asked how his trip was going. Shocked officers realized he had somehow slipped past them. Desperate to find him, officers called Sicurella's pager and punched in his home telephone as the callback number, hoping the telephone's call display would tip them to where Sicurella was. When Sicurella returned the call nine minutes later, however, it came back as an unpublished number. It took two hours for the RCMP to get the information from Bell Canada that the call had been placed from Montreal's Bar Le Corner on Bernard Street. At 4:36 p.m., surveillance officers found Sicurella and watched him throughout the night—during which he met twice with Sciortino—and the next day, when Sciortino and Sicurella met briefly in a Burger King parking lot. Taking no chances after so many slip-ups and scares, an air surveillance team in a helicopter tracked Sicurella's car as it wove through the city's busy streets.

Shortly before 5:00 p.m. on August 1, Sicurella and Sciortino met again, parking their cars close together near Sciortino's Beaubien neighborhood home. Sciortino pulled a white shopping bag out of his trunk and handed it to Sicurella, who then placed it on the passenger side of his car before quickly driving off. At 5:07 p.m., police moved in and arrested Sicurella. Inside the shopping bag they found $200,000 in $50 and $100 bank notes, neatly bundled with rubber bands. One of the $100 bills was counterfeit. The next day, an arrest warrant was issued for Sciortino and others. Sciortino turned himself into the RCMP at their Cornwall detachment on August 22, where he was charged with conspiracy to import cocaine.

Making matters worse for the traffickers, the drug courier who had stumbled with the Gran Fury—setting the entire investigation in motion—agreed to become a government witness and was cooperating with authorities in exchange for a reduced sentence for himself and charges being dropped against his wife. It was a rare display of government cooperation by someone who had worked with the Sixth Family. Most of the conspirators pleaded guilty.

Named as the ringleaders, Girolamo Sciortino and Joe Sicurella faced serious drug charges in Canada and the United States, leading to an unusual joint prosecution. They pleaded guilty, three months apart, in both countries and were handed 12½ years in Canada and 10 years in the United States for the cocaine conspiracy. The men were then whisked back to Canada, where they were allowed to serve their sentences. For Sicurella, it was a particularly advantageous move. As a first-time federal offender charged with drug trafficking, which the National Parole Board does not consider a crime of violence, he was eligible for accelerated parole. In 2001, he was granted day parole, and full parole in 2003. Sciortino, however, did not fare as well. In 2002, three years after his imprisonment, he was convicted for drug trafficking yet again and sentenced to an additional 32 months. When he applied for parole in February 2007, the parole board was unimpressed.

"According to information supplied by police, you were far more involved in drug trafficking than you led people to believe," the parole board told Sciortino. "You are affiliated as a member of the Montreal Mafia," the board said, also noting Sciortino's denials: "You insist that your crimes had nothing to do with the clan," the record says.

"The interveners believe that you chose crime in full knowledge and out of contempt for legal and social norms—all this under the guise of your pro-social values and legal activities as a restaurateur over the years," the board said. "Your turning to illicit activities was a life choice, taken in the course of business dealings where you did a cost-benefit analysis before committing yourself unconditionally."

In the end, Richard Southwick, the U.S. prosecutor, marvels at the large case and how it all spun out from the traffic stop of the cabbie. If they had hired a second courier to share the driving back from Texas, it could have ended differently, he said.

"If they hadn't been so darned cheap, they probably would not have gotten caught."

CHAPTER 27

MONTREAL, DECEMBER 1993

It is always cold in Canada at Christmas. Just as it also has sunny, warm summers, winters across most of the country are typically long and icy, an event celebrated by some with winter festivals and outdoor ice skating. For Oreste Pagano, who was acutely acclimatized to the south—having been born in the city of Naples, in southern Italy, and residing for years in sweaty South American cities and then in Miami—it was bone-numbing weather that greeted him on this visit to Montreal. This trip, his first to Canada, stretched from Christmas 1993 into the New Year. Although snow was all around him, it was a very different sort of white powder that was on Pagano's agenda in Montreal. Like Vito Rizzuto and Alfonso Caruana, Pagano was a busy man and, for Pagano, "business" seemed to always mean arranging cocaine shipments of the highest order. Bullish and almost bald, Pagano was a member of the Camorra, the Mafia of Naples. He had been introduced to Alfonso Caruana in 1991, while they both enjoyed Venezuela's tourist mecca of Margarita Island, a place where the Rizzutos have also repeatedly visited in recent years for meetings and travel aboard someone else's private jet.

Pagano had fled to South America from the authorities in Italy and, after hooking up with Alfonso, was shopping for 400-kilo loads, or more, of cocaine secured from Colombian cartel contacts made during his year of living in Bogotá. It became a frequent and profitable relationship for both Pagano and the Caruanas and, in return, Pagano was drawn close into the bosom of the Sixth Family.

On this Christmas, Pagano came to Montreal seeking answers from Alfonso Caruana. He wanted to know when he could expect to receive the substantial sum of money owed to him and his Colombian cartel suppliers for arranging a staggeringly huge cocaine shipment from Venezuela to Italy, a 5,466-kilo load. Despite the unsavory nature of their dealings, Pagano did not ignore the spirit of the season and brought with him a gold watch as a Christmas present for Alfonso. Alfonso had a gift, of sorts, for Pagano, as well. The two men had taken rooms at the same Montreal hotel and, on one of the seemingly unending chilly days, Alfonso announced to him that they were having dinner that evening with a *compare*, Pagano said. *Compare* is an Italian word that can mean "Godfather" or "kinsman." Whatever meaning Alfonso was attaching to the word, he made it clear to Pagano that they were going to be meeting a person of importance.

At about seven o'clock, Vito Rizzuto arrived at their hotel.

"This gentleman arrived, a very tall gentleman with a distinguished appearance," Pagano said of his first impressions of Vito. "He picked us up with his car and all three of us went out to dinner."

The world of Pagano and Alfonso was an extremely secretive one. Neither spoke carelessly of the other's business. Of all their secrets, their extensive drug-trafficking activity was their most sacred and closely guarded. So when, at dinner, Pagano realized that Vito seemed to know all about what he had been up to, it was an important signal.

"When Alfonso brought me to Vito Rizzuto and I had come to learn that Vito Rizzuto knows already what Alfonso and I were doing, I understood that Vito Rizzuto was the head of the Mafia, who is above Alfonso," Pagano said. "Because, otherwise, why would Alfonso have to tell him what we were doing?" As such, any business ventures that might be suggested by Vito would seem, to Pagano, to be promising propositions indeed. When Pagano later discreetly checked Vito out, he found Vito's reputation impeccable.

"From what I know, he is head of the Mafia, leader of the Italian Mafia that is here in Canada," Pagano said. "Alfonso told me." No matter what authority, power, connections or wealth the Caruana–Cuntrera family carried around the world, in Canada, they could not exceed the authority of Vito Rizzuto, as the head of the Sixth Family, Pagano added. "After the Rizzutos, it is the Caruana family that counts the most, that has more of a voice in any discussion. The number of Alfonso's family is number two." Pagano approached other references, all easily vouching for Vito. "Besides Alfonso, other people had told me, who knew me, and told me that he was the Mafia leader of everything."

The dinner conversation that evening between Vito, Alfonso and Pagano was not just small talk.

"We spoke in terms of business," Pagano said. They started cooking up a new way to get cocaine shipped into North America and Vito also offered Pagano a portion of a large hashish load, Pagano alleged: "I also spoke with Vito ... about a drug trafficking deal that we were going to do together."

The plan seemed simple enough by drug trafficking standards, Pagano recalled. Vito had a contact with a Canadian industrialist who owned a mining operation in Venezuela. Several times a year, the company shipped the extracted minerals to Canada, where they were processed. In the shipments, cocaine could easily be hidden for a secret journey into Canada, Pagano was told. The regular shipments from a large, legitimate company meant the chances of it being targeted for interception were minimal.

"Vito Rizzuto sent me to speak to [his contact]. He lived in Venezuela and he had a mine in Venezuela but he was Canadian," Pagano said. "He told me to send this 100 kilos to this person from the city of Bolivar and said that we could begin to do some work with them. I went to the city of Bolivar personally and gave him 100 kilos of coke." The delivery took place some months later when Pagano had a lull in his business with the Caruanas after a shipment had been seized in Miami.

"I had sent 100 kilos in October of '94 in Venezuela. The person that I had to send it to, the person I was told to send it to, this person had said that the merchandise should arrive in Canada by Christmas," Pagano said. "I had spoken with Vito Rizzuto, telling him that I was sending him the hundred kilos." So, again around Christmastime, a year after his first visit to Montreal when he said he had met Vito for dinner, Pagano flew to Canada to see how their venture had worked out. This time, the mood of the men in Canada matched the chill in the air. The news from Venezuela was not good.

PUERTO CABELLO, VENEZUELA, DECEMBER 1994

It was shortly before Christmas and spirits might well have been high among workers in Puerto Cabello, a bustling old seaport to the west of Caracas. Puerto Cabello was once considered among the best deep-water ports in the New World and was the departure point for cocoa, coffee and cotton heading to Europe. In the 1700s, this seafaring activity attracted pirates who roamed the Caribbean Sea, prompting the construction of extensive fortifications along the coast, called the Fortín de San Felipe but often nicknamed the "Castle of the Liberator." The fort was later used to jail political dissidents and the messages of its desperate occupants, scrawled on stone walls, are still decipherable. And just as the stone fortifications remain visually dominant, so remains the importance of shipping in this city, which is considered Venezuela's primary commercial and military port. While fear of marauding sea pirates has receded over the centuries, Puerto Cabello has retained its attraction to organized criminal elements.

Cocaine comes to Venezuela from its neighbor. The country is linked to Colombia by the Pan-American Highway and smaller spur roads that carry the heavy traffic of buses, cars and trucks through two official border crossings. Both the highway crossings and clandestine border crossing points are used to shuttle drugs. The quantities are large and, often, stockpiled to ensure a smooth and steady supply not dependent on border interdictions.

"Methods of shipment and concealment are sophisticated, similar to those used in Colombia, and traffickers often establish 'front' companies using false documents. Traffickers use key urban and port centers around Maracaibo, Maracay, Caracas, Barquisimeto and Puerto Cabello to temporarily store drugs, then evade local law enforcement by shipping them from these poorly monitored ports," according to a report by the U.S. Department of State. Puerto Cabello is further described by the U.S. Embassy in Caracas as: "a known embarkation point for multi-ton containerized shipments of cocaine to the U.S."

Increasing pressure on Venezuela from the American government had brought an incremental increase in narcotics seizures and arrests. Corruption, however, was still rampant. About the time that Pagano said he was arranging a test shipment of cocaine to Canada at the behest of the Sixth Family, President Carlos Andrés Pérez was on trial on charges of embezzlement, and a scandal was emerging after arrest warrants against more than 35 money launderers connected to the Cali cocaine cartel were dismissed by a corrupt judge, according to the U.S. Department of State. "Corruption poses a threat to the Government of Venezuela's democratic institutions and is a significant impediment to effective narcotics control programs," the State department concluded in its narcotics report that year.

In these uncertain times, officers with the Guardia Nacional, one of three Venezuelan federal agencies sharing drug-enforcement responsibilities, swooped down on a shipping facility in Puerto Cabello and arrested seven people who were loading 12 barrels containing mined magnesium into a shipping container destined for Montreal. When authorities inspected the shipment, mixed in with the metal was 543 kilograms of cocaine, with an estimated value of $100 million.

Among those arrested was Stephan Zbikowski, 32, of Longueuil, Quebec, a suburb of Montreal on the south shore of the St. Lawrence River. Zbikowski is the son of a wealthy mining engineer in Quebec who shares his name. The elder Zbikowski was involved in mining operations in Venezuela and had a leadership role in a firm with exploration rights over 8,600 acres in Venezuela from where it hoped to discover gold. The arrest threw the Zbikowski family into turmoil. His mother flew twice to Venezuela to make representations on her son's behalf. By March 1997, the younger Zbikowski was still being held without a conviction in a tough Venezuelan prison. The case prompted questions in the Canadian Parliament by two Quebec politicians, Stéphane Bergeron and Philippe Paré. In 1997, Bergeron presented a petition to the prime minister, signed by close to 2,500 people, asking the government to implore the Venezuelans to release Zbikowski.

The family's situation did not improve, however. A year after the arrest of the young Zbikowski, the father was himself arrested on drug charges in Canada after a joint probe by the U.S. Drug Enforcement Administration, New York State Police and the Quebec provincial police. Officers seized 75 kilos of cocaine and issued arrest warrants against 12 people; along with the elder Zbikowski, then 58 years old, police issued an arrest warrant against the Sixth Family's Emanuele Ragusa. Zbikowski was deemed a leader in the network that involved the United States, Canada, Mexico and Venezuela, according to government documents. He was later sentenced to 13 years in prison.

"You were one of the directors of this criminal plan. Your role consisted of planning, controlling, directing, financing, coordinating and taking charge of the transportation of cocaine," National Parole Board records say of his crime. Two notes in his file linked him to the Mafia.

MONTREAL, JANUARY 1995
News of the Puerto Cabello arrests and cocaine seizure reached Canada at about the same time, coincidentally, as Oreste Pagano. The prodigious trafficker arrived in Montreal to meet with Vito and Alfonso and to find out how their test scheme had gone. The seizure seemed to have happened while he was en route and he was unaware of what had occurred in Venezuela.

"Vito Rizzuto handed me a newspaper that was talking about the seizure. And the newspaper said that 500 kilos were seized," Pagano said. "I told him that this was not the merchandise that I sent. I handed over a hundred kilos, not 500." Somewhere, someone seems to have gotten greedy. It was not the first time such a thing had upset Pagano's carefully made plans. The alleged 100-kilo shipment had been substantially boosted and eventually became so overloaded it tipped. The mobsters were spun into some confusion. Whose drugs had been seized? Who was responsible? Was it really their shipment that had been found? Or someone else's? Was their smaller shipment still on the way? Everyone had questions for the others.

"He was sending someone to find out how it was seized," Pagano said of what he claimed was Vito's plan to sort things out. "And he was saying that he didn't know how [or] from where this gentleman had gotten the other 400 kilos. ... They said that they did not know and that they would find out; that they would make the person pay for the shipment and the [lost] earnings as well," Pagano said. He was told to "have a little patience," and that Vito "would be sending the money to me." The seizure, of course, did not upset only the gangsters.

"After finding out about his son's arrest ... [the young Zbikowski's father] worried that he also may be arrested. He had gotten himself admitted to a clinic in Montreal," Pagano said. "To have an alibi," he claimed.

Pagano continued to work closely with Alfonso, but his relationship with Vito waned over the screw-up on their first job together, Pagano said. Vito and Pagano met a few times more after that. Both were at the wedding of Alfonso's daughter in Toronto on April 29, 1995, at which Vito was cordial toward him and even invited Pagano to a wedding in his own family two months later.

Pagano waited without word on the investigation into what went wrong in Venezuela and, more importantly, without receiving the money he had fronted the consortium in buying the 100 kilos of lost product. Pagano wanted to make one last approach to Vito about getting reimbursed, he said, when he next had a chance to meet with him. And he now had his invitation to an event where Vito was guaranteed to be present.

MONTREAL, JUNE 3, 1995

On the day of his wedding, Vito's oldest son, Nicolò, looked as dapper as his father. Named for his grandfather, Nicolò was 27, with dark hair and his father's brooding, furrowed brow but a wider, more robust face. His wedding was cause for family celebration. Making matters even more comfortable for all concerned was his choice of bride: Eleanora Ragusa. In a perfect example of the family's tight-knit structure, Vito's son's bride was the daughter of Emanuele Ragusa, a longtime family confidant. Ragusa's other daughter, Antonina, had married Luigi Vella, who was Alfonso Caruana's cousin. Emanuele Ragusa's sister similarly married into the Sciascia family.

The wedding, at the Sheraton Centre Hotel in downtown Montreal, was formal and impressive, attended by "people of the family, the entire Mafia clan," Oreste Pagano said. Vito had invited Pagano to attend, likely out of respect for his close association with Alfonso Caruana. Although decidedly uninvited, police thought it impressive as well. It did not take long for intelligence officers to learn of the impending nuptials as the RCMP were in the midst of Project Choke, yet another large operation targeting the Rizzuto organization. Officers were probing a conspiracy to import large loads of heroin and cocaine from South America and were keeping close tabs on Vito and many of his associates. Police interest in the family made such private events as weddings and funerals prime targets for surveillance by intelligence officers looking for fresh photographs and clues to who was friendly with whom. There seemed to be less of a frenzy by police over the marriage on June 19, 1999, of Vito's other son, Leonardo, to Maria Tutino, a chartered accountant.

For the wedding of Vito's son Nicolò, the RCMP and Laval police mounted an extensive operation to monitor the celebration, taking possibly as many photographs of the guests as any official wedding photographer. Many of the Sixth Family members were there as were other relatives: Emanuele Ragusa, Domenico Manno, Agostino Cuntrera, Francesco Arcadi, Frank Campoli and many others. Although invited to attend such an important family event, Pagano clearly never became personally close to Vito; during an early police debriefing after Pagano agreed to cooperate with authorities, Pagano mistakenly recalled Vito's name as "Paolo Rizzuto."

Pagano wisely chose to refrain from confronting Vito about the overdue payment on that day, a day when Vito likely would not have his mind on such matters.

"I wanted to, because I still had not received the money," Pagano said. But he waited—until the next morning.

"The morning after the wedding, we met at the hall and he told me to remain calm and that he would be sending me the money, which I never received," Pagano said. "I never got it." That sour start to their business relationship halted any further dealings between Pagano and Vito, he said.

"This drug-trafficking deal went bad because the drugs were seized. … It was later broken off because the job, the first job, went bad and I lost trust. And even the people that had sent me the merchandise lost—not having received the money—lost their trust." Pagano was merely reiterating an old mafioso maxim: "Lose my money, lose my trust."

Pagano told Canadian police of the cocaine scheme during secret debriefings in early 1999, and then again in more detail in late 1999. He obviously felt it was something the authorities could or should act upon.

"What I want her to understand," he said to the translator during one of his debriefing sessions, referring to the female RCMP officer asking him questions, "is that everything that I am saying is not hearsay, because, as [for] hearsay, I could tell you lots of things, but I prefer to speak of things that I know directly."

Could this spark another investigation and possible charges against Vito? The grounds seemed compelling. There was evidence from Venezuela of the arrests and the seizure of the drugs in the mining company barrels, coupled with Pagano's testimony of personally making the arrangements to send drugs to Vito and, later, personally delivering them to the mining official in Venezuela. More than eight years later, no such charges had been laid.

Other deals for the Rizzuto organization, many others, went far smoother than the mining scheme. Still, the Sixth Family had their share of slip-ups and bad luck as they diversified their holdings from heroin to cocaine to hashish to counterfeit currency, continually seeking to maximize profit.

For the leading members of the Sixth Family, the dirty days seemed far behind them. The messy murders in Montreal in the 1970s of the Violi brothers and the prison terms served by their kin in return, the bold, frightening purge of the rebellious Bonanno captains in New York in the early 1980s, the uncertainty that came with Vito's serious drug charges in the late 1980s and the unpleasantness of Nick Rizzuto's incarceration in Venezuela that stretched into the early 1990s—the memories of such turmoil were fading into the past. Business was booming.

CHAPTER 28

NEW YORK AND MONTREAL, 1994

The Sixth Family was unmoved by the failure of the occasional new venture or the lengthy sentence issued against a senior member, even one as close to their core as Domenico Manno, and refused to retreat from the fervent cross-border movement of drugs. Around the same time as Manno's South Florida escapade, Girolamo Sciortino's corn-wall cocaine blues and the cocaine debacle in Venezuela, another core member of the Sixth Family was similarly busy expanding the franchise. This operation was built on sound economic theory: the law of supply and demand.

Cocaine had become so plentiful in North America that the price was steadily dropping. At the same time, Europe was awash in cheap heroin, thanks to bumper crops in Afghanistan. The Montreal mafiosi saw an easy business model for enhanced profit; all they needed to do was get their cocaine to Europe to sell at a premium and, in return, move their heroin to sell in the United States with a similar markup.

For this scheme, the Sixth Family relied on Emanuele Ragusa, according to U.S. law enforcement and court files. Ragusa worked with the family's trusted drug intermediary, Sammy Nicolucci. This time, rather than a Hispanic family linked to Colombia or a biker gang or native criminals, the Sixth Family formed an alliance with the Big Circle Boys, an Asia-based crime syndicate, and the 'Ndrangheta, the Mafia of Italy's Calabria region.

For the Sixth Family and the Big Circle Boys to work together was a meeting of two seemingly perfect criminal entities. The organizations are strikingly similar. Both hark back to the tradition of their ethnic criminal roots. The Big Circle Boys, who take their name from the circle of prisons around the Chinese city of Canton, come from the traditions of the Triads of China. Both groups, however, recognize the weaknesses of a rigid hierarchical structure and the vulnerability it creates and adjust their structure accordingly. Like the Sixth Family, the Big Circle Boys' motive is purely one of profit, and at the root of their power and wealth is the global heroin trade. Like the Sixth Family, the Big Circle Boys are active in dozens of countries around the world, in both legitimate and illicit activities and, like the Sixth Family, they are master networkers. The Big Circle Boys' chief representatives in their venture with the Sixth Family were Cheung Wai Dai, known by the street name "Ah Wai," and Chung Wai Hung, known as "Thai Gor Hung."

Also in on their scheme was Emanuele LoGiudice, a New York–based Sicilian mafioso who was working to distribute whatever heroin the Sixth Family could get him. Ragusa and Nicolucci held several meetings with their Asian heroin connections, according to police. The conspiracy they mapped out was for the Big Circle Boys to bring in heroin from Asia to Canada, which the Sixth Family would buy and ship to New York. Once there, a portion would be sold to LoGiudice for the Mafia to distribute and the remainder sold to the Kung Lok Triad, another Asian crime group with its roots in Hong Kong. Further, cocaine would then be bought in Florida by the Sixth Family and shipped to Canada where some of it would be sold to the Big Circle Boys for resale and the rest shipped to Italy to the Sixth Family's own trafficking contacts.

At a meeting at the Great Wall Tea House in Montreal in the early 1990s, Nicolucci and Ah Wai finalized the narcotics trading post.

For the Sixth Family, it was a perfect win-win plot. As middle-men—the prime position for the organization—they would profit simply by taking the heroin from the Chinese and passing it to traffick-ers in New York. Similarly, the price markup on their cocaine in Europe was a substantial jump that more than made up for the risks and costs of the transatlantic journey. The business model came together in late 1991 and operated for several years. With so many criminals involved, however, it was not long before the drug trafficking came to the atten-tion of the RCMP. The first slip came from the Big Circle Boys. Officers in Canada learned that Chung Wai Hung was playing an increasing role in the drug world and, by 1993, police had placed wiretaps on his phone lines.

On May 6, 1993, a package containing 3 kilograms of cocaine—which had been mailed by some of the targets of the police probe and destined for 'Ndrangheta members in Siderno, Italy—was seized in Brooklyn. With the international scope of the operation growing, the Polizia di Stato, the Italian national police, joined the probe. It was soon discovered that this package was not the first to have been sent. Colombian gangsters in Bogotá were identified as the original source of the cocaine that was being bought in Florida. In November 1993, a shipment of 167 kilograms of cocaine that was destined for Rome was seized in Colombia.

By early 1994, despite these seizures, the operation was running full tilt. Chung Wai Hung had brought in heroin that had quickly been sold and, in typical Big Circle Boy fashion, he had reinvested his profits in the underworld. He created a wide criminal organization in Canada involving drugs, counterfeiting, gambling and credit-card fraud.

"He even discussed the prospect of opening a prostitution business," said Zachary W. Carter, the United States Attorney for Brooklyn at the time, who prosecuted the case.

LoGiudice, working from his base in New York, was the eventual recipient of much of the heroin. He was an old-timer in the drug business. In 1981 he was caught accepting heroin brought to him from Europe by a Belgian smuggler. He was also well connected with some of the most active Sicilian traffickers, including Michele Modica, a mafioso who would become infamous in Canada after a failed attempt by a Sixth Family associate to assassinate him in a Toronto restaurant in 2004 left a bystander paralyzed. After LoGiudice was released from jail, he fell into old habits and became a prime heroin customer of the Sixth Family.

To sell it, he relied on men such as William Zita, a street player who had been arrested for assaulting a policeman in 1960 and for selling untaxed cigarettes in 1968. For the next two decades, Zita worked as a bookie and loan shark while maintaining a legitimate job at the John F. Kennedy Airport—a position that provided him with a steady stream of stolen goods to be fenced. He soon realized bigger returns came from drug sales and ended up dealing in heroin. Zita was caught in 1981 and sent to prison. After his release, he worked with LoGiudice, whom he called "Manny."

Transport of the drugs was left to the Sixth Family, who had become experts. The family maintained a regular run from Montreal to New York and then to Florida and back—mirroring the Manno conspiracy. The trucks carried heroin south into New York and then pressed on to Florida, where they picked up cocaine and headed north, often stopping again outside New York to collect cash from drug sales before heading back across the border into Canada.

"That truck, I think, was on a run, an automatic run. It passed ... every couple of weeks," said Zita. "I think it was going to Florida. It was a Montreal, Canada situation to Florida. That was the run it was making." There always seemed to be a truck on the move, on one leg of the journey or another.

LoGiudice was constantly caught in a financial squeeze, despite the flow of drugs, and Zita received only small amounts of cash for his considerable work selling the heroin, always with the promise of more money once LoGiudice formalized an ongoing relationship with the Sixth Family.

LoGiudice realized the power and wealth that could flow from working closely with the Rizzuto organization. It gave him incentive to ignore problems along the way. Trouble came, for instance, in the autumn of 1994 when a kilogram of heroin of inferior quality arrived at LoGiudice's door. Despite the slight, LoGiudice felt he needed to maintain his business relationship with Montreal and ordered Zita to work harder to sell it.

"Manny has a problem selling this heroin," Zita said. "He couldn't move it and he owed money, somewhere between $100,000 and $150,000. He told me, 'Listen, I can't give you anything on this but there is a shot that we can open the door here and we can make some money in the future. ... When this whole thing is over, I will give you something.'" Once the heroin was sold, "the people in Montreal" would give them more to sell but, Zita said, you had to be careful who you bought your heroin from in Canada.

"Manny said that he knew people, other people, up in Canada, that he could get it [from], but it wasn't a smart thing to do. ... I would assume that they let him know that he was responsible to [the Sixth Family] and that he should do business with them and nobody else." And so the crummy heroin was ground down to a fine powder to make it look to be of better quality before it could be resold.

"I was a little surprised that somebody was going to take a kilo of this stuff," Zita said. It was going to Canada, Zita was told. The story seemed preposterous.

"Nobody wanted it and it was going to Canada? Come on. *Canada*? They got the real stuff, you know. This stuff was Mickey Mouse stuff." The suggestion that inferior heroin could be offloaded to Canadian traffickers was enough to arouse suspicion in any experienced dealer. Sending bad heroin to Canada was like sending wilted tulips to

Holland. Zita immediately smelled a rat and he was right. By the time they figured out that their operation had been compromised, however, it was too late.

––––––––

It was not long after Ragusa and Nicolucci had arranged their innovative drug scheme that the RCMP stumbled into the middle of it, according to court and police documents. A joint RCMP–FBI investigation was launched. Wiretaps and surveillance were placed on the Big Circle Boys, and the Combined Forces Special Enforcement Unit (CFSEU), a joint anti-mob police team in Canada, loaned an informant—a former criminal named Gino who worked with police for cash—to the FBI. Gino was to infiltrate the distribution end in New York. The operation was called Project Onig—Gino spelled backwards—and it ran from 1991 until 1997.

When the police operation was brought to a close, a dozen traffickers were arrested in the United States and more than 40 in Calabria, Italy. In New York, several of the Big Circle Boys' associates and many of LoGiudice's men—including William Zita—all betrayed their bosses and agreed to cooperate with the government to reduce their own sentences. No one linked to the Sixth Family, however, said a word.

Onig was an eye-opener for law enforcement officials in several countries. It proved that formerly separate groups, usually suspicious of each other and protective of their turf, had found a way to conduct mutually beneficial criminal operations without violence or jealousy. The reward for such cooperation was enhanced profit.

Colombian cartels, Hispanic Florida drug gangs, New York mobsters, Sicilian mafiosi, Chinese Triads, the Big Circle Boys, the 'Ndrangheta, the Hells Angels—all were working seamlessly with the Sixth Family, an organization that had grown into a truly global criminal enterprise. Across the United States, court files were being littered with references to members of the clans of the Sixth Family. No one, however, seemed to be pulling it together to realize that these cases involving New York, Florida, Pennsylvania, Los Angeles, Buffalo, Detroit, Italy, Colombia, Montreal and Toronto were not disparate strands but, rather, part of a single organization based in Canada, where it was largely immune to the increasing efforts of American law enforcement to crush the Mafia. Few fully recognized the growing influence of the

Sixth Family on international affairs and fewer still understood that what was once a small, outpost of subservient gangsters had grown into an independent and powerful entity that could hold its own in any underworld, on any continent.

"The most significant aspect of this investigation was in the revealing of the depth of cooperation between [Mafia] groups and other major organized crime groups," says an FBI report on the success of Project Onig. The Bureau pointed to the investigation as a landmark probe against international organized crime.

The only disappointment from Project Onig for the FBI, the report notes, was that Emanuele Ragusa, one of the prime targets of the operation, remained in Canada, beyond their grasp. Unlike Manno, when this enterprise collapsed, Ragusa managed to escape.

———

Emanuele Ragusa was born on October 20, 1939, in Cattolica Eraclea. Like so many of the Sixth Family, he emigrated to Canada and settled comfortably in Montreal where he mingled with mafiosi in both the Rizzuto family and the Caruana–Cuntrera clan. Police on three continents would document his ties to both families.

Italian authorities say they have been trying to get their hands on Ragusa for years. In 1983, he was convicted *in absentia* for his role in a drug-trafficking scheme tied to Francesco Mafara, a Sicilian Man of Honor who, in 1977, was among the first to sell heroin from refineries in Sicily. Mafara confessed to his involvement as a top heroin man and was murdered shortly afterward by some of the mobsters he betrayed. Italian police also noted that Ragusa had been found in the home of Giuseppe Cuffaro, the money launderer, with Leonardo Caruana, the mafioso who shuttled between Montreal and Sicily. Alfonso Caruana and his wife, Giuseppina, also used a cellular telephone with a Montreal area code that was registered in Ragusa's name. On November 11, 1993, when Venezuelan police raided the Caruanas' villa they found an invoice for Ragusa's cellphone, according to the Italian government.

In 1996, Ragusa, at age 56, was sentenced to 12 years in prison in Canada for a conspiracy to import drugs—a charge unrelated to the Project Onig case. It was his first criminal conviction in Canada. In prison, officials took note that the RCMP had declared him an important leader in the Sicilian Mafia with many years of close association with the Rizzutos. As a mitigating factor, it was noted that he had never been linked to crimes of violence.

During his incarceration, Ragusa faced down two extradition requests, first from the United States for the Project Onig conspiracy, and later from the Italians for Mafia association. Prison officials were alerted to the U.S. extradition request in April 1998. Despite that, he was allowed out on day parole a month later to perform community service at the Mission Bon Accueil, a Montreal charitable shelter for the homeless. Supervisors at the shelter were pleased with his work until they noticed steaks were missing. A search found two slabs of meat in Ragusa's bag. He was asked not to return to the shelter. He later faced stern denunciation from members of the National Parole Board for the "immoral" act of stealing from the disadvantaged people he was supposed to be helping. While he was slapped on the wrist for the steak heist, his greater concern of a U.S. extradition was settled in his favor when it was ruled that the American case was too circumstantial to merit his being sent to New York, according to government documents.

Just as that was being resolved, however, the Italian government joined the queue to get a piece of Ragusa. The courts in Italy were prepared to imprison him for Mafia association. In true Sixth Family style, this, too, ended in his favor when a court ruled that the Italian request be denied because, at the time, Mafia association was not a crime in Canada, according to Ragusa's parole records.

During his stay in prison, Ragusa was rarely a problem prisoner, although guards once found him with a stash of 66 packets of cigarettes hidden in his cell, suggesting either an entrepreneurial streak or a tobacco addiction. He rebuffed suggestions by the authorities that he was a mafioso, declaring to parole officials that he was erroneously associated with the Mafia because of his Italian ancestry. Officials, however, noted his close personal ties to the Sixth Family. Parole records cite the marriage of Ragusa's daughter to Vito's son, Nick, going so far as to say: "Your son-in-law is the son of the reported chief of the Sicilian Mafia in Montreal." Ragusa was denied permission in 2000 for a leave from prison to participate in the baptism of his grandchild, the offspring of his daughter and Vito's son, on the grounds that Vito would also be participating in the service. Another important family event, a wedding, caused Ragusa problems as well.

On July 12, 2002, prison officials were informed that Ragusa's son, Pat, was getting married the next day to Elena Tortorci, a woman whose family, not surprisingly, is from Cattolica Eraclea. The cream of the Sixth Family had been invited, including Vito, his father, Nick, and Agostino Cuntrera. Prison staff found that Ragusa had requested and received a pass for a temporary absence for that day. Suspicious officials questioned him about his plans for his leave before his departure. Ragusa said he had nothing special in mind; he was going to stay at home and relax. Police and prison security agents secretly monitored the wedding and noted Ragusa among the guests, trying to duck out of wedding photos. That night, while the wedding reception was in full swing, police stopped by Ragusa's house and found it in darkness. No one answered their knock at the door. Ragusa later admitted that he had deliberately kept his son's wedding from prison officials for fear of not being allowed to attend, as he had been refused two years earlier when he requested permission to attend the baptism.

Disappointed prison officials then canceled future passes, keeping him in prison until his statutory release—a questionable law in Canada that automatically lets nonviolent prisoners out of prison after serving only two-thirds of their sentence. On November 11, 2004, the National Parole Board ordered him to provide officials with statements of income and expenses during his release to allow some monitoring of his activities. Having previously handed parole officials a psychiatric evaluation that said he was suffering from "burnout" from criminal activities and saying he was finished with crime, he planned to use his freedom to work in a corner store.

Despite published reports that Ragusa was the Emanuele who allegedly joined Vito in gunning down the three captains in 1981, there has been no known attempt by American authorities to request his extradition to face trial on the matter.

The FBI's interest in Ragusa and other Canadians allegedly involved in the intrigue of the Bonanno Family is evident in an internal note from March 2004, after another debriefing session by agents of Frank Lino. Titled "Canadian Pictures," the report says that Lino was shown a photograph of Ragusa and asked about him.

"[Lino] did not know Emanuele Ragusa's name but remembered meeting him. [Lino] did not recall whether he had met him in Canada or the United States."

Because of the Onig informant and the cross-border police cooperation, Ragusa's Sixth Family venture faltered; such failure, however, was rare. Ragusa, Manno, Sciortino—police were able to pick away at the edges of the Sixth Family but the core remained intact. The organization, as a whole, was flush with success.

With each successful shipment, each new enterprise and every new revenue stream, their resources swelled, their abilities grew and their strength increased. Fewer and fewer organizations were capable of mounting a challenge. As long as the money kept flowing, there was little need for more wars. And the money did flow, in great gushing streams; which, of course, can create problems of its own.

A FAMILY AFFAIR

VITO RIZZUTO (top, on the right) stands solemnly with his father, Nicolò, and mother, Libertina, at the marriage of Vito's eldest son in 1995. Vito is recognized as the current leader of the Sixth Family, a powerful Mafia organization more than a century old. Vito typically wears appropriate attire as the head of a corporate-like Mafia, such as in 1998 (bottom left) and more recently (bottom right).

FAMILY ROOTS

THE SIXTH FAMILY'S ROOTS are in Cattolica Eraclea, a remote village of 6,000 in the south-west of Italy's island of Sicily, the birthplace of the Mafia. The roadside sign (above) alerts the few visitors who come to wander these narrow streets (below).

A FIRST GENERATION of the Sixth Family moved to America in 1925, including Vito Rizzuto (left), who provided a name and an outlaw culture to a grandson who would become notorious on three continents. With him was Calogero Renda (right), his brother-in-law, whose descendants would remain at the Rizzuto family's side. They moved quickly to New York, where the American Mafia was forming. Once there, Rizzuto met a messy end and sparked a U.S. visa fraud scandal.

THE VITO RIZZUTO of this generation was working his way through school in Montreal while his father, Nicolò, built formidable criminal ties in Canada, Europe and South America. Vito, well-dressed and smiling, is in the middle of the back row in this high school photograph.

NEW YORK LOOKS NORTH: Joe Bonanno, who gave his name to the Bonanno Family (far left) took an early interest in Canada. Carmine Galante, his underboss, (top, middle) secured Montreal for the family, an interest later maintained by subsequent Bonanno bosses, including Philip Rastelli (top, right). Joe Bonanno's son, Bill, (below, second from left) met with Luigi Greco (below, far left) while in Canada with a group of New York gangsters for Vito's wedding in 1966, a visit ending in their arrest. The men are seen at their arraignment in a Montreal Court, below.

EVOLUTION

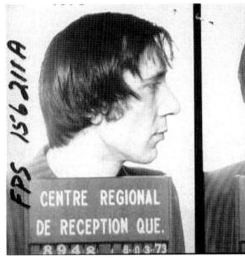

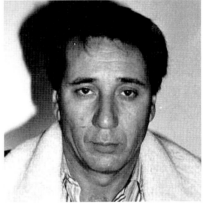

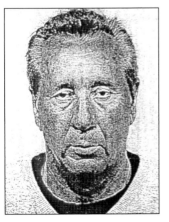

VITO'S STYLE and fashion has changed with the times, as seen in his police booking shots. From 1973 (top) when in jail for a botched arson; 1982 (middle left) when charged with hashish importation; 1986 (middle right) during another drug arrest; and finally, (left) in a photo taken in 2004 when he was arrested for drunk driving. This photo was used by U.S. authorities in their request for his extradition. Despite the arrests, Vito has not been convicted of any crimes since 1972—until he faced American justice 35 years later.

OPPOSITION IN MONTREAL came from two men, Vic Cotroni (top left), the old Godfather, and Paolo Violi (top right) his street boss. Violi's mob secrets were aired at a public crime commission and he was called to testify, as seen above. Despite his refusal to cooperate, he was killed soon after (below), securing Montreal for the Sixth Family.

"THE ZIPS"

THE BONO WEDDING in 1980 was a meet-and-greet for drug barons; when photographs from the wedding were seized by the FBI, it was an intelligence coup. (top) Vito, Joe LoPresti and Gerlando Sciascia pose at the Sixth Family's table (with police-adhered name tags stuck on the photos). Santo Giordano, a fellow "Zip," is seated at the far left of the photo in a light-gray suit. (middle) Cesare Bonventre and Baldo Amato (standing above Bonventre) at their table. Sal Catalano, the Zips' Brooklyn street boss (left), was among the hundreds of guests, not all of whom were involved in crime.

THE THREE CAPTAINS

Alphonse "Sonny
Red" **INDELICATO**

Philip "Philly
Lucky" **GIACONNE**

Dominick "Big Trinny"
TRINCHERA

A NEW YORK REBELLION was led by "Sonny Red" Indelicato (seen in the bottom picture, in briefs, walking with his son, Bruno) supported by "Philly Lucky" and "Big Trinny." Sonny Red's faction, seen at the Bono wedding (middle), was an early distributor of the Sixth Family's heroin in New York. Their relationship soured, however, and members of the Sixth Family then joined with Joe Massino in plotting to quell the rebellious group.

AFTERMATH

THE DAY AFTER the three captains were massacred in Brooklyn, the FBI caught Vito Rizzuto (middle, with garment bag and cigarette) leaving a motel in the Bronx with Joe Massino (far right), Gerlando Sciascia (left) and Giovanni Ligamarri, another Zip involved in their drug ring.

WEEKS LATER, Sonny Red's body was found in a vacant lot in Queens. He had been shot and dumped in a shallow grave. His slaying would not be solved for more than 20 years.

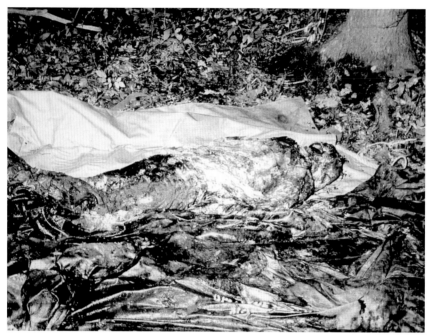

SONNY BLACK was found dead and rotting outdoors after his New York colleagues learned that Donnie Brasco, the supposed crook he was pushing for Mafia membership, was actually an undercover FBI agent. He refused the government's protection and embraced his underworld death sentence: "Hit me one more time; make it good," he said, after being shot and wounded by his mob pals. They complied.

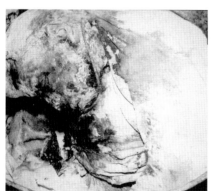
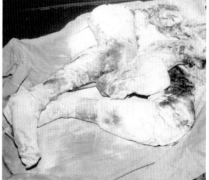

CESARE BONVENTRE fared no better, despite his standing as a leader among the Zips and a friend of the Sixth Family. In 1984, just as he was about to be arrested in the Pizza Connection case, he was also brutally killed by his colleagues. When police found his body in a New Jersey warehouse it was in two pieces, each half in a different metal drum.

DRUGS FLOWED into North America by plane, train, boat and truck, thanks to the Sixth Family. In 1987, police seized the trawler *Charlotte Louise* (above) on the east coast of Canada and eventually found a load of hashish hidden in its water tanks (left). Police suspect it was one of many.

TOO MUCH MONEY was a problem. To launder some of their cash, the Sixth Family turned to Joe Lagana, a Montreal lawyer, who used what he thought was a crooked money exchange service but was really an undercover RCMP operation. Lagana (above middle, in suit) and another lawyer (right) meet with undercover officers as they launder $91 million, some of which is seen on the exchange service's desk (left).

"GEORGE FROM CANADA"

GERLANDO SCIASCIA was the Sixth Family's man in New York, earning him the nickname "George from Canada" and attracting intense interest from federal agents (seen in FBI pictures above) until Bonanno boss Joe Massino felt threatened. It meant a messy end for Sciascia in 1999 (below), an attack Massino was desperate to hide from Vito and would lead to Massino's downfall.

VITO'S FATHER, Nicolò Rizzuto, was clearly unhappy during his arrest in Venezuela in 1988 (left) although he appears far happier a few years later, below. At bottom, as he is often seen on the streets of Montreal, well dressed and wearing a fedora. He is seen here walking with Paolo Renda, Rocco Sollecito, Pietro Triassi and Francesco Arcadi in 1999.

FECHA   12 02 88   CARACAS   A 10 12 286

FRIENDS AND FAMILY

Domenico **MANNO**

Paolo **RENDA**

Emanuele **RAGUSA**

Agostino **CUNTRERA**

Joseph **LOPRESTI** (middle) with Vito and Giuseppe **BONO** in 1980 (with police labels).

FRIENDS AND FAMILY

Leonardo **RIZZUTO**

Nick **RIZZUTO**

Francesco **DEL BALSO**

Lorenzo **GIORDANO**

Alfonso **CARUANA**

Giacinto **ARCURI**

Frank **CAMPOLI**

Gaetano **PANEPINTO**

Giuseppe **TORRE**

Photos by Adrian Humphreys

VITO AND HIS FAMILY lived a comfortable life in Montreal. Vito's mansion (bottom) features a three-port garage. In a row on the same short street are the homes of his father, Nicolò (top), and brother-in-law, Paolo Renda (middle).

RIZZUTO HEADQUARTERS is a café in Montreal that, despite its name, is decidedly unwelcoming to outsiders (top). For decades, police have watched Vito from afar: (middle left) with Antonio and Roberto Papalia, businessmen in Vancouver, in 2001; (middle right) at a boxing match in 1983; (bottom) on the phone while walking with Claude Sénécal (2) and Anthony Volpato (3) in 1991.

GROWING PAINS

SHOWING RESPECT in 2000 at the funeral of Gaetano Panepinto, one of Vito's men in Ontario. Walking down the church steps are (left to right in white shirts) Francesco Arcadi, Rocco Sollecito, Joe Renda and Paolo Renda. Panepinto's murder was one of several stumbles as the Sixth Family absorbed Ontario.

VITO RIZZUTO (seated, left) with Juan "Joe Bravo" Fernandez (seated, right) and Frank Campoli (standing, right). Fernandez was later arrested and Vito's ties to Campoli were revealed.

THE RATS OF NEW YORK

"Big Joey" **MASSINO**

"Good-Looking Sal" **VITALE**

Frank "Curly" **LINO**

Frank **COPPA**

"Goldie" **LEISENHEIMER**

"Shellackhead" **CANTARELLA**

UNDER SEIGE

Photo by Ryan Remiorz, Canadian Press

VITO RIZZUTO leans in close to listen to one of his lawyers, Jean Salois, after a court appearance in Montreal on February 6, 2004, following his arrest on U.S. charges that he was a gunman in the Brooklyn purge of three rival Mafia captains. After spending 16 nights in jail, Vito looked tired and weary from the ordeal, but it was far from over. He and his team of lawyers fought hard for more than two years to remain in Canada, taking his case to the Supreme Court of Canada—but to no avail. As soon as the Supreme Court declined to hear his case, Vito was removed from his cell and placed on board a waiting airplane. That afternoon he appeared for the first time in a Brooklyn court, where he pleaded not guilty and was whisked to a crowded detention center, where he again waited while his lawyers worked.

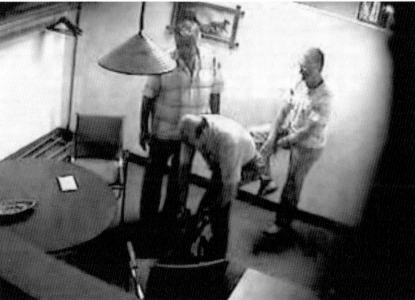

INNER SANCTUM: Many members of the Sixth Family apparently felt safe behind the closed doors of their semi-private Montreal headquarters, the Club Social Consenza. Little did they know that police were secretly watching and listening, such as (top) when Paolo Renda, Nick Rizzuto, Frank Arcadi, Rocco Sollecito and a visitor allegedly divided up money; and (below) when Nick allegedly stuffed money down his socks.

PROJECT COLISÉE

THE RCMP HAILED their efforts in 2006 against the Sixth Family as "one of the most important police operations in the history of Canada" that challenged "the pinnacles of organized crime." The four-year, joint operation led to charges of gangsterism, drug trafficking, illegal gambling, attempted murder, extortion, the corruption of public servants and the possession of illegal guns. Police say they also tracked the cross-border movement of drugs and money, including those pictured above. Code named Project Colisée, French for "Colosseum," the famous ampitheatre of Ancient Rome, the operation was hugely expensive.

POLICE ACTION came swift for men Canadian police allege were among the top bosses of the Rizzuto organization. While Vito was fighting charges in the United States, his father, Nicolò (top left), brother-in-law, Paolo Renda (top right), Frank Arcadi (bottom left) and Rocco Sollecito (bottom right) were arrested in Project Colisée. They were awaiting trial in Montreal as 2007 came to a close.

A NEW YORK MINUTE

Illustration by Elizabeth Williams

PLEAS OF POVERTY from Vito (second from right) as he was sentenced for his role in the gangland massacre of the three captains drew the ire of U.S. Judge Nicholas Garaufis (far left) in May 2007. Vito said he was broke and unable to pay a fine to accompany his 10 years of prison. Federal prosecutor Greg Andres (second from left, arms behind back) said the claim was absurd. "Like everyone in the mob, his relatives hold all the assets," he said in court. The judge agreed and ordered him to pay the maximum fine allowed under law: $250,000. In this courtroom sketch, Vito stands between his two U.S. lawyers, John Mitchell on his left and David Schoen on his right. It could well be Vito's last public appearance before his release, scheduled for October 6, 2012.

CHAPTER 29

LUGANO, SWITZERLAND, AUGUST 1994

Through a narrow opening in the facade of the cobblestoned water-front streets of Lugano, guests staying in just the right rooms of the Hotel Nassa Garni have a pleasing view of the cerulean waters of Lake Lugano. The city is nestled low on the south-facing shore and framed on both sides by the heavily wooded sub-alpine peaks of San Salvatore and Monte Brè. Beyond them are the snowcapped peaks of the Alps. That backdrop contrasts nicely with the bright terracotta rooftops of the city's old buildings, blessing Lugano with views tailor-made for postcards and travel brochures.

This scenery, however, can be better viewed from better hotels.

The Hotel Nassa Garni is a modest three-star facility that must have had one of its stars affixed merely for its location, being on Via Nassa, the heart of Lugano's shopping district and in the midst of a stretch sometimes called "the luxury mile." On this surprisingly narrow street, meticulously maintained stores offering the famous Italian fashion brands of Armani, Gucci and Versace vie for the wallets of passing visitors with equally tidy stores offering famous Swiss luxury watch brands such as Breguet, Patek Philippe and TAG Heuer. That blend of culture typifies Lugano. In the southernmost canton of Switzerland, lying just 14 miles north from its border with Italy, the largely Italian-speaking city boasts wide piazzas, tree-lined promenades and relaxed cafés, giving it a decidedly Mediterranean flavor and making it a popular destination for travelers from Italy.

It was the Hotel Nassa Garni where Libertina Rizzuto, the doting mother of Vito and faithful wife of Nick, checked in on August 31, 1994, after arriving alone on a connecting flight from Montreal. It was not for the shopping, however, that she had come to Lugano. Like most visitors, the stores and the views were mere trappings for Libertina; the real reason Lugano consistently attracted a wealthy clientele was that, despite a population of less than 50,000, it maintained more than 100 full-service banks. This gave the city one of the highest banks-per-capita rates in the world, more than twice that of Zurich.

On the evening of her arrival, after checking into the hotel, Libertina walked around the corner and across the Plaza Carlo Battaglini to the seven-story Hotel Excelsior. At the time, the Excelsior, a waterfront property with tasteful lakeside palms, was the finer of the two hotels, known for its spectacular view of the waterfront and its lounge's well-stocked bar.

In front of the Excelsior, as had been arranged, she met Luca Giammarella, a 47-year-old Montreal Realtor who lived directly across the road from Nick and Libertina on Antoine-Berthelet Avenue. The Rizzuto and Giammarella families had been close for more than a decade and Nick and Libertina showed that familiarity and affection by always calling Luca Giammarella by a nickname—"Nino." Giammarella arrived in Lugano the day before Libertina, having flown from Montreal to Milan and then taking the popular 90-minute train ride across the border, arriving at Lugano's train station, which overlooks the town from the west. Once in Switzerland's third-largest banking center, he checked into Room 415 of the Excelsior.

That evening, as the tourist season was waning, Libertina and Giammarella met to discuss the best way for them to retrieve the contents of an account in a private Swiss bank. After agreeing to meet outside the Credit Suisse Trust the next afternoon, they bade each other good night and Libertina returned to her room in the Nassa.

Shortly after 2 p.m. on September 1, 1994, Libertina met Giammarella again, this time in front of the modern offices of the Credit Suisse Trust, a branch of the century-old bank. It is a meandering one-and-one-half-mile walk or a short taxi ride to the bank from the Hotel Nassa; slightly less from the Excelsior.

"I met Nino in front of the Credit Suisse bank and I went inside. Nino had a small plastic handbag in which he would have put all the money we could withdraw in cash," Libertina said, shortly after her visit to the bank. "If the operation had worked, I would have deposited the money in another bank in Lugano."

The neat modern offices of the Credit Suisse Trust are just a few hundred yards from the waterfront and staffed by 16 employees skilled in the diverse languages and banking requirements of its international clientele. It is one of those storied Swiss banks, the fodder for many a movie and novel, one offering, as it advertises, "a full range of fiduciary and administrative services," specializing in "setting up and administering offshore companies, Anglo Saxon Trusts, Panama and Liechtenstein Foundations, holding bankable and non-bankable assets."

It was here that Giammarella maintained account No. 312413, opened on May 25, 1988. On the day of Libertina and Giammarella's visit to Lugano, the account maintained a balance of 820,000 Swiss francs, worth about US$718,000 at the time.

Inside the Credit Suisse branch, Giammarella—his blue bag in hand—said he wished to close the account and to have the balance turned over in cash, Swiss authorities were told. A banking representative asked him about the bag that he carried and he said he was going to stuff the cash in it and take it with him. The banker asked him to wait in a small room for another official.

"In the bank, Nino learned that the directors would not give him the money in cash, whereby he asked—at my suggestion—that they give him two checks in my name," Libertina later said.

"A few moments later," Giammarella added, "the police arrived and they accompanied me and Mrs. Rizzuto to the Lugano police station."

———

Libertina Rizzuto and Luca Giammarella were kept apart in police custody, after being escorted to the Lugano police headquarters, and it was a little before 4:30 p.m. when Inspector D. Bianchi entered one interrogation room, where he greeted Libertina, and Inspector Renato Pagani entered another to interview Giammarella. When the two officers later emerged from their questioning and compared their notes they found striking contradictions.

"A week ago, my husband and I decided that I should come to Lugano to withdraw all the money in an account under the name of our close friend Luca Giammarella—who is also a resident of Canada—but in fact is our property," Libertina said, in Italian, according to a transcript of her interrogation made by Swiss authorities. She explained that she had arranged to meet Giammarella at the bank and was in the midst of a simple financial transaction when they were arrested.

The money, she insisted, was the proceeds from the family's legitimate business holdings in Venezuela—primarily from powdered milk, cheese, industrial chicken production and furniture manufacturing. She and her husband, Nick, had asked for the money to be deposited in Giammarella's name about 10 years earlier for business reasons, she told police. They now wanted to clean up their financial affairs.

"He had to deposit the money because he wanted to declare it in Canada," she said. "I came to Lugano to withdraw our money from Giammarella's account, leave it here [in another bank] and inform the Canadian government that it was here, to pay the taxes, on the day my husband was to receive his Canadian residency." Her husband could not come to do the transfer himself, she said, because he was ill and unable to travel.

"Why did your husband send you, a senior, to Lugano and not your son or daughter?" Inspector Bianchi asked, a suggestion that seemed to insult Libertina, who was a fit and capable 67-year-old matriarch.

"Because I came," she said bluntly.

"But why this sudden trip after leaving this important matter for years and years in the hands of a third person, an outsider?" the officer asked.

"We just decided to. And also because on October 27, 1994, my husband will undergo another operation," she answered, telling officials that Nick was in Montreal awaiting surgery but that he still maintained his primary residence in Venezuela. He was in the process of again obtaining permanent resident status in Canada after his lengthy stay in South America, she said, although she appears to have made no mention of his recent incarceration there.

"What does this matter now?" she asked. "I just want to point out that I was with Nino at the Credit Suisse bank making a legal transaction."

Her version of events was strikingly different in almost every detail from what Giammarella was, at that moment, telling Inspector Pagani in a neighboring room. During his questioning, Giammarella said he was not at the bank with Libertina, that he did not know she was in Switzerland and that he had in fact no plans to withdraw any money from his account but was merely there to ask for some credit information from a banking official named Battista Petrini.

"I was alone. They had me wait for Mr. Petrini in a small room. Then they asked me to move to another room, and that's when I ran into Mrs. Libertina Rizzuto, a woman I've known for many years as a neighbor in Montreal. I had no idea she was there," he said.

"The money in the account is yours?" Inspector Pagani asked.

"Yes, it's my money," Giammarella insisted.

"Does Mrs. Rizzuto factor into the information you were seeking at the Credit Suisse bank?" the officer asked.

"No. As I said earlier, I met her by chance in a room at the bank. I didn't even know she was there. As I said, I'm staying at the Excelsior. As for Mrs. Rizzuto, I don't know if she is passing through Lugano or if she is staying at a hotel." Again he was asked if the money was his.

"Again, the money, which I believe to be about 500,000 Swiss francs, is mine, and Mrs. Rizzuto was not with me. I only met her by chance." Giammarella also denied telling bank officials that he had brought the empty blue handbag with him for carrying the money he was there to withdraw. Police interrupted their interrogation of Giammarella for an hour while officers searched his hotel room at the Excelsior. After the search, Giammarella was allowed to collect his personal belongings, pay his hotel bill and return to police custody, where the questions became even more uncomfortable.

In Giammarella's room, police had found two notes. The first read: "Poplare—Flavia Alberti MICA 23910 tel 587111 via Vigezzi N.1."

"It's the Banque Populaire Suisse—I have some interests in that place. I'd rather not get into specifics," Giammarella explained, naming another bank branch in Lugano.

"On another note found in your possession are the words 'Signor Muller B. di Roma Piazza S. Carlo,'" Inspector Pagani said.

"That's the Banca di Roma of Lugano. I have contacts at that bank, too, that I'd rather not go into here," Giammarella countered.

While he was not forthcoming about these other banking "contacts" and "interests," as he called them, further investigation by Swiss authorities found that account No. 23910, assigned the code name "MICA" at the Banque Populaire Suisse, was held in Giammarella's name. After he transferred Cdn$500,000 and 1,100,000 Swiss francs to personal and business accounts controlled by Joe Lagana, a Montreal lawyer who was a close confidant and relative of Vito Rizzuto's, the account retained a balance that day of Cdn$225,000. Similarly, account No. 61002, assigned the code name "ASPARAGINA" at the Banco di Roma, was also in Giammarella's name and contained Cdn$1 million and another 1,100,000 Swiss francs, funds that were then blocked by Swiss authorities. All three accounts were opened over two days, on May 24 to 25, 1988.

Large as they were, these figures were just the tip of the iceberg of what was at play in Lugano that day. There were plenty of clues for the

Swiss investigators. Clearly, one of the problems of juggling so much money in so many accounts is keeping track of the banking information. Few have the head for so many numbers and so, time and again, authorities found people in incriminating circumstances carrying slips of paper that referred to Lugano bank accounts that the Swiss linked to the Rizzutos. Along with the notes Giammarella had in his hotel room investigators also seized from Libertina her datebook and personal address book, which she was carrying with her when she was taken into custody. Inside, investigators found similar cryptic references to other bank accounts and notations about certain people, Beniamino Zappia and Joe Lagana among them.

When Swiss authorities started sifting through the banking records of the names they now had, they found at least 14 accounts in Lugano alone that could easily be linked to the Rizzutos.

"During the investigation, we discovered another series of Lugano bank accounts belonging to [or] having belonged directly to the Rizzuto family or to other individuals related to the family, notably Giuseppe LoPresti, who died under circumstances that remain unknown, [and] Beniamino Zappia," as well as other relatives by blood and by marriage of the Rizzutos, says a report by Swiss police on the money trail.

"The Rizzutos have, in the majority of the cases, a proxy on these accounts," the report concludes.

Meanwhile, Libertina was growing impatient. She wanted to know why police were taking such an interest in her visit to Lugano.

"Because you didn't simply open an account at the Credit Suisse bank and have the money transferred internally," Inspector Bianchi told her, referring to the more acceptable form of moving such large sums of money around. It looked to police like someone was trying to hide the source of the money or erase any paper trail linking its withdrawal to its future deposit.

Although walking in with a blue handbag ready to take 820,000 Swiss francs out of a bank did amount to suspicious activity—even in Switzerland—it was not the real reason why Giammarella's request to withdraw the assets in his account was declined and police were so quickly and quietly called. He and Libertina did not know it, but the day before they arrived at the Credit Suisse branch—just as Libertina was arriving in Lugano, in fact—the accounts were being frozen on the order of Switzerland's Public Minister, at the request of the Office of the Federal Police. That request, in turn, had come from Canada.

Neither was this the first time the Rizzutos had come to the attention of Swiss authorities. A separate investigation had already been launched by Carla Del Ponte, the chain-smoking public prosecutor from Lugano, who became the country's attorney-general and, more recently, made headlines as the controversial war crimes prosecutor at The Hague's International Criminal Tribunal for the Former Yugoslavia, where she led the prosecution against Slobodan Milosevic, the former Yugoslav leader who died in March 2006. Before taking on suspected war criminals, Del Ponte earned the hatred of the Sicilian Mafia in the late 1980s when she worked with Giovanni Falcone to uncover the transit through Switzerland's banks of cash proceeds from the huge Pizza Connection drug ring. For her efforts, the Mafia not only referred to her spitefully as *la puttana*—"the whore"—but also, in 1988, placed a half ton of explosives in the foundation of her home, which was discovered before its detonation.

Undeterred, Del Ponte crusaded against the infamous secrecy of the Swiss banking establishment, which earned her more hatred, but also brought eventual banking reform—the very changes that allowed authorities to track the money trail of the Rizzutos and block the accounts in Lugano that Libertina and Giammarella were trying to gain access to when they were arrested.

It was in 1990, as part of Del Ponte's sweeping probe of the massive laundering of drug money by international criminals and the revelations over the movement of cash from the Pizza Connection case, that the prosecutor opened a secret file on the Rizzutos. During her probe she was told by Judge Falcone that in 1986 a Quebec man named Christian Deschênes had been arrested after police seized two truckloads of tightly packed hashish. The hashish, worth an estimated $100 million, had been offloaded from a fishing vessel on the remote shores of Cape Breton, on Canada's eastern seaboard. It was, police believed, yet another load arriving under the auspices of the Sixth Family. When arrested, Deschênes was carrying a slip of paper on which was written information about a Lugano bank account. That account—No. 650.068, held in the name of Beniamino Zappia at the Union des Banques Suisses—was the same one Libertina had written in her datebook, Swiss authorities say.

A fascinating window was opened on the immense financial end of the Sixth Family empire. The tracing of the accounts by the Swiss authorities seems to have been limited to those held in Lugano with a Rizzuto family member directly listed as the account holder or with authorized access to it, plus those accounts easily found to have money moved into accounts controlled by Joe Lagana. As with any facet of the Sixth Family, it formed a complicated tangle.

The Swiss probe through this financial web, however, started simply enough when a Montreal lawyer paid a visit to a more-than-respectable-looking foreign currency exchange company on one of the busiest corners in Montreal's business district.

MONTREAL, EARLY SEPTEMBER 1990

The convenience of the new foreign currency exchange counter must have seemed a godsend for Joe Lagana when the almost chic-looking retail space opened its doors at the corner of Peel Street and de Maisonneuve Boulevard West in downtown Montreal. The Centre International Monétaire de Montréal (Montreal International Currency Center) was directly across the street from Lagana's seventh-floor law office. The street-level facility was clean, neat and well staffed. It had obvious security features, including bulletproof windows, and touches of class, such as polished hardwood paneling, brand-new office furniture and reliable money-counting machines.

Far more important to Lagana and two other lawyers employed at his firm, however, was that the facility was willing to accept large piles of small, crumpled bills that were brought in and dumped out of sacks, hockey equipment bags, shoe boxes and shopping bags and, in return, send the client off with easily bankable checks, large denomination U.S. banknotes and successful off-shore wire transfer receipts—all without awkward questions or apparent reports to the authorities. It was just what Lagana was looking for, as it is often difficult to get rid of all the cash generated from large drug sales.

The Centre International Monétaire had been incorporated on August 17, 1990, with fictitious names listed as its management. There were five employees who staffed the counter and handled the cash. They had each been trained by the staff of a prominent Canadian bank just weeks before. The exchange office was then opened to the public early in September. Over the next four years, from that unannounced and unadvertised start, the company would process Cdn$141.5 million in known and suspected drug money from clients walking in off the street. Of that amount, $91 million would come from Lagana and his associates, most of it brought into the exchange office by him directly or by Richard Judd and Vincenzo Vecchio, two other lawyers who worked in Lagana's law firm. Lagana's interest, however, started cautiously. He watched the exchange house for almost a year before actually sending any money to it, and even then his first transaction was a small one, just $10,000, as a test.

Over time, Lagana, who was married to another lawyer, became increasingly comfortable with his new business associates at the Centre International Monétaire. Over the course of his visits, he would find that the staff not only did not ask embarrassing questions about where the money came from, but were perfectly accepting of the fact that it was the proceeds from large-scale cocaine deals. The men he worked with at the exchange counter would later, in fact, step in and directly help, not only moving the money, but shipping the actual cocaine.

What went unnoticed during these transactions, however, were some special features of the Centre Internationale Monétaire that would have caused Lagana, and almost all of its customers, considerable concern: hidden video cameras and audio recording equipment had been strategically placed to capture a clear record of the transactions. Even more surprising was the fact that the exchange office was staffed entirely by undercover officers with the RCMP. The Centre Internationale Monétaire, it would later be revealed, was the centerpiece of Operation 90-26C, a police "reverse sting" operation codenamed "Operation Contract."

It was an innovative scheme designed to uncover the flow of drug money. The idea stemmed from the simple fact that there were just far too many foreign currency exchange facilities in Montreal for all of them to be earning a legal living from servicing tourists and legitimate businessmen. Police knew some of these facilities were aiding drug traffickers by cleaning and moving their dirty money. What they did not know was how immensely popular their own undercover financial services would become once word of it spread through the underworld.

"The money started rolling in. Big hockey bags of cash, bundles of money, some counted, some not counted. We were overwhelmed. We were counting millions every day," said Michel Michaud, who worked undercover at the exchange for three years, convincing drug traffickers and money launderers he was a crooked businessman rather than a dedicated RCMP constable. "We usually worked at the exchange counter from nine-to-five. Then we started going out for dinner with the bad guys. Lagana would always pick the restaurant. At Milos, on Parc Avenue, I don't know how many bottles of wine we had but we ended up paying the bill of over $800. Sometimes we spent lots of money in night clubs with them. When we got home we had hours of notes and reports to write. Each meeting and telephone conversation with a bad guy had to be written up ASAP—we could not fall behind in our notes; our notes were going to be crucial," he said.

Within its four years of operation, the facility would launder drug money on behalf of 25 criminal organizations. Its services were in such demand, however, that the few officers assigned to the investigation were soon in over their heads. Police were understaffed, underfunded and without adequate technical equipment to follow up on the dizzying number of new contacts being made from underworld clients walking in off the street, and so most customers were walking out of the office after their transactions without triggering any further police investigation.

On September 24, 1992, for example, a man entered the Internationale Monétaire at 11:23 a.m. carrying with him $959,720 in Canadian banknotes. After the bills fanned through the money-counting machines, he was issued 16 bank drafts made out to five different names for that amount in the equivalent value of U.S. dollars, minus the company's processing fee. When the man left, there was no officer available to follow and identify him. It was all too much for at least one officer. Shortly after that mysterious figure left the office with his underworld financial needs having just been satisfied by police agents, Constable Mike Cowley, an RCMP investigator working on the case, wrote a confidential internal memo to his supervisors complaining of the lack of attention being given the important operation: "Without the necessary resources, it seems like our undercover officers are simply offering a money laundering service for drug traffickers," he wrote on October 16, 1992. His concern seemed justified.

What the investigators did know, however, was that the money they were processing was moving quickly around the globe. The bank drafts they issued and U.S. banknotes they were releasing seemed to be turning up everywhere. A man arrested in Montgomery, Alabama, was found carrying 110 kilograms of cocaine, as well as cash that had been issued by the International Monétaire. Other marked bills were found on drug suspects in Toronto and Vancouver. Bank drafts issued by the company were later deposited into banks in the Bahamas, Panama, Netherlands, Belgium, Florida, New York and Miami. To make the money easier to trace, the officers started convincing as many customers as they could to take checks rather than cash. Most times the crooks did not care in whose name the checks were made out to—as long as it was not their own. The investigators started writing huge checks out in the names of cartoon characters, such as Fred Flintstone and hockey greats, including Bobbie Orr, Larry Robinson and Frank Mahovlich. Even politicians were invoked, although more cautiously: the names "Pierre Mulroney" and "Brian Trudeau" found their way onto checks.

Of the 25 criminal organizations that did business at the exchange office, the RCMP mustered the resources to properly investigate only two of them. Unfortunately for Joe Lagana, he was the frontman for one of them. As the largest volume mover of the clandestine cash, Lagana was an obvious target. His open candor with the men running the exchange did not help him duck scrutiny; the fact that he was a lawyer and that some officers believed he was a relative of Vito Rizzuto's—a contention one of Vito's longtime lawyers disputes—might well have been the clincher.

After watching Lagana pass large loads of cash across their counter, police finally settled in, on June 26, 1993, to watch and listen to Lagana interact with his associates. One man he repeatedly spoke to was Vito Rizzuto. Lagana soon emerged in investigators' eyes as the intermediary between Vito and other associates. Over secretly installed wiretaps, police heard numerous conversations between the two discussing what were clearly financial matters, but the men spoke in a mutually understood code that made it "impossible to determine their exact nature," a police report notes. In each case, police say, Vito spoke in "an amicable and familiar tone." The two also met in person. On January 18, 1994, during police surveillance, officers watched Vito pull up in a Jeep Cherokee in front of a 12-story Peel Street office building, one packed with financial and travel companies. He then waited until Lagana emerged from the building and hopped into the Jeep. On February 4, 1994, police watched Vito meet at the same building with Lagana and Luis Cantieri, an experienced drug importer who was still on parole for a 1986 narcotics conviction. Vito and Cantieri also met without Lagana. Months earlier, on September 23, 1993, police watched Vito and Cantieri eat together at Montreal's Latini restaurant.

Despite the chronic shortage of investigative resources, the officers made some solid progress. They had gained the trust of several of their regular underworld clients who were connected to the Rizzutos and would socialize with them, discussing mob gossip and criminal plans. One client, Dominico Tozzi, was a 52-year-old jetsetting businessman who was ostensibly involved in an import-export business and as a nightclub owner. He was also a mob associate of the Rizzutos, who rented an office across from the exchange house, one floor above Lagana's law office, and dabbled in both cocaine conspiracies and high-value money laundering. Tozzi bragged to an undercover officer working at the exchange company about his contacts in law enforcement, both the Montreal city police and the Montreal office of the federal RCMP. His contacts were not as plugged-in as Tozzi might have hoped.

On March 29, 1993, one of the undercover RCMP officers working at the covert currency exchange counter met with Tozzi at a downtown Montreal restaurant. Tozzi, of course, took the man to be an underworld colleague who had worked for almost three years in moving the organization's drug money through the exchange.

Over lunch, Tozzi, a business associate of Joe Lagana's, spoke of their mutual interest—the movement of lots of dirty cash. Tozzi was in need of laundering services for about $2 million, he said. As the lunch stretched on and the wine flowed, Tozzi started talking more than he should have, according to police reports filed on the meetings. He said the "big boss" was Italian. The boss was the one who made the major decisions, he said. Going further, he confided that the boss's name was Vito Rizzuto.

Tozzi had, in fact, met with Vito just the day before, he boasted, and Vito was the one who was calling the shots on the $2 million he was looking to process at the currency exchange. Likely leaning in a little closer and lowering his voice, Tozzi then told the agent that the "big Italian boss" never directly got his hands dirty in such affairs. The boss refused to "touch anything," Tozzi said. The boss was very well known to police and could not risk being caught by them or else he would surely find himself in prison, Tozzi said. The investigators were thrilled, stoking their hopes that the Tozzi slip and their other efforts in the operation would make those words prophetic. This time, officers were certain, Vito would be nabbed.

The undercover officer later mentioned Tozzi's name to Lagana. Lagana said that if Tozzi were ever arrested and told police all he knew, half of the people in Montreal might end up in jail. Lagana then warned him to be careful what he said around Tozzi. The officer replied that Tozzi might find himself killed if he was so dangerous.

"I'm surprised it hasn't already happened," Lagana replied.

The interactions between the undercover officers and their new criminal customers went beyond such gossip. In 1994, they were approached with an additional business proposition. Could they help "take care" of a cocaine shipment from Colombia into the United States and Canada? The agents readily agreed. This was the chance they had been waiting for, to be able to conclusively connect the masses of cash to illegal drugs. As the plans for moving the drugs unfolded, they revealed the seamless way the Sixth Family worked with both Colombian cocaine cartels and members of the Hells Angels Motorcycle Club.

COAST OF COLOMBIA, AUGUST 17, 1994

An ocean-going freighter steered slowly south toward the warm coastal waters off the Colombian coast, not far from the city of Barranquilla, one of the four major industrial centers of Colombia and among South America's busiest ports. The ship had been secretly leased by RCMP officers working with agents from U.S. Customs and the Drug Enforcement Administration, and was being passed off as an underworld asset in the control of the supposedly crooked men behind the International Monétaire.

On August 17, 1994, as the ship slowed to a halt offshore, near the mouth of the Magdalena River, its covert police crew was met by Norman Rosenblum, a wealthy and enthusiastic businessman from Vancouver who, despite his expensive tastes for designer clothes and high-end watches, was not above doing some of the heavy lifting himself. When the freighter arrived at the rendezvous point, Rosenblum shot from the Colombian beach and helped push aboard 14 bales of cocaine, weighing in at 558 kilograms. The freighter then headed north, stopping first in Miami, then making its way along Canada's eastern seaboard and down the St. Lawrence Seaway to Montreal.

Once it arrived at the Port of Montreal, the drugs were supposed to be transshipped to England. In London, two Quebec members of the Hells Angels waited to collect the load for distribution in Europe. But the drugs never made the journey across the Atlantic. Police removed the cocaine from the freighter in Montreal and held it as a key piece of evidence in their four-year-long money-laundering investigation, the needed proof that the cash coming into the Centre International Monétaire was, in fact, drug money.

With the seizure, police could finally start to wrap up their frantic money-laundering operation. Working with federal prosecutors, officers started sorting out who should—and could—be arrested. Police were anxious to place Vito Rizzuto under arrest for what investigators saw as his obvious role in the background of so many of the key money and drugs players. Government lawyers were not so sure.

Debate ensued while the investigation was ending.

MONTREAL, AUGUST 30, 1994

At 6 a.m. on August 30, 1994, police officers who had literally synchronized their watches started moving in on more than 40 suspects in coordinated raids on homes, businesses and financial institutions across Montreal and in other Canadian cities, including Quebec City, Trois-Rivières and Vancouver. About 480 officers from federal, provincial and city police forces participated in the sweep. One of the accused lawyers, Vincenzo Vecchio, was arrested as he dropped his six-year-old son off for his first day of school.

"It was all done very discreetly," his wife said. "My children didn't know what was happening. I told them he was just going off somewhere with a client." The two Hells Angels who were waiting patiently in London for the cocaine to arrive were arrested by British police.

By mid-morning, the RCMP's Quebec headquarters in Westmount was flush with accused gangsters, drug dealers, illicit money movers and excited police officers. To handle the crowd, the gymnasium was partitioned into 40 temporary holding areas where suspects were questioned and processed separately.

The arrests cut close to the bone for the Sixth Family. Emanuele Ragusa, who was described as "the banker" for the network, was scooped up by police, as was one of the family's most trusted drug contractors, Sammy Nicolucci. Lagana, Vito's lawyer and a relative, and two other lawyers in Lagana's law firm were also arrested. Vincenzo "Jimmy" DiMaulo, a longtime friend of Vito's, who, a dozen times a year or more, would be included in Vito's foursome in a round of golf, was among those taken to RCMP headquarters. Rosenblum, who was described as the network's "transportation manager," was picked up in Vancouver. Cantieri and Tozzi were also caught in the dragnet.

Nowhere among the downcast throng, however, was Vito Rizzuto.

At the insistence of federal prosecutors who had evaluated the extensive evidence gathered by investigators—including 3,500 recorded conversations and videotaped meetings—Vito could not be charged. Police had to satisfy themselves with naming Vito as an unindicted co-conspirator, offering him bad publicity rather than a judicial fight. He would not be arrested, nor would he face the courts. While search warrants and affidavits filed in the case openly refer to the "Vito Rizzuto group," his name was glaringly absent from the list of those arrested or wanted for arrest. Vito's name was also included on the search warrant authorizing officers to enter Joe Lagana's law office; Vito was one of 26 people and 34 companies whose records could be seized if any were found there. All were alleged to have been involved in the Rizzuto organization's drugs and dirty money enterprise.

"We know that he is part of the conspiracy but, because of legal principles, we cannot file this evidence against Mr. Rizzuto," prosecutor Danielle Côté said at the time. Once again, Vito walked away. Police tried to mask their disappointment.

"We've seized their dope and we've frozen their homes and bank accounts. We left them 25 cents for a phone call. It's going to hurt them a lot," said Sergeant Claude Lessard, a chipper RCMP spokesman, when announcing the sweeping arrests. He should have known better.

Vito and his associates were left with far more than 25 cents.

BERN, SWITZERLAND, AUGUST 31, 1994

There was little diplomatic fanfare when a representative of Canada's embassy in Switzerland arrived at the Federal Police headquarters in Bern on the morning after the Montreal arrests. He was there on urgent business and in need of their help. Presenting official requests received from the RCMP, the ambassador was seeking "urgent judicial assistance" from Swiss authorities.

The undercover police operation against the Rizzuto organization in Canada had apprehended some of the men, but did little to capture the money. The RCMP was anxious to recover the money it had laundered for the traffickers. The ambassador presented the Swiss Federal Police with the names of those who were charged with moving the drug money through the RCMP's currency exchange, with a request that their banking activities in Switzerland be examined and accounts frozen. The Swiss quickly focused on Joe Lagana's role. A number of accounts that had either sent or received transfers from Lagana's numerous business or personal accounts were blocked from further activity with a notification that, should anyone try to gain access to the funds, police were to be called immediately. Three of those accounts were listed in the name of Luca Giammarella. One was at the Credit Suisse Trust in Lugano.

Wasting no time, after the covert money-laundering sting in Montreal had been revealed, Libertina Rizzuto and Giammarella headed to their banks in Lugano. They arrived one day too late. Police in Switzerland were already sifting through the accounts and banking records, tracking the international movement of huge amounts of money in several foreign currencies through personal and corporate accounts. The Credit Suisse Trust branch had already received the government order of August 31 and immediately informed the Public Minister of the presence of Libertina and Giammarella. This is what led to their arrest.

A curious pattern of account openings and closings was emerging for Swiss investigators, experienced in tracking money; they noted three distinct "phases" in which Rizzuto money was cycled every few years through a fresh set of bank accounts.

"It can be said that the moving from one phase to another was done in order to create difficulties for any future investigations," the Swiss authorities concluded.

Luca Giammarella can be excused for having to write down the names and addresses of the banks in Lugano in which he nominally held title to huge amounts of cash, for there is little evidence to suggest he had much to do with them between the time he opened them in late May 1988 and the time he apparently came with Libertina Rizzuto to drain them, six years later.

On May 24, 1988, Giammarella visited the Banque Populaire Suisse, a financial institution that holds art exhibitions as part of its cultural contribution to the city, and opened the "MICA" account, the first of what would be three Swiss bank accounts in his name later traced by authorities. That same day he visited the Banca di Roma, a Lugano branch of a Rome-based commercial bank, to open a second, the "ASPARAGINA" account. The next day, he was off to the Credit

Suisse to open the third account, the one he was trying to get into in 1994 when arrested. All told, into these three accounts over those two days, he had deposited 4,646,100 Swiss francs, according to Swiss authorities. That was worth about US$3 million at the time.

Giammarella was not alone in Lugano on that visit, and if he was inexperienced in setting up Swiss accounts, there was another Rizzuto associate in the city who had plenty of experience in such matters. According to the registration of a customs notice at the Chiasso border station on the Italian–Swiss frontier, where the busy rail lines stretching from Lugano to Milan are monitored, Beniamino Zappia also crossed into Switzerland on May 24. Swiss financial records show that Zappia was also conducting banking business in Lugano on the same day Giammarella was opening his accounts. Zappia personally made a withdrawal from an account at the Banca Privata Rothschild in Lugano—account No. 603.154, assigned the code name "SEBUCAN"—in which he shared signing authority with Paolo Renda, Vito's brother-in-law. The Zappia/Renda "SEBUCAN" account had been bloated, just two months before, by a series of five consecutively numbered high-value checks, each drawn from the same Montreal bank.

That Zappia and Giammarella both found themselves in Lugano at the same time was no more a coincidence than Giammarella and Libertina's simultaneous visits years later, authorities believe. Zappia was playing a key role in moving the Rizzutos' riches.

What Swiss police believed Zappia and Giammarella were up to that May was the transferring of funds from the second phase of the Rizzutos' complicated banking cycle, into the third phase.

The first phase of the money's run in Switzerland had typically seen members of the Rizzuto family directly opening accounts in their own names with multiple family members having signing authority over them. There were four accounts, for instance, each in a different Lugano bank, opened between October 30, 1980, and August 25, 1981, in the name of Libertina Rizzuto, or jointly in the name of Libertina and Nick. On all four accounts, most of the immediate family had signing authority, granting each of them access to the cash. Two of the accounts granted signing authority to both Nick's son and daughter—Vito Rizzuto and Maria Renda—as well as their respective spouses, Giovanna Cammalleri and Paolo Renda. Two other accounts dropped Paolo Renda from the list. During this phase, Joe LoPresti also opened a Swiss account, with signing authority granted to LoPresti's wife, Rosa, and to Libertina Rizzuto. Another account was listed strictly in Beniamino Zappia's name—the "PRETORIA" account—from which more than US$55,000 was transferred to LoPresti's "BOUCHERVILLE" account.

This first phase of the money's run ended when most of these accounts were closed, one by one, in May, June and July of 1985. Only one of the joint Rizzuto accounts, No. O-5722.089, given the code name "MARACAI" at the Société de Banque Suisse, to which all of the immediate family members had authorized access, remained open with a modest balance. It was, in fact, the smallest of the accounts when authorities froze the Cdn$109,000 and US$820 found in it.

By the summer of 1985, the Rizzutos were moving their cash holdings away from accounts listed in their own names, signaling the start of phase two of the money shuffle, according to the Swiss.

These accounts were entrusted to extended family members—and to Beniamino Zappia, whom police found had spent his youth in Cattolica Eraclea, the Rizzuto clan's hometown in Sicily.

The account listed in one family member's name was still open at the time of the 1994 investigation and authorities froze the balance of approximately 2 million Swiss francs.

Three other phase-two accounts, each opened at a different Lugano bank, were in the name of Beniamino Zappia. One of them retained Nick Rizzuto as an authorized signing officer; another, Paolo Renda; and on a third, a Giorgio Bissi was listed, the Swiss authorities say. These accounts were kept flush with transfers from the Fédération des Caisses Populaires Desjardins, a financial institution in Montreal that maintains two branches a few blocks apart on either side of the Club Social Consenza, the Rizzutos' Montreal headquarters. Between December 11, 1986, and March 29, 1988, more than 5,412,000 Swiss francs, US$1,306,715 and Cdn$500,000 flowed from the Montreal Caisses Populaires into these three accounts.

The money's third phase was launched when Giammarella went in May 1988 to open his accounts, according to the Swiss. Authorities believed that Zappia was secretly arranging things behind the scenes in Switzerland on behalf of the Rizzutos. The Swiss prosecutor's office noted that the total number of Swiss francs sent to Zappia's accounts from Montreal was just slightly more than the amount Giammarella deposited when opening the three accounts—4,646,100 Swiss francs.

"It is suspected that the funds deposited by Giammarella come from the transfers in Switzerland into the bank accounts of Beniamino Zappia, from [the] Canadian bank," a Swiss police report says.

The substantial balance in two of Giammarella's accounts was then slowly siphoned off through repeated transfers into accounts connected to Joe Lagana, the Montreal lawyer who was handling the Rizzuto organization's drug money in Canada. On December 23, 1992, Cdn$500,000 was moved into account No. 001124870, code named "PINO" at the Banque Cantrade in Lausanne, Switzerland, which was in Lagana's name. The following year, on November 29, 1993, 500,000 Swiss francs were transferred to the same account. On April 28, 1994, another 600,000 Swiss francs were sent to a Banque Cantrade business account in the name of Biolight S.A., a firm that belonged to Lagana. Similarly, on February 20, 1992, 500,000 Swiss francs were moved from the Credit Suisse to an account at the Banca Commerciale Italiana in Geneva. The holder of this account was Shield Enterprises, S.A., a company the Swiss said "seemingly belonged" to Lagana.

"It is important to emphasize the transfers from Giammarella's accounts to Giuseppe [Joe] Lagana's accounts, for a total of approximately 2,500,000 Swiss francs," a report by the Swiss prosecutor's office says. "According to the arguments presented by Mrs. Rizzuto's legal counsel, Lagana would have immediately returned most of this amount to the Rizzutos. They have, therefore, admitted to a business relationship between the Rizzutos and Lagana." With Lagana now a charged and soon-to-be-convicted launderer of drug money in Canada, that was a precarious relationship to have.

When Libertina and Giammarella were stopped at the Credit Suisse, apparently trying to drain the account, Swiss police believe it was another move in the Sixth Family's money dance.

"It seems clear that at the moment of their arrest, Mrs. Libertina Rizzuto intended to open a fourth phase, after the closing of the Giammarella accounts," the Swiss authorities concluded.

———

Switzerland and its neighbor to the east, the tiny principality of Liechtenstein, were awash in Sixth Family money. Switzerland was the early global leader in the secret money field, having offered financial services to European aristocrats for centuries. Bank secrecy was a

Swiss law in the 1930s, making it an offense to disclose any information about an account, even to the government. The two nations, which have a customs and monetary union, expanded their international reputation as havens for cash and other assets during the Second World War when both remained neutral. Postwar, they built on that trade by offering easy business incorporation, low taxes and limited banking regulatory oversight. It spawned outstanding growth in the financial sector, but brought condemnation from the international community for facilitating massive laundering of criminal proceeds. The crackdown in Switzerland that had been urged on by Carla Del Ponte was later matched in Liechtenstein, which implemented new anti-money-laundering legislation and, more recently, concluded a Mutual Legal Assistance Treaty with the United States. The changes mean that those who wish to hide vast capital must be more imaginative and engage in far greater subterfuge—or avoid the Old World financial centers altogether, seeking out fringe nations who seek to replicate the unlikely economic prosperity of Liechtenstein, which has wealth beyond anything that could be expected from a doubly landlocked nation of just 62 square miles with little in the way of natural resources.

From the 1970s through to the late 1990s, however, the two European states were Sixth Family favorites. Alfonso Caruana had been stopped by Swiss Customs officials in November 1978 and fined for a currency violation relating to the US$600,000 he was carrying. The Caruana–Cuntreras, who were establishing a heroin and cocaine pipeline in Europe, based largely in Germany and England, were also building a money pipeline to Switzerland and Liechtenstein as a corollary enterprise to handle the profits. The arrangements were frequently handled by Giuseppe Cuffaro, the mafioso who emigrated to Montreal just before the Rizzutos and forged an early alliance between their clans.

Like their friends, the Rizzutos, the Caruana–Cuntrera clan used extended family members, hastily arranged businesses and corporate accounts to shuffle their money between North America, Europe and South America. In 1996, as Alfonso Caruana was being investigated by police in several countries, he continued to use an effective combination of Canadian-based companies and U.S.–based banks to get his drug money where he needed it.

"Information recently has surfaced which indicates that several millions of dollars originating from cocaine trafficking which [Alfonso] Caruana is a part of, has been forwarded to the City Bank of New

York," says a secured diplomatic transmission, sent in April 1996 from the RCMP's liaison officer at Canada's embassy in Rome, to police in Toronto, who were probing Caruana's activities. The New York account was in the name of Bedford House International Ltd., with an address in Etobicoke, a district in the west end of Toronto. Similarly, money transfers linked to Caruana's cocaine sales in Italy were tracked by Italian and Dutch authorities through a Holland-based company called Marshall Compton, S.A., to an account at the Schweizerische Bankverein in Zurich, held by Experta Trustee Comp. Ltd., according to another diplomatic note from that year. A Swiss investigation showed Experta Trustee to be a firm operating a Zurich bank account on behalf of other companies, including Hifalia Inc., formed in Montreal.

The Swiss were keenly aware of the possible implications of the types of suspicious financial activities they found occurring under the Rizzuto name: the large cash transactions; the seemingly dubious explanations of the funds' origins; the involvement of known drug traffickers such as Joe LoPresti and Christian Deschênes; the involvement of accused money launderers such as Joe Lagana; connections between the primary account holders and confirmed drug seizures; the allegations in several countries of the Mafia interests and drug-trafficking role of the Rizzutos; their close association with the Caruana–Cuntrera and the Mafia clans investigated in the Pizza Connection case. There was an inescapable suspicion for Swiss authorities that the bank balances they were tracking represented the proceeds of crime, likely from international drug trafficking. And now they had a principal holder of the original phase-one accounts—Libertina Rizzuto—in their custody. They were as intent on seizing the Rizzuto assets as the Montreal officers running the currency exchange had been on laying charges against Libertina's son.

"According to the information provided by the Italian authorities to Mrs. Del Ponte, Guiseppe (Joe) LoPresti was connected to organized crime in the United States and in Canada, notably in regards to individuals such as Nick Rizzuto, husband of Libertina Rizzuto, and Gerlando Sciascia, all of which come from Cattolica Eraclea in Sicily," notes a Swiss government report on the Rizzuto financial dealings. "It is also obvious that the owners of these funds did everything possible to prevent being discovered (accounts in the names of third parties, periodic changes of account) and to cover the trace of the money (deposits and withdrawals in cash)," the report says.

There was one crucial piece of the puzzle missing before the Swiss could thunder down on the jailed Rizzuto matriarch—evidence of drugs. Or, for that matter, evidence of any other crime.

"As far as the charge of participating or supporting organized crime, concrete evidence would have to be found proving that the Rizzuto family makes up a criminal organization or belongs to a criminal organization," the Swiss prosecutor's office concluded. "It obviously remains to be proven that the funds in question, particularly those deposited into the three bank accounts held by Luca Giammarella, are the result of illicit activities, notably narcotics trafficking."

Because it was money, not drugs, that investigators found moving freely through Switzerland, evidence of a narcotics conspiracy would have to come from somewhere else. The Swiss authorities turned to Canada. Just as Canada had requested judicial assistance from the Swiss, leading to Libertina's arrest in Lugano, the Swiss authorities formally issued their own "request for urgent judicial assistance" to Canadian officials, seeking their help in finishing the job that the undercover RCMP officers at the currency exchange office had started.

On December 16, 1994, with Libertina and Giammarella still in custody, Fabrizio Eggenschwiler, the assigned public prosecutor with the Public Ministry of the canton of Tessin in Switzerland, asked the Canadian government to tell them what they could about the Rizzutos. Eggenschwiler sought "anything that would demonstrate that the members of the Rizzuto family are a criminal organization or belong to such an organization," as well as evidence of the criminal origin of the money. Details of the evidence gathered by investigators against Joe Lagana, particularly information on "all the possible connections between this procedure and the Rizzuto family," would also be helpful.

"The assigned public prosecutor emphasizes the urgent nature of this request due to the present custody of Libertina Rizzuto and Luca Giammarella," Eggenschwiler concluded. The Rizzutos once again turned to Jean Salois. His mandate was to gain the pair's freedom. He was unimpressed with the materials the RCMP were feeding to the Swiss.

"Canadian authorities were impressed upon to transmit everything that concerned the Rizzutos in their files, as well as various documents and various information that were often equivocal, based on the opinions or the conclusions of the police or simply suspicions that would never be admissible in a court," according to Salois. When he complained of this to the RCMP, officials were aghast that the Swiss had shared the Canadian submissions with the lawyer for the accused. Salois feels the RCMP were trying to take advantage of the different rules of the European judicial process to admit evidence that would not be acceptable in Canada.

"Canadian authorities were caught out at their own game," Salois said.

MONTREAL, MARCH 1995

The Swiss case against a Rizzuto—this time Libertina—like so many others mounted against the family, quickly fizzled. Libertina and Giammarella were released not long afterward. About six months after their arrest, Libertina and Giammarella were granted bail and allowed to return to Canada. The Rizzuto matriarch was met in Montreal by a relieved and welcoming family. It was an emotional greeting. The situation was sorted out in time to allow Libertina to be present, in a black dress and big jewelry, at the wedding of her grandson, Nick.

Her release, however, did not go without suspicion and controversy. In March 1995, Michel Bellehumeur, a member of Parliament with the Bloc Québécois party, rose in Canada's Parliament and publicly questioned the government's inability or unwillingness to help the Swiss.

"It seems their release came as a result of the half-hearted assistance the RCMP gave Swiss police authorities. Could the prime minister explain why the RCMP failed to give the Swiss authorities their full cooperation when they refused to provide information crucial to legal proceedings in Switzerland?" Bellehumeur asked. "What explanation does the prime minister have for the fact that the only officer familiar with the case involving Mrs. Rizzuto and Mr. Giammarella was on holiday when the Swiss authorities had to release these two individuals?" The government promised to look into the matter. Two weeks later, Bellehumeur asked for an update. Herb Gray, a venerable government defender who was Canada's solicitor general, said the Bloc MP was "mistaken."

"I have been informed that the Swiss authorities are quite satisfied with the support they received from the RCMP," Gray assured the country. Almost three years after the arrests, on July 11, 1997, the Swiss officially ended their interest in the case, according to Salois.

The treatment accorded Vito's mother—having been held in jail for months in a foreign country—was distressing and upsetting for Vito, said Oreste Pagano, who, at the time of Libertina's troubles, said he was working on the deal with Vito that went afoul in Puerto Cabello. For his mother, who had given Vito his height, his high cheekbones and downcast eyes, Vito would spare no expense in obtaining legal counsel abroad to protect her rights, argue for her innocence and push for her release. His mother's incarceration was a constant distraction for Vito, and the Montreal boss bemoaned the situation personally to Pagano.

"At that moment he was having difficulties, that his mother was also in prison in Switzerland," Pagano said.

Pagano also said that there was much more money at stake than the Swiss investigators, diligent as they were, discovered.

"She had gone to withdraw money from a bank in Switzerland, where there was, I believe, around $5 million, and there she was stopped and she ended up in prison in Switzerland." And even that amount was a mere pittance compared to the $91 million that the officers laundered in Montreal at a single currency-exchange office—money, investigators say, that was from the Rizzuto organization.

Both Libertina's visit to Switzerland and the covert Montreal operation—just two snapshots of a specific time and place—hint at the tremendous wealth and financial resources the Rizzutos have had at their disposal, offering compelling proof that they formed a sophisticated, successful and multinational organization.

What's more, their money remained largely untouched.

If police only ever catch an estimated one-tenth of the supply of illegal drugs, surely their record on finding dirty money is even worse. If this was the supply of cash uncovered in a single probe, imagine the size of the whole pot at the Sixth Family's command.

The few failed franchise efforts made by Manno, Ragusa, Sciortino and Zbikowski were clearly not debilitating to the organization as a whole. Even with these colleagues charged by police and their drug networks exposed, police believe there was ample product for the Sixth Family to wield. In 1997, police surveillance teams watched Nick Rizzuto meet with Gerlando Caruana, Agostino Cuntrera and Joe Renda, according to police reports. Investigators believed the meeting was called by Nick to regulate the price of cocaine. Such an ability would be one of the key advantages of owning the franchise rights. As the Sixth Family expanded its range of activities—with the flood of hashish coming into Canada along the East Coast, with heroin and cocaine coming in from South America, Florida, Texas and Italy and with its money searching for sanctuary abroad—the organization was growing beyond recognition.

It was growing beyond New York.

CHAPTER 30

QUEENS, JUNE 1991

Philip "Rusty" Rastelli did not look particularly healthy even before he was ravaged by cancer, so it was a surprise to no one when the Bonanno Family rank and file received orders to show up for the wake and funeral of their boss. Over three days, starting on June 25, 1991, New York gangsters of all stripes filed through to pay their respects to the emaciated corpse of the dead Bonanno boss as he lay at a funeral home not far from Sal Vitale's Grand Avenue social club. Cadillacs and Lincolns clogged the roadway and a stream of gangsters, almost all of them wearing white shirts, ties and dark suits, wandered into the funeral home, chatted with each other, greeted Rastelli's family and then crept outside for a cigarette.

It was a significant sign of respect, although much of it duplicitously given by gangsters who had long been begging for the boss to move aside so that Joe Massino could salvage the sagging fortunes of the family.

"Everyone showed up," Vitale said. Everyone also knew that Rastelli had been a mere figurehead within the family for years, and there was little question over who would replace him. After the murder of Carmine Galante and the purge of the three captains, Rastelli's power was only as secure as Massino wanted it to be. While Rastelli was in jail, Massino ran the show, Vitale said. Even members of Rastelli's own administration took a back seat to Massino. Nicholas "Nicky Glasses" Marangello was the underboss and Stefano "Stevie Beef" Cannone was the *consigliere*, but neither stood up to Massino.

"I don't think Nicky Glasses and Stevie Beef really wanted the position. They didn't want to butt heads with a strong captain, a strong individual, like Joe Massino. Anything that Joe wanted to do, Joe could do," Vitale said. "Phil Rastelli wanted to step down the day he got home," Vitale said of Rastelli's release from prison in 1983. "When he got out of jail, he really wanted to retire. He wanted to give everything to Mr. Massino. He just wanted to live his life out peacefully." The signs of Rastelli's impotence were everywhere.

"If Mr. Rastelli would have given me an order, I would have checked it with Joe Massino before I accepted," Vitale said. Massino was in no hurry to have the boss stand down. There was little reason for him to move against Rastelli so long as he maintained his favored status in the family; he enjoyed the insulation it afforded him from federal agents. Massino knew a family's boss was always the government's top target.

When Rastelli's death was imminent, however, Massino did not leave his succession to chance. The position, while bringing huge risks, also brought immense profit. Before Rastelli died, he mapped out exactly what was to happen.

"When Phil dies, make Anthony Spero call a meeting. Elect me boss. Have someone second the motion, whether it be you, Big Louie, whoever, make me boss," Massino said to Vitale. It happened precisely as he ordered. After the burial of Rastelli, Spero called to order a meeting of Bonanno captains at a Staten Island home.

"Regretfully, Phil Rastelli has died. But it's now time that we elect a new boss," Spero said to the gathering.

"Why don't we make Joe Massino [boss]?" one of the captains said, as if it were a spur-of-the-moment idea. There was no dissent. A new era in the Bonanno Family history had begun.

"At that time, most of the people were dead. There weren't any people to challenge," said Frank Lino, a Bonanno captain. Massino— and federal indictments—had cleared away some potential competition, particularly from the Zips. Sal Catalano, as street boss of the Zips in New York, had once been seen as a possible contender. At one point during Rastelli's incarceration, Catalano had been elevated to the position of acting boss of the family, a move that probably drew considerable heat from other bosses, if not officially from the entire Commission.

"They were looking to make him boss and I think they were pushing Phil Rastelli aside, but he couldn't be [boss] because he was already made in Italy," Vitale said. "You can't have allegiance with two—you are either all Italy or all United States." The issue of how Sicilian Men of Honor would fit into the American Mafia was still causing problems. The rule Vitale spoke of, however, seemed to apply only to holding the top post, as boss, because plenty of Zips in America and Canada had been inducted into the Bonanno Family as soldiers and elevated to captain. Any remaining claim Catalano might once have had evaporated when he was sentenced to 45 years in prison for his part in the Pizza Connection case in 1987. Another Zip who had ambition, street smarts and charisma, Cesare Bonventre, had been killed in 1984, on Massino's orders, on the eve of the Pizza Connection arrests.

As for Gerlando Sciascia, he, like Catalano, had been made in Sicily, apparently precluding him from contention. After helping Massino to orchestrate the purge of the three captains and becoming wealthy through the Sixth Family's drug trade, Sciascia had also been sidelined for five years, the time between his arrest in Canada for the drug conspiracy and his acquittal on the charges in New York in 1990. After a jurer was bribed and Sciascia walked free, however, he tried to pick up where he had left off. Six months after his acquittal, an FBI report noted: "It is believed that Sciascia continues to be an active and influential figure in the narcotics trade."

As long as he could ply Sixth Family drugs, Sciascia seemed content to remain near the top echelons of Bonanno Family power, having the ear of Massino and Vitale, while retaining his zeal for selling narcotics. Sciascia seemed to be a key supporter of Massino's bid to take over the Bonanno Family, suggesting that the Sixth Family approved of where New York was going. Sciascia's place in the Bonanno Family seemed secure under the new administration. The Sixth Family's previous deal with Massino to topple the three captains and keep the drugs flowing remained in effect.

"He was well respected," Vitale said of Sciascia. "I liked George. George was a good man." And yet Sciascia seemed ill at ease.

In July 1991, just weeks after Massino was named the official boss, Sciascia, along with his wife and daughter, applied for permanent resident status in Canada, sponsored by his son, Joseph, who was a Canadian citizen. Sciascia seemed to be wearing out his welcome in New York.

"George would speak his mind, if he had anything on his mind. He believed in our life. If he felt something was wrong, he would tell you," Vitale said. Sciascia, for example, had taken a dislike to Anthony "TG" Graziano, a Bonanno veteran who had served as captain and *consigliere*, because he thought Graziano was using illicit drugs.

Sciascia, Vitale and Graziano had a meeting to discuss family business in which TG appeared glassy-eyed, unfocused and unsteady on his feet. After Graziano left, Sciascia turned to Vitale, stunned.

"TG is a captain," Sciascia said in alarm to Vitale. "You're supposed to be representing your family and you're walking around high?

You're going to other, outside, families and making a fool of yourself? It reflects on the family," he said. "Every time I see this guy, he's stoned," Sciascia griped, an odd complaint from one of the biggest drug dealers in New York. Vitale said he would bring it up with Massino. Sciascia said he certainly would as well. Graziano, one of Massino's favorite underlings, had a friend in the boss, however. Massino looked into it. Graziano said he was on prescription medication for a stomach ailment and not dipping into street drugs, swearing: "On my children's eyes, I'm not getting high." Massino bought the explanation. Sciascia still kept his distance, and their animosity festered.

Sciascia had also apparently found himself in a dispute with Marty Rastelli, brother of the old boss, Philip Rastelli. Marty felt that he was owed money by Sciascia, who refused to acknowledge the debt. When Marty pressed the matter, Sciascia spurned him in no uncertain terms, screaming: "You got nothing coming. I'm going to war tomorrow, if you want to." Sciascia was making more people nervous.

LOWER MANHATTAN, MAY 1992

The spring of 1992 brought yet another crisis to the Bonanno Family, and Sal Vitale reached out to Sciascia for help, although it looked more like a test of loyalty than anything else. The Bonanno Family's long-term scams in the circulation department of the *New York Post*, a tabloid that enjoyed splashing sensational mob stories across its pages, were falling apart. Several Bonanno soldiers and associates had been on the payroll of the *Post* but did little or no work, an arrangement overseen by Robert Perrino, the newspaper's delivery superintendent. When an electronic bug was found in Perrino's office and the mobsters learned of a New York State Police investigation into their shenanigans, they feared that Perrino, who was more white-collar crook than hardcore gangster, would not hold up under the pressure.

"They felt that he would blow the whistle on the whole operation," Vitale said. "He could do a lot of damage." It was decided that Perrino had to die. Vitale and Anthony Spero met to discuss the situation while Massino was in prison.

"George is always volunteering shooters from Montreal. Let's put him to the test and let him take care of it," Spero said. Over coffee, Vitale put the idea to Sciascia.

"I will get you two shooters from Montreal," Sciascia quickly promised. The reception to the plan in Montreal, however, does not seem to have been enthusiastic. One suspects that Montreal mobsters quickly dismissed taking such a risk when their drug franchise was not under threat. There seemed little interest in doing New York's dirty work just to gain brownie points. At a subsequent meeting with Vitale at the Stage Diner on Queens Boulevard, Sciascia got around the awkwardness by presenting an alternative plan.

"Instead of me getting shooters from Canada, Montreal—it's hard to come across the border—use Baldo," Sciascia said, presenting Baldassare Amato, one of the Zips, who had been Cesare Bonventre's right-hand man and who had come to New York through Canada. Amato was a Bonanno soldier but, according to the Bonanno Family structure, was in the crew of Louie Ha-Ha, who had assumed control of Bonventre's crew after he was killed. Despite the breach in mob etiquette—Sciascia offering another captain's soldier—Vitale approved of the replacement. (It was a breach that did not sit well with Massino, who later told Vitale off for letting Sciascia disrespect Amato's captain that way. It showed how the Zips continued to work together outside the official hierarchy of the family, a situation that was increasingly upsetting to Massino.) The murder of Perrino was scheduled to coincide with Vitale's son's birthday party, and the underboss opted for fatherly, rather than family, duties, and asked another gangster to stand in for him at the murder. It fell to Michael "Mickey Bats" Cardello to walk Perrino to his death.

Perrino was the son-in-law of Nicky Marangello, a former Bonanno underboss, but if Perrino felt that pedigree protected him from Bonanno bloodletting, he grossly overestimated gangster sentimentality; he was last seen on May 5, 1992, leaving his daughter's house and heading for a meeting with mob associates. Perrino was shot as planned; Frank Lino, however, was not impressed by the abilities of Amato, the shooter. When Lino and his crew came to clean up the body, they found Perrino was not quite dead, and another gangster had to stab him before the body was taken away for disposal, Lino said.

"Next time your shooter leaves a body," an annoyed Lino later told Vitale, "make sure it's dead."

———

Although they took a pass on killing Perrino, the Montreal-based mobsters of the Sixth Family did get involved in one scheme Vitale put to them, although Vitale was only acting as a middleman for the DeCavalcante Family, a Mafia organization based in New Jersey. Vitale had by this time been inducted into the Bonanno Family after his work in the messy Bonventre murder, and Massino had made him his underboss. It was as the Bonanno underboss that Vincent "Vinny Ocean" Palermo—the acting boss of the DeCavalcante Family—solicited Vitale's help in reaching out to the Bonanno men in Montreal. Vito Rizzuto, Gerlando Sciascia and Joe LoPresti had socialized with members of the DeCavalcante Family in the past. The boss of the family, John Riggi, his *consigliere*, Stefano "Steve" Vitabile, and leading captain, Giuseppe "Pino" Schifilliti, had all attended Giuseppe Bono's 1980 wedding.

"He knew we had Montreal," Vitale said of Vinny Ocean. "When the United States put embargoes on Persian rugs, Canada does not have an embargo. If we buy them in Canada, he had a buyer in Manhattan that would buy all of the rugs off us." A cross-border rug pipeline was quickly set up.

"We send people to Canada to buy Persian rugs and smuggle them across the border," Vitale said. An associate of the Montreal gangsters who was nominally involved in the carpet scheme said the perpetrators in Canada thought it hilarious to be involved in moving something so benign across the border. They developed an ongoing joke about it, a short skit that imagined one of them being caught red-handed at the border with the carpets: "I said I was a *rug* smuggler, not a *drug* smuggler," the joke went. They drew great hilarity from simply replacing "rug" for "drug" in any number of ways: rug cartels, rug trafficking, rug mules … it was as if the puns alone were worth the risk. But, of course, it was the illicit profit that was the true draw. The scheme was surprisingly lucrative, as the appetite of Manhattan's wealthy residents for the opulent rugs was nearly insatiable. Vitale's cut as a middleman between the Canadian and Jersey gangsters was about $20,000, he said.

Despite the success of this penny-ante scheme, the deterioration in the relationship between the Bonanno administration and the Sixth Family leadership was becoming more acute. To head it off, Massino sent men north to talk with Vito.

MONTREAL, JULY 1991

It was agreeable weather in Montreal on Canada Day, 1991, with a cooling breeze, hardly a cloud and no hint of rain. As a day for baseball, it approached perfection. The bright sky, however, did little to lighten the sour mood of fans inside Olympic Stadium. Starting on that holiday Monday and continuing for most of the week, the New York Mets swept the Montreal Expos four games straight, the close of an 11-game losing streak. For a group of tough visitors from New York City sitting in the stands, the Mets' victory was cause for celebration, another boost during a raucous trip to Montreal that included the city's famously daring strip clubs and wild discos.

Despite the banalities of their itinerary, however, this was not the usual group of tourists and their convivial hosts in Montreal were also extraordinary: emissaries from the Bonanno Family, sent by Joe Massino, had come north to talk business with their Canadian friends. Anthony Spero, the Bonanno *consigliere*, headed the group of goodwill ambassadors for this visit north. Joining him was Frank "Curly" Lino, Frank "Big Frank" Porco and at least two other New Yorkers. The visit went unnoticed at the time, but when details the group's alleged itinerary was revealed more than a decade later, it would cause a sporting scandal in New York and a political scandal in Canada.

The gangsters enjoying the baseball at the Olympic Stadium snagged their tickets from Mets pitcher John Franco, considered one of baseball's great closers and a New York sports icon, said Lino. The Brooklyn-born left-hander even had the gangsters visit with him in the clubhouse, according to statements Lino made to the FBI. Several of the mobsters also went out on the town with members of the Mets, Lino said. Such a party would be memorable for the mobsters, as Franco was the standout player in the series. When news emerged in 2004 that Franco and his colleagues had socialized with gangsters, it was greeted with concern in professional baseball circles, where fraternization between professional athletes and those involved in bookmaking and illegal gambling is highly frowned upon. When the media went to Franco for comment, confirmation or denial, his response was ambiguous: He declined to address "the specifics" of Lino's allegations but said he was "proud to be an Italian–American and have lived my life in a respectable fashion." Later that year, the Mets did not renew his contract and he signed for a year with the Houston Astros. The gangsters met others in Canada, as well. When details of Lino's other allegations later emerged, it made the brouhaha over John Franco pale in comparison.

This Canada Day weekend visit was not Frank Lino's first visit to Montreal to speak with Vito on behalf of the Bonannos. More than a decade earlier, just a couple of months after the 1979 murder of Carmine Galante, Lino had been sent to Montreal along with his captain, Bruno Indelicato—the son of Sonny Red and one of Galante's killers—and Thomas "Tommy Karate" Pitera, another soldier in Bruno's crew.

"We went to see, you know, [about] a closer relationship with the Montreal faction," Lino said of that first visit. The Bonanno administration seemed to recognize Montreal's value and feared that the murder of Galante, who had retained close ties to Montreal and was often referred to in New York as the head of the Montreal crew, might have alienated the Canadian wing. One night in a restaurant during that trip, Bruno introduced Lino to Vito Rizzuto, saying Vito was a soldier in the Bonanno Family. He was also introduced to several other men, whom he described as "a crew" of members in "the Canadian faction of the Bonanno Family." Bruno, Lino and Tommy Karate stayed in Montreal for several days and during their visit they saw Vito four or five times. While there, Joe LoPresti, who knew the New Yorkers through his work arranging heroin sales with Sciascia, told Lino that Vito "was very powerful in Canada." (It was a curious delegation. Less than two years after this first visit, Indelicato and Lino would be the two survivors of the deadly ambush of the three captains at the hands Vito and his Montreal colleagues.)

Lino was asked to return to Montreal in 1991, a decade after the captains' purge. The second visit, the one in which the New Yorkers enjoyed their baseball win over the Expos, featured a larger and more important entourage that carried a more urgent message. The New Yorkers seemed to be politely received in Montreal this time around as well. Vito and LoPresti escorted them around the city's sites and famous nightlife, Lino said. Between the nightclubs and the baseball, however, there was serious business to be discussed and, as is often the case with *mafiosi*, much of it was done over dinner. As a formal welcome for the Americans, Montreal's gangsters threw a feast in their honor.

"[Lino] remembers meeting with a group of Canadian Bonanno members at a catering hall," says an FBI report prepared in December 2003 when FBI Special Agents Christine Grubert and Jay Kramer secretly debriefed Lino after he agreed to cooperate with the government.

"At this meeting, the Canadian Bonannos were informed of Massino's new position as boss of the Bonanno Family," the report says.

The date of the visit to Montreal was a little fuzzy for Lino: "While we were there I saw Joe LoPresti. I didn't pay attention what year it was, it was '91, '88, '89. It's no big deal to me."

Lino insisted LoPresti was at the meetings in Montreal. Lino would have remembered him since he was one of the few Montrealers Lino knew. LoPresti had been in Lino's bar in New York many times and Lino recognized him easily when photographs of LoPresti were later shown to him. If the Bonanno entourage came with news that Massino had been made the new boss, and LoPresti was there at the time, it means the excursion to Montreal took place after Rastelli's death, on June 24, 1991, but before LoPresti's murder, on April 30, 1992.

This, in turn, means that—if Lino is to be believed—the visit likely occurred during the four-game series between the Mets and the Expos, from July 1 to 4, 1991. (There was only one other Expos–Mets series in Montreal between the time of Rastelli's and LoPresti's deaths, an April 17 to 19, 1992 match-up in which the Mets took two of the three games. This would have been almost a year after Rastelli's death but only 11 days before LoPresti's murder. This alternative date is tantalizing, since it is so close to LoPresti's death that it leads to speculation that the Montrealer committed some indiscretion during the meetings, or that the New Yorkers brought news or a complaint against him that needed addressing. It is, however, likely too long after Rastelli's death. It did not take a year for Massino to install himself in the job and he likely did not wait long afterwards to reach out to Canada.)

The Sixth Family's party in a Montreal catering and banquet hall was quite an affair, with the closest of the Rizzutos' friends and family invited. It was a dinner for "made members" only, Lino told the FBI in one of his debriefing sessions, meaning that outsiders and associates were not a part of the festivities. Lino also spoke of the Montreal visits, with less precision, under oath in a Brooklyn courtroom.

"We met with George [Sciascia], Joe LoPresti, Vito Rizzuto. We had a dinner with about 30, 40 people," Lino said in court. LoPresti and Sciascia would have been busy during the dinner; as the only two who knew everyone from both cities, they would be preoccupied with introducing the diners to one another. Introductions are important to mobsters. They are carefully constructed and carefully observed. As a secret society, it takes three mobsters for any two of them to officially meet, according to Mafia tradition. A member cannot reveal his membership to anyone outside the fraternity, so he cannot announce to a stranger, even one he is pretty certain has also been made, that he is an inducted member. Only a third made man can formally introduce two other made members to each other; the third person must confirm to each that the other has also been inducted into the Mafia.

"When you say somebody is *amico nostra* ["a friend of ours"], you know he's a made man. If you just say he's a friend, he's just a friend," Lino explained. In accordance with that policy, it would have fallen upon Sciascia and LoPresti to do most of the introductions at the dinner party. They would have been among the few people in the room who could confirm that both people being introduced, from both cities, were, in fact, Mafia members.

Lino told the FBI that he was formally introduced to a Montrealer who bore a special distinction, one worth bragging about. LoPresti said the man Lino was meeting was both a Bonanno soldier and a politician, according to the FBI documents. Lino said the man was Alfonso Gagliano, an allegation the veteran former Canadian politician vehemently denies.

"[Lino] was shown a picture of Alfonso Gagliano," says an FBI debriefing report. To protect their identities, informants' names are not used in these reports, and the word "Individual" replaces the informant's name. It is clear from the notes, however, that it was Lino making the statements, a point confirmed later in court. "[Lino] stated that he recognized Gagliano from his trip to Montreal, Canada, in the early 1990s. [Lino] advised that Gagliano was introduced to him as a soldier in the Bonanno Family by Joe LoPresti, another Bonanno member in Canada. At a dinner, LoPresti bragged to the individual that the Montreal Bonannos had such extensive connections, including that of Gagliano, a politician," the report says. Lino also "socialized with Gagliano when he was hanging out with Vito Rizzutto [*sic*]." The statement is shocking. Alfonso Gagliano played an important and prominent part in Canada's political life for two decades. He was first elected to Parliament to represent the people of Montreal's Saint-Léonard neighborhood in 1984 and held the riding through four straight elections, a tenure during which he became a powerful politician. He was in charge of the important Liberal Party caucus for the province of Quebec and was named to Cabinet in 1996, and to the post of Minister of Public Works in 1997. He later said his move into the federal Cabinet was delayed because of an RCMP investigation into his past associations. After leaving politics, he was named Canada's ambassador to Denmark, but was recalled in 2004 amid the scandal of a damning report by the country's Auditor-General documenting inappropriate government expenditures in a $332-million sponsorship program that Gagliano oversaw for a time. A monumental inquiry headed by Judge John Gomery found that the program amounted to "an elaborate kickback scheme," that funneled money to the Quebec wing of the Liberal Party of Canada and to Liberal-friendly advertising executives. Judge Gomery's report said that $147 million in public money went directly from the sponsorship program to the agencies as commissions and fees.

Lino's allegations about Gagliano, first reported in the New York *Daily News*, created a furor in Canada. On the day the allegations became public, it was raised in Parliament by Stephen Harper, then the leader of the Opposition and now the Prime Minister.

"The report claims that in the 1990s he was a 'made' member of the Brooklyn-based Bonanno crime family. My question is simple: Since Mr. Gagliano was in Cabinet and ambassador during this period, was the government aware of this information and when did it become aware of these allegations?" Harper asked. The then prime minister Paul Martin replied: "Let me simply say that these are very serious allegations and everyone should be very careful about accepting or repeating such allegations." The Opposition was unsatisified with the response, and Peter MacKay, a senior Opposition member said: "It is a very serious matter. ... Prior to his appointment as ambassador to Denmark, Mr. Gagliano filled a number of Liberal Cabinet positions until the year 2002. Again, my question for the government, for the prime minister, for the minister responsible, is what steps did the Privy Council Office and the Department of the Solicitor General take to ensure that proper security clearances were obtained prior to Mr. Gagliano being admitted to Cabinet?" This question was responded to by Anne McLellan, the deputy prime minister at the time: "I have no intention of commenting on these allegations. If the honorable member is asking about the operational activities of the RCMP, I suggest that the honorable member more appropriately direct his question to the Royal Canadian Mounted Police," she said.

For his part, Gagliano has firmly denied Lino's allegations explicitly and repeatedly.

"I was a very popular member of Parliament," Gagliano told reporters, saying he might inadvertently have met some of the gangsters named by Lino in the course of glad-handing and politicking. "As a politician I might have—in social events, in public events, during an election campaign going door-to-door—I might have met some of those people. But really, it doesn't mean that I know [them] personally." He said he never attended a dinner with mafiosi and was never involved in criminal behavior.

"I'm not a member of a Mafia," Gagliano said. In the annals of things that politicians feel they have to say to defend themselves, this surely ranks above even the famous denial by Richard Nixon, the former U.S. president: "I am not a crook."

———

It was not the first time Gagliano had had to brush aside allegations of questionable ties to known *mafiosi* and organized crime figures. When it was revealed that he was the former bookkeeper for a business owned by Agostino Cuntrera, who helped to kill Paolo Violi in 1978, he said it was "an error in judgment." Cuntrera and Gagliano shared another link. The Association de Siciliana, a cultural group in Montreal founded and presided over by Gagliano, was later run by Cuntrera, who was named president a few years after Gagliano gave up the post. Another bookkeeping client of Gagliano's was Dino Messina, who was found during court proceedings over a stock fraud to be a financial representative of Vito Rizzuto's. Another man with unsavory links, Filippo Vaccarello, a drug trafficker linked to the Sixth Family, was under surveillance when officers watched him walk into Gagliano's bookkeeping office a year after he was first elected into federal office. Gagliano told police he did not know Messina or Vaccarello. And in 2001, Gaetano Amodeo, an accused Mafia assassin from Cattolica Eraclea who was wanted for murder and attempted murder in Italy and Germany, was arrested in Montreal, where he had been living for almost five years. Several Canadians had traveled back to Cattolica Eraclea for Amodeo's 1986 wedding to Maria Sicurella. One of the crimes Italian courts blamed on Amodeo was the shooting of a Carabinieri officer who was probing the Mafia in Agrigento province. The Canadian public was outraged that the government knew Amodeo had been in Canada for two years before he was arrested; the RCMP had even sent Italian authorities a surveillance photo of Amodeo meeting with Nick Rizzuto. Indeed, Gagliano's office had sent a letter to Canada's immigration department seeking information on behalf of Maria Sicurella di Amodeo, Amodeo's wife, who was applying to become a landed immigrant. She later sponsored her husband for entry to Canada. Before he was sent back to face justice in Italy, Amodeo made a statement that would later be echoed by Gagliano: "I was never part of the Mafia."

———

Another mobster has also secretly suggested to police that the Montreal Mafia had direct access to a friend in the Canadian government. These statements, never before revealed, add to the allegations of the Montreal Mafia's political ties.

Drug trafficker Oreste Pagano agreed to cooperate with authorities after he was charged alongside Alfonso Caruana for conspiracy to import drugs. During one of Pagano's secret debriefing sessions, he spoke of the value to the mob of having contacts in the government. In Italy, he said, the Mafia was well entrenched in political circles.

"You have to realize that the Mafia in Italy, let's say, in the last 40 years, were much supported by the politicians. By important politicians," he said. The cooperation in granting huge government public works contracts was immensely profitable for both sides, the only illicit scheme that could compete with drug trafficking in terms of its financial return.

"The most important investments where they can profit are the government investments. So then there was a strong connection between the Mafia and the government. For every investment of, for example, $100 million, the profit on $100 million was $30 million in profit. Fifteen million dollars would go to the Mafia and $15 million would go to the government," Pagano said.

He was then asked by an officer with the RCMP's Integrated Proceeds of Crime Unit in Toronto if the Mafia had a similar relationship with the government in Canada. Pagano was not as sure.

"I couldn't tell you. I was not living in Canada," he answered. But, Pagano was asked, did Alfonso Caruana ever speak to him about such relationships?

"We spoke once about it, that there was a person who was going into the Canadian government and was from the same village as

Alfonso [Caruana]. From Siciliana," Pagano said in a September 21, 1999, interview.

"He was from the same village as Alfonso [Caruana]. ... I don't know this person," Pagano said. This was the kind of information that the Sicilian Men of Honor liked to keep secret from outsiders. And, although Pagano was one of Alfonso Caruana's closest business partners, he was neither family nor a Sicilian and that made him an outsider.

"They don't talk about it. It's like I told you, these are things they keep to themselves," he said. Investigators could not help but note that Alfonso Caruana's family was based in Siciliana, a small Sicilian town in Agrigento province. Alfonso Gagliano is from Siciliana as well.

Mobsters are certainly more likely to claim access to a politician than an elected official is to acknowledge an association with gangsters. It may have been only an empty boast.

These scandals over Gagliano and John Franco, the ball player, that would later emerge from the Bonannos' visit to Montreal were never envisioned by the gangsters at the time. The troubles stemmed, after all, from allegations of mere social—non-criminal—interaction. Of more importance to the Bonanno representatives at the time was the message they had for Vito from Massino, who continued to watch in dismay as the Sixth Family distanced itself even further from the Bonanno Family.

What was the purpose of their visit to see Vito?

"Well, to make them understand that they still had ties with New York," Lino said. "That you [need to bring] the family closer together because, I guess, they might have lost ties."

MANHATTAN, FEBRUARY 1995

Despite the warm reception in Montreal extended to the New York gangsters, relations between the Sixth Family and the Bonanno Family were growing chilly. Montreal continued to withdraw from Bonanno affairs. Accordingly, life for Sciascia in New York was becoming similarly unpleasant. Increasingly at odds with the Bonanno Family leadership, he also had to contend with the notoriety of the drug case he had faced with LoPresti. Even with his acquittal, the charges and the Angelo Ruggiero tapes had given him an unwanted high profile among American and Canadian police. Although he often visited Canada while carrying out his drug-trafficking schemes, he had never obtained Canadian citizenship, remaining both a citizen of

Italy and a permanent resident in the United States. His application to legally relocate to Canada was a tough sell. The process dragged on until February 1995, when Susan Burrows, an official at the Canadian Consulate in New York, notified Sciascia's lawyers that she wanted to interview Sciascia in person.

Burrows had been well briefed on the Sixth Family and their business associates, and if Sciascia thought he was to face a test of his knowledge of Canadian history or to recount his investment potential as an immigrant, he was in for a surprise.

"Do you know Salvatore Ruggiero?" Burrows began.

"Yes," a cautious Sciascia replied. "We met in the pizza place. His seven children used to hang out there," he said of his California Pizza franchise at the Green Acres Mall. "We were friends. He was always ordering pizzas ... that's where my problems started."

And, Burrows asked, how about Cesare Bonventre?

"I may have met him a few times," Sciascia said, "through [Sal] Catalano."

"Baldo Amato?" Burrows continued.

"I am the godfather of Mr. Amato's daughter. I knew his father in Italy," Sciascia said. "I see him once in a while—at his daughter's birthday, etc."

"Do you know Giuseppe LoPresti?"

"We were friends in Italy," Sciascia responded. "He was a godfather at my daughter's confirmation. He passed away." No mention of murder; no mention of his involvement in it.

"Okay, Mr. Sciascia," Burrows continued, "do you know Giuseppe Bono?" Again he nodded.

"Yes, he lived near my house. He asked my daughter to be his flower girl. I haven't seen [the Bonos] since they were married and went back to Italy," he said.

"Do you know Nicolò or Nick Rizzuto?"

"Yes, he was my *paesano* in our town of 5,000 in Italy. He lived on the same block, about 10 houses away from me. I met him once in Canada when my niece got married, then I used to see him at weddings. I haven't seen him in a long time." Burrows asked him about the circumstances of Nick being stopped at the border by U.S. Customs agents with documents for Sciascia's Peugeot in his possession. Sciascia said it was "a mistake" that Nick had the papers.

Moving on, Burrows next asked about Vito Rizzuto.

"I know all the family," Sciascia answered. "I have nothing to do with him. I see him at weddings and funerals."

What about Paolo Renda?

"He lived across the street," Sciascia said, adding that Renda was Vito's brother-in-law. "I saw him a few times at family gatherings, nothing else."

Six months later, Burrows notified him of the decision: "Having investigated further the responses to the questions which you gave me at your interview, I must confirm that I do consider you inadmissible to Canada." She said she believed that Sciascia was a member of the Mafia and a danger to the public. On September 8, 1995, Joseph Sciascia, on his father's behalf, appealed Burrows's decision. Six weeks later, the immigration department certified that Sciascia was a danger to the Canadian public.

"George from Canada" remained in America.

CHAPTER 31

LONG ISLAND, MARCH 1999

At a silver wedding anniversary party for the nephew of Sal Vitale, held at a family-owned restaurant in Hempstead, Long Island, Joe Massino—who had arrived late to the festivities—pulled his underboss aside. Sitting down together at the end of one of the tables, Massino told him shocking news.

"George has got to go." This was Massino's simple way of issuing a death sentence against Gerlando Sciascia, the Sixth Family's representative in New York. The news was not received well by Vitale, who was fond of Sciascia and his old-school ways. Vitale knew better than to question his boss but he could not hide the look of distaste on his face.

"If you have any problems with it, I'll get other people. I don't need you," Massino snapped.

"Whatever you want to do, Joe," Vitale said, throwing his hands in the air in an overt sign of surrender. Vitale knew the rules: "I don't have no right to know nothing," he said later.

Massino then told Vitale to contact Patrick "Patty from the Bronx" DeFilippo, another Bonanno captain, to arrange the hit and, if they needed anything in the way of a car or a van to do the job, to call Anthony "TG" Graziano. DeFilippo was one of the Bonanno men who had traveled to Canada in 1966 for Vito Rizzuto's wedding, only to be arrested by Montreal police.

Massino was a cunning boss. To carry out this sensitive piece of business, he had tapped two gangsters that he knew had their own motivation to whack Sciascia. Graziano was something of a nemesis to Sciascia, after Sciascia pressed his complaints over his drug use, and he would happily help to topple his rival. DeFilippo, too, had an on-going beef with Sciascia over a large marijuana deal and would benefit if he were to be removed from the equation. As with the assassination of Bonventre—and any hostile move against the Zips—killing Sciascia required special handling.

The plan called for Sciascia's death to be made to look like a drug deal gone awry—and nothing to do with the Bonannos. Sciascia's body would be dumped on the street in the Bronx rather than made to disappear, as is typically the case in mob hits.

"It would look like George got caught up in his own dirt," said Vitale. Massino also had made plans for the timing of the murder, one that showed how sensitive it was and how anxious he was for it not to point back to him. Massino was leaving the following morning for St. Maarten, a Dutch-run tropical island in the Caribbean.

"Try to get it done before I come home," he said. He wanted to keep the fact that he had ordered Sciascia's death from two organizations. "Number one, law enforcement wouldn't know, and two, Montreal wouldn't know," Vitale said.

Keeping it from Vito and the Sixth Family was crucial, said Vitale, for the simple reason that they feared him.

"They have, like, 19 people; we didn't want to get involved in a war," he said of the official strength of the Montreal allotment of made Bonanno soldiers. The strength of the Sixth Family, of course, could not be measured in such a narrow way. As Vito would soon personally show Vitale and Massino, New York's rigid structure meant little to him.

BROOKLYN, MARCH 1999

It was with more secrecy than is typical of a mob hit that Massino and his handpicked men mapped out a plan of attack on Sciascia.

Two weeks earlier, Massino met directly with DeFilippo in Danny's Chinese Restaurant on Cross Bay Boulevard, not far from the boss's Howard Beach home. It was there that Massino assigned him this "piece of work," as he typically referred to the murders he was ordering. DeFilippo, a decidedly inexperienced assassin, then started scheming and by the time Vitale met with him to discuss it, he had the plot thoroughly mapped out.

Outside DeFilippo's York Avenue apartment in Manhattan's upscale East Side, he and Vitale walked the streets as they spoke in private, Vitale said.

"Joe sent me. You know what we got to do?" Vitale asked him.

"I'm all set up," DeFilippo replied.

"You need a car? I could get a car," Vitale said.

"I don't need a car," DeFilippo said.

"Patty, do you need a car?" Vitale repeated. DeFilippo insisted he did not.

"How are you going to do this? Explain it to me," said Vitale.

"I'm going to kill him in Johnny Joe's truck," DeFilippo said, naming John "Johnny Joe" Spirito, a trusted Bonanno associate. DeFilippo was going to use his ongoing dispute with Sciascia as a crafty way to lure him to his death. Sciascia was to be told that another mobster was ready to mediate a sit-down between them to settle their beef, and to meet DeFilippo in Manhattan and from there he would be driven to the meeting. Like Bonventre, Sciascia was a suspicious and crafty man. DeFilippo felt sure Sciascia would not get into a strange car, so they would use a vehicle familiar to him to put him at ease—a white Mercury Mountaineer sport utility vehicle driven by Spirito.

"He'll be comfortable getting into Johnny Joe's truck. He knows Johnny Joe," DeFilippo told Vitale. Once Sciascia was dead, Spirito would drive the body to the Bronx and dump it in the street, DeFilippo said. For that he would earn his membership into the Bonanno Family. DeFilippo had the plot carefully arranged, including asking Michael "Nose" Mancuso to be nearby in his gold Nissan Altima as a back-up shooter if anything went wrong, Vitale said.

The next day, at the York Grill near DeFilippo's home, Vitale passed two guns and a silencer to DeFilippo.

"Does it work? Did you try it?" asked an anxious DeFilippo.

"No," replied Vitale. "You want to try it? Let's go for a ride." The two hopped into a black Lincoln Town Car and Vitale drove through the streets of midtown Manhattan while DeFilippo fired a few rounds through the open sun roof. As they left the car to return to the diner, Vitale grabbed hold of DeFilippo to ensure he had his attention for an important message.

"Joe told me to tell you: Hit him high, hit him low," Vitale said, meaning, in gangster parlance, to alternate between firing bullets into the head and into the chest—up and down, up and down—to leave no mistake about the outcome.

"I got it. Don't worry," said DeFilippo. Test-firings, silencers, back-up shooters, instructions on inflicting maximum damage—again, special precautions.

On the day DeFilippo intended to strike, he called Throgs Neck Jewelers on East Tremont Avenue—a store where Sciascia could often be found, run by John Chiazzese, a relative of Sciascia's known by some as "John the Jeweler"—and left what was meant to seem like a conciliatory message: "We will work out our differences," DeFilippo said and asked Sciascia to meet him at the intersection of 79th Street and First Avenue in Manhattan at 9 p.m.

When Sciascia arrived at the jewelry store, nothing in his demeanor suggested he suspected this day would be the last day of his life. He jotted down on a slip of paper, in his unsteady handwriting, where he was to meet DeFilippo: "PAT D. 79 ST AV 1." That evening, he parked his black Jeep Cherokee on the east side of Second Avenue between 79th and 80th streets, walking the block and a half to his rendezvous with DeFilippo. At the intersection, Spirito pulled his Mountaineer to a stop and Sciascia settled into the luxury interior of the SUV's rear seat. In the front passenger seat was DeFilippo. At some point during the ride, seven .25-caliber bullets, fired from the front and just inches away, ended Sciascia's life a month after his 65th birthday.

"I was in the truck when he was killed," Spirito said. "I drove a vehicle to Boller Avenue, got out of the vehicle, opened the door and pulled the body of George Sciascia out—may he rest in peace."

Vitale made sure he was in the area of the hit that night, arriving half an hour before DeFilippo's meeting with Sciascia. He drove aimlessly about for an hour before stopping across the street from DeFilippo's apartment, where there was a pay phone. He called him.

"Hello?" DeFilippo said, answering his phone.

"Patty, what's up?" an anxious Vitale said. "Come on downstairs," he added, for such a delicate thing could never be spoken of over the telephone. DeFilippo came trotting down from his apartment and crossed the road to meet with Vitale. Again the two walked and talked.

"What's going on?" Vitale asked.

"It is done. It is over," DeFilippo said.

Vitale had one more task to perform in this unpleasant business. He called Joe Massino and spoke a prearranged signal: "I picked up the dolls for the babies." The code meant that Sciascia was dead.

―――――

Shortly after 11 p.m. on March 18, 1999, a man leaving his girlfriend's home on Boller Avenue, near the Hutchinson River Parkway, watched in horror as what appeared to be a man's body was tossed out of a truck, landing rudely on the pavement, face up and sprawled, beside a chain-link fence. Returning indoors, he called 9-1-1 and asked for police and an ambulance. Medical assistance was not in order. Sciascia lay dead on the street, where police found him dressed in a red-and-black argyle sweater, gray dress pants, black socks and shoes and a black leather jacket. His silver hair was streaked with blood and a grimace was frozen on his punctured face. His head and body had been riddled with bullets that perforated his brain, lungs, liver and pancreas. He was indeed hit high and hit low. This time, the discovery of the body was not a concern to the Bonannos. It was part of the plan, so that it would not look like a mob hit but rather a drug dispute gone awry. In Sciascia's wallet, police found a business card for a Montreal jewelry shop run by the wife of Gaetano Amodeo, the Mafia hitman from Cattolica Eraclea who was later found hiding in Montreal. Also found was the note he made of his planned meeting with DeFilippo and other scrawled phone messages, including several from Canada, with the names and phone numbers of Montreal associates.

A New York City police officer tucked the first parking ticket onto the windshield of Sciascia's Jeep promptly at 8:00 the following morning. Eight more tickets would pile up before rush hour was over as parking enforcement officers, unaware the owner was in no position to move it, grew increasingly annoyed. The Jeep was eventually towed and, when it was linked to the body found hours before, became the focus of much police scrutiny. It yielded nothing.

There was an unexpected hitch for Sciascia's killers, however. The next morning, Vitale's pager beeped. DeFilippo's number popped up and Vitale promptly returned the call from the nearest pay phone.

"I have to meet you. It is important," DeFilippo said.

"Okay. The usual spot," Vitale answered. The usual spot was a diner near a busy highway exit. This time it was DeFilippo who seemed anxious.

"You got to get rid of the truck for me. There is too much blood in the truck. They can't clean it up," he said.

As DeFilippo and Vitale were fretting over the blood-soaked Mountaineer, police were breaking the heart-wrenching news to Sciascia's family. His wife, Mary, then called Baldo Amato, who could hardly believe it. He quickly arranged a meeting with Vitale at the Blue Bay Diner on Francis Lewis Boulevard in Queens, saying it was "very important." Vitale was sitting waiting in the diner when Amato arrived. He was a wreck.

"They killed my *goombah*," Amato wailed, using Sicilian mob slang for a close friend.

"They did what?" Vitale replied, already working Massino's ruse by feigning surprise.

"They killed my *goombah*," Amato repeated, his eyes filling with tears.

"What the hell's going on?" Vitale replied.

"I don't know," Amato said. "They kill my *goombah*."

"Baldo," said Vitale, sympathetically. "Wait for the chief to come home and we'll discuss it with him. I don't know what's going on, Baldo, I don't know."

When Massino returned from his Caribbean island holiday, he was briefed on the murder. He heard grisly descriptions from the gangsters who chopped up the truck.

"The truck was filled with blood. It was completely filled with blood and at that point Joe Massino said that this poor George must have bled to death," Vitale said.

Massino also heaped rewards on the men who had rid him of the perceived threat from Sciascia. Spirito was inducted as a made man into the Bonanno, sponsored for membership by DeFilippo. Massino also ordered Vitale to erase the $54,000 debt DeFilippo owed him, the amount left after he worked furiously to pay down the $150,000 he had borrowed. Vitale tore DeFilippo's page out of his "shy book," where he tracked their loan sharking debts, and ripped it into pieces. Mancuso was later elevated to a position where he allegedly sat as acting boss of the Bonanno Family when Massino was incapacitated.

WHITE PLAINS, NEW YORK, MARCH 1999

Joe Massino was emphatic that his role in killing Sciascia not be known, even to those within the family whom he typically trusted. To that end, he ordered Vitale and every Bonanno captain to attend Sciascia's wake at a White Plains funeral home. Even those mobsters not in town were told to show up.

"I was in Las Vegas and I was called to go to his funeral," said Frank Lino, who was a Bonanno captain. "They want me to fly there to go to the funeral." At the wake, Vitale was busy further bolstering the subterfuge by asking the captains to investigate Sciascia's murder.

"On Mr. Massino's order, I asked every captain in our family," Vitale said. "I said the administration had nothing to do with this murder. He was like a brother to us. We want to know what's going on. If you find anything out, bring it to our attention. ... We want to know who killed George."

Lino remembered being pulled aside by Vitale. "Keep your ear to the ground. No one knows who killed George," Vitale told him.

It was all designed, said Vitale, to "put up a smokescreen, a diversion." When a mobster is killed in battle or dies of natural causes, there is a traditional show of strength and respect from his underworld kin. Mobsters and their associates typically show up en masse at the funeral and wake and lavish flowers and gifts on the grieving family. But if a gangster dies in what is called a "sanctioned hit"—one approved by the family leadership for what is considered a legitimate breach of the underworld code—the fallen comrade is typically shunned, even in death. His fellow gangsters avoid the funeral and wake, unless they had particular blood or close personal ties. When Carmine Galante was murdered, for example, word went out that his funeral was to be a no-show for New York wiseguys. When Sciascia was killed, Massino wanted to deflect suspicion from himself, so he wanted Sciascia's wake and funeral packed with New York gangsters. Over two days, agents watching the event documented more than 40 members and associates of the Bonanno Family in attendance, including Anthony "Tony Green" Urso, then listed by the FBI as the *consigliere*, and Vitale, the underboss. At least one Montreal representative was also there: Joe Renda, described by Vitale as a "goodfellow in our family" and as Vito Rizzuto's nephew, but he is, in fact, Sciascia's nephew.

Massino's charade did not work on the Sixth Family, although it certainly worked on police and the press, who started to dismiss the theory that it was a sanctioned hit because of the turnout at the funeral.

MONTREAL, 2001

Massino made one last attempt to bring the Sixth Family back into line. If the elimination of Sciascia had been meant to head off some threat or challenge he thought Sciascia posed, it had also severed New York's direct link to Montreal. Massino's first emissary had been Frank Lino. His second was Anthony Spero, his *consigliere*. This time, around 2001, it was an even greater sign of respect for the importance of the Sixth Family; he sent Vitale, his underboss, and Anthony Urso, who had been made the acting *consigliere*—it was the entire Bonanno administration, save for Massino, who had long since stopped participating in public mob meetings, now calling on Vito. With such powerful New York figures heading north, clearly Vito had no interest in crossing the border into America to meet them in New York.

"Mr. Massino sent me there," Vitale said, "to familiarize ourselves with them. Joe Massino wanted me to go up there to speak with Vito, to get what was going on, to familiarize ourselves with what was going on in Canada now that George was dead. ... He wanted to feel their pulse, to see what they were thinking about the murder." Sciascia's death seemed to be a sore spot for Vito.

"He was very hurt by what happened to George," said Vitale.

Sciascia's murder had alienated Massino from the Sixth Family, physically and emotionally, and, with Sciascia and LoPresti both deceased, the Sixth Family no longer had an official representative in New York, in the eyes of the Bonanno Family administration. Massino wanted Vitale and Urso to also take care of a housekeeping matter—Massino wanted to officially name Vito as the head of the Montreal faction of the Bonanno Family. Massino felt the offer of being made a captain was a flattering one, a privilege any of his New York gangsters would kill for—and, in fact, many of them had. But Massino, like most people, grossly underestimated Vito's international presence and far-reaching underworld interests and overestimated Vito's interest in the streets of New York. Just as Massino had enjoyed a layer of insulation under Rastelli's leadership—maintaining the power without drawing the added attention of being a boss—so, too, did Vito benefit from keeping his name off the charts and weekly reports of the FBI's Bonanno Squad.

The meeting, over lunch, between Vito and Vitale was an awkward one; one that belies the FBI's official designation of Vito as a mere soldier, and even the Bonanno administration's ranking of Vito as an acting captain. The meeting did not run as Massino had hoped and certainly was not the reception Vitale was used to receiving as underboss, where he dictated orders and compliant gangsters did his bidding; doubly so for soldiers being offered a coveted promotion. For a meeting between a soldier and the family's underboss, it is noteworthy that Vitale—the underboss—was the one who seemed nervous, unsure of himself and deferential. Vitale, it turned out, was no match for Vito.

"I meet with Vito," Vitale said. "First, he was very annoyed that no one told him about George. I don't think he believed that it was a drug deal going astray." Vitale, giving false assurances on the matter, moved on to the second item on the Bonanno Family's agenda: naming a new Montreal captain to replace Sciascia.

"Who do they respect up here? Who is 'the man' up here?" Vitale asked Vito, expecting Vito to step up and declare his obvious dominance. Vito remained aloof.

"We are all brothers. We are all equals," Vito replied. Vitale tried again, this time more directly.

"Who do the men respect? Who could be a good captain?"

"My father," Vito replied.

The answer frustrated Vitale. The Bonannos were not about to name the 77-year-old Nick, no matter what his background and experience, as the new captain. They wanted Vito. But Vitale seemed nervous to force the issue.

"That isn't the way to go," Vitale said later, although not to Vito's face. "He knew where I was heading and he didn't want to become a captain … We wanted him to take the position and he avoided the question and I felt it best to leave it alone."

Vitale and Urso returned to New York with the question of a new captain of the "Montreal crew" unresolved. Massino was unimpressed with their report. "I should have forced you to make him official captain," Massino snapped.

The indifference the New York emissaries encountered from Vito in Montreal seemed to mark the severing of ties between Montreal and New York, a connection that up until then had remained solid since Carmine Galante claimed Montreal as Bonanno turf more than 50 years earlier. The ignorance of Vitale, Urso and Massino to the reality of their Montreal brethren was sweeping. When one considers that a crew of Bonanno soldiers usually numbered fewer than 10 soldiers—"A captain is supposed to have 10; we don't have enough men," Vitale said, so a captain could have as few as three soldiers—it must have seemed like a fool's offer to Vito, who commanded twice as many "made" Bonanno soldiers in Canada and perhaps hundreds of made men in the Sicilian tradition carrying the Sixth Family's influence throughout the world.

When asked by Vitale about the strength of the Montreal group, Vito told him that, with Sciascia now dead, 19 made men stood with him. This number included only the inducted American Mafia members—the few Montrealers who maintained dual membership in the Sixth Family, in accordance with the rules of the Sicilian Mafia, and in the Bonanno Family, in accordance with the rules of the American Mafia. The strength of the Montreal faction of the Bonannos, in fact, seems to have been set in stone at 20. In 1974, Paolo Violi, the former street boss of Montreal, was recorded as saying that he had 20 full members in the Bonanno organization. Nearly 30 years later the number remained the same. Vito seemed to use New York's rigid view of Mafia membership to hide his organization's true strength from Massino.

Vitale's question about strength, however, shows the independence and control Vito had over affairs in Canada. It suggests that it was Vito, not Massino, who held the power over membership in his "crew." Had the Montreal members been Bonanno soldiers in the traditional New York sense, their names would need to have been brought to Massino's attention beforehand. Massino or his predecessors would have chosen which, if any, names received one of the valuable and sparse number of memberships available. The normal course of membership into the Bonanno Family was for Massino to pick and choose.

"The only one to approve a person being inducted is the boss," Vitale said. Massino would tell Vitale, as his underboss, whom he wanted to bring into the family, and Vitale would pass the names on to other Bonanno captains so each one could be checked out. Any complaints, suspicions or concerns would be addressed. Then the names that remained unchallenged would go out to the other New York families. Since new members could only be brought in to replace members who had died—a strategy designed to keep the strength of each family steady in a bid to prevent one from moving to dominate— the other families would be given the names of proposed members in one column and the names of the dead gangster they were replacing in another, Vitale said.

"We ask the other people in our family, 'What do you know about the individual?' Then we propose him. We take his name, put him on four pieces of paper and send out the people to the other families, to shop the families. If we don't hear from them within two weeks, we know it's okay to 'straighten him out.'" Had Vito's men gone through such a process, presumably Massino and Vitale would know how many members there were in Montreal. Although, it could just have been that there had been so much tumult in the Bonanno Family over the years that such institutional knowledge had been lost and the ebb and flow of membership had not been carefully tracked. Regardless, it shows how little the Bonanno administration knew of the internal affairs of the Canadian operation and how much they eyed it with suspicion.

As with all mob business, Vitale's visit to Montreal on Massino's behalf closed with a quick discussion about money.

"I laid out the money for the hotel, for the food, for me and Tony [Urso] and when I got back, Joe said 'How much did you lay out?' and I said $900. He gave me the $900," Vitale said.

It was a small investment by Massino in trying to reclaim what he appears to have lost after his murder of Sciascia. The Sixth Family seemed to have stopped paying their traditional tribute money to New York.

"I think the last time I was in their presence when they brought money down was approximately '98, '99," Vitale said of the Montreal gangsters. He said Montreal might have continued with the traditional tribute arrangement but he had no evidence of this and could not be sure. An internal report by the RCMP suggests that the financial relationship between the Sixth Family and the Bonanno Family ended with Massino's sneak attack on Montreal's man in New York: "After the murder of Sciascia, the envelopes [of money] stopped coming from Canada," the recent report says.

Their tie to the Bonanno Family was becoming less and less important as the Sixth Family's enterprises grew. With the intense attention paid to the Mafia by the FBI, the relationship was also something of a liability for the Montrealers. The relationship with Massino and his gangsters was becoming irrelevant to the modern business structure that Vito had been building. It was a bit like a waning reliance on the postal system with the advent of the Internet.

Vito made it clear to Vitale that the ascendant Sixth Family had outgrown its subservience to the Bonanno Family in New York. Vito's words to Vitale, spoken during their awkward lunchtime chat, were shocking in their clarity.

"We're our own little family," Vito said, according to Vitale. "There's about 18, 20 of us, and we stay by ourselves and everybody respects everybody else." The words were couched in politeness, as expected from such a gracious host, but New York had just been told to get lost. Vitale understood and dutifully carried Vito's message back to New York, reporting to Massino: "They have their own little splinter group."

The Sixth Family had not only eclipsed the wealth and strength of the Bonanno Family in New York, they now seemed to have extricated themselves from the family hierarchy and were truly setting themselves apart from any of the Five Families in New York.

CHAPTER 32

MONTREAL, 1990

The sign, erected near the corner of Jean-Talon East and Buies streets in Montreal, should have blended easily into the neighborhood's cluttered landscape as just another banal part of urban life: "Coming Soon—Pizza Hut." As the first outlet in Quebec for the world's largest pizza franchise, famous elsewhere for their deep pan pizzas, the planned Montreal opening in late 1990 was to be a beachhead, of sorts. A businessman in Quebec with a track record of success had secured the master franchise rights for the entire Island of Montreal, giving him the exclusive right to open and run dozens of Pizza Hut restaurants to feed the population of more than 3 million. It seemed only natural to locate the flagship outlet in Saint-Léonard—Montreal's "Little Italy"—where it would be surrounded by the very people whose culture had made pizza a popular international dish. The corner lot seemed ideal.

The sign announcing the pending arrival of Pizza Hut, however, enraged at least one neighbor.

Despite the transfer of power that had come to the underworld of Montreal after the deaths of Paolo Violi and Vic Cotroni, it seemed some things had not changed under the leadership of the Sixth Family. Just as Mauro Marchettini, the would-be pool hall owner under Violi's reign, had learned, the Pizza Hut owner would soon realize there were peculiarities to doing business in Saint-Léonard. The passage of three decades had changed little for the workaday mobsters on the streets of Montreal. With Vito and Nick Rizzuto in strict command, the mob men still considered themselves to be above the law and, in Saint-Léonard, at least, the makers of it. As such, the new Pizza Hut, located just across the street from Mike's Submarines, which was owned by Agostino Cuntrera, was regarded as a flagrant offense, Montreal police officers said. Agostino Cuntrera had been convicted for his role in the slaying of Violi and was a thoroughly integrated part of the Sixth Family enterprise.

"Agostino doesn't handle competition well," said a former organized crime investigator who probed the mob for decades in Montreal. A simple message was conceived for the businessman, police allege.

"He hires a couple of neighborhood kids to burn down the sign," the officer said. The next morning, the would-be pizza proprietor was greeted by a charred stump where his "Coming Soon" sign had stood. His response, however, was not what the mobsters expected. Had the Pizza Hut been run by a street-savvy Italian, the message of a burnt sign in Saint-Léonard might have been better understood as a not-so-subtle warning of ruffled mob feathers. This owner, however, was not Italian.

"Now, he is Jewish, so he doesn't understand for nothing when it comes to the mob," an officer said. "He doesn't get the message. He responds the way he has always responded to such things—he goes and puts up a bigger sign."

Work continued apace on the new restaurant and the frustration of the gangsters grew. Near the end of July, a more menacing message was sent. This time, it was not the sign but the building that was set ablaze. By mob standards, it was small-fry arson; the flames were doused before irreparable damage was caused. Only the bathroom area, where the fire was set, was hard hit. It was a setback for the opening, but the owner bravely pressed ahead. The restaurant, after all, represented an investment of approximately $1.2 million.

"We were focused on getting that place open and just running it as a business as best we could, like everyone else," said a former senior manager of the company. "He [the owner] wanted to open the store and, I guess, innocently in whatever way, he just figured you are opening a business, you got the franchise license, you paid your lease, you've got a deal with your landlord, you put your building up and off you go, right? And then, after you open, you expect to compete at a level with respect to what you have to offer. The customers then either come to you or they go to a competitor. That's business, and we were businessmen," he said.

"I guess not everyone plays by the rules," he added. Indeed not.

It was 2:37 a.m. on February 12, 1991, just a few days before the Pizza Hut was set to open, when an explosion erupted on Jean-Talon, waking neighbors and bringing the fire department rushing to the red-roofed brick building. This time, a serious player—a longtime member of the Hells Angels Motorcycle Club—had been brought in with instructions to do serious damage, police say. The fire department was soon joined by police officers and, in the morning, *Le Brigade des incendies criminels*, the Montreal police arson squad.

Evidence gathered by investigators showed that two explosive charges—made up of sticks of dynamite—had been assembled outside the building, one at the rear and the other at the side, strategically placed near natural gas pipes. The dynamite was hooked up to a detonator and 250 feet of wire, suggesting that the bomber had been there to set it off, at a safe distance, before fleeing. Had the gas line caught fire, the resulting explosion and fire would likely have leveled the premises completely. As it was, there was a powerful explosion but little flame. There was significant damage to the walls, roof, gas lines and the bathrooms—again—but the building remained standing and salvageable. Defiantly, the rebuilding began that very day, likely driving anyone from across Jean-Talon into fits of rage. Stunned staff gathered at the pizzeria the next day, gossiping among themselves and wondering what was going on.

"We have never had any threats. It has nothing to do with revenge. Truly, we have absolutely no idea who would want to do something like this to us," a company spokesperson said. Some staff soon left the firm, a reaction to the trouble at the flagship outlet, a former manager said. It was not only the local employees who were asking questions. The insurance company, too, was concerned over the fateful history of a business that had not yet opened its doors to customers. Awkward questions were also coming from the head office of Pizza Hut, which was owned at the time by powerful PepsiCo, the makers of Pepsi-Cola and one of the world's largest food and beverage companies. It was a significant ownership group, with annual revenues of $29 billion.

"There were certainly problems with respect to the store and the opening," a former manager said. "At one point, what happened was the insurance [company] didn't want to cover us any more, so we had to ask for assistance, for PepsiCo to support us, which they did. But try to explain this. Pizza Hut has restaurants all over the world and I'm not so sure they've encountered anything like that anywhere else. You can imagine, from an insurance perspective, what do you say? What's going on there? It was something very particular to that area."

What happened next was even more remarkable.

"PepsiCo is a big company, and they go and make a pointed inquiry as to what is going on in Montreal," said a retired police officer who was involved with the case. "When they first started asking, the response was: 'You're trying to open a pizzeria in Saint-Léonard—are you crazy?'" That answer only infuriated the company. From the head office of PepsiCo, a stern letter was sent to the chief of police demanding intervention, the officer said. In the letter, the company put the force decidedly on the spot by asking: Who is in charge of Saint-Léonard, the Mafia or the police? The chief knew such a challenge could not go unanswered. Equally, he knew, the answer had better be the police, or more than just business would be lost.

Officers knew they needed to send a message to Vito Rizzuto. Police in Montreal have a history of turning to creative means to get the attention of bad guys. When it came to getting the Mafia to listen, they knew the language best spoken was money. A devious plan was hatched, although no one officially takes credit for concocting it. At the time, organized crime investigators knew that a lucrative means of illicit profit came to the mafiosi through black-market video gambling machines. This was before the government recognized what the mob had long known and took over the running of the gambling devices, pouring the profit into its own coffers instead of the mob's. Two men associated with the Rizzuto organization were well known on the street for their string of gambling machines, set up in social clubs, cafés and bars throughout the city. Nicodemo Cotroni and Vincenzo DeSantis made a small fortune allowing Quebecers a fast and easy way to throw away their money, police said. Both men had ties to organized crime: Nicodemo was the eldest son of mob boss Frank Cotroni and had shown his own savvy by beating several gambling-related charges and another for assault; DeSantis was known by the nickname "Jimmy Rent-a-Gun" and earned an immediate place in the underworld by being the bartender at the Reggio Bar, Violi's old headquarters. Each of the poker machines they had placed was earning between $500 and $600 a week, providing a steady stream of revenue to be divided up.

"We started visiting these establishments and seizing the video gambling machines and saying to [the club and bar owners] as we left each one: 'Tell Vito it's because of Pizza Hut'," said a former police officer in Montreal.

"After about 30 or 40 of these visits, we phoned up Jean Salois [Vito's longtime lawyer] and say we would like to speak with Vito. Jean Salois comes in with Vito Rizzuto to the police station and Vito—through his lawyer—says he only came to assure us that he had no involvement in any of it. We said: 'We understand that you have no involvement, but we want it to end.'

"And it did," the former officer said. (Salois, it should be noted, says he was never contacted by police on this matter and he and Vito did not meet with officers about it: "Never, during all the years that I have represented Mr. Rizzuto, have I gone with him to a police station or elsewhere to meet with them," he said. "It is a blatant lie.")

That first Pizza Hut outlet would eventually open and meet with success, both in Saint-Léonard and across Montreal. By the spring of 1991, PepsiCo announced it was expanding its franchise deals into other areas of Quebec and, by September 1991, the Montreal franchisee had four outlets open, three more scheduled to open before the end of the year and another 15 planned for 1992. There seemed to be an odd hunger for the distinctive pizzas that Pizza Hut was offering; Montreal, despite its robust Italian population, generally seems to have trouble producing great pizza. In 2005, Pizza Hut was popular enough to be voted the second-best pizza in the city by the readers of the *Mirror*, a tabloid newspaper. That was a drop from the top spot, a rank it held in the poll's previous four years. The Pizza Hut case was a rare victory over the powerful Mafia on its own turf, although it came at a high emotional price.

"It was very difficult," said the man who was the Pizza Hut franchise owner at the time. (It has since changed hands more than once.) "I just know the repercussions; I don't know anything leading up to it," he said. He dismisses the notion that he is a brave figure who set an example of how honest citizenry can defeat the mob.

"I would look at it another way—incredibly stupid. You have to look at it both ways. If something would have happened, then it was incredibly stupid. Really, the heroes in this are the police. The heroes are the anti-gang squad and the heroes are the arson squad. That's it. That's it. There are no other heroes."

The moves against Pizza Hut show the duality of the organization that the Sixth Family had become as it moved into the 1990s. It had wrested control over a traditional mob city in order to gain a prominent foothold in the international drug trade, which it ran with a modern corporate sensibility, but at the same time it could not ignore its traditional roots as a village Mafia clan. It had an overarching mandate to move drugs, but various arms and cells of the organization reached out to take care of business in all its many forms. While the Bonanno Family in New York suffered from repeated federal indictments of its leadership, as well as deadly wars and assassinations among factions, the Sixth Family maintained a policy of growth, diversification and a careful avoidance of such messy affairs.

As it had with its drug schemes—cooperating with bikers, Asian and Colombian gangs, cornering the hashish market and moving into cocaine—the Sixth Family expanded into other criminal frontiers. From stock market swindles in Western Canada to petty extortion in Montreal; from a colossal counterfeiting operation producing U.S. currency to trying to recover the hidden gold of a deposed Asian dictator, the Sixth Family seemed to have a hand in every imaginable nook and cranny of global crime.

TORONTO, APRIL 1993

In the age of Enron, WorldCom and Martha Stewart, Penway Explorer Ltd. is a relatively minor flimflam, one of those periodic stories of charlatans squeezing an undeserved profit out of the stock market.

In the investment community, they call it "wash trading," when traders simultaneously buy and sell shares in the same company. It unfairly makes it look like there is interest in a company's stock when in fact the sales are a wash—no additional investment is made. Another scheme is called the "pump-and-dump," whereby unscrupulous salesmen convince unsophisticated investors to buy an unworthy stock to boost its price and then, when the price reaches a prearranged target, those in the know suddenly sell their shares. It was a combination of these schemes that was planned for Penway Explorers, an obscure mining company being traded on the Alberta Stock Exchange. Penway held mining claims in Northern Ontario in the late 1980s. Worth only pennies a share under normal conditions, large blocks of the stock were bought cheaply and parked while co-conspirators artificially inflated the stock's value, pumping it up to $6 a share.

A key salesman of Penway stocks was Arthur Sherman, who worked for McDermid St. Lawrence Securities Ltd., a Toronto brokerage firm. That Sherman was a problem trader was no secret. His supervisor, John Shemilt, described him as being "up to no good" from the moment he was hired. On May 8, 1988, Sherman vanished.

Twelve days later, he telephoned his boss and said he was in Aruba and would return at the end of the month. When Sherman failed to show up, he was fired. The fact that Sherman was missing left several of his clients checking their accounts. Many found their Penway stock was missing, totaling 530,400 shares. Sherman, it was found, had sold them before vanishing, presumably with the money. He appears to have dumped the stock before the conspirators had planned, beating them to the punch. His sudden purge of so much Penway stock sank the share value to around 30 cents. The investors figured they had been cheated out of $3.5 million by Sherman and took the missing broker and his former brokerage firm to court. Lawyers for the firm, however, took issue with the investors—a seedy bunch, including a disbarred lawyer and a shady stock promoter from Montreal who dealt in stolen securities. The brokerage argued that the investors were not the "sole and exclusive beneficial owners" of the stock. Something was fishy with Penway beyond Sherman's disappearance.

All of this would have been of little interest outside the investment community if it were not for revelations at a civil trial that the actual owners of the shares seemed unwilling to come forward. The investors who launched the lawsuit, lawyers for the brokerage claimed, were fronts for other people described as a "shadowy" Montreal group. Suddenly, a petty fraud case took on the trappings of a mystery novel. During 45 days of hearings, held sporadically between April 1992 and April 1993, Judge George Adams heard that the Penway swindle was where the markets and the Mafia met.

The dirty nature of Penway's transactions seemed obvious to Lise Ledesma, a receptionist at the brokerage firm. She was the poor soul people had to go through to reach Arthur Sherman before he disappeared. Ledesma said she received rude and demanding telephone calls from two people using the name Rizzuto who wanted to talk to Sherman. One of the calls was a long-distance connection placed by a Spanish-speaking operator—this was at a time when Nick Rizzuto was under arrest in Venezuela on the cocaine charge and, apparently, in need of cash to pay his legal fees. Vito then came to the offices of McDermid St. Lawrence in Toronto to see Sherman. Ledesma said he was accompanied by "two very large and frightening thugs." The visit and the calls were not well received. Sherman became "visibly anxious and nervous when it came to Mr. Rizzuto," she said.

The Penway transactions all led back to the Montreal Mafia. Robert Campbell, a disbarred lawyer and convicted forger, had bought his Penway shares through a firm in Toronto called Mercore Securities Inc., which seemed to trade nothing but Penway stock. Campbell was purchasing shares for Vito, who held meetings over the scheme in Montreal and Toronto, the court heard. Campbell had "the full confidence" of Vito and there was a large cash loan made from Vito, or his associate Dino Messina, court heard. The checks being exchanged throughout the stock deals also came from people linked to the Rizzutos. One of them, for $80,000, was made out to Rocco Sollecito, whom police had frequently seen meeting with Vito and other members of the Sixth Family.

Checks, however, were the least of the problems at Penway. Staff at a brokerage in Montreal reported their irritation with $40,000 to $50,000 payments for the stock being made in $10 and $20 bills. Gennaro Scaletta, who was arrested with Nick Rizzuto in Venezuela on cocaine charges in 1988, showed up in deposit records, along with Messina, Sollecito and Libertina Rizzuto, Vito's mother. Even these people were declared to be yet another layer of insulation around the real owner, the judge ruled: "On the evidence, I find the only person acting as a true owner was Vito Rizzuto." The transactions were subject to "the aggressive scrutiny of Roméo Bucci and the presence of Frank Campoli," the judge said. At that time, Bucci was a name from the mob's past and Campoli from its future. Bucci was the mobster who had previously been sent to New York by Paolo Violi to register Montreal's vote in the Bonanno Family leadership selection; Frank Campoli, described at the trial as "Vito's man in Toronto," married into the Cammalleri family and would surface years later in a probe into Vito's involvement in another controversial company.

Judge Adams dismissed the lawsuit. Unconvinced that Sherman had absconded with the Penway money, he suggested another possibility: that Sherman's disappearance was the result of "the wrath of Mr. Rizzuto."

The bad publicity for Vito from the Penway trouble was not over. By 1995, officials at Revenue Canada—the federal tax department—had pored over evidence from the proceedings. The question they had was that if Vito had been the beneficiary of all those stock purchases, why had none of this money been claimed on his tax returns? The taxman wanted his share of the $1.4 million in revenue that was traced to Vito through the stock transactions and issued a tax judgment against him. In addition to the unpaid taxes and a hefty interest payment, the government sought a $127,000 fine. Vito appealed the decision to the Tax Court of Canada. The department then threw itself into the case with surprising zeal. It appeared almost personal. The government's lawyers planned to introduce into evidence the school records of Vito's three children, evidence from Nick's arrest in Venezuela at the time of the swindle and records from Vito's arrests in the hashish cases. Also to be entered was a document titled "Associations of Vito Rizzuto with the Criminal Element in Canada and Elsewhere," and the criminal records for Vito and 28 of his associates, a collection of drug traffickers, money launderers, killers—and Maurice "Mom" Boucher, a leader of the Hells Angels Motorcycle Club, who qualified as all three. Also entered into the record was a statement of facts that included this line: "The applicant is known as 'the Godfather' of the Italian Mafia in Montreal." From then on, the designation would be repeated in the media whenever Vito found his way into news stories. The aggressive tactics seemed to take Vito and his lawyers by surprise.

Vito, always publicity shy, was suddenly reluctant to fight the tax bill and, after a frenzy of private meetings in August 2001, between his lawyer and government attorneys, an out-of-court settlement was reached just days before the hearings were scheduled to start.

"We felt like we had a strong case, but we wanted to avoid the media circus that was sure to happen," said Paul Ryan, Vito's tax lawyer, who said the government's emphasis on Vito's criminal connections was unusual. The terms of the settlement were not released.

According to government sources, Vito agreed to pay $400,000 to settle his case behind closed doors and avoid further public scrutiny, a sum that Vito himself has since confirmed. The suddenness and secretiveness of the settlement caused some alarm. John Williams, chairman of the government's Public Accounts Committee, filed a motion in Parliament demanding "copies of all agreements and related documents and/or correspondence, including reports, minutes of meetings, notes, e-mail, memos and correspondence, entered into between the government and Mr. Vito Rizzuto." Somebody seemed to think it was fishy. The government responded that tax matters were private and declined to make any information public. The payment of the fine was likewise done in private. The $400,000 settlement appears to have been a communal effort by the Rizzuto family, with several members sending large sums of money over the course of a year to Jean Salois, who set up an account to handle the inter-family loans. The flow started on January 21, 2002, with a $50,000 deposit by Vito's wife, Giovanna. She matched that deposit five months later and added another $75,000 in September. Vito's son, Nick, rose to the occasion with a $125,000 deposit into the account on May 15, and another $95,000 a month later. Vito's daughter, Bettina, kicked in $50,000 on February 5, leaving Vito needing to add only $5,000 of his own to the kitty. It was a communal approach that had been used by the family before. In a legal account apparently established to fund the fight against the government's tax case, $93,000 was accumulated through various deposits from Vito, his mother, his wife and his son Leonardo, according to accounting documents prepared by Salois, Vito's lawyer.

———

In the early 1990s, investigators watching Vito were also perplexed by a seemingly improbable venture that saw him traveling to Switzerland, Hong Kong and the Philippines. The travel was part of an attempt to get his hands on gold ingots from the fortune of Ferdinand Marcos, the deposed (and deceased) president of the Philippines. Vito claimed to have a mandate from the family of a Filipino general, who was a close associate of the former president, to retrieve assets from the Marcos estate on their behalf; it was believed to be hidden in Swiss and Hong Kong banks, the RCMP said. The talk of the gold stash surfaced during Project Bedside, another police operation investigating Vito for suspected drug activities. Officers found Vito in near constant contact with two brothers, twins, in Vancouver; their talk was not of Libyan hash, but Filipino gold.

Roberto and Antonio Papalia had once worked in Montreal night-clubs with Vito, when all three were young men. An older brother, Adolfo, was a co-owner, with Paolo Renda, of Complexe Funéraire Loreto, a Montreal funeral home that Vito had listed as his place of employment for several years, until 2001. (These Papalias are not related to the Ontario gangsters of the same last name.) After moving to Vancouver, the twins became controversial figures, making a name for themselves through several stock market deals and corporate ventures that ran afoul of market regulators. Roberto has been banned for life from being a director of any U.S. public company by the Securities and Exchange Commission, for defrauding investors; police have recorded

Antonio, known as "Tony," talking with Vito about a stock transaction in 1996 and was, until recently, in contact with Vito on a weekly basis, according to police. The Papalias reportedly controlled a small gold and iron-ore mine on Texada Island, a stretch of land 32 miles long and 6 miles wide that lies in the Strait of Georgia, about 190 miles north of Seattle. The mine might explain their interest in the Marcos gold plan or, conversely, why Vito might have sought their input.

Police in Canada were at a loss as to what to do when they realized what was under discussion. There was no easy evidence of a crime, certainly not one in Canada, and any investigation of such a global scheme would be an expensive venture. One thing they could do was alert the Philippines government to Vito's interest.

"We were telling people in the Philippines that he's arriving in Manila Tuesday, you should follow him from the airport, see where he is going, who he meets with," said a Montreal police officer involved in the case. "And they said, 'You have to pay us if you want us to tail him.' We couldn't believe it, we were like, 'Hey, it's your national treasury being pilfered, not ours'." It is unknown if Vito's attempt to act as an intermediary was successful.

SAINT-DONAT, QUEBEC, FEBRUARY 1995

The repetitive clunking sound coming from a cramped basement laundry room could easily have passed as a washing machine on its spin cycle, as unexpected visitors arrived at a chalet on a secluded lake near Saint-Donat, about a 90-minute drive north of Montreal. Instead of laundry facilities, a reconditioned printing press was found churning out counterfeit $100 U.S. banknotes. Piles of them. As police gathered the boxes containing sheets of uncut banknotes, which would later be tallied at some $15 million in face value, other officers arrested the man operating the press. In addition to being surprised by the sudden arrival of agents with the U.S. Secret Service, the RCMP and Montreal police, Lebanese-born Joseph Baghdassarian was frazzled from a cocaine binge. His erratic state only added to the marvel agents had for the quality of his work.

"He is a master craftsman," said Paul Laurin, a counterfeiting specialist with the RCMP who led the raid. "I have to say that this man was a counterfeiter who put his heart into his work. There aren't too many printers so good who go bad." The key to the work of Baghdassarian, who became known by the nickname "the Artist," was his ability to replicate the red and blue fibers that are embedded in genuine Federal Reserve bills. The Artist worked his magic with the printer, but it was the Sixth Family that moved his merchandise. The clan had long valued bogus banknotes and, as early as 1972, had been selling bulk loads of counterfeit notes and even using them to pay some of their bills. The notes from the Artist's press, sold for about $15 each, were recovered in Albany, Buffalo, Boston, Cincinnati, Miami, Honolulu, Houston, Los Angeles, Reno, San Francisco, Toronto and Vancouver. No less than $24 million had recently rolled off that press, and this was by no means the first batch. After the chalet raid, seven people were arrested and charged with counterfeiting, conspiracy and possession of counterfeit bills. The authorities boldly named the Montreal Mafia as the bankrollers and distributors of the counterfeit bills but, again, no member of the Sixth Family was ever indicted.

The stock swindles and gold deals, bogus money and extortion kept various Sixth Family members busy and well fed over the years, but such activities were never designed to replace their primary business. Drugs remained the priority, and in that, they would soon encounter a new underworld force that was both collaborator and challenger.

CHAPTER 33

MONTREAL, 1995

Maurice "Mom" Boucher was an ambitious, charismatic and seemingly fearless leader within the Hells Angels Motorcycle Club in Montreal, who headed a particularly bold and vicious chapter of the world's largest and most notorious biker gang. Boucher's Hells Angels chapter was the Quebec Nomads, a name denoting that they were, like the Sixth Family, not tied to a geographic territory. Also like the Sixth Family, the Nomads were obsessed with the staggering profits that the drug trade could bring. Mom Boucher's first targets in Montreal were rival bikers and independent drug dealers, many of whom he beat into submission, drove into retirement or had killed. He was buying drugs in bulk and working hard to have all street dealers sell only drugs bought through him. Boucher soon wielded considerable clout throughout the province of Quebec, controlling a significant and growing drug-trafficking enterprise.

For Boucher, that was not nearly enough. Again like the Sixth Family, Boucher wanted to build his own monopoly, to become his own brand and run his own drug franchise. Quietly, he was planning for the day when he was strong enough to replace Vito Rizzuto at the top of the underworld, but he knew that time had not yet come. Meanwhile, he faced a challenge that demanded his more immediate attention. Not all of the street distributors in the area were interested in dealing with Boucher. A number of dealers, bar owners and distributors got together and went looking for a better deal, and they found it in the Sixth Family. When Boucher learned his monopoly was being challenged by a group calling themselves the Alliance, who had secured a source through the Sixth Family, he was furious.

"The Hells Angels complained like hell about it to the Italians," said a longtime drug investigator in Montreal. He, like many police officers in Canada, even the Italian-born ones, used the word "Italians" as shorthand for the Mafia when talking about organized crime, just as

"Russians" is used for Eastern European crime groups, and "Jamaicans" for the criminal posses of immigrants from Jamaica.

"The Italians said to the Hells Angels, 'We will sell to whomever we want; we don't ask permission for anything. If we have a buyer we will sell it to that buyer and if you have a problem with that, then work it out amongst yourselves,'" the investigator said. The Nomads, under the leadership of Boucher, took the mob at its word. If they could not stop the flow of drugs to their competition at its source, then they would stop it at the retail end. When the rival gang—which had by then formalized its structure and changed its name to the Rock Machine—refused to restrict where and from whom they bought their drugs, the war was on. The Hells Angels were unrelenting; the Rock Machine, unyielding. The violence of the biker war in Quebec was unprecedented in Canada. Beginning in earnest in 1994, the war would claim more than 160 lives. It was a battle that the Hells Angels were winning, a fact not lost on the Sixth Family.

For his part, Vito appears to have recognized the impressive breadth of the Nomads' drug distribution network and the determination of its leader. Boucher came to represent a one-stop retail outlet. His reach was dominant in Quebec and Atlantic Canada and growing steadily across Canada. Like an oil-patch baron meeting a gas-station magnate, the two found good reason to talk. Never friends, but typically treating each other with courtesy, the Hells Angels and the Sixth Family started to hammer out an arrangement. The Sixth Family was the only criminal check on Boucher's ambition and power, and Vito could do that through reputation alone. While violence filled the streets of Montreal, precious little of it involved the Sixth Family.

"They basically signed contracts to be the sole supplier," said André Bouchard, the former head of the Major Crimes Unit of the Montreal police. "The Italians had the contacts in South America and the bikers didn't, not at that point. The Italians said to the Hells, 'We'll bring it into the port, you arrange to get it out of the port and it's yours to distribute in the province,'" Bouchard said of the early deal that set out the primary roles of the Mafia, the West End Gang and the Hells Angels. The West End Gang, an Irish-based mob, had a foothold in the Port of Montreal and, for a price, which might just as easily be a share of the drug shipment, they would make sure a load made it off a ship and into the hands of the Hells Angels, without anyone in the Sixth Family having to touch the drugs. Handling the bulk importation exposed the Mafia to the least risk of arrest. An agreement was formed between the three criminal organizations to control the supply and price of drugs, a forum called the Consortium.

By the summer of 1995, the deal was such that the supply of drugs was restricted considerably for most dealers—but not for Mom Boucher. Dany Kane, a biker well placed with senior Hells Angels who became an informant, told his police handlers on June 20, 1995, that the "drought continued" among drug dealers not tied to Boucher. The other Hells Angels realized that the Sixth Family was freezing them out, declining to sell to anyone but Mom Boucher. Boucher had formed an internal board of control for drug distribution, consisting of himself and four other Nomads, called *La Table*, "the table." Most Hells Angels in Quebec were forced to buy their drugs through *La Table*.

On the streets of Montreal, the dealers realized they had two real options for supply, the Mafia or the Hells Angels. As these middlemen worked their schemes to move the drugs around the province and into the bars, cafés and nightclubs where they were sold, they developed a simple hand sign to alert the people on the other end of the transaction as to just whose product they were dealing. A flash of a V with the fingers, like the peace sign given backwards, with the knuckles facing out, meant it was Vito's load; a twisting motion of the fist at the wrist, mimicking the turning of the throttle on a motorcycle's handbar, meant it was Mom Boucher's. Conversely, they might use two sets of letters.

"People will also say 'V-R' to refer to him. They will say, 'This is coming from V-R' or 'This is coming from the 'H-A,'" a Montreal gangster said, referring to the initials of Vito Rizzuto and the Hells Angels. Vito was also well-known by his nickname "The Tall Guy."

The Hells Angels generated a lot of fear on the street, but a February 1997 incident is a telling display of Vito's reputation. Dany Kane told his police handlers that two or three bikers, including Donald Magnussen, the right-hand man of a powerful Hells Angel, beat up Vito's youngest son, Leonardo, outside a St-Laurent Boulevard bar. It was not meant as a challenge to Vito's authority but simply a case of mistaken identity—the bikers just did not know who it was they were pounding. Talk rippled through the underworld of Vito wanting revenge and Magnussen, normally a thundering, murderous presence himself, cowered in fear. He refused to go out alone. Not long after the incident, he was calling his biker buddies looking for someone to go to the gym with him, Kane said. Few were willing to help out. Magnussen had also upset fellow bikers with an intemperate killing of a biker from the Los Brovos motorcycle gang, a group of bikers from Winnipeg that the Hells Angels were courting to join them. Whether one or the other enemy caught up with Magnussen, in 1998, he was found dead, floating in the St. Lawrence River. He had been savagely beaten before being killed. A Quebec criminal with long ties to organized crime said he doubts Vito would have gone after Magnussen.

"He was probably more upset with his son. He probably gave his son shit for getting into that kind of trouble; for causing a disturbance and allowing himself to be in that position. Vito likes to avoid that sort of thing," the underworld source said.

"They are very, very, very conservative people. Extremely conservative. Anytime there was any commotion or any attention, that was a bad thing. Things you wouldn't think would be a problem were—if you saw them in a restaurant and called them out by name, that would be a problem. If you were drunk and loud in a bar and saw them and came over to them, that would be a problem. They are actually very boring people," he said of the Sixth Family's inner core.

MONTREAL, APRIL 2000

The more it looked like the Hells Angels were winning the war for control of drug distribution in Quebec, the more the Sixth Family extended its hand in friendship to the gang. By 2000, they were working closely together, coordinating activities, prices and manpower and, in April of that year, senior Nomads and their closest associates were meeting with Vito's son Nick, according to Kane. Normand Robitaille, a Nomad member and a favorite of Mom Boucher's, was the gang's main liaison with the mob. Kane would often stand guard outside their meetings. The interaction, apparently, did not need to be hidden: a meeting between Nick, Robitaille and other Nomads on April 10, 2000, was held in a Montreal restaurant's bar; another, between Nick and Robitaille, on May 25, was in the parking lot of a Kentucky Fried Chicken, Kane told his handlers. From the Sixth Family's end, Antonio "Tony" Mucci acted as something of a go-between with the bikers, Kane said. Mucci gained notoriety when, in 1974, he walked into the newsroom of *Le Devoir*, a Montreal newspaper, and shot crime reporter Jean-Pierre Charbonneau, who had been writing about mob activity. Charbonneau survived and continued to expose the Mafia's activities and later became a popular politician.

By late May, the meetings between the Sixth Family and Hells Angels bore more fruit. A cartel had been formed that set a uniform price for cocaine at all levels: at the bulk rate it was to be $50,000 per kilo, a huge jump from its price of $32,000 a few years earlier, and at the street level it was to be sold for $25 for a one-quarter gram. By mid-June, the bikers and other dealers who were left out of both the Consortium and *La Table* were complaining of the price-fixing. They were losing customers because of the price. The Consortium did not seem to care. They insisted that the price could not be lowered, no matter what.

The mob's relationship with the bikers was working so well they started talking about other cooperative ventures, such as a telemarketing scam that involved phoning Americans to inform them they had won a car in a lottery; all the victims had to do was pay the taxes. Those foolhardy enough to pay the money would only kick themselves, not the tires of a new car. Kane told his police handlers that he was promised a cut of the telephone scam just for standing watch over the organizational meetings. The scheme was expected to clear $1 million each week.

The alliance with the Hells Angels caused some ruffled feathers within the Mafia, just as it had for bikers who were left out of *La Table*. Salvatore Gervasi, for instance, was a big man, not only because of his 300-pound frame but because his father, Paolo Gervasi, was a mafioso with close ties to Vito. Paolo Gervasi also owned Cabaret Castel Tina, a Saint-Léonard strip club popular in the Montreal underworld. The elder Gervasi was believed to be a made man in Vito's Mafia, or, as some in Montreal's underworld say, he had "hot hands," a reference to the burning picture of a saint that Mafia members hold in their hands during their induction ceremony. In the mid-1980s, Vito used Gervasi's club as a base, making frequent phone calls from its office. A decade later, it remained a great place for conducting illicit business. Salvatore, 32, was using his father's club as his base when he started into a criminal career.

"Salvatore used to hang around with the Rock Machine at the club. They wore their patches in the club and he furnished them, through his contacts, with narcotics," said André Bouchard, the retired Montreal police commander. "It didn't go over well with the Hells Angels because the Hells Angels were dealing directly with the Italians and the Italians weren't supposed to be working with the Rock Machine." After the Hells Angels complained to the Mafia leadership, Paolo Gervasi was told to keep his son in line. The warnings became graver but Salvatore's relationships with the Rock Machine continued.

"The night of Salvatore's murder, we found him in the trunk of a car. They parked the Porsche in front of his father's home in Saint-Léonard. His father arrived and came crashing into the crime scene; we had to tackle him to keep him away from the trunk," Bouchard said of the April 2000 murder of the young Gervasi.

"So the old man got pissed. He got really angry at the Italians when he found out that they killed his son and he said he was going to get rid of the club. The Italians offered to buy the club from him and he told them to go fuck themselves and he actually got up on a bulldozer and tore down his own club. It was his way of getting back at them. He built condominiums over top of the club, and a parking lot. That really pissed the Italians off and that was the first time they shot him." Four months after his son's murder, Gervasi was shot repeatedly as he walked out of a bank. The bullets were not meant to kill, unless the gunman was incompetent. The message, however, was ignored by Gervasi, a tough and hot-headed man who, in response, did the un-imaginable—he went after Vito himself.

Police learned of the plot and, for weeks, watched two men who had been hired as hitmen. Investigators also felt it was necessary to warn the targets—Vito Rizzuto and Francesco Arcadi—according to an RCMP report. On July 13, 2001, police were watching the alleged assassins, who were driving in different vehicles and seemed to be converging on Vito's Consenza headquarters. Fearing imminent gun-play, police stopped both vehicles and arrested two men. Although neither was armed, a search of one of their homes turned up an AK-47 automatic rifle, a .357-caliber magnum revolver, two 9mm pistols, two bulletproof vests, walkie-talkies and ammunition clips, police said. The tension was not over. On February 25, 2002, a pass-erby reported a suspicious object underneath a Jeep Grand Cherokee parked near the Consenza club. Police do not believe Vito was the target of that bomb plot, investigators say in internal documents; it was meant for Paolo Gervasi. The old mobster's luck would not hold forever. He would later be killed, caught in a flurry of gunfire as he sat behind the wheel of his Jeep, but that final chapter for Gervasi was not yet played out when the Hells Angels and the Mafia were dividing their spoils.

On June 21, 2000, Robitaille had nothing but warm regards for the Sixth Family, gushing over Vito and Tony Mucci to Kane. Affairs between the two groups had been tense in the past, but, Robitaille told Kane, they were now one big team. Robitaille's confidence stemmed from a meeting earlier that day at a restaurant in Laval, across the river from Montreal. Vito, Mucci and two of their associates met with Robitaille and two senior members of the Hells Angels Nomads.

"Norm told me that Vito was very nice and it wasn't pretense," Kane wrote in his diary of a conversation with Robitaille. "He told me that the Italians were strong and that if they were at war with them, the Hells Angels would have more trouble with them than they had with the Rock Machine." On July 31, Kane again stood watch over a meeting between the organizations. The St-Laurent Boulevard restaurant was closed, so Kane could hear some of the chatter between Vito's son, Nick, and Robitaille, he told his handlers. Nick said that 250 kilos of cocaine a week were moving through Montreal. At the new fixed rate, that meant $12.5 million in revenue each and every week.

Along with letting others do the more dangerous hands-on work of selling the drugs in Canada, the Sixth Family's business model offered other benefits as well, investigators said.

"Vito never brings anything in that isn't already sold. He wouldn't bring in 5,000 kilos if he had only sold 1,200 kilos. The stuff is bought and paid for in advance and his job was to bring it to the Port of Montreal or the Port of Vancouver or the Port of Halifax—whatever port you want," André Bouchard said. An experienced drug investigator agreed that Vito was a master of financing.

"Vito never put a dime of his own money into a deal. It was always somebody else's money but he would end up with 60 percent of the product. He would take no risk but imprisonment—and that was remote with his level of insulation—and if the deal worked out he puts $50 to $60 million in his pocket, and if it didn't work out, well, other people lose their money," the officer said. "He is a very clever man."

The bikers meant more to Vito than just men to push his dope. The nagging war between the Hells Angels and the Rock Machine drew the attention of the police and the public, making the bikers the number-two criminal organization but the number-one police target in Quebec and, later, in all of Canada.

"We didn't really have enough time for the Italians. All the time, it was the bikers," Bouchard said. This meant Vito went about his business largely unimpeded by city and provincial police. It had nothing to do with corruption, Bouchard said. It had to do with the in-your-face nature of the war waged by the rival biker gangs that left bodies in Montreal streets.

"The Italians played it very smart," Bouchard said. "[Police] put all of their money and all of their eggs in one basket and said, 'We have to attack the motorcycle gangs. They're the ones making the most noise.' If you throw enough money at something, you can get things done. My guys were working 16-hour days for years on the bikers." There was little left over to keep an eye on the Sixth Family. During the biker war, Vito got an easy ride in Montreal.

"During that whole period, from 1992 to 2001, nobody touched the Italians. The police didn't go after them. We didn't check on them, we didn't wiretap them. And any information that came in largely came from other police departments. They said, 'Watch out for this guy, watch out for that guy.' The Italians sat back, made all their money, bought up businesses, laundered their money. They became specialists in laundering money," said Bouchard, who added he regrets not having the resources to focus on both organizations.

The sparks from the biker war soon grew too hot, even for the Sixth Family. Innocents were getting caught in the crossfire. First, in 1995, an 11-year-old boy was killed by shrapnel from a car bomb. Two years later, two Quebec prison guards were killed in a bid to destabilize the justice system. Then, in 2000, Montreal's best-known crime reporter, Michel Auger, was shot in the parking lot of his newspaper, the popular tabloid *Le Journal de Montréal*. Despite six bullets in his back, Auger survived, but the outrage over the bold attack was palpable. Protest marches were held and demands made for tougher anti-gang legislation to tackle this criminal audacity. Politicians started talking about an American-style racketeering law. Suddenly, the biker war was putting a crimp in the Sixth Family's quiet existence.

"Vito did sit down with Mom Boucher and say, 'You have to stop these things, it's hurting everyone,'" Bouchard said.

Even a crime boss as powerful and as aggressive as Mom Boucher needed to listen when Vito spoke. Vito could make peace as well as war.

MONTREAL, MARCH 2001

In the early hours of March 28, 2001, authorities mustered some 2,000 police officers from numerous federal, provincial and municipal forces for what would be the largest police assault against organized crime in Canada. After years of investigation by police using a number of informants—one who had been murdered when his cover was blown, killed while still wearing his police wire, ghoulishly capturing his own death on tape, and another, Dany Kane, who committed suicide—a stack of arrest warrants had been assembled as part of a major police operation for targets in Quebec and Ontario. By the end of the day, 128 people had been arrested in what was called Operation Springtime 2001. All of them were bikers or biker associates. The members of the Hells Angels Nomads were pinched; their puppet gangs and assassins, their money launderers and drug runners were arrested.

The Hells Angels, by taking on society so openly and defiantly, had drawn all of the heat and now faced all of the repercussions.

Their partners, the Sixth Family, once again skipped over the carnage and went on with its business.

CHAPTER 34

TORONTO, JANUARY 2001

Before the police toppled the most aggressive of the world's Hells
Angels, Vito Rizzuto and his Sixth Family kin were already planning a
strategy to deal with the growing strength of the bikers. He recognized
them as a threat at the same time he accepted them to sit at his table,
likely with an eye to the old adage about keeping your friends close
and your enemies even closer.

In the months before Operation Springtime 2001 largely settled the
matter, Vito was working to do with the Mafia what the Hells Angels
had managed to accomplish with the bikers. The Hells Angels had recently accepted several veteran motorcycle gangs in Ontario into their
fold, dramatically waiving their own rules on membership and granting full-patch membership status to all of the bikers in the independent
gangs who agreed to bury their own gang colors. It had been a bold
move that gave the Hells Angels coast-to-coast coverage of the prime
drug markets of Canada. Vito wanted to do the same for the Mafia
clans, uniting them all under his banner, a move that would give him
unprecedented power and position.

In late January 2001, some of the province's most plugged-in police investigators started hearing whispers of a gathering of Mafia clans
from across the country. A meeting was either being called or had
already been held north of Toronto as an apparent attempt to forge an
alliance among quarreling Mafia clans from Ontario, Quebec, British
Columbia and possibly New York State. The aim was to present a united front to the internationally linked and newly unified biker gang.

"The Hells Angels are now in Ontario forming a unity with the
Hells Angels in Montreal. Is that a threat to them? I'd say so," said a
Toronto police officer who investigates organized crime. "It seems it's
time for the Italians to put their differences aside, and if they perceive
the bikers as a threat, then they have incentive," he said of the Mafia
clans. Police believed the meeting was chaired, or was planned to be

chaired, by Vito. It was a strategic move to use the threat of the bikers as an excuse to let him have Ontario; as opposed to conquerer, he was branding himself as protector.

Despite the dense population of notable mobsters in the province of Ontario, clustered mainly in and around Toronto, Hamilton and Niagara Falls, there was a distinct leadership vacuum. On the last day of May 1997, Johnny "Pops" Papalia, who had thrown his lot in with the Magaddino Family in Buffalo early in life and parlayed it into a four-decades long career as one of Canada's leading crime figures, had been shot dead. Papalia had, like Vic Cotroni in Montreal, struck a deal with an American Mafia organization to be their representative in Canada. It made him strong when the Buffalo mob was strong and he then went on to outlive his American contemporaries. The demise of Papalia, at the age of 73, left the province without a central mob figure. The Sixth Family was anxious to fill that void but, in keeping with its tradition, it acted with caution. Investigators could not shake the belief that the Sixth Family's ambition played a role in the demise of Papalia, a murder preceded by the slaying of his man in Toronto, Enio Mora—at the hands of Sicilian mobsters—and followed by the slaying of Papalia's man in Niagara Falls, Carmen Barillaro. It seemed a purge of the old American Mafia presence in Ontario, as had occurred in Montreal two decades before. (Giacinto Arcuri was charged with killing Mora, but was acquitted.)

The gunman who killed Papalia and Barillaro was caught and told police and the court that he was acting on the orders of the Musitano Family, a rival mob clan in Hamilton. Police suspicions over Sixth Family involvement, however, were not allayed when, in the middle of the night, investigators secretly tailed Pasquale "Pat" Musitano, the young boss of his family, to a restaurant in Woodbridge, north of Toronto. There, on October 23, 1997, exactly three months after Barillaro was murdered and five months after Papalia was killed, Musitano and his cousin, Giuseppe "Pino" Avignone, had a lengthy meeting with Vito and Vito's hulking enforcer in Toronto, Gaetano "Guy" Panepinto. What, investigators wondered, was the connection?

Panepinto had long been a fixture on the Southern Ontario crime scene and had grown from a street rowdy into a middle-level player, but had difficulty leaving the adrenaline rush of thuggery behind; bombings, arsons, loan sharking and extortion were his stock-in-trade. His connections with professional hijacking crews made him a ready supplier of weapons, stolen cars, motorcycle parts, steroids, cocaine and other drugs.

"Guy was the go-to guy if you had something physical that needed to be done, or something with some risk attached. He was this huge motherfucker, but had a great smile. He knew everybody. The bikers loved him; the Italian guys always had a kind word for him. He wasn't afraid to be a real criminal," said a biker associate of Panepinto's. At the same time, he was moving to a higher level of sophistication, establishing his own front companies and legitimate sources of income, including a Toronto franchise of Casket Royale, a storefront outlet in Toronto's Little Italy that offered discount coffins and funeral merchandise. His caskets ran from $295 for thin pressboard to $4,900 for a bronze luxury model. He offered designer themes—such as denim-covered caskets with cowboy-themed decorations—and used, as a somber marketing ploy, an offer of "free" children's caskets.

"Guy had a great sense of humor. When he opened the casket store he said he'd become his own best customer," said a longtime underworld friend.

Panepinto quickly swore his sword to Vito. In Ontario, Panepinto joined a mix of old-time Sicilian Men of Honor, Calabrian gangsters, motorcycle gangs and other proven career criminals, who were attracted to Vito and his Sixth Family organization.

Vito was far from being alone in Ontario when he made moves on the province. The Sixth Family had many friends there: Vito's in-laws, who, according to police, had long been a presence in Ontario under the leadership of Antonio Cammalleri, who was Vito's wife's uncle; Peter Scarcella, a Sicilian mobster to whom Vito had been introduced to back in the 1960s when Vito was courting his wife, who later asked Vito to be the godfather to his daughter and went on to become a mobster of note in Toronto; Giacinto Arcuri, who had fled from Cattolica Eraclea after the murder of the town's mayor and kept close to Montreal and New York allies of both the Rizzutos and Gerlando Sciascia. Arcuri is a man of note to Toronto's underworld, pegged by police as above even Scarcella within the Sicilian coterie. Other men who had made a name for themselves but had largely managed to avoid the scrutiny of police were also with Vito. And their old allies, the Caruana–Cuntreras, had also relocated to Ontario in the early 1990s, with Alfonso Caruana running his drug empire from his new base north of Toronto, where he and other family members bought homes and businesses.

Also in Ontario was Frank Campoli, who had married Vito's wife's cousin, who was a Cammalleri. Campoli was named in court as Vito's "man in Toronto" in the Penway stock scam in Ontario in 1988, but he had greater business success with OMG Media Inc.

OMG, originally called Olifas Marketing Group, was a Toronto-area firm that in the late 1990s came up with a way to blend the recycling craze with paid advertising; large metal bins would be placed on street corners where passersby could deposit their recyclable bottles or fast-food containers, and dispose of litter. The containers would display advertising. OMG urged municipalities and cities to sign contracts that would permit placement of the bins on busy thoroughfares. The more bins, the higher the advertising revenues. For OMG, ads were crucial to its revenue. Up-front expenses were considerable in that the container bins had to be built and trucked to the agreed locations. Yet the pitch to cities and schools seemed oddly to favor those clients.

OMG normally paid its municipal and institutional clients approximately $10 for each container that it was allowed to place. OMG would then pay for the manufacturing of each bin (approximately $1,500 each), its shipping and installation costs, and then ongoing maintenance costs. In some cases, OMG was even responsible for collecting the weekly recyclables and refuse. In return, OMG was granted the right to sell and place advertisements on two faces of the bin. Most deals allowed the municipalities a certain number of bin faces for its own advertising, such as public-service announcements, for free.

OMG had signed agreements with the city of Montreal, and in Ontario, the cities of Toronto, Ottawa, Hamilton, London, Markham and Windsor. It also moved into the educational market, placing boxes or signing agreements with universities, colleges and elementary schools, including McMaster University in Hamilton and the Toronto District School Board. In 2003, OMG signed its largest contract in the United States with the Board of Education for the City of New York. It was a deal to place some 2,700 bins on school property. OMG also looked abroad, working on agreements in Italy, Eastern Europe, Malaysia, Barbados and Trinidad and Tobago.

In its early days, OMG had several men involved in the business. Frank Campoli, Giancarlo Serpe and Salvatore Oliveti among them. Campoli was in contact with Vito Rizzuto on a weekly basis, according to police. Serpe had been seen by police meeting with many mobsters over the years, notably murdered mafioso Enio Mora. According to court documents, Serpe was "the last witness to have seen Mora alive." Serpe was also seen with Giacinto Arcuri, who would later be charged and acquitted of killing Mora. OMG's Quebec division was headed by Michael Strizzi, who had been a close personal friend of Vito's for more than 20 years. These connections appear to have gone unnoticed by, or were of no concern to, city staff and politicians as OMG was negotiating its public contracts.

The pitch to the city of Toronto, the company's largest Canadian contract, was backed by Joe Foti, a Liberal fundraiser who held considerable sway before his death. He was famous for his annual barbecue, which attracted notable politicians, including Jean Chrétien, then Canada's Prime Minister. OMG also hired a high-powered lobbyist, Paul Pellegrini, president of the Sussex Strategy Group, to help attract federal government advertising. Pellegrini registered as a lobbyist on OMG's behalf on December 19, 2001, to make telephone calls, arrange meetings and conduct "informal" communications with government departments, including Canadian Heritage, National Defence, Revenue Canada, and Public Works, Pellegrini said. (Pellegrini said his relationship with OMG was short-lived and neither he nor his firm retains any connection to the company.)

OMG's proposal was well received in Toronto. Turning its back on a staff recommendation, the city's public works committee voted to give OMG a 10-year contract without putting it out to public tender; this decision was later overturned by city council. When the bids from several companies were received, OMG was selected as the best. By 2003, it had placed 2,797 bins on Toronto's streets, at an estimated cost to OMG of $4 million.

As the recycling trend became rooted in the public consciousness, the company positioned itself to profit. In 2003, OMG budgeted for $8 million in revenue. Its public relations efforts with city politicians and staff were working wonders. As Lou Gallucci, OMG's vice-president at the time, said in a sworn affidavit: "OMG is dependent on the goodwill of the municipalities in which it operates, as OMG requires the consent and approval of the municipalities in order to provide its services."

––––––––

Altogether, Ontario was looking a lot friendlier to the Sixth Family than ever before. By October 2000 it had a fast-rising stake in the distribution of cocaine throughout Southern Ontario. With Johnny Papalia and the most powerful and volatile of his cronies out of the way, there seemed little appetite among the Ontario-based clans to give the Rizzutos much grief. The lucrative nature of their cooperation with the Hells Angels in Quebec bought them the immediate good graces of the independent biker gangs in Ontario that were being heavily courted by the Quebec Hells Angels.

Following the successful strategy his father had used in Montreal when the Sixth Family began to raise its voice against Paolo Violi and strengthened his claim through an alliance with the Caruana–Cuntrera clan, Vito searched for a strong group with an impeccable pedigree with whom to forge an alliance with in Ontario. Shunning the Sixth Family's traditional fondness for keeping their affairs closely Sicilian, he found the perfect coupling in the Commisso family. Based around three brothers, Cosimo, Rocco Remo and Michele, the Commissos had immigrated to Toronto from Calabria in 1961 and were about as street strong in Toronto as any mob clan could expect. The stage seemed set for the Sixth Family to make its move.

From night clubs to fitness clubs, strip bars to fast-food outlets, drugs were being moved at the retail level in Toronto and surrounding cities, replicating the cocaine distribution system that had made Quebec gangsters rich. Legitimate businesses and corporate investments were in place and its Ontario manpower was not insignificant. The time had finally come for the Sixth Family to absorb its neighbor.

"Was it a takeover? Yes," said one of the Toronto police's top organized crime investigators. "That was their intention."

"Vito was making his way here much more often. It was on a weekly basis to show his face and make his presence known. He was here in person to show people that maybe it was finally time for him to take control, that it was time to do things his way," said another top anti-Mafia investigator. "He wanted to unite all of the Italian groups, just as the bikers united in Ontario. Vito was doing the same thing with the Italians. The bikers came together under the Hells Angels, and the Italians fell in under Vito."

Vito was hard to miss in Toronto, as he was always with at least two other men, apparently bodyguards, a contrast to his routine in Montreal, where he typically traveled alone, and drove his own car.

"He walks with authority. He looks very distinguished. He dresses very businesslike. Most of the time I've seen him he is wearing a suit and tie," said a police officer who worked surveillance shifts monitoring Vito's visits to Ontario. "Not only does he play the part, he looks the part."

Toronto's gangsters were largely recognizing his authority, if not exactly his control; but his position in Ontario was hardly comparable to the hegemony he maintained in Quebec.

"Although Vito is the one who happens to be in charge, in Toronto, he really doesn't seem to have a hold on his people in the same way as in Montreal," said an organized crime investigator. "There are people who are affiliated with him, people who are related to him, people who are running things on his behalf or in his name or using his name. As long as they have his blessing and he basically knows what they are doing and he gets his cut from it, he is happy enough with the situation. He would come in once in a while to check on his friends and to check on his family. That's all he has to do, show up. He has the standing, the name recognition." Officers monitoring wiretaps that were running on some of the Sixth Family's people in Ontario said the reporting structure was kept loose.

"Although he is part of his family, there was no weekly reporting or monthly reporting. Not even really a quarterly report," said an officer, speaking about Peter Scarcella, a leading Sixth Family ally in Toronto. "He would visit him—Vito is godfather to his daughter—but the conversations with his associates show the way the family works here in Toronto is a lot different from how it works in Montreal. There is still a lot of respect within the families in Montreal. They still have that respect, they still follow the hierarchy, they still tell the boss what they're up to, and it is understood that when or if anything does happen the people at the top will get their cut. They don't have to ask for it. In Toronto, it is not so smooth. There is not such respect within their families."

Vito appears not to have wanted to clamp down too tightly, perhaps as an opening strategy to gain further acceptance as a force to be embraced rather than resented or repelled.

"The purse strings have opened up," said one Mafia-linked career criminal of the new business model in Ontario. "There is now more money to go around. John [Papalia] kept things pretty tight."

In order to bring about some discipline, however, Vito started to directly place more of his own men in Ontario, with two setting up in Hamilton and others in Toronto and its suburbs.

Giuseppe "Joe" Renda, a nephew of Gerlando Sciascia, was sent from Montreal to Toronto to work with Gaetano Panepinto, Frank

Campoli and others to solidify the Sixth Family's hold.

Taking advantage of the new opportunities and manpower in Ontario, the Rizzuto organization established a sports betting enterprise that used Internet hook-ups and BlackBerries to register hundreds of millions of dollars in bets placed at video stores, gas stations and other small retail outlets in Toronto, Ottawa and Hamilton. They found a willing and hungry clientele; one man placed a $100,000 bet on a single football game. It quickly became one of the largest betting rings in Canada.

The moves put Vito at the top of his game. His reach was unchallenged. His territory was staggerly large, not only in geographic size but in its population and economic might. Toronto and its surrounding suburbs offered almost 5 million people and Montreal another 3½ million. Vito also had outposts of friends and colleagues in other Canadian cities as well, particularly in Vancouver. The Sixth Family, noted a recent RCMP report, had "taken over the criminal underworld with the help of their associates across the country."

With Ontario falling under the Sixth Family's shadow, an alarm was sounded by intelligence officers working with the Combined Forces Special Enforcement Unit (CFSEU), a joint police unit of several police agencies under the leadership of the RCMP. Staffed by some of Canada's foremost anti-Mafia investigators, the CFSEU was analyzing intelligence reports, tidbits of mob gossip from investigators and street snitches and slowly saw the pieces falling into place.

The Sixth Family, a secret intelligence report noted, was dominating "not only the province of Quebec but the province of Ontario as well, making this organization one of the most influential and powerful traditional organized crime groups in North America."

That kind of alarm is difficult to ignore.

"Unfortunately for Vito," said a police investigator, "it started to fall apart."

CHAPTER 35

TORONTO, JULY 15, 1998

The first clear sign that Ontario was not the same sort of place as Montreal for the Sixth Family and its friends came on July 15, 1998, before Vito Rizzuto and his kin had even fully brought the province into their confederacy. The message was a harsh one: police cruisers closed down a quiet suburban street in Woodbridge, just north of Toronto, at 7:05 a.m., letting nothing but police vehicles through. A police convoy then snaked past the large detached homes and well-manicured lawns. Two minutes later, an RCMP officer rang the doorbell at 38 Goldpark Court. Inside, officers arrested Alfonso Caruana, the boss of the Caruana–Cuntrera clan, which, for four decades, had been a firm ally and friend of the Rizzutos'. Also arrested that day were Alfonso's two brothers, Gerlando in Montreal and Pasquale in Toronto, and other members of their drug network. In Cancun, the clan's key drug facilitator, Oreste Pagano, was nabbed by Mexican police and flown to Canada.

The case would unfold as the most successful investigation into the Sicilian Mafia in Canada, but it began humbly, with a comment caught on a wiretapped telephone in 1995, made by Enio Mora, a longtime gangster in Toronto. Mora, who was nicknamed "Pegleg" because he had lost part of one leg in a shootout, was heard discussing an upcoming wedding. Toronto police intelligence officers Bill Sciammarella and Tony Saldutto discovered the date, time and location of the wedding and the detectives and other officers with the Combined Forces Special Enforcement Unit (CFSEU) watched guests arrive for the celebration at Toronto's Sutton Place Hotel. The Sixth Family was well represented: Vito himself came, wearing a gray suit jacket; Rocco Sollecito, Francesco Arcadi and Frank Campoli were also there. Between the April 1995 wedding and the 1998 arrests of the Caruana brothers and associates, Canadian police ran Project Omertà, spending an estimated $8.8 million to capture the mobsters.

Concern among the Sixth Family at the news of the arrests was palpable; there had been a high degree of interaction between Alfonso Caruana and Vito and other family members and associates. Extensive records filed in court as part of Project Omertà revealed calls to pizzerias tied to drug traffickers involved with the Rizzutos, cafés that doubled as meeting places for the Sixth Family, lawyers linked to the family and car dealerships suspected of shipping cocaine into Ontario stashed in vehicles. In one call, Nick Rizzuto was heard talking to one of the Caruana brothers, telling him to bring two traffickers to a meeting. In another, police heard drug traffickers talking about "the old man." According to a police summary of the conversation: "The 'old man' was identified through surveillance as Nicolò Rizzuto ... [the traffickers say] not to speak to him because he talks too much and to go and speak to his son, believed to be Vito Rizzuto." Surveillance teams following Project Omertà suspects from Toronto to Montreal took several photographs of Nick attending meetings. In all, more than a dozen members of the Sixth Family were observed interacting with the Project Omertà targets. Some were sent into the United States to transfer money or drugs—although no leading figures, including Caruana, Nick and Vito, felt comfortable crossing the border into America.

The obvious relationship between the Rizzutos and the Caruanas, coupled with their longstanding alliance, prompted one of Canada's leading organized crime investigators to suggest they were two parts of the same operation. "I've long wondered how separate they really are," he said, illustrating his point by weaving the fingers on both of his hands together.

Although Project Omertà uncovered extensive interplay between the Sixth Family and the Caruana drug network, and despite the overt accusations made against Vito by Oreste Pagano to police, once again no charges were laid.

TORONTO, SUMMER 2000

Problems for the Sixth Family in Ontario did not stem only from aggressive law enforcement. The century-old traditions of the Mafia also conspired to damage its new assets, namely Gaetano Panepinto, its hulking enforcer who was moving cocaine and discount coffins in Toronto. Panepinto was pleased with his lot in life as Vito expanded his presence and power in Toronto. As an early adopter of the Rizzuto brand, he was using his association to its full extent and the aggrandizing feeling of power it endowed seemed to cause him to forget that he was not truly a member of its inner circle. In the underworld, such oversight is often tragic.

Like any active gangster, Panepinto disliked competition, which is why he was incensed when two newly arrived Calabrian mafiosi started to cut into his action. The two men were 'Ndranghetisti who had fled police in their hometown of Siderno, on southern Italy's Ionian coast. Toronto was a good place for such men to hide, as a significant number of mafiosi from Siderno had, for generations, settled in and around the city, establishing what an Italian judge recently called the most important "colony" of the Sidernese 'Ndrangheta. When these two fugitives, who were believed to be cousins, left Italy, Toronto 'Ndrangheta leaders were told to expect them. The fugitives were welcomed, given permission to work in the city and, in accordance with their underworld code, came under the protection of the Toronto colony.

These two fugitives immediately looked around for ways to make money and found it by placing illegal slot machines. It was of little concern to them that their fledgling gambling business was in direct competition with a similar enterprise run by Panepinto. Vito's man immediately complained that the Calabrian newcomers were squeezing him. As a major earner, supporter and contributor to the Sixth Family's cause, Panepinto felt he could deal directly with the Sidernese.

"Remember, Guy was never made. He acted made—he had guys around him, a crew of his own just like a made guy, but he never won the jackpot," a well-connected Toronto criminal said. Another man, who managed a gym Panepinto had a financial interest in, said Panepinto raised his complaints at a "sit-down" with a powerful organized crime figure north of Toronto.

"They told him there was nothing they could do," the manager said. "They'd try to see that he got an end [a portion of the profits], but he basically could kiss his machines goodbye. The Siderno guys were the real thing and Panepinto wasn't; he wasn't made. In spite of everything, he was a link between the Rizzutos who brought in the drugs and the bikers and guys who distributed them. He might have got made eventually, but who knows? I'm told he went to Montreal; he went to Vancouver to discuss the situation with some bikers out there, maybe to get some muscle to bring east. But he got nothing. Montreal didn't care about his machines or his grabs [truck hijackings]; they just wanted to move their drugs through him."

The Sidernese likely tolerated Panepinto's audacity in bringing the matter directly to them, despite his inferior underworld standing, because of his link to the Sixth Family, but that could carry him only so far.

Frustrated in his failed efforts at repelling the fugitives, Panepinto took a chance. He lured the two men to the basement of his St. Clair Avenue West casket business, where, with at least one other shooter, he gunned them down, police believe. The bodies were removed and have never been found. A fire was deliberately set to destroy evidence of the slayings. Panepinto then went about his business.

It did not take long for the lack of contact from the Sidernese fugitives to cause alarm among the 'Ndrangheta families, who then investigated the disappearances. The signs quickly pointed to Panepinto. The Sixth Family leadership was apprised of their concerns, according to police investigators. It was a serious problem because, within the Mafia, a made man is accorded protection under an underworld code that is surprisingly uniform on this point.

"When you join, it's like getting a license," a Toronto gangster said. "You get opportunities, you get protection and you get support. You get organization. No one can come and earn where you earn. You won't find a card game opening on the same street; you won't have a free-for-all when you're moving dope, guys undercutting you. Whether it's the Calabrese, the Sicilians, the American Mafia, you join so you can earn and you can earn safely. When you're made, you're like a god." It is what puts the organization in organized crime.

One of the Mafia's most important rules is that made men cannot be killed without permission from higher-ups. It was a rule that caused much grief for the Sixth Family when it wanted to push Paolo Violi aside in the 1970s. For a non-made man, no matter how powerful or productive, to murder an initiated member of a family is a transgression that cuts through finance, connections and underworld stature. Panepinto felt his financial contributions made him immune from this basic foundation of the Mafia. For a terrified, fleeting moment, he might have realized how wrong he was. Also conspiring against Panepinto were the ingrained traditions of the men he had insulted. The 'Ndrangheta operates under a code of conduct that is rigid and unforgiving. This mindset embraces honor, manliness, personal power and the *faida*, "the vendetta." *Faida* is an important part of 'Ndrangheta culture. It was inconceivable to the Sidernese that this slight could be left unanswered.

"Panepinto took it upon himself to do these guys," said a police officer involved in the investigation. "The people he killed belonged to other families. They probably approached Vito and said, 'Why did you do that to our guys?' Vito would say, 'I didn't do anything. I didn't have anything to do with it. Handle it any way you wish. Do whatever you have to do to make amends.'" It was bad timing for Panepinto. If the traditional rules of the mob did not persuade Vito that he had to let Panepinto go, the efforts he was making to unify the mobsters in Ontario gave him a more pragmatic reason to step aside and not aggravate the influential Sidernese gangsters any further.

"Vito was trying to amalgamate the Italian families. Whatever it took, whatever had to be done to maintain the peace," another officer said.

TORONTO, OCTOBER 3, 2000

Panepinto was only a few blocks from his home in an upscale west Toronto neighborhood when a van pulled up beside his burgundy Cadillac. From the van came a fusillade of gunfire. Panepinto suffered numerous bullet wounds and his car veered from the roadway and crashed to a stop, where his body was found slumped over the steering wheel by neighbors who had heard gunfire and screeching tires. In his car, police found blueprints for a nightclub in Barrie, a city north of Toronto, and a book about organized crime in Canada. Homicide detectives called it "a professional, organized hit" and immediately ran into a wall of silence from the victim's friends and associates.

Mourners soon gathered at Panepinto's house. Among the cars parked outside was a vehicle registered to Frank Campoli. If Toronto needed any reminder of the disparate underworld connections of Panepinto, it came seven days later at his funeral. The exhaust from 50 Harley-Davidson motorcycles rose from the street, as bikers, many of whom would soon trade in their own gang patches to become members of the Hells Angels, formed an honor guard for Panepinto's hearse. Through the blue haze, police intelligence officers watched as Vito Rizzuto arrived at the church, walking in close quarters with five men who had traveled with him from Montreal, an entourage that included Paolo Renda, Francesco Arcadi and Rocco Sollecito—three of Vito's top men.

"We expected some sort of turnout but this is beyond what we thought Panepinto rated," an intelligence officer said. A biker at the funeral had little to say about the murder. "We're here to show strength," he said. "We'll take him to rest and let things sort themselves out." There seemed little to sort out. Panepinto's blood erased the insult against the Siderno mobsters and the Sixth Family wrote off his loss as the cost of doing business in Ontario.

Such losses were mounting, however. In April 2001, RCMP Chief Superintendent Ben Soave, who headed the CFSEU, unveiled Project Oltre, a joint police operation targeting the Rizzutos' large, new gambling network: 54 people were arrested in Toronto, Ottawa, Hamilton and Montreal, among them Joe Renda. Police said the ring took in $200 million in bets. Over 140 days, police could document $20 million placed on NFL, NHL, NBA and college sports games as well as horse racing. In keeping with Sixth Family tradition, dozens of low-level bookies pleaded guilty; large fines and asset forfeitures were accepted with little argument, including Joe Renda's $50,000 Lincoln Navigator, in return for charges against the top players being dropped. Renda and some of his key associates in Toronto left court free men. With all of the attention and obvious police heat in Ontario, Renda moved back to Montreal.

To compensate for the setbacks, the Sixth Family sent a new hands-on representative to Toronto.

WOODBRIDGE, ONTARIO, OCTOBER 2001

Juan Ramon Fernandez is a muscular man with a strong jaw, black hair and dark eyes. His Spanish features sometimes draw comparisons to Antonio Banderas, the movie actor, but his actions spoke more to the movie character Tony Montana, the murderous drug lord in Brian DePalma's film *Scarface*. People who have watched Fernandez operate say he acts and talks like the tough, maniacal Cuban character depicted by Al Pacino. As a Spaniard, Fernandez would not have been an inducted member of the Sixth Family, but as a trusted operative with a proven criminal aptitude, he was accepted as a loyal associate.

Born on Boxing Day in 1956, Fernandez emigrated to Canada from Spain with his family when he was five and settled in Montreal. As he grew, he built a strong street persona, gaining a reputation for being efficient with his fists. It was a calling card that helped him earn a position that, traditionally, is considered a stepping stone to greater things in the underworld; he became a driver for a leading mobster, in his case, Frank Cotroni. Fernandez fit in perfectly; he was polite to his betters, loyal to his friends and unyielding to his enemies. In 1979, when he was 21, Fernandez demanded that his girlfriend, a 17-year-old stripper, have sex with one of his associates. When she refused, he struck out, punching her hard in the throat. She later died in hospital. Fernandez was convicted of involuntary manslaughter and sentenced to 12 years in prison. His prison file shows numerous complaints against him, including threatening other inmates. Ever the entrepreneur, Fernandez was a prominent drug dealer within the prison walls and sent associates around the prison to collect drug debts from fellow prisoners. He forced a prisoner to smuggle hashish into prison when he returned from an outside visit. Prison staff did not feel much safer; one female guard complained that Fernandez told her he knew her home address, and he told another employee: "You don't know what I'm capable of." A rumor persists that he also successfully seduced a smitten female prison guard inside his cell.

His ability to impose his will over a tough prison brought him to the attention of the Sixth Family. When released from prison, Fernandez was ordered deported by Canadian authorities, but he managed to fight the order for 12 years. By January 1990, he was selling Jaguar automobiles and working at a nightclub under the Sixth Family's supervision. Eighteen months later, he was arrested again when police found him with $32,000 in cash and three kilograms of cocaine. He pleaded guilty to drug charges and was sentenced to 42 months in prison. While serving this sentence he was married in the prison chapel; he invited Vito and Sixth Family drug trafficker Raynald Desjardins to attend. Vito was denied admittance by prison officials. In 1999, Fernandez's options in Canada expired and he was finally removed. Canadian authorities assumed they had seen the last of him, but not long after, he was found in a café in Woodbridge, Ontario, and deported a second time. He did not travel as far as authorities hoped. Fernandez moved to Florida, where he stayed at a Miami condominium that was linked to his then-lawyer, Carmine Iacono, before returning north on a false Canadian passport. By the summer of 2001, he had established himself on the streets around Toronto as an imposing figure named Joe Bravo.

"Bravo was closer to Vito than Panepinto," an investigator said. "He was doing things for him directly. He was sent out to collect and to make sure that Vito gets his end. He was the eyes and ears for Vito and he reported back to him. He'd tell Vito: 'These guys are doing good; these guys are doing nothing.' And Vito would say: 'It'd be nice if these guys gave us a piece of it,' and then Bravo would go back and try to collect it for Vito. Bravo was doing Vito's work directly. He didn't really have any businesses here of his own. Plus, he was to keep peace with the bikers." Bravo was often seen walking at Vito's side, shorter than the boss but broader at the shoulders and thicker in the arms, and was often respectfully one step behind. As with other initiatives, this move by the Sixth Family in Ontario was set to stumble.

———————

Now that the Quebec biker war was curtailed, police in Montreal were starting to turn their attention to the Sixth Family. A civilian agent, a former drug courier, had agreed to work with authorities in return for money and a judicial break. He was mingling with people associated with the Sixth Family. Using the informant as their linchpin, Montreal police and the RCMP launched a joint investigation, code-named Project Calamus. The prime target was Vito, with secondary objectives set at any high-level operative associated with the Sixth Family. There were plenty of leads to chase.

When the former drug courier told police that he met in Montreal with an alleged Colombian drug supplier named Abraham Nasser in 2001, the project took on another focus. Also at the meeting, the informant said, was José Guede, an old friend of the informant's from a Spanish social club who was also a criminal defense lawyer working in the law firm of Loris Cavaliere, who was one of Vito's lawyers. The law firm was of interest to police because it also employed two of Vito's children, his younger son, Leonardo, and his only daughter, Bettina, who are both lawyers. Guede socialized on occasion with Vito, playing high-stakes poker games with him and others. Nasser, the Colombian contact, gave the informant his business card, which he signed on the back, and told him if he came to Bogotá to present the card at any of his restaurants and he could arrange to buy cocaine. The informant told police that when he mentioned this to Guede, the lawyer said to bring back as much as he wanted and he could move it through his contacts. The drugs, the informant said in court, were destined for Antonio Pietrantonio, a Montreal man with a previous drug conviction who earned his nickname "Tony Suzuki" because of his proprietorship of a large car dealership. Police have repeatedly documented Pietrantonio socializing with members of the Sixth Family and meeting with Vito, but he was not charged with any involvement in the informant's drug scheme. This all came out in court after Guede was charged by police with conspiracy to import cocaine. A Quebec judge later ordered a stay of proceedings in the charges against Guede when it was found that an RCMP officer lied during his testimony in an attempt to bolster the credibility of the undercover informant. The informant also met with Fernandez, who was starting to shift his attention to Ontario but was still involved in affairs in Montreal. The two spoke of how best to smuggle the cocaine the informant was planning to bring from Colombia. They discussed registering an import company in Montreal and another in Venezuela to help mask the anticipated cocaine shipments.

"If the first container arrives, sure, the customs guy will check," the informant said. "But if the containers go through all the time, after a couple of months they'll still check, but not as much. If we imported fruit 10 times, on the 11th time you put in coke and the chances of them checking would be much less." The informant, Fernandez and others quibbled over what kind of companies to start and were think-ing of textile firms, but when arrangements were ready, the informant called Fernandez.

"Okay, man, good news. Our friend says it's a fruit store," he told Fernandez. "Yeah, he has mangos to sell and everything."

"Beautiful," Fernandez replied. As Fernandez started spending more time in Toronto than he did in Montreal, the informant headed east with him, with his police handlers keeping watch.

———

In York Region, a suburban area north of Toronto that includes the town of Woodbridge, where several mobsters live hidden amongst the large popu-lation of honest Italians, police officers had been busy probing changes in the underworld that came with the Sixth Family's re-invigorated pres-ence. They had noticed the increasing swagger of Gaetano Panepinto and had started setting up a probe of him and his associates when the cas-ket salesman was murdered. This gave York police the code name for their case, Project R.I.P., for "rest in peace," a phrase usually reserved for tombstones. Officers running Project R.I.P looked into Panepinto's old crew—and found Fernandez running the show—at about the same time that officers with Project Calamus were following Fernandez west from Montreal and finding him in Woodbridge. A joint police effort was launched, with Vito and his son Nick the prime targets of one of many strands of investigation that were emerging, according to police.

In 2001, police uncovered an alleged extortion plot involving a Toronto car dealer who owed $500,000 to Frank Martorana, a Montreal luxury car dealer. According to police, Martorana happened to owe a similar amount to a third luxury car dealer, also based in Montreal. Police believe that this third dealer approached Vito about getting his money out of Martorana, who had previous dealings with the Montreal Mafia and boasted a mild criminal past, including a conviction in 1999 when he visited an art gallery, took a liking to the works on the walls and walked off with them. When the Toronto car dealer who was at the end of the debt chain was visiting Montreal, he was greeted by four men: Vito; his son Nick; a member of the Caruana family; and a fourth man who did business with the Rizzutos, according to police. The Toronto car dealer was allegedly told that the debt would now have to be paid—not to Martorana—but to them, which was certainly a more alarming debt to be holding. Police believe the money was soon turned over to a lawyer who had links to Vito, but when the disgusted Toronto car dealer made a remark about contacting the Quebec bar association, which regulates lawyers in the province, the money was returned. Rather than face possible exposure, the Montreal men immediately stepped away from the deal. This was not the way it was supposed to happen; rarely did things turn so sour in Montreal.

In an interview, the Toronto car dealer declined to talk about the matter in any detail, saying the incident was "a personal matter." He acknowledged that he had met the Rizzutos, Carmelo Caruana, and another man over money but would not discuss it further.

"I made a report to the police," he said. "That's behind me now." And perhaps it is; none of the details was ever made public. It was, however, another sign that Ontario was not playing by the rules of engagement that the Sixth Family had grown comfortable with in Quebec. No charges were ever laid in the matter, and, in fact, when it became clear that neither Vito nor his son would be criminally prosecuted for any alleged involvement in the car dealer's debt, Montreal's Project Calamus wrapped up.

Another effort to catch Vito and his family involved in a crime had crumbled. The Project Calamus informant, however, who was by then moving with Fernandez about Toronto, remained in Ontario and continued to work with the Project R.I.P. officers.

TORONTO, MAY 2002

The Montreal police informant had gained the trust of Fernandez, which did not appear to be an easy task. That the informant was not a nervous wreck dealing so closely and precariously with him is a wonder. Almost everyone else was petrified of Fernandez. From outlaw motorcycle gang members to other mobsters, veteran drug traffickers to Eastern European crime figures, a common theme to their conversations was nervousness about upsetting Fernandez. Conversations between tough underworld figures reveal their obsequiousness when speaking with him, their obvious attempts at flattering and their determination to keep him happy.

As Fernandez set about inserting himself in Ontario's underworld on behalf of the Sixth Family, he had some assistance from an unexpected quarter: members of two police agencies. A municipal police officer and a federal officer seemed to be secretly helping the Sixth Family. One officer tried to track down the name of an informant who was leaking information about Fernandez to police; tipped the mobsters off that a building they used was under secret police surveillance; let them know when search warrants were issued by a judge; and ran a records check for them on the central police computer from his squad car. One of Fernandez's key associates in Toronto said he had a cousin who was a member of York Regional Police drug squad and another cousin working with the RCMP in Milton, west of Toronto, according to claims made by the mobsters, captured on tape and quietly filed in court.

"They've got surveillance set up at Fabulous Fitness," a close associate of Fernandez told him on December 20, 2001.

"For?" asked Fernandez.

"Well I don't know. He was assigned to work it and to photograph everybody coming and going outta there," the associate said. "He doesn't know why. He was uh, he was assigned to do it and he had to work it last night."

"Who told you this?" asked Fernandez.

"My little cousin and he works for York Region," answered the mob associate. "They started it two days ago."

"Okay then, anyways, just keep your uh, ears open for me, okay?" said Fernandez. The associate also said he had his cellphone checked by his cousin through the Canadian Police Information Centre (CPIC), the central records database for Canada's police agencies. When Fernandez suggested that a cellphone might be bugged, his associate said he knew it was clear.

"I have my little cousin run it through CPIC, through his computer," the associate bragged. "He actually came down with his car just to come fuckin' talk to me about it."

On March 7, 2002, the police source passed additional information to the mobsters, information Fernandez needed to ferret out a snitch, according to the conversations. Someone had been telling police about Fernandez's presence in Ontario in a bid for leniency on charges after he and several friends were arrested.

"I talked to my cousin," the associate said. "He doesn't know exactly who it is ... but they're [the police] under the impression that you're somewhere in the Woodbridge area. ... Now, he says he wasn't one of the arresting officers," the associate continued, "but there was something that happened about a month ago. ... He says there were four people that were picked up on this issue."

"Yeah?" said Fernandez.

"Now one of them, okay, had said that you were back in town," he said, adding the snitch was "looking for leverage" on a minor charge.

"Can you get the names?" asked Fernandez.

"He said he'll get them for me when he's back on duty."

"All I need are the names of the people that got stopped," said Fernandez. "Understand?"

"Yeah."

"And I'll take it from there," Fernandez added ominously.

On April 24, 2002, his underling again had information from his police source: "There were a number of search warrants issued out on that same day," the associate said to Fernandez. "It's a huge investigation with Metro, Peel and York Region," he said. "He says he's only got a little glimpse of it because he's on the drug task force. ... But on April the second, he says there were ten search warrants issued out by the same judge all for the same purpose."

On May 15, 2002, Fernandez called his friend in an uncharacteristic frenzy: "This morning something happened that it really stinks," began Fernandez. He had spotted undercover surveillance officers but was not sure if they were after him or someone else. "Is there a way that you could find out?"

"Yeah, yeah, there is," said his associate. "I got another cousin that works for Milton dispatch, RCMP," he said. "Joe, I will check. ... Give me about a half hour, okay?"

The cat-and-mouse game of infiltration—the police into the mob and the mob into the police—was a complicated one.

Also chronicled by the informant and police officers were meetings and conversations between Vito and Fernandez and many friendly personal chats between Fernandez and Frank Campoli, one of the men then involved with OMG. During one such call between Fernandez and Campoli, the OMG executive asked him if he wished to speak with "our buddy." Campoli then handed the cellphone to Vito, who had a brief chat with Fernandez, according to a recording of the phone call. Fernandez and Campoli also discussed using an OMG truck to move a large load of tiles. Fernandez was also heard claiming that he had some financial involvement with OMG, or would at least profit when the firm was sold to Spanish interests. (His involvement led police investigators to suggest the government try to seize the firm as a proceeds of crime asset. No such move ever materialized.)

Meanwhile, the informant had learned of plans by Fernandez to bring in a large shipment of cocaine and he passed the information on to his police handlers. The officers were trying to nail down exactly when and where it was to land. It was then, in May 2002, that the undercover informant was called in for another meeting with Fernandez.

When the two men had a moment of privacy, Fernandez passed a dirty woolen work sock to the informant, its sides bulging with a large pistol and a handful of bullets inside. Fernandez told him to take the gun and use it to kill Constantin "Big Gus" Alevizos. Big Gus stood six-foot-six and weighed 450 pounds, leaving little wonder as to how he got his nickname. Big Gus had upset Fernandez; a rumor placed him as a likely suspect in the disappearance of a duffel bag of cash from Panepinto's home after his murder. Fernandez seemed to think the money was rightfully owned by the Sixth Family. The murder contract put police in an awkward situation. If they shut down the investigation, they would lose all hope of tracking the cocaine shipment. If they did not withdraw their informant, he risked being fingered by Fernandez as a rat. And even if the informant had simply declined the murder contract, officers feared Fernandez would have asked another of his minions to pull it off. They could not allow that to happen.

Shortly after the passing of the loaded sock, police shut down Highway 407, a major expressway north of Toronto, while heavily armed police officers stopped a sport-utility vehicle. Fernandez was hiding inside. When he was arrested, police found him in possession of several pieces of false identification and a credit card in the name of Carmine Iacono, the Toronto-area lawyer in whose Miami condominium he had stayed. It was surprising, because Iacono was an active member of the community, having unsuccessfully run as a Progressive Conservative candidate in the Vaughan–King–Aurora riding in the previous provincial election. Iacono declined to comment when asked about his involvement with Fernandez.

Four months later, Project R.I.P. was concluded with raids by police on businesses and homes around Toronto, on Canada's East Coast, and in New York State. Thirty-two people were arrested, charged variously with dealing in drugs, fraudulent credit cards, stolen goods, weapons offences and violence.

It was as close to the Sixth Family as Project Calamus and Project R.I.P. ever got. The family's rocky reception in Ontario, however, was not yet over.

MONTREAL, MAY 30, 2002

A blue 2001 Jeep Grand Cherokee with a beige interior was heading west on Maisonneuve Boulevard West in downtown Montreal when the driver was signaled to the side of the road by a police officer. It was 3:45 a.m., and the officer apparently detected signs of impairment, but when he asked the driver to take a breath test, the driver allegedly refused. It was a normal part of patrolling Montreal's downtown streets. The fact that the driver was Vito Rizzuto, and the Jeep was not his, made this a traffic stop of note.

Vito was placed under arrest and informed of his rights. Half an hour later, lawyer Jean Salois had been roused and informed of his client's status and, not long after, Vito was released on a promise to appear in court two days later. It must have made any police officer curious as to why a Montrealer as well known as Vito was driving a Jeep with Ontario license plates. After running the plate number, officers found that it was registered to an Ontario company: OMG Media Inc.

It took six months for the connection between Vito and OMG's Jeep to become public, but when it did, it was a scandalous affair. The head of the City of Toronto's public works department called for police to investigate possible links between OMG and the Mafia, and city officials in Ottawa and Montreal started reexamining their contracts and asking for legal opinions from city solicitors. OMG officials played down the incident. OMG owned eight vehicles; seven of them were in

Ontario and one, the Jeep, was in Quebec. That Jeep had been given to Michael Strizzi, the head of the company's Quebec division, for company use, said Salvatore Oliveti, president and founder of OMG. It was that Jeep Vito was driving.

"I really think this is all about me being Italian and speaking with a big accent," Oliveti said. Not everyone agreed. Strizzi said he had lent the Jeep to Vito a month or so earlier. Under intense pressure to distance himself and his company from the controversy, Oliveti accepted Strizzi's offer to resign.

Vito, however, did not see what the uproar was about. In an uncharacteristic chat with a reporter, he explained why he was behind the wheel of the OMG Jeep.

"OMG Media Inc. does business in Montreal. There's a friend of mine who works for OMG Quebec, has been working there for four years, five years, I don't know how long. His name is Michael Strizzi. He's the designated driver for this truck, and once in a while I go out with him and once in a while he lends me the truck," Vito said, adding he had been friends with Strizzi for 20 years. "That's the way it is," Vito added.

"I don't know why they're making a big fuss out of this thing just because I was driving the truck," he said. "All they got to do is just go see the company and ask them what do I have to do with the company."

Despite Vito's nonchalance over the public link between him and OMG, the effect on the company was devastating. A forecast of $8 million in revenue dwindled to $3 million, according to a letter sent from Salvatore Oliveti to officials with a firm that had been in negotiations to purchase half of OMG.

"The events of this past February have caused us severe and possibly irreparable damage," Oliveti wrote on June 24, 2003, of the public revelation of Vito's traffic stop. "Now, months after the news coverage that involved people associated with OMG, the true extent of the damage is being realized." The company was forced "to pursue extensive public relations exercises with city councils," and still the stigma of organized crime remained. "There are many agencies that simply will not associate with the current OMG ownership," he wrote to officials with potential investors, Corporacion Americana de Equipamientos Urbanos S.L., of Mexico. "Needless to say, this has affected our relationships with different cities and we have worked very hard to regain their confidence." Oliveti also feared that the problem could, "at any given time," become larger. For Lou Gallucci, OMG's vice-president, the embarrassment was personal.

"OMG's staff have all suffered terribly as a result of these allegations. My children have been asked if I am involved in the mob. I will not forget the day I returned home and my child asked me what the mob was and whether I was a member. My experience was common to other members of OMG's staff," Gallucci wrote in an affidavit.

OMG needed about $10 million in order to fulfill its existing contracts to install recycling bins and, to raise it, OMG turned to other outside investors. In April 2003, OMG started negotiating with Torstar Corporation, which owns Canada's largest daily-circulation newspaper, *The Toronto Star*. Torstar was offering $6 million for OMG's assets, except for the New York school board contract and OMG's European and Asian subsidiaries, which OMG's investors—chief among them the Campoli family—was holding on to. The deal was mired in civil lawsuits when competing investors questioned the other's right to buy the firm.

Eventually, new ownership of the OMG assets was found. A Spanish firm, Eucan Urban Equipment of Canada Inc., a branch of the Spanish conglomerate Cemusa, bought what remained of OMG and pressed ahead with new contracts for a new style of recycling bin—with even larger advertising space. The new group of company directors, through their lawyers, deny they have any links to Vito, Campoli or any organized crime figure.

The incident cost Vito's friends a lot of money and further exposed the involvement of some of Vito's key people in Ontario.

Vito, meanwhile, pleaded not guilty to impaired driving.

When the Sixth Family had taken control of Montreal, it had meant toppling a single monolithic figure, the rival mobster Paolo Violi. In Ontario, they were suffering from a thousand tiny cuts, wounds that would continue to bleed to this day.

CHAPTER 36

MONTREAL, MAY 21, 2003

From the sidewalk, the repetitive hip-hop beat of dance music throbbed through the doors of the Joy Club, on La Montagne Street, one of many nightclubs in Montreal's crowded downtown. The music became an ear-splitting roar when Mitchell Janhevich pulled open the doors and stepped inside. Janhevich, a Montreal city policeman, was one of several officers patroling downtown nightclubs, keeping tabs on street gang members and drug dealers who were filling the void left by the arrest of the Hells Angels leadership. Tuesdays are typically slow for the clubs, but it was the Joy's busiest night. Billed as "staff night," it was an opportunity for those who made a living by giving others a good time each weekend to relax and enjoy themselves. Tuesdays brought bartenders, bouncers, strippers, waitresses and busboys from many other clubs to party at Joy.

By the time Janhevich walked into the club, Tuesday night had become Wednesday morning hours before, but the place was still hopping. Several customers caught the officer's attention: standing at the bar was one of the few men closely associated with the biker war who remained free; nearby were two men from a street gang he had arrested for firearm possession a few weeks before. Then, through the dim light, Janhevich saw five men huddled together in a raised and separate area of the club, the VIP section. He had to look twice to make sure, but there was Vito Rizzuto and four other men, sitting and talking.

"It was strange. You walk in and there is one of the last people from the Hells Angels and then some street gangs and then him—it was like the jackpot for a police officer," Janhevich said. "He looked to be in a little meeting with them. I thought, 'What the hell is he doing here?' It was not the type of place you'd expect to see him. I thought this was strange. I went out and checked his name and when you check his name, the computer almost blows up—you have to call the intelligence unit and give them the details." Janhevich and his team watched the club from outside. Vito and his friends soon walked out and climbed into a Mercedes, Vito into the front passenger seat beside the driver and three men into the back. The car pulled away but had not gone far before Janhevich pulled it over and approached the driver.

"Is there a problem?" the driver asked, handing over his driver's license and registration.

"No, I just want to check things out," replied Janhevich, who then noticed that one of the passengers in the backseat was not wearing a seatbelt. "That is an infraction. I'm going to have to see some ID," he said to the man. The passenger refused, Janhevich said.

"Listen, if you don't identify yourself, plain and simple, we're going to arrest you. Whether it takes one guy or 10 guys, you are going to get arrested and we're going to identify you," Janhevich said, but the passenger continued to refuse. At that point, Vito climbed out of the front seat of the car and walked toward Janhevich.

"What the fuck is going on? What the fuck did we do? Why are you harassing us?" Vito said, according to Janhevich. "What the fuck are you guys doing? Why are you fucking with us?" Vito continued. Janhevich has a policy when policing the city's streets: he is polite to a fault until he meets with obscenity; then he meets swear word for swear word.

"First of all, stop fucking swearing because if you want to make a show, I'll make a show, that's no problem. There is no need to fucking talk to me like that. I have a job to do, so stand back and let me do my job," Janhevich said.

Vito seemed surprised. The two men, both tall and slim, were facing each other, inches apart, and their voices were getting louder. Passersby had stopped to watch; other officers watched with wide eyes.

"Do you have any idea who I am?" Vito said.

"Yeah. Do you have any idea who I am?" the officer shot back. "This is my street. When you're in your business or in your home, you do your stuff. When you are on my turf, you go by my rules. And right now you're in my territory. It's my show. It's my game here."

Vito seemed to suddenly relax. A slight smirk fell across his face, as if he liked the argument and the firm response from the officer.

"Okay, okay, take it easy, take it easy," Vito said.

Janhevich then arrested the man in the backseat. Vito asked what would happen next, and when he was told that his friend would be taken to a local police station to be identified, he tried to intervene.

"Well, okay. I'll give you his name," Vito said. He was Vincenzo Spagnolo, Janhevich was told. With no identification forthcoming however, the officer still took the man into custody. Vito wanted to know where he would be taken and if he could go there to help Spagnolo out. Janhevich told him they were heading to the police operations center on Guy Street. When Janhevich arrived, the officers at the front desk called to him, saying in amazement that Vito Rizzuto was there to see him.

"I went out in the lobby and he put his hand out to shake my hand and said: 'You remind me a bit of me. You stick up for your men, I stick up for mine. I respect that. I like the way you handled my men. I handle them the same way.'"

His men. Vito had plenty of those.

The tall, almost patrician, mafioso, standing in the brightly lit lobby of the police office, had come a long way. So, too, had the family he had become the leader of—not the "boss," but the natural-born leader. His men, under Vito's tutelage and that of his father, Nick, formed a criminal unit that far outstripped the position the Sixth Family held in official American organized crime charts. By 2003, the Rizzuto organization was variously listed in FBI and DEA files as merely "the Canadian crew of the Bonanno Family" or the "Montreal faction of the Bonannos." The reality is far different. The territory under its control is huge—more than a million square miles of Quebec and Ontario directly fall under its influence, an area larger than one-quarter the size of the entire United States. It includes major cities, the busiest border crossings between the U.S. and Canada, and many mature Mafia clans that are, by and large, cooperating under the Sixth Family's banner.

Where American Mafia bosses controlled criminal activity in portions of a city or a New York borough or the criminal activity in an industrial or commercial sector—such as construction or New York's garment district—the Sixth Family was an enterprise with a true global reach. The Sixth Family had outpaced any crew in the Bonanno Family and, indeed, man-for-man, dollar-for-dollar, had eclipsed the family as a whole.

Vito could step onto an airplane and fly to any of a dozen countries where he would be immediately recognized and respected. He spoke to associates in several different languages—English, French, Italian and Spanish. He fit in at the highest levels of commerce and industry without embarrassment or social allowances. While the turf of an American Mafia crew might expand street by street into a neighborhood, or into new criminal ventures, the Sixth Family expanded into countries and across continents, penetrating diverse economies and reaping untold reward. The 20 men the Bonanno administration considers to be Montreal's membership are but a pale shadow of what the Sixth Family has become.

It is no surprise that Sal Vitale admitted the Bonanno administration feared a war with Montreal after the slaying of Gerlando Sciascia in 1999.

The Sixth Family's organization is awesome.

––––––––––

The Sixth Family blends the traditions of the Sicilian Mafia with a modern corporate structure, building a rugged, durable, ever-expanding corporate Mafia. It maintains the secretiveness of the mafiosi tradition but keeps its inner circle far more tightly controlled than in the American Mafia. The Sixth Family has shed the old militaristic organizational structure of the Five Families—which has soldiers answering to captains who answer to a boss. It has been replaced with a structure that is even more ancient—the family. It is not merely a Mafia initiation ceremony that binds its core, but rather, almost without exception, marriage vows and blood ties. It is far more effective at engendering loyalty and trust; for protecting the organization from betrayal and infiltration. It is one thing for an informant to turn on friends, neighbors and colleagues, but quite another to turn on brothers, uncles and cousins. An informant from within the Sixth Family would need to sever all ties with their kin.

The Sicilian Mafia has been compared to an octopus, because it is a malleable, multi-tentacled beast that reaches out and grabs its prey but, when one arm is lost, another soon grows to replace it. It is a reasonable analogy. Beyond comparisons to the world of business, other criminal organizations and the animal kingdom, however, perhaps the best comparison of the Sixth Family is to a cult. From birth, its members are separated from mainstream society—intellectually, morally and culturally—and incubated in an insular world where each lives in accordance with the family's special rules, values and beliefs. It demands total commitment and loyalty. Members are taught that the end justifies the means. It breeds an explicit and highly polarized us-versus-them mentality. It is not accountable to the rest of society. It is preoccupied with making money and benefiting the group even at the expense of an individual member. There are threats and consequences to leaving.

The cult model has served the organization well. Protected by its insular nature, made wealthy through drug transactions and powerful through its street presence, the Sixth Family has developed a dominant place in the underworld, with a commanding physical presence, forcing its fingers into all aspects of street life, politics, finance and crime, both sophisticated and petty. It is a blending of the old and the new, the best of the traditional Sicilian Mafia and the best of the American Mafia, to form an almost perfect criminal enterprise. Flexible, adaptable and rapacious, it finds a way of working around any obstacle, always consuming whatever lies in its path while at all times protecting its core. That core, for now, is formed by the Rizzutos, which provides the Sixth Family's leadership.

"There is no crowning, no vote to make a leader in the clans you call the Sixth Family. The leader naturally emerges and he is more of a steward, guiding the interests and activities of several blood relatives and in-laws," said an Italian police investigator who has studied the Sixth Family clans. "He doesn't take power and he isn't bestowed power. Power flows to him naturally. Not every interest is of the criminal. He is involved in or knows intimately the marriages; the marriages that are in trouble; the births of the children; the status of the older generation. He consults with the older generation, who may be retired but are still very knowledgeable of the Mafia and have connections and relationships of their own."

Within the Sixth Family, for now at least, that head is Vito Rizzuto. He is an impressive leader. Had he not been brought up confined within the Mafia, he would likely have succeeded in legitimate business or perhaps politics; he is charismatic, efficient, energetic, intelligent and ambitious.

"Vito Rizzuto heads the family as a business," says an RCMP report on the organization.

As a leader, Vito's presence and name have meant much in the underworld, but his hands-on links are carefully hidden. He declares modest salaries on his income tax but drives luxury automobiles. He once maintained a Lincoln, a Mercedes-Benz, a Jaguar and three Corvettes, one of them a vintage 1959 model. He has led a busy and hectic life but one that rarely—if ever—involves steady nine-to-five employment. He played golf more than 100 times a year, often using the private time on the links to discuss intimate organizational details with other members of his carefully selected foursome. It is a gentleman's version of the mob boss's traditional "walk-and-talks," where a gangster would go for a brisk walk with criminal associates to avoid having the chat caught by police microphones. Vito maintained a presence at the Club Social Consenza and three other clubs and cafés that were part of his regular routine. His job was largely to show up, to just show his face and lend his name. Transactions rarely took more than that. His father had prepared him well.

———

Vito has long relied on his father, Nick, as his most senior and trusted advisor, police say.

Nick spends much of his time at the Club Social Consenza, jovially playing cards with close friends behind a large window that looks out on to the public walkway of the strip mall where the club is located. He is invariably neatly dressed and often formally attired in shirt, jacket and tie when he moves about the city. He evokes a distinctive gangster chic with his penchant for wearing a fedora to cover his almost bald head and sunglasses as a bid, perhaps, at greater anonymity.

In his younger days, Nick could look menacing and forceful. He walked with confidence and could flash a look of disapproval that associates quickly learned to recognize and appease at the earliest opportunity. As a senior citizen, his image has muted considerably. He has shed much of his bulk and his facial features have been softened by time and frequent flashes of a teeth-baring smile. His grin might be provoked by what police say happens when many of these associates meet with him. At the Consenza, or other restaurants that he frequents in Montreal, such as the Roma, police say he has quiet discussions with visitors who outline plans and schemes; Nick then gives those plans that meet with his approval the family's blessing, police believe. Nick then often leaves with a packet of money, what is referred to in French as *cote d'argent*—literally, "dues money," but more accurately what American mobsters call "tribute money," profit flowing up the hierarchy of the organization. Police say he hides the money in his jacket, topcoat or other articles of clothing until he can unload it. Most suitable for a man of his position and esteem, this is not money that Nick "collects," but rather, money he "accepts." His role, police say, is of utmost discretion. Vito would not want it any other way.

Nick's leisurely routine, however, does not mean he is removed from the family's affairs. He is a frequent ambassador at important meetings. Almost daily, Nick meets at the Consenza club with Paolo Renda and Francesco "Frank" Arcadi, described by police as a leading Rizzuto captain. Arcadi was convicted of operating an illegal gaming house in 1984, but came to fuller police attention when he was seen at Vito's side at the funeral of Joe LoPresti in 1992. He then started spending time with Vito, turning up in cars with Vito when they were stopped by police and during police surveillance of family weddings and funerals, including the Toronto funeral of Gaetano Panepinto. Police believe that Arcadi is taking over supervision of much of the street level action on behalf of the family and has responsibility for both the Saint-Léonard and Rivière-des-Prairies areas of Montreal.

Paolo Renda is himself now a senior citizen, although a robust and often dapper-looking man with his hair graying and thinning at the front. A quiet operator, Renda has been at the Rizzutos' side all his life. He is Nick's cousin and went on to marry Maria, his daughter. As Vito's brother-in-law, he bonded with Vito and the men's friendship was baptized by fire in the botched arson in their early days.

Renda has been given little attention by police over the years, despite at one time being a suspect in the killing of Paolo Violi. Renda is a businessman. He runs a construction company, Renda Construction Inc., that at one time had Vito listed as a secondary shareholder, vice president and administrator. Its office address was in the same strip plaza as the Consenza social club, where Renda is seen most days. The firm was not a flourishing success, police documents show: in 2001, the company declared just $21,008 in earnings; the following year that dropped to $8,031, before bouncing back, in 2003, to a declared $34,032. Renda is involved in other companies as well, including a second construction firm, a motel, a bistro and a restaurant in Longueuil, Quebec. His wide business involvement has led police to suspect that he runs the financial wing of the family.

Police have also followed the careers of Vito's sons. Investigators have pegged Leonardo, Vito's youngest son, as the most capable of achieving leadership of the family enterprise. Leonardo is bright, having attended the University of Ottawa's law school, and is now a lawyer in Quebec. Along with his sister, Bettina, he works at the law firm of Loris Cavaliere, which often represents Vito. Leonardo causes tremendous grief for police investigating Vito and his associates because of his special legal standing. Leonardo, police say, has frequently sat in on meetings between family members, including his father and brother—extending to the meetings the protection of lawyer–client privilege. Police have been reluctant to listen in on such conversations because these intrusions, as was shown when the RCMP previously bugged the dinner conversations of Vito's lawyer, are viewed dimly by the courts.

Nick, Vito's first-born son, is more of the hands-on guy in the family, police allege. He frequently meets with someone before that person is allowed to meet with Vito. An astute man with street smarts, he checks out strangers wishing to get close to the family; he often speaks on his family's behalf. He and a key associate also run a Longueuil real estate firm.

Beyond this core leadership, the Sixth Family's ranks—the men under Vito's command—are expansive.

"The nucleus of the Montreal-based Sicilian Mafia ... [comprises] hundreds of soldiers and associates," says a Canadian police report drafted in 2004. Those who merely do business with the Sixth Family or work with them in short-term ventures are not included in this. Neither, generally, are the businessmen who do mostly non-criminal favors for the organization. Enumerating the strength of a secret organization is fraught with difficulty. Some members, no doubt, manage to keep below the radar of police and other observers of organized crime. Some members die—some of natural causes, others killed in disputes—and others are imprisoned. The jailed members will, for the most part, remain associated with the group, both inside and outside of the institution, but hardly count when calculating the street strength of an organization while they are away. There are also many fringe players who, for convenience, safety or profit, pledge fealty to the organization but are not a part of it. This applies to a growing number of street gang members in Montreal who have taken up the slack in the Hells Angels drug distribution.

There is evidence to suggest the number of people who are a routine and continuing part of the Rizzuto criminal organization, those who appear to have a formal role, a specific job and a designated reporting mechanism within the network's enterprises and are considered to be members by police, exceeds 500 people. For instance:

- A recent internal police report on those considered to be the leading targets for investigation as part of the Rizzuto criminal organization in the city of Montreal shows three large *cellules*, or "cells," of the organization, two of them comprising roughly 50 people, and a third, 30 people.

- Each of the cells has its own reporting structure and leadership. Three people supervise each of the two large cells and one leader oversees the smaller one. These seven bosses, who have for decades been among the most prominent men of the Sixth Family, are shown as reporting to Vito.

- The Sixth Family's Montreal-based operations also have two smaller satellite cells, comprising about a half-dozen members each, one based on the South Shore, the communities across the St. Lawrence River from Montreal, and the other in Cornwall, Ontario, a small border city linking Quebec, Ontario and Massena, New York. There is another outpost linked to the Kahnawake native reserve, also on the South Shore.

- A dossier on Vito, compiled by the Montreal police, documents some of his meetings and telephone conversations with alleged associates, recorded during police operations into organized crime activities. Taking only those people listed in meetings since 1985, after the death of Vic Cotroni, and removing frivolous or apparently purely social gatherings, the list exceeds 75 names. Most have criminal records and most are well known in the underworld. Only 14 of the names also appear on the above lists.

- A classified chart prepared by the RCMP's Criminal Analysis Branch maps out "Vito Rizzuto's Criminal Affiliations by Kinship and Intermarriage." It traces the marriages and blood ties between Vito and 10 other families, comprising some 40 people, most of whom form the innermost core of the Sixth Family. Almost all of them have family members who have faced drug arrests or other criminal charges and all of them have members who appear in criminal intelligence files as organized crime members or associates.

- Yet another confidential police report tracks the organization's leadership in Montreal in 1997. It shows a spider web of lines linking "sub-organizations" and "henchmen" back to Vito and his father Nick. It shows 13 cells, each headed by a senior underworld player who reports directly to Vito. Another three key men are shown separately as also reporting to Vito. Another four separate cells—the remnants of the old Cotroni and Violi organization, including some of the most venerable mobsters in Montreal—are shown as reporting to Vito, with the now-deceased Frank Cotroni acting as an intermediary. Another four cells are shown reporting to Nick through Agostino Cuntrera. Other core members of the Sixth Family are noted individually on the chart, with most linked to Vito through Nick.

- A recent report on the Sixth Family's chief operatives in Ontario shows 15 key men, most of whom run their own powerful Mafia organizations in the Toronto area. These groups range in size from a crew of five or six to a sprawling organization of several dozen, typically related, members that is, itself, an impressive Mafia organization. Also in Ontario, police allege, are four or five active and successful businessmen with no criminal records who work intimately on Vito's behalf.

- The Sixth Family has other branches or operatives, smaller in size, in other Canadian cities, most notably Vancouver, a large city on Canada's west coast, where there is a "Western Front" documented by police.

- There is a separate group of Sixth Family members that police refer to as the "new generation," which is generally made up of the sons, nephews and younger cousins of older Sixth Family members. Rizzuto, Sciascia, Manno, LoPresti, Renda and Cuntrera are all last names that cascade through the generations while continuing to find their way into police files.

Internationally, as well, the Sixth Family's interests are extensive. Beyond its numerous activities in Canada and the United States, its trafficking enterprises in Venezuela and Colombia and its relatives who remained in Cattolica Eraclea and surrounding Sicilian villages, an unreleased analysis by Canada's Department of Justice tracked financial holdings and connections from the Sixth Family to 16 other countries. They include:

- money laundering, investments and financial transfers through Switzerland, Germany and Great Britain. The family also has at least one operative located in London, England;

- investments in Saudi Arabia achieved with the suspected involvement of a member of the Saudi Royal family;

- importation of wood products and wood flooring from, and financial investments in, China;

- financial investment ventures in Algeria, a North African nation, and in the United Arab Emirates, an oil-rich Middle Eastern country on the Persian Gulf;

- investments in Cuba, along with periodic visits and extended stays in the country;

- drug transactions, meetings and visits in Mexico;

- alleged infiltration of public works projects in Italy. Also, at least one family operative is based in Rome and another in Milan;

- drug importation and involvement in airport servicing in Haiti;

- gambling enterprises in Belize, a small Central American country that borders Mexico;

- family members and associates traveling to and attending meetings in Panama, Aruba, Bahamas and the Dominican Republic.

Perhaps the most alarming aspect of police allegations concerning the Sixth Family's fulsome ranks is that it has a "Lawyer's Branch," one of its most protected, secretive and valued divisions. Police claim that practicing lawyers are involved in the family's enterprises to such an extent that a small proportion of them is considered by investigators to be a distinct branch of the organization. Police believe that the main cells of the organization each have their own designated lawyers. This would be a key distinction from other criminal organizations that maintain above-board but ongoing professional relationships with lawyers. Investigators suspect that the legal branch is not acting solely as judicial participants. There are no fewer than 11 lawyers from different law firms in Quebec that have raised police suspicions. Another has been identified by police as working closely with the family's business in Ontario. They have played varying roles in the family's enterprises, police suggest. But by no means are all lawyers who have acted for members of the Sixth Family implicated in improper activities; in fact, most are not.

One lawyer is dubbed "the Messenger" by police investigators. They say he carries messages: for instance, from Montreal he went to New York City; from New York City he went to Toronto; from Toronto he went to a jail north of the city. Along the way, the Quebec attorney spoke softly and passed along advice and warnings, according to police. He spoke to members of the Sicilian faction and other members of the Bonanno crew in New York, many of them in jail or out on bail, an investigator said. In Toronto he met with lawyers representing the Sixth Family's associates who were facing charges in that city. In a visitor's room in an Ontario prison, police say he met with a senior member of the Caruana–Cuntrera Family.

Police have found that lawyer–client privilege is being used as a prime defense by the Sixth Family. One lawyer, police have marveled, seems to have the job of sitting in on family meetings, bringing down the veil of legal privacy to discussions, as his daily activity. The lawyers' jobs are often simple: keep the lines of communication open, and prevent Vito's name and affairs from being brought up in court. Combative, aggressive men facing organized crime charges have meekly made the best deal they could and pleaded guilty, at the behest of Montreal. One suspect, believing he could beat drug charges, told his own lawyer to tell a certain Quebec lawyer that he had a good shot in court.

"This isn't about him," the Quebec lawyer allegedly told the accused man's counsel. "This is about the big guy. Don't make beating the charge the saddest day of your client's life."

Informants have talked about investing money through a law firm, about the office being used as a safe meeting place for critical discussions and about escrow accounts being used to launder drug money. Sometimes a lawyer is present for a meeting; at other times he absents himself to another room. Wiretaps on Sixth Family targets that have made their way into the court record have captured loose talk of questionable relationships with some of their lawyers. One gangster spoke of trying to pay his lawyer for certain services but being told the lawyer could not take the cash; the lawyer then said he could sure use a new computer. Others speak of using lawyers to help in getting false travel papers, to unearth personal information about people and other irregular duties. There was the lawyer who was allegedly involved in receiving the payment from the Toronto car dealer on Vito's behalf. That the substantial sum was returned when the businessman raised the possibility of exposing the lawyer's involvement suggests the value placed on the branch's secrecy.

Some other clues have emerged. Meetings allegedly about large cocaine shipments during which José Guede, a Montreal lawyer, was present are outlined in a Montreal police report filed in open court. (The charges against Guede were later dropped.) Similarly, the odd connections between Ramon Fernandez, Vito's man in Toronto, and lawyer Carmine Iacono emerged during the Project R.I.P. prosecution. Earlier, Joe Lagana, a lawyer for Vito, and three junior lawyers from the same firm, pleaded guilty to laundering drug money after the RCMP's sting operation at the money exchange house.

"The lawyers are a tricky part of getting at the Rizzuto family," an organized crime investigator said. "When we're up on the wires [running wiretaps], the minute we know it's a lawyer, we have to minimize [shut the recorders off]." With Vito and his key administrators keeping so many lawyers around them, that leads to a lot of minimizing.

"We're in a Catch-22 situation," said another officer. "If we want to put in an affidavit [requesting a judge's permission to intercept phone conversations] on a lawyer, we have to say that we have reason to believe that the lawyer is involved in crime. But you don't have that evidence because you can never listen in on their conversations. We need someone to come forward and tell us that they have evidence of a crime so we can move forward."

Several senior and experienced police investigators say they suspect lawyers are used in a number of different ways to thwart police monitoring of conversations.

"If you are on the wires and a lawyer comes into the conversation, the authorization says you have to cut out. The lawyer comes on the phone and clearly identifies himself as a lawyer and then says, 'OK, now turning to the case you and I are involved with.' And you have to stop listening. *You have to stop.* If the guy is involved in crime, we don't get to hear it," said an officer involved in extensive investigation of Sixth Family targets.

Some phone numbers are known by police to be a number for a lawyer's office and so officers realize a call is likely being made to a lawyer before any conversation even takes place. More often than not, officers turn off the wire without even waiting for a connection in a scrupulous bid to adhere to the court authorization allowing the wiretap which explicitly forbids intercepting calls between lawyers and their clients. Some officers believe, however, that this situation is being exploited. Investigators say some lawyers are registering cellular telephones in their names and then giving the phone to members or associates of the Sixth Family to use.

"You now have a bad guy carrying the phone of a lawyer. These guys know we can't listen to a lawyer. We don't want to taint the case so we cut out when the call is made," said an investigator. In the old days, officers might listen to conversations they should not be hearing and then erase the tapes later and pretend it never happened. In a digital age where the calls are exhaustively logged and recorded, there is a permanent record that cannot be hidden.

"They'll know if we breach the court order. Is it worth it? No. It is extremely frustrating," said an officer. At all times, the poor track record of previous investigations against Vito looms large.

Officers also suspect that some lawyers do third-party transfer of telephone calls. A target of an investigation may call a lawyer, engage in a conversation that would be covered by lawyer–client privilege and then—when they are pretty sure police would have cut out of the conversation—transfer the call to a third person, to allow them to engage in an unmonitored chat.

"We need some help from the Justice Department," said an investigator. "We need some ability in certain cases to listen in and see, to just see if it is a legitimate lawyer–client call or something else."

———

As the new millennium dawned, Vito headed an unprecedented criminal organization, the likes of which Canada had never seen. As law enforcement beat back the Five Families in New York, the Sixth Family, safely operating from its base in Canada, steadily expanded its wealth and position. Those two opposite trajectories—the near collapsing of the American Mafia organizations and the growth of the Rizzuto organization—have seen the Sixth Family eclipse the families of the New York Mafia.

It has forged an organization few criminal cartels in any of the Americas can overshadow.

Even with all that police were learning about the Sixth Family and its power, wealth and substantial holdings, there were still many secrets; and many surprises to come.

CHAPTER 37

MONTREAL, JANUARY 20, 2004

Wearing a bathrobe pulled over his pajamas, Vito Rizzuto followed his wife to the front door of their Montreal home after a sharp knock woke them at precisely 6:15 a.m. Outside, Sergeant-Detective Pietro Poletti and Detective Nicodemo Milano, both officers with the Montreal city police, stood on the wide front porch of the Rizzutos' immense Tudor-style mansion at 12281 Antoine-Berthelet Avenue.

With its impressive cut-stone facade, three-port garage and lead-ed window panes, the house, near the waterfront of the Rivières des Prairies, is an enviable sight. Poletti and Milano, two dedicated Italian–Canadian officers who had worked on the force's organized crime squad, had maintained an interest in investigating the Mafia despite the force's preoccupation with the warring motorcycle gangs. It was more reward for their efforts than strategic necessity that saw these two selected as the ones to knock on Vito's door that morning. Lurking nearby were four uniformed police officers discreetly placed a little far-ther from the house in idling squad cars; Montreal police were making an effort to ensure the arrest was handled with civility, but were not prepared to risk it becoming an ignoble spectacle.

The two detectives politely greeted Giovanna Rizzuto, Vito's wife, at the door when she opened it a crack. They apologized for the early intrusion and then explained to Vito, in English and in French, that he was being arrested and charged in connection with three murders, based on indictments issued in New York. Twenty-two years and eight months after the May 5, 1981, slayings of Alphonse "Sonny Red" Indelicato, Philip "Philly Lucky" Giaccone and Dominick "Big Trinny" Trinchera, U.S. authorities were formally alleging that Vito, now a 57-year-old grandfather of five, was the one who led the way out of the Brooklyn social club's closet and started the massacre.

Vito did not seem surprised by the news, or even by the early morn-ing interruption. He was cooperative, at all times acting the gentleman.

His wife remained composed. Poletti accompanied him to his bedroom to allow him to dress. Vito picked out a camel-colored turtleneck, dress pants and a sports jacket, eschewing a tie, apparently aware that ties are removed from prisoners before being placed in police cells for fear they will be used to commit suicide. Within 15 minutes, Vito was inside an unmarked police car with the pair of detectives and on his way to a police holding cell.

After his booking, Vito was whisked to court; the discretion with which he was removed from his home had by now evaporated. Word of the arrest had spread quickly in Montreal and it was with lights flashing and sirens wailing that a convoy of police cars sped past a growing sprawl of television cameras and newspaper photographers who jostled for a better view of the captured don. At his perfunctory three-minute appearance in Montreal's large, modern courthouse that afternoon, a tanned Vito listened somberly to his lawyer, Loris Cavaliere, who asked the judge for more time to study the U.S. government's extradition papers. Outside court, Cavaliere described his client as "very confident" and said a decision had not yet been made on whether to seek bail while fighting extradition. Vito was then promptly returned to his cell.

Vito was the only Canadian arrested that day. In New York, however, FBI agents, state and city police were moving through the city's boroughs arresting 26 people accused in 15 murders and murder conspiracies. It was a concerted effort to strike hard at the Bonanno Family, the culmination of considerable effort to eradicate one of the most famous of the Five Families of New York.

The U.S. government's first target had been Vito Rizzuto.

BROOKLYN, DECEMBER 31, 2003

Three weeks earlier, on New Year's Eve, 16 members of a grand jury in New York's Eastern District courthouse met and concurred with the prosecutor's allegations, outlined in a seven-page indictment, that Vito Rizzuto—alone—should be charged with a racketeering conspiracy.

"At various times the defendant, Vito Rizzuto, was a soldier or associate in the Bonanno Family," the indictment alleged, stating that from February 1, 1981, through December 2003, Vito engaged with others in a pattern of racketeering activity affecting interstate and foreign commerce, namely the murders of the three captains. The indictment was then neatly signed by the jury foreman and the case against Vito assigned the court file number 03-CR-1382, a file that would later swell to magnificent size. An arrest warrant was issued against Vito that same day, signed by a Brooklyn judge who also issued a limited unsealing order, allowing the government to provide the indictment to the relevant U.S. and Canadian authorities for the purpose of pursuing Vito's arrest and extradition. The arrest warrant commanded any authorized police officer to arrest Vito, but no officers got a chance to see it, let alone act on it. The warrant and indictment were immediately placed in a white 10-by-15-inch envelope, sealed, labeled *U.S.A. v. John Doe* and filed in court with instructions that it not be listed on the court's public docket. Prosecutor Greg Andres then left to enjoy his New Year's festivities.

Soon after the holiday, Nicolas Bourtin, an assistant United States attorney, finished drafting the "Record of the Case for the Prosecution," a 13-page typed document that in concise, clearly worded and numbered paragraphs outlined the allegations against Vito and revealed the existence of four confidential cooperating witnesses, each a former member or associate of the Bonanno Family who was prepared to take the stand and testify against him. The document was a necessary start to the potentially lengthy extradition process. Bourtin had to convince Canadian authorities—both judicial and political—that there was enough evidence against Vito to merit removing a Canadian citizen from his home and sending him to face American justice. In Canada, with its generous Charter of Rights and Freedoms and firm institutional culture of providing numerous safeguards and multiple legal appeals, it is not always an easy task or quick process.

Bourtin gathered the evidence together and began to explain the rudiments of the case against Vito.

"The government will establish Rizzuto's association and membership in the Bonanno Family and his role in the conspiracy to murder, and the murders of, Indelicato, Giaccone and Trinchera through, among other evidence, the testimony of a cooperating witness, the testimony of law-enforcement officials, the testimony of an organized crime expert, surveillance evidence, crime scene evidence and the testimony of the medical examiner," Bourtin wrote. In the document, prepared weeks before any of the arrests, the names of the cooperating witnesses were concealed—Sal Vitale, for instance, is disguised as CW#1, short for the first "cooperating witness."

Bourtin then attached two photographs of Vito—one taken at the Giuseppe Bono wedding and the other a recent mug shot originally provided by Canadian authorities—some crime scene photographs from the recovery of Sonny Red's body and the intriguing FBI surveillance photograph of Vito leaving the Capri Motor Lodge with Gerlando Sciascia, Joe Massino, the Bonnano boss, and Giovanni Ligammari, their Zip ally. These pictures were offered as evidence that Vito associated with known gangsters and, more importantly, placed him in New York around the time of the murders. Also, as supporting documents, Bourtin included an autopsy report from the 1981 examination of a body unearthed on Ruby Street, and a certificate, signed by Sonny Red's son-in-law, identifying the deceased. These confirmed that at least one of the people Vito was accused of killing was in fact dead and, more to the point, dead as a result of three gunshot wounds to the face, chest and back.

Bourtin then attached a cover letter, dated it—January 5, 2004—and signed it with graceful swoops at the top of the N and the bottom of the B. That very day, the package was received by the Canadian government, along with a diplomatic note, only the third such communication between America and Canada of the new year. Traditionally these inter-governmental communications take on the formal air of a wedding invitation: "The Embassy of the United States of America presents its compliments to the Department of Foreign Affairs and International Trade and has the honor to request the extradition of Vito Rizzuto from Canada," it begins.

Later, a superseding indictment—a fresh set of charges that replaced the original one—was issued, adding 26 names to Vito's original indictment in case 03-CR-1382.

MONTREAL, JANUARY 2004

On Monday, January 12, eight days before Vito was to be arrested, Sergeant-Detective Poletti was quietly watching Vito's house when a gray 2002 Mercedes ML500 pulled out of the driveway at 9:15 p.m. Poletti followed it a short distance, and while the car was waiting to turn from Antoine-Berthelet Avenue on to Gouin Boulevard West, he pulled his own car close. Turning his head quickly toward the Mercedes, Poletti saw that Vito was indeed its driver. Two days later, at 10:31 a.m., Benoît Poirier of the Montreal police watched a blue Jeep Grand Cherokee, registered to Vito's wife, pull out and away from the driveway. The officer radioed the news to his colleague Josée Poitras, who picked up the tail and followed the Jeep until the officer similarly confirmed that Vito was inside, driving alone. Then, 23 minutes later, Réal Lepine watched Vito park the Jeep and enter an office building on St-Laurent Boulevard.

The stepped-up surveillance of Vito was not accidental. By the second week of January, a select few members of the Montreal police had been told of the U.S. government's intention to have Vito prosecuted in New York. In anticipation, officers in Montreal started keeping closer tabs on him, watching for signs he might be preparing to flee, confirming he still lived at his longtime residence and appraising the relative difficulty or danger of an arrest. Surveillance officers set up outside to watch Vito's house, although it is difficult to imagine that their vigil went unnoticed on a street where many neighbors are so close to the Rizzutos.

If Vito, who is an extremely astute man, did not catch on to the increased attention being paid him by police, his concerns for his future must have been heightened courtesy of the press. As early as February 2001, Vito would have learned, if he did not already know it, that American authorities were convinced he played a hand in the murders of the three captains. In a large investigative profile of Vito in Canada's *National Post*, the FBI's incriminating photograph of Vito, Sciascia, Massino and Ligammari leaving the Capri Motor Lodge was detailed. As well, excerpts from a confidential FBI report, alleging that Vito was involved in the shooting, were also revealed.

Vito's own sources may have also alerted him to possible trouble coming from New York. A year earlier, the arrests of Joe Massino and Sal Vitale likely raised a red flag. Shortly after the arrests of the top two Bonanno bosses, Vito boarded a plane with his wife and left Canada for two weeks abroad, destination unknown.

On March 2, 2003, not long after a Bonanno informant had notified his lawyer, John Mitchell, that he no longer required his services because he was now cooperating with the government, again by coincidence or by design, Vito left Canada, this time flying alone on a Skyservice jet and arriving back in Montreal eight days later. He was soon on a plane again, on a March 21 flight with Cubana de Aviación to Havana with his wife, where they stayed for about six weeks, according to customs declarations filed with Canada Border Services Agency. Police sources suspected that Vito chose Cuba for this trip because he was aware that Cuban and American officials do not cooperate well together, and his presence there might insulate him from any U.S.

prosecution. Government authorities, however, do not work as quickly as one might think.

Vito had long been back in Canada when, on January 14, 2004, in utmost secrecy, Irwin Cotler, then Canada's Minister of Justice, authorized Canadian officials to proceed with arresting Vito. But an arrest needed to be coordinated with the FBI. Despite the secrecy attached to these developments, a week before Vito and his co-accused were set to be arrested, a surprising item headlined "Eyeing Canadian Club" appeared in the *New York Sun* and on the popular organized crime Web site, www.ganglandnews.com. Jerry Capeci, a noted New York organized crime reporter and columnist, had been tipped to the FBI's interest in Vito.

"Federal prosecutors in Brooklyn are looking north and eyeing the reputed Mafia boss of Canada in the grisly 1981 murders of three Bonanno capos," Capeci's January 15, 2004, exclusive began. The veteran mob-watcher quoted unnamed law enforcement sources about their interest in the "wealthy Bonanno capo," who was compared in the piece to John Gotti. Capeci clearly had solid sources; his scoop was published on the same day that the Eastern District grand jury returned a sealed, and supposedly secret, 20-count superseding indictment against Vito and his New York co-accused. The story, however, escaped the notice of Canadian investigators. The day of its appearance, a story on the American interest in Vito was being prepared by a reporter in Canada, who called police officials and confidential sources for comment and confirmation. Investigators were thrown into panic, asking if a copy of Capeci's story could be faxed to them immediately. The confirmation was then published coast-to-coast in Canada. Two stories, one on each side of the border, had been published that might have alerted Vito. American and Canadian officials, who had been planning a coordinated sweep of all of the men indicted in both countries, faced a quandary: if they did not move quickly to arrest Vito, he might flee to Cuba, where he could well be out of their reach. On the other hand, if they moved early against Vito, they risked warning his alleged co-conspirators in New York. After much hand-wringing, investigators decided that surveillance on Vito should be stepped up considerably, but they would stick to the schedule and not move against him. This decision would be reevaluated if investigators turned up evidence he was preparing to flee.

Vito, however, had no interest in running.

NEW YORK AND MONTREAL, JANUARY 20, 2004

As Poletti and Milano knocked on Vito's front door in Montreal to arrest him, approximately 150 FBI agents, New York State Police investigators and New York City Police detectives were making similar calls across New York. Officials to the south were likewise flush with success. Most of those named in the indictment were picked up, early and easily, when officers arrived at their homes and known haunts on the morning of January 20, 2004.

The mood of the American authorities was one of jubilation as the indictment against 27 accused Bonanno gangsters—including much of the family's leadership—was finally unsealed and announced to the media.

Roslynn R. Mauskopf, the U.S. Attorney for the Eastern District of New York, called the arrests "the broadest and deepest penetration ever of a New York City–based organized crime family." It was not a point drawing contradiction.

"The entire leadership, acting leadership and virtually every criminal leader in the Bonanno Family stands either convicted or under indictment. With unprecedented access to the inner workings of the Bonanno Family's administration, we had front-row seats, listening as these career criminals described murdering innocent victims in a desperate effort to salvage their crumbling criminal enterprise," Mauskopf said.

Raymond Kelly, commissioner of the New York City Police Department, as a policeman rather than a lawyer, put it more succinctly: "The Bonanno Family [is] an endangered species."

Vito's precise position within the Bonanno Family created some confusion for authorities. Officially, they stuck to the formal nomenclature of New York's Five Families and, since Vito was considered to be a made guy but one who never accepted the offer of being named captain, they adopted his rank as a mere Bonanno soldier. But his power, prominence and distinctive service clearly deserved more notation. In a press release, U.S. authorities hinted at his greater standing: "Bonanno Family soldier Vito Rizzuto, referred to by Canadian law enforcement and the Canadian press as the 'Godfather of the Italian Mafia in Montreal,' is the most influential Bonanno Family member in Canada," the release says.

At a crowded press conference, the first name spoken by Pasquale "Pat" D'Amuro, assistant director-in-charge of the FBI in New York, was the name of the man he did not yet have his hands on.

"Among the many accomplishments of this investigation are the clearance of numerous homicides which were committed in the New York City metropolitan area over the past two decades and, with the arrest of Vito Rizzuto, the incarceration of the Godfather of organized crime in Canada," D'Amuro said. More recently, the FBI posted a bulletin summarizing its key moves in controlling organized crime. In it, the bureau named Vito as one of its top three catches in the operation. The other two were the acting boss and acting underboss of the Bonanno Family: Anthony "Tony Green" Urso, who authorities say was the acting boss, standing in for Joe Massino while he was before the courts, and Joseph "Joe Saunders" Cammarano, the acting underboss filling in for Sal Vitale, who was likewise fighting a charge. The pair were said to have ordered the murder of Anthony Tomasulo, a Bonanno associate who was found wrapped in a body bag in the rear seat of his own car in May 1990 for refusing to pay a portion of the proceeds from his illegal joker-poker gambling machines to the Bonanno bosses.

Louis "Louie Ha-Ha" Attanasio, at one time an acting underboss, was also indicted that day, but when agents went looking for him they came up empty-handed. Louie Ha-Ha faced life in prison for allegedly shooting Cesare Bonventre in the back of the head while Vitale drove the Zip leader to his death. Louie Ha-Ha was enjoying the warm bayfront property of his winter home on the Caribbean island of St. Maarten. For almost a year he remained out of the government's reach, reveling in an island law that protects permanent residents with a favorably short statute of limitations on crime, even murder. Local authorities, however, bowing to U.S. pressure, revoked his legal resident status on the grounds he gained it on false pretenses, apparently having declared he did not have a criminal record. He was then arrested and returned to New York, a move his lawyer, Larry Bronson, declared to be a "kidnapping."

Seven alleged Bonanno captains or acting captains were also named in the same indictment, along with 16 Bonanno soldiers and associates, including Vito's fellow Zip and Sixth Family friend Baldassare "Baldo" Amato. Baldo is accused of being the man who shot Robert Perrino, the superintendent of delivery at the *New York Post*, at the urging of Gerlando Sciascia, in lieu of bringing in Montrealers to do the job. Baldo's second murder accusation is over the death of Sebastian "Sammy" DiFalco, an associate of Baldo's. On March 17, 1992, DiFalco's body was pulled from the trunk of his own car, found in the parking lot of a Dunkin Donuts in Queens.

Along with 15 other soldiers and associates, it was a significant haul, one that continued the government's assault against the Bonanno Family. Between March 2002, and the unsealing of Vito's indictment, the U.S. government had prosecuted more than 70 members and associates of the Bonanno crime family who were alleged to have been involved in 23 murders, murder conspiracies and attempted murders, government records show.

"In little more than one year, the government has dismantled successive administrations of the Bonanno Family. Today, virtually the entire family leadership of the Bonanno Family has been incapacitated, with only a few family captains remaining unindicted," the government crowed in its 21-page press release announcing the sweep. The time frame the government boasted of—"little more than one year"—was, in reality, a gentle fraud. It ignored the fact that the law-enforcement efforts of several agencies at various levels of government and in two countries had been directed at the family for decades, almost fruitlessly, before these inroads were made.

The joy that the officials could not contain on the day of the arrests was born of the frustration and humiliation they had lived with for years.

CHAPTER 38

NEW YORK, 2001

It had been more than 20 years since the FBI had done serious damage to the Bonanno Family although, it must be said, the attack back then was so spectacular and devious it has lived on in legend. For six years, FBI Special Agent Joseph D. Pistone had assumed his undercover guise as Donnie Brasco and been accepted as an associate into the family. Once his duplicity was revealed, Pistone's evidence in court deeply shook the family with some 200 indictments and 100 convictions—but it did not extinguish the Bonannos. Pistone's work toppled many a gangster, but Joe Massino—who was charged with aiding in the murders of the three captains at a 1987 trial featuring Pistone as the star witness—managed to beat the rap. Even after the indictments stopped flowing from Pistone's evidence, the stinging wounds remained for the Bonannos, as his exploits were documented in a bestselling book and then a popular movie, *Donnie Brasco*, starring Al Pacino and Johnny Depp. In response to the breach of security, the family lost its seat on the Commission and had become something of a Mafia pariah.

Since then, however, the FBI's success against the Bonanno Family had been slim. The Bonanno Squad was struggling and, all the while, the family was rebuilding. As the leaders in New York's other Mafia families wobbled and toppled, the Bonannos seemed impervious to serious prosecution. It became a point of pride for the gangsters and, over the years, served to regenerate the family. The humiliation over the Brasco infiltration was slowly being erased.

In 1986, Carmine Persico, boss of the Colombo Family, was convicted on racketeering charges and sentenced to life imprisonment. In 1992, John Gotti, the famously flamboyant boss of the Gambino Family, was finally convicted of racketeering and handed a life sentence, after three acquittals. That same year, Vittorio "Little Vic" Amuso, boss of the Lucchese Family, was sentenced to life imprisonment for racketeering. In 1997, Vincent "Chin" Gigante, a Mafia old-timer who was head of the

Genovese Family, was imprisoned for racketeering. By the late 1990s, the leadership of four of New York's Five Families was in disarray.

Lending proof to the adage that what does not kill you makes you stronger, Joe Massino had learned much from evaluating how Donnie Brasco had got so close to so many in his family. Massino also weighed the failures of other bosses who were convicted and the methods used to ensnare them. He even studied the FBI personnel who were assigned to investigate him and then took pleasure in letting them know it; he often congratulated agents on any in-house promotions and sometimes mentioned in passing their educational background or past accomplishments.

The Bonanno Family, under Massino, was experiencing a distinct renaissance, remaining surprisingly buoyant in an era of gangland disarray. This fact was not lost on the media. Reporters and columnists picked up on Massino's status as the only official New York boss who was not imprisoned and dubbed him "The Last Don." The name was a ringing endorsement of Massino's enterprising ways as a gangster. It was also more than a little frustrating for the men and women who had been trying to topple him.

———

The Bonanno Squad had reassessed its progress in 1998. The unit, which has the official FBI designation of Squad C-10, an abbreviation for Criminal Investigative Unit Number Ten, had a lot on its plate. Its workload was the most divided of all of the squads assigned to the Five Families in New York. Along with monitoring and investigating the Bonanno Family's activities in the city, Squad C-10 was responsible for the DeCavalcante Family based in neighboring New Jersey, the Teamsters union and also—in a nod to the Bonannos' peculiar relationship with gangsters in Canada and Sicily—international organized crime linked to New York.

As Sal Vitale's discovery of the FBI's bug in the ceiling of Massino's club highlighted, electronic eavesdropping had not yielded the same success against the Bonannos as had, for example, the bug in the home of Angelo "Quack Quack" Ruggiero, one of the Sixth Family's Gambino partners. And despite making generous offers to a number of Bonanno members facing charges, authorities had not convinced a single one to cooperate. While the FBI and federal prosecutors were increasingly aware of the effectiveness of mob turncoats in securing difficult convictions, particularly in the face of the testimony of Salvatore "Sammy Bull" Gravano, the Bonanno men had remained steadfast.

Even those gangsters who faced certain death from their colleagues for vouching for Donnie Brasco refused to cooperate, despite overt offers from the government. Sonny Black refused to accept even an agent's telephone number. Instead, he handed his jewelry to the bartender at the Motion Lounge social club, said he might not be coming back and glumly went to meet mob colleagues who, as he suspected, had orders to kill him. On orders from Sciascia and Massino, Frank Lino lured Sonny Black to a meeting at a fellow mobster's house and then pushed him down a flight of stairs. At the bottom, he was shot, but the gunman's weapon jammed. As he lay on the floor wounded, Sonny Black looked up at his friends and implored them, "Hit me one more time; make it good." They complied.

Bonanno gangsters were smug in the knowledge that no made Bonanno member had ever become a rat. It was a point Joe Massino would emphasize at the induction ceremonies for members into his family.

"During the ceremony, Mr. Massino would tell us his family were the only family that never had any informants in history. We had two individuals in the electric chair in the Fifties, but never had a rat in the family," Sal Vitale said. The resuscitation of the Bonanno Family was enough for the organization to regain its seat on the Commission, and then raised Massino to the pinnacle of American crime as the Commission's senior member.

"The other four families, all their bosses were in jail. Who is actually going to these [Commission] meetings were an underboss or an acting underboss. So Joe felt it was beneath him for him to attend, so he would send me," said Vitale. Oh, how the mighty Commission had fallen.

Massino continued his evolution from street tough to wily mob boss, even if the organization, as a whole, was becoming a shadow of its former self. By late 1993, his longevity and success at avoiding serious prosecution led him to quietly re-christen the entire crime family in his honor.

"We turned it into the 'Massino Family,'" Frank Lino said. The gangsters were anxious to bury their association with their namesake Godfather.

"Joe Bonanno, he wrote a book about the Commission. They just wanted to do away with his name," Lino said. "They said he betrayed, you know, the family."

Vitale confirms the change: "Joe Bonanno wrote a book. He was the founding father of the Bonanno Family. He wrote a book. I think it was called *A Man of Honor*, and since he wrote that book, he disrupted our life. So we don't want to be known as the Bonanno Family. So, behind closed doors, we were known as the Massino Family," Vitale said. "Mr. Massino felt that it should not be called the Bonanno [Family]," said Vitale. "We are not open for publication, public knowledge. It is not for the average person to know who we are. By him writing the book, it brought us all to the surface, so that is why we felt he disrespected us." News of the change in the family's name slowly filtered out to Bonanno members.

"We didn't go around making it public knowledge to our captains, but during our ceremony, or during a meeting, we would say, you know, the 'Massino Family,'" Vitale said.

By the mid-1990s, there was a new way of conducting business in the family. In fact, Massino tried to move the organization closer to its roots, as the Mafia had largely remained in Montreal. He initiated a rule, through the Commission, insisting that new Mafia members be "full Italian," meaning both parents had to trace their ancestry back to the birthplace of their secret society. For years, as long as a crook could bring in cash and had a father who hailed from the old country, he was prime American Mafia material. Massino also recognized the strength that came from the bonds of family—true family—and encouraged his members to induct their sons.

"He felt that he knew the bloodline; he felt that if it was good enough for the father it should be good enough for the son," said Vitale.

Massino also moved to insulate himself from prosecution. He ordered that the gangsters' social clubs, which had long formed an integral part of the New York Mafia mystique, be shut down to limit opportunities for police investigators to monitor their activities. Massino himself stopped attending mob-linked wakes, weddings and funerals—once a staple of a mob boss's routine. He wanted to reduce his public exposure. Talking about anything of substance over a home or cell phone was banned. To compensate, Vitale assigned each of his 15 captains a two-digit number as a code. Sciascia's was 02. When any of them needed to reach the Bonanno administration, they would call

Vitale's pager from a public pay phone and leave the phone booth's number, followed by the captain's two-digit code. Vitale would then go to another public pay phone and return the call.

"I would know who I am speaking to by the last two digits," said Vitale. Massino even tried to erase his own name from FBI wiretaps, recordings he assumed—he knew—were secretly being made all around him.

"You were told not to use his name," Lino said. Massino's men were supposed to use a hand gesture, touching their ear or grabbing their earlobe, in place of speaking his name out loud when referring to him in conversation. At a meeting at Massino's Casa Blanca Restaurant, the boss told Lino that the soldiers and captains needed to protect him as the boss, or "our family would probably disintegrate." The men generally went along with the directives, since they acknowledged that they indeed had an interest in protecting Massino, so long as he was a productive and successful boss, protecting their profits and their dealings with the other Five Families.

"You are only as strong as your boss to the other families," Vitale noted.

———

Massino's intense insulation meant the FBI needed also to evolve. Around 1999, a different strategy was emerging, an approach that mimicked the advice given by the Nixon-era informant Deep Throat to investigative journalists: "Follow the money." The probe that would threaten to topple the Bonanno Family bosses became a decidedly unromantic paper chase, one relying not so much on action-oriented cops but on careful, nitpicking accountants. The new breed of agents painstakingly tracked how, and from whom, the Bonanno Family was drawing revenue and where that money was going.

Kimberly McCaffrey and Jeffrey Sallet were two FBI Special Agents attached to Squad C-10 who were also trained forensic accountants. They started sifting through documents—tax returns and financial records—tracing the flow of Massino's illicit cash.

"In those days, everyone was going out on surveillance, while we would be going through each paper in a stack of boxes," McCaffrey said. "We'd find a K-1 financial statement and get excited, and people would joke, 'you guys are such geeks.'" The plodding work by the FBI's "geeks" recognized that much of the mob's activities qualified more as white-collar crime than crude shakedowns.

"We looked into sources of income and expenses and at the hierarchy of the family, looking for financial associations, financial crimes," McCaffrey said. "We used grand jury subpoenas, interviews, surveillances, reviewing bank documents, financial records."

"This phase of our investigation of the Bonanno Family began with a non-traditional approach to fighting organized crime," the FBI's Pat D'Amuro said. "A team of forensic accountants followed the money and identified patterns of connection and criminal activity."

A new, intricate probe was launched—not into unsolved mob murders or international heroin deals, but into parking lot receipts. The K-1 reports McCaffrey and Sallet studied were statements of joint partnerships and earnings submitted with tax returns. They showed that Massino and Vitale were earning money from several New York parking lots in a business arrangement with the wife of Richard "Shellackhead" Cantarella, a Bonanno captain. By 2000, the probe of that arrangement had led to Barry Weinberg, a businessman who loved socializing with mobsters and who, in return for the excitement, helped them in their business pursuits. Agents felt they had found their weak link.

McCaffrey and Sallet confronted Weinberg in January 2001, when they had his Mercedes pulled over in midtown Manhattan by New York City police, who then hustled him into an unmarked van. The agents threatened to charge him with tax evasion and other offenses and, within minutes, the man crumpled. A timorous, white-collar criminal to the core, Weinberg had no interest in even a short stay in jail and agreed to cooperate in the Bureau's hunt for bigger fish. Weinberg spent the next year meeting with Shellackhead and Frank Coppa, another Bonanno captain, while wearing a secret recording device, the first such infiltration of the Bonannos since Donnie Brasco hung up his wires. With that investigation beginning to gain traction, the Bonannos were hit from another direction.

BOCA RATON, FLORIDA, MARCH 2002

On March 19, 2002, Anthony "TG" Graziano, the 61-year-old gangster whom Gerlando Sciascia had grown to despise and who, by then, had become the Bonanno *consigliere*, was indicted for racketeering in New York. The indictment was linked to a second indictment filed against him the next day in Florida, one that hinted at the value of financial investigations like McCaffrey and Sallet's. The New York case was about low-brow murder, drugs and extortion, while the Florida case was over a sophisticated investment swindle. In New York, it involved torturing a wayward colleague with a blowtorch, dragging another around a room at the wrong end of a noose and burning a third with a cigarette lighter. In Florida, it was about smooth-talking financial bamboozling through high-pressure telephone sales pitches seeking investors in bogus foreign exchange markets. Between them, the two indictments against Graziano presented the twin faces of the modern mob and illustrated the need for a new and more flexible approach in the FBI's organized crime investigations.

Graziano's eventual conviction and 11-year sentence would also serve, in the months ahead, as a potent reminder to his Bonanno colleagues of the steep consequences of an indictment under the Racketeer Influenced and Corrupt Organizations (RICO) Act. Arrested alongside Graziano in the Florida case—an investigation that saw a Tampa police officer working undercover, posing as a money launderer—was John J. Finkelstein, a Montreal businessman who relocated to Boca Raton and oversaw four "boiler rooms" where fraudsters bilked investors across North America, many of them seniors, out of US$11.7 million on behalf of the Bonanno Family. Finkelstein, described by his lawyer as a devout Jew and family man, had a distinctly undesirable nickname among his underworld colleagues. They called him "Fink."

Such nicknames might have fed Massino's paranoia over informants coming close to him. He followed the cases of each of his mob associates with careful diligence, seeking hints of their cooperation with the government, such as defendants suddenly changing lawyers, irrationally pleading guilty or receiving light sentences. Any underling who fit any of these criteria was immediately suspect. The boss routinely had New York lawyer Matthew Mari, who has a long association with the Bonannos through representing several members and associates, check court files for updates on the status of prosecutions against Massino's colleagues, prosecutors claimed in a memorandum filed in court. No one seemed above suspicion, not even Sal Vitale, Massino's brother-in-law. Massino suspected Vitale was a "rat" long before Vitale had actually decided to become one. He voiced his concerns and his growing dislike of Vitale to fellow gangsters. He went so far as to suggest Vitale would be killed. Fellow Bonanno members reportedly started calling Vitale "Fredo," the name of the weak brother who betrayed the boss in *The Godfather: Part II*. In the film, Fredo was killed for his disloyalty.

It was a gross strategic blunder on Massino's part. With so many informants and wiretaps aimed his way, it did not take long for this loose talk to come to the attention of the FBI, and astute agents were later able to put it to good use. With federal agents squirreling away any piece of potential evidence against the Bonanno inner circle, even Massino's considerable efforts to protect himself would soon prove to be in vain. Betrayal loomed large.

BROOKLYN, OCTOBER 2002

Frank Coppa was not a typical member of the Mafia. For starters, he finished high school and even started college. Then there was his appearance; a rotund man with a round, balding head, he looked more like a parish priest than a fierce gangster. Just a year after his induction into the Mafia in 1977, Coppa was set apart again when he was injured in a car explosion, a victim of a rare bombing among American mobsters, who generally prefer the more personal approach of a gun. Coppa's greatest distinction, however, was yet to come. Coppa knew well the ramifications of the oath of *omertà*, something he had sworn before Carmine Galante himself. When he accepted the offer of membership, he swore his silence.

"That means you live by the gun and you die by the gun," he said.

Coppa was 61 years old and a few months into a five-year sentence for stock manipulation when he was hit again with a racketeering indictment that could lead to 20 years' imprisonment. Never a hard man, despite having a hand in several gangland murders, Coppa considered himself something of a gentleman bandit, and prison was not an environment he was thriving in. He reportedly burst into tears in front of disgusted inmates early in his incarceration. Contrary to his earlier assessment of living by the gun and dying by the gun, Coppa was facing a slow, languishing end as a frightened man in a prison cell. FBI agents could practically smell his fear and zeroed in on him, offering salvation to the priestly-looking figure.

In November 2002, Coppa did what no inducted member before him in the storied history of the Bonanno Family had ever done; he agreed to become a cooperating witness for the government against his Mafia colleagues.

"I didn't want to do no more time," was his simple explanation. His subsequent revelations, during secret debriefings, amazed agents on Squad C-10 as they listened to him unravel once-perplexing mob mysteries. He recounted in detail the murders of Sonny Black, Robert Perrino and Tony Mirra, all the while implicating Joe Massino, Sal Vitale, Frank Lino, Richard "Shellackhead" Cantarella and other leading Bonanno members. Coppa's information and promised testimony in court was hailed by the government as a "landmark achievement." On its own, it was certainly an important development and, for the hard-pressed Squad C-10, a point of gratification. Coppa's true importance, however, stemmed primarily from the domino effect it caused after news of his cooperation rippled through the underworld. In that, he was nothing less than historic.

When word of Coppa's defection reached Massino, the news chilled him. He sent for Vitale. Despite Vitale being monitored with an electronic ankle bracelet while awaiting trial and strictly banned from communicating with Massino, the dutiful Vitale answered the call. Massino's message was short and sobering.

"Frankie Coppa went bad," he said.

When the rest of the Bonanno leadership learned of Coppa's break from them, Shellackhead, who had been indicted alongside Coppa for racketeering, realized his chances of beating a conviction had just evaporated. When Shellackhead was arrested, police also charged his wife and son, Paul. His son had also been inducted into the Bonanno Family. Always a bright man whose ability to exploit a deal had made him one of the Bonannos' wealthiest New York gangsters, Shellackhead quickly applied his gambler's wits to calculating the odds of regaining his freedom. The odds were against him. In December 2002, just one month after Coppa turned, the Cantarella family also placed its faith in the government. Shellackhead's insights into the Bonanno operations were far greater than Coppa's because he had long had special access to the boss. Once a week, from 1996 until 2002, he had dinner with Massino at the Casa Blanca Restaurant in Queens. The two covered a lot of material over pasta and wine. Massino was grooming him for a position of power within the family and using him to fulfill the traditional job of the underboss—without the title—by placing him as the main liaison between the boss and his captains. It was a move to further insulate Massino from prosecution and also reflected his growing mistrust of Vitale. That move left Vito Rizzuto as one of the select few who could talk directly to Massino—if he had anything to say to him, Vitale said.

With Shellackhead and Coppa now onside, prosecutors leaned heavily on their proffered testimony to draft indictments against their top two Bonanno targets—the boss and the underboss of the Bonanno Family. On January 8, 2003, a grand jury in the Eastern District of New York returned a 19-count indictment against Massino and Vitale. The RICO indictment named Massino in the slaying of Sonny Black, and Vitale in the Perrino killing. Also named in the same indictment, for his role in Sonny Black's death, was Frank Lino.

The next day, the government said it had 20 criminals willing to testify on the government's behalf to the existence of the Bonanno Family, 15 of whom would further name Massino as the boss. In court filings that followed, what Massino had already known was confirmed publicly by the government—two of those cooperating witnesses were made Bonanno members. To his surprise, Vitale was not one of them.

Officials kept Massino and Vitale in separate prisons as they started their journeys through the courts. Away from Massino, agents alerted Vitale to the fact that Massino was targeting him as a weak link and they offered him a deal. Vitale was ripe for such maneuvers. Already upset at the downturn in his mob fortunes under the reorganized Bonanno enterprise, Vitale had for months been pondering his future. His wife had even visited Massino to personally ask him if he intended to kill her husband, an approach that was greeted with much guffawing by gangsters who later heard about it. Massino had already broken the news to Vitale that most of the men "despised" him. And, although Massino left Vitale with the official title of underboss, he directly undermined him by relying on Shellackhead instead.

"He put a wedge, in that period of time, between me and the captains, leaving me in a very vulnerable position," Vitale said. "He took the captains away from me; they weren't allowed to call me, they weren't allowed to give me Christmas gifts. ... I had the position as underboss but the captains couldn't call me, couldn't associate with me. The captains couldn't make me earn any money. I was more or less ... shelved. You might have the title but you are not doing anything, you are just, for lack of a better word, you are a figurehead."

When Vitale was earlier charged, in 2001, no one called his wife to offer support. When he had a health scare, only one soldier visited him in hospital. Feeling alienated and vulnerable, Vitale made his decision and sent word, through one of his son's friends, who was a lawyer, that he was willing to discuss cooperation. He was whisked to a safer prison facility and started talking to federal prosecutors.

"I felt that my wife and kids were going to be left in the street. That's why I decided to do what I'm doing," Vitale said of his decision. He showed his affection for Massino by describing their split in a term usually reserved for the end of a romantic relationship: "We broke up."

Now, feeling betrayed and vulnerable, he offered damning information that profoundly threatened Massino and the Bonanno Family. Vitale also had plenty to say about Canada.

As with the other turncoats, Vitale began lengthy debriefings during which he tore down the curtains that had long blocked the government's view of Joe Massino, the modern incarnation of the Bonanno Family and the men who made it powerful, including Vito Rizzuto.

———

If Coppa's action was the opening trickle, Vitale's decision to join him opened the floodgates. Bonanno members and associates, suddenly facing substantial prison terms, began to fear they would be the ones caught out. No one wanted to be the sad gangster left to face the full wrath of the courts without a cooperation agreement and with the fingers of their former colleagues-in-arms—men who were equally guilty or, in some cases, substantially more so—all pointing at them in court. With news or rumors of each new turncoat, Bonanno mobsters quietly cataloged in their minds what that person might have on them, and then weighed the danger they faced of being incriminated. When the odds looked particularly grim, they were increasingly switching sides.

Confirmation of Vitale's defection, although not really taking the Bonanno leadership by surprise after Massino's public musings, hit the gangsters hard. Frank Lino found it deeply distressing, for he knew that Vitale would considerably bolster the case against him for the Sonny Black murder by corroborating the expected testimony from his old friend Frank Coppa. Worse, Vitale could pin other murders on him.

Throughout his Mafia career, Lino proved time and again that he had an uncanny instinct for self-preservation. Escaping what was meant to be certain death in 1981, when the three captains were massacred in front of him, was perhaps the most dramatic example of his unnatural longevity. His quick willingness to set his loyalty to Sonny Red aside—once it was clear Massino was winning the power struggle—was another. Likewise, in early 2003, with life imprisonment hovering over him, Lino did it again, this time abandoning his oath of *omertà*. It was not just his crime family he needed to turn against, however. As a lifelong criminal and longtime underworld player, he was required by the government to catalog all of his past crimes, who he committed them with and to list all of the made members of the mob and its associates that he was aware of. This meant turning in his son, Joseph, who was also a made man in the Bonanno Family, and other relatives. Even Duane "Goldie" Leisenheimer, Massino's loyal acolyte, who had gone to prison in the past to protect the boss, turned on the mob and became yet another cooperating witness for the government. The array and rank of Bonanno informants climbing onboard surprised investigators.

"The number of so-called 'made members' of the Bonanno Family who have abandoned the oath of *omertà* and cooperated actively with the investigation, and who have indicated a desire to cooperate, is truly unprecedented," said the FBI's Pat D'Amuro. "Instead of beating people up, they are beating down our doors in an effort to cooperate."

Some of the informants, including Joseph "Joey Mook" D'Amico and James "Big Louie" Tartaglione agreed to wear wires when they met with fellow gangsters, secretly recording their conversations, another first in the government's assault against the Bonannos. The government would record veteran gangsters discussing serious underworld business, including family administration meetings and sitdowns with members of three of New York's Five Families: the Gambino, Colombo and Genovese families. In one recording, made during a meeting in September 2003, when the Bonanno Family was really feeling the heat from news of the informants, Anthony Urso, the acting boss at the time, was heard suggesting one way to stem the flood of rats.

"You gotta throw somebody in the streets—this has got to stop. Fuck it, he can do it, I can do it. This is how they should have played and they might have done this before: [if] you turned [informant], we wipe your family out," he said. "How would Sal feel if I killed one of his kids?" Urso asked Big Louie. "Why should the rat's kids be happy where my kids or your kids should suffer because I'm away for life? If you take one kid—I hate to say it—and do what you gotta do, they'll fuckin' think twice."

It would be a reprehensible thing for anyone to suggest, let alone a family man such as Urso. In a bid to aid Urso in obtaining a release on bail after he too was arrested, his own son, Steven Craig Urso, an associate professor at Nassau Community College in Garden City, New York, wrote to the judge: "I would like you to know that my father is a kind and considerate man. ... My dad has also taught me so much—honesty, respect and the value of hard work. ... Despite his many challenges and his physical injuries, he has always maintained a healthy and modest lifestyle. He also taught me how to respect both my mind and body and how to meet life's challenges with both courage and dignity." The elder Urso himself seemed to have a change of heart—or at least told the judge he had—when he renounced his life in the Mafia.

"I still battle with my demons over this young man's death almost every day of my life. I wish there had been something I could have done to save him," he wrote to Judge Nicholas Garaufis of the Bonanno associate he had killed. "I have made some bad choices in life, but sometimes by the time you realize that you made a mistake, it's too late to walk away. Now that I am finally free of that life of crime, all I can hope and pray for is the opportunity to live out the last years of my life in peace with my loved ones."

Although Urso was dissuaded from going after the family of "rats" by his fellow gangsters, it suggested the desperation the Bonanno gangsters were feeling. It also highlighted the potential danger of becoming a government informant. This was underscored by Lino, who said informants like him faced a death sentence on the streets: "If I was not cooperating, I would be killing the witnesses," Lino said.

Along with fear of the turncoats, conversations among the senior members of the Bonanno administration—the men chosen to fill in while Massino was incarcerated—reveal their attempts at protecting the remaining Bonanno assets. With "Big Louie" Tartaglione, a veteran Bonanno captain, secretly recording the conversations for the government, the senior New York mobsters refer to "them up there," according to transcripts of the recordings. "Up there" is code for Canada, Tartaglione later said.

"When he's got a case going, he don't wanna show them, like now, [that] we got Canada too," Joseph "Joe Saunders" Cammarano said during one conversation. Tartaglione later decoded the chat; Joe Massino did not want his men discussing New York's relationship with Montreal while the FBI was all over them.

"They don't want [people] saying… 'Canada this and that.' Leave it alone so maybe you don't let the cat out of the bag," Tartaglione explained. After Cammarano said they all needed to protect the Canadian contingent, Anthony Urso said it was likely too late. The rats, he said, will have already blabbed.

"You think he didn't say he was out there with me, with all those people?" Urso said, a reference to Urso's trip to Montreal with Vitale a few years earlier, when they met Vito and some of his men.

The Bonanno mobsters who remained unindicted grew increasingly resigned to the outcome of the demise of *omertà* within their ranks. In a frank assessment, Vincent "Vinny Gorgeous" Basciano predicted how it would turn out.

"At the end of the day, we're all gonna be in jail," he said.

It was not long after those words were spoken that Vito Rizzuto and his New York colleagues were arrested.

―――――――

On February 13, 2004, Vito's co-defendants—those who had been arrested on the same day as him in the sweep through New York—got their first tangible look at the strength of the government's case against them. The first installment of the government's evidence was turned over to defense lawyers, in accordance with the rules of disclosure. Included in that early batch were 250 exhibits and more than 70 audio recordings—the result of the informants' having secretly worn wires while striking up conversations with associates.

"Additional discovery will follow," Greg Andres, the prosecutor, added dryly. The volume and extent of the evidence proffered from so many informants, each adding a layer of corroboration to the other, presents a daunting challenge for any defendant. A jury could easily turn away in disgust from one unsavory turncoat, or, under clever cross-examination, two of them could be made to appear too unreliable to base a conviction on. But six or more cooperating informants sticking largely to the same story would be considerably persuasive.

For Vito, however, his judicial prospects would only get worse—potentially much worse—when another unexpected and almost inconceivable informant stepped out from the shadows.

CHAPTER 39

BROOKLYN, JULY 30, 2004

After nine weeks of spirited trial, the foreman of an anonymous 12-member jury stood before Judge Nicholas Garaufis and announced their findings. Joseph Massino, then 61 and the boss of the Bonanno Family, was found guilty of ordering seven gangland murders. It left him facing a mandatory life sentence. Among the murders he was found to have orchestrated were the May 5, 1981, ambush of the three captains, as well as the slayings of Sonny Black and Anthony Mirra for letting Donnie Brasco near the family. At the trial, Greg Andres and his assistant attorneys, Robert Henoch and Mitra Hormozi, had led six former Bonanno underlings of Massino's to the stand to point their finger incriminatingly at the boss.

"For the first time in the history of organized crime prosecution, members of the Bonanno Family who once took the oath of *omertà* took the oath of a witness," a U.S. Department of Justice official said, after the convictions.

The government's record against the Bonannos was now unparalleled. Joe Massino brought to 30 the number of Bonanno defendants convicted after trial or pleading guilty to federal indictments. That total included the boss, the underboss, the *consigliere*, four members of the family's ruling committee, 10 captains or acting captains and seven made members who were soldiers. Further, 33 additional members and associates were under indictment and facing justice, including Vito Rizzuto.

The U.S. government lost little time in noting one measure of its achievement: the official bosses of all Five Families of New York were now behind bars serving substantial prison sentences. Massino's troubles were not over; he still faced a second indictment—this one for ordering the execution of Gerlando "George from Canada" Sciascia.

This charge was different from the others for one ominous reason—the murder had taken place in 1999, five years after the death penalty for a racketeering murder was placed on the books. The law had been passed despite quiet, behind-the-scenes lobbying of politicians by gangsters. The gangsters' fear was well placed. The Massino case proved that the government would not flinch from sending a mob boss to face execution. This case against Massino was now a matter of life or death.

In November 2004, prosecutors made it official: if Massino was convicted, they would seek to execute him for ordering Sciascia's death. The announcement, however, was attacked by Judge Garaufis, the trial judge, as being an uncalled for parting shot from John Ashcroft, the U.S. Attorney General, who had already announced his retirement from office when he issued the call for the mob boss's execution.

"While it is apparent that the outgoing Attorney General has the authority to render the decision announced here in open court today, Mr. Ashcroft's choice to make such a sobering and potentially life-ending decision now, after several delays, and only after tendering his resignation to the President and announcing to the country that he no longer wishes to preside over the Department of Justice, is deeply troubling to this court," Judge Garaufis said from the bench. "It is my hope and expectation that the incoming Attorney General, presumably Judge Alberto R. Gonzales, will, upon taking office, conduct a careful review of Mr. Ashcroft's decision in the final moments of his tenure."

John Nowacki, a spokesman for the Department of Justice, defended the prerogative of the Attorney General to seek to have Massino executed: "The death penalty is the law of the land, provided for as the ultimate punishment for heinous crimes, and this administration is committed to the fair implementation of justice."

The tactic against Massino, however controversial, worked wonders. Massino now faced almost certain death. With the crime family he had worked tirelessly to rebuild and rejuvenate—even rebranding it under his own name—falling again into tatters; after facing betrayal after betrayal as he sat in the courtroom staring at his former associates testifying against him; after having his personal family torn asunder by the cooperation of Sal Vitale, his own brother-in-law; and after being handed a life sentence and now facing possible execution, Joseph Massino did something he would never have thought possible. He offered his own cooperation to the government.

The news was as stunning as it was exciting to the few officials who were let in on one of the biggest secrets in law enforcement since Donnie Brasco roamed the streets of New York. Never before had the top boss of one of the Five Families become a cooperating government informant. His input and insight could prove invaluable. Although imprisoned, Massino had maintained his position as the boss of the family. He had continued to hear reports and give instructions from prison through intermediaries, including his wife and one of his criminal lawyers. He was in a position to provide the most accurate and detailed account of some of the most important decades in Mafia history.

"There are some things that only Joey knows," said a law enforcement official involved in the Bonanno investigations. It did not take long for Massino's cooperation to pay dividends. He agreed to be wired up so that officials could record his supposedly clandestine jailhouse chats with Vincent Basciano, whom the government said was the acting boss of the Bonanno Family. In one recording, Basciano is heard telling Massino that he ordered the December 2004, shooting of Randolph Pizzolo, a mob associate. When Massino asked him why the young man was killed, Basciano had a ready answer.

"Because he is a fucking dangerous kid that don't fucking listen," Basciano said, according to documents filed in court. "I thought [killing] this kid would have been a wake-up call for everybody."

What was even more disturbing for justice officials, however, was Basciano's alleged proposal to kill Greg Andres, the federal prosecutor who was leading the legal charge against the Bonanno organization, and Judge Garaufis, who had been hearing all of the Bonanno trials— and meting out stiff sentences. Talk of that plot was also captured on tape when Basciano was talking to his boss, prosecutors claim. Massino had other secrets to offer as well.

QUEENS, FALL 2004

On October 4, 2004, 23 years after Sonny Red's body had been pulled from the blackened soil, FBI agents, New York City Police detectives and forensic staff from the New York Medical Examiner's Office returned to the vacant lot on Ruby Street. This time, they brought cadaver-sniffing dogs and heavy earth-moving equipment. Despite the opulence suggested by the area's street names—Ruby is joined by Amber, Emerald and Sapphire streets—the passing of time has made the neighborhood only more desolate: a low-rise vista of ramshackle properties, dotted with abandoned rusting cars and threadbare tires, gives way to imposing apartment complexes. "Quick cash closing—Top dollar paid," reads a sign not far from the lot, providing a phone number for remaining residents who wish to sell their land. Developers now eye the mob's old turf near John F. Kennedy Airport, with the police activity having done little for property values on Ruby. Armed with a search warrant, police erected blue wooden barriers and yellow crime-scene tape around the same lot where Sonny Red was found. The ground had not yet given up all of its secrets.

Authorities, led back to the site by Massino's information, dug for three weeks, tearing deep into the marshy, rancid soil, ripping through weed trees and smashing concrete slabs that covered portions of the ground.

After three weeks of digging and sifting through the soil, investigators uncovered pieces from two corpses. The first sign they were not on a wild-goose chase was the discovery of a severed foot and attached shinbone, still wrapped in a black shoe, a testament to the durability of sensible footwear. Other bones soon surfaced. Resting with one set of remains was the same expensive Piaget wristwatch that Philly Lucky was wearing when he disappeared; with the other was a credit card stamped with Big Trinny's name. After DNA drawn from the bones was compared to samples provided by their families, the identity of the two missing captains was confirmed.

News of Massino's cooperation with the government came as a shock to everyone. Among those most dismayed were his relatives.

"He is a bitter, tortured man who now stands alone," Massino's 43-year-old daughter, Adeline, told Anthony DeStefano at *Newsday*. "My mother, my sister and I [know] no reason why he is doing this and probably never will. Maybe he himself doesn't know that answer.... We supported my dad through the trial but now feel it impossible to support or condone his actions any further," she said, adding that it went against his oft-spoken belief of never hurting friends.

On June 23, 2005, Joe Massino, then 62 years old, stood in court before Judge Garaufis and, with his hands folded in front of him, spoke astounding words.

"As the boss of the Bonanno Family, I gave the order," Massino said in a hoarse half-whisper.

"And the order was to do what?" Judge Garaufis asked.

"Kill George from Canada," Massino answered. The boss had realized that Sciascia, and perhaps the Sixth Family, was a threat. Massino said in court that he ordered Sciascia's slaying in order to maintain or increase his position within the Bonanno Family.

"It was done by Sal Vitale, Johnny Joe, Michael Nose and Patty DeFilippo," he added, immediately becoming the first boss of a New York Mafia family to testify against some of his most loyal underlings, men who had killed their friend at his request.

His admission, guilty plea and cooperation led the government to rescind its controversial request for the death penalty and, instead, Massino was handed a life sentence. Donna, Gerlando Sciascia's daughter, was present in the courtroom to see justice done and had written a letter to the judge about her family's loss, but asked that it not be read aloud in court. She left without speaking to reporters. In court, Massino stood silently while a letter from Laura Trinchera, daughter of Big Trinny, was read. "Joseph Massino took away a 'Big' part of our lives, my father, who was absolutely the best father anyone could have asked for," she wrote. "I will never forget that day when we were all informed that my father will not be coming back."

Massino's defection to the government must have jolted Vito Rizzuto, who knew that if he was to face Judge Garaufis's court, Massino was in a position to point a convincing finger right at him. Massino had proved the reliability of his evidence already, by leading agents to the remaining Ruby Street bodies. His cooperation certainly raised interest in the photograph used by U.S. authorities to help in their extradition case, the 1981 picture of Vito, Massino, Sciascia and Giovanni Ligammari leaving a New York motel the day after the murders of the three captains.

Ligammari died in a most unconventional manner; police found both him and his son, also a Bonanno member, hanging together in their home. Their deaths were ruled as suicides, but suspicion and accusations of underworld involvement linger.

With Sciascia and Ligammari both dead, only two men truly knew what they were doing at the motel that day. Now one of them is talking.

Vito suddenly faced the prospect of going on trial in New York with Massino being called as the government's star witness against him in a dramatic courtroom spectacle—the longtime boss of the Bonanno Family pointing his finger at the organization's most successful asset.

CHAPTER 40

BROOKLYN, MAY 2004

The familiar shape of the soaring neo-Gothic granite towers and the swooping cables of the Brooklyn Bridge, spanning New York's turbulent East River, poke above the mature trees that line Cadman Plaza, an urban park forming a wide promenade outside the United States Courthouse in Brooklyn. The building features a central glass rotunda with rising towers of courtrooms and offices to each side. Inside, visitors, lawyers and court staff alike are greeted by federal marshals for a thorough security search before being allowed to enter.

On the sixth floor, through tall wooden doors, was Courtroom 11.

Against a backdrop of floor-to-ceiling green marble sat U.S. District Judge Nicholas Garaufis. Before him stretched two long wooden tables, one used by the defendants and their lawyers and the other by the prosecutors. To one side sat the jury, in large wooden chairs generously upholstered in brown. Beyond that is the public gallery, where spectators crammed into achingly austere wooden benches in five long rows. This room was as much the personal fiefdom of Judge Garaufis as New York's Maspeth district ever was for Joseph Massino, or Montreal's Saint-Léonard for Vito Rizzuto.

It was in this courtroom that a five-by-seven-inch color photograph, a clear, bright and sharply focused image of the face of a man with neatly coifed dark hair and a tight, crooked smile, was displayed for a jury and shown to a heavy-set witness who had been called to the stand in the prosecution of Massino, the Bonanno boss.

"I am going to show you some photographs and I am going to ask you if you recognize the individual," Greg Andres, the federal prosecutor, said to Frank Lino, who was under oath and on the stand testifying for the government against Massino. It was May 24, 2004, the first day of testimony by Lino, who was the first Bonanno turncoat to be willingly called to the stand.

"Tell us who it is and what position, if any, they have in the Bonanno

Family," Andres continued. After flipping through a number of photographs—of Philip Rastelli, Joe Massino, Cesare Bonventre, Sal Catalano, Sal Vitale and Gerlando Sciascia, among others—Andres came to the photo of a man in a black suit flashing a smile.

"Government Exhibit 2-VV, who is that?" Andres asked.

"That looks like Vito Rizzuto from Montreal," Lino said.

"Did he hold a position in the Bonanno Family?" Andres asked.

"I met him, he was a soldier," Lino answered. The next day, Lino, again on the stand, told the court of his visit to Canada to meet with the family's crew in Montreal, meeting and socializing with Vito.

Similarly, on June 29, 2004, on the second day of the highly anticipated testimony by Sal Vitale, the underboss turned informant, the interest of the New York court was again drawn northward.

"Sir," Andres began, addressing Vitale, "does the Bonanno Family operate outside of the United States?"

"Yes," answered Vitale.

"Where else does it operate?" Andres asked.

"We have a group in Montreal, Canada," Vitale said.

"Do you know if there is a member of the Bonanno Family that controls Canada or that area?"

"Today?" Vitale clarified.

"Yes," Andres said.

"Vito Rizzuto," Vitale answered.

"Do you know what position he holds?"

"Acting *capo-regime*," Vitale said, using the Italian designation for an acting captain, a reference to the fact that Vitale recognized Vito as being in charge of Montreal but not having accepted the invitation from Massino to officially be named a captain.

"When was the last time you saw Mr. Rizzuto?" Andres asked.

"Approximately three years [ago]," Vitale said. Andres then asked if he had gone to Canada for the meeting with Vito.

"Mr. Massino sent me there," Vitale answered.

One of the government's exhibits shown to the jury was a large poster board of row after row of photographs of men's faces. Many were mug shots, some were police surveillance photos while others were from the 1980 wedding of Giuseppe Bono. The board, labeled "Soldiers," was a follow-up to a similar board featuring other photographs, this one labeled "Bonanno/Massino Organized Crime Family (1975–2004)—Administration/Acting Administration." On the board showing Bonanno soldiers was a photograph of Vito, a close-up from one of the Bono wedding photos. Underneath the picture is the label "Vito Rizzuto" and the suggestion that his nickname for some was "Vito from Canada." Vito's face was placed between a mug shot of the thuggish Thomas "Tommy Karate" Pitera with his nose swollen and cut, suggesting he was not arrested peacefully, and a surveillance shot of Benjamin "Lefty" Ruggiero, the gangster who achieved celluloid immortality when he was depicted by Al Pacino in *Donnie Brasco*. Also sharing that row of photos was Tony Mirra, who was murdered for his real-life introduction of Donnie Brasco into the mob family.

This is the type of evidence that would begin any prosecution against Vito in New York. The same prosecutors would lead the same cooperating witnesses, with the probable addition of Joe Massino, through their purported experiences with "Vito from Canada." It must have been a chilling prospect for a secretive man such as Vito. His mob business had never before received such public judicial scrutiny.

OTTAWA, 2005

Vito had no intention of ever facing that gang of turncoats.

"I maintain my innocence of all charges," he declared. He decided, however, to claim his innocence in Canada rather than in Garaufis's courtroom for as long as he could.

Vito's battle against being extradited to the United States was well funded, multipronged and well organized. At a court hearing in Quebec to argue against his extradition, he had no fewer than five lawyers working on his case, not including his youngest son, Leonardo, and daughter, Bettina, who are both lawyers and took a keen interest in the case. He also retained an experienced New York criminal lawyer, John Mitchell, who was Sal Vitale's lawyer on two racketeering indictments and was representing the Bonanno underboss until Vitale decided to cooperate with the government. Mitchell provided legal advice and legal briefs on American law and procedures on Vito's behalf.

Retaining so much legal muscle is not an inexpensive proposition. After Vito's arrest in Montreal, the need for a substantial war chest to pay the mounting fees in this legal battle was quickly realized. As it had done to weather the Tax Court case against Vito, members of the Rizzuto family started setting money aside. On February 10, 2004, Vito's wife, Giovanna, started an account at the office of their lawyer, Jean Salois, with a $50,000 deposit. Vito's son Leonardo would kick in $40,000 and

Vito's daughter, Bettina, $25,000. Vito's mother and father, Nick and Libertina, would add $50,000, according to an accounting of the fund by Salois. The lawyers started putting their case together.

"The Canadian extradition proceedings allege offences for which I am not wanted in the U.S. and for which I have not been indicted," Vito declared in a sworn affidavit, filed in the Federal Court of Canada in Ottawa, as part of an appeal against being shipped to the United States. "I am not accused of murder in the United States," he said of the RICO Act indictment against him, which names acts of murder as part of the racketeering conspiracy and not as separate criminal charges. He did not like the way Canadian prosecutors seemed to suggest he faced a murder charge. He felt it was a purposeful conspiracy to spirit him out from under the protection of the Canadian Charter of Rights and into the hands of hungry American law-enforcement officials.

"The confusion between the offences is intentional," Vito has declared in an affidavit. His arguments were not well received in Canadian courts.

If Vito was feeling abandoned by his government, at least one person in a position of power has been looking out for him. Noël A. Kinsella, a Conservative senator from New Brunswick, who was the leader of the Opposition in the Senate of Canada, rose in the Senate chambers to ask about the decision by Justice Minister Irwin Cotler to order the extradition of Vito, a man he described as "a presumed Mafia operative in Montreal." His question for the government: "The honorable leader in this place knows that Canadian laws are in place respecting the extradition of persons to jurisdictions where the death penalty could be sought for murder. Would the minister advise this house whether the Minister of Justice has been given any assurances that the death penalty will not be sought?"

Jack Austin, the Senate leader, said that he understood that such assurance had been "sought and obtained."

Vito's pending drinking-and-driving charge, meanwhile, which was also before the courts, was put on hold until his more substantial problem could be settled.

MONTREAL, AUGUST 6, 2004

In one of the interconnecting labyrinthine hallways of Montreal's Palais de Justice, the city's busy courthouse, a graying, bespectacled attorney walked slowly toward one of the many courtrooms. His wide smile and ruffled hair were instantly recognizable to passing lawyers and report-ers, although many had to quiz others nearby to actually put a name to the face. The appearance of Alan M. Dershowitz, the famed Boston lawyer and Harvard law professor, known for representing such celeb-rity clients as O.J. Simpson and Mike Tyson, was causing something of a celebrity moment himself, brightening up the dry legal proceedings at Vito's bail hearing before the Quebec Superior Court.

Dershowitz had been engaged to come to Montreal to provide tes-timony on behalf of Vito on points of American law. His testimony was to bolster the contention, argued by Vito's lawyers, that the chances of successful prosecution in New York was slight and so it would be in the best interests of justice to release Vito on bail while he awaited decisions over his various appeals, made to both the Quebec Court of Appeal and the Federal Court of Canada.

It was a surprising appearance and Dershowitz was mobbed by reporters anxious for a sound bite. They seemed disappointed when he stuck so closely to his script of arcane legal facts.

"The charges in this case are very specific and very narrow and they end in 1981, so, under a traditional statute of limitation analysis, he would have had to be prosecuted by 1986," Dershowitz told reporters. His appearance, however, suggested the lengths to which Vito would go to defend himself. But even Dershowitz could not prevail. Nor could five citizens of Montreal who offered their homes and businesses as sureties against Vito fleeing if released on bail: the owner of a supermarket in the plaza beside the Club Social Consenza; a woman from Cattolica Eraclea and her husband, close neighbors of the Rizzutos, who run a Laval submarine-sandwich shop and own several buildings in Montreal; another former resident of Cattolica Eraclea who has known Vito since childhood and offered his catering business as a surety; and yet another former resident of Vito's hometown who offered his small chain of bakeries. The bail request and appeal were led by Pierre Morneau, the same lawyer in-volved in the Newfoundland case when his dinner table was bugged by the RCMP.

Vito's bail request was turned down and, in November 2005, a panel of three judges with the Quebec Court of Appeal unanimous-ly rejected his appeal of the extradition order. Since he had already withdrawn an appeal to the Federal Court of Canada, his options were narrowing.

On December 22, 2005, Vito appealed to the Supreme Court of Canada, the highest court in the country, to overturn the government's decision to send him to face trial in the United States.

BROOKLYN, 2005

In New York, meanwhile, Vito's co-accused were not facing such delays and had started to trickle through the justice system. Few were faring well. The government had moved immediately for permanent orders of detention against 16 of the accused, including Vito—who had already been called dangerous and a flight risk in court documents, though he was not yet before a U.S. court. It was a hurdle for many just to make bail. Some never did.

Bail climbed to $6 million for Patrick "Patty Muscles" Romanello, described as a long-standing associate of the Bonanno Family who was facing life imprisonment. Romanello was accused in the 1983 murder of Enrico Mazzeo, a former deputy commissioner of the New York City Marine and Aviation Department who was moonlighting as a Bonanno associate when shot, wrapped in a plastic bag and placed in the trunk of his rental car. Before closing the trunk, a Bonanno soldier stabbed Mazzeo eight to 10 times in the neck to make sure he was dead.

Romanello was also charged with the 1990 murder of Louis Tuzzio, a Bonanno associate who was killed on orders from Sal Vitale, after demands for his blood were made by John Gotti. Tuzzio drew the wrath of the Dapper Don when he was involved in a hit aimed at Gus Farace, a Bonanno associate. Farace was ordered killed because he had murdered Special Agent Everett Hatcher, an undercover DEA officer; the ensuing police outrage brought a wave of unwanted pressure on the mob. During the sloppy Farace hit, Tuzzio and two colleagues shot and injured the son of an influential Gambino Family soldier. Similarly, the slaying of Tuzzio was not a smooth piece of work. When detectives found him dead in the driver's seat of his car in Brooklyn, there were clear signs of a struggle: he had cuts across his face and head, and his right leg was resting on the car's dashboard, suggesting he was trying to kick out the front windshield when he died. In his hand was a clump of hair yanked from an attacker. Romanello would eventually plead guilty.

Romanello's bid for bail took an unusual twist after he offered up property listed in the names of his wife and mother-in-law as sureties that he would not flee. The government questioned how much influence his wife really had over Romanello. Prosecutors then revealed that Romanello had a second family that his wife did not know about.

"If this stands in the way of being granted bail, Mr. Romanello has authorized counsel to acknowledge the fact before his wife and children in open court," Romanello's lawyer replied. Observers pondered which would be a worse punishment for Romanello—incarceration at the crowded Metropolitan Detention Center or house arrest under the watchful eye of a wife who would just be learning of her husband's extensive extramarital activities.

Notwithstanding Romanello's obvious virility, looking at the medical dossiers of many of Vito's other co-defendants—and ignoring their criminal allegations—it hardly seemed a robust group assembled before the courts. The number of medical ailments they complained of, brought to the attention of the judge to boost their bids for bail or a loosening of their strict bail provisions, could have filled a medical textbook.

"He's in very poor physical health," James Frocaro, lawyer for accused 70-year-old gangster Louis Restivo, said in court. "I actually had to write down what he suffers from because there is so much. And they're all serious," he said, before listing them: diabetic neuropathy, heart disease, high blood pressure, kidney disease, eye disease, gangrene in his foot, a crippling lower back condition and open heart surgery three years before. Others cataloged their often arcane ailments and maladies for the court's consideration.

The Sixth Family's old friend, Baldassare "Baldo" Amato, had problems of a different sort. Amato was already in prison from a robbery conviction when he was rearrested on the racketeering indictment. For Amato, in particular, the prospects look grim.

"More than 10 cooperating witnesses will testify to Amato's association with, and position in, the Bonanno Family," prosecutors said in court filings. "Amato has been observed by surveillance agents for more than 20 years at organized-crime–related locations and events," the government continued. More perturbing for Amato, however, was his predicament over a racketeering-robbery charge against him that was included in the indictment. Amato was charged with ordering the violent armed robbery of patrons and employees of Café Vienna in Queens, in March 1997. Two of the men who went with baseball bats, sledgehammers and a gun to the underground gambling den to force those inside to turn over their money and jewelry were prepared to testify that they were sent by Amato as retaliation for the proprietors' audacity in competing with one of his gambling joints. This charge against Amato was easy pickings for the prosecutors, because on July 13, 2000, Amato pleaded guilty to organizing the heist in a deal described as a sweetheart of an offer at the time. In hindsight, it was disastrous for him. It is an oddity of the Racketeering-Influenced and Corrupt Organizations (RICO) Act that past criminal convictions can be used against a defendant a second time if the act is later shown to be part of a criminal enterprise. The government planned to enter Amato's guilty plea as evidence of his complicity in ongoing racketeering. Their job was already half done.

"To prove Amato's participation in a 'pattern of racketeering activity,' the government need only prevail on one of the remaining four racketeering acts, the evidence of each of which is strong," prosecutors said. Amato faced life imprisonment if convicted. As an Italian-born immigrant who never obtained U.S. citizenship, he also faced deportation to Italy at the conclusion of any sentence. Perhaps that pressure took its mental toll on the weary gangster. Or, alternatively, perhaps it gave him incentive to pursue creative defense strategies. Regardless, Amato had a rocky time in court. He went through several appearances unrepresented by legal counsel. He was eventually assigned a public defender but this did not seem to lessen his torment. His new lawyer, Michael Hueston, quickly began pushing for extensive testing—psychological, neurological and physical. After one early court appearance, Amato complained that he had become ill during transit from his cell to the courtroom and asked to be excused from future routine court appearances for medical reasons.

"It appears the defendant may or may not be able to stand trial," said Judge Garaufis, who then ordered that a prison neurologist examine Amato. There was clearly some concern over the legitimacy of his complaints, but the proposition of delaying the trial against others while Amato's tests were completed was unacceptable. Amato was quickly severed from his co-accused to face justice later if he was found fit to face trial. Amato was not letting his defense rest during his medical examinations, however. A private investigator working for him was at the U.S. Archives in New York poring through boxes of records from old drug trials, including the famed Pizza Connection. He was anxious to read, among other things, the testimony of Tommaso Buscetta, the Sicilian Mafia turncoat.

Federal prosecutors felt Amato's weak position could be exploited. They had asked him so many times to cooperate that he wrote to Judge Garaufis directly, begging him to tell the government lawyers to stop pestering him to turn on Vito and other co-accused. "I told my attorney the first time," Amato wrote after another try by the government, "that I was not interested in cooperating. I pray to your honor to not allow the [prosecutor] to discuss with my attorney about me co-operating." He won that battle, perhaps his last victory. Forced to face trial in the summer of 2006, a jury heard the long chronicle of his life in crime and even witnessed firsthand the fear Amato could instill. Francesco Fiordilino, a Bonanno associate from Castellammare del Golfo, who had known Amato for much of his life, had joined the tide of informants, even testifying at the trial of Joey Massino, the family boss. After taking the stand at Amato's trial, however, Fiordilino made a surprise announcement.

"Your Honor, I ain't testifying," he said.

"What's that?" Judge Garaufis said, clearly stunned.

"I ain't testifying."

The prosecutor, John Buretta, explained Fiordilino's predicament: "The witness is scared of Baldo Amato." Over the lunch break, Fiordilino was convinced to uphold his end of the deal, but the drama did nothing to convince the jury that Amato was a man wrongfully accused. He was duly found guilty after a six-week trial. In October, 2006, the 54-year-old mobster who was once a frequent visitor to Canada was given a life sentence and a tongue-lashing from Judge Garaufis: "Mr. Amato, you're just a plain, wanton murderer and a Mafia assassin. The sentence I'm going to give you, as far as I'm concerned, is a gift."

The professed frailty of some of the defendants was largely a red herring, prosecutors insisted. Those who prosecute the Mafia with the frequency of New York's government attorneys are well aware that mobsters typically develop serious medical conditions when facing trial, ailments that miraculously seem to clear up upon acquittal or imposition of a light sentence.

Robert Henoch, an assistant prosecutor working with Greg Andres, argued eloquently that advanced age or weakening physical prowess do not correspond to a reduction in the power or relative dangerousness of someone involved in the Mafia.

"Ronald Reagan was 78 years old when he was the president of the United States and I probably could have beat him in arm wrestling, but that doesn't mean that he wasn't the most powerful man in the world."

Amato's spirited defense against his charges was a rarity in New York in recent years. In May 2006, on the eve of jury selection for their racketeering case, five more accused gave up, including Michael "Mickey Bats" Cardello, who had walked the *New York Post* supervisor to his death at the hand of Amato. He accepted 10 years in prison with his guilty plea.

All of Vito's co-accused—those arrested in the same January 2004 sweep—eventually opted for guilty pleas or government deals, or received guilty verdicts at trial.

From the sprawling indictment, 03-CR-1382, that began with Vito Rizzuto and expanded to 27 people, only Vito's case remained un-settled. This may well have been exactly where his defense team wanted him to be.

CHAPTER 41

LAVAL, QUEBEC, MARCH 2005

The clean cubist décor of the 9,000-square-foot split-level Moomba Supperclub in Laval, just across the river from Montreal, is even more eye-catching than the fashionable clientele who pack the place each night. By the spring of 2005, the club was gaining a niche in the crowded entertainment scene with its trendy supper-club concept, offering decent dinner service followed by DJs, dancing and drinking until 3 a.m. With its enforced dress code and valet parking, the Moomba attracted a crowd that was a little more upscale than was found in many of Montreal's downtown bars and clubs.

It was a little past 2 a.m. on March 10, 2005, when the sound of gunfire cut through the beat of a Latin track that was blasting the Moomba's dance floor, sending patrons diving for cover and scattering from the crowded club. By the time the 250 guests had cleared out and police officers and ambulance attendants had arrived, two men had been found gravely injured. Lying inside the bar was Mike LaPolla, 36, an olive-skinned man with a long face and shaved head who had worked with the Sixth Family as an enforcer for several years and had a recent drug conviction. Outside the Moomba, police found Thierry Beaubrun, 28, a black man with short dark hair and a small goatee. Beaubrun was heavily involved with the Crack Down Posse, an aggressive Montreal street gang, and the 67s, another of the city's street gangs, according to a police report. Both LaPolla and Beaubrun were shot after an apparent fistfight escalated into a shootout; hours later, both men died in hospital.

Sixth Family leaders quickly gathered to discuss what had happened and how it might impact business. Lorenzo Giordano, described by police as an aggressive street boss within the Sixth Family organization, had been in the Moomba when the shooting broke out and was closely questioned by his seniors. Rocco Sollecito, originally from Grumo Appula in Southern Italy who is close to the Rizzutos, said he had been told the killing of LaPolla was "an isolated incident," but Rocco's son, Giuseppe Sollecito, warned that the dead rival, Beaubrun, was a "captain of the blacks" and there would be blood on the streets because of it.

"The blacks are not people you can sit down and reason with," Giuseppe Sollecito allegedly said. "They are not like [us]. They are animals." It was not only the friends of LaPolla who worried about where the slayings might lead. Police were nervous the gunfight signaled emerging underworld tension between the Mafia and the largely black street gangs, perhaps a brewing war that would go far beyond two hotheads who refused to back down.

Prison officials were similarly concerned and decided not to take any chances with one of their highest-profile prisoners. Immediately after the Moomba slayings, Vito was moved into protective custody, meaning solitary confinement, at Ste-Anne-des-Plaines prison, a federal facility north of Montreal. Prison staff worried that members of the street gangs, who have a significant presence in the prison system, might try to avenge Beaubrun's death by attacking Vito. Prison was one of the few places in Quebec where the Sixth Family was outnumbered by rivals.

Incarceration in Canada for Vito, as he fought extradition to the United States, had offered ups and downs. He was held for a period in the Rivières-des-Prairies provincial detention center not far from his home. There he lived in a grim cell with a simple cot, porcelain sink and a tiny desk built into the wall. Vito could touch the green walls on either side if he stretched his arms out when standing on the worn black floor of his cell. When his release on bail was denied, he was granted his request for a transfer to Ste-Anne-des-Plaines prison, where he had a little more room to roam until his placement in protective custody, a move he did not like but one that was relatively brief, a longtime friend of Vito's said.

While in both facilities, Vito was kept well informed on affairs outside the prison walls. He had family visits from his father, children and grandchildren and telephone calls with close associates. In prison, he also enjoyed the benefits of having two children who were lawyers. Since both Leonardo and Bettina were helping with their father's case, they had lengthy and frequent access to him.

There has been plenty of news for them to bring Vito since his arrest.

MONTREAL, MAY 2005

Two months after the Moomba shootout, another sign of underworld unrest surfaced in the form of four burly men who rushed into a Saint-Léonard barbershop. Inside, they tussled with Frank Martorana—enough to bloody him up—and then forced him into a waiting sport utility vehicle. Martorana, a luxury car dealer in Montreal, has had long ties with the Sixth Family. The bold kidnapping in broad daylight sparked concerns for Martorana's safety and a frantic search. Police found his late-model Mercedes-Benz S55 AMG, valued at about $130,000, parked nearby. Six days later, however, Martorana returned home, apparently safe and unharmed. He made a courtesy call to the Montreal police to tell them to call off their search but did not explain his absence, press any charges or file any official complaint.

It was the start of an odd pattern. Several other men, most with links to the underworld, were kidnapped for a short period of time—ranging from hours to weeks—before being released. One man, Nicola Varacalli, the father of a Montreal night club owner, Mario Varacalli, was grabbed from his Montreal home on Halloween night in 2005 by four men who knocked on his door wearing costumes to hide their faces. His kidnappers allowed him to make several telephone calls to associates, imploring them that they "must stop the junk on the street." On December 8, Varacalli, who has cocaine convictions, contacted police through a lawyer; like Martorana, he was no longer being held against his will but was uninterested in pursuing the matter with the authorities.

As disturbing as Varacalli's kidnapping might have been to those who knew him, it was only a symptom of a greater problem facing the Sixth Family, part of a growing dispute with the D'Amico clan from Granby, about an hour's drive east of Montreal. The D'Amico organization, which felt wronged by Arcadi, presented a rare display of open defiance towards the Sixth Family's hegemony. On December 1, 2005, Luca D'Amico arrived at the Club Social Consenza to deliver a letter addressed to "Uncle Cola," an anglicized version of a common nickname for Nick. The letter presented to the Rizzuto patriarch the D'Amicos' side of the dispute. It sought a negotiated settlement that only Nick could arrange, the letter said. The D'Amicos did not appear to have faith in Arcadi handling this matter. Nick needed a little more prodding to get involved and the D'Amicos soon offered a bold show of strength.

On December 23, Luca D'Amico and two colleagues walked into the Consenza, paused for a moment and then left, with D'Amico signaling with his right hand as he walked out. A cavalcade of vehicles then pulled up to collect the trio and the procession of eight SUVs and Mercedes cars accompanied the visitors away from the Sixth Family headquarters. What could have happened, had the intent been directly hostile rather than a display of strength and determination, was not lost on the Sixth Family bosses. Arcadi quickly phoned his colleagues, warning them to be careful, saying: "The insane guy is in the neighborhood." Arcadi was clearly spooked by the D'Amicos' obstinacy and was seen carrying a pistol on his right hip.

Other actions on the street while Vito was indisposed had grimmer results—Montreal police were dealing with a string of unsolved slayings with underworld links.

"Now that Vito's not running the show, all of the guys who are owed money or who had scores to settle but were held in check are free to act," said André Bouchard, the former commander of Montreal police's Major Crimes Unit. "If Vito told them they were not going to get paid, they weren't going to get paid and they had to accept that. But now he isn't here and they are saying, 'Fuck him, I want my money.' There is a lot of unrest right now. When Vito Rizzuto was on the streets, everyone paid attention to him. Now that Vito isn't on the street, nobody is afraid any more. There have been three or four hits recently. I don't think in normal times that these guys would have been taken out. This would never have happened when Vito was around."

Indeed, several experienced underworld figures in Montreal said that, before his arrest, Vito Rizzuto often played the role of mediator to others in the underworld, whether they were involved with the bikers, the Mafia, the Irish gangs or were independent operators. Everyone seemed to feel they were under some obligation to listen to Vito.

"They help to resolve disputes. They keep the peace," an underworld source said of the Sixth Family's leadership. "You need that. Mind you, someone gets fucked out of money each time but you can't go to court so there isn't much option. The option is to shoot it out and be ostracized by everyone else. No one ever wants to go to a meeting [with Vito] because you know you're going to get fucked out of your money."

The meetings were often quick and casual, a far cry from how such sit-downs are portrayed in popular culture, an underworld source said. Those involved often do not even sit down.

"People can't be seen meeting together—especially someone like Vito. Some people don't want to be seen meeting with Vito and Vito doesn't want to be seen meeting with a lot of people. It draws heat for both of them," the source said. "When they talk about having a meeting or a sit-down, it isn't like in the movies—a big powwow at a table in a darkened basement or in a private room at a restaurant. Mostly, they would arrange a meeting in the Pharma Plus [a large drug-store chain] or some other public place; it's arranged so that the guy Vito's meeting with just happens to be walking down the same aisle at the same time as Vito is. He gets a one-minute talking-to and then Vito moves on down the aisle." To anyone watching, it appears to be a chance meeting of little consequence and, for police, there was little chance of hearing the chat.

Vito had the authority to listen to both sides of a dispute and pass judgment; he could tell someone he had to pay a fine or some-one else that he was to wipe a debt off his books without payment, the underworld source said. Since most criminals took heed of Vito's pronouncements, it was an effective way to settle disputes without bloodshed.

"It's a culture of bullshit and as long as you believe in it, it works," a gangster said. With Vito removed from the streets there were fewer and fewer believers.

ROME, FEBRUARY 2005

In Italy—particularly in the south—government contracts offer a steady source of income for the Mafia. During large construction projects, Sicily's Mafia is an invisible but ubiquitous partner. The plundering be-gins even before a project's conception, through the accumulation of land. It quickly ramps up into the labor and construction fields, security for work sites, provision of organized labor and heavy machinery, pay-ments to acquire permits and, finally, a piece of the management of the completed project and perhaps a share of the profits from it. Politicians and mafiosi have long divided this revenue between them.

In Calabria and in Sicily, organized crime groups are so pervasive in building and development activities that many companies in the north—where Italy's financial sectors lie—try to avoid doing business there. Firms that do undertake projects budget vast sums for extortion payments and bribes. Traditionally, those that failed to accommodate the Sicilian Mafia or the 'Ndrangheta in Calabria have been beset

by endless "bad luck" with their projects: executives have been kidnapped, trucks and machinery damaged, destroyed or stolen, permits
and licenses delayed and labor problems not resolved.

Between the two mob strongholds of Sicily and Calabria is the Strait
of Messina, a stretch of water two and a quarter miles wide. Vehicles
and trains cross it by ferry and, during holidays, lineups can last more
than 10 hours as vehicles wait for a spot on the vessels. A bridge-link
from Sicily to the mainland has been dreamed about and argued over
for more than a century but it was only in the past 25 years that serious study was undertaken. Supporters believe it will open the door to
development on the relatively poor island of Sicily. Opponents point to
the region's history of active volcanoes, the anticipated environmen-
tal damage and dangerously high winds as reason to scratch the plan.
Then there is the cost, estimated at about $6 billion. Setting aside the
ancient legend of a sea monster living in the strait, all sides of the
bridge debate were keenly aware of another beast waiting to feast on
the huge public contract to build such an immense structure: the Mafia.

With the Sicilian Mafia based at one end of the proposed bridge
and the 'Ndrangheta at the other, it was impossible to expect organized
crime not to try to claim a significant portion of what promised to be
the largest public-works project in Southern Italy's history. As such,
when the government announced in 2002 that it would proceed with
the ambitious eight-lane suspension bridge, a special task force was
established to root out any Mafia involvement.

On February 11, 2005, news that surprised no one finally broke:
government investigators said they had uncovered a plot by organized crime to control the consortium selected to build and maintain
the bridge. At a press conference in Rome, senior officers with the
Direzione Investigativa Antimafia, the federal force targeting organized
crime, announced the arrest of a wealthy construction engineer and
the issuing of arrest warrants against four other men accused of trying
to infiltrate the bidding process.

The DIA then managed to elicit surprise: at the head of the criminal consortium, officials announced, was Vito Rizzuto.

Arrested at his home in Rome hours before the announcement
was Giuseppe "Joseph" Zappia, born in 1925 in Marseilles, to parents
originally from Calabria. Zappia had earlier moved to Canada and is
best remembered as the controversial contractor responsible for building the Olympic Village in Montreal for the 1976 Summer Olympic

Games. The job was mired in scandal: in 1988, he was cleared of fraud charges related to the work only after two key witnesses died. Zappia then shuttled between Canada and the Middle East—where he was involved in several large development projects—before settling in Rome in 1997. In 2001, he bragged that he had formed a friendship with Silvio Berlusconi, then the Italian prime minister. At the press conference announcing Zappia's arrest and the arrest warrants against Vito and three business associates, a police spokesman said Zappia had established a construction company called Zappia International that was used as a front for Vito's bid to build the bridge.

"Vito Rizzuto tried to participate in the tender for the construction of the Messina Bridge between Sicily and Calabria. Of course, Rizzuto himself cannot come here to Italy and say 'OK, I'd like to build the Messina Bridge'," said Silvia Franzè, a chief superintendent with the DIA. "In Italy, everybody knows of the Rizzuto Family. And so according to our legislation, a Mafia family cannot participate in a public tender to get a public works contract. Even if he doesn't have a charge in Italy, everybody in Italy knows that he is connected with Caruana–Cuntrera and so on and so on. We know in Italy who Vito Rizzuto is."

To help Vito in his bid to profit from the bridge project, he turned to his old friend Zappia, police say.

"Zappia was the president of a company that asked to participate in the tender and he had a lot of meetings with people to have this public work, it is a huge public work. He was the clear face of the Rizzuto Family," said Franzè. A confidential Canadian police report on the investigation says that Vito and Zappia have known each other since the 1970s and that Zappia was well aware of police interest in Vito. That was why he tried to limit direct contact between them, preferring instead to deal with intermediaries.

"Vito Rizzuto and Zappia spoke together directly only twice," said Franzè. One of those chats came on November 1, 2002.

"Everything is going smoothly. All the plans have been accepted," Zappia said, according to a transcript of the conversation.

"So we have a good chance, no?" Vito responded.

"Not only a good chance, but a guarantee as well."

"Good, good," Vito said.

Most of the dealings documented by police, however, came through three intermediaries who looked out for Vito's interests, Italian court documents say.

Filippo Ranieri, born in Montreal in 1937, was a business consultant and described by police in Italy as "a broker." Canadian police describe him as a longtime associate of Vito's. Italian police say Ranieri was the main liaison between Vito and Zappia. Hakim Hammoudi, born in Algeria in 1963 and dividing his time between Paris and Montreal, was another business consultant whose name appears on a confidential Canadian police chart listing Vito's associates. Both Ranieri and Hammoudi dealt with Zappia by phone, fax and in person. A police report alleges that both men met with Zappia in Rome several times during the course of the bridge bidding process. Also involved, the authorities announced, was Sivalingam Sivabavanandan, born in 1953, a Sri Lankan businessman living in London, England, who goes by the nickname "Bavan." Both Sivabavanandan and Hammoudi were accused of helping Vito invest his vast wealth.

"They were two businessmen, the guys who kept the contacts with the bank to find others who wanted to put money to invest. They were following all of the economic interests of Vito Rizzuto. They were brokers working for Vito Rizzuto. The Messina Bridge was only one of the investments that Vito Rizzuto was involved in," said Franzè. Hammoudi and Zappia were working on ventures in Algeria, Saudi Arabia and the United Arab Emirates that promised to provide Vito a substantial profit that was, in turn, to be reinvested in a large oil venture based in London, England, according to authorities. The Italian government is working to trace some of that money and investigators asked the Swiss to again look into the family's banking records.

Prosecutor Adriano Iasillo in Rome charged that the group had more than $6 billion ready to invest in the project.

The probe began in October 2002 and investigators said the illicit consortium submitted a preliminary tender, regarding technical qualifications, two years later. It had already invested more than $4.3 million in the proposal, authorities estimated. At the time of the arrest announcement, police executed search warrants in several European cities and gathered a mountain of documents. The centerpiece of the government's evidence is hundreds of wiretap conversations, some made in Canada and some in Italy, including one in which a conspirator says that, if all goes well, they will be able to build the bridge on behalf of a friend—whom investigators say is Vito—and then handle the accounting necessary to satisfy both "the Mafia and 'Ndrangheta."

Arrest warrants were issued in Italy against Vito, Ranieri, Hammoudi and Sivabavanandan. Soon after, Sivabavanandan was arrested in France and extradited to Italy. He was sentenced to two years in jail after pleading guilty to Mafia association. He then caught a lucky break; about halfway through his sentence the Italian government, struggling with overcrowded prisons, decreed that all prisoners serving less than three years be released. On gaining his freedom, he returned to England. Italy requested Ranieri's extradition from Canada, a request the Canadian government has declined to act on thus far, likely because he is charged only with Mafia association, which is not a crime in Canada, Italian authorities said. Hammoudi is likewise unavailable for prosecution. Neither the Italian nor the Canadian government knows precisely where he is, Franzè said.

Meanwhile, a lawyer for Zappia said his client is innocent of the charge. He suggested that Zappia is a victim of mistaken identity, saying there is someone else with the same last name who is involved with the Rizzutos, likely a reference to Beniamino Zappia, the man who Swiss authorities say set up several of the Rizzutos' Lugano bank accounts.

"He says he doesn't know Vito Rizzuto at all and is not involved in the case. We have some conversations on tape. During the trial these conversations will be produced and the judge will decide about it. We are waiting for that," said Franzè.

Any extradition of Vito to Italy would have to come second to the claim against him by U.S. authorities. In Italy, if convicted of being the head of a Mafia association, he could face seven years in prison.

The sheer scale of the Sixth Family's investment and leadership role in one of the largest public-works projects in Europe suggests the immense wealth and power resting in the hands of Vito and his organization; he had, authorities contend, found his way to the head of the mob's most sought-after plum in the homeland of both the Sicilian Mafia and the Calabrian 'Ndrangheta—and controlled a $6-billion investment, among others.

"Vito Rizzuto has a lot of money," said Franzè.

For anyone questioning the power of the Sixth Family, the allegations from the Strait of Messina Bridge, if true, are an eye-opener. The arrest warrants for Vito and the others were no doubt disturbing to the Sixth Family, but had they known how Italian authorities first caught wind of the suspicions they would have been petrified. They would not find that out, however, for another 21 months.

———

"Problems are slowing them down," a leading police Mafia investigator said of the Sixth Family's status in 2006. "They know there have been several major investigations going on, from 1996, really, until now. A lot of intelligence has come out and they know it. Everything has come to a standstill. The understanding is that, because of him being in jail and until the extradition thing goes through, nothing is really going to happen."

In the meantime, Vito Rizzuto waited behind bars.

The empire he worked so hard to establish was fraying around the edges. His organization, at the highest levels, was the target of intense police attention and the victim of increasing underworld unrest. Vito was disappointed by his failure to win a release on bail that would have allowed him to reestablish some sense of order in an underworld left confused and unruly. His jailing prevented him from enjoying his status as one of the world's superbosses. But, despite these setbacks on the street, he seemed to rather desperately prefer the inside of a Canadian prison over an American courtroom.

For in New York, the rats were waiting.

NEW YORK, AUGUST 17, 2006

Vito's winning streak in the courts had already taken a bruising by the time the Supreme Court of Canada came to decide whether or not it would hear the mobster's appeal of his extradition order. In the two and a half years since his arrest, despite his legal firepower, he had lost his motions and appeals in the Quebec Superior Court and the Quebec Court of Appeal, withdrawn his appeal to the Federal Court of Canada, and had the Supreme Court of Canada decline to hear his appeal over being denied bail. By the summer of 2006, it must have been difficult for Vito to retain much optimism that the Supreme Court would agree to intervene at the eleventh hour to prevent his extradition and, as expected, the justices in Canada's highest court were just as cool to Vito's legal arguments as their lower court colleagues.

Almost immediately after the court declared that it would not hear his appeal, Rizzuto was whisked from jail and escorted by Montreal police officers to Pierre Elliott Trudeau International Airport, where an aircraft supplied by the U.S. government was waiting for him.

Three hours later, he finally appeared in an American court. Facing Judge Nicholas Garaufis, Vito pleaded not guilty to his racketeering charge for the murder of the three captains and was ordered to be held in custody. For the Sixth Family, this was the most serious crisis it had faced since Vito's father Nick was imprisoned in Venezuela.

There was more anguish to come.

CHAPTER 42

LAVAL, QUEBEC, SEPTEMBER 14, 2006

Intruders found a stash of money crammed inside a sports bag and hidden under the basement stairs of a Laval home. Wads of hundred-dollar bills—more than 28,000 of them—and one lonely fifty-dollar bill were bundled and banded. The trespassers took their time removing the haul of almost $3-million. They knew that they would find serious cash here, in a comfortable home connected to a Sixth Family drug trafficker. They also knew that they had the house to themselves, since the residents were on holiday in Las Vegas, unaware that they were losing far more at home than they could ever hope to win at the casinos.

When the man who had hidden the money flew home the following day and discovered his loss, he was petrified. Some of the money was his—that was bad enough—but a large chunk belonged to Giuseppe "Pep" Torre, one of the Rizzutos' closest associates and accused prolific drug trafficker. The victim gathered his wits and called Torre on the telephone with this alarming news.

"Pep, I'm finished," he said.

"Don't tell me this," Torre warned.

"I feel like crying, man," he replied. He suspected the cash had been stolen by his brother-in-law, one of the few people who knew where it was.

"I'm going to fucking choke the guy," he told Torre. "I'm gonna kill him," he said, before storming out of the house with a gun.

It was one more in a series of unexpected upsets for the Sixth Family. A bookmaker who ran a $1-billion gambling operation in Ottawa and Montreal left his car parked on the street for a moment while he visited a betting shop. When he returned, a suitcase stuffed with $43,000 in cash had been pilfered from the trunk. Another of their drug dealers found that $280,000 had been looted from a metal safe in his home.

The rash of thefts did not go unnoticed by Sixth Family bosses. Even with Vito Rizzuto, their chief, in jail while fighting his New York charges, the organization was not short of leadership. Meetings were held to ponder who could be behind these thefts and how to safeguard their cash. Mobsters moved bags of money to safer locations. Suddenly, fewer and fewer people were trusted.

For police, this confusion was all good. The frenzied chatter about missing money must have brought mischievous smiles to some in Montreal because the anger and accusations brought carelessness to men who were unaccustomed to being victims; they spewed a wealth of information about the inner workings of their organization as they tried to pinpoint who had turned bad.

"We're getting busted every day," Lorenzo Giordano, a leading Sixth Family henchman, complained to his colleagues. "I'm calling everybody every morning to see if everybody's okay." In hindsight, such calls were not a good idea. Unbeknownst to the drug traffickers, money launderers, gangsters and bookies, a select team of police investigators had an unusual vantage point from which to watch and listen to this underworld chaos. For police, the best part of this situation was that they already knew exactly who had taken the money from the basement in Laval, from the trunk of the bookmaker's car and from the metal safe—police officers had.

Taking the money was a tactic designed to spark exactly the sorts of phone calls, meetings, whispers and suspicions that were taking place. It was all part of a daring police plan that had been years in the making.

If the Sixth Family bosses thought Vito Rizzuto's trouble in the U.S. was their biggest worry in 2006, they were wrong. What the gangsters did not know was that representatives of several law-enforcement agencies had gathered together four years before to meticulously start pulling threads from the broad tapestry of criminal conspiracies that were the domain of the Sixth Family.

The police efforts would eventually be codenamed Project Colisée and mushroom into the largest coordinated attack on any Canadian Mafia group in history. In the 1990s, a tightly focused operation, Project Omertà, had taken out the leadership of the Sixth Family's close allies, the Caruana–Cuntrera clan, sending to prison several of its world-class drug traffickers, including the family head, Alfonso

Caruana. Police hoped Project Colisée could do the same—and more—to the Sixth Family. For decades, the organization had proven virtually untouchable. They had shed a member here or there to police enforcement—Domenico Manno, Emanuele Ragusa, Girolamo Sciortino and Gaetano Amodeo among them—and even fewer to gangland intrigue, most notably Gerlando Sciascia, Joe LoPresti and Vito's grandfather generations before. In each case, however, the core of the organization remained strong. Could that dismal enforcement record ever be undone? The task was daunting. At least 10 previous RCMP-led projects in several provinces, all aimed at putting Vito and his senior mob colleagues behind bars, had ended in failure. This time, however, police had a particularly intriguing base to build a case on, although, ominously, it came from another failure.

Project Calamus, the RCMP's operation set up in 2001 to probe a $500,000 loan between car dealers, had wrapped up without charges against Vito, his son Nick, or anyone else. Project Calamus's sister investigation in Ontario, however, codenamed Project R.I.P., was continuing to gather intelligence. Information about the attempts to recover the $500,000 enabled York Regional Police, located north of Toronto, to obtain court authorization to conduct secret electronic surveillance that came dangerously close to the Sixth Family.

"We ran our lines into Montreal," said an Ontario investigator, a reference to police wiretaps.

On September 23, 2002, based on evidence from the Project R.I.P. recordings, a Quebec judge gave police in Montreal some wiretaps of their own to monitor. The timing was perfect. After the 2001 arrests of the leading Hells Angels, police in Quebec could finally pull their attention and resources away from the deadly biker war. A secret police team was established, bringing together investigators from the RCMP, Montreal city police, the Sûreté du Québec, Laval police, Canada Customs, Canada Border Services Agency and the Canada Revenue Agency. Called the Combined Forces Special Enforcement Unit (CFSEU)—or, to its many francophone officers, the Unité mixte d'enquête sur le crime organizé (UMECO)—it was modeled on the successful CFSEU in Toronto that had been the bane of mobsters for decades. It was the Toronto CFSEU that put the Caruanas in prison. The Montreal CFSEU divided its meager resources between two investigations. One team, using the codename Project Calvette, targeted Raymond Desfossés, a West End Gang veteran running a burgeoning drug empire. The other took the codename Project Cicéron, the original codename for Project Colisée. Both the Cicéron and Colisée monikers— the first a nod to the great orator of ancient Rome and the other to the Colosseum, the iconic Roman amphitheatre—allude to their target: the primarily Italian gangsters of the Sixth Family.

Project Cicéron's wiretaps first targeted Vito and 12 of his close associates. Hope among the few officers who knew of it was high. The objective was ambitious: to seriously destabilize the Montreal Mafia by charging Vito and senior members of his organization with violating Canada's anti-gang laws. To do that, however, they needed to penetrate the inner sanctum of the Sixth Family. For generations, that had proved impossible.

The investigators knew exactly where they should start.

MONTREAL, JUNE 2003

There is little in the way of beauty in the back room of the Club Social Consenza. Cream-colored walls bordered by green; a single picture— of a running animal—hung on a wall in an oddly shaped wooden frame. The furniture is spartan: a long metal coat rack against one wall with a dozen unmatched hangers dangling from it; a small television propped in a corner; a round cherry wood table topped by a green ceramic ashtray and surrounded by steel tube-frame chairs. The table is lit by a conical lamp overhead, casting a theatrical spotlight over the men who sit hunched around it. Outsiders do not make it into this back room. Out front, the Consenza is technically open to the public. As a café in a commercial strip mall at 4891 Jarry Street East in Montreal's Saint-Léonard neighborhood, it offers espresso, cappuccino and café au lait. The large men near the entrance who glower at all strangers, however, make it an uncomfortable place for a leisurely drink. Since the 1980s, this had been the home base for older members of the Sixth Family.

When Nick Rizzuto arrived at the Consenza, as he did most days, he would nod a greeting to those already inside, hang his trench coat and fedora on the coatstand near the entrance and take a seat at a table with friends for a leisurely game of cards. He would then disappear into the back office when those close to him arrived, including Paolo Renda, Frank Arcadi, Rocco Sollecito and, until his arrest for the murders of the three captains, his son Vito. It was clear to police that these five men were the absolute top of the organization.

When someone arrived at the Consenza who wanted to talk to one of the bosses, the visitor would wait in the front section, perhaps ordering an espresso, while one of the men with slicked-back hair who spent their days watching over the club walked to the door of the back room, gently knocked and told the bosses who was here. The visitor would typically be escorted in and the door then closed behind him. The Project Cicéron investigators knew they needed to peer behind that door. From the beginning of their investigation, the Consenza was identified as the headquarters of the senior bosses and if investigators were to make any serious progress they needed to see and hear what happened when Vito, Nick and their colleagues gathered around that table.

By June 2003, investigators had gathered the evidence needed to secure a judge's approval to secretly intercept private conversations taking place at the Consenza. Next, they needed to actually get their gadgets inside without anyone knowing. That was not an easy task. When it came time to wire up the Consenza, investigators working on Project Cicéron left nothing to chance. As many as 50 officers were divided into carefully coordinated specialist units: locksmiths skilled at getting through any door; alarm wizards who could bypass security systems; technical experts who knew how to set up miniature lenses and transmitting microphones; and dozens of physical surveillance teams.

On the night of the planned penetration, police needed to know with certainty where everyone who had keys to the club was at all times. The last thing they needed was one of their suspects arriving at the Consenza to find police technicians fiddling with wires inside. Included in those having to be watched was a caretaker who often showed up at 4 a.m. to tidy the café before the start of the next business day. Each target was given a code name. Eschewing the drama of movies and television, the names were bland; every suspect in the growing files of Project Cicéron was assigned a number and a letter, starting at A-1. The list would stretch to A-205. From early in the evening, all key-holders were put under tight surveillance by officers who watched their assigned targets as they went about their business and eventually retired at night.

"A-12 has settled in," a surveillance officer would report over a secure radio.

"A-3 is now home," another would report. One by one, the surveillance teams checked in until none of the targets were still out prowling. As an added precaution, a perimeter of plain-clothed officers with a list of license plates and descriptions of Sixth Family vehicles sat in unmarked police cars watching everything that came within five blocks of the Consenza. These officers were authorized to take extreme measures to stop a suspect from reaching the club—including crashing into a target's car in a staged accident.

When everyone was accounted for, the commanding officer finally gave his technical teams permission to start their spycraft. To reduce the chances of being noticed, technicians planned to push their lenses and microphones through the ceiling from a neighboring office in the commercial strip rather than going through the front door of the club. While the techies worked for more than two hours, surveillance officers across the city kept their lonely vigils, constantly watching their targets to make sure no one started making unexpected moves towards Jarry Street.

The plan called for three miniature video cameras and several audio probes to monitor the Consenza. One camera was placed outside, aimed at the front doors. Another captured most of the goings-on inside the main portion of the café and the third, the most important, was pointed directly at the round table in the small back office. Some 30 times over the next two and a half years the cameras needed to be adjusted, when the focus was off, for instance, or when the round table was moved to the other side of the back office. Each time, the same elaborate procedure and precautions were required. Sometimes, when not all of the targets could be accounted for, the operation was scrubbed at the last minute and rescheduled for another night.

When the cameras and microphones were finally switched on, to be monitored around-the-clock by officers in a secret wire room, it was a significant coup for Project Cicéron. There was elation within police ranks. The Sixth Family had never before been so exposed. Police could finally see and hear what they had been missing.

———

"*Sette, otto, nove,*" Nick Rizzuto said, counting in Italian. "*Uno, due, tre, quattro,*" said another man with him in the back office of the Consenza, who joined in the counting of a bundle of cash, about an inch and a half thick. The counting went on laboriously. "*Ventisette, ventotto, ventinove.*"

"That's half," the man said.

"Twelve and twelve is twenty-four, no?" replied Nick. He then lifted up his pant leg and stuffed his share of the money into one of his socks. It was a Wednesday afternoon but it could well have been any day, for there always seemed to be counting going on in the back office of the Consenza and much dividing of thick piles of cash. People routinely arrived at the Consenza offering *cote d'argent*, tribute money. Despite the gifts, their reception was often gruff.

"How much is it?" Nick would say, getting right down to the nitty-gritty. Sometimes, the bearer was invited to sit with the bosses at the back room table.

On May 11, 2005, after lunch, Moreno Gallo arrived at the Consenza and slipped into the back room with Nick, Renda, Arcadi and Sollecito. In his cream-colored jacket, Gallo, a veteran mobster on parole from a life sentence for a 1973 murder, stood out from the other men, who all wore dark clothing. Before Nick could even settle into his seat at the round table, Gallo pulled a large bundle of cash from the inside breast pocket of his jacket and held it aloft for Arcadi, who sat across from him, to gawk at. Arcadi beamed his broad, toothy smile. Gallo placed the bundle on the table in front of Renda, who then counted it and separated it into five piles. Renda quickly put Vito's share into one pocket of his stylish grey suit jacket and his own share into another. Nick, Arcadi and Sollecito also grabbed a pile each. As Nick proceeded to recount his portion, as he typically did no matter who had handed him the money, the other men chatted. Renda smiled congenially at Gallo. After a few minutes, when Nick had finally sorted his money, they all got up and left. The scene would become routine. The person passing over the money would change from day to day, but the pattern was clear. Cash came in, was counted and divided into five piles, and the recipients happily stuffed their share into their pockets or socks or wallets. After Vito was arrested on the American charge, Nick or Renda would take Vito's share, presumably for safekeeping. Police documented 191 occasions when substantial sums of money were delivered to the back room of the Consenza and divided at the table of five.

The men were not shy about the split. On May 23, 2005, the wires picked up Sollecito explaining it to Beniamino Zappia, the man who had decades before helped the Rizzutos set up their bank accounts in Switzerland.

"When they do something—and it doesn't matter when they do it—they always bring something here so it can be divided up among us five: Me, Vito, Nicolò and Paolo," he said. Unspoken but understood was that the fifth share went to Arcadi, who had become the street boss for many of the activities of the organization, police allege.

Money flowed in from across the country: from Montreal traffickers, from gangsters in Toronto and from smugglers on Native reserves; from extortions and gambling in most major Canadian cities; from enforcers and runners who made collections on behalf of the Sixth Family; and from criminals who sent bundles of cash without being asked—just because they thought it was the thing to do. Mike LaPolla, the man who would later be gunned down in the Moomba supper club, delivered packages of cash to the back room. Antonio "Tony" Mucci, a longtime mobster who gained notoriety in 1973 for shooting *Le Devoir* crime reporter Jean-Pierre Charbonneau, turned over money.

The flood of information being gathered by Project Cicéron investigators was immense. Officers identified a huge Mafia enterprise composed of many cells. The leaders of each of these cells kept in daily contact with the senior bosses.

Key secondary players who were involved in the hands-on running of a multitude of criminal ventures were soon identified, police say. Two men in particular drew their attention: Lorenzo Giordano, a muscular man known as "Skunk" because of the white strips through his black hair, and Francesco Del Balso, a heavy-set man with a taste for expensive cars. Police allege that these two men collectively acted as the right hand of Arcadi, supervising drug importations, sports betting, and contact with other criminal groups, and as leaders of a crew of aggressive enforcers who instilled a climate of fear for the Mafia on the streets of Montreal. These younger men—Giordano was born in 1963 and Del Balso in 1970—had a regular hangout of their own, the Bar Laennec, in a strip mall at 2004 Boulevard René-Laennec in Laval. In February, 2005, the Laennec was also wired by police.

The joy of finally peering into these inner sanctums of the Sixth Family, however, came with a growing sense of panic for police. The operation was moving faster than the team could efficiently manage. Officers were struggling to keep up with thousands of conversations spoken over telephones and in clubs in English, French and Italian, often all within the same chat. Some 1,200 conversations each week had to be listened to, transcribed and analyzed. Many chats were about criminal operations and others were just run-of-the-mill gossip and the daily trivia of living. For the officers on Project Cicéron, the conversations started backing up, suspects were going unidentified and surveillance photographs were left unsorted and unlabeled. The over-time logged by the too-few investigators was extensive. When officers finished a shift of live monitoring of the wiretaps they often moved right on to a second shift processing the backlog of recorded calls. Just as the investigators who had worked on the RCMP's currency exchange operation in the 1990s had felt, there were fears that Project Cicéron would collapse under the weight of its own success.

The growing unease over the sprawling nature of the investigation—an officer described it as like "holding a tiger by his toenail"—was further fuelled by slips, leaks and screw-ups.

———

It was about 3 a.m. on a freezing cold night when plain-clothes police officers started working furtively in the dark to pick the lock on the front door of a modest tavern in Montreal's Saint-Léonard neighbor-hood. It did not take them long to crack open the door, allowing a team of police specialists to slip inside with microphones and min-iature cameras. Another penetration of a secretive club, believed by investigators to be yet another rallying point for Sixth Family members, was under way by the Project Cicéron team.

By now their moves were well-practiced. Many of the surveillance officers had become comfortable with their targets and knew their rou-tines. There was little difficulty picking up their trail and, one by one, each surveillance team had checked in that their target was settled in for the night. Officers in unmarked cars were also in place, watch-ing the club from the outside. This bugging operation was going like clockwork.

Then someone slipped up. The alarm inside the club had not been properly disabled and just as the technical team was preparing to get to work, an alarm was flashing at a private security firm and the club's proprietor of record was being woken up with news of a suspected break-in. The proprietor, who lived just a few blocks away, quickly jumped into his car to investigate. The surveillance officer watching him immediately reached for his radio to send a warning that his tar-get was on the move. In a case of compounding bad luck, the officer's warning went out just as another officer had clicked his radio on to say something else. The surveillance officer's warning was never heard by his colleagues at the club. It was not until the proprietor had pulled his car into the club's parking lot that startled surveillance officers at the scene were able to radio a warning.

"He's here, he's here," came a frantic call. As the proprietor got out of his car and walked towards his club, the officers inside dove for cover, awkwardly trying to hide under tables and chairs, yanking bags of tools and electronic equipment with them. The proprietor had walked up to the front of his club and was reaching out with his keys towards the door—which had been left unlocked by the officers inside—when a Montreal city police cruiser with its lights flashing screeched to a halt behind him.

"Don't touch the door, there's a bomb threat here," the officer bellowed, getting out of his cruiser.

"No, no, I want to go in and check on my place," the man protested, reaching up once more with his keys.

"No, there's a bomb threat. You have to leave immediately. Don't touch that door." There was, of course, no bomb threat. It was hastily enacted crisis control, a way of stopping the man in his tracks, hopefully without him seeing or suspecting what was going on inside. Maintaining the ruse, city police roped off several city blocks around the club under the guise of public safety. In reality, the wide perimeter gave the Project Cicéron techies the time and space needed to crawl out from under the tables and slink away from the club. Before the "bomb threat" was declared "unfounded" and the area opened to the public, however, police had one last trick to pull. They erased the video tape from the club's security camera that had captured the bungled entry and frantic hiding.

Scrubbing clean the tape did not erase the tavern owner's suspicions, however. Not long afterwards he called in private electronics experts to scan the club for wires and bugs.

There were other scares as well. A microphone hidden in a couch at the club was discovered one day by a surprised Consenza regular. The entire couch was quickly disposed of. Later, the dowdy club was given a makeover. Police heard of the plans for fresh paint, new furniture, new window signs advertising its espresso and, in a quiet re-christening, a large new name to be posted above its door. Just before the renovation was scheduled to begin, an urgent police operation went into play to secretly remove all of their cameras and microphones to prevent them from being discovered. When the paint was dry and the

Club Social Consenza had become the Associazione Cattolica Eraclea, an homage to the Rizzuto's hometown in Sicily, another elaborate police operation was undertaken to put the wires back in.

Trouble of a different sort came to Project Cicéron when a newspaper reporter who had stumbled upon some elements of the Rizzuto investigation called the RCMP seeking official confirmation and comment. The reporter had used the probe's supposedly secret codename in his query: Project Cicéron. Worries over the leak were not eased by the fact that the reporter was a veteran, well known and trusted by many of the officers. As a precaution, "Cicéron" as a codename was retired. The investigation, which was by then moving into its final phase, was renamed Project Colisée. Along with the new name, what was now known as Project Colisée got a boost in manpower. As the CFSEU's other operation, Project Calvette, successfully wrapped up with arrests and seizures in late 2004, bringing the drug schemes of Raymond Desfossés to a close, officers from that investigation were reassigned to the Sixth Family probe. The team grew to include about 100 full-time officers, plus another 10 investigators from the Canada Revenue Agency who were tracing assets of the key suspects.

Project Colisée was also given a new commanding officer, one who had, as a young constable a decade before, worked undercover to tackle the Sixth Family's cocaine importing schemes at the Travelodge Hotel in Cornwall. Back in 1994, the RCMP's Michel Aubin had played a modest but important role in the drug case. Having steadily been promoted to the rank of Inspector, he was now calling the shots. It was his job to ensure that Project Colisée did not join the long list of case files that tried but failed to seriously debilitate the Sixth Family. Aubin had the unenviable task of plotting the endgame. Unlike other operations that had targeted the Mafia in Canada, Project Colisée was evolving into a broad, multi-faceted probe. It did not narrow its focus to concentrate on a single revenue stream, such as drugs or gambling, or on a specific incident, such as a murder. Nor did it seek to only scoop up the top bosses—it was casting its net wide. The Sixth Family as a whole was put under the microscope and Aubin and his Colisée colleagues were building an American-style racketeering case. They were finding murders, murder plots, shootings, bribery and corruption of government officials, drug shipments and drug conspiracies, multi-million-dollar gambling rings, money laundering, extortions and gun offenses on which to gather evidence.

The bill for the investigation was likewise exploding. The global reach of the Sixth Family meant investigators needed to travel the world to investigate it: the Unites States, Italy, England, Germany, Colombia, Cuba, Mexico, Haiti, Jamaica, the Dominican Republic, Belize, Aruba, Venezuela, Switzerland and the Bahamas.

Three times the date of the planned sweep of arrests had to be postponed. There was much work still to be done, but time was clearly running out.

MONTREAL, AUGUST 30, 2006

A Cadillac pulled to a stop at the intersection of Henri-Bourassa Boulevard East and Rodolphe-Forget Boulevard in Montreal's Rivière-des-Prairies district, an ominous location for the Sixth Family—if they thought of such things—as it was where the body of Joe LoPresti, their close colleague and kin, had been discovered by police in 1992. Two men riding on a Japanese-made motorcycle pulled up beside the Cadillac shortly before 3:20 p.m.; the passenger, dressed in black and wearing a full motorcycle helmet that hid his face, hopped off and immediately opened fired into the passenger side of the car. The shooter then climbed back on the motorcycle and the pair sped away.

The driver, Mario Iannitto, was only slightly injured. Taking the brunt of the bullets was the Cadillac's passenger, Domenico Macri, who died from his wounds. Macri, born in 1970, was a gifted and intelligent man who left a wife and young son. He was known to police as a Sixth Family confidant, an up-and-coming gangster from the Calabrian wing of the organization who, in 1993, pleaded guilty to possession of heroin. Of chief concern to the Sixth Family, however, was the fact that Macri was frequently Arcadi's driver and bodyguard and at the time of his murder was, in fact, on his way to Arcadi's house to collect him.

Within minutes, word spread among Macri's Montreal colleagues as dozens of cell phones, already bugged by police, started chirping and bleating around the city.

"Yeah, bro, they shot D.M.," Giordano told Del Balso, who was stunned by the news. Giordano could barely contain his shock. "He's dead! He's dead! What happened? What are we going to do now?"

Arcadi's immediate reaction was that he must have been the intended target. He knew he had angered a rival by double-crossing him in a recent transaction. He wondered, aloud and in horror, about what might have happened had he been in the car with his family at the time of the attack. The Bar Laennec buzzed with activity as people came and went, whispering and hugging. Iannitto, the injured driver, was roused from his recovery and hauled in for questioning by leading Sixth Family soldiers. He was then summoned to meet directly with Renda, Sollecito, Arcadi, Giordano and Del Balso to give his account. Clearly, this was serious business. At a meeting in the Bar Laennec the following day, Sollecito, Renda and Arcadi met to discuss the murder.

"We are already starting to study the situation. As far as I'm concerned, it's a big fucking problem," Sollecito assured Arcadi. Renda said he would ask about the incident at a meeting he was having the next day with a man who he felt might have some answers. Arcadi, however, was anxious for action.

"Here we are, father, son and holy spirit," Arcadi said, evoking the religio-criminal mindset of the Mafia. "I agree that it's things that we have to reason out; things have to be measured, things have to be evaluated. But when it gets to a certain point, and we are touched by some stupidities, the discussions have to be short."

Believing Arcadi to have been the intended target in the murder, Renda suggested he leave town. "See, what you gotta do now: find an island, take your wife and leave." Arcadi was unsure. He did not like the idea of people thinking he was fleeing.

"I have to decide if I go or don't go," he said. "Maybe I go to Italy with my brothers." He then declared that he would triumph in any war. "Nobody is going to get rid of me, but we are looking. We are looking for that pig; we are looking for him because he's a sea of problem," he said in frustration. "What do we do—us? What do we do—us—when one of *us* has been killed? To tell you the truth, we do what we have to."

The visitation and funeral of Macri was a set-piece of Sixth Family solidarity. Macri's family and friends mingled with the cream of the Montreal underworld as they gathered for two days of visitation at the Loreto funeral home on Boulevard des Grandes-Prairies, a swank parlor owned by members of the Rizzuto and Renda families. At Macri's large funeral on September 5, 2006, at Marie Auxiliatrice Catholic Church, just a two-minute drive from where he had been shot, mobsters spanning the generations were out in force. Paolo Renda stood with his son, Charlie. Old-timer Agostino Cuntrera, who had helped murder Paolo Violi back in 1978, stood within arm's reach of Frank Cotroni, Jr., the son of the last of the old Cotroni bosses to die. Vito's son, Nick, was there. Lorenzo Giordano, looking smart in a black shirt, black tie and black suit jacket, walked beside Giuseppe Torre. Iannitto, the driver of Macri's Cadillac, watched somberly, knowing how close he had come to also being in a casket. Francesco Del Balso was included as a participant in the service. Wearing a black leather coat over a black shirt unbuttoned at the neck, he was one of several who held a quivering white dove to be released into the heavens.

Despite the doves of peace, the Sixth Family was preparing for war. Police surveillance teams spotted Giuseppe Fetta, Danny Winton, Martinez Canas and Charles Edouard Battista—pegged by officers as Mafia bodyguards—as they checked out and tested a silenced pistol in a garage, police say. Battista fired a shot into the ground to test the efficiency of the silencer. Police saw Battista give a machine gun to Fetta, while putting together a second automatic weapon. An arsenal was assembled: two AR-15 semi-automatic assault rifles, a machine gun, a shotgun, bulletproof vests and ammunition.

Del Balso called Streit Manufacturing, an armored vehicle company north of Toronto, and told a sales agent he needed a "high-level" vehicle that was "full bullet proof" and available immediately. He wanted a certified protection rating of B-5, which would stop bullets from an AK-47, have a grenade-proof floor and inserts in the tires that allowed it to drive on flats. Del Balso rejected a bone-white Cadillac as being "too flashy." After hearing the other options, Del Balso said he would take two sport utility vehicles, a Toyota 4Runner and a Nissan Armada, provided they were dark-colored and available immediately.

The senior Sixth Family members started traveling with bodyguards. Men with guns were stationed in cars outside the Consenza. Guns seemed to be on everyone's mind and never far from reach. Del Balso and one of his bodyguards, Ennio Bruni, compared weapons one day inside the Bar Laennec.

"What you have?" Del Balso asked.

"A .38," Bruni replied.

"That fucking old cop [gun]" Del Balso said dismissively. Bruni was a fan of the weapon.

"That's the best one, that's the best one," Bruni said, showing how it handled. "Like this. Look! How you gonna miss? It's dead. You crank it one time." A loud shot rang out.

Del Balso was impressed: "That's what I want."

Police fretted about the increasing signs of violence. Senior officers felt that Project Colisée needed to wrap up soon or their cameras and microphones would be recording a bloodbath. There were also signs that some police targets were restless in other ways.

MONTREAL AND LAVAL, NOVEMBER 6, 2006

A "For Sale" sign at a mansion in Laval's tony Val-des-Brises development was noticed by investigators two days after it was hammered into the immaculately landscaped front lawn. With an in-ground pool, hardwood floors, doors imported from Italy, heated ceramic tiles in the fully finished basement and a superb fireplace in the living room, the home was called a "a real jewel" by the Realtor, with a selling price of $999,000 to match. The house was owned by Giuseppe Torre, who police say managed the Sixth Family's drug importation schemes through Montreal's Pierre Elliot Trudeau International Airport. When Torre and his wife bought it in 2004, a year when the couple declared a combined income of $87,384, the house had already come to the attention of tax investigators.

About 10 agents with the Canada Revenue Agency had been added to the Project Colisée team to help the government track down and secure assets of the top targets. Officers watching their secret videos knew the look of joy on the faces of the bosses as they collected their cash. They knew that loyalty and blood made the Sixth Family strong but revenue was what made it happy.

"I can tell you one thing, if you want to discourage organized crime people and let them know clearly that Canada is not a good place to do business, seize their assets," said RCMP Deputy Commissioner Pierre-Yves Bourduas. "These people get involved in organized crime above all to acquire assets."

The lavish home that appeared to be beyond the means of the Torres's incomes was not the only incongruence tax agents found. Torre and his wife, a former Air Canada flight attendant, had claimed almost $100,000 in personal expenditures in 2001 on declared combined income of $30,562. Credit card receipts showed that $1,902 had recently been spent on lingerie at Victoria's Secrets. There were painful hair transplants for Torre—more than a thousand grafts; second-row seats at the World Cup in Germany; trips to New York and Alberta to see hockey games; flights to Acapulco, Mexico City, Frankfurt, San Francisco and Los Angeles. There were gambling binges—on a single day Torre lost $100,000 on sports bets. Despite the luxury, his wife complained about having to drive a BMW M3 because Torre refused to buy her a Porsche.

Similar contrasts were found when the tax agents looked at Nick Rizzuto. In 2001, for instance, Nick was a pensioner living on $26,574 in old age security and income from his investment portfolio, according to his tax returns. Yet he lived in a mansion, had a condo in Milan, almost $2-million in blue chip stocks, cruised around in a 1987 Jaguar XJ12 and a 2001 Mercedes E430 and pampered his wife, Libertina, with furs and jewels. And while Nick and Libertina did not list any off-shore accounts in their tax returns, investigators believed they had more than $5-million in Swiss banks. Nick's investment accounts showed cash injections from the money-laundering capital of Panama. A constant fear haunted investigators that their targets would liquate their assets and move the money beyond the government's reach.

"Nick Rizzuto could, without any constraints whatsoever, liquidate his investments that he holds at RBC Dominion Securities, National Bank Financial and National Bank of Canada by transferring his assets to Panama," Jean-Pierre Paquette, one of the tax investigators, wrote in an affidavit filed in court.

What was of most concern for the Project Colisée team, however, was the "For Sale" sign on Torre's home. When they looked at his other assets they found that two income properties, rental units owned by Torre and his wife, were also on the market.

"Giuseppe Torre is actually in the process of emptying his assets and his real estate holdings," tax investigator Benoit Martineau wrote in an affidavit. The liquidation came just as police were winding down Project Colisée and planning arrests. Could it mean there had been another leak? Were the subjects of their investigation preparing to flee?

Just a few weeks before, Del Balso had left for Acapulco, causing some concern. Upon his return to Montreal, his luggage was checked by border agents at the airport. Del Balso mocked their efforts. He could "buy this fucking airport if he felt like it," he quipped.

"You're wasting your time checking me out when all the drugs in the world are passing under your nose," he said. He should know, officers thought.

———

Investigators worked frantically with federal prosecutors to sort out who they could charge, who would be arrested for what and who would be let go, perhaps for another day. With Vito facing American justice, he was, for the moment, no longer a Canadian concern. The sprawling lists of hundreds of suspects began to be whittled down.

There were the senior leaders—Nick Rizzuto, Paolo Renda, Rocco Sollecito and Francesco Arcadi—who police claim orchestrated and profited from a vast array of criminal enterprises. There were the street bosses—Lorenzo Giordano and Francesco Del Balso—who allegedly supervised the activities of the family. There were 38 people allegedly working to smuggle drugs into Canada through the Montreal airport, including Giuseppe Torre, the suspected manager of the ring, a female customs officer with the Canada Border Services Agency and a dozen airline and airplane food service workers. There were others alleged to have arranged cocaine importation from South America and the Caribbean by way of shipping containers, including another female border guard. There were 10 people alleged to be running a large Internet betting service through a computer server located first in Belize and then moved in 2005 to the Kahnawake native reserve. (Court documents say they took in $391.9-million in less than a year.) There was a separate group of 24 men and women who allegedly exported marijuana to Florida through the Akwesasne reserve and brought money from its sale back into Canada. There were those accused of specific acts of violence and several bodyguards accused of firearms offenses.

The rest would have to wait. As with past investigations, there were leading subjects of investigation that police wanted to arrest but that prosecutors declined to charge. In the end, the Project Colisée bosses settled on securing arrest warrants for 91 people, most of them in Montreal, but others in Toronto and Halifax.

MONTREAL, NOVEMBER 22, 2006

By 5 a.m., more than 700 officers with the RCMP, Montreal and Laval police and agents with the Canada Revenue Agency were marshaled together in several staging areas and briefed on the basics of why they had been roused this early. To maintain security, just 90 of them knew who the targets were to be when the raiding teams started swooping down on almost a hundred homes, businesses and offices. Rather than a television-style smash-and-grab of suspects, officers were instructed to take a "passive approach" to the arrests and the targets responded in kind; all were arrested without incident. In most cases, their capture came with an early morning knock at the front door of their home.

At Nick's mansion, police allowed the old mafioso to dress in his trademark gangster chic: knee-length designer coat and snappy fedora. His wife, however, was so distraught that officers called an ambulance. Nick was then led from their home, his hands bound in front with plastic handcuffs. Seeing the media's cameras, Nick forced a toothy smile. Project Colisée was finally going public.

On the same street, police went to Renda's to arrest him and Vito's house to search for evidence. Sollecito was also arrested quietly at his home. Arcadi was found in the Hemmingford area, south of Montreal, just about to head out on a hunting expedition. He was brought back to Montreal still dressed in camouflage. Most of the 91 suspects were found easily. By the end of the day, the only major target still unaccounted for was Giordano, who fled to Toronto; he was arrested there almost six months later. Six men and one woman remain fugitives, all wanted on drug charges.

The RCMP quickly declared Project Colisée to be "one of the most important police operations in the history of Canada."

"I have to admit that over the 32 years that I've been in this organization, the Rizzuto organization has been on our radar screen for most of my service. So it was quite a feat," said Deputy Commissioner Bourduas. "The Rizzuto family syndicate has been operating in Canada since the 1950s and has implications in all parts of the world. When you tackle these types of organizations, there's a price tag and if I quoted the price for Colisée, it would be in the millions of dollars. It's staggering, but it's a price we all have to pay."

The cost of the project will undoubtedly exceed $50 million. Nearly $35 million of confirmed expenses have been tracked, with many of the biggest bills still unaccounted for. The RCMP had, by far, the largest share of the costs, with its expenses leading up to the arrests in 2006 of $32,084,823. That includes more than $26 million in salaries and $4 million in overtime, according to the RCMP. The Sûreté du Québec picked up $1,628,269 of the cost. The Sûreté's expenses started in 2003, with $228,937 in costs and peaked in 2005 when $504,957 was spent, according to documents provided by the force. The Canada Revenue Agency spent $752,640 in the short time it was involved, starting in May 2005; most of it in salaries to its agents, according to the agency. The accounting is far from complete, however. One of the largest partners in Project Colisée, the Montreal city police, could not provide an accounting of its costs, but did give as an example that it had

1,015 hours of overtime to pay its officers just for November 21, the day of the Colisée arrests. Laval police, likewise, declined to provide information on its share of expenses. Canada Border Services Agency, named as a Colisée partner, has declared that it incurred no expenses for the operation. And then there are the significant costs of the prosecution and the incarceration of the accused after the arrests. The legal bills for the government will be immense.

Inspector Aubin, Project Colisée's commanding officer, said success should be measured by more than just what it will do to the Sixth Family. Aubin believes that "With Project Colisée, we have cut to the core of traditional organized crime. If we were successful in striking this organization where they thought to be safe, we could do the same against other criminal groups. With the dismantling of this organization, we can safely say that no criminal organization will be able to rest easy."

What is more, officers say, their work is not done.

"It has been a very large investigation," said a veteran Project Colisée investigator. "After this there will no doubt be Colisée 2, Colisée 3 and 4."

"It was like my wife knitting a sweater," another investigator said. "Gather, gather, gather. You drop a stitch here, you pick it up and you keep on unrolling the wool. Well, we dropped a stitch or two but when we finished the sweater was a quilt." He laughed.

"And we still have a little wool left, eh?"

Chapter 43

BROOKLYN, MAY 4, 2007

"Okay. Mr. Rizzuto, how do you plead to the charge contained in count one of the superseding indictment, guilty or not guilty?" The question, put to Vito Rizzuto by Judge Nicholas Garaufis in a spacious Brooklyn courthouse on the morning of May 4, 2007, brought the wealthy and powerful mafioso to a crossroads. Remarkably, despite being the leader of the Sixth Family, the biggest name in Canadian crime and a global superboss, he had avoided answering such questions in the negative for 35 years. And for 26 years—minus one day—he had also avoided admitting his involvement in a mob massacre, the storied shooting of the three Bonanno captains.

Now, dressed in a baggy prison uniform rather than the designer suit he would have preferred, with his usually well-coifed hair shorn unfashionably short by a prison barber, and with his unease revealing itself in the repetitive jiggling of his legs as he stood before Judge Garaufis, Vito hesitated in his answer just long enough for the clutch of reporters to wonder what surprise maneuver might save him this time. And then he answered in a steady but slightly raspy voice.

"Guilty," he said, his hands clasped meekly in front of him.

"Are you making this plea of guilty voluntarily and of your own free will?" asked the judge.

"Yes, Your Honor."

Vito then needed to tell the court what he had done wrong, a way for Judge Garaufis to weigh the appropriateness of the five-page plea agreement that had been hammered out by Vito's attorneys and Greg Andres, the federal prosecutor, and signed by Vito earlier that day, stipulating that in return for his guilty plea Vito would be handed a 10-year prison term. For this, Vito put on a pair of reading glasses and turned to a scrap of paper on which one of his lawyers had crafted a bare-bones outline of his admission.

"Between February 1, 1981 and May 5, 1981, I conspired with others to conduct the affairs of an association, in fact, enterprise through a pattern of racketeering activity. Specifically, on May 5, 1981, acting with others in Brooklyn, New York, I committed the racketeering acts of conspiracy to murder and the murder of Alphonse Indelicato, Philip Giaccone and Dominick Trinchera," he said. The awkwardness of the statement, sounding more like a government indictment than an honest admission of guilt, brought a moment of silence to the courtroom. Judge Garaufis, who had overseen dozens of court proceedings against the Bonanno Family, was unimpressed.

"You haven't told me anything about what he did," the judge said, visibly becoming more annoyed as he spoke. "I want to know more about it. This is not some game. I am the judge. It is unacceptable. Was he the driver? Was he one of the shooters?" the judge asked. "Why should I accept his plea and accept a 10-year sentence when he could be sentenced to 20 years? People have gone to jail for the rest of their lives, as a practical matter, because of their involvement in these crimes. If he's got something more to tell me, I'd like to hear it before I accept this plea."

Vito's New York lawyer, John Mitchell, was taken aback.

"May I have a moment, Your Honor?" he asked. During a short break, Vito and Mitchell had an animated exchange. Gone was the meek Vito who had been addressing the judge. Here was the Vito of old, the man in control. Motioning sharply with his hands as he spoke quietly to his lawyer, Vito had opinions, apparently, about what he would and would not admit to and he seemed to be accepting little debate about it. One suspects he was making it clear that he would not admit that he was a member of the Mafia. When court reconvened, Vito was prepared with a less scripted account of his crime.

"Well, I was one of the guys who was to participate in this," Vito began. "My job was to say, 'It's a holdup,' when I went in the room, 'so everybody stand still.' This moment the other people came in and they started shooting the other guys."

"You were armed?" asked Judge Garaufis.

"I was armed," said Vito.

It then fell to Andres to explain why he was settling for a 10-year sentence for such an atrocity.

"Given this crime happened over 26 years ago, given that it gives some finality in part to the victims, it allows us to return some of the evidence at least to some of the victims, and given the time passage, while that's no excuse it's certainly one of the things that factors into the government's calculation as to how to dispose of the case," he said.

A few weeks later, on May 25, 2007, Vito appeared once more before Judge Garaufis for his official sentencing. Here, he tried to dodge a hefty fine by presenting financial statements claiming he was broke. His only assets, he said, were $3,000 in cash and the $468,000 value of his one-third stake in Construction Renda, Inc., a family-owned Montreal firm. That was more than erased, he claimed, by his $475,300 in debts—money he owed to family members: $103,300 to his youngest son, Leonardo; $92,000 to his only daughter, Bettina; and $280,000 to his mother, Libertina. The claims were preposterous.

"His net worth is absurdly and conveniently equal to his liabilities," Andres said. "Like everyone in the mob, his relatives hold all the assets."

Judge Garaufis seemed to agree: "The court is not convinced that the information provided regarding his liabilities can be considered reliable. We have a businessman from Canada who doesn't own his own house. His only asset is a share of this company—it's not much to show for 30 years in business and I'm not convinced that the representations are complete or accurate."

Vito's pleas of poverty, in fact, almost derailed the sentencing agreement. The annoyed judge handed Vito the stiffest fine the law allowed: $250,000. Even then, Vito's lawyers asked that it be paid in installments, angling for a payment plan that would have stretched beyond the end of his prison sentence. They then resisted having the fine secured by Vito's shares in the construction firm. They pushed too hard. Displaying a flash of anger, the judge ordered the payment within 90 days.

"Today marks the final chapter in the sad story of the execution of three people some 26 years ago in the pursuit of power and money," Judge Garaufis said. "As the history of this event unfolded in this courthouse, it is apparent to the court that such a sordid and cynical act deserves only our scorn and condemnation. It is impossible to measure the human misery left in its wake. Our city is scarred by each and every such occurrence. I hope, but do not see much promise, that we will not see such wanton lawlessness and inhumanity in our future."

Despite the added burden of the fine, it was, in reality, a sweetheart of a deal. Going to trial would have been expensive and embarrassing, publicly revealing more about the Montreal Mafia than had been uncovered since the days of Paolo Violi and his indiscretions. The parade of cooperating witnesses would have been overwhelming and, at the end of the day, Vito's chances of beating the charge were slim. Not one of the 27 people named in the original indictment had won. If Vito lost at trial, he would have certainly been handed a 20-year sentence. What is more, with his guilty plea, the U.S. Bureau of Prisons was accepting the starting date for Vito's sentence as January 20, 2004, the morning he was arrested inside his Montreal mansion. Under U.S. regulations, he will likely be released after serving 87 percent of his sentence. His projected release date is October 6, 2012. He will be 66 years old.

Vito, however, could find he is free even sooner. As a Canadian citizen he is eligible to apply to serve his sentence in Canada—where his prison time would be cut even shorter under statutory release rules that effectively reduce sentences by one-third or perhaps even two-thirds if the National Parole Board does not consider racketeering a crime of violence (just as it does not consider drug trafficking or drug importation to be a violent crime). Further, because he was sentenced in the United States, the order from Judge Garaufis for three years of supervision following the completion of his prison term would have no force. Vito would be free.

There is some irony in the outcome. Had Vito not been arrested and extradited to the United States, he would surely have been arrested in the Project Colisée sweep. Given the seriousness of the charges his family members and colleagues now face in Canada, and the apparent strength of the government's evidence, Vito could well be back on the streets of Montreal before many of those charged only in Canada.

It is safe to say that although he did not beat the charge this time, he certainly beat the odds.

As Vito's father and the others face the start of their legal battles in Canada, Vito is settling into life as a prisoner in America. His lawyers had requested that Vito be placed in Ray Brook prison in upstate New York, just 115 miles south of Montreal, to allow easy visits from his family. Instead, from Brooklyn's crowded Metropolitan Detention Center, he was flown to a prison transfer facility in Oklahoma and then, some days later, to his assigned prison: the medium-security Florence Federal Correctional Complex in Florence, Colorado, 1,945 miles from home.

ROME, OCTOBER 23, 2007

Just when Vito was settling in to the relatively anonymous routine of a federal inmate, Italian authorities gathered in Rome to make an announcement that would again thrust him into the headlines around the world: Bankers, businessmen, investment brokers and a man linked to the royal family of Italy were arrested in Europe, accused of being part of a prodigious underworld financial empire. In a series of raids in Italy, Switzerland and France, police froze $730-million worth of assets, seized 22 companies and charged 17 men. The group used several firms listed on German and American stock markets, including one registered in Vancouver and linked to gold mines in Canada and Chile, authorities alleged.

The controlling mind behind it all, authorities said, was Vito Rizzuto. Once again Italian authorities issued a warrant for his arrest as the boss of a Mafia association, and expressed a desire to have him extradited to face trial in Italy. Arrest warrants were also issued against Vito's father, Nick, and the inner core of the Sixth Family: Paolo Renda, Frank Arcadi and Rocco Sollecito. It was not lost on investigators that all of these men were currently in custody.

"We believe that even from jail they are able to control the organization," said Silvia Franzè, with the Direzione Investigativa Antimafia in Rome. "We blocked a lot of bank accounts and money. We have seized many companies and hundreds of millions of Euros all around the world because we believe that behind these companies is Vito Rizzuto. We found there were cells here in Italy controlled by Vito Rizzuto. We found out the links between the chiefs of those cells and the companies allegedly involved in financial crimes and in acquiring land for development."

Also arrested was Mariano Turrisi, 53, the president and founder of Made in Italy Inc., an import-export marketing group. He is heard on wiretaps speaking with Vito in 2002 and 2003, police said. Turrisi's arrest is particularly noteworthy—he was the senior deputy of a political movement founded by Prince Emanuele Filiberto, an heir to the Italian throne when the monarchy ended in 1946. The political movement, called "Values and Future" in English, was founded when Prince Filiberto returned from exile in 2002 after a constitutional amendment allowed male members of the royal family, called the Royal House of Savoy, to re-enter Italy.

It all presented a decidedly white-collar face of the Mafia. Links to such people show the level of influence that the Rizzuto name carries around the world, police said.

Also among those charged in Italy were: Roberto Papalia, the controversial Vancouver businessman and Rizzuto associate, who was arrested in Milan; Beniamino Zappia, who decades earlier had helped the Rizzutos move money through Lugano banks, was also arrested in Milan; and Felice Italiano, a LaSalle, Quebec businessman who had charges dropped against him more than a decade ago after one of Canada's largest drug seizures. Italiano owns Ital-Peaux, a Quebec company that exports raw animal hides. Italian authorities allege Italiano used animal hides to mask the smell of narcotics from drug-sniffing dogs. He was on holiday in Rome with his wife when police arrested him in his hotel room just two hours before his return flight to Canada. Other Canadians and Italians are still wanted in the case.

Italian legal documents in the case dramatically portray Vito as a global superboss. The Rizzutos "gave birth to a transnational society" that worked to unite the Italian mafias and create "overseas cells," a document from the Rome anti-Mafia prosecutor's office alleged. The organization sought to "manage and control the economic activities connected to the acquisition of contracts in public works" and to "commit a series of crimes—killings, international drug trafficking, extortion, frauds, smuggling, stock-market manipulation, insider trading and criminal transfer of securities."

For the Sixth Family, bad news kept rolling in.

———

The sentencing of Vito Rizzuto in the United States, the arrests of so many of his colleagues in Canada and the uncertainty over pending charges in Italy presents a serious and significant setback for the Sixth Family, the likes of which it has never before had to overcome. The organization apparently had a contingency plan in place to ensure a smooth transition should Vito or another senior leader be removed from the game. The Project Colisée recordings show its robust "table of five" leadership model. It is doubtful, however, that there was much anticipation of such deep Canadian losses following so soon on the heels of Vito's arrest. The organization is significantly weaker. The dismantling of several of its lucrative revenue streams and the underworld embarrassment of being so thoroughly penetrated by police compound its losses. The evidence gathered by Project Colisée investigators will haunt Montreal mobsters for years, with those compromised by their visits to the Club Social Consenza but not arrested feeling vulnerable and wondering what might befall them in the future. The talk of Project Colisée 2 and 3 will be making crooks and mobsters nervous from coast to coast.

All is not lost for the Sixth Family, however.

There are many important, respected and skilled members of several clans in the Sixth Family organization left untouched by the arrests. Of the 205 subjects tracked by Project Colisée officers—of which approximately 130 were designated as primary and secondary targets—only 91 actually faced arrest when the probe wrapped up. Some of those who remain free were considered by investigators to carry significant leadership responsibility and authority. Vito's associated clans and allies in Toronto and some in Vancouver continue to operate. Although some cash, drugs, guns, houses and other assets were seized by police in Project Colisée, the Sixth Family's vast wealth remains largely undisturbed. And, perhaps most important, none of the dozen or so men and women labeled by police as forming the "new generation" of the Sixth Family were arrested.

The clans, while made up of people, are held together by bonds that give the organization a tensile, almost irresistible strength. Like the octopus the Mafia is often compared to, new tentacles appear whenever old ones are lost. The arrest of a single player, even one with Vito's obvious ability, charisma, respect and incomparable contacts will be but a speed bump in a history that stretches back more than a century. The Sixth Family, in its historical battle for survival, is greater than any single leader and greater, even, than any of the individual clans it encompasses. The family has proved itself to be a durable entity, much like a resilient counterculture or a virus. New players—many of them the children of current members of its inner circle—are already being groomed for their roles and will one day emerge, ready to carry on the cult-like criminal traditions they have been born into; just as the Famiglia Manno became the Rizzuto organization which became the Sixth Family. Who knows which of the clan names will become dominant in the years to come?

Removing Vito Rizzuto from the leadership of the Sixth Family is not like cutting the head off a beast. It is more like yanking a clump of hair from its head. The rest of the strands remain, grow and prosper; the spot left by the absent strands soon overgrown.

And eventually forgotten.

Epilogue

FLORENCE, COLORADO, OCTOBER 5, 2012

It was breakfast time for inmates at the Florence Federal Correctional Complex, but inmate 04307-748 had little interest in food; for him it was moving day. By 7:07 a.m. his paperwork was complete, his release formalized and inmate 04307-748 was ready to once again become Vito Rizzuto. While his prison sentence for his role in the 1981 murders of the three Bonanno captains was finally complete, he was not yet a free man. As a foreign national convicted of a serious crime, he was handed directly to U.S. Immigration and Customs Enforcement agents and held under guard while preparations were made for his immediate deportation. For most deportations it takes days or weeks to formalize the plan, but by dinnertime that same day he was escorted onto an Air Canada jet at Denver airport and shown to a seat at the back of the plane along with a four-agent escort. A journalist with Radio-Canada approached Vito. Wearing a pair of half-frame reading glasses to fill out his customs declaration form and sipping coffee, Vito looked into the reporter's cellphone camera and held up his left hand. Rather than a bold pronouncement of his intent, however, Vito uttered a plea to be allowed to fly in peace.

When the plane landed in Toronto at 10:41 p.m., Vito and his escorts were the last to disembark. Preparations had also been made in Canada. Waiting in the arrivals lounge was a posse of heavily armed police in body armor, the expected entourage to greet the return of the biggest name in Canadian crime. There was an interview of sorts, an attempted debriefing by the airport special squad, composed of officers from the municipal police, Canada Border Services Agency and RCMP. Vito was congenial but uninformative. He was a free man and he was looking forward to being reunited with his family, he told the customs agents. As a Canadian citizen with the right to enter his country, there was little the agents could do but ask him a few questions. They all knew this and everyone kept to the script. Once cleared of customs, Vito was warmly greeted by his youngest son, Leonardo, along with a man from New York and an associate from Montreal. Police later suspected the New Yorker was there as a guarantor, a sort of hostage to ensure nothing untoward happened to Vito upon arrival, given recent events.

RCMP surveillance teams were ready to follow him but Vito climbed into an SUV and promptly disappeared, somehow slipping through the net. Police later found the SUV at a hotel close to the Toronto airport, but Vito was nowhere to be seen. For a couple of weeks, he was like a ghost—rumors spread of him being spotted at a store in Saint-Léonard, a café in Woodbridge, Ontario, or a restaurant in Hamilton. A week after his arrival, police confirmed he attended a dental appointment in Montreal. The truly important meetings, however, were held in stricter secrecy. First came deep debriefings, sources say. His key people would have laid out the enormity of all that had happened since his extradition. While he had been frequently updated on family and gangland highlights while he was in prison, not everything could be said in that environment. Vito knew his conversations were being monitored; fine details had to be held back or spoken in code and not always precisely interpreted.

There was much to discuss.

It had been more than eight years since Vito Rizzuto had walked the streets. Since the morning at the start of 2004 when he was led to the back of a Montreal police car, he had been held in continuous custody. Much had changed, likely more than he could ever have imagined. His peremptory grip on Canada's underworld had been lost and his rivals, who had long been forced to cower, had finally found their trigger fingers.

Vito knew the police had been the first to erode his organization. By the fall of 2008, most of the leading figures arrested by police in Project Colisée had pleaded guilty in order to avoid a revealing and embarrassing trial. Even so, details included in summaries of police evidence exposed the depth and breadth of the Sixth Family's enterprises in Montreal, from massive drug smuggling to a coffee monopoly; from extortion of businessmen to vicious collection of gambling debts; from collecting *pizzo* (an illicit tax on businesses) to committing large-scale tax fraud.

In keeping with Mafia tradition, the plea deals most benefited the bosses—seniority within the Sixth Family was revealed by the sentencing. Faring best was Vito's father, Nicolò, who, after pleading guilty to possession of the proceeds of crime and concealing criminal proceeds for the benefit of a criminal organization, was sentenced to four years in prison. After the court subtracted twice the two years he had spent in custody awaiting trial, a Canadian judicial practice, he was released on the same day he was sentenced. Paolo Renda, Vito's brother-in-law, pleaded guilty to proceeds of crime possession, gangsterism and weapons charges for guns found in his house when he was arrested. He was given a six-year sentence but, when his time served was subtracted, only two years remained before he was eligible for parole. Rocco Sollecito received eight years; Francesco Arcadi and his two top street enforcers, Lorenzo Giordano and Francesco Del Balso, were each sentenced to 15 years. Others cut the best deal they could, with varying degrees of success. Project Colisée was an unprecedented encroachment on the Sixth Family's core strength but, given the legal and enforcement costs, the effort and years of investigation, it can just as easily be seen as a judicial failure, especially when the project's rewards are compared to the crippling effects of similar—or lesser—operations in the United States.

After police and the courts took their swipes at the clan it was the turn of gangland rivals. They were not as lenient. The year the inner circle pleaded guilty, 2008, also saw Rizzuto-linked bookies and traffickers robbed and kidnapped, and Rizzuto friends, allies and business partners, including reputed Mafia stalwart Tony Mucci, narrowly escaping assassination. The year ended with someone grabbing Mario "Skinny" Marabella when he stopped for gas in Laval. His car was later found, torched, but neither the man nor his body have been seen again. As a longtime mob associate of Agostino Cuntrera, who was considered one of the most senior Sixth Family loyalists remaining free, Skinny's disappearance seemed portentous. The new year brought new wounds: in January 2009, Sam Fasulo, a drug trafficker who sold crack cocaine and heroin out of Montreal's Italian cafés and answered to Arcadi, was shot and killed while driving and dozens of Italian cafés were besieged by firebomb attacks. It seemed that after years of being unable to raise a complaint, let alone a fist, against the decrees of the Sixth Family, the collective leash on aggrieved criminals had snapped.

The bloodshed next hit closer to home for the Sixth Family. Frederico Del Peschio, whose connections to the Mafia stretched back to the Vic Cotroni era and who, in the 1980s, served time in a

Venezuelan prison with Nicolò Rizzuto, Vito's father, was shot in the back on August 29, 2009, as he arrived at the parking lot of La Cantina, his Montreal restaurant that had been a favorite of Vito's. He was 59 years old. His body was prepared at the Loreto funeral home, owned by Rizzuto family members, and his funeral mass conducted at the Church of the Madonna della Difesa. Both facilities, with frightful regularity, would continue to make unwelcome intrusions into the lives of the Rizzuto family.

Three days after Christmas 2009, Nick Rizzuto, Vito's eldest son, was shot dead at close range in broad daylight beside his black Mercedes in Montreal's Notre-Dame-de-Grâce neighborhood. Witnesses described a lone gunman with dark skin, wearing jeans and with his head obscured by a hood, firing four to six times. Nick was 42 years old. He had been nicknamed "The Ritz" by many on the street, suggesting resentment in some quarters over his position as the dauphin, the wealthy and privileged eldest son of the boss and the presumed heir. As police marked off shell casings on the pavement and interviewed witnesses who described a sound like firecrackers going off, other officers could be seen walking into the nearby office of FTM Construction, a firm owned by Tony Magi, who was involved in real estate deals with young Nick. No charges have been laid in the slaying and Magi issued a statement objecting to any insinuation he was involved in Nick's slaying. Vito received the devastating news by telephone at his Colorado prison and contemplated seeking compassionate leave to be at the funeral, but he didn't attend. Instead, on January 2, 2010, Nick's gold-colored casket was escorted by his namesake grandfather, Nicolò, and grandmother, Libertina; his mother, Giovanna; his brother, Leonardo, and sister, Bettina; his widow, Eleanora (the daughter of Emanuele Ragusa, an old and trusted Rizzuto confident); and, most mournful, Nick and Eleanora's two sons, including his eldest, named Vito in keeping with the family's naming convention, on whose birthday Nick's murder took place. "Forgive us our sins and lead us to eternal salvation. ... Nicolò was promised eternal joy at his baptism. ... Now he is in good hands with God," said the priest, Father Jacques du Plouy, in Italian to the large congregation inside the Church of the Madonna della Difesa. The church's name, known in English as Our Lady of Defence, was taking on an unintentionally appropriate resonance.

Four months after Nick's funeral, a National Parole Board of Canada panel convened to warn Paolo Renda against seeking revenge for the murder of young Nick—his godson—before releasing him on parole from his Project Colisée sentence. If Renda did not already believe it, Nick's funeral showed him he had enemies far more frightening than police. And so it likely elicited annoyance but not fear when, on May 20, 2010, his gray Infiniti sedan was pulled over on Gouin Boulevard by a car with flashing lights. He was on his way home after a round of golf and stopping at a butcher's shop to buy four steaks for a family dinner. As two men wearing Montreal police jackets approached his car, he appears to have rolled down his car window anticipating questions and probably ready to show his license. He would not have known it, but the position of the stop seems to have been carefully selected. Video surveillance dotting the streetscape ended a short distance behind his car and the view of the next camera did not start until farther ahead, a police investigator said. He likely had a bone-chilling realization soon after stopping: the men were not really police officers. Renda, the Sixth Family's *consigliere*, has not been heard from since. He was 70 years old. His disappearance and, eventually, his presumed death, became particularly revealing to investigators pondering the barrage of attacks on the Sixth Family, and, likely, to Vito himself. Renda could have simply been shot dead at the wheel of his car, his body left as another public pronouncement of the Rizzutos' growing vulnerability and waning power; instead, he was kidnapped. Mobsters and investigators both asked the same question—why?—and came up with the same answer: because Renda was the family's main money man. Taking him alive suggested not only revenge but also a deeper purpose. Someone was trying to take over. Renda knew who was paying out to whom, how much and how often. He knew who was doing the collecting and where the money was going. He knew about the family's banking, accounts, stashes of cash, assets, reserves, routines, passwords, debts and bribes; he knew who their people in positions of influence were, who was dirty and who was not. These are the very things someone supplanting the Sixth Family would need to know to ensure a smooth transition. Investigators believe Renda faced an unpleasant end, likely under torture, as such information was extracted from him.

Suddenly, being seen as a leader within the Sixth Family had become the most dangerous job in the land. One thing about old-school mafiosi, however, is they do tend to cling to a sense of duty. It was with reluctance and an epithet that Agostino Cuntrera stepped in to answer the call. Someone needed to represent the clan on the street while Vito's time in prison ticked down. Few men in Montreal laid claim to a richer piece of the city's gangland history. Cuntrera was a cousin of Alfonso Caruana, the great Sicilian drug-trafficking ally of the Sixth Family, and had directly helped kill Paolo Violi in 1978, an act that thrust the Sicilian faction into power. Cuntrera's new, interim job came with an armored car and a trusted bodyguard. That protection was not enough. Perhaps by intent or curious coincidence, his murder on June 29, 2010, outside his Montreal food-distribution business mirrored his own attack on Violi: both men were shot in the head at close range with a shotgun.

The symmetry between the bloodshed of the Sixth Family's rise and the attempt to bring it down was even more apparent in the next shocking attack. The Rizzutos' war of ascension under Nicolò's leadership had ended in 1980 when the last of the Violi brothers, Rocco, joined his family at the kitchen table of their Saint-Léonard home for a meal. A single bullet from a sniper's rifle punched through a window and struck him in the head. After so long, it is uncertain if Nicolò recalled the details of that outrageous assassination, but others did. On November 10, 2010, the patriarch joined his wife and daughter for dinner in the kitchen of their mansion on Antoine-Berthelet Avenue. It was about 5:40 p.m., and darkness was falling across the house that backed onto a heavily wooded lot edged by high cedars. To enjoy the relaxing woodland vista, Nicolò had constructed a bright solarium along the back of his house, and it was through the double panes of glass in the solarium that a sniper was peering at the legendary Mafia figure through his scope. A single shot was fired with precision, striking Nicolò high in the neck. He slumped to the floor, dead, in front of his stunned family. He was 86 years old.

Members of the Sixth Family's core gathered for Nicolò's funeral mass in a grieving vigil, once again at the Church of the Madonna della Difesa, along with close to 800 others, on November 15, 2010, watched closely by police and journalists. Beefy private security guards tried to keep journalists and those not deemed to be in a suitable state of respect outside. As the church's bell rang out at the end of the ceremony, it seemed to also toll the end of the Sixth Family.

If this was a war, the casualties were piling up on only one side and as blood continued to run, investigators started weaving together strands that helped explain much, but not all, of it. From street informants, wiretaps, surveillance and educated surmises, attention started to fall on a new face in town. Of course, in prison, Vito had already been informed of the arrival of an influential New York mob boss. The last thing the destabilized underworld in Montreal needed was another gangster added to the mix. This one, though, came courtesy of the U.S. government.

Salvatore Montagna was a man of three countries. Born in Montreal on May 11, 1971, one of three sons of Italian immigrants, the family returned to Sicily when he was still an infant. Over the years, they shuttled back and forth. When he was 15, they moved to New York.

Sal Montagna followed in his father's footsteps, becoming an ironworker and starting his own company. He built Matrix Steel Co., of Brooklyn, into a multimillion dollar enterprise, eliciting his rather sober nickname, "Sal the Ironworker." In New York, he married an American-born Italian woman and the couple had three daughters. His marriage allowed him to become a legal permanent resident of the United States. Somewhere in between those milestones, he also became active in the Bonanno crime family. Managing to maintain a low profile, seemingly just one of dozens of players littering police charts of Mafia family structures, Montagna eventually came up in a minor bookmaking investigation. Among those arrested was Patrick "Patty from the Bronx" DeFilippo, who was the prime suspect in the 1999 murder of Gerlando Sciascia, Vito's man in New York. Clearly, the Ironworker was moving in the right circles for promotion.

That bookmaking beef should have been just a minor inconvenience. In 2001, however, just as Montagna was preparing to apply for U.S. citizenship, he was subpoenaed to testify before a grand jury about the case. The prosecutor was unsatisfied with Montagna's obstinate testimony and charged him with criminal contempt. In 2003, he pleaded guilty and was sentenced to five years of probation. That hardly corralled the ambitious man. In 2006, the FBI secretly recorded New York gangsters in an intimate conversation during which Michael Cassese announced that Montagna was now the family's acting boss, according to court documents. "There's nobody in between. That's it," the gangster said of Montagna's new position as the family's top authority. Not long after, Montgana was yanked out of the shadows and thrust onto the front page of New York's *Daily News*, which revealed his unexpected ascent and colorfully dubbed him the "Bambino Boss" because of his youth, just 36 years old. The Bonanno clan, of course, was a fragment of its former self: Montagna's predecessors Joseph "Big Joey" Massino and Vincent "Vinny Gorgeous" Basciano had been arrested and convicted; Massino had turned informant and Basciano was serving life in prison for murder. Wealthy, strong, stable, low-key, having displayed *omertà* in the face of a grand jury and with Sicilian roots and Canadian ties, Montagna had many attractive qualities as a mobster. His biggest selling point, however, was that he had little intimate contact with the Bonanno mafiosi who had become government informants. The family needed a fresh beginning and someone like Montagna was necessary to finally break the chain of high-ranking turncoats fingering the boss and the boss then fingering his inner circle who, in turn, fingered the emerging replacement boss. Only someone outside the clique could stop that destructive cycle. Despite his youth, Montagna was old school, retaining a sense of what he had seen in Montreal and Sicily, and the Montagna family's hometown in Sicily was about as good a lineage as it gets in the Bonanno clan: Castellammare del Golfo, the home of Joseph Bonanno, who gave his name to the New York clan.

Being a Mafia boss has many benefits but one distinct drawback is that it makes you an enormous target for police. With no informant to provide direct evidence on Montagna in their bag of tricks, authorities looked for other weaknesses and discovered that Montagna was not actually an American citizen. This was important, because his conviction for contempt of court was enough to make any foreign national ineligible for U.S. residency. In April 2009, the Bambino Boss was arrested in New York and deportation proceedings started. He had a choice of where he could land: Canada, where he was born, or Italy, where his parents were born. Montagna chose Montreal. Just about six hours' drive north of New York, it wasn't impossible for him to run the family from there. And Canada had possibilities. Montagna knew of the upheaval in Montreal. He knew that where there is chaos there can be opportunity. Or disaster.

In Montreal, Montagna had rules to follow, in keeping with Mafia convention. He had to visit the resident bosses and explain why he was on their turf. He could operate, but only in conjunction with the locals. It was a replay of the tension a generation before when Paolo Violi complained about Nicolò Rizzuto arriving in Montreal. Montgana visited the big shooters in the Canadian underworld, not just in Montreal, but also in Toronto and Hamilton. The Ontario cities, he found, were hotbeds of anti-Rizzuto sentiment. He was greeted with the respect that comes with being the head of a New York Mafia family. He met Sicilian and Calabrian gangsters and the remnants of the old American La Cosa Nostra. Montagna knew not to ask too much and not to be judgmental. He understood the Sicilian proverb that the mouth is for eating. Everything started smoothly.

As the murderous violence reduced the Sixth Family, almost everyone else in Montreal's underworld saw their relative value and strength rise by default. Gangsters move to fill any vacuum. When an emboldened Montagna met with Nicolò to convince the old man that a new reality was at work in the underworld, that New York was ready to settle things down, Nicolò was reportedly cold and dismissive; Montagna had Sicilian roots but he was still just a man of the American Mafia from a discredited underworld family. Further, Nicolò, like an aging dynastic emperor, seemed unable to contemplate his own family's fall. Many others, however, were agitating for just such an outcome. Police intelligence officers tried to keep up with this new wild card. Working with wiretaps and informants, a theory emerged that Montagna had aligned himself as part of a consortium that was formed, at first, to find a new leader who could keep Montreal under control. The others thought to be in on the scheme included longtime Rizzuto loyalist Raynald Desjardins and his brother-in-law, Mafia veteran Joe DiMaulo, who had weathered more than a half-century in underworld intrigue.

With so much at stake and with competing interests and emotions, the consortium soon crumbled into internecine feuding. DiMaulo and Desjardins' familial connection might have made Montagna feel increasingly isolated. Part of the discomfort may have come from claims that, in direct conflict with accepted Mafia standards, Vito had personally inducted Desjardins, a French-Canadian without Italian lineage, into the organization alongside another loyal non-Italian, Juan Ramon Fernandez, the enforcer known as Joe Bravo, who was a Spaniard. Such a breach would never play well with a Sicilian traditionalist. Or, at least, be cynically used to sow seeds of discontent with other mafiosi. In September 2011, Desjardins escaped an assassination attempt.

Suspicion fell on Montgana, who seemed to run with the New York strategy of trying to kill first. Having failed, however, the reaction was Montreal style: kill better.

On November 24, 2011, Montagna went to a meeting at a home in Charlemagne, a North Shore suburb of Montreal. If he didn't know he was marked for death when he walked through the door, he certainly did when he left through a window; bleeding from bullet wounds, he fled from his attackers through the deep snow. Robust, he reached the narrow, frigid water of the Assomption River and somehow managed to swim to the other side. When police, alerted by neighbors who heard the sound of gunfire, arrived, they found the well-dressed Montagna clinging to life in the bloodstained snow on the riverbank, but their resuscitation efforts failed. He was 42 years old. Several men were subsequently arrested in the slaying, Desjardins prominent among them. As of spring 2014 he had not yet faced trial.

Hearing of such intense internal dissent from men Vito had expected only loyalty, or at least obedience, from must have burned in his mind as he plotted his return from prison. His woes, however, were not confined to mere bullets and blood. As if he did not have enough to cope with, word also reached him of a brewing political scandal in his home province that threatened to expose his empire even more.

––––––––

Project Colisée had been damaging to the Sixth Family, but that police operation was limited in scope, focusing on drugs, violence and gambling. In fact, the Sixth Family leadership might well have breathed a sigh of relief when told what information was contained in the prosecutors' evidence. Other crimes that inevitably stumbled into the investigators' frame had been purposely overlooked. Corruption, kickbacks, collusion—it was all set aside as "non-pertinent information," the commission heard, despite evidence of millions of dollars being siphoned out of the construction industry and ending up in the Sixth Family's coffers.

A police probe for drug trafficking would be expected by the Sixth Family and factored in as a cost of doing business; what came next, however, was likely not something ever anticipated. The rampant corruption was almost overlooked—as it usually is—until the autumn of 2011 when the Liberal premier of Quebec, Jean Charest, squeezed by damning news exposés and opposition rhetoric, agreed to establish a commission of inquiry to get to the bottom of the potentially inappropriate relationship between developers, builders, politicians and gangsters in the province. The Commission of Inquiry on the Awarding and Management of Public Contracts in the Construction Industry was born but its wordy name ensured it would be known as the Charbonneau Commission, after the remarkable woman chosen to chair it: Justice France Charbonneau of the Superior Court of Quebec.

The Charbonneau commission was not a roundtable of chin-wagging experts contemplating a theoretical problem. Under Charbonneau's firm hand, it became a full-on crusade with the power to subpoena witnesses, conduct searches and seize documents and private records. As the commission began its inquiry, it immediately came across the Sixth Family and, after the public hearings began on May 22, 2012, the Mafia's poisonous role in public affairs took center stage.

Getting that compelling evidence—the so-called "non-pertinent information" that had been set aside during Project Colisée—out of the RCMP's hands and onto the public record, however, was bizarrely difficult, requiring the commission to fight the RCMP in court. After winning access to the footage, hours of it was broadcast, playing live online and winning endless repeats on newscasts. Not only were the secret surveillance videos of magnates paying money and respect to mobsters not pursued criminally by the RCMP, in some cases the hidden microphones were actually shut off—so the conversations were not recorded—because the subjects were not of interest to the RCMP, a representative of the federal force testified at the commission. Even with that difficult limitation it was clear there was a long line of developers attending the secretive back room of the Sixth Family's social club. Video of the men turning over stacks of cash to the gangsters and of Nicolò then stuffing it into his socks riveted the nation and became an Internet meme. People ogled secret police video of a Sixth Family Christmas party, where businessmen exchanged two-cheek kisses with mafiosi. The commission heard that Quebec businessmen paid the Sixth Family 2.5% of the value of the public works contracts their firms were awarded.

The commission then called many of the businessmen to appear under oath before it to explain what was going on. Among the reluctant witnesses were the formerly merry men of Cattolica Eraclea. In fact, the Rizzutos' obscure Sicilian hometown became central to the alleged corruption plot. Most of the Montreal contractors working on sewer and sidewalk projects had direct ties to the town. The commission was told of a corporate cartel that divided lucrative and inflated public works contracts amongst themselves in a bid-rigging scheme. Lino Zambito, a Montreal construction boss who became a star witness, said he was allowed entry into the cartel because his father, Giuseppe, was from Cattolica Eraclea. Many of the businessmen accused of consorting with the Rizzutos had Cattolica ties, including Domenico Arcuri, the owner of a decontamination company who is the son of an alleged mobster from Cattolica; Accursio Sciascia, a paving company boss who was vice-president of Montreal's Association Cattolica Eraclea; Frank Catania, founder of a road construction firm, who is another Cattolica émigré; and others. Nicolo Milioto, a former construction boss, also from Cattolica Eraclea, was described by witnesses as a middleman who helped exchange cash between the Mafia and the construction world. Milioto was nicknamed "Mr. Sidewalk" because of his dominance in that construction specialty, although he steadfastly denied any collusion, even though the RCMP had tracked him making 236 visits to the Rizzutos' café.

One construction boss testified that Vito appeared unexpectedly at a meeting in a Laval restaurant to tell him not to bid on a $25-million public contract. The commission heard that Vito took city officials, including engineers Gilles Surprenant and Luc Leclerc, on free trips to the Dominican Republic, where they played golf. In return, they were expected to fiddle with the value of city construction projects that Vito's friends were getting. Appearing before the commission, Surprenant testified he accepted more than $700,000 in cash bribes from various construction bosses in return for help rigging bids; Leclerc testified he received at least $500,000 in kickbacks.

The repercussions of the evidence gathered at the Charbonneau Commission and a renewed push against corruption shook the province of Quebec. City halls and political offices were raided. In November 2012, Gilles Vaillancourt, the mayor of the city of Laval, resigned after police searched his home, municipal buildings and safety deposit boxes, although he denied wrongdoing. Six months later he was arrested and charged with gangsterism. He is fighting the charges, and at the time of writing the trial had not yet taken place. Montreal mayor Gérald Tremblay also resigned in November after the commission heard that his party, Union Montreal, received a 3% kickback on city sewerage rehabilitation contracts allegedly awarded to the mob-backed cartel. Although insisting he had done nothing wrong, he said he was stepping aside for the greater good of the city.

Montreal's political crisis did not abate: Tremblay's replacement, Michael Applebaum, was forced to resign in June 2013, after his arrest on 14 charges, including fraud, conspiracy and breach of trust, not in connection with mob collusion, but over two real estate transactions. He maintains his innocence and vowed to clear his name at a forthcoming trial.

The insidious nature of the Mafia in Montreal was slowly being revealed. Citizens who once shrugged at mob antics that did not seem to hurt them were getting a look at the true predatory nature of the Sixth Family. Those who were indifferent to gangsters killing each other suddenly learned that the mobsters' corrupting influence was said to have inflated the price of public works projects by as much as 30%. Taxpayers then also heard that the commission's spotlight had already saved them money by forcing the mob's "tax" to be cut in half.

"We'd heard that 30% was billed and now that number is 15%," Sergent-Détective Eric Vecchio of the Montreal police, who was seconded to the commission, testified. Public scrutiny was cutting into Vito's profits. Businessmen who had once felt safe dealing with the Sixth Family realized that contact could one day ruin their reputation. In many ways, the Charbonneau Commission was hurting the Sixth Family more than Project Colisée had. Without the private bonds that were being described at the commission, the Sixth Family could not be the power it was because, ultimately, such relationships in the realms of business, politics, the justice system and the church are what separate the Mafia from street gangs. Drug routes could be rebuilt much more easily than such deep-seated connections to the upper world.

Further, the timing of the Charbonneau revelations could not have been worse for Vito. Just weeks before he was set to be released, former FBI agent Joseph Pistone, better known as Donnie Brasco—the alias he used for years while infiltrating the Bonanno family in New York—took the stand at the Charbonneau Commission. Pistone was undercover at the time of the three captains' murders for which Vito was imprisoned. Pistone's evidence about the way the Mafia works elicited international headlines. Next, RCMP Corporal Linda Féquière testified that the Mafia's Calabrian faction seemed to be back on top. "I'm not saying the Sicilian faction has completely disappeared, but there is a return of the Calabrian faction that happened after the arrest and extradition of Vito Rizzuto," she said.

And finally, as Vito was packing his few things in prison for his return to Canada, the Charbonneau Commission was preparing a subpoena to force him to answer questions. Vito knew his old nemesis, Paolo Violi, once faced the same fate. Violi's refusal to cooperate sent him to jail for contempt. Vito had had enough of bars.

———

As Vito received this unremittingly bad news while he was in prison, it must have brought an immense weight of bitterness, sorrow and anger. If he had not been arrested, if he had been on the street, it would have all played out differently, regardless of whether he decided to broker peace or wage war. Police officers realized Vito's dilemma and tried to turn his family's misfortunes into an opportunity. Investigators from Canada and the United States repeatedly visited him in his Colorado prison during the turmoil. They arrived with a list of questions they wanted answered, offering protection for him and his family in return. Despite the stakes, the offers were rejected. He showed no interest. His sole emotion was one of annoyance at the interruptions. He didn't need police help, he needed only his freedom. And that day was getting closer.

Everyone braced for what might happen upon his release. Police prepared for his revenge. Gangland rivals did too. Journalists started writing Vito's obituary. His friends were anxious about what they might be asked to do and fearful of whether even Vito could turn the tide. There was underworld chatter of a hit squad of loyal Rizzuto triggermen gathering in Hamilton to prepare for whatever the boss wanted them to do. Police in Montreal were on high alert for unexpected movement by underworld figures of both high and low rank. Adding to the uncertainty was news that the comfortable mansion in Montreal where Vito and his wife, Giovanna, had lived for 30 years, where their children had been raised and where Vito had been arrested, was on the market, for just under $2 million. "This beautiful stone residence was custom built to the highest quality standards and is now being sold for the first time by the original owner," said the real estate listing. Liza Kaufman, the sales agent, said Vito's wife's circumstances had changed: "It is a typical case of an empty nester. I know she wants to downsize." Many wondered if this meant that Vito was abandoning Montreal. Or even Canada.

"If you look at the TV or read the news, you have the impression Mr. Rizzuto will come out of jail with two machine guns and a tank and two revolvers around his belt," Jean Salois, Vito's longtime lawyer, who retired before Vito was even extradited, said before Vito's release date, trying to dampen expectations of violence. "It must be a very hard time for him. To lose a son, his father, his brother-in-law would be a big burden. You read the news, and Mr. Rizzuto will come out of jail and avenge the loss of his father and his son and so on and so forth. This is kind of ridiculous." But even Salois acknowledged the reality: "He is not the kind of man to hide if there is a problem."

MONTREAL, OCTOBER 5, 2012

He may not have precisely been hiding, but Vito spent his first few weeks of freedom in relative privacy, with much of it spent living at the homes of friends and relatives in the Toronto area. In Montreal, he avoided his mansion, still on the market at the time, for a condominium where loyal soldiers stayed in units nearby.

At secure, well-guarded homes in both Toronto and Montreal, Vito summoned people for one-on-one audiences with the returning boss. It is a truism of the Mafia that when the boss calls you in, you have to go. To ignore the summons would be a death sentence or, at least, an iridescent flare that you no longer accepted Vito as the boss, which could amount to the same thing. Many would have gone to the meeting knowing it was an open question whether they would come out alive.

"A lot of them thought they were going to be killed. One of the greatest moves Vito made was to call people into a meeting and tell them he was in charge. He just stated the fact," said a source with knowledge of the meetings. Vito's face was more fearsome to many than a rival's gun. "You need to have an air of terror about you," the source added. Vito wanted to know: How far did you go to help "the family"? It's one thing to have kept your business going, but how far did each man who was called in to account for his actions go to help the family? How far did each go to betray the family?

"Sit down, tell me," Vito told them, his voice and face calm, cool, the source said. Spoken or unspoken, the follow-up was understood: "Then I'll decide if you live or die."

Many saw Vito's seeming disappearance as a sign of his weakness and fear. It was really a quiet prelude before the storm. He needed to know who was with him, who was against him and who was declining to take a side. He was surveying the battlefield, inspecting his troops, assessing his assets and liabilities. Anyone thinking he was retiring was delusional.

"He's not running or retiring. He's a mobster until they put him in the ground," an organized crime investigator, who was watching Vito closely, said at the time. One large gambling operation in Toronto that had stopped paying a cut to Montreal after Vito's extradition—handing it instead to gangsters of Calabrian descent in Toronto—came back into the Sixth Family fold when Vito returned. "Everyone made a ton of money with Vito. Making money is the fundamental fact of organized crime and they knew they would continue making money with Vito," the investigator said.

The fundamental question Vito needed to answer was not who had attacked his family and his business; he surely knew that. His fundamental question was why the Sixth Family faltered so catastrophically while he was away. Maybe Vito had not prepared his men for leadership because nobody, including himself, believed he wouldn't be there to be the boss. Maybe Project Colisée took out too many of his senior guys at the same time. Perhaps too many of the Sixth Family leaders only knew how to lead in a time of peace and had not trained to be gangsters in a time of war. When a mobster comes of age always getting what he wants just by asking, how does he perform when all of a sudden he needs to take it by force? Perhaps times had changed. Or perhaps the underworld needed Vito Rizzuto more than anyone realized.

It took one month for Vito to act, although with events so recent and raw and no judicial accounting of what happened, everything described next is based on fragmentary evidence.

On November 4, 2012, a month after Vito's release and a week before the anniversary of Nicolò's murder, shots were fired in Blainville, a suburb of Montreal. An ambulance was called to a large home on a wide street nestled along the woods of a golf course, where almost every home has a swimming pool. There, Joe DiMaulo, the veteran mobster, was found dead in his driveway. He was 70 years old. When news of the murder first broke, the initial reaction was that the attacks against the traditional powers of the mob were continuing, but DiMaulo's murder is now pegged as the start of Vito's battle to retain his crown. DiMaulo was part of the unsanctioned consortium trying to settle Montreal's leadership quandary while Vito was away, along with Desjardins and Montagna. Cooperating in that ill-fated venture was seen as casting his lot in with the renegade faction. It was DiMaulo trying to do what he had always done best—back the winning side in any dispute, just as he had done when the Sixth Family seized Montreal—but this time getting it wrong. When the Sixth Family—and indeed Vito's direct kin—needed him most, DiMaulo had failed to answer the call. It was a notable place for Vito to start. For those looking for such things, there was the added symbolism that DiMaulo being shot in the head at home in the evening, left to be discovered by his distraught wife, was all strikingly similar to Nicolò's demise.

It looked a shrewd and chilling strategy: don't lunge at the enemies who had always hated you and continued to hate you, but rather first kill your friends who had not done enough to support you or had betrayed you. It suggests that to Vito, disloyalty was the cardinal sin.

BAGHERIA, SICILY, APRIL 9, 2013

If there was anyone Vito needed in a time of war, it might have been Juan Ramon Fernandez, his rock-ribbed, loyal henchman known in Ontario by the assumed named Joe Bravo. Morally cold and physically strong, he had the proven parts to kill and a passionate, demonic presence that instilled fear in almost everyone. Fernandez, who led Vito's expansion into Ontario, had paid the price for his fierce brand of gangsterism with prison time although incarceration did not have the same effect on him as it did on most. In prison, he was at the top of the inmate food chain. While in maximum security he still managed to arrange hash shipments from Jamaica, tamper with a witness testifying against him and orchestrate attacks on inmates at other prisons. Upon his release in April 2012, he was immediately deported to his native Spain but as the war against the Sixth Family continued, there was high expectation he would return to Canada to extract his boss's revenge.

Fernandez did not stay long in Spain but he didn't return to Canada, instead settling in Bagheria, a Mafia stronghold outside Sicily's capital of Palermo, the very heart of the Sicilian Mafia. He chose the city because at least ten mafiosi living there had close ties to Canada, most with the Sixth Family. It was police in Canada who learned of his resettlement and tipped off Italian investigators as to who it was strutting through town and meeting with traditional mafiosi as if he himself were a Man of Honor. Part of Fernandez's appeal to the gangsters was his ability to arrange lucrative shipments of oxycodone pills from Sicily into Canada, and cocaine to Sicily and Canada from Ecuador and Colombia.

"Fernandez lived in Sicily, but his heart and his mind were in Toronto. He thought every day of the business of Toronto. His business was still there, every day he was in contact with his men in Toronto," said Lieutenant-Colonel Fabio Bottino, commander in Palermo of the Carabinieri ROS, the special paramilitary police unit that probes sophisticated organized crime and transnational crime. "And Canadian men came to Italy to meet with him and talk to him about his business in Toronto and in Montreal." Police in Sicily started an intensive investigation of Fernandez and the mafiosi he was mingling with. There was much upheaval in Bagheria, similar to that in Montreal. Just as they had done in Canada, police in Italy secretly listened as Fernandez spoke with both Sicilian and visiting Canadian gangsters. Fernandez's hubris once again made him vulnerable. The Carabinieri had his BMW X5 and his phones. Some of what they heard was shocking.

Declaring that Vito "makes the fucking rules" regardless of what Mafia bosses in Sicily thought, Fernandez vociferously asserted his right to sit at the table with the Men of Honor. "Vito 'made' me and my *compare*, Raynald," he said, a shocking claim that Vito had officially inducted two non-Italians into the Mafia.

"You're not Italian," replied the bewildered man he was speaking with.

"No, no. Me and my *compare*," Fernandez insisted, were "made" men despite their lineage. When faced with further disbelief, Fernandez started bellowing and pounding his fist against his thigh as if he wanted to pound them into his visitor instead.

"Show some respect. I sit at the right hand of God, that's how close I am," he said of his relationship with Vito.

"But I thought that . . ." the man stammered and then stopped, apparently comprehending the dangerous look in Fernandez's eyes. The man's voice turned quiet and meek as he added, "I just thought you couldn't because you're not Italian."

Along with the shocking notion of Vito breaking the centuries-old law of the Mafia by admitting non-Italians as members—and of Fernandez having the stones to openly talk about it in Sicily—police also uncovered his drug network and the power struggle within the

Bagheria Mafia with Fernandez at its center. They also tracked regular phone calls from a lawyer in Canada who seemed to be relaying instructions to Fernandez, Italian police said. In fact, police allege, the lawyer was in close contact with both sides in the internal Bagheria dispute. Then, as police in Sicily prepared to move against the conspiring mobsters, Fernandez's voice completely disappeared from the wires. Had he been tipped to the police probe? Had he returned to Canada to stand at Vito's side? Neither.

On April 9, 2013, Fernandez, with a friend from Canada, Fernando Pimentel, drove to a meeting to close a marijuana deal with two brothers, Pietro and Salvatore Scaduto, authorities allege. The brothers, born in Sicily, had moved to Canada in 1989 after their father, a Mafia boss in Bagheria, was killed. Pietro Scaduto was deported back to Italy after he was involved in the botched Toronto mob shooting in 2004 that left Louise Russo, an innocent mother, paralyzed. Fernandez was heard many times on the wiretaps extolling their friendship. Fernandez and Pimentel arrived at the meeting in an isolated field outside Bagheria, where Fernandez was told a large marijuana crop was being harvested. As they got out of the car, the pair was met with a fusillade of bullets which killed them both. It was the sort of planned ambush that would be needed to kill someone as feared as Fernandez. Before their bodies were rolled to the side of the dirt road and set ablaze, the gold Rolex watch on Fernandez's wrist was removed.

It was not only a valuable piece of jewelry. Investigators in Canada believe the watch was given to him by Vito. Italian police had heard him say it was the only piece of his jewelry not confiscated by police in Canada. "He loved that watch. Every day he wore this watch. Every day," said Lieutenant-Colonel Bottino. Days later, someone was caught selling that Rolex for 3,000 euros. In a police sweep that followed, 21 men were arrested for various charges, including the Scadutos, who were charged with the two murders. When police searched Fernandez's home in Bagheria, they found that the Rolex was not the only memento he brought with him from Canada; among his possessions were two first-edition copies of this book, one in English and one in Italian, which he had inscribed and signed in the front cover.

The case in Italy shed light on the war in Canada. Italian investigators say that even though Fernandez spoke passionately about Vito's power, he was reluctant to support him in the underworld war if it meant going against Desjardins. Fernandez had told associates in Sicily he was close to Vito but also close to Desjardins, whom he named as leading the rebel faction in Canada, police in Italy said. "He didn't want to take a side in the dispute. He wanted to stay neutral," said Bottino. In Vito's new world order, there was no place for neutrality, no matter where one lived. But a purge of deserters was not the only part of Vito's plan.

WOODBRIDGE, ONTARIO, JULY 12, 2013

It was around 1 a.m. when Salvatore Calautti left a large bachelor party at the Terrace Banquet Centre, an opulent rental hall in Vaughan, just north of Toronto, with his pal and underworld associate, James Tusek. Calautti climbed into his black BMW X6 in the parking lot. The lot is within sight of a police station but that proximity provided no deterrence to the gunman who came up to Calautti and opened fire, killing him in his seat with a bullet to his head before shooting Tusek, who was hit in his stomach and chest and left to die. Calautti was 41 years old; Tusek, 35.

The death of Calautti took guests at the stag by surprise but to many who knew of his past, it seemed a fitting end. Calautti was a suspect in so many slayings and attempted murders that he was seen as something of a mob hitman; almost all of those he was accused of attacking were ambushed in their cars or vans.

Among the slayings Calautti was likely involved in was that of Gaetano Panepinto, Rizzuto's man in Ontario who ran a discount-coffin shop before his 2000 shooting. Calautti was also rumored to have been involved in the slaying of Nicolò Rizzuto. Whether he was in Montreal at the time is not yet known, but with rumors flying and his reputation as a triggerman for the Calabrian 'Ndrangheta leaders in Toronto, it seemed at least plausible. It is rumored that several 'Ndrangheta clans had a representative in Montreal for the slaying, to share the credit—or spread the blame if it went awry. Calautti also had his own beef with the Sixth Family. In recent times he had found himself under pressure over a large gambling debt owed to a Rizzuto-allied bookmaker. Calautti had turned to members of the *camera di controllo*, the Toronto 'Ndrangheta's board of control, for protection and support. The Calabrian mobsters were ready to help because of Calautti's constant willingness to throw his muscle around on the street on their behalf, collecting debts and settling scores. Calautti and Tusek also had ties to Vincenzo "Jimmy" DeMaria, named by authorities as an important 'Ndrangheta boss in Toronto, and to DeMaria's cousin, Nicola

Cortese, who himself had been caught up in the intrigue of the sniper attack on Nicolò when he was arrested in a Canadian Tire store in Montreal three days after the patriarch was shot. He was caught trying to shoplift a handgun holster, an ammunition pouch for 12-gauge shotgun shells, a black balaclava and a rubber car part that could double as a silencer, all while carrying a roll of $100 bills totaling $3,000. Police questioned Cortese about Nicolò's shooting and wanted to know why Cortese returned to Canada from Italy only days before the attack, but found no evidence linking him to it.

Vito's information on the death of his father was likely more fulsome than anyone's and if he had concluded Calautti was somehow involved, it is an easy explanation for the gunshots outside the stag. And if it was not about avenging Nicolò's murder, Calautti's willingness to fearlessly attack on the Calabrians' behalf still provided good reason why Vito might want to draw a line in the sand with Calautti's blood between himself and Toronto's belligerent Calabrian gangsters.

ACAPULCO, MEXICO, NOVEMBER 10, 2013

Moreno Gallo was dining with a friend at the Forza Italia restaurant in Acapulco, a popular eatery with two levels of seating and an outdoor patio, when two men dressed in black came up to him and shot him several times in the head and chest at close range. The professional-style hit left him no chance of survival. He was 68 years old.

Those trying to envision who might step in to fill Vito's void had often mentioned Gallo's name. He had well-regarded diplomatic skills and longevity in the mob as one of the old-timers who effortlessly moved to the Rizzuto faction once it was clear Montreal's Calabrian faction had lost the 1970s war. He was a good earner who dutifully brought a sizable wad of cash as tribute to the Sixth Family. And he had killed—a drug-related murder in 1974—which is always a plus in the Mafia. His great weakness, however, was that after his conviction for the killing he remained on lifetime parole, which restricted whom he could associate with and where he could travel. During the recent troubles in Montreal, Gallo was said to have acted as something of a go-between or arbiter. He seemed to share sympathies with the recently slain DiMaulo.

Any chance of a promotion, however, was trampled when police used a 2005 Project Colisée video of him handing over a stack of cash to Nicolò as proof of a parole violation to send him back to prison. Things took a stranger turn for him when the renewed scrutiny uncovered a clerical error made during his original incarceration in the 1970s. Gallo had moved to Canada from Italy when he was nine years old but never became a Canadian citizen, yet when he was sent to prison he was mistakenly labeled a Canadian, meaning deportation was not an issue. After his parole revocation in 2007, that mistake was spotted and authorities deported him as a foreign national convicted of a serious crime. He left Canada in 2012 and moved to Mexico. He was fighting in court for the right to return to Canada but the gunmen at the Forza Italia put an end to that.

Once again, it seemed Vito had ignored the low-hanging fruit to select a target who was expected to have remained loyal to his clan. And once again, with the murder falling on the very anniversary of Nicolò's assassination, it was a hit offering tantalizing symbolism.

Taken as a whole, the Sicilian defense—whether Vito's passionate revenge or his dispassionate strategy to reclaim his underworld throne—came in well-selected precision strikes, not in a wanton bloodbath. He struck in Quebec, in Ontario, in Sicily and in Mexico. Vito knew the Mafia lesson taught by his father: you punish one to teach a thousand. His message was received. Montreal seemed to more or less return to its subservient state; Toronto seemed cowed and silent, unwilling or unable to finish the job of toppling the Sixth Family.

By the end of 2013, just 12 months after returning from a foreign prison to again take the helm of a crippled and humbled organization, he had improbably reclaimed his crown. It was perhaps his most stunning achievement. What could possibly stop him?

MONTREAL, DECEMBER 23, 2013

To the outside world, Vito Rizzuto was back on top of his game, free, triumphal and feared, but he carried a secret that only those closest to him knew: he was suffering from lung cancer. He had complained of chest ailments in 2007 when he pleaded guilty, with his lawyers telling New York Judge Nicholas Garaufis that he recently had an X-ray that showed a spot on his lung. At the time, he had been waiting two months for a CAT scan to determine what it was. His complaint was not given much weight; officials believed it was a ploy for judicial sympathy, perhaps with an eye to gaining an early prisoner transfer back to Canada or easier accommodations while incarcerated.

The media and police suddenly remembered that old complaint when news broke that Vito had collapsed in his home early Sunday morning. In a panic, his wife, Giovanna, called an ambulance and Vito was taken to Sacré-Coeur Hospital where, at 4 a.m. on Monday, December 23, 2013, he died. The cause of death was pneumonia as a complication of his lung cancer, said his old lawyer, Jean Salois. Cancer: a foe even more unrelenting than the Mafia.

Vito Rizzuto was 67 years old.

It seemed almost unbelievable. The man who was born into a gang-ster clan in Sicily, who took a burgeoning underworld empire forged by his father and transformed it into an unparalleled, made-in-Canada criminal brand, had died at a relatively young age of natural causes. He had become the biggest name in crime and likely the most powerful criminal boss Canada will ever know.

"Mr. Rizzuto would never talk about how powerful he was, if he really was; he would never talk about that to anyone. That is not the type of man he was," Salois said. "He was a very likable guy. He was polite. He was a polyglot. He could talk business, politics, whatever you wanted to discuss. If you did not know that he was Vito Rizzuto, I could present him to you and you would think he is the president of a big company."

News of his death elicited disbelief.

"Here was a man driven—driven by plans, by objectives, driven by power, driven by his family name, someone who was a part of the underworld royalty internationally, I can't believe this is the end," said a police officer who spent years investigating Vito. "He has survived so much. Who would think his body would fail him?" And an underworld figure who once hung around daily with the Montreal Mafia declared: "I'm not counting Vito out 'till I see his body myself. Then I'm going to poke him, just to be sure." There really was no doubt although, bi-zarrely for a man such as he, there was no autopsy performed.

Over two days, hundreds of mourners shuffled through the Loreto funeral home, filling its upper and lower floors. The entire facility had been set aside for Vito's farewell; one room was filled, nearly floor to ceiling, with dozens of ornate and intricate floral arrangements. In a second large room, Giovanna and her and Vito's surviving chil-dren, Leonardo and Bettina, stood with other family members greeting mourners near his casket. Bravely, they gave kisses, hugs and thanks to those who came, offering comfort instead of expecting it from others.

As news cameras jostled to capture the solemn grandeur of Vito Rizzuto's funeral on December 29, the bell atop the Church of the

Madonna della Difesa once more issued a slow toll for the Rizzuto family. Inside, to a packed crowd—despite several journalists and others not deemed family or friends being ejected—Monsignor Igino Incantalupo led a Catholic funeral mass in Italian, just as he had done for Vito's father. Afterwards, the solemn, sonorous sound of the church bell accompanied the gold-colored casket, followed by Vito's family, down the front steps of the church built by Italian immigrants to serve their countrymen in Canada's oldest Italian community. Inside the church are spectacular frescoes, including one striking image of fascist dictator Benito Mussolini mounted on a steed, painted before the Second World War. Outside, mourners filed past a statue commemorating the victims of war. The sculptor may not have envisioned this type of war, a dirty street battle for criminal supremacy, but the statue seems appropriate as no other church in North America has sent more mobsters to the great beyond than this.

The magnificent outline of the church was a comforting façade for a grieving family but, in death, provided one last controversy: Why was the Catholic Church providing such pageantry for a man who had become synonymous with organized crime in this community? And what message was it sending to the eagerly watching community?

"I think mafiosi should not be granted the sacraments and, on the occasion of their funerals, should be restricted solely to the blessing of the coffin, with no homilies," Nicola Gratteri, Italy's best-known anti-mob prosecutor, said after the spectacle. "The risk is to legitimize the strength and power of mafiosi within the territory. The funeral pomp ensures maximum visibility and legitimacy. They should be avoided. The Mafia often communicates with a non-verbal language. . . . Funerals and weddings have always been functional to power."

Monsignor Incantalupo defended his actions, saying: "He was a Christian and he had the right to have a funeral in the church. Now, I know that everyone is not in agreement with that but the church cannot refuse a baptized person. We don't have to judge so that is why we make the funeral of that guy and to make the funeral of his father two years ago and of his son more years ago. It's not my problem. I don't have to judge anybody. I don't know even if before he died if he didn't ask [for] confession. I don't know. I don't judge. The family asked for a service and we did it. The church doesn't refuse anybody."

That was not always the case, however. After the 1997 murder of Mafia boss Johnny "Pops" Papalia, the old don from Hamilton, the city's bishop said a funeral mass was out of the question. Instead, the family's priest gave a simple blessing in a private funeral chapel. And in Sicily, recently, church leaders declared that convicted mobsters would be refused a church funeral, with Bishop Antonino Raspanti declaring: "Being a Christian is incompatible with having links to Mafia organizations."

While clerics and theologians contemplated how funerals of such notorious figures might best be handled in the future, wider attention turned to a conundrum of a more worldly nature. With Vito now well and truly gone, how might the immense void be filled?

Answers will not come easily.

It is difficult to see any one man fully replacing him. There will certainly be a new boss anointed, likely a relative of some kind, and, if not, a proven member from one of the trusted clans the Rizzutos have long been close to. The Sixth Family will not disappear with Vito. It has been a resilient, organic entity for generations. The new leader, however, is unlikely to retain the hegemony Vito built. It is difficult to foresee Canada ever again having such a single, dominant boss.

Maybe the Calabrian gangsters of Toronto will retreat to their former insular ways, again splitting the country's underworld between Montreal and Toronto. Maybe a Calabrian boss will try to run the show as Vito's replacement or maybe there will be a board of control, mimicking the *camera di controllo* model of the 'Ndrangheta. After all, Canada is a multicultural country always willing to experiment with new ideas, even unnatural ones.

For the Sixth Family, a period of retraction and retrenchment seems likely.

And, one day, regrowth.

Principal Sources and References

PROLOGUE:

The murder of the three captains is drawn from the trial testimony of a number of former Bonanno members who agreed to cooperate with the government, particularly that of Salvatore Vitale and Frank Lino, in *U.S.A. v. Joseph Massino* (02-CR-307, Eastern District of New York) in 2004 and *U.S.A. v. Vincent Basciano* (03-CR-929, Eastern District of NY) in 2006; internal FBI reports of earlier debriefings of the same men; "Record of the Case for the Prosecution," filed in Quebec Superior Court in support of the U.S. request for extradition of Vito Rizzuto; autopsy results by the New York Medical Examiner's Office; and visits to the locations involved. Early suspicion of Vito's involvement comes from "La Cosa Nostra in Canada," a Federal Bureau of Investigation internal report prepared in March 1985. The extent of Sixth Family holdings comes from multiple court files, internal American and Canadian law enforcement reports and interviews.

CHAPTER 1:

Information on Cattolica Eraclea and Agrigento comes from several visits from 2004 to 2006. Additional details were provided by the Comune di Cattolica Eraclea, the town's administration. The life story of Vito's namesake grandfather was uncovered by the authors in old, previously secret—and sometimes crumbling—government files and old passenger manifests, including records from the U.S. Citizenship and Immigration Services, U.S. Department of State, the National Archives and Records Administration and the Ispettorato Dell'Emigrazione in Italy. Other details come from Italian genealogical records; law enforcement reports and briefings from Italy, the United States and Canada; interviews and family charts.

CHAPTER 2:

The early Rizzuto activities in America, the arsons, the visa frauds and the messy demise of Vito's grandfather come from several of the old files listed above, along with records from the County of Putnam District Attorney's Office, the coroner's report and contemporary news articles from *The Putnam County Courier* and *The New York Times*.

CHAPTER 3:

The Rizzutos' early life comes from Italian genealogical records, law enforcement reports and briefings from Italy, the United States and Canada, passenger manifests, interviews and family charts. "The Rothschilds of the Mafia on Aruba" by Tom Blickman (*Transnational Organized Crime*, Vol. 3, No. 2, Summer 1997) was helpful. Details on the murder of the mayor and its fallout comes from court documents from the Corte di Assise di Agrigento and the Corte di Appello di Palermo, confidential Canadian police reports and contemporary news accounts in several Italian newspapers. The quote from the Agrigento judge comes from *Mafioso* by Gaia Servadio (Sever & Warburg Ltd., London, 1976).

CHAPTER 4:

The Sixth Family's relocation comes from records of the Canada Border Services Agency and other law enforcement agencies, including a private briefing by the RCMP on the Sixth Family and a dossier on Vito prepared by Montreal police filed in Quebec Court of Appeal, June 29, 2004 (No. 500-10-002800-041), translated from French. Further details come from Port of Halifax records held by the National Archives of Canada. Cross-border travel by Sixth Family stalwarts comes from sources in the border security sector. Montreal's early criminal milieu is drawn from a study of several files held by the U.S. National Archives and Records Administration and the National Archives of Canada, law enforcement reports, interviews with both underworld figures and retired investigators and contemporary news accounts. A better understanding of the early organization of the Montreal mob, as well as direct quotes, come from author interviews with former senior mafioso Bill Bonanno in 2007. A huge number of documents on Carmine Galante were released by the FBI under the Freedom of Information (FOI) Act. *The Canadian Connection* by Jean-Pierre Charbonneau (Optimum, Montreal, 1976) was an invaluable reference.

CHAPTER 5:

Description of the Grand Hôtel comes from visits to Palermo; the facility's historical information is courtesy of hotel management. Details on the Mafia summits come from: testimony of Tomasso Buscetta, a Sicilian mafioso turned informant; law enforcement reports; the President's Commission on Organized Crime *Record of Hearing V*, February 20–21, 1985, Miami, Florida; interviews with police analysts in several countries; and several dozen credible media reports. *Octopus* by Claire Sterling (Norton, New York, 1990) was helpful. French Connection details come from numerous court files and U.S. Drug Enforcement Administration files. Galante's drug dealing comes from court documents filed in *U.S.A. v. William Bentvena, et al* (319 F.2d 916, United States Court of Appeals Second Circuit) and *R. v. Cotroni*. Details on Vito's early life in Montreal come from Vito's admissions in U.S. court in 2007, police files, interviews and sworn testimony by Vito in *R. v. Morielli* (1995, Quebec Superior Court), translated from French. More information on Canadian involvement in the French Connection is in *The Enforcer* (HarperCollins, Toronto, 2004) by Adrian Humphreys.

CHAPTER 6:

The Boucherville arson comes from contemporary newspaper accounts supported by the criminal record of Vito and Paolo Renda. The Sixth Family's relationships come from confidential police and FBI files, interviews and documents filed in *R. v. Caruana, et al* (F-0383, Ontario Superior Court). Bill Bonanno's arrest comes from police files, an interview with Bonanno, a newspaper account and photographs of the event examined by the authors; Vito's wedding and citizenship information from the Montreal police dossier; his pre-nuptial contract from documents filed in court; and Cammalleri family history from an internal report on the "Lake Muskoka Conference" by police intelligence officers in 1985 and a 1986 RCMP report entitled "Traditional Organized Crime, Ontario." The NK 2461-C wiretap comes from police files; information on more recent phone calls to Montreal by Joe Bonanno is from an interview with a retired federal agent and confirmed by Bill Bonanno.

CHAPTER 7:

The Marchettini shake-down, some details on Paolo Violi's interaction with New York and the Quebec crime commission quotes come from the report of the *Commission d'enquête sur le crime organize* (CECO) (Éditeur official du Québec, Quebec City, 1977). Details on Greco's life come from interviews with Bill Bonanno and police and FBI files; details on his death come from contemporary newspaper accounts. *The New York Times* quote is from a May 9, 1967 story. FBI, DEA and RCMP files added context to the Sicilian–Calabrian feud; interviews with current and retired investigators and underworld figures were also helpful.

CHAPTER 8:

Understanding the downfall of Violi, here and elsewhere, was aided by discussions with Robert Menard, a retired Montreal policeman who lived undercover above the Reggio Bar for six years in an operation that placed and monitored secret microphones. Violi's trip to Italy is documented in *Men of Dishonor* by Pino Arlacchi and Antonino Calderone (William Morrow & Co., New York, 1992). Nick Rizzuto's cross-border travels are from border sources. Violi's drug interest comes from court documents in Reggio Calabria, Italy, in *Sentenza contro Paolo De Stefano + 59*, filed in 1979, translated from Italian. Some information on Settecasi's intervention and interest in drugs, here and elsewhere, comes from the Tribunale Civile e Penale di Palermo in *Lucia Beddia + 12*, filed in 1996, and Canadian police reports.

CHAPTER 9:

The visits to Montreal by New York intermediaries are documented in the CECO reports and Italian court files, and captured for posterity on the Reggio Bar recordings. The testimony from Cuffaro comes from Italian and American intelligence reports from the "Big John" case. Information on the Arcuris comes from interviews with police and family sources, FBI reports and Italian and American court documents, including *U.S.A. v. Baldassare Amato*. The chat between Nick and Violi is from the Reggio recordings.

CHAPTER 10:

Activities in Venezuela come from: a visit to the locations involved; interviews with officials in Venezuela, the United States, Italy and Canada; police and law enforcement files; the Buscetta testimony; and three volumes of debriefings of mob turncoat Oreste Pagano, including *Disclosure Re: Statement of Oreste Pagano* (April 7, 1999); *Project Omertà: Pagano Interview/Statement* (September 21, 1999); and *Transcript, Project Omertà* (November 18, 1999). Major Lauretti's remarks are from his testimony in Ontario Provincial Court on September 25, 1998, observed by the authors. Other information comes from police files and interviews.

CHAPTER 11:

Recent RCMP files, CECO reports, the Reggio Bar recordings and FBI documents released under the FOI Act were helpful in understanding the Calabrian–Sicilian feud. Sphinx quote is from *Blood Brothers* by Peter Edwards (Key Porter, Toronto, 1990) and archival footage was useful in describing people and events.

CHAPTER 12:

Information on Licata's murder and the changes in Brooklyn's underworld comes from testimony of turncoat Luigi Ronsisvalle at the President's Commission on Organized Crime, 1985; contemporary media accounts; court files; interviews; and a visit to locations involved. Information from Kenneth McCabe, a legendary New York organized crime investigator who recently passed away, was helpful. Vitale's, Lino's and Frank Coppa's words come from their testimony in 2004. The "highest American boss" quote comes from interviews with an underworld source by the authors in 2005. Falcone's quotes, here and elsewhere, come from *Men of Honour* by Giovanni Falcone (Warner, London, 1993) and Tripodi's quotes, here and elsewhere, from *Crusade* by Tom Tripodi and Joseph P. DeSario (Brassey's, McLean, 1993). *Last Days of the Sicilians* by Ralph Blumenthal (Simon & Schuster, New York, 1989) was also helpful.

CHAPTER 13:

Information on Pietro Sciarra and the downfall of the Violis comes from interviews with police officers who were involved, law enforcement files (particularly the FBI's March 1985 report and the RCMP's "The Mafia: A Canadian Update, 1990"), CECO, archival footage and police crime scene and surveillance photos. Manno's statement and police contact with Violi's killers come from the Montreal police dossier. Information on the wreath from Bonanno is from Edwards. The "pig" phone calls come from a television documentary directed by Daniel Creusot. Pizza Connection information comes from police files, interviews and documents filed in *U.S.A. v. Gaetano Badalamenti, et al* (84-CR-236, Southern District of NY) a.k.a. "the Pizza case," and its subsequent appeal (887 F.2d 1141/1989). Information on the Sixth Family's enclave in Montreal comes from several visits to the area over many years and a study of aerial photographs. The "key that turns the lock of America" quote and other information comes from a lengthy

PRINCIPAL SOURCES AND REFERENCES

author interview in 2006 with a ranking Carabinieri officer in Italy, who requested anonymity.

CHAPTER 14:

The Brasco and Lefty quotes come from *Donnie Brasco* by Joseph D. Pistone and Richard Woodley (Signet, New York, 1987) and Pistone's testimony in court in several related criminal cases, particularly *U.S.A. v. Joseph Massino* (81-CR-803, Southern District of NY). The authors were aided by interviews and discussions with former FBI agent Pistone in 2004. Massino's criminal career and his interaction with Galante and Rastelli come largely from sworn testimony by Bonanno turncoats, particularly Vitale. The Green Acres surveillance comes from police testimony given in the Pizza case. Galante's murder is told from court testimony and FBI debriefings of Bonanno turncoats, particularly Lino, and government reports and documents, much of it filed in *U.S.A. v. Anthony Salerno, et al* (85-CR-139, Southern District of NY) and in the Pizza case.

CHAPTER 15:

The Bono wedding comes from myriad police reports from American, Canadian and Italian authorities, a study of dozens of photographs taken at the event and a visit to locations involved. Sterling provided the dollar values. Additional details on Bono come from *Republic of Italy and Minister of Justice v. Alfonso Caruana* (C-42781, Ontario Court of Appeal). Charles Rooney's testimony comes from *U.S.A. v. Massino* (2003). Bonventre's and Amato's mad dash to Canada is documented in the Pizza case files. Law enforcement files, both public and private, were again invaluable.

CHAPTER 16:

The Bucks County murder comes largely from contemporary news accounts and a study of crime scene photos; the significance of it comes from law enforcement files and interviews with agents and officers. The early Sixth Family incursion into Detroit is from old U.S. Citizenship and Immigration Services and U.S. Department of State files. The early heroin seizures are from Bureau of Narcotics and Dangerous Drugs (BNDD) files and the later ones are from the Pizza case files. For more information on America's early war on drugs, read *The Strength of the Wolf* by Douglas Valentine (Verso, New York, 2004).

CHAPTER 17:

Information on Phil Rastelli and the Bonanno leadership comes from numerous case files and court documents, including the various court testimonies of Vitale and Lino and interviews with gangsters and cops. The graveyard encounter comes from author interviews during a visit to Cattolica Eraclea in 2004. Sciascia's personal information comes from: a transcript of his interrogation by Canadian consular officials; his affidavits, letters and documents filed in the Federal Court of Canada (IMM-61-96); law enforcement files in the U.S., Italy and Canada; and interviews with police and U.S. Homeland Security officials.

CHAPTER 18:

The dispute with Sonny Red comes from court testimony by Bonanno turncoats, particularly Vitale and Lino; law enforcement files; a study of dozens of surveillance photographs; and interviews with lawyers and federal agents. Some biographical details on Sonny Red come from the files of mob historian Andy Petepiece. Details on the murders, here and elsewhere, comes largely from testimony of Vitale, Lino, Duane Leisenheimer and James Tartaglione in *U.S.A. v. Massino* (2002) and *U.S.A. v. Basciano*, supported by law enforcement reports, court filings and visits to locations involved.

CHAPTER 19:

Vito's statements about the three captains' murders come from his allocution in Brooklyn court in 2007. The clean-up comes from informant testimony and from interviews with Pistone. The shooting of Santo Giordano was colorfully told by Gaspare Bonventre and Dr. Ed Salerno during the 1987 racketeering trial of Massino. The hospital encounter is from Blumenthal. The Capri surveillance is from testimony of Special Agent William Andrew in 2004, a study of his photos and various law enforcement reports filed over two decades. The discovery of Sonny Red's body comes from police incident reports prepared at the time, the medical examiner's report, crime scene photos, a summary of evidence filed in Quebec court and court testimony of Vitale and Lino. Information on "Donnie Brasco" coming out from undercover is from interviews with Pistone, his court testimony and his book. Vitale's search for bugs comes from his testimony; Colgan's quote is from "The Last Don" by Richard Corliss and Simon Crittle, *Time* magazine, March 29, 2004. Lefty's quote on drugs comes from recordings secretly made by Pistone.

CHAPTER 20:

Details on the Ruggiero plane crash come from the National Transportation Safety Board, *Aircraft Accident Report NTSB / AAR-83-01*, Washington D.C. Heroin usage rates are from Sterling. Information on the Sixth Family's heroin distribution in New York comes from interviews with law enforcement and legal sources, FBI reports, wiretap recordings of Sciascia and Joe LoPresti in action from the "Quack Quack" tapes, filed in *U.S.A. v. Angelo Ruggiero, et al* (83-CR-412, Eastern District of NY) and the 341-page sealed complaint against the traffickers in the Pizza case. Vito Agueci's Mafia induction is from BNDD files.

CHAPTER 21:

The FBI's assault on Sciascia is from the Bureau's extensive case notes compiled over several years and released under the FOI Act, supplemented by DEA and RCMP records, the testimony of agent Charles Murray in *U.S.A. v. Gerlando Sciascia, et al* (Eastern District of NY) and of Rooney and McCabe in *U.S.A. v. Massino* (2004). The investigation into Nick Rizzuto is contained in Polizia di Stato files. Cesare Bonventre's death is detailed in testimony by Vitale, Leisenheimer and Tartaglione; the discovery of his body from Joseph Keely, a former New Jersey State Trooper.

CHAPTER 22:

LoPresti's capture is detailed in his arrest report. His personal history comes from FBI, RCMP and Montreal police files and interviews with current and former investigators. Sciascia's fight to stay in Canada comes from his extradition case file; the quote about his arrest is from "Why the Mob Loves Canada," by Jerry Capeci, *Financial Post Magazine*, February 1, 1992. Details on the legal proceedings are from the records in *U.S.A. v. Sciascia*. The jury bribe is from the FBI's debriefing notes of Salvatore Gravano. LoPresti's interaction with Vito is largely from the Montreal police dossier and his murder from police files and interviews with officers involved in its investigation. Sciascia's declarations on LoPresti's murder are from Vitale's testimony.

CHAPTER 23:

The "fish" investigation is from Tripodi, supported by Italian police records. Vito and Sabatino Nicolucci's trip to Caracas is from the Montreal police dossier and the Aruba hotel stay is from Blickman.

Nicolucci's history comes from a criminal records check, the Montreal dossier, National Parole Board records and interviews with a former colleague. The expatriate Mafia in South America material comes largely from Pagano's statements to police and from a visit to locations involved. Information on Nick's arrest comes from Cuerpo Técnico de Policía judicial records and FBI and RCMP files. Information on consular contact and visits during Nick's incarceration comes from an author interview with a diplomatic source in 2001. Material on the impact of Nick's arrest is from U.S. Department of Justice records, the Montreal police dossier and RCMP files. Tozzi's claims are from the Montreal police dossier and interviews with investigators involved in the case; his denial comes from an author interview with his close relative in 2001.

CHAPTER 24:

Information on Ireland's Eye is from Memorial University's Maritime History Archive and conversations with area residents and visitors. The Montreal Mafia's involvement in Lebanon, Pakistan and Libya comes from interviews with former drug investigators, the Montreal police dossier and "Death Merchants" by William Marsden in *The Gazette* (Montreal), February 5, 1989. The *Charlotte Louise* case comes from interviews with former RCMP officers, including Michel Michaud, who helped search the boat; and police records. Marsden revealed the Table 6 yarn in "Mounties bug lamp but fate pulls switch," *The Gazette*, December 19, 1990. The hashish smuggling fiascos come from interviews, contemporary media accounts and police files; Dupuis quotes come from his sworn affidavit filed in Quebec court and additional details on the case are from Jean Salois, Vito's longtime lawyer, in correspondence with the authors.

CHAPTER 25:

Conversations between Manno and his co-conspirators come from extensive wiretap recordings in the United States and Canada, filed in *U.S.A. v. Domenico Manno, et al* (94-CR-6042, Southern District of Florida). The Mafia's interests in Miami comes from the Pagano statements. Background on Manno comes from genealogical records, police files, court exhibits and his statements made in court; his cross-border travel comes from confidential border files. The Florida caper comes from copious evidence and testimony filed in the case, information from FBI Special Agent William Douglas, the case agent, and visits to the locations involved.

CHAPTER 26:

The story of Girolama Sciortino's cocaine blues comes from extensive interviews with police officers and prosecutors on both sides of the U.S.–Canada border, court records and the Agreed Statement of Facts for "Project Office" obtained under the Access to Information Act. His criminal record and some background information comes from the parole records, police files and municipal records; his son's record from the Montreal police dossier.

CHAPTER 27:

Pagano's trips to Canada, meetings with Vito and involvement in the cocaine scheme come from his statements given to police as part of his cooperation agreement. Information on Venezuelan drug routes comes from "International Narcotics Control Strategy Report," April 1993, Bureau of International Narcotics Matters, U.S. Department of State and statements from the U.S. Embassy in Caracas. Prison information comes from interviews with an investigator and "Punishment Without Trial: Prison Conditions in Venezuela," March 1997, by Human Rights Watch. The arrests in Puerto Cabello come from contemporary news accounts supported by police files. Information on Zbikowski's troubles and the intervention of Quebec politicians comes from *Hansard*, the official record of the Canadian parliament. The arrests in Canada and the U.S. come from police files; Zbikowski's business interests come from corporate press releases issued prior to his arrest and his criminal interests from National Parole Board records. Details on the Rizzuto childrens' weddings comes from the *Amended Motion to Institute Proceedings* filed by Leonardo and Bettina Rizzuto against the authors in 2007 (500-17-033610-067, Quebec Superior Court).

CHAPTER 28:

The Sixth Family's drug scheme with the Big Circle Boys comes largely from testimony and other evidence filed in *U.S.A. v. Emanuele LoGiudice, et al* (97-CR-660, Eastern District of NY). The Project Onig details come from interviews with officers involved in the case, supported by private police files and public FBI records. William Zita's statements are from his sworn court testimony. Ragusa's personal history comes from genealogical records, police files and parole records; his family's weddings are from the Montreal police dossier. Italy's interest in Ragusa comes from Italian court records, particularly information prepared by the Guardia di Finanza, and the Tribunale Civile e Penale di Palermo in *Beddia + 12*, translated from Italian. Information on the FBI's investigation of Ragusa comes from internal notes on the debriefing of Lino.

CHAPTER 29:

The visit to Lugano by Libertina Rizzuto and the movement of money through Swiss banks is documented in detail in the "Request for Urgent Judicial Assistance" by the Public Prosecutor from the Canton of Tessin, Switzerland, dated December 16, 1994 (Inc. MP n. 6129/94), translated from French; and the "Verbale Di Interrogatorio" of Rizzuto and Luca Giammarella, translated from Italian. Additional information comes from Salois, a Rizzuto lawyer. A visit to locations involved aided the story. Bank statistics come from *The Laundrymen* by Jeffrey Robinson (Simon & Schuster, London, 1998). Information on Operation 90-26C is assembled from interviews with Michaud, who worked undercover at the exchange counter; internal police documents; court files; other interviews and contemporary news stories. Particularly useful was a series of investigative stories by Andrew McIntosh for *The Ottawa Citizen* in June 1998. Vito's interaction with Joe Lagana and Luis Cantieri are documented in the Montreal police dossier and with Nicolucci in parole board records. The Caruanas involvement in Switzerland and Liechtenstein comes from records filed in *R. v. Caruana, et al.* Police suspicions over transactions between American banks and Canadian companies come from secured diplomatic transmissions obtained by the authors. Questions by politicians come from *Hansard* transcripts and Vito being worried for his mother was recounted by Pagano.

CHAPTER 30:

Information on Rusty Rastelli and the rise of Joe Massino comes from FBI surveillance reports and files, photos, and Vitale's testimony. The beef with Anthony Graziano was detailed by Vitale in testimony in *U.S.A. v. Patrick DeFilippo* (03-CR-0929, Eastern District of NY) in 2006. The DeCavalcante Family's attendance at the Bono wedding comes from a study of photographs of the event. The carpet smuggling comes from both Vitale's testimony and an interview with a Montreal gangster. Trips to Montreal by Bonanno representatives come from the court testimony and secret FBI debriefings of Lino. Historical scheduling of Major

League Baseball games is from www.baseball-reference.com. Alfonso Gagliano's background is from *Canadian Parliamentary Guide, 1985* (Normandin, Ottawa, 1985) and *Canadian Parliamentary Guide, 2001* (Gale Group, Farmington Hills, 2002); concern in Canada's parliament over Lino's allegations is from *Hansard* and denials by Gagliano come from contemporary media reports. Amodeo's departure from Canada comes from Immigration and Refugee Board records, interviews with family members, *Hansard* and contemporary reporting, including that of the authors. The new information on a claimed Mafia link to government comes from an unreleased Pagano debriefing. Sciascia's interview by consular officials is transcribed in his immigration file.

CHAPTER 31:

Plans to kill Sciascia were recounted by Vitale in both FBI debriefings and court testimony, particularly in *U.S.A. v. Patrick DeFilippo* in 2006. Massino's involvement and the "dolls" code come from a summary of Massino's "302" information—his FBI debriefings. Spirito's admissions are from his court appearance and plea in 2005 in *U.S.A. v. John Spirito* (03-CR-929, Eastern District of NY). The discovery of Sciascia's body and its condition come from police reports, crime scene photos and the medical examiner's report, obtained by the authors. Massino's entreaty to Vito to be made *capo-regime* was told by Vitale and supported by confidential police files. The strength of the Montreal contingent under Violi was revealed in the Reggio Bar recordings. The end of the tribute from Montreal to New York comes from a private RCMP briefing. The statements from Vito about Montreal being "our own little family" were revealed by Vitale in *U.S.A. v. Vincent Basciano* on March 1, 2006.

CHAPTER 32:

The Pizza Hut troubles come from interviews with police investigators, a former senior company manager and the former franchise owner, who was not anxious to revisit these events. The bombing details come from contemporary news accounts with additional details from an interview with an investigator. Corporate information comes from contemporary company press releases that were unrelated to the events recounted here. Salois's rebuttal comes from his correspondence with the authors. Penway shenanigans are from *Campbell v. Sherman* (30594/88, Ontario Court of Justice). Vito's tax woes are from *Vito Rizzuto v. The*

Queen (98-2497-IT-G, Tax Court of Canada), the undisclosed settlement from a well-placed government source (later confirmed by Vito) and the lawyer's quote from *The Gazette*. The suspicion by John Williams is contained in Canada's parliamentary "Notices of Motions for the Production of Papers (No. 3)," October 2, 2002. The family's "war chest" to fund the tax fight is revealed in sworn statements of account presented in court but not made public and information on the Papalia twins comes from interviews, police files and Securities and Exchange Commission records. The Marcos gold affair comes from an interview with a former Montreal police officer and the counterfeiting case comes from *U.S.A. v. Joseph Baghdassarian* (95-CR-209, Northern District of NY) and contemporary news accounts.

CHAPTER 33:

The Hells Angels interaction with the Sixth Family comes from interviews with former Montreal city and Quebec provincial police officers, police files, the diaries of biker turncoat Dany Kane (filed in *R. v. Sebastien Beauchamps* and *R. v. René Charlebois* in Quebec Superior Court) and author interviews with an underworld source. Information on the Gervasi family troubles comes from an interview with former police commander André Bouchard and the RCMP's "Criminal Intelligence Brief Vol. 9, No. 2," dated April 2, 2002, obtained under the Access to Information Act. This brief, as well as interviews with several police officers in 2001, was also helpful on the murder plot against Vito. There are a number of recent books of substance exploring the biker war, including *The Biker Trials* by Paul Cherry (ECW, Toronto, 2005), *Hell's Witness* by Daniel Sanger (Viking, Toronto, 2005) and *The Road to Hell* by Julian Sher and William Marsden (Knopf, Toronto, 2003).

CHAPTER 34:

The Sixth Family's overtures in Ontario come from author reporting from 2001 to 2005, including interviews with: former Detective-Constable Bill Sciammarella, who retired in May 2006 from the Toronto police force after years of chasing some of the most significant mobsters; Detective-Inspector Paul Sorel, the officer in charge of York Regional Police's investigative services; other York police officers; RCMP Chief Superintendent Ben Soave; former Detective-Sergeant Mike Davis, of the Toronto homicide squad; Sergeant Robert Thibault, of the organized crime investigations unit of the Sûreté du Québec; Detective Inspector Larry Moodie, with the Ontario Provincial Police's illegal gaming unit; a mob-linked career criminal in Toronto; a Toronto mobster; a biker friend of Panepinto's who attended his funeral; the manager of a Toronto-area gym that Panepinto invested in; and a longtime trusted associate of an active Mafia family in Hamilton, Ontario. Interviews were supported by multiple police files. The spate of Mafia murders in Ontario come from author interviews and research from 1997 to 2006. The meeting between Vito and the Musitanos is from the Montreal police dossier. OMG's corporate information comes from documents filed in *Corporacion Americana de Equipamientos Urbanos S.L. v. Olifas Marketing Group Inc., et al* (03-CV-252398CM1, Ontario Superior Court) and registration papers filed with the Ontario government in 2001, 2003, 2004 and 2006. Giacinto Arcuri and Giancarlo Serpe's contact with Enio Mora is from *R. v. Arcuri* and the subsequent appeal to the Supreme Court of Canada (2001 SCC 54, File No. 27797). Information on OMG lobbying comes from the Public Registry of Lobbyists and an interview with the lobbyist; City of Toronto's involvement with OMG comes from interviews with city staff, corporate documents and internal correspondence. The CFSEU assessment of the power of the Sixth Family comes from secret police intelligence reports obtained by the authors.

CHAPTER 35:

The Sixth Family's stumbles in Ontario come from many of the above noted sources. The family's appearance in Project Omertà comes from the Crown's disclosure filed in *R. v. Caruana, et al*. For further details on the rise and fall of the Caruana–Cuntreras, read *Bloodlines* by Lee Lamothe and Antonio Nicaso (HarperCollins, Toronto, 2001). The Siderno Group is documented in *Vincenzo Candido + 23* from the Tribunale di Reggio Calabria (Judgement No. 230/01, June 27, 2001). The death of the Calabrian fugitives comes from interviews with both homicide and organized crime investigators and the attendance of the Sixth Family at Panepinto's funeral from author observation. The gambling pinch comes from the arrest sheets at the time of the raids. Juan Fernandez's background comes from interviews with sources noted for Chapter 31, as well as documents filed in *R. v. Fernandez* (Ontario Court of Justice, 2004), parole records and author observation of Fernandez. His involvement with José Guede, informant testimony and the wiretap transcripts come from *R. v. Guede* in Quebec court and *R. v. Fernandez* in Ontario court. The car dealer scenario comes from confidential police files and an interview with the dealer involved, whom the authors have chosen not to name as he appears to be more a victim than anything. The police corruption conversations come from the Project R.I.P. recordings; the soundtrack of Fernandez's arrest was also captured by police over an audio probe secretly placed in his SUV. Vito's appearance in the OMG Jeep comes from the Montreal police arrest report; the fallout from it comes from author interviews with company officials and letters and affidavits filed in the OMG suit. Quotes from Vito come from "Alleged Mobster: No City Link" by George Christopoulos, *Toronto Sun*, February 4, 2003 and the statement that the new owners of OMG's assets have no links to organized crime comes from documents and letters sent by the company's lawyers in response to a telephone inquiry.

CHAPTER 36:

The Joy Club face-off comes from an interview with Montreal police Sergeant Mitchell Janhevich, supported by a police incident report and a visit to the locations involved. The "no crowning" quote comes from an interview with a Carabinieri officer. The organizational structure and expanse of the Sixth Family comes from a synthesis of dozens of police reports and intelligence files, aided by author observations, numerous interviews with police, legal and civilian sources and author visits. Vito's automobile interest comes from the Tax Court files and his golf routine comes from his testimony in *R. v. Morielli.*

CHAPTER 37:

Arrest details come from an interview with an arresting officer, the charges and related information from *U.S.A. v. Vito Rizzuto* (03-CR-01382, Eastern District of NY) and "Record of the Case for the Prosecution." The pre-arrest police surveillance of Vito comes from an affidavit by Montreal police detective Nicodemo Milano, dated January 15, 2004. Vito's pending arrest was revealed in "Eyeing Canadian Club" by Jerry Capeci in the *New York Sun*, January 15, 2004, also published on Capeci's Web site www.ganglandnews.com, followed by "FBI probes Canadian Mafia 'Godfather'" by Adrian Humphreys, *National Post*, January 17, 2004. The post-arrest glee comes from U.S. Department of Justice press releases and press conference. Louie Ha-Ha's fugitive flight is from "Long arm of the law nabs wiseguy" by John Marzulli, New York *Daily News,* December 30, 2004.

CHAPTER 38:

The Bonanno Family's renaissance under Massino comes largely from trial testimony of five Bonanno turncoats—Vitale, Lino, Frank Coppa, Richard Cantarella and James Tartaglione. Vitale was particularly insightful in *U.S.A. v. Basciano.* Information on Squad C-10 comes from interviews, the testimony of Special Agent Gregory Massa and contemporary news accounts. Agent McCaffrey's quotes are from her court testimony and *Secrets of the Dead: Gangland Graveyard* broadcast on PBS, November 16, 2005. The turning of Barry Weinberg comes from court records, government exhibits and *Five Families* by Selwyn Raab (St. Martin's, New York, 2005), where the "Fredo" story also comes from. Anthony Graziano's Florida crimes come from *U.S.A. v. Graziano, et al* (02-CR-60049, Southern District of Florida) and his New York crimes from *U.S.A. v. Cosoleto, et al* (02-CR-307, Eastern District of NY) and an interview with lawyer Paul McKenna. The conversations of the Bonanno wiseguys were secretly recorded by turncoat mobsters who agreed to work for the government.

CHAPTER 39:

Information here is culled from both of Massino's recent racketeering cases (CR-02-307 and CR-03-929), interviews with and releases by officials with the U.S. Department of Justice, a statement from Judge Nicholas Garaufis provided by his office, an interview with a federal agent involved in the case and visits to the locations involved. Massino's family's quotes are from "Family spurns mob boss leak to feds" by Anthony M. DeStefano, *Newsday,* January 30, 2005. Contemporary news accounts helped with trial color.

CHAPTER 40:

The Bonanno informants' identification of Vito comes from court transcripts, a visit to the courtroom and an examination of the government exhibits. Vito's quotes come from his sworn affidavit filed in *Vito Rizzuto v. Minister of Justice of Canada* (T-316-04, Federal Court of Canada). Vito's legal arguments come, in part, from legal memos prepared by John W. Mitchell for Vito's defense. The "war chest" collections are from sworn accounts filed in court but not publicly released. Noël Kinsella's quotes are from *Hansard.* The evidence against Baldo Amato comes from a prosecutor's memoranda filed in court; his plea to be left alone and Fiordilino's hesitant appearance are captured in the files of *U.S.A. v. Amato*. Amato's private investigator was encountered by the authors.

CHAPTER 41:

The Moomba clash comes from police reports, photographs and a visit to the area. Vito's prison stay comes from an interview with a long-time friend of his. The Sixth Family's response to the Moomba deaths, the Varacalli kidnapping and the D'Amico confrontation is document-ed in RCMP search warrant applications (500-26-042048-060, Quebec Superior Court). Other kidnapping information comes from interviews as part of contemporary reporting by authors and an interview with former police commander Bouchard. Vito's place in the Montreal un-derworld comes from a lengthy interview with a veteran gangster. The press conference by anti-Mafia authorities in Rome was covered by Italian newspapers and the past of Giuseppe Zappia is largely from police files and Canadian news accounts. Quotes from Silvia Franzè are from author interviews in 2007. Details on Vito's alleged co-con-spirators on the bridge come from RCMP files in Canada and Direzione Investigativa Antimafia files in Italy, and case files in *Richiesta di Rinvio a Giudizio* (Nr. 12417/03, Tribunale di Roma). The post-arrest assessment comes from an interview with a senior police investigator in 2006.

CHAPTER 42:

The Project Cicéron / Project Colisée assault on the Sixth Family comes from documents filed in Quebec court in support of the RCMP search warrant applications; subsequent charge sheets; interviews with sever-al investigators; confidential law enforcement reports; releases from the RCMP; the Parliamentary Standing Committee on Justice and Human Rights (February 1, 2007); a study of photographs; and surveillance and visits conducted by the authors. The financial information comes from *Loi de l'impot sur le revenu c. Giuseppe Torre* (T-1951-06, Federal Court of Canada) and *Loi de l'impot sur le revenu c. Nick Rizzuto* (ITA-13069-06, FCC).

CHAPTER 43:

The downfall of Vito came in two court appearances in Brooklyn, at-tended by the authors. His prison movement from the U.S. Bureau of

Prisons and information on the remaining strength of the organization is from police files. The new charges from Italy come from the Direzione Investigativa Antimafia in Rome.

EPILOGUE:

The updated story of Vito's criminal legacy is mostly original reportage and analysis by the authors, drawing on a pantheon of sources. Some of the material first appeared in news stories by Adrian in the *National Post*. Media accounts from a strong group of Montreal journalists, who serve the public so well, helped with additional details. The Charbonneau Commission is commended for making its documentation available, and thanks to Jean Salois for tolerating our intrusions. We drew heavily on Monique Muise's coverage of Vito's visitation in the *Gazette*; as well, Paul Cherry and Antonio Nicaso were helpful.

Acknowledgments

Far-reaching geography and the vast stretch over time of the events covered here were only two of the many challenges we faced in researching and writing this piece of underworld history. A host of kind-hearted people—and the occasional mercenary figure—stepped up to help ease our burden. We extend our appreciation to all.

Out of respect for their underworld code or a fear of aggrieved colleagues, numerous people within the criminal milieu spoke with us on the condition that we not identify them. Similarly, on the other side of the law, several law enforcement and legal sources requested their name not appear in this book. Their reasons were strangely similar: fear of institutional reprimand and castigation from a boss. The men and women in both of these categories are among the most valued contributors to what has become The Sixth Family.

Interviews and research for this project was conducted in several countries. In that regard, some of the most appreciated assistance came from guides, translators and research assistants, almost all of who did not wish to be publicly named. We express our gratitude regardless of anonymity.

Some who have helped us in our continuing curiosity on organized crime include: Detective-Constable Anthony Saldutto and former Detective-Constable Bill Sciammarella of the Toronto Police Service; Montreal Police Sergeant-Detective Pietro Poletti; former RCMP Staff Sergeant Larry Tronstadt; RCMP Staff Sergeant Reginald King; former Special Agent Bruce Mouw, who led both the FBI's Bonanno Squad and Gambino Squad; former RCMP Constable Michel Michaud; former RCMP Chief Superintendent Ben Soave, who was the head of the Combined Forces Special Enforcement Unit; RCMP Inspector Glenn Hanna; former Montreal Police Commander André Bouchard; former FBI Special Agent Joseph Pistone (a.k.a. "Donnie Brasco"); former RCMP intelligence analyst Pierre de Champlain; Chief Superintendent Silvia Franzè of the Direzione Investigativa Antimafia; former Montreal

Police Sergeant-Detective Robert Menard; former Ontario Provincial Police Detective-Constable Ron Seaver, who passed away in 2005; York Regional Police Detective David Stilo; and Sergeant Robert Thibault, organized crime unit, Sûreté du Québec.

At the office of the United States District Attorney, Eastern District of New York, Robert Nardoza, Samantha Ward, Samuel D. Noel and Pietro Deserio were helpful. Investigative reporters, writers and journalists who were gracious with their time, include: Paul Cherry, Michel Auger, Daniel Sanger, Alexander Norris, André Cédilot, Allison Hanes and Graeme Hamilton, in Montreal; Anthony M. DeStefano, Claudio Gatti and Jerry Capeci in New York; Robert Benzie, Antonio Nicaso and John Greenwood in Toronto; and Daniel Nolan in Hamilton.

Marian L. Smith, historian at the U.S. Citizenship and Immigration Services History Office; Sallie Sypher, deputy Putnam County historian; John Celardo and Aloha South at the U.S. National Archives and Records Administration; and Sue Swiggum and Marj Kohli of www.theshipslist.com aided us greatly. Staff at the FBI's Freedom of Information–Record Dissemination Section in Washington, D.C. was generally true to their name and the National Parole Board in Canada is a model of how a government agency can provide a timely release of relevant information while still complying with privacy legislation. Clerks at the various courts we visited around the world were generally helpful despite themselves.

For translation work, additional research in various countries and other support we thank: Dr. F. and A. Miosi, D. and V. Hearn, N. and G. Robinson, Andy Petepiece, Martin Patriquin, Les Perreaux, Kim McNairn, Ian Stuart, Steve Meurice, Jennifer Kirk, Natalie Alcoba, Melissa Leong, Scott Maniquet, Anne Marie Owens and Stewart Bell. In terms of the book's creation, we benefited from the considerable talents of Elizabeth Schaal, Don Loney, Julien Béliveau, Jean-Louis Morgan, Pam Vokey and Brian Rogers.

And above all, thanks to Paula and company and Lucy for letting the Sixth Family take us away from our first families.

INDEX

About the Authors

Adrian Humphreys covers organized crime for the *National Post* and is the author of *The Enforcer*, the best-selling biography of Johnny "Pops" Papalia, one of North America's longest-reigning Mafia bosses. He was the principal consultant for History Television's popular series "Mob Stories" and has written on crime for the *Chicago Sun-Times*, Britain's *Daily Telegraph* and *Reader's Digest*. He can be contacted at humphreys@canada.com.

Lee Lamothe is the author of the bestseller *Bloodlines: The Rise and Fall of the Mafia's Royal Family; Global Mafia: The New World Order of Organized Crime; Angels, Mobsters & Narco-Terrorists; and The Last Thief*, a novel about the Russian Mafia. As a journalist and writer, he has covered organized crime across North America, Europe, South America and Asia.